Expert F# 2.0

P.S for download code location

Text Processing $5 ft 2ft ft ?

Don Syme, Adam Granicz,
and Antonio Cisternino

Apress®

Expert F# 2.0

ISBN-13 (pbk): 978-1-4302-2431-0

ISBN-13 (electronic): 978-1-4302-2432-7

Printed and bound in the United States of America 9 8 7 6 5 4 3 2 1

Distributed to the book trade worldwide by Springer-Verlag New York, Inc., 233 Spring Street, 6th Floor, New York, NY 10013. Phone 1-800-SPRINGER, fax 201-348-4505, e-mail orders-ny@springer-sbm.com, or visit www.springeronline.com.

For information on translations, please e-mail rights@apress.com, or visit www.apress.com.

Apress and friends of ED books may be purchased in bulk for academic, corporate, or promotional use. eBook versions and licenses are also available for most titles. For more information, reference our Special Bulk Sales–eBook Licensing web page at www.apress.com/info/bulksales.

The source code for this book is available to readers at www.apress.com. You will need to answer questions pertaining to this book in order to successfully download the code.

This book is dedicated to the memory of James Huddleston,
the editor at Apress who initiated this book project and
encouraged the authors with his insights, loyalty, enthusiasm, and humor.
Jim passed away in February 2007, an enormous loss to his family,
Apress, and the authors.

Contents at a Glance

Contents

Foreword

According to Wikipedia, "Scientists include theoreticians who mainly develop new models to explain existing data and experimentalists who mainly test models by making measurements—though in practice the division between these activities is not clear-cut, and many scientists perform both." The domain-specific language that many scientists use to define their models is mathematics, and since the early days of computing science, the holy grail has been to close the semantic gap between scientific models and executable code as much as possible. It is becoming increasingly clear that all scientists are practicing applied mathematics, and some scientists, such as theoretical physicists, are behaviorally indistinguishable from pure mathematicians. The more we can make programming look like mathematics, the more helpful we make it to scientists and engineers.

John Backus wrote the design for the "IBM Mathematical Formula Translating System," which later became the language FORTAN, in the early 1950s. Still today, FORTRAN is popular within the scientific community for writing efficient numeric computations. The second oldest programming language, Lisp, was invented by John McCarthy in 1958. Like FORTRAN, Lisp was also inspired by mathematics, in this case by Alonzo Church's lambda calculus. Today, Lisp is still popular in the scientific community for writing high-level symbolic computations.

Interestingly, despite their common roots in mathematics, one can consider FORTRAN as the mother of all imperative and object-oriented languages and Lisp as the mother of all declarative languages. Their differences can be accounted to point of view: FORTRAN starts close to the machine with numbers and moves upward toward the mathematics, adding layers of abstraction where possible. Lisp starts with the mathematics with symbols and grows downward to the machine, peeling off layers of abstraction when necessary. But just as the previous quote remarks that the division between theoretical and experimental scientists is not clear-cut, in practice many programming problems require both imperative and declarative aspects.

Functional programming today is a close-kept secret amongst researchers, hackers, and elite programmers at banks and financial institutions, chip designers, graphic artists, and architects. As the grandchildren of Lisp, functional programming languages allow developers to write concise programs that are extremely close to the mathematical models they develop to understand the universe, the human genome, the pricing of options, the location of oil, the serving of advertisements on web pages, or the writing of fault-tolerant distributed systems. However, to the uninformed developer, functional programming seems a cruel and unnatural act, effete mumbo jumbo. The academic and mathematical origins of functional programming plays up in scary big words such as *type inference*, *structural types*, *closures*, *currying*, *continuations*, *principal types*, *monads*, *inference*, *impredicative higher-ranked types*, and so on. Even worse, most pure functional languages today are not well integrated with mainstream professional tools and IDEs, libraries, and frameworks.

Imperative programming today is the tool of choice for scientific programmers who simulate fluid dynamics, chemical reactions, mechanical models, and commercial software developers who write operating systems, enterprise applications, and shrink-wrapped software such as word processors, spreadsheets, games, media players, and so on. Imperative languages typically have great tool support, debuggers, profilers, refactoring editors, unit test frameworks, and so on, and large standard numeric libraries that have been perfected over decades by domain experts. As grandchildren of FORTRAN, they focus on machine operations first and build abstractions upward. Compared to functional languages, their syntax is unnecessarily verbose, and they lack modern features emerging from the mathematics of computing itself, such as closures, type inference, anonymous and structural types, and pattern matching. These features are essential for the kind of compositional development that makes functional programming so powerful.

F# is unique amongst both imperative and declarative languages in that it is the golden middle road where these two extremes converge. F# takes the best features of both paradigms and tastefully combines them in a highly productive and elegant language that both scientists and developers identify with. F# makes programmers better mathematicians and mathematicians better programmers.

Erik Meijer

About the Authors

■ **DON SYME** is a Principal Researcher at Microsoft Research, and the main designer of F#. Since joining Microsoft Research in 1998, he has been a seminal contributor to a wide variety of leading-edge projects, including generics in C# and the .NET Common Language Runtime, F# itself, F# asynchronous programming and Units of Measure in F#. He received a Ph.D. from the University of Cambridge Computer Laboratory in 1999.

■ **ADAM GRANICZ** is the CEO of IntelliFactory, the leading provider of F# training, development and consulting services, and technologies that enable rapid functional, reactive web development. He has over six years of experience applying F# in commercial projects, and works on WebSharper, IntelliFactory's web development platform that offers unrivaled productivity, a uniform programming model based on F#, and the fastest way to develop robust, client-based Rich Internet Applications. Adam is an active F# evangelist, a regular author in online F# media and speaker at development conferences and industry partners, and serves on the steering committee of the Commercial Users of Functional Programming (CUFP) Workshop, representing the F# segment.

■ **ANTONIO CISTERNINO** is assistant professor in the Computer Science Department of the University of Pisa. His primary research is on meta-programming and domain-specific languages on virtual-machine-based execution environments. He has been active in the .NET community since 2001, he recently developed VSLab, a Visual Studio add-in designed to add the ability of creating dynamic tool-windows, and he also contributed to the development of Octopus, a scheduler of virtual machines running on Hyper-V. He teaches F# in the Programming Graphical Interfaces course at the University of Pisa. Antonio has a Ph.D. in Computer Science from the University of Pisa.

About the Technical Reviewer

■ **ANDRÉ VAN MEULEBROUCK** has been using Microsoft technologies since the early days of COM. He has written white papers and articles on functional programming and theoretical computer science. He also has a background in Scheme, which is a language that F# draws influence from. Once he discovered F#, he began using F# as a beta tester and quickly read all available materials cover to cover.

He lives in Southern California, and works as a .Net developer.

Acknowledgments

We would like to thank Dominic Shakeshaft, Anita Castro and Jonathan Hassell from Apress, who have worked with us and kept us on track for publication. Likewise, we thank André van Meulebrouck and Tomáš Petříček who acted as technical reviewers on the two editions of the book, and whose comments were invaluable in ensuring that the book is a comprehensive and reliable source of information.

The drafts and first edition of this book were read and commented on by many people, and the book has benefited greatly from their input. In particular, we would like to thank Ashley Feniello whose meticulous reviews proved invaluable, as well as John Bates, Nikolaj Bjorner, Luca Bolognese, Laurent le Brun, Richard Black, Chris Brumme, Andrew Herbert, Ralf Herbrich, Luke Hoban, Jason Hogg, Anders Janmyr, Paulo Janotti, Pouya Larjani, Julien Laugel, Richard Mortier, Enrique Nell, Gregory Neverov, Raj Pai, Ravi Pandya, Phil Trelford, Dave Waterworth, Dave Wecker and Onno Zoeter, to name but a few.

We also thank Microsoft Research, without which neither F# now this book would have been possible, and we are very grateful for the interactions, help and support given by other researchers language designers, including Byron Cook, Anders Hejlsberg, Xavier Leroy, Simon Marlow, Erik Meijer, Malcolm Newey, Martin Odersky, Simon Peyton Jones, Mads Torgersen and Phil Wadler.

Finally we thank our families and loved ones for their long-suffering patience. It would have been impossible to complete this book without their unceasing support.

CHAPTER 1

Introduction

F# is a typed functional programming language for the .NET Framework which allows you to write simple code to solve complex problems. It combines the succinctness, expressivity, and compositionality of typed functional programming with the runtime support, libraries, interoperability, tools, and object model of .NET. The aim of this book is to help you become an expert in using F# and the .NET Framework.

Functional programming has long inspired researchers, students, and programmers alike with its simplicity and expressive power. Applied functional programming is booming: a new generation of typed functional languages is reaching maturity; some functional language constructs have been integrated into languages such as C#, Python, and Visual Basic; and there is now a substantial pool of expertise in the pragmatic application of functional programming techniques. There is also strong evidence that functional programming offers significant productivity gains in important application areas such as data access, financial modeling, statistical analysis, machine learning, software verification, and bio-informatics. More recently, functional programming is part of the rise of declarative programming models, especially in the data query, concurrent, reactive, and parallel programming domains.

F# differs from many functional languages in that it embraces imperative and object-oriented (OO) programming. It also provides a missing link between compiled and dynamic languages, combining the idioms and programming styles typical of dynamic languages with the performance and robustness of a compiled language. The F# designers have adopted a design philosophy that allows you to take the best and most productive aspects of these paradigms and combine them while still placing primary emphasis on functional programming techniques. This book helps you understand the power that F# offers through this combination.

F# and .NET offer an approach to computing that will continue to surprise and delight, and mastering functional programming techniques will help you become a better programmer regardless of the language you use. There has been no better time to learn functional programming, and F# offers the best route to learn and apply functional programming on the .NET platform.

F# now a supported language from Microsoft through tools such as Visual Studio, making functional programming is now a viable choice for many mainstream and professional programming activities. The lead designer of the F# language, Don Syme, is one of the authors of this book. This book benefits from his authority on F# and .NET and from all the authors' years of experience with F# and other programming languages.

The Genesis of F#

F# began in 2002, when Don Syme and others at Microsoft Research decided to ensure that the ML approach to pragmatic but theoretically based language design found a high-quality expression for the

.NET platform. The project was closely associated with the design and implementation of Generics for the .NET Common Language Runtime. The first stabilized, supported version of F# is F# 2.0, and this is the version of the language described in this book and is also the version included with Visual Studio 2010.

F# shares a core language with the programming language OCaml, and in some ways it can be considered an OCaml for .NET. F# wouldn't exist without OCaml, which in turn comes from the ML family of programming languages, which dates back to 1974. F# also draws from Haskell, particularly with regard to two advanced language features: *sequence expressions* and *workflows*. Strong connections still exist between the designers of these languages, and their user communities overlap.

Despite the similarities to OCaml and Haskell, programming with F# is quite different. In particular, the F# approach to type inference, OO programming, and dynamic language techniques is substantially different from all other mainstream functional languages. Programming in F# tends to be more object-oriented than in other functional languages. Programming also tends to be more flexible. F# embraces .NET techniques such as dynamic loading, dynamic typing, and reflection, and it adds techniques such as expression quotation and active patterns. We cover these topics in this book and use them in many application areas.

F# also owes a lot to the designers of .NET, whose vision of language interoperability between C++, Visual Basic, and the language that eventually became C# is still rocking the computer industry. Today, F# draws much from the broader community around the Common Language Infrastructure (CLI). This standard is implemented by the Microsoft .NET Framework, Mono, and Microsoft's client-side execution environment Silverlight. F# is able to leverage libraries and techniques developed by Microsoft, the broader .NET community, the highly active open source community centered around Mono, and open source and cross-platform implementation of the ECMA CLI standard that works well on Windows, Mac, and Linux environments. These include hundreds of important libraries and major implementation stacks such as language-integrated queries using Microsoft's LINQ.

About This Book

This book is structured in two halves: Chapters 2 to 10 deal with the F# language and basic techniques and libraries associated with the .NET Framework. Chapters 11 to 19 deal with applied techniques ranging from building applications to software engineering and design issues.

Throughout this book, we address both *programming constructs* and *programming techniques*. Our approach is driven by examples: we show code, and then we explain it. Frequently, we give reference material describing the constructs used in the code and related constructs you may use in similar programming tasks. We've found that an example-driven approach helps bring out the essence of a language and how the language constructs work together. You can find a complete syntax guide in the appendix, and we encourage you to reference this while reading the book.

The book's chapters are as follows:

Chapter 2, "Getting Started with F# and .NET," begins by introducing F# Interactive, a tool you can use to interactively evaluate F# expressions and declarations and that we encourage you to use while reading this book. In this chapter, you use F# Interactive to explore some basic F# and .NET constructs, and we introduce many concepts that are described in more detail in later chapters.

Chapter 3, "Introducing Functional Programming," focuses on the basic constructs of typed functional programming, including arithmetic and string primitives, type inference, tuples, lists, options, function values, aggregate operators, recursive functions, function pipelines, function compositions, pattern matching, sequences, and some simple examples of type definitions.

Chapter 4, "Introducing Imperative Programming," introduces the basic constructs used for imperative programming in F#. Although the use of imperative programming is often minimized with F#, it's used heavily in some programming tasks such as scripting. You learn about loops, arrays, mutability mutable records, locals and reference cells, the imperative .NET collections, exceptions, and the basics of .NET I/O.

Chapter 5, "Mastering Types and Generics," covers types in more depth, especially the more advanced topics of generic type variables and subtyping. You learn techniques that you can use to make your code generic and how to understand and clarify type error messages reported by the F# compiler.

Chapter 6, "Working with Objects and Modules," introduces object-oriented programming in F#. You learn how to define concrete object types to implement data structures, how to use OO notational devices such as method overloading with your F# types, and how to create objects with mutable state. You then learn how to define object interface types and a range of techniques to implement objects, including object expressions, constructor functions, delegation, and implementation inheritance.

Chapter 7, "Encapsulating and Packaging Your Code," shows the techniques you can use to hide implementation details and package code fragments together into .NET assemblies. You also learn how to use the F# command-line compiler tools and how to build libraries that can be shared across multiple projects. Finally, we cover some of the techniques you can use to build installers and deploy F# applications.

Chapter 8, "Mastering F#: Common Techniques," looks at a number of important coding patterns in F#, including how to customize the hashing and comparison semantics of new type definitions, how to precompute and cache intermediary results, and how to create lazy values. You also learn how to clean up resources using the .NET idioms for disposing of objects, how to avoid stack overflows through the use of tail calls, and how to subscribe to .NET events and publish new .NET-compatible events from F# code.

Chapter 9, "Introducing Language-Oriented Programming," looks at what is effectively a fourth programming paradigm supported by F#: the manipulation of structured data and language fragments using a variety of concrete and abstract representations. In this chapter, you learn how to use XML as a concrete language format, how to convert XML to typed abstract syntax representations, how to design and work with abstract syntax representations, and how to use F# active patterns to hide representations. You also learn three advanced features of F# programming: F# computation expressions (also called *workflows*), F# reflection, and F# quotations. These are used in later chapters, particularly Chapters 13 and 15.

Chapter 10, "Using the F# and .NET Libraries," gives an overview of the libraries most frequently used with F#, including the .NET Framework and the extra libraries added by F#.

Chapters 11 to 19 deal with applied topics in F# programming. Chapter 11, "Working with Windows Forms and Controls," shows how to design and build graphical user interface applications using F# and the .NET Windows Forms library. We also show how to design new controls using standard OO design patterns and how to script applications using the controls offered by the .NET libraries directly.

Chapter 12, "Working with Symbolic Representations," applies some of the techniques from Chapters 9 and 11 in two case studies. The first is symbolic expression differentiation and rendering, an extended version of a commonly used case study in symbolic programming. The second is verifying circuits with propositional logic; you learn how to use symbolic techniques to represent digital circuits, specify properties of these circuits, and verify these properties using binary decision diagrams (BDDs).

Chapter 13, "Reactive, Asynchronous, and Parallel Programming," shows how you can use F# for programs that have multiple logical threads of execution and that react to inputs and messages. You first learn how to construct basic background tasks that support progress reporting and cancellation. You then learn how to use F# asynchronous workflows to build scalable, massively concurrent reactive programs that make good use of the .NET thread pool and other .NET concurrency-related resources. This chapter concentrates on message-passing techniques that avoid or minimize the use of shared memory. However, you also learn the fundamentals of concurrent programming with shared memory using .NET.

Chapter 14, "Building Web Applications," shows how to use F# with ASP.NET to write server-side scripts that respond to web requests. You learn how to serve web-page content using ASP.NET controls. We also describe how projects such as the WebSharper Platform let you write Ajax-style, client-based Rich Internet Applications in F#.

Chapter 15, "Working with Data," looks at several dimensions of querying and accessing data from F#. You first learn how functional programming relates to querying in-memory data structures, especially via the LINQ paradigm supported by .NET and F#. You then look at how to use F# in conjunction with relational databases, particularly through the use of the ADO.NET and LINQ-to-SQL technologies that are part of the .NET Framework.

Chapter 16, "Lexing and Parsing," shows how to deal with concrete language formats in addition to those already discussed in Chapter 9. In particular, you learn how to use the F# tools to generate lexers and parsers from declarative specifications and how to use combinator techniques to build declarative specifications of binary format readers.

Chapter 17, "Interoperating with C and COM," shows how to use F# and .NET to interoperate with software that exports a native API. You learn more about the .NET Common Language Runtime, how memory management works, and how to use the .NET Platform Invoke mechanisms from F#.

Chapter 18, "Debugging and Testing F# Programs," shows the primary tools and techniques you can use to eliminate bugs from your F# programs. You learn how to use the .NET and Visual Studio debugging tools with F#, how to use F# Interactive for exploratory development and testing, and how to use the NUnit testing framework with F# code.

Chapter 19, "Designing F# Libraries," gives our advice on methodology and design issues for writing libraries in F#. You learn how to write vanilla .NET libraries that make relatively little use of F# constructs at their boundaries in order to appear as natural as possible to other .NET programmers. We then cover functional programming design methodology and how to combine it with the OO design techniques specified by the standard .NET Framework design guidelines.

The appendix, "F# Brief Language Guide," gives a compact guide to all key F# language constructs and the key operators used in F# programming.

Because of space limitations, we only partially address some important aspects of programming with F#. It's easy to access hundreds of other libraries with F# that aren't covered in this book, including Managed DirectX, Windows Presentation Foundation (WPF), Windows Communication Foundation (WCF), Windows Workflow Foundation (WWF), Irrlicht, the Mono Unix bindings, the Firebird.NET database bindings, several advanced SQL Server APIs, and mathematical libraries such as Extreme Optimization and NMath. There are also hundreds of open-source projects related to .NET programming, some with a specific focus on F#. F# can also be used with alternative implementations of the CLI such as Mono and Silverlight, topics we address only tangentially in this book. Quotation meta-programming is described only briefly in Chapter 9, and some topics in functional programming such as the design and implementation of applicative data structures aren't covered at all. Also, some software engineering issues such as performance tuning are largely omitted. Many of these topics are addressed in more detail in *Beginning F#* by Robert Pickering, also published by Apress, and originally titled *Foundations of F#*. The first edition of this book was published under the title *Expert F#*, and the title was revised at the suggestion of the publisher.

Who This Book Is For

We assume you have some programming knowledge and experience. If you don't have experience with F#, you'll still be familiar with many of the ideas it uses. However, you may also encounter some new and challenging ideas. For example, if you've been taught that OO design and programming are the only ways to think about software, then programming in F# may be a reeducation. F# fully supports OO development, but F# programming combines elements of both functional and OO design. OO patterns such as implementation inheritance play a less prominent role than you may have previously experienced. Chapter 6 covers many of these topics in depth.

The following notes will help you set a path through this book, depending on your background:

C++, C#, Java, and Visual Basic: If you've programmed in a typed OO language, you may find that functional programming, type inference, and F# type parameters take a while to get used to. However, you'll soon see how to use these to be a more productive programmer. Be sure to read Chapters 2, 3, 5, and 6 carefully.

Python, Scheme, Ruby, and dynamically typed languages: F# is statically typed and type-safe. As a result, F# development environments can discover many errors while you program, and the F# compiler can more aggressively optimize your code. If you've primarily programmed in an untyped language such as Python, Scheme, or Ruby, you may think that static types are inflexible and wordy. However, F# static types are relatively nonintrusive, and you'll find the language strikes a balance between expressivity and type safety. You'll also see how type inference lets you recover succinctness despite working in a statically typed language. Be sure to read Chapters 2 to 6 carefully, paying particular attention to the ways in which types are used and defined.

Typed functional languages: If you're familiar with Haskell, OCaml, or Standard ML, you'll find the core of F# readily familiar, with some syntactic differences. However, F# embraces .NET, including the .NET object model, and it may take you a while to learn how to use objects effectively and how to use the .NET libraries themselves. This is best done by learning how F# approaches OO programming in Chapters 6 to 8 and then exploring the applied .NET programming material in Chapters 10 to 19, referring to earlier chapters where necessary. Haskell programmers also need to learn the F# approach to imperative programming, described in Chapter 4, because many .NET libraries require a degree of imperative coding to create, configure, connect, and dispose of objects.

We strongly encourage you to use this book in conjunction with a development environment that supports F# directly, such as Visual Studio 2005 or Visual Studio 2008. In particular, the interactive type inference in the F# Visual Studio environment is exceptionally helpful for understanding F# code: with a simple mouse movement, you can examine the inferred types of the sample programs. These types play a key role in understanding the behavior of the code.

■ **Note** You can download and install F# from www.fsharp.net. You can download all the code samples used in this book from www.expert-fsharp.com; they were prepared and checked with F# 2.0. As with all books, it's inevitable that minor errors may exist in the text. An active errata and list of updates will be published at www.expert-fsharp.com.

CHAPTER 2

■ ■ ■

Getting Started with F# and .NET

This chapter covers simple interactive programming with F# and .NET. To begin, you should download and install a version of the F# distribution from www.fsharp.net. You may also have a version on your machine already. The sections that follow use F# Interactive, a tool you can use to execute fragments of F# code interactively and a convenient way to explore the language. Along the way, you see examples of the most important F# language constructs and many important libraries.

Creating Your First F# Program

Listing 2-1 shows your first complete F# program. You may not follow it all at first glance, but we explain it piece by piece after the listing.

Listing 2-1. Analyzing a String for Duplicate Words

```
/// Split a string into words at spaces
let splitAtSpaces (text: string) =
    text.Split ' '
    |> Array.toList

/// Analyze a string for duplicate words
let wordCount text =
    let words = splitAtSpaces text
    let wordSet = Set.ofList words
    let numWords = words.Length
    let numDups  = words.Length - wordSet.Count
    (numWords,numDups)

/// Analyze a string for duplicate words and display the results.
let showWordCount text =
    let numWords,numDups = wordCount text
    printfn "--> %d words in the text" numWords
    printfn "--> %d duplicate words" numDups
```

You can paste this program into F# Interactive, which you can start by using the command line, by running fsi.exe from the F# distribution, or by using an interactive environment such as Visual Studio. If you're running from the command line, remember to enter ;; to terminate the interactive entry – you don't need to do this in Visual Studio or other interactive environments.

```
C:\Users\dsyme\Desktop> fsi.exe

Microsoft (R) F# 2.0 Interactive build 4.0.30319.1
Copyright (c) Microsoft Corporation. All Rights Reserved.

For help type #help;;

> <paste in the earlier program here> ;;

val splitAtSpaces : string -> string[]
val wordCount : string -> int * int
val showWordCount : string -> unit
```

Here, F# Interactive reports the type of the functions splitAtSpaces, wordCount, and showWordCount (you learn more about types in a moment). The keyword val stands for *value*; in F# programming, functions are just values, a topic we return to in Chapter 3. Also, sometimes F# Interactive shows a little more information than we show in this book (such as some internal details of the generated values); if you're trying out these code snippets, then you can ignore that additional information. For now, let's use the wordCount function interactively:

```
> let (numWords,numDups) = wordCount "All the king's horses and all the king's men";;
val numWords : int
val numDups  : int

> numWords;;
val it : int = 9

> numDups;;
val it : int = 2

> numWords - numDups;;
val it : int = 7
```

This code shows the results of executing the function wordCount and binding its two results to the names numWords and numDups, respectively. You can examine the values by entering each as a single expression, which assigns the result to a value called it and displays the value. Examining the values shows that the given text contains nine words: two duplicates and seven words that occur only once. showWordCount prints the results instead of returning them as a value:

```
> showWordCount "Couldn't put Humpty together again";;
--> 5 words in the text
--> 0 duplicate words
```

From the output you can more or less see what the code does. Now that you've done that, let's go through the program in detail.

■ **Tip** You can start F# Interactive in Visual Studio by selecting View ➤ Other Windowsand then selecting F# Interactive. A tool window appears, and you can send text to F# Interactive by selecting the text and pressing Alt+Enter.

Documenting Code Using XMLDocs

Let's start with the definition of the wordCount function in Listing 2-1. The first line of the definition isn't code but a comment:

```
/// Analyze a string for duplicate words
```

Comments are either lines starting with // or blocks enclosed by (* and *). Comment lines beginning with three slashes (///) are XMLDoc comments and can, if necessary, include extra XML tags and markup. The comments from a program can be collected into a single .xml file and processed with additional tools or can be converted immediately to HTML by the F# command-line compiler (fsc.exe). Chapter 7 covers using the F# command-line compiler in more detail.

Using let

Now, look at the first two lines of the function wordCount in Listing 2-1. These lines define the function wordCount and the local value words, both using the keyword let:

```
let wordCount (text: string) =
    let words = ...
```

let is the single most important keyword you use in F# programming: it's used to define data, computed values, functions, and procedures. The left of a let binding is often a simple identifier but can also be a pattern. (See the "Using Tuples" section for examples.) It can also be a function name followed by a list of argument names, as in the case of wordCount, which takes one argument: text. The right of a let binding (after the =) is an expression.

Values and Immutability

In other languages, a local *value* is called a local *variable*. However, in F#, you can't change the immediate value of locals after they've been initialized unless the local is explicitly marked as mutable, a topic we return to in Chapter 4. For this reason, F# programmers and the language specification tend to prefer the term *value* to *variable*.

As you'll see in Chapter 4, data indirectly referenced by a local value can still be mutable even if the local value isn't; for example, a local value that is a handle to a hash table can't be changed to refer to a different table, but the contents of the table itself can be changed by invoking operations that add and remove elements from the table. But many values and data structures in F# programming are completely *immutable*; in other words, neither the local value nor its contents can be changed through external mutation. These are usually just called *immutable values*. For example, all basic .NET types such as integers, strings, and System.DateTime values are immutable, and the F# library defines a range of immutable data structures such as Set and Map, based on binary trees.

Immutable values offer many advantages. At first it may seem strange to define values you can't change. However, knowing a value is immutable means you rarely need to think about the value's *object identity*—you can pass such values to routines and know they won't be mutated. You can also pass them between multiple threads without worrying about unsafe concurrent access to the values, discussed in Chapter 13.

Understanding Types

F# is a typed language, so it's reasonable to ask what the *type* of wordCount is. F# Interactive has shown it already:

```
val wordCount : string -> int * int
```

This indicates that wordCount takes one argument of type string and returns int * int, which is F#'s way of saying "a pair of integers." The keyword val stands for *value*, and the symbol -> indicates that wordCount is a *function*. No explicit type is given in the program for the type of the argument text, because the full type for wordCount is *inferred* from its definition. We discuss type inference further in the "What Is Type Inference?" sidebar and in more detail in later chapters.

Types are significant in both F# and .NET programming more generally for reasons that range from performance to coding productivity and interoperability. Types are used to help structure libraries, to guide you through the complexity of an API, and to place constraints on code to ensure that it can be implemented efficiently. Unlike in many other typed languages, F#'s type system is both simple and powerful because it uses orthogonal, composable constructs such as tuples and functions to form succinct and descriptive types. Furthermore, type inference means you almost never have to write types in your program, although doing so can be useful.

Table 2-1 shows some of the most important type constructors. Chapters 3 and 4 discuss all these types in more detail.

Table 2-1. Some Important Types and Type Constructors and Their Corresponding Values

Family of Types	Examples	Description
int	int	32-bit integers. For example: -3, 0, 127.
type option	int option, option<int>	A value of the given type or the special value None. For example: Some 3, Some "3", None.
type list	int list, list<int>	An immutable linked list of values of the given type. All elements of the list must have the same type. For example: [], [3;2;1].
type1 -> type2	int -> string	A function type, representing a value that accepts values of the first type and computes results of the second type. For example: (fun x -> x+1).

Family of Types	Examples	Description
type1 * ... * typeN	int * string	A tuple type, such as a pair, triple, or larger combination of types. For example: (1,"3"), (3,2,1).
type []	int[]	An array type, indicating a flat, fixed-size mutable collection of values of type type.
unit	unit	A type containing a single value (), akin to void in many imperative languages.
'T	'T, 'a, 'Key, 'Value	A variable type, used in generic code.

Some type constructors, such as list and option, are *generic*, which means they can be used to form a range of types by instantiating the generic variables, such as int list, string list, int list list, and so on. You can write instantiations of generic types using either prefix notation (such as int list) or postfix notation (such as list<int>). Variable types such as 'a and 'T are placeholders for any type. Chapters 3 and 5 discuss generics and variable types in more detail.

What Is Type Inference?

Type inference works by analyzing your code to collect constraints. These are collected over the scope of particular parts of your program, such as each file for the F# command-line compiler and each chunk entered in F# Interactive. These constraints must be consistent, thus ensuring that your program is well-typed; you get a type error if not. Constraints are collected from top to bottom, left to right, and outside in. This is important because long identifier lookups, method overloading, and some other elements of the language are resolved using the normalized form of the constraint information available at the place where each construct is used.

Type inference also *automatically generalizes* your code, which means that when your code is reusable and generic in certain obvious ways, it's given a suitable generic type without your needing to write down the generic type. Automatic generalization is the key to succinct but reusable typed programming. Chapter 5 discusses automatic generalization.

Calling Functions

Functions are at the heart of most F# programming. It's not surprising that the first thing the wordCount function does is call a function—in this case, the splitAtSpaces function, which is the first function defined in the program:

```
let wordCount (text: string) =
    let words = splitAtSpaces text
```

Let's first investigate the splitAtSpaces function by running F# Interactive:

```
> splitAtSpaces "hello world";;
val it : string list = [ "hello"; "world" ]
```

You can see that splitAtSpaces breaks the given text into words, splitting at spaces.
    In the earlier code, you can also see examples of the following:

- Literal characters such as ' ' and 'a'

- Literal strings such as "hello world"

- Literal lists of strings such as the returned value ["hello"; "world"]

Chapter 3 covers literals and lists in detail. Lists are an important data structure in F#, and you see many examples of their use in this book.

Lightweight Syntax

The F# compiler and F# Interactive use the indentation of F# code to determine where constructs start and finish. The indentation rules are very intuitive; we discuss them in the appendix, which is a guide to the F# syntax. Listing 2-2 shows a fully qualified version of the wordCount function.

Listing 2-2. A Version of the wordCount Function Using Explicit "in" Tokens

```
/// Analyze a string for duplicate words
let wordCount text =
    let words = splitAtSpaces text in
    let wordSet = Set.ofList words in
    let numWords = words.Length in
    let numDups  = words.Length - wordSet.Count in
    (numWords,numDups)
```

Double semicolons (;;) are still required to terminate entries to F# Interactive. However, if you're using an interactive development environment such as Visual Studio, then the environment typically adds them automatically when code is selected and executed. We show the double semicolons in the interactive code snippets used in this book, although not in the larger samples.
    Sometimes it's convenient to write let definitions on a single line. You can do this by separating the expression that follows a definition from the definition itself using in. For example:

```
let powerOfFour n =
    let nSquared = n * n in nSquared * nSquared
```

Here's an example use of the function:

```
> powerOfFour 3;;
val it : int = 81
```

Indeed, let pat = expr1 in expr2 is the true primitive construct in the language, where pat stands for *pattern* and expr1 and expr2 stand for *expressions*. The F# compiler inserts the in if expr2 is column-aligned with the let keyword on a subsequent line.

■ **Tip** We recommend that you use four-space indentation for F# code. Tab characters can't be used, and the F# tools give an error if they're encountered. Most F# editors convert uses of the Tab key to spaces automatically.

Understanding Scope

Local values such as words and wordCount can't be accessed outside their *scope*. In the case of variables defined using let, the scope of the value is the entire expression that follows the definition, although not the definition itself. Here are two examples of invalid definitions that try to access variables outside their scope. As you can see, let definitions follow a sequential, top-down order, which helps ensure that programs are well-formed and free from many bugs related to uninitialized values:

```
let badDefinition1 =
    let words = splitAtSpaces text
                                ^^^^   error: text is not defined
    let text = "We three kings"
    words.Length;;
```

gives

```
    let words = splitAtSpaces text
-----------------------------^^^^

stdin(19,31): error FS0039: The value or constructor 'text' is not defined
```

---

and

```
let badDefinition2 = badDefinition2+1;;
```

gives

```
let badDefinition2 = badDefinition2+1
------------------^^^^^^^^^^^^^^

stdin(21,19): error FS0039: The value or constructor 'badDefinition2' is not defined
```

Within function definitions, you can *outscope* values by declaring another value of the same name. For example, the following function computes (n*n*n*n)+2:

```
let powerOfFourPlusTwo n =
    let n = n * n
    let n = n * n
    let n = n + 2
    n
```

This code is equivalent to the following:

```
let powerOfFourPlusTwo n =
    let n1 = n * n
    let n2 = n1 * n1
    let n3 = n2 + 2
    n3
```

Outscoping a value doesn't change the original value; it just means the name of the value is no longer accessible from the current scope.

Because let bindings are only one kind of expression, you can use them in a nested fashion. For example:

```
let powerOfFourPlusTwoTimesSix n =
    let n3 =
        let n1 = n * n
        let n2 = n1 * n1
        n2 + 2
    let n4 = n3 * 6
    n4
```

Here, n1 and n2 are values defined locally by let bindings within the expression that defines n3. These local values aren't available for use outside their scope. For example, the following code gives an error:

```
let invalidFunction n =
    let n3 =
        let n1 = n + n
        let n2 = n1 * n1
        n1 * n2
    let n4 = n1 + n2 + n3      // Error! n3 is in scope, but n1 and n2 are not!
    n4
```

Local scoping is used for many purposes in F# programming, especially to hide implementation details that you don't want revealed outside your functions or other objects. Chapter 7 covers this topic in more detail.

Using Data Structures

The next portion of the code is as follows:

```
let wordCount (text : string) =
    let words = splitAtSpaces text
    let wordSet = Set.ofList words
    ...
```

This gives you your first taste of using data structures from F# code. The last of these lines lies at the heart of the computation performed by wordCount. It uses the function Set.ofList from the F# library to convert the given words to a concrete data structure that is, in effect, much like the mathematical notion of a set, although internally it's implemented using a data structure based on trees. You can see the results of converting data to a set by using F# Interactive:

```
> Set.ofList ["b";"a";"b";"b";"c" ];;
val it : Set<string> = seq [ "a"; "b"; "c" ]

> Set.toList (Set.ofList ["abc"; "ABC"]);;
val it : string list = [ "ABC"; "abc" ]
```

Here you can see several things:

- F# Interactive prints the contents of structured values such as lists and sets.

- Duplicate elements are removed by the conversion.

- The elements in the set are ordered.

- The default ordering on strings used by sets is case sensitive.

What Is Set in Set.ofList?

The name Set references the F# module Microsoft.FSharp.Collections.Set in the F# library. This contains operations associated with values of the Set<_> type. It's common for types to have a separate module that contains associated operations. All modules under the Microsoft.FSharp namespaces Core, Collections, Text, and Control can be referenced by simple one-word prefixes, such as Set.ofList. Other modules under these namespaces include List, Option, and Array.

Using Properties and the Dot-Notation

The next two lines of the wordCount function compute the result you're after—the number of duplicate words. This is done by using two properties, Length and Count, of the values you've computed:

```
let numWords = words.Length
let numDups = words.Length - wordSet.Count
```

F# performs resolution on property names at compile time (or interactively when you're using F# Interactive, where there is no distinction between compile time and runtime). This is done using compile-time knowledge of the type of the expression on the left of the dot—in this case, words and wordSet. Sometimes, a type annotation is required in your code in order to resolve the potential ambiguity among possible property names. For example, the following code uses a type annotation to note that inp refers to a list. This allows the F# type system to infer that Length refers to a property associated with values of the list type:

```
let length (inp : 'T list) = inp.Length
```

Here, the 'T indicates that the length function is generic; that is, it can be used with any type of list. Chapters 3 and 5 cover generic code in more detail.

As you can see from the use of the dot-notation, F# is both a functional language and an object-oriented language. In particular, properties are a kind of *member*, a general term used for any functionality associated with a type or value. Members referenced by prefixing a type name are called *static members*, and members associated with a particular value of a type are called *instance members*; in other words, instance members are accessed through an object on the left of the dot. We discuss the distinction between values, properties, and methods later in this chapter, and Chapter 6 discusses members in full.

■ **Note** Type annotations can be useful documentation and, when used, should generally be added at the point where a variable is declared.

Sometimes, explicitly named functions play the role of members. For example, you could write the earlier code as follows:

```
let numWords = List.length words
let numDups = List.length words - Set.count wordSet
```

You see both styles in F# code. Some F# libraries don't use members at all or use them only sparingly. However, judiciously using members and properties can greatly reduce the need for trivial get/set functions in libraries, can make client code much more readable, and can allow programmers who use environments such as Visual Studio to easily and intuitively explore the primary features of libraries they write.

If your code doesn't contain enough type annotations to resolve the dot-notation, you see an error such as the following:

```
> let length inp = inp.Length;;

  let length inp = inp.Length;;
  ----------------^^^^

stdin(1,17): error: Lookup on object of indeterminate type. A type annotation may
be needed prior to this program point to constrain the type of the object. This
may allow the lookup to be resolved.
```

You can resolve this by adding a type annotation as shown earlier.

Using Tuples

The final part of the wordCount function returns the results numWords and numDups as a *tuple*:

```
let numWords = words.Length
let numDups  = words.Length - wordSet.Count
(numWords,numDups)
```

Tuples are the simplest but perhaps most useful of all F# data structures. A tuple expression is a number of expressions grouped together to form a new expression:

```
let site1 = ("www.cnn.com",10)
let site2 = ("news.bbc.com",5)
let site3 = ("www.msnbc.com",4)
let sites = (site1,site2,site3)
```

Here, the inferred types of site1 and sites are as follows:

```
val site1 : string * int
val sites : (string * int) * (string * int) * (string * int)
```

Tuples can be decomposed into their constituent components in two ways. For pairs—that is, tuples with two elements—you can explicitly call the functions fst and snd, which, as their abbreviated names imply, extract the first and second parts of the pair:

```
> fst site1
val it : string = "www.cnn.com"

> let relevance = snd site1
val relevance : int

> relevance;;
val it : int = 10
```

The functions fst and snd are defined in the F# library and are always available for use by F# programs. Here are their simple definitions:

```
let fst (a,b) = a
let snd (a,b) = b
```

More commonly, tuples are decomposed using *patterns*, as in the following code:

```
let url,relevance = site1
let site1,site2,site3 = sites
```

In this case, the names in the tuples on the left of the definitions are bound to the respective elements of the tuple value on the right, so again url gets the value "www.cnn.com" and relevance gets the value 10.

Tuple values are typed, and strictly speaking there are an arbitrary number of families of tuple types: one for pairs holding two values, one for triples holding three values, and so on. This means if you try to use a triple where a pair is expected, you get a type-checking error before your code is run:

```
> let a,b = (1,2,3);;
error: this pattern matches values of type 'int * int' but is here used
with values of type 'int * int * int'. The tuples have different lengths.
```

Tuples are often used to return multiple values from functions, as in the wordCount example earlier. They're also often used for multiple arguments to functions, and frequently the tupled output of one function becomes the tupled input of another function. Here is an example that shows a different way of writing the showWordCount function defined and used earlier:

```
let showResults (numWords,numDups) =
    printfn "--> %d words in the text" numWords
    printfn "--> %d duplicate words" numDups

let showWordCount text = showResults (wordCount text)
```

The function showResults accepts a pair as input, decomposed into numWords and numDups, matching the results of wordCount.

Values and Objects

In F#, everything is a *value*. In some other languages, everything is an *object*. In practice, you can use the words largely interchangeably, although F# programmers tend to reserve *object* for special kinds of values:

- Values whose observable properties change as the program executes, usually through the explicit mutation of underlying in-memory data or through external state changes

- Values that refer to data or state that reveals an identity, such as a unique integer stamp or the underlying .NET object identity, where that identity may differ from otherwise identical values

- Values that can be queried to reveal additional functionality, through the use of casts, conversions, and interfaces

F# thus supports objects, but not all values are referred to as objects. Chapter 4 discusses identity and mutation further.

Using Imperative Code

The showWordCount and showResults functions defined in the previous section output results using a library function called printfn:

```
printfn "--> %d words in the text" numWords
printfn "--> %d duplicate words" numDups
```

If you're familiar with OCaml, C, and C++, printfn will look familiar as a variant of printf— printfn also adds a newline character at the end of printing. Here, the pattern %d is a placeholder for an integer, and the rest of the text is output verbatim to the console.

F# also supports related functions such as printf, sprintf, and fprintf, which are discussed further in Chapter 4. Unlike C/C++, printf is a type-safe text formatter, where the F# compiler checks that the subsequent arguments match the requirements of the placeholders. There are also other ways to format text with F#. For example, you can use the .NET libraries directly:

```
System.Console.WriteLine("--> {0} words in the text", box(numWords))
System.Console.WriteLine("--> {0} duplicate words", box(numDups))
```

Here, {0} acts as the placeholder, although no checks are made that the arguments match the placeholder before the code is run. The use of printfn also shows how you can use sequential expressions to cause effects in the outside world.

As with let ... in ... expressions, it's sometimes convenient to write sequential code on a single line. You can do this by separating two expressions with a semicolon (;), and again this is a primitive construct of the language. The first expression is evaluated (usually for its side effects), its result is discarded, and the overall expression evaluates to the result of the second. Here is a simpler example of this construct:

```
let two = (printfn "Hello World"; 1+1)
let four = two + two
```

When executed, this code prints Hello World precisely once, when the right side of the definition of two is executed. F# doesn't have statements as such: the fragment (printfn "Hello World"; 1+1) is an expression, but when evaluated, the first part of the expression causes a side effect, and its result is discarded. It's also often convenient to use parentheses to delimit sequential code. The code from the script could in theory be parenthesized with a semicolon added to make the primitive constructs involved more apparent:

```
(printfn "--> %d words in the text" numWords;
 printfn "--> %d duplicate words" numDups)
```

■ **Note** The token ; is used to write sequential code within expressions, and ;; is used to terminate interactions with the F# Interactive session. Semicolons are optional when the individual fragments of your sequential code are placed on separate lines beginning at the same column position.

Using .NET Libraries from F#

The true value of F# lies not just in what you can do inside the language but also in what you can connect to outside the language. For example, F# doesn't come with a GUI library. Instead, F# is connected to .NET and via .NET to most of the significant programming technologies available on major computing platforms. You've already seen one use of the .NET libraries, in the first function defined earlier:

```
/// Split a string into words at spaces
let splitAtSpaces (text: string) =
    text.Split ' '
    |> Array.toList
```

Here, text.Split is a call to a .NET library instance method called Split defined on all string objects.

To emphasize this, the second sample uses two of the powerful libraries that come with the .NET Framework: System.Net and System.Windows.Forms. The full sample is in Listing 2-3 and is a script for use with F# Interactive.

Listing 2-3. Using the .NET Framework Windows Forms and Networking Libraries from F#

```
open System.Windows.Forms

let form = new Form(Visible=true,TopMost=true,Text="Welcome to F#")

let textB = new RichTextBox(Dock=DockStyle.Fill, Text="Here is some initial text")
form.Controls.Add textB

open System.IO
open System.Net

/// Get the contents of the URL via a web request
```

```
let http (url: string) =
    let req = System.Net.WebRequest.Create(url)
    let resp = req.GetResponse()
    let stream = resp.GetResponseStream()
    let reader = new StreamReader(stream)
    let html = reader.ReadToEnd()
    resp.Close()
    html

let google = http "http://www.google.com"
textB.Text <- http "http://news.bbc.co.uk"
```

This example uses several important .NET libraries and helps you explore some interesting F# language constructs. The following sections walk you through this listing.

Using open to Access Namespaces and Modules

The first thing you see in the sample is the use of open to access functionality from the namespace System.Windows.Forms:

```
open System.Windows.Forms
```

Chapter 7 discusses namespaces in more detail. The earlier declaration means you can access any content under this path without quoting the long path. If it didn't use open, you'd have to write the following, which is obviously a little verbose:

```
let form = new System.Windows.Forms.Form(Visible=true,TopMost=true,
                                         Text="Welcome to F#")
```

You can also use open to access the contents of an F# module without using long paths. Chapter 7 discusses modules in more detail.

More About open

Using open is an easy way to access the contents of namespaces and modules. However, there are some subtleties. For example, open doesn't actually load or reference a library—instead, it reveals functionality from already-loaded libraries. You load libraries by referring to a particular DLL using #r in a script or -r as a command-line option.

Libraries and namespaces are orthogonal concepts: multiple libraries can contribute functionality to the same namespace, and each library can contribute functionality to multiple namespaces. Often, one particular library contributes most of the functionality in a particular namespace. For example, most of the functionality in the System.Windows.Forms namespace comes from a library called System.Windows.Forms.dll. As it happens, this library is automatically referenced by F#, which is why you haven't needed an explicit reference to the library so far. You can place your code in a namespace by using a namespace declaration at the top of your file, as discussed further in Chapter 7.

If two namespaces have types, subnamespaces, and/or modules with identical names, then when you open these, you can access the contents of both using the same shortened paths. For example, the namespace System contains a type String, and the namespace Microsoft.FSharp.Core contains a module String. In this case, long identifier lookups such as List.map search the values and members under both of these, preferring the most recently opened if there is an ambiguity.

Finally, if you ever have name collisions, you can define your own short aliases for modules and types, such as by using module MyString = My.Modules.String and type SysString = System.String.

Using new and Setting Properties

The next lines of the sample script use the keyword new to create a top-level window (called a *form*) and set it to be visible. If you run this code in F# Interactive, you see a top-level window appear with the title text *Welcome to F#*:

```
let form = new Form(Visible=true,TopMost=true,Text="Welcome to F#")
```

Here, new is shorthand for calling a function associated with the type System.Windows.Forms.Form that constructs a value of the given type—these functions are called *constructors*. Not all F# and .NET types use constructors; you also see values being constructed using names such as Create or via one or more functions in a related module such as String.init or Array.init. You see examples of each throughout this book.

A form is an *object*; that is, its properties change during the course of execution, and it's a handle that mediates access to external resources (the display device, mouse, and so on). Sophisticated objects such as forms often need to be configured, either by passing in configuration parameters at construction or by adjusting properties from their default values after construction. The arguments Visible=true, TopMost=true, and Text="Welcome to F#" set the initial values for three properties of the form. The labels Visible, TopMost, and Text must correspond to either named arguments of the constructor being called or properties on the return result of the operation. In this case, all three are object properties, and the arguments indicate initial values for the object properties.

Most properties on graphical objects can be adjusted dynamically. You set the value of a property dynamically using the notation obj.Property <- value. For example, you could also construct the form object as follows:

```
open System.Windows.Forms
let form = new Form()
form.Visible <- true
form.TopMost <- true
form.Text <- "Welcome to F#"
```

Likewise, you can watch the title of the form change by running the following code in F# Interactive:

```
form.Text <- "Programming is Fun!"
```

Setting properties dynamically is frequently used to configure objects, such as forms, that support many potential configuration parameters that evolve over time.

The object created here is bound to the name form. Binding this value to a new name doesn't create a new form; rather, two different handles now refer to the same object (they're said to *alias* the same object). For example, the following code sets the title of the same form, despite its being accessed via a different name:

```
let form2 = form
form2.Text <- "F# Forms are Fun"
```

Values, Methods, and Properties

Here are the differences between values, methods, and properties:

- *Simple values:* Functions, parameters, and top-level items defined using `let` or pattern matching. Examples: `form`, `text`, `wordCount`.

- *Methods:* Function values associated with types. Interfaces, classes, and record and union types can all have associated methods. Methods can be overloaded (see Chapter 6) and must be applied immediately to their arguments. Examples: `System.Net.WebRequest.Create` and `resp.GetResponseStream`.

- *Properties:* A shorthand for invoking method members that read or write underlying data. Interfaces, classes, and record and union types can all have associated properties. Examples: `System.DateTime.Now` and `form.TopMost`.

- *Indexer properties:* A property can take arguments, in which case it's an *indexer property*. Indexer properties named `Item` can be accessed using the `.[_]` syntax. Examples: `vector.[3]` and `matrix.[3,4]`.

The next part of the sample creates a new `RichTextBox` control and stores it in a variable called `textB`:

```
let textB = new RichTextBox(Dock= DockStyle.Fill)
form.Controls.Add(textB)
```

A control is typically an object with a visible representation—or, more generally, an object that reacts to operating system events related to the windowing system. A form is one such control, but there are many others. A `RichTextBox` control is one that can contain formatted text, much like a word processor.

Fetching a Web Page

The second half of Listing 2-3 uses the `System.Net` library to define a function `http` to read HTML web pages. You can investigate the operation of the implementation of the function by entering the following lines into F# Interactive:

```
> open System;;
> open System.IO;;
> open System.Net;;

> let req = WebRequest.Create("http://www.microsoft.com");;
val req : WebRequest

> let resp = req.GetResponse();;
val resp : WebResponse

> let stream = resp.GetResponseStream();;
```

```
val stream : Stream

> let reader = new StreamReader(stream);;
val reader : StreamReader

> let html = reader.ReadToEnd();;
val html : string

> textB.Text <- html;;
```

The final line sets the contents of the text-box form to the HTML contents of the Microsoft home page. Let's look at this code line by line.

The first line of the code creates a WebRequest object using the static method Create, a member of the type System.Net.WebRequest. The result of this operation is an object that acts as a handle to a running request to fetch a web page—you could, for example, abandon the request or check to see whether the request has completed. The second line calls the instance method GetResponse. The remaining lines of the sample get a stream of data from the response to the request using resp.GetResponseStream(), make an object to read this stream using new StreamReader(stream), and read the full text from this stream. Chapter 4 covers .NET I/O in more detail; for now, you can test by experimentation in F# Interactive that these actions do indeed fetch the HTML contents of a web page. The inferred type for http that wraps up this sequence as a function is as follows:

```
val http : string -> string
```

■ **Note** *Static members* are items qualified by a concrete type or module. Examples include System.String.Compare, System.DateTime.Now, and List.map. *Instance members* are methods, properties, and values qualified by an expression. Examples include form.Visible, resp.GetResponseStream(), and cell.contents.

XML Help in Visual Studio

In a rich editor such as Visual Studio, you can easily find out more about the functionality of .NET libraries by hovering your mouse over the identifiers in your source code. For example, if you hover over `Dock` in `textB.Dock`, you see the XML help shown here:

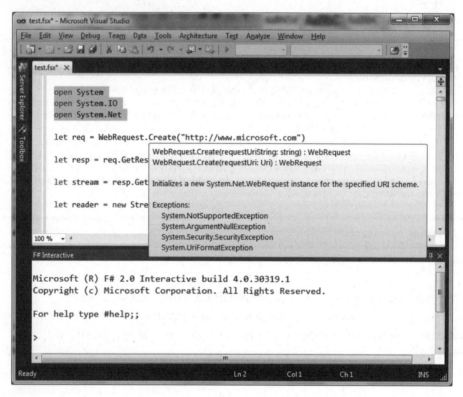

Summary

This chapter looked at some simple interactive programming with F# and .NET. Along the way, you met many of the constructs you use in day-to-day F# programming. In the next chapter, you take a closer look at these and other constructs that are used to perform compositional and succinct functional programming in F#.

■ **Note** In Chapter 3, you use some of the functions defined in this chapter. If you're using F# Interactive, you may want to leave your session open as you proceed.

CHAPTER 3

■ ■ ■

Creating Your First F# Program—Introducing Functional Programming

F# is effective and productive primarily because it's built on the tried and tested constructs of functional programming. This chapter covers the core building blocks of functional programming with F#, including simple types and function values, pattern matching, lists, options, and sequences; as well as how to declare some of your own simple types. Chapters 4 through 6 cover imperative programming, generics, and object-oriented programming.

Getting Started with F# Arithmetic

We first cover the most common base types of data manipulated in F# code, beginning with the basics of F# arithmetic.

Basic Literals

Table 3-1 lists the basic numeric types used in F# code and their corresponding literal forms. The table also lists the non-numeric types bool and unit.

Table 3-1. Basic Types and Literals

Type	Description	Sample Literals	.NET Name
bool	True/false values	true, false	System.Boolean
byte	8-bit unsigned integers	0uy, 19uy, 0xFFuy	System.Byte
sbyte	8-bit signed integers	0y, 19y, 0xFFy	System.SByte
int16	16-bit signed integers	0s, 19s, 0x0800s	System.Int16

Type	Description	Sample Literals	.NET Name
uint16	16-bit unsigned integers	0us, 19us, 0x0800us	System.UInt16
int, int32	32-bit signed integers	0, 19, 0x0800, 0b0001	System.Int32
uint32	32-bit unsigned integers	0u, 19u, 0x0800u	System.UInt32
int64	64-bit signed integers	0L, 19L, 0x0800L	System.Int64
uint64	64-bit unsigned integers	0UL, 19UL, 0x0800UL	System.UInt64
nativeint	Machine-sized signed integers	0n, 19n, 0x0800n	System.IntPtr
unativeint	Machine-sized unsigned integers	0un, 19un, 0x0800un	System.UIntPtr
single, float32	32-bit IEEE floating-point	0.0f, 19.7f, 1.3e4f	System.Single
double, float	64-bit IEEE floating-point	0.0, 19.7, 1.3e4	System.Double
decimal	High-precision decimal values	0M, 19M, 19.03M	System.Decimal
bigint	Arbitrarily large integers	0I, 19I	Math.BigInt
bignum	Arbitrary-precision rationals	0N, 19N	Math.BigNum
unit	The type with only one value	()	Core.Unit

Arithmetic Operators

Table 3-2 lists the most commonly used arithmetic operators. These are overloaded to work with all the numeric types listed in Table 3-1.

Table 3-2. *Arithmetic Operators and Examples*

Operator	Description	Sample Use on int	Sample Use on float
+	Unchecked addition	1 + 2	1.0 + 2.0
-	Unchecked subtraction	12 - 5	12.3 - 5.4
*	Unchecked multiplication	2 * 3	2.4 * 3.9
/	Division	5 / 2	5.0 / 2.0
%	Modulus	5 % 2	5.4 % 2.0
-	Unary negation	-(5+2)	-(5.4+2.4)

The behavior of these and other operators can be extended for user-defined types, a topic covered in Chapter 6. In F#, addition, subtraction, and multiplication over integers are unchecked; that is, if overflow or underflow occurs beyond the representable range, then wraparound occurs. For example, 2147483647 is the largest representable 32-bit integer of the int type:

```
> 2147483647+1;;
val it : int = -2147483648
```

You can access checked versions of arithmetic operators that raise System.OverflowException exceptions by opening the Microsoft.FSharp.Core.Operators.Checked module. If avoiding overflow is a priority, then using the decimal, bigint, and bignum types is recommended. Division by zero raises a System.DivideByZeroException exception, except in the case of floating-point numbers, where it returns one of the special floating-point numbers Infinity and -Infinity. Operator overloading interacts with type inference—if a use of an overloaded operator isn't otherwise constrained to work on a particular type, then F# assumes it works on 32-bit integers.

To constrain a use of an operator to a particular type, you must give a type annotation that has the effect of telling the compiler the type on the left of the two arguments to the binary operator. For example, in the absence of additional type information, the following function is assumed to work with integers:

```
> let squareAndAdd a b = a * a + b;;
val squareAndAdd : int -> int -> int
```

A single type annotation on a is sufficient to indicate that a * a is an operation on float values and thus returns a float value, and that a * a + b is also an operation on float:

```
> let squareAndAdd (a:float) b = a * a + b;;
val squareAndAdd : float -> float -> float
```

If you want, you can also give full type annotations for the arguments and return type of a function:

```
> let squareAndAdd (a:float) (b:float) : float = a * a + b;;
val squareAndAdd : float -> float -> float
```

Bitwise Operations

All the integer types listed in Table 3-1 support bitwise manipulations on their underlying representations. Table 3-3 shows the bitwise manipulation operators.

Table 3-3. Bitwise Arithmetic Operators and Examples

Operator	Description	Sample Use	Result
&&&	Bitwise "and"	0x65 &&& 0x0F	0x05
|||	Bitwise "or"	0x65 ||| 0x18	0x7D
^^^	Bitwise "exclusive or"	0x65 ^^^ 0x0F	0x6A
~~	Bitwise negation	~~~0x65	0xFFFFFF9a
<<<	Left shift	0x01 <<< 3	0x08
>>>	Right shift (arithmetic if signed)	0x65 >>> 3	0x0C

The following sample shows how to use these operators to encode 32-bit integers into 1, 2, or 5 bytes, represented by returning a list of integers. Integers in the range 0 to 127 return a list of length 1:

```
let encode (n: int32) =
    if   (n >= 0    && n <= 0x7F)   then [ n ]
    elif (n >= 0x80 && n <= 0x3FFF) then [ (0x80 ||| (n >>> 8)) &&& 0xFF;
                                           (n &&& 0xFF) ]
    else [ 0xC0; ((n >>> 24) &&& 0xFF);
                 ((n >>> 16) &&& 0xFF);
                 ((n >>> 8)  &&& 0xFF);
                 (n          &&& 0xFF) ]
```

Here's an example of the function in action:

```
> encode 32;;
val it : int32 list = [32]

> encode 320;;
val it : int32 list = [129; 64]

> encode 32000;;
val it : int32 list = [192; 0; 0; 125; 0]
```

Arithmetic Conversions

Numeric types aren't implicitly converted—conversions between different numeric types must be made explicitly. You do this by using overloaded conversion operators. These work the same way as overloaded infix operators such as + and *. Table 3-4 shows the primary conversion operators.

Table 3-4. Overloaded Arithmetic Conversions and Examples

Operator	Description	Sample Use	Result
sbyte	Convert/truncate to sbyte	sbyte (-17)	-17y
byte	Convert/truncate to byte	byte 255	255uy
int16	Convert/truncate to int16	int16 0	0s
uint16	Convert/truncate to uint16	uint16 65535	65535us
int/int32	Convert/truncate to int32	int 17.8	17
uint32	Convert/truncate to uint32	uint32 12	12u
int64	Convert/truncate to int64	int64 (-100.4)	-100L
uint64	Convert/truncate to uint64	uint64 1	1UL
float32	Convert to float32/single	float32 65	65.0f
float	Convert to float/double	float 65	65.0

These conversions are all unchecked in the sense that they won't raise exceptions. Again, the Microsoft.FSharp.Core.Operators.Checked module has corresponding definitions of these operators. An alternative is to use the .NET static methods contained in the type System.Convert, such as System.Convert.ToDouble( ). These do perform checking, which means they raise an exception if the source number can't be represented within the numeric range of the target type. As with many .NET constructs, uses of System.Convert methods may require type annotations to resolve overloading, discussed further in Chapters 5 and 6.

Arithmetic Comparisons

When used with numeric values, the binary comparison operators =, <>, <, <=, >, >=, min, and max perform comparisons according to the natural ordering for each particular numeric type. You can also use these operators on other data types, such as to compare lists of integers, and you can customize their behavior for new types you define. Chapter 5 discusses generic comparison in detail, and Chapter 8 discusses customizing generic comparison.

When used with floating-point values, these operators implement the IEEE semantics for NaN (Not a Number) values. For example, (NaN = NaN) is false, as are (NaN <= NaN) and (NaN < NaN).

Overloaded Math Functions

The module Microsoft.FSharp.Core.Operators includes the definition of a number of useful overloaded math operators. These are shown in Table 3-5 and are overloaded either on a suitable range of integer types or on the basic floating-point types.

Table 3-5. *Overloaded Math Functions and Examples*

Function	Description	Sample Use	Result
abs	Absolute value of signed numeric types	abs (-10.0f)	10.0f
cos, sin, tan	Trigonometric functions	cos 0.0	1.0
cosh, sinh, tanh	Hyperbolic trigonometric functions	cosh 1.0	1.543080635
acos, asin, atan, atan2	Inverse trigonometric functions	acos 1.0	0.0
ceil, floor	Round up, round down	ceil 1.001	2.0
truncate	Round toward zero	truncate 8.9	8.0
exp, log, log10	Exponent, logarithm, base-10 logarithm	exp 1.0	2.718281828
(**)	Power	2.0 ** 4.0	16.0

Introducing Simple Strings

The F# type string is an abbreviation for the .NET type System.String and represents a sequence of Unicode UTF-16 characters. The following sections briefly introduce strings and the most useful functions for formatting them.

Working with String Literals and Primitives

Table 3-6 shows the different forms for writing string literals.

Table 3-6. *String and Character Literals*

Example	Kind	Type
"Humpty Dumpty"	String	string
"c:\\Program Files"	String	string
@"c:\Program Files"	Verbatim string	string
"xyZy3d2"B	Literal byte array	byte []
'c'	Character	char

Table 3-7 shows the escape characters you can use in strings and characters.

Table 3-7. Escape Characters in Nonverbatim Strings

Escape	Character	ASCII/Unicode Value	Examples
\n	New line	10	"\n"
\r	Carriage return	13	"\r"
\t	Tab	9	"\t"
\b	Backspace	8	
\NNN	Trigraph	NNN	"\032" *(space)*
\uNNNN	Unicode character	NNNN	"\u00a9" (©)
\UNNNNNNNN	Long Unicode character	NNNN NNNN	"\U00002260" (_)

As shown in Table 3-6, a literal form is also available for arrays of bytes: the characters are interpreted as ASCII characters, and non-ASCII characters can be embedded using escape codes. This can be useful when you're working with binary protocols:

```
> "MAGIC"B;;
val it : byte [] = [|77uy; 65uy; 71uy; 73uy; 67uy|]
```

Verbatim string literals are particularly useful for file and path names that contain the backslash character (\):

```
> let dir  = @"c:\Program Files";;
val dir : string
```

You can also use multiline string literals:

```
> let s = "All the kings horses
- and all the kings men";;
val s : string
```

The operator .[] is used to access the elements of a string, and the property Length retrieves its length:

```
> let s = "Couldn't put Humpty";;
val s : string

> s.Length;;
val it : int = 19

> s.[13];;
val it : char = 'H'
```

The operator .[index..index] can be used to take substrings:

```
> let s = "Couldn't put Humpty";;
val s : string

> s.[13..16];;
val it : string = "Hump"
```

Strings are immutable; that is, a string value can't be modified after it's built. For example, the Substring method on the string type doesn't modify the original string but returns a new string representing the result. As mentioned in Chapter 2, immutability is a key concept for many F# values, and you encounter it many places in this book. If you attempt to mutate a string, you get an error like the one shown here:

```
> let s = "Couldn't put Humpty";;
val s : string = "Couldn't put Humpty"

> s.[13] <- 'h';;

  s.[13] <- 'h';;
  ^^

stdin(75,0): error: FS0001: Type error in the use of the overloaded operator
'set_Item'. The type 'string' does not support any operators named 'set_Item'
```

Building Strings

The simplest way to build strings is via concatenation using the + operator:

```
> "Couldn't put Humpty" + " " + "together again";;
val it : string = "Couldn't put Humpty together again"
```

You can also build strings using objects of the .NET type System.Text.StringBuilder. These objects are mutable buffers that you can use to accumulate and modify text, and they're more efficient than repeated uses of the + operator. Here's an example:

```
> let buf = new System.Text.StringBuilder();;
val buf : System.Text.StringBuilder

> buf.Append("Humpty Dumpty");;

> buf.Append(" sat on the wall");;

> buf.ToString();;
val it : string = "Humpty Dumpty sat on the wall"
```

■ **Note** For compatibility with OCaml, the ^ operator can also be used for string concatenation, although it's generally used only when cross-compiling code with OCaml.

Working with Lists and Options

Some of the foundational data structures of F# coding are tuples, lists, and options. The following sections discuss these and some related topics by example.

Using F# Lists

F# lists are a common data structure used in functional programming. You saw some examples of concrete lists in Chapter 2. Table 3-8 shows the primitive constructs for building lists.

Table 3-8. Some List-Related Language Constructs and Operators

Operator/Expression	Description	Examples
[]	The empty list	[]
expr :: expr	"Cons" an element with a list	1 :: [2; 3]
[expr; ...; expr]	A list value	[1; 2; 3]
[expr .. expr]	A range of integers	[1 .. 99]
[for x in list …]	A generated list (see end of chapter)	[for x in 1..99 -> x * x]
expr @ expr	Concatenates two lists	[1; 2] @ [3]

Here are some basic list values:

```
let oddPrimes = [3; 5; 7; 11]
let morePrimes = [13; 17]
let primes = 2 :: (oddPrimes @ morePrimes)
```

The value and type of primes are as follows:

```
val primes : int list = [2; 3; 5; 7; 11; 13; 17]
```

Lists are immutable: the cons :: and append @ operations don't modify the original lists; instead, they create new lists. You can see this in the following interactive session:

```
> let people = [ "Adam"; "Dominic"; "James" ];;
val people : string list

> people;;
val it : string list = [ "Adam"; "Dominic"; "James" ]

> "Chris" :: people;;
val it : string list = [ "Chris"; "Adam"; "Dominic"; "James" ]

> people;;
val it : string list = [ "Adam"; "Dominic"; "James" ]
```

Note that people has not been changed by the construction of a new list using the cons operator. F# lists are represented in memory as linked lists; each F# list value is a cons cell containing a value plus a pointer to the next chain in the list, or else it's a special nil object. When you create a new list using the :: operator, then the tail of the new list points to the old list, which ensures that the inner memory associated with lists is often reused as part of multiple list values.

You can decompose lists from the head downward by using *pattern matching*. You saw some simple examples of pattern matching on tuples in Chapter 2, and we look at pattern matching in more detail in "Getting Started with Pattern Matching" later in this chapter. Here is an example of using pattern matching with lists:

```
let printFirst primes =
    match primes with
    | h :: t -> printfn "The first prime in the list is %d" h
    | [] -> printfn "No primes found in the list"
```

```
> printFirst oddPrimes;;
The first prime in the list is 3
val it : unit = ()
```

The first line after the match is a pattern-matching rule that matches the input primes against the pattern h :: t. If primes is a nonempty list, then the match is successful, and the first printfn is executed with h bound to the head of the list and t to its tail. The second line considers the case where primes is an empty list. Note that the :: and [] symbols can be used both to build up lists in expressions and to decompose them in pattern matching. The F# library also includes a module List that contains some useful functions related to programming with lists. You see many of these functions in the next section and throughout this book. Table 3-9 shows some of them.

F# lists aren't appropriate for all circumstances; for example, very large data structures should probably be represented using arrays or other data structures or even managed by an external tool such as a relational database. We discuss a number of immutable data structures in the "Some Common Immutable Data Structures" sidebar.

Table 3-9. *Some Sample Functions in the List Module*

Function	Type	Description
List.length	'T list -> int	Returns the length of the list.
List.head	'T list -> 'T	Returns the first element of a nonempty list.
List.tail	'T list -> 'T list	Returns all the elements of a nonempty list except the first.
List.init	int -> (int -> 'T) -> 'T list	Returns a new list. The length of the new list is specified by the first parameter. The second parameter must be a generating function that maps list indexes to values.
List.append	'T list -> 'T list -> 'T list	Returns a new list containing the elements of the first list followed by the elements of the second list.
List.filter	('T -> bool) -> 'T list -> 'T list	Returns a new list containing only those elements of the original list where the function returns true.
List.map	('T -> 'U) -> 'T list -> 'U list	Creates a new list by applying a function to each element of the original list.
List.iter	('T -> unit) -> 'T list -> unit	Executes the given function for each element of the list.
List.unzip	('T * 'U) list -> 'T list * 'U list	Returns two new lists containing the first and second elements of the pairs in the input list.
List.zip	'T list -> 'U list -> ('T * 'U) list	Returns a new list containing the elements of the two input lists combined pairwise. The input lists must be the same length; otherwise, an exception is raised.
List.toArray	'T list -> 'T[]	Creates an array from the given list.
List.ofArray	'T[] -> 'T list	Creates a list from the given array.

Here are examples of how to use some of the functions from Table 3-9. The last two examples use *function values*, which we cover in more detail in "Introducing Function Values" later in this chapter.

```
> List.head [5; 4; 3];;
val it : int = 5

> List.tail [5; 4; 3];;
val it : int list = [ 4; 3 ]

> List.map (fun x -> x*x) [1; 2; 3];;
val it : int list = [ 1; 4; 9 ]

> List.filter (fun x -> x % 3 = 0) [2; 3; 5; 7; 9];;
val it : int list = [ 3; 9 ]
```

Some Common Immutable Data Structures

Data structures are generally divided between *mutable* and *immutable*, a distinction touched on in Chapter 2 and covered in more detail in Chapter 4. Immutable data structures are sometimes called *persistent* or simply *functional*. Here are some of the immutable data structures commonly used with F#:

- *Tuple values and option values:* These are immutable and are basic workhorses of F# programming.

- *Immutable linked lists of type* 'T list: These are cheap to access from the left end. They're inefficient for random-access lookup because the list must be traversed from the left for each lookup—that is, random-access lookup is O(n), where n is the number of elements in the collection. The full name of this type is Microsoft.FSharp.Collections.List<'T>.

- *Immutable sets based on balanced trees:* Chapter 2 shows some example uses of immutable sets, and an implementation is provided via the type Set<'T> in the F# library namespace Microsoft.FSharp.Collections. These are cheap to add, access, and union, with O(log(n)) access times, where n is the number of elements in the collection. Because the type is immutable, internal nodes can be shared between different sets.

- *Immutable maps based on balanced trees:* These are similar to immutable sets but associate keys with values (that is, they're immutable dictionaries). One implementation of these is provided via the F# library type Map<'Key,'Value> in Microsoft.FSharp.Collections. As with sets, these have O(log(n)) access times.

Chapter 4 covers imperative programming and mutable data structures.

Using F# Option Values

Like lists and tuples, option values are simple constructs frequently used as workhorses in F# coding. An option is simply either a value Some(v) or the absence of a value None. For example, options are useful for returning the value of a search where you may or may not have a result. You see in the section "Defining Discriminated Unions" that the option type is defined in the F# library as follows:

```
type 'T option =
    | None
    | Some of 'T
```

The following is a data structure that uses options to represent the (optional) parents of some well-known characters:

```
> let people = [ ("Adam", None);
                 ("Eve" , None);
                 ("Cain", Some("Adam","Eve"));
                 ("Abel", Some("Adam","Eve")) ];;
val people : (string * (string *string) option) list
```

Pattern matching is frequently used to examine option values:

```
> let showParents (name,parents) =
      match parents with
      | Some(dad,mum) -> printfn "%s has father %s, mother %s" name dad mum
      | None          -> printfn "%s has no parents!" name;;
val showParents : (string * (string * string) option) -> unit

> showParents ("Adam",None);;
Adam has no parents
val it : unit = ()
```

The F# library also includes a module Option that contains useful functions for programming with options. Table 3-10 shows some of these. Although it's easy to code them by hand using pattern matching, it can also be useful to learn and rely on the standard definitions.

Table 3-10. Some Sample Functions in the Option Module

Function	Type	Description
Option.get	'T option -> 'T	Returns the value of a Some option; otherwise raises an exception.
Option.isNone	'T option -> bool	Returns true for a None option.
Option.map	('T -> 'U) -> 'T option -> 'U option	Given None, returns None. Given Some(x), returns Some(f x), where f is the given function.
Option.iter	('T -> unit) -> 'T option -> unit	Applies the given function to the value of a Some option; otherwise, does nothing.

Using Option Values for Control

You can use option values for both data and control; they're often used to represent the success or failure of a computation. This can be useful when you're catching an exception, as shown in the following example (which uses the function http from Chapter 2):

```
let fetch url =
    try Some (http url)
    with :? System.Net.WebException -> None
```

Chapter 4 describes exceptions in more detail—what matters here is that if a network error occurs during the HTTP request, the exception is caught, and the result of the fetch function is the value None. Successful web page requests return a Some value. Option values can then be discriminated and decomposed using pattern matching, as shown here:

```
> match (fetch "http://www.nature.com") with
  | Some text -> printfn "text = %s" text
  | None -> printfn "**** no web page found";;
text = <HTML> ... </HTML>  (note: the HTML is shown here if connected to the web)
val it : unit = ()
```

Working with Conditionals: && and ||

A basic control construct in F# programming is if/then/elif/else. Here's an example:

```
let round x =
    if x >= 100 then 100
    elif x < 0 then 0
    else x
```

Conditionals are really shorthand for pattern matching; for example, the previous code could be written like this:

```
let round x =
    match x with
    | _ when x >= 100 -> 100
    | _ when x < 0    -> 0
    | _               -> x
```

Conditionals are always guarded by a Boolean-valued expression. You can build them using && and || (the "and" and "or" operators) as well as any library functions that return Boolean values:

```
let round2 (x, y) =
    if x >= 100 || y >= 100 then 100,100
    elif x < 0 || y < 0 then 0,0
    else x,y
```

The operators && and || have the usual short-circuit behavior in that the second argument of && is evaluated only if the first evaluates to true, and likewise, the second argument of || is evaluated only if the first evaluates to false.

Defining Recursive Functions

One of the fundamental building blocks of computation in F# is recursion. The following code shows a simple, well-known recursive function:

```
> let rec factorial n = if n <= 1 then 1 else n * factorial (n-1);;
val factorial : int -> int

> factorial 5;;
val it : int = 120
```

This example shows that a recursive function is simply one that can call itself as part of its own definition. Recursive functions are introduced by let rec. Functions aren't recursive by default, because it's wise to isolate recursive functions to help you control the complexity of your algorithms and keep your code maintainable. It may help to visualize the execution of factorial 5 in the following way (note that in reality, F# executes the function using efficient native code):

```
factorial 5
= 5 * factorial 4
= 5 * (4 * factorial 3)
= 5 * (4 * (3 * factorial 2))
= 5 * (4 * (3 * (2 * factorial 1 )))
= 5 * (4 * (3 * (2 * 1)))
= 5 * (4 * (3 * 2))
= 5 * (4 * 6)
= 5 * 24
= 120
```

As with all calls, the execution of the currently executing instance of the function is suspended while a recursive call is made.

Many of the operators you've encountered so far can be coded as recursive functions. For example, the following is one possible implementation of List.length:

```
let rec length l =
    match l with
    | [] -> 0
    | h :: t -> 1 + length t
```

Likewise, many functions such as List.iter are often implemented using recursive functions.

Recursion is sometimes used as a means of programming particular patterns of control. For example, the following code repeatedly fetches the HTML for a particular web page, printing each time it's fetched:

```
let rec repeatFetch url n =
    if n > 0 then
        let html = http url
        printfn "fetched <<< %s >>> on iteration %d" html n
        repeatFetch url (n-1)
```

Recursion is powerful but not always the ideal way to encode either data manipulations or control constructs, at least if other techniques are readily available. For example, the previous program could be implemented using a for loop, as explained in Chapter 4, which would be clearer. Likewise, you should typically avoid explicit recursion if an operator is available that captures the pattern of recursion being used. For example, many explicit loops and recursive functions can be replaced by uses of functions such as List.map and Array.map.

A typical error with recursion is to forget to decrement a variable at the recursive call. For example, we incorrectly entered the following nonterminating function when writing this chapter:

```
let rec badFactorial n = if n <= 0 then 1 else n * badFactorial n
```

You should always check your recursive calls to ensure that the function is tending toward termination—that is, that the arguments are approaching the base case. This is called *well-founded recursion*.

You can define multiple recursive functions simultaneously by separating the definitions with and. These are called *mutually recursive functions*. For example:

```
let rec even n = (n = 0u) || odd(n-1u)
and     odd n = (n <> 0u) && even(n-1u)
```

This gives the following types:

```
val even : uint32 -> bool
val odd : uint32 -> bool
```

Of course, a more efficient, nonrecursive implementation of these is available!

```
let even (n:uint32) = (n % 2u) = 0u
let odd  (n:uint32) = (n % 2u) = 1u
```

You must sometimes take care with recursive functions to ensure that they're *tail recursive*, or else the computation stack of your program may be exhausted by large inputs. This is particularly important for library functions or functions that operate over large data structures with very large numbers of recursive calls. Indeed, the implementation of length shown previously isn't tail recursive. Chapter 8 discusses tail recursion in depth.

Introducing Function Values

This section covers the foundational building block of F# functional programming: function values. We begin with a simple and well-known example: using function values to transform one list into another.

One of the primary uses of F# lists is as a general-purpose, concrete data structure for storing ordered input lists and ordered results. Input lists are often transformed to output lists using aggregate operations that transform, select, filter, and categorize elements of the list according to a range of criteria. These aggregate operations provide an excellent introduction to how to use function values. Let's take a closer look at this in the following code sample, which continues from the definition of http from Listing 2-2 in Chapter 2:

```
> let sites = [ "http://www.live.com";
                "http://www.google.com" ];;
val sites : string list

> let fetch url = (url, http url);;
val fetch : string -> string * string

> List.map fetch sites;;
val it : (string * string) list
= [ ("http://www.live.com", "<html>...</html>");
    ("http://www.google.com", "<html>...</html>"); ]
```

The first interaction defines sites as a literal list of URLs, and the second defines the function fetch. The third calls the aggregate operation List.map. This accepts the function value fetch as the first argument and the list sites as the second argument. The function applies fetch to each element of the list and collects the results in a new list.

Types are one useful way to help learn what a function does. Here's the type of List.map:

```
> List.map;;
val it: ('T -> 'U) -> 'T list -> 'U list
```

This says List.map accepts a function value as the first argument and a list as the second argument, and it returns a list as the result. The function argument can have any type 'T -> 'U, and the elements of the input list must have a corresponding type 'T. The symbols 'T and 'U are called *type parameters*, and functions that accept type parameters are called *generic*. Chapter 5 discusses type parameters in detail.

■ **Tip** You can often deduce the behavior of a function from its type, especially if its type involves type parameters. For example, look at the type of List.map. Using type parameters, you can observe that the type 'T list of the input list is related to the type 'T accepted by the function passed as the first parameter. Similarly, the type 'U returned by this function is related to the type 'U list of the value returned by List.map. From this, it's reasonable to conclude that List.map calls the function parameter for items in the list and constructs its result using the values returned.

Using Anonymous Function Values

Function values are so common in F# programming that it's convenient to define them without giving them names. Here is a simple example:

```
> let primes = [2; 3; 5; 7];;
val primes : int list

> let primeCubes = List.map (fun n -> n * n * n) primes;;
val primeCubes: int list

> primeCubes;;
val it : int list = [8; 27; 125; 343]
```

The definition of primeCubes uses the *anonymous function value* (fun n -> n * n * n). Such values are similar to function definitions but are unnamed and appear as an expression rather than as a let declaration. fun is a keyword meaning function, n represents the argument to the function, and n * n * n is the result of the function. The overall type of the anonymous function expression is int -> int. You could use this technique to avoid defining the intermediary function fetch in the earlier sample:

```
let resultsOfFetch = List.map (fun url -> (url, http url)) sites
```

You see anonymous functions throughout this book. Here is another example:

```
> List.map (fun (_,p) -> String.length p) resultsOfFetch;;
val it : int list = [3932; 2827 ]
```

Here you see two things:

- The argument of the anonymous function is a tuple pattern. Using a tuple pattern automatically extracts the second element from each tuple and gives it the name p within the body of the anonymous function.

- Part of the tuple pattern is a wildcard pattern, indicated by an underscore. This indicates that you don't care what the first part of the tuple is; you're interested only in extracting the length from the second part of the pair.

Computing with Aggregate Operators

Functions such as List.map are called *aggregate operators*, and they're powerful constructs, especially when combined with the other features of F#. Here is a longer example that uses the aggregate operators Array.filter and List.map to count the number of URL links in an HTML page and then collects stats on a group of pages (this sample uses the function http defined in Chapter 2):

```
let delimiters = [| ' '; '\n'; '\t'; '<'; '>'; '=' |]
let getWords (s: string) = s.Split delimiters
let getStats site =
    let url = "http://" + site
    let html = http url
    let hwords = html |> getWords
    let hrefs = html |> getWords |> Array.filter (fun s -> s = "href")
    (site,html.Length, hwords.Length, hrefs.Length)
```

Here, you use the function getStats with three web pages:

```
> let sites = [ "www.live.com";"www.google.com";"search.yahoo.com" ];;
val sites : string list

> sites |> List.map getStats;;
val it : (string * int * int * int) list
  = [("www.live.com", 7728, 1156, 10);
     ("www.google.com", 2685, 496, 14);
     ("search.yahoo.com", 10715, 1771, 38)]
```

The function getStats computes the length of the HTML for the given web site, the number of words in the text of that HTML, and the approximate number of links on that page.

The previous code sample extensively uses the |> operator to *pipeline* operations, discussed in the "Pipelining with |>" sidebar. The F# library design ensures that a common, consistent set of aggregate operations is defined for each structured type. Table 3-11 shows how the same design patterns occur for the map abstraction.

Table 3-11. A Recurring Aggregate Operator Design Pattern from the F# Library

Operator	Type
List.map	('T -> 'U) -> 'T list -> 'U list
Array.map	('T -> 'U) -> 'T [] -> 'U []
Option.map	('T -> 'U) -> 'T option -> 'U option
Seq.map	('T -> 'U) -> seq<'T> -> seq<'U>

You may see types that define methods such as Map that provide a slightly more succinct way of transforming data. For example, this might allow you to write a transformation like so:

```
site.Map getStats
```

This may require the use of a type annotation. Both styles are used in F# programming, depending on the methods and properties available for a particular data type.

Pipelining with |>

The |> forward pipe operator is perhaps the most important operator in F# programming. Its definition is deceptively simple:

```
let (|>) x f = f x
```

Here is how to use the operator to compute the cubes of three numbers:

```
[1;2;3] |> List.map (fun x -> x * x * x)
```

This produces [1;8;27], just as if you had written this:

```
List.map (fun x -> x * x * x) [1;2;3]
```

In a sense, |> is function application in reverse. However, using |> has distinct advantages:

- *Clarity:* When used in conjunction with operators such as List.map, the |> operator allows you to perform the data transformations and iterations in a forward-chaining, pipelined style.

- *Type inference:* Using the |> operator lets type information flow from input objects to the functions manipulating those objects. F# uses information collected from type inference to resolve some language constructs such as property accesses and method overloading. This relies on information being propagated left to right through the text of a program. In particular, typing information to the right of a position isn't taken into account when resolving property access and overloads.

For completeness, here is the type of the operator:

```
val (|>) : 'T -> ('T -> 'U) -> 'U
```

Composing Functions with >>

You saw earlier how to use the |> forward pipe operator to pipe values through a number of functions. This was a small example of the process of *computing with functions,* an essential and powerful programming technique in F#. This section covers ways to compute new function values from existing ones using compositional techniques. First, let's look at function composition. For example, consider the following code:

```
let google = http "http://www.google.com"
google |> getWords |> List.filter (fun s -> s = "href") |> List.length
```

You can rewrite this code using function composition as follows:

```
let countLinks = getWords >> List.filter (fun s -> s = "href") >> List.length
google |> countLinks
```

You define countLinks as the composition of three function values using the >> forward composition operator. This operator is defined in the F# library as follows:

```
let (>>) f g x = g(f(x))
```

You can see from the definition that f >> g gives a function value that first applies f to the x and then applies g. Here is the type of >>:

```
val (>>) : ('T -> 'U) -> ('U -> 'c) -> ('T -> 'c)
```

Note that >> is typically applied to only two arguments: those on either side of the binary operator, here named f and g. The final argument x is typically supplied at a later point.

F# is good at optimizing basic constructions of pipelines and composition sequences from functions—for example, the function countLinks shown earlier becomes a single function calling the three functions in the pipeline in sequence. This means sequences of compositions can be used with relatively low overhead.

Building Functions with Partial Application

Composing functions is just one way to compute interesting new functions. Another useful way is to use *partial application*. Here's an example:

```
let shift (dx,dy) (px,py) = (px + dx, py + dy)
let shiftRight = shift (1,0)
let shiftUp    = shift (0,1)
let shiftLeft  = shift (-1,0)
let shiftDown  = shift (0,-1)
```

The last four functions are defined by calling shift with only one argument, in each case leaving a residue function that expects an additional argument. F# Interactive reports the types as follows:

```
val shift : int * int -> int * int -> int * int
val shiftRight : int * int -> int * int
val shiftLeft  : int * int -> int * int
val shiftUp    : int * int -> int * int
val shiftDown  : int * int -> int * int
```

Here is an example of how to use shiftRight and how to apply shift to new arguments (2,2):

```
> shiftRight (10,10);;
val it : int * int = (11,10)

> List.map (shift (2,2)) [ (0,0); (1,0); (1,1); (0,1) ];;
val it : int * int list = [ (2,2); (3,2); (3,3); (2,3) ]
```

In the second example, the function shift takes two pairs as arguments. You bind the first parameter to (2, 2). The result of this partial application is a function that takes one remaining tuple parameter and returns the value shifted by two units in each direction. This resulting function can now be used in conjunction with List.map.

Using Local Functions

Partial application is one way in which functions can be computed rather than simply defined. This technique becomes very powerful when combined with additional local definitions. Here's a simple and practical example, representing an idiom common in graphics programming:

```
open System.Drawing;;
let remap (r1: Rectangle) (r2: Rectangle) =
    let scalex = float r2.Width / float r1.Width
    let scaley = float r2.Height / float r1.Height
    let mapx x = int (float r2.Left + truncate (float (x - r1.Left) * scalex))
    let mapy y = int (float r2.Top + truncate (float (y - r1.Top) * scaley))
    let mapp (p: Point) = Point(mapx p.X, mapy p.Y)
    mapp
```

The function remap computes a new function value mapp that maps points in one rectangle to points in another. F# Interactive reports the type as follows:

```
val remap : Rectangle -> Rectangle -> (Point -> Point)
```

The type Rectangle is defined in the .NET library System.Drawing.dll and represents rectangles specified by integer coordinates. The computations on the interior of the transformation are performed in floating point to improve precision. You can use this as follows:

```
> let mapp = remap (Rectangle(100,100,100,100)) (Rectangle(50,50,200,200));;
val mapp : Point -> Point

> mapp (Point(100,100));;
val it : Point = X=50,Y=50

> mapp (Point(150,150));;
val it : Point = X=150,Y=150

> mapp (Point(200,200));;
val it : Point = X=250,Y=250
```

The intermediate values scalex and scaley are computed only once, despite the fact that you've called the resulting function mapp three times. It may be helpful to think of mapp as a function object being generated by the remap function.

In the previous example, mapx, mapy, and mapp are *local functions*—functions defined locally as part of the implementation of remap. Local functions can be context dependent; in other words, they can be defined in terms of any values and parameters that happen to be in scope. Here, mapx is defined in terms of scalex, scaley, r1, and r2.

■ **Note** Local and partially applied functions are, if necessary, implemented by taking the *closure* of the variables they depend on and storing them away until needed. In optimized F# code, the F# compiler often avoids this and instead passes extra arguments to the function implementations. Closure is a powerful technique that is used frequently in this book. It's often used in conjunction with functions, as in this chapter, but is also used with object expressions, sequence expressions, and class definitions.

Using Functions as Abstract Values

The function `remap` from the previous section generates values of type `Point -> Point`. You can think of this type as a way of representing "the family of transformations for the type `Point`." Many useful concepts can be modeled using function types and values. For example:

- The type `unit -> unit` is frequently used to model actions: operations that run and perform some unspecified side effect. For example, consider the expression (`fun () -> printfn "Hello World"`).

- Types of the form *type* `-> ` *type* `-> int` are frequently used to model comparison functions over the type type. You also see `type * type -> int` used for this purpose, where a tuple is accepted as the first argument. In both cases, a negative result indicates less than, zero indicates equals, and a positive result indicates greater than. Many collection types accept such a value as a configuration parameter. For example, the F# `compare` function performs generic comparison on values (see Chapter 5).

- Types of the form `type -> unit` are frequently used to model *callbacks*. Callbacks are often run in response to a system event, such as when a user clicks a user interface element. In this case, the parameter sent to the handler has some specific type, such as `System.Windows.Forms.MouseEventArgs`.

- Types of the form `unit -> type` are frequently used to model *delayed computations*, which are values that, when required, produce a value of type type. For example, a threading library can accept such a function value and execute it on a different thread, eventually producing a value of type type. Delayed computations are related to lazy computations and sequence expressions, discussed in "Using Sequence Expressions."

- Types of the form `type -> unit` are frequently used to model *sinks*, which are values that, when required, consume a value of type type. For example, a logging API may use a sink to consume values and write them to a log file.

- Types of the form `type1 -> type2` are frequently used to model *transformers*, which are functions that transform each element of a collection. You see this pattern in the `map` operator for many common collection types.

- Types of the form `type1 -> type2 -> type2` are frequently used to model visitor *accumulating functions*, which are functions that visit each element of a collection (type `type1`) and accumulate a result (type `type2`). For example, a visitor function that accumulates integers into a set of integers has type `int -> Set<int> -> Set<int>`.

■ **Note** The power of function types to model many different concepts is part of the enduring appeal of functional programming. This is one of the refreshing features F# brings to object-oriented programming: many simple abstractions are modeled in very simple ways and often have simple implementations through orthogonal, unified constructs such as anonymous function values and function compositions.

Iterating with Aggregate Operators

It's common to use data to drive control. In functional programming, the distinction between data and control is often blurred: function values can be used as data, and data can influence control flow. One example is using a function such as List.iter to iterate over a list:

```
let sites = [ "http://www.live.com";
              "http://www.google.com";
              "http://search.yahoo.com" ]
```

```
sites |> List.iter (fun site -> printfn "%s, length = %d" site (http site).Length)
```

List.iter simply calls the given function (here an anonymous function) for each element in the input list. Here is its type:

```
val iter : ('T -> unit) -> 'T list -> unit
```

Many additional aggregate iteration techniques are defined in the F# and .NET libraries, particularly by using values of type seq<type>, discussed in "Getting Started with Sequences" later in this chapter.

Abstracting Control with Functions

As a second example of how you can abstract control using functions, let's consider the common pattern of timing the execution of an operation (measured in wall-clock time). First, let's explore how to use System.DateTime.Now to get the wall-clock time:

```
> open System;;
> let start = DateTime.Now;;
val start : DateTime

> http "http://www.newscientist.com";;
val it : string = "<html>...</html>"

> let finish = DateTime.Now;;
val finish : DateTime

> let elapsed = finish - start;;
val elapsed : TimeSpan

> elapsed;;
val it : TimeSpan = 00:00:01.9799671
```

Note that the type `TimeSpan` has been inferred from the use of the overloaded operator in the expression `finish - start`. Chapter 6 discusses overloaded operators in depth. You can now wrap up this technique as a function `time` that acts as a new control operator:

```
open System
let time f =
    let start = DateTime.Now
    let res = f()
    let finish = DateTime.Now
    (res, finish - start)
```

This function runs the input function f but takes the time on either side of the call. It then returns both the result of the function and the elapsed time. The inferred type is as follows:

```
val time : (unit -> 'T) -> 'T * TimeSpan
```

Here `'T` is a *type variable* that stands for any type, and thus the function can be used to time functions that return any kind of result. Note that F# automatically infers a generic type for the function, a technique called *automatic generalization* that lies at the heart of F# type inference. Chapter 5 discusses automatic generalization in detail. Here is an example of using the `time` function, which again reuses the `http` function defined in Chapter 2:

```
> time (fun () -> http "http://www.newscientist.com");;
val it : string * TimeSpan = ...    (The HTML text and time will be shown here)
```

Using .NET Methods as First-Class Functions

You can use existing .NET methods as first-class functions. For example:

```
> open System.IO;;
> [@"C:\Program Files"; @"C:\Windows"] |> List.map Directory.GetDirectories;;

val it : string [] list =
  [ [|"C:\\Program Files\\Adobe"; "C:\\Program Files\\Apoint";
      "C:\\Program Files\\CA"; "C:\\Program Files\\CE Remote Tools"; ...]; ... ]
```

Sometimes you need to add extra type information to indicate which overload of the method is required. Chapter 6 discusses method overloading in more detail. For example, the following causes an error:

```
> open System;;
> let f = Console.WriteLine;;

C:\misc\test.ml(11,8): error: FS0041: The method WriteLine is overloaded.
Possible matches are shown below. Resolve the overloading by adding further
type annotations to the arguments.

Possible overload: 'Console.WriteLine(bool value) : unit'.

Possible overload: 'Console.WriteLine(char value) : unit'.
...
```

However, the following succeeds:

```
> let f = (Console.WriteLine : string -> unit);;
val f : string -> unit
```

Getting Started with Pattern Matching

One important tool in F# programming is *pattern matching*, a general construct that combines decomposition and control. In the previous sections, you got a taste of how you can use pattern matching with tuple, list, and option values. However, you can also use pattern matching in many other situations. You see many other examples of pattern matching in this book, but let's start with some simple pattern matching over strings and integers. As you've already seen, pattern matches on explicit values are introduced using the match ... with ... construct:

```
let urlFilter url agent =
    match (url,agent) with
    | "http://www.control.org", 99 -> true
    | "http://www.kaos.org"   , _  -> false
    | _, 86 -> true
    | _ -> false
```

The inferred type of the function is as follows:

```
val urlFilter : string -> int -> bool
```

The expression (url,agent) after the keyword match is a tuple of type (string*int). Each rule of the match is introduced with a | followed by a pattern, then ->, and then a result expression. When executed, the patterns of the rules are used one by one, and the first successful pattern match determines which result expression is used. In the previous example, the first pattern matches if url and agent are "http://www.control.org" and 99, respectively. The next matches if url is "http://www.kaos.org". The third pattern matches if agent is 86. The last three rules all use *wildcard* patterns represented by the underscore character; these match all inputs.

The overall conditions under which urlFilter returns true can be determined by reading through the pattern match: agent 99 can access "http://www.control.org", no one can access "http://www.kaos.org", and, excluding the latter, agent 86 can access anything.

Patterns are a rich and powerful technique for simultaneous data analysis and decomposition. Table 3-12 summarizes all the ways to form patterns in F#; many of these involve building up patterns from other patterns. The sections that follow look at some of these constructs, and Chapter 9 covers active patterns.

Table 3-12. Different Ways to Form Patterns

General Form	Kind	Example
(pat, ... ,pat)	Tuple pattern	(1,2,("3",x))
[pat; ... ;pat]	List pattern	[x;y;z]
[| pat; ...; pat |]	Array pattern	[| "cmd"; arg1; arg2 |]
{ id=pat; ...; id=pat }	Record pattern	{ X=1; Y=2 }
Tag(pat, ... ,pat)	Tagged union or active pattern	Point(x,y)
pat | pat	"Or" pattern	[x] | ["X";x]
pat & pat	"And" pattern	[p] & [Point(x,y)]
pat as id	Named pattern	[x] as inp
id	Variable pattern	x
_	Wildcard pattern	_
Any literal	Constant pattern	36, "36", 27L,System.DayOfWeek.Monday
:? type	Type test pattern	:? string
null	Null test pattern	null

Matching on Structured Values

Pattern matching can be used to decompose structured values. Here is an example where you match nested tuple values:

```
> let highLow a b =
    match (a,b) with
    | ("lo", lo), ("hi", hi) -> (lo,hi)
    | ("hi", hi), ("lo", lo) -> (lo,hi)
    | _ -> failwith "expected a both a high and low value";;
```

The match examines two pairs and looks at the strings in the first element of each, returning the associated values:

```
> highLow ("hi",300) ("lo",100);;
val it : int * int = (100,300)
```

The first rule matches if the first parts of the input pairs are the strings "lo" and "hi", respectively. It then returns a pair made from the respective second parts of the tuples. The second rule is the mirror of this in case the values appeared in reverse order.

The final cases of both of the previous examples use wildcard patterns to cover remaining cases. This makes the patterns *exhaustive*. Frequently, no wildcard is needed to ensure this, because for many input types F# is able to determine whether the given set of rules is sufficient to cover all possibilities for the given shape of data. However, if a match isn't exhaustive, a warning is given:

```
> let urlFilter3 url agent =
      match url,agent with
      | "http://www.control.org", 86 -> true
      | "http://www.kaos.org", _ -> false;;

   match url,agent with
   ^^^^^^^^^^^^^^^^^^^^
warning: Incomplete pattern matches on this expression. ...
```

In these cases, it may be necessary to add an extra exception-throwing clause to indicate to the F# compiler that the given inputs aren't expected:

```
let urlFilter4 url agent =
    match url,agent with
    | "http://www.control.org", 86 -> true
    | "http://www.kaos.org", _ -> false
    | _ -> failwith "unexpected input"
```

Nonexhaustive matches are automatically augmented by a default case where a MatchFailureException is thrown. Chapter 4 discusses exceptions.

F# is frequently able to determine whether pattern-matching rules are redundant, such as if a rule can never be selected because previous rules subsume all such cases. In this case, a warning is given. For example:

```
> let urlFilter2 url agent =
      match url,agent with
      | "http://www.control.org", _ -> true
      | "http://www.control.org", 86 -> true
      | _ -> false;;

   | "http://www.control.org", 86 -> true
   ^^^^^^^^^^^^^^^^^^^^^^^^^^^^^^^^^^^^^^^^
warning: This rule will never be matched.
```

■ **Tip** Use wildcard patterns with care. F# can often determine whether a match is exhaustive, and the use of wildcard patterns effectively disables this analysis for any particular pattern match. Sometimes it's better to write out the extra cases of a match as explicit patterns, because you can then adjust your code when new kinds of input data are introduced.

Guarding Rules and Combining Patterns

Individual rules of a match can be guarded by a condition that is executed if the pattern itself succeeds. Here is a simple use of this mechanism to record the three clauses of computing the sign of an integer:

```
let sign x =
    match x with
    | _ when x < 0 -> -1
    | _ when x > 0 ->  1
    | _ -> 0
```

You can combine two patterns to represent two possible paths for matching:

```
let getValue a =
    match a with
    | (("lo" | "low") ,v) -> v
    | ("hi",v) | ("high",v) -> v
    | _ -> failwith "expected a both a high and low value"
```

Here, the pattern ("lo" | "low") matches either string. The pattern ("hi",v) | ("high",v) plays essentially the same role by matching pairs values where the left of the pair is "hi" or "high" and by binding the value v on either side of the pattern.

■ **Note** Individual patterns can't bind the same variables twice. For example, a pattern (x,x) isn't permitted, although (x,y) when x = y is permitted. Furthermore, each side of an "or" pattern must bind the same set of variables, and these variables must have the same types.

Getting Started with Sequences

Many programming tasks require the iteration, aggregation, and transformation of data streamed from various sources. One important and general way to code these tasks is in terms of values of the .NET type System.Collections.Generic.IEnumerable<type>, which is typically abbreviated to seq<*type*> in F# code. A seq<*type*> is a value that can be *iterated*, producing results of type type on demand. Sequences are used to wrap collections, computations, and data streams and are frequently used to represent the results of database queries. The following sections present some simple examples of working with seq<type> values.

Using Range Expressions

You can generate simple sequences using *range expressions*. For integer ranges, these take the form of
seq {n .. m} for the integer expressions n and m:

```
> seq {0 .. 2};;
val it : seq<int> = seq [ 0; 1; 2; ]
```

You can also specify range expressions using other numeric types, such as double and single:

```
> seq {-100.0 .. 100.0};;
val it : seq<double> = seq [ -100.0; -99.0; -98.0; ... ]
```

By default, F# Interactive shows the value of a sequence only to a limited depth. seq<'T> values are
lazy in the sense that they compute and return the successive elements on demand. This means you can
create sequences representing very large ranges, and the elements of the sequence are computed only if
they're required by a subsequent computation. In the next example, you don't actually create a concrete
data structure containing one trillion elements but rather a sequence value that has the *potential* to yield
this number of elements on demand. The default printing performed by F# Interactive forces this
computation up to depth 4:

```
> seq {1I .. 1000000000000I};;
val it : seq<bigint> = seq [1I; 2I; 3I; 4I; ... ]
```

The default increment for range expressions is always 1. A different increment can be used via range
expressions of the form seq { n .. skip .. m }:

```
> seq { 1 .. 2 .. 5 };;
val it : seq<int> = seq [ 1; 3; 5 ]
```

```
> seq { 1 .. -2 .. -5 };;
val it : seq<int> = seq [ 1; -1; -3; -5 ]
```

If the skip causes the final element to be overshot, then the final element isn't included in the result:

```
> seq { 0 .. 2 .. 5 };;
val it : seq<int> = seq [ 0; 2; 4 ]
```

The (..) and (.. ..) operators are overloaded operators in the same sense as (+) and (-), which
means their behavior can be altered for user-defined types. Chapter 6 discusses this in more detail.

Iterating a Sequence

You can iterate sequences using the for ... in ... do construct, as well as the Seq.iter aggregate operator discussed in the next section. Here is a simple example of the first:

```
> let range = seq {0 .. 2 .. 6};;
val range : seq<int>

> for i in range do
      printfn "i = %d" i;;
i = 0
i = 2
i = 4
i = 6
```

This construct forces the iteration of the entire seq. Use it with care when you're working with sequences that may yield a large number of elements.

Transforming Sequences with Aggregate Operators

Any value of type seq<type> can be iterated and transformed using functions in the Microsoft.FSharp.Collections.Seq module. For example:

```
> let range = seq {0 .. 10};;
val range : seq<int>

> range |> Seq.map (fun i -> (i,i*i));;
val it : seq<int * int> = seq [ (0, 0); (1, 1); (2, 4); (3, 9) ... ]
```

Table 3-13 shows some important functions in this library module. The following operators necessarily evaluate all the elements of the input seq immediately:

- Seq.iter: This iterates all elements, applying a function to each one.

- Seq.toList: This iterates all elements, building a new list.

- Seq.toArray: This iterates all elements, building a new array.

Most of the other operators in the Seq module return one or more seq<type> values and force the computation of elements in any input seq<type> values only on demand.

Table 3-13. Some Important Functions and Aggregate Operators from the Seq Module

Operator	Type
Seq.append	: seq<'T> -> seq<'T> -> seq<'T>
Seq.concat	: seq< seq<'T> > -> seq<'T>
Seq.choose	: ('T -> 'U option) -> seq<'T> -> seq<'U>
Seq.delay	: (unit -> seq<'T>) -> seq<'T>
Seq.empty	seq<'T>
Seq.iter	: ('T -> unit) -> seq<'T> -> unit
Seq.filter	: ('T -> bool) -> seq<'T> -> seq<'T>
Seq.map	: ('T -> 'U) -> seq<'T> -> seq<'U>
Seq.singleton	: 'T -> seq<'T>
Seq.truncate	: int -> seq<'T> -> seq<'T>
Seq.toList	: seq<'T> -> 'T list
Seq.ofList	: 'T list -> seq<'T>
Seq.toArray	: seq<'T> -> 'T[]
Seq.ofArray	: 'T[] -> seq<'T>

Which Types Can Be Used as Sequences?

Table 3-13 includes many uses of types such as seq<'T>. When a type appears as the type of an argument, the function accepts any value that's compatible with this type. Chapter 5 explains the notions of subtyping and compatibility in more detail; the concept should be familiar to OO programmers because it's the same as that used by other .NET languages such as C#, which itself is close to that used by Java. In practice, you can easily discover which types are compatible with which by using F# Interactive and tools such as Visual Studio: when you hover over a type name, the compatible types are shown. You can also refer to the online documentation for the F# libraries and the .NET Framework, which you can easily search using the major search engines.

Here are some of the types compatible with seq<'T>:

- *Array types:* For example, int[] is compatible with seq<int>.

- *F# list types:* For example, int list is compatible with seq<int>.

- *All other F# and .NET collection types:* For example, System.Collections.Generic.SortedList<string> is compatible with seq<string>.

The following types aren't directly type compatible with seq<'T> but can be converted readily into sequences when needed:

- Some .NET types are compatible with a somewhat deprecated nongeneric .NET 1.0 construct called System.Collections.IEnumerable (note the absence of any generic parameter) but aren't compatible with the newer .NET construct System.Collections.Generic.IEnumerable<type>, called seq<type> in F# code.

- Some .NET types such as System.Text.RegularExpressions.MatchCollection support only a GetEnumerator method and can't be used directly as values of type seq<type>. However, you can convert them into sequences by using them in conjunction with the sequence expression syntax mentioned earlier, such as seq { for x in matchCollection -> x } or for x in matchCollection do ....

Expressions of the form for pat in seq are described in the section "Using Sequence Expressions" and in Chapter 4.

Using Lazy Sequences from External Sources

Sequences are frequently used to represent the process of streaming data from an external source, such as from a database query or from a computer's file system. For example, the following recursive function constructs a seq<string> that represents the process of recursively reading the names of all the files under a given path. The return types of Directory.GetFiles and Directory.GetDirectories are string[]; and as noted earlier, this type is always compatible with seq<string>:

```
open System.IO
let rec allFiles dir =
    Seq.append
        (dir |> Directory.GetFiles)
        (dir |> Directory.GetDirectories |> Seq.map allFiles |> Seq.concat)
```

This gives the following type:

```
val allFiles : string -> seq<string>
```

Here is an example of the function being used on one of our machines:

```
> allFiles @"c:\WINDOWS\system32";;
val it : seq<string> =
    = seq ["c:\\WINDOWS\\system32\\$winnt$.inf";
           "c:\\WINDOWS\\system32\\12520437.cpx";
           "c:\\WINDOWS\\system32\\12520850.cpx";
           "c:\\WINDOWS\\system32\\6to4svc.dll"; ...]
```

The allFiles function is interesting partly because it shows many aspects of F# working seamlessly together:

- *Functions as values:* The function allFiles is recursive and is used as a first-class function value within its own definition.

- *Pipelining:* The pipelining operator |> provides a natural way to present the transformations applied to each subdirectory name.

- *Type inference:* Type inference computes all types in the obvious way, without any type annotations.

- *NET interoperability:* The System.IO.Directory operations provide intuitive primitives, which can then be incorporated in powerful ways using succinct F# programs.

- *Laziness where needed:* The function Seq.map applies the argument function lazily (on demand), which means subdirectories aren't read until required.

One subtlety with programming with on-demand or lazy values like sequences is that side effects such as reading and writing from an external store shouldn't in general happen until the lazy sequence value is consumed. For example, the previous allFiles function reads the top-level directory C:\ as soon as allFiles is applied to its argument. This may not be appropriate if the contents of C:\ are changing. You can delay the computation of the sequence by using the library function Seq.delay or by using a sequence expression, covered in the next section, where delays are inserted automatically by the F# compiler.

Using Sequence Expressions

Aggregate operators are a powerful way of working with seq<type> values. However, F# also provides a convenient and compact syntax called *sequence expressions* for specifying sequence values that can be built using operations such as choose, map, filter, and concat. You can also use sequence expressions to specify the shapes of lists and arrays. It's valuable to learn how to use sequence expressions:

- They're a compact way of specifying interesting data and generative processes.

- They're used to specify database queries when using data-access layers such as Microsoft's Language Integrated Queries (LINQ). See Chapter 15 for examples of using sequence expressions this way.

- They're one particular use of *computation expressions*, a more general concept that has several uses in F# programming. Chapter 9 discusses computation expressions, and we show how to use them for asynchronous and parallel programming in Chapter 13.

Creating Sequence Expressions Using for

The simplest form of a sequence expression is seq { for value in expr .. expr -> expr }. Here, -> should be read "yield." This is a shorthand way of writing Seq.map over a range expression. For example, you can generate an enumeration of numbers and their squares as follows:

```
> let squares = seq { for i in 0 .. 10 -> (i,i*i) };;
val squares : seq<int * int>

> squares;;
val it : seq<int * int> = [ (0,0); (1,1); (2,4); (3,9); ... ]
```

The more complete form of this construct is seq { for pattern in seq -> expression }. The pattern allows you to decompose the values yielded by the input enumerable. For example, you can consume the elements of squares using the pattern (i,iSquared):

```
> seq { for (i,iSquared) in squares -> (i,iSquared,i*iSquared) };;
val it : seq<int * int * int> = [ (0,0,0); (1,1,1); (2,4,8); (3,9,27); ... ]
```

The input seq can be a seq<type> or any type supporting a GetEnumerator method. (The latter is supported because some important types from the .NET libraries support this method without directly supporting the seq interface.)

Enriching Sequence Expressions with Additional Logic

A sequence expression often begins with for ... in ..., but you can use additional constructs. For example:

- *A secondary iteration:* for pattern in seq do seq-expr

- *A filter:* if expression then seq-expr

- *A conditional:* if expression then seq-expr else seq-expr

- *A* let *binding:* let pattern = expression in seq-expr

Secondary iterations generate additional sequences, all of which are collected and concatenated together. Filters let you skip elements that don't satisfy a given predicate. To see both of these in action, the following computes a checkerboard set of coordinates for a rectangular grid:

```
let checkerboardCoordinates n =
    seq { for row in 1 .. n do
            for col in 1 .. n do
                if (row+col) % 2 = 0 then
                    yield (row,col) }
```

```
> checkerboardCoordinates 3;;
val it : seq<(int * int)> = seq [(1, 1); (1, 3); (2, 2); (3, 1); ...]
```

Using let clauses in sequence expressions allows you to compute intermediary results. For example, the following code gets the creation time and last-access time for each file in a directory:

```
let fileInfo dir =
    seq { for file in Directory.GetFiles dir do
            let creationTime = File.GetCreationTime file
            let lastAccessTime = File.GetLastAccessTime file
            yield (file,creationTime,lastAccessTime) }
```

In the previous examples, each step of the iteration produces zero or one result. The final yield of a sequence expression can also be another sequence, signified through the use of the yield! keyword. The following sample shows how to redefine the allFiles function from the previous section using a sequence expression. Note that multiple generators can be included in one sequence expression; the results are implicitly collated together using Seq.append:

```
let rec allFiles dir =
    seq { for file in Directory.GetFiles dir do
              yield file
          for subdir in Directory.GetDirectories dir do
              yield! allFiles subdir }
```

Generating Lists and Arrays Using Sequence Expressions

You can also use range and sequence expressions to build list and array values. The syntax is identical, except the surrounding braces are replaced by the usual [ ] for lists and [| |] for arrays (Chapter 4 discusses arrays in more detail):

```
> [ 1 .. 4 ];;
val it: int list = [ 1; 2; 3; 4 ]

> [ for i in 0 .. 3 -> (i,i*i) ];;
val it : (int * int) list = [ (0,0); (1,1); (2,4); (3,9) ]

> [| for i in 0 .. 3 -> (i,i*i) |];;
val it : (int * int) [] = [ (0,0); (1,1); (2,4); (3,9) ]
```

■ **Caution** F# lists and arrays are finite data structures built immediately rather than on demand, so you must take care that the length of the sequence is suitable. For example, [1I .. 1000000000I] attempts to build a list that is one billion elements long.

Exploring Some Simple Type Definitions

F# is a typed language, and you often need to declare new shapes of types via type definitions and type abbreviations. This chapter covers only some of the simpler type definitions that are useful and succinct workhorses for functional programming. F# also lets you define a range of sophisticated type definitions related to object-oriented programming, discussed in Chapter 6. However, these aren't often required in basic functional programming.

Defining Type Abbreviations

Type abbreviations are the simplest type definitions:

```
type index = int
type flags = int64
type results = string * TimeSpan * int * int
```

It's common to use lowercase names for type abbreviations, but it's certainly not compulsory. Type abbreviations can be generic:

```
type StringMap<'T> = Microsoft.FSharp.Collections.Map<string,'T>
type Projections<'T,'U> = ('T -> 'U) * ('U -> 'T)
```

Type abbreviations aren't concrete, because they simply alias an existing type. They're expanded during the process of compiling F# code to the format shared between multiple .NET languages. The difference can, for example, be detected by other .NET languages; because of this, a number of restrictions apply to type abbreviations. For example, you can't augment them with additional members, as can be done for concrete types such as records, discriminated unions, and classes. In addition, you can't truly hide a type abbreviation using a signature (see Chapter 7).

Defining Records

The simplest concrete type definitions are records. Here's an example:

```
type Person =
    { Name: string;
      DateOfBirth: System.DateTime; }
```

You can construct record values by using the record labels:

```
> { Name = "Bill"; DateOfBirth = new System.DateTime(1962,09,02) };;
val it : Person = { Name="Bill"; DateOfBirth = 09/02/1962 }
```

Should there be a conflict between labels among multiple records, you can also construct record values by using an explicit type annotation:

```
> ({ Name = "Anna"; DateOfBirth = new System.DateTime(1968,07,23) } : Person);;
val it : Person = { Name="Anna"; DateOfBirth = 23/07/1968 }
```

Record values are often used to return results from functions:

```
type PageStats =
    { Site: string;
      Time: System.TimeSpan;
      Length: int;
      NumWords: int;
      NumHRefs: int }
```

This technique works well when returning a large number of heterogeneous results:

```
let stats site =
    let url = "http://" + site
    let html,t = time (fun () -> http url)
    let hwords = html |> getWords
    let hrefs = hWords |> List.filter (fun s -> s = "href")
    { Site=site; Time=t; Length=html.Length;
      NumWords=hwords.Length; NumHRefs=hrefs.Length }
```

Here is the type of stats:

```
val stats  : string -> PageStats
```

Here is how F# Interactive shows the results of applying the function:

```
> stats "www.live.com";;
val it : PageStats = { Site="www.live.com"; Time=0.872623628;
                       Length=7728, NumWords=1156; NumHRefs=10; }
```

Handling Non-Unique Record Field Names

Record labels need not be unique among multiple record types. Here is an example:

```
type Person =
    { Name: string;
      DateOfBirth: System.DateTime; }

type Company =
    { Name: string;
      Address: string; }
```

When record names are non-unique, constructions of record values may need to use object expressions in order to indicate the name of the record type, thus disambiguating the construction. For example, consider the following type definitions:

```
type Dot = { X: int; Y: int }
type Point = { X: float; Y: float }
```

On lookup, record labels are accessed using the dot (.) notation in the same way as properties. One slight difference is that in the absence of further qualifying information, the type of the object being accessed is inferred from the record label. This is based on the latest set of record labels in scope from record definitions and uses of open. For example, given the previous definitions, you have the following:

```
> let coords1 (p:Point) = (p.X,p.Y);;
val coords1 : Point -> float * float

> let coords2 (d:Dot) = (d.X,d.Y);;
val coords2 : Dot -> int * int

> let dist p = sqrt (p.X * p.X + p.Y * p.Y);; // use of X and Y implies type "Point"
val dist : Point -> float
```

The accesses to the labels X and Y in the first two definitions have been resolved using the type information provided by the type annotations. The accesses in the third definition have been resolved using the default interpretation of record field labels in the absence of any other qualifying information.

Cloning Records

Records support a convenient syntax to clone all the values in the record, creating a new value with some values replaced. Here is a simple example:

```
type Point3D = { X: float; Y: float; Z: float }
let p1 = { X=3.0; Y=4.0; Z=5.0 }
```

```
> let p2 = { p1 with Y=0.0; Z=0.0 };;
val p2 : Point3D
```

The definition of p2 is identical to this:

```
let p2 = { X=p1.X; Y=0.0; Z=0.0 }
```

This expression form doesn't mutate the values of a record, even if the fields of the original record are mutable.

Defining Discriminated Unions

The second kind of concrete type definition discussed in this section is a discriminated union. Here is a very simple example:

```
type Route = int
type Make = string
type Model = string
type Transport =
    | Car of Make * Model
    | Bicycle
    | Bus of Route
```

Each alternative of a discriminated union is called a *discriminator*. You can build values by using the discriminator much as if it were a function:

```
> let nick = Car("BMW","360");;
val nick : Transport

> let don = [ Bicycle; Bus 8 ];;
val don  : Transport list

> let james = [ Car ("Ford","Fiesta"); Bicycle ];;
val james  : Transport list
```

You can also use discriminators in pattern matching:

```
let averageSpeed (tr: Transport) =
    match tr with
    | Car _ -> 35
```

```
    | Bicycle -> 16
    | Bus _ -> 24
```

Several of the types you've already met are defined as discriminated unions. For example, the 'T option type is defined as follows:

```
type 'T option =
    | None
    | Some of 'T
```

Discriminated unions can include recursive references (the same is true of records and other type definitions). This is frequently used when representing structured languages via discriminated unions, a topic covered in depth in Chapter 9:

```
type Proposition =
    | True
    | And of Proposition * Proposition
    | Or of Proposition * Proposition
    | Not of Proposition
```

Recursive functions can be used to traverse such a type. For example:

```
let rec eval (p: Proposition) =
    match p with
    | True -> true
    | And(p1,p2) -> eval p1 && eval p2
    | Or (p1,p2) -> eval p1 || eval p2
    | Not(p1) -> not (eval p1)
```

The F# type of immutable lists is defined in this way:

```
type 'T list =
    | ([])
    | (::) of 'T * 'T list
```

A broad range of tree-like data structures are conveniently represented as discriminated unions. For example:

```
type Tree<'T> =
    | Tree of 'T * Tree<'T> * Tree<'T>
    | Tip of 'T
```

You can use recursive functions to compute properties of trees:

```
let rec size tree =
    match tree with
    | Tree(_,l,r) -> 1 + size l + size r
    | Tip _ -> 1
```

Here is the inferred type of size:

```
val size : Tree<'T> -> int
```

Here is an example of a constructed tree term and the use of the `size` function:

```
> let small = Tree("1",Tree("2",Tip("a"),Tip("b")),Tip("c"));;
val small : Tree<string>

> small;;
val it : Tree<string> = Tree ("1",Tree ("2",Tip("a"),Tip("b")),Tip("c"))

> size small;;
val it : int = 5
```

Chapters 8, 9, and 12 discuss symbolic manipulation based on trees.

■ **Note** Discriminated unions are a powerful and important construct and are useful when modeling a finite, sealed set of choices. This makes them a perfect fit for many constructs that arise in applications and symbolic analysis libraries. They are, by design, nonextensible: subsequent modules can't add new cases to a discriminated union. This is deliberate: you get strong and useful guarantees by placing a limit on the range of possible values for a type. Extensible types can be defined through the use of records of functions and object interface types, discussed in Chapters 5 and 6.

Using Discriminated Unions as Records

Discriminated union types with only one data tag are an effective way to implement record-like types:

```
type Point3D = Vector3D of float * float * float
let origin = Vector3D(0.,0.,0.)
let unitX  = Vector3D(1.,0.,0.)
let unitY  = Vector3D(0.,1.,0.)
let unitZ  = Vector3D(0.,0.,1.)
```

These are particularly effective because they can be decomposed using succinct patterns in the same way as tuple arguments:

```
let length (Vector3D(dx,dy,dz)) = sqrt(dx*dx+dy*dy+dz*dz)
```

This technique is most useful for record-like values where there is some natural order on the constituent elements of the value (as shown earlier) or where the elements have different types.

Defining Multiple Types Simultaneously

Multiple types can be declared together to give a mutually recursive collection of types, including record types, discriminated unions, and abbreviations. The type definitions must be separated by the keyword and:

```
type Node =
    { Name : string;
      Links : Link list }
and Link =
    | Dangling
    | Link of Node
```

Summary

F# is a multiparadigm language, and this chapter looked at the core language constructs used for functional programming. The next chapter explores how to use F# for imperative programming: how to use mutable state, raise and handle exceptions, and perform I/O.

CHAPTER 4

■■■

Introducing Imperative Programming

In Chapter 3, you saw some of the simple but powerful data types and language constructs that make up F# functional programming. The functional programming paradigm is strongly associated with "programming without side effects," called pure functional programming. In this paradigm, programs compute the result of a mathematical expression and don't cause any side effects, except perhaps reporting the result of the computation. The formulas used in spreadsheets are often pure, as is the core of functional programming languages such as Haskell. F# isn't, however, a pure functional language. For example, you can write programs that mutate data, perform I/O communications, start threads, and raise exceptions. Furthermore, the F# type system doesn't enforce a strict distinction between expressions that perform these actions and expressions that don't.

Programming with side effects is called imperative programming. This chapter looks more closely at a number of constructs related to imperative programming. It describes how to use loops, mutable data, arrays, and some common input/output techniques.

If your primary programming experience has been with an imperative language such as C, C#, or Java, you may initially find yourself using imperative constructs fairly frequently in F#. However, over time, F# programmers generally learn how to perform many routine programming tasks within the side-effect-free subset of the language. F# programmers tend to use side effects in the following situations:

- When scripting and prototyping using F# Interactive

- When working with .NET library components that use side effects heavily, such as GUI libraries and I/O libraries

- When initializing complex data structures

- When using inherently imperative, efficient data structures such as hash tables and hash sets

- When locally optimizing routines in a way that improves the performance of the functional version of the routine

When working with very large data structures or in scenarios where the allocation of data structures must be minimized for performance reasons

Some F# programmers don't use any imperative techniques except as part of the external wrapper for their programs. Adopting this form of pure functional programming for a time is an excellent way to hone your functional programming techniques.

■ **Tip** Programming with fewer side effects is attractive for many reasons. For example, eliminating unnecessary side effects nearly always reduces the complexity of your code, so it leads to fewer bugs. Another thing experienced functional programmers appreciate is that the programmer or compiler can easily adjust the order in which expressions are computed. A lack of side effects also helps you reason about your code: it's easier to visually check when two programs are equivalent, and it's easier to make radical adjustments to your code without introducing new, subtle bugs. Programs that are free from side effects can often be computed on demand as necessary, often by making very small, local changes to your code to introduce the use of delayed data structures. Finally, side effects such as mutation are difficult to use when data is accessed concurrently from multiple threads, as you see in Chapter 13.

Imperative Looping and Iterating

Three looping constructs are available to help simplify writing iterative code with side effects:

- Simple for loops: `for var = start-expr to end-expr do expr`
- Simple while loops: `while expr do expr`
- Sequence loops: `for pattern in expr do expr`

All three constructs are for writing imperative programs, indicated partly by the fact that in all cases the body of the loop must have a return type of unit. Note that unit is the F# type that corresponds to void in imperative languages such as C, and it has the single value (). The following sections cover these three constructs in more detail.

Simple for Loops

Simple for loops are the most efficient way to iterate over integer ranges. This is illustrated here by a replacement implementation of the repeatFetch function from Chapter 2:

```
let repeatFetch url n =
    for i = 1 to n do
        let html = http url
        printf "fetched <<< %s >>>\n" html
    printf "Done!\n"
```

This loop is executed for successive values of i over the given range, including both start and end indexes.

Simple while Loops

The second looping construct is a while loop, which repeats until a given guard is false. For example, here is a way to keep your computer busy until the weekend:

```
open System

let loopUntilSaturday() =
    while (DateTime.Now.DayOfWeek <> DayOfWeek.Saturday) do
        printf "Still working!\n"

    printf "Saturday at last!\n"
```

When executing this code in F# Interactive, you can interrupt its execution by using Ctrl+C.

More Iteration Loops over Sequences

As discussed in Chapter 3, any values compatible with the type seq<type> can be iterated using the for pattern in seq do ... construct. The input seq may be an F# list value, any seq<type>, or a value of any type supporting a GetEnumerator method. Here are some simple examples:

```
> for (b,pj) in [ ("Banana 1",true); ("Banana 2",false) ] do
      if pj then printfn "%s is in pyjamas today!" b;;
Banana 1 is in pyjamas today!
```

The following example iterates the results of a regular expression match. The type returned by the .NET method System.Text.RegularExpressions.Regex.Matches is a MatchCollection, which for reasons known best to the .NET designers doesn't directly support the seq<Match> interface. It does, however, support a GetEnumerator method that permits iteration over the individual results of the operation, each of which is of type Match; the F# compiler inserts the conversions necessary to view the collection as a seq<Match> and perform the iteration. You learn more about using the .NET Regular Expression library in Chapter 10:

```
> open System.Text.RegularExpressions;;
> for m in (Regex.Matches("All the Pretty Horses","[a-zA-Z]+")) do
      printf "res = %s\n" m.Value;;
res = All
res = the
res = Pretty
res = Horses
```

Using Mutable Records

The simplest mutable data structures in F# are mutable records. In Chapter 3, you saw some simple examples of immutable records. A record is mutable if one or more of its fields is labeled mutable. This means record fields can be updated using the <- operator: that is, the same syntax used to set a property. Mutable fields are generally used for records that implement the internal state of objects, discussed in Chapters 6 and 7.

For example, the following code defines a record used to count the number of times an event occurs and the number of times the event satisfies a particular criterion:

```
type DiscreteEventCounter =
    { mutable Total: int;
      mutable Positive: int;
      Name : string }

let recordEvent (s: DiscreteEventCounter) isPositive =
    s.Total <- s.Total+1
    if isPositive then s.Positive <- s.Positive+1

let reportStatus (s: DiscreteEventCounter) =
    printfn "We have %d %s out of %d" s.Positive s.Name s.Total

let newCounter nm =
    { Total = 0;
      Positive = 0;
      Name = nm }
```

You can use this type as follows (this example uses the http function from Chapter 2):

```
let longPageCounter = newCounter "long page(s)"

let fetch url =
    let page = http url
    recordEvent longPageCounter (page.Length > 10000)
    page
```

Every call to the function fetch mutates the mutable record fields in the global variable longPageCounter. For example:

```
> fetch "http://www.smh.com.au" |> ignore;;
val it : unit = ()

> fetch "http://www.theage.com.au"  |> ignore;;
val it : unit = ()

> reportStatus longPageCounter;;
We have 1 long page(s) out of 2
val it : unit = ()
```

Record types can also support members (for example, properties and methods) and give implicit implementations of interfaces, discussed in Chapter 6. Practically speaking, this means you can use them as one way to implement object-oriented abstractions.

Mutable Reference Cells

One particularly useful mutable record is the general-purpose type of mutable reference cells, or ref cells for short. These often play much the same role as pointers in other imperative programming languages. You can see how to use mutable reference cells in the following example:

```
> let cell1 = ref 1;;
val cell1 : int ref = {contents = 1;}

> !cell1;;
val it : int = 1

> cell1 := 3;;
val it : unit = ()

> cell1;;
val it : int ref = {contents = 3;}

> !cell1;;
val it : int = 3
```

The key type is 'T ref, and its main operators are ref, !, and :=. The types of these operators are as follows:

```
val ref  : 'T -> 'T ref
val (:=) : 'T ref -> 'T -> unit
val (!)  : 'T ref -> 'T
```

These allocate a reference cell, mutate the cell, and read the cell, respectively. The operation cell1 := 3 is the key one; after this operation, the value returned by evaluating the expression !cell1 is changed. You can also use either the contents field or the Value property to access the value of a reference cell.

Both the 'T ref type and its operations are defined in the F# library as simple record data structures with a single mutable field:

```
type 'T ref = { mutable contents: 'T }
let (!) r = r.contents
let (:=) r v = r.contents <- v
let ref v = { contents = v }
```

The type 'T ref is a synonym for a type Microsoft.FSharp.Core.Ref<'T> defined in this way.

Which Data Structures Are Mutable?

It's useful to know which data structures are mutable and which aren't. If a data structure can be mutated, then this is typically evident in the types of operations you can perform on that structure. For example, if a data structure Table<'Key,'Value> has an operation like the following, then in practice you can be sure that updates to the data structure modify the data structure itself:

```
val add : Table<'Key,'Value> -> 'Key -> 'Value -> unit
```

That is, the updates to the data structure are destructive, and no value is returned from the operation; the result is the type unit, which is akin to void in C and many other languages. Likewise, the following member indicates the data structure is almost certainly mutable:

```
member Add : 'Key * 'Value -> unit
```

In both cases, the presence of unit as a return type is a sure sign that an operation performs some side effects. In contrast, operations on immutable data structures typically return a new instance of the data structure when an operation such as add is performed. For example:

```
val add : 'Key -> 'Value -> Table<'Key,'Value> -> Table<'Key,'Value>
```

Or for example:

```
member Add : 'Key * 'Value -> Table<'Key,'Value>
```

As discussed in Chapter 3, immutable data structures are also called functional or persistent. The latter name is used because the original table isn't modified when adding an element. Well-crafted persistent data structures don't duplicate the actual memory used to store the data structure every time an addition is made; instead, internal nodes can be shared between the old and new data structures. Example persistent data structures in the F# library are F# lists, options, tuples, and the types Microsoft.FSharp. Collections.Map<'Key,'Value> and Microsoft.FSharp.Collections.Set<'Key>. Most data structures in the .NET libraries aren't persistent, although if you're careful, you can use them as persistent data structures by accessing them in read-only mode and copying them where necessary.

Avoiding Aliasing

Like all mutable data structures, two mutable record values or two values of type 'T ref may refer to the same reference cell—this is called aliasing. Aliasing of immutable data structures isn't a problem; no client consuming or inspecting the data values can detect that the values have been aliased. However, aliasing of mutable data can lead to problems in understanding code. In general, it's good practice to ensure that no two values currently in scope directly alias the same mutable data structures. The following example continues from earlier and shows how an update to cell1 can affect the value returned by !cell2:

```
> let cell2 = cell1;;
val cell2 : int ref = {contents = 3;}

> !cell2;;
val it : int = 3

> cell1 := 7;;
val it : unit = ()

> !cell2;;
val it : int 7
```

Hiding Mutable Data

Mutable data is often hidden behind an encapsulation boundary. Chapter 7 looks at encapsulation in more detail, but one easy way to do this is to make data private to a function. For example, the following shows how to hide a mutable reference within the inner closure of values referenced by a function value:

```
let generateStamp =
    let count = ref 0
    (fun () -> count := !count + 1; !count)
```

```
val generateStamp: unit -> int
```

The line `let count = ref 0` is executed once, when the `generateStamp` function is defined. Here is an example of the use of this function:

```
> generateStamp();;
val it : int = 1

> generateStamp();;
val it : int = 2
```

This is a powerful technique for hiding and encapsulating mutable state without resorting to writing new type and class definitions. It's good programming practice in polished code to ensure that all related items of mutable state are collected under some named data structure or other entity such as a function.

Understanding Mutation and Identity

F# encourages the use of objects whose logical identity (if any) is based purely on the characteristics (for example, fields and properties) of the object. For example, the identity of a pair of integers (1,2) is determined by the two integers themselves; two tuple values both containing these two integers are for practical purposes identical. This is because tuples are immutable and support structural equality, hashing, and comparison, discussed further in Chapters 5 and 8.

Mutable reference cells are different; they can reveal their identities through aliasing and mutation. However, not all mutable values necessarily reveal their identity through mutation. For example, sometimes mutation is used just to bootstrap a value into its initial configuration, such as when connecting the nodes of a graph. These are relatively benign uses of mutation.

Ultimately, you can detect whether two mutable values are the same object by using the function `System.Object.ReferenceEquals`. You can also use this function on immutable values to detect whether two values are represented by the physically same value. But in this circumstance, the results returned by the function may change according to the optimization settings you apply to your F# code.

Using Mutable Locals

You saw in the previous section that mutable references must be explicitly dereferenced. F# also supports mutable locals that are implicitly dereferenced. These must either be top-level definitions or be local variables in a function:

```
> let mutable cell1 = 1;;
val mutable cell1 : int = 1

> cell1;;
val it : int = 1

> cell1 <- 3;;
val it : unit = ()

> cell1;;
val it : int = 3
```

The following shows how to use a mutable local:

```
let sum n m =
    let mutable res = 0
    for i = n to m do
        res <- res + i
    res
```

```
> sum 3 6;;
val it : int = 18
```

F# places strong restrictions on the use of mutable locals. In particular, unlike mutable references, mutable locals are guaranteed to be stack-allocated values, which is important in some situations because the .NET garbage collector won't move stack values. As a result, mutable locals may not be used in any inner lambda expressions or other closure constructs, with the exception of top-level mutable values, which can be used anywhere, and mutable fields of records and objects, which are associated with the heap allocated objects themselves. You learn more about mutable object types in Chapter 6. Reference cells and types containing mutable fields can be used instead to make the existence of heap-allocated imperative state obvious.

Working with Arrays

Mutable arrays are a key data structure used as a building block in many high-performance computing scenarios. The following example illustrates how to use a one-dimensional array of double values:

```
> let arr = [| 1.0; 1.0; 1.0 |];;
val arr : float[]

> arr.[1];;
val it : float = 1.0

> arr.[1] <- 3.0;;
val it : unit = ()

> arr;;
val it : float[] = [| 1.0; 3.0; 1.0 |]
```

F# array values are usually manipulated using functions from the Array module; its full path is
Microsoft.FSharp.Collections.Array, but you can access it with the short name Array. Arrays are created
either by using the creation functions in that module (such as Array.init, Array.create, and
Array.zeroCreate) or by using sequence expressions, as discussed in Chapter 3. Some useful methods are
also contained in the System.Array class. Table 4-1 shows some common functions from the Array module.

Table 4-1. Some Important Functions and Aggregate Operators from the Array Module

Operator	Type	Explanation
Array.append	: 'T[] -> 'T[] -> 'T[]	Returns a new array containing elements of the first array followed by elements of the second array
Array.sub	: 'T[] -> int -> int -> 'T[]	Returns a new array containing a portion of elements of the input array
Array.copy	: 'T[] -> 'T[]	Returns a copy of the input array
Array.iter	: ('T -> unit) -> 'T[] -> unit	Applies a function to all elements of the input array
Array.filter	: ('T -> bool) -> 'T[] -> 'T[]	Returns a new array containing a selection of elements of the input array
Array.length	: 'T[] -> int	Returns the length of the input array
Array.map	: ('T -> 'U) -> 'T[] -> 'U[]	Returns a new array containing the results of applying the function to each element of the input array
Array.fold	: ('T -> 'U -> 'T) -> 'T -> 'U[] -> 'T	Accumulates left to right over the input array
Array.foldBack	: ('T -> 'U -> 'U) -> 'T[] -> 'U -> 'U	Accumulates right to left over the input array

F# arrays can be very large, up to the memory limitations of the machine (a 3GB limit applies on 32-bit systems). For example, the following creates an array of 100 million elements (of total size approximately 400MB for a 32-bit machine):

```
> let (r : int[]) = Array.zeroCreate 100000000;;
val r : int [] = ...
```

The following attempt to create an array more than 4GB in size causes an OutOfMemoryException on one of our machines:

```
> let (r : int[]) = Array.zeroCreate 1000000000;;
System.OutOfMemoryException: Exception of type 'System.OutOfMemoryException'
was thrown.
```

■ **Note** Arrays of value types (such as int, single, double, int64) are stored flat, so only one object is allocated for the entire array. Arrays of other types are stored as an array of object references. Primitive types such as integers and floating-point numbers are all value types; many other .NET types are also value types. The .NET documentation indicates whether each type is a value type or not. Often, the word struct is used for value types. You can also define new struct types directly in F# code, as discussed in Chapter 6. All other types in F# are reference types, such as all record, tuple, discriminated union, and class and interface values.

Generating and Slicing Arrays

In Chapter 3, you saw in passing that you can use sequence expressions as a way to generate interesting array values. For example:

```
> let arr = [| for i in 0 .. 5 -> (i,i*i) |];;
val arr : (int * int) [] =
  [|(0, 0); (1, 1); (2, 4); (3, 9); (4, 16); (5, 25)|]
```

You can also use a convenient syntax for extracting subarrays from existing arrays; this is called slice notation. A slice expression for a single-dimensional array has the form arr.[start..finish], where one of start and finish may optionally be omitted, and index zero or the index of the last element of the array is assumed instead. For example:

```
> let arr = [| for i in 0 .. 5 -> (i,i*i) |];;
val arr : (int * int) [] =
  [|(0, 0); (1, 1); (2, 4); (3, 9); (4, 16); (5, 25)|]

> arr.[1..3];;
val it : (int * int) [] = [| (1, 1); (2, 4); (3, 9); |]

> arr.[..2];;
val it : (int * int) [] = [| (0, 0); (1, 1); (2, 4); |]

> arr.[3..];;
val it : (int * int) [] = [| (3, 9); (4, 16); (5, 25) |]
```

Slicing syntax is used extensively in the example "Verifying Circuits with Propositional Logic" in Chapter 12. You can also use slicing syntax with strings and several other F# types such as vectors and matrices, and the operator can be overloaded to work with your own type definitions. The F# library definitions of vectors and matrices can be used as a guide.

■ **Note** Slices on arrays generate fresh arrays. Sometimes it's more efficient to use other techniques, such as accessing the array via an accessor function or object that performs one or more internal index adjustments before looking up the underlying array. If you add support for the slicing operators to your own types, you can choose whether they return copies of data structures or an accessor object.

Two-Dimensional Arrays

Like other .NET languages, F# directly supports two-dimensional array values that are stored flat: that is, where an array of dimensions (N, M) is stored using a contiguous array of N * M elements. The types for these values are written using [,], such as in int[,] and double[,], and these types also support slicing syntax. Values of these types are created and manipulated using the values in the Array2D module. Likewise, there is a module for manipulating three-dimensional array values whose types are written int[,,]. You can also use the code in those modules as a template for defining code to manipulate arrays of higher dimension.

Introducing the Imperative .NET Collections

The .NET Framework comes equipped with an excellent set of imperative collections under the namespace System.Collections.Generic. You've seen some of these already. The following sections look at some simple uses of these collections.

Using Resizeable Arrays

As mentioned in Chapter 3, the .NET Framework comes with a type `System.Collections.Generic.List<'T>`, which, although named `List`, is better described as a resizeable array. The F# library includes the following type abbreviation for this purpose:

```
type ResizeArray<'T> = System.Collections.Generic.List<'T>
```

Here is a simple example of using this data structure:

```
> let names = new ResizeArray<string>();;
val names : ResizeArray<string>

> for name in ["Claire"; "Sophie"; "Jane"] do
      names.Add(name);;
val it : unit = ()

> names.Count;;
val it : int = 3

> names.[0];;
val it : string = "Claire"

> names.[1];;
val it : string = "Sophie"

> names.[2];;
val it : string = "Jane"
```

Resizable arrays use an underlying array for storage and support constant-time random-access lookup. In many situations, this makes a resizable array more efficient than an F# list, which supports efficient access only from the head (left) of the list. You can find the full set of members supported by this type in the .NET documentation. Commonly used properties and members include `Add`, `Count`, `ConvertAll`, `Insert`, `BinarySearch`, and `ToArray`. A module `ResizeArray` is included in the F# library; it provides operations over this type in the style of the other F# collections.

Like other .NET collections, values of type `ResizeArray<'T>` support the `seq<'T>` interface. There is also an overload of the `new` constructor for this collection type that lets you specify initial values via a `seq<'T>`. This means you can create and consume instances of this collection type using sequence expressions:

```
> let squares = new ResizeArray<int>(seq { for i in 0 .. 100 -> i*i });;
val squares : ResizeArray<int>

> for x in squares do
      printfn "square: %d" x;;
square: 0
square: 1
square: 4
square: 9
...
```

Using Dictionaries

The type System.Collections.Generic.Dictionary<'Key,'Value> is an efficient hash-table structure that is excellent for storing associations between values. The use of this collection from F# code requires a little care, because it must be able to correctly hash the key type. For simple key types such as integers, strings, and tuples, the default hashing behavior is adequate. Here is a simple example:

```
> open System.Collections.Generic;;

> let capitals = new Dictionary<string, string>(HashIdentity.Structural);;
val capitals : Dictionary<string,string> = dict []

> capitals.["USA"] <- "Washington";;
val it : unit = ()

> capitals.["Bangladesh"] <- "Dhaka";;
val it : unit = ()

> capitals.ContainsKey("USA");;
val it : bool = true

> capitals.ContainsKey("Australia");;
val it : bool = false

> capitals.Keys;;
val it : KeyCollection<string,string> = seq["USA"; "Bangladesh"]

> capitals.["USA"];;
val it : string = "Washington"
```

Dictionaries are compatible with the type seq<KeyValuePair<'key,'value>>, where KeyValuePair is a type from the System.Collections.Generic namespace and simply supports the properties Key and Value. Armed with this knowledge, you can use iteration to perform an operation for each element of the collection:

```
> for kvp in capitals do
      printf "%s has capital %s\n" kvp.Key kvp.Value;;
USA has capital Washington
Bangladesh has capital Dhaka
val it : unit = ()
```

Using Dictionary's TryGetValue

The Dictionary method TryGetValue is of special interest because its use from F# is a little nonstandard. This method takes an input value of type 'Key and looks it up in the table. It returns a bool indicating whether the lookup succeeded: true if the given key is in the dictionary and false otherwise. The value itself is returned via a .NET idiom called an out parameter. From F# code, three ways of using .NET methods rely on out parameters:

- You may use a local mutable in combination with the address-of operator &.

- You may use a reference cell.

- You may simply not give a parameter, and the result is returned as part of a tuple.

Here's how you do it using a mutable local:

```
open System.Collections.Generic

let lookupName nm (dict : Dictionary<string,string>) =
    let mutable res = ""
    let foundIt = dict.TryGetValue(nm, &res)
    if foundIt then res
    else failwithf "Didn't find %s" nm
```

The use of a reference cell can be cleaner. For example:

```
> let res = ref "";;
val res: string ref = {contents = "";}

> capitals.TryGetValue("Australia", res);;
val it: bool = false

> capitals.TryGetValue("USA", res);;
val it: bool = true

> res;;
val it: string ref = {contents = "Washington"}
```

Finally, here is the technique where you don't pass the final parameter, and instead the result is returned as part of a tuple:

```
> capitals.TryGetValue("Australia");;
val it: bool * string = (false, null)

> capitals.TryGetValue("USA");;
val it: bool * string = (true, "Washington")
```

Note that the value returned in the second element of the tuple may be null if the lookup fails when this technique is used. null values are discussed in the section "Working with null Values" at the end of this chapter.

Using Dictionaries with Compound Keys

You can use dictionaries with compound keys such as tuple keys of type (int * int). If necessary, you can specify the hash function used for these values when creating the instance of the dictionary. The default is to use generic hashing, also called structural hashing, a topic covered in more detail in Chapter 8. If you want to indicate this explicitly, you do so by specifying Microsoft.FSharp.Collections.

HashIdentity.Structural when creating the collection instance. In some cases, this can also lead to performance improvements, because the F# compiler often generates a hashing function appropriate for the compound type.

Here is an example that uses a dictionary with a compound key type to represent sparse maps:

```
> open System.Collections.Generic;;
> open Microsoft.FSharp.Collections;;

> let sparseMap = new Dictionary<(int * int), float>();;
val sparseMap : Dictionary <(int * int),float> = dict []

> sparseMap.[(0,2)] <- 4.0;;
val it : unit = ()

> sparseMap.[(1021,1847)] <- 9.0;;
val it : unit = ()

> sparseMap.Keys;;
val it : Dictionary.KeyCollection<(int * int),float>  = seq [(0,2); (1021; 1847)]
```

Some Other Mutable Data Structures

Some of the other important mutable data structures in the F# and .NET libraries are as follows:

- System.Collections.Generic.SortedList<'Key,'Value>: A collection of sorted values. Searches are done by a binary search. The underlying data structure is a single array.

- System.Collections.Generic.SortedDictionary<'Key,'Value>: A collection of key/value pairs sorted by the key, rather than hashed. Searches are done by a binary chop. The underlying data structure is a single array.

- System.Collections.Generic.Stack<'T>: A variable-sized last-in/first-out (LIFO) collection.

- System.Collections.Generic.Queue<'T>: A variable-sized first-in/first-out (FIFO) collection.

- System.Text.StringBuilder: A mutable structure for building string values.

- Microsoft.FSharp.Collections.HashSet<'Key>: A hash table structure holding only keys and no values. From .NET 3.5, a HashSet<'T> type is available in the System.Collections.Generic namespace.

Exceptions and Controlling Them

When a routine encounters a problem, it may respond in several ways, such as by recovering internally, emitting a warning, returning a marker value or incomplete result, or throwing an exception. The following code indicates how an exception can be thrown by some of the code you've been using:

```
> let req = System.Net.WebRequest.Create("not a URL");;
System.UriFormatException: Invalid URI: The format of the URI could not be
determined.
```

Similarly, the GetResponse method also used in the http function may raise a System.Net.WebException exception. The exceptions that may be raised by routines are typically recorded in the documentation for those routines. Exception values may also be raised explicitly by F# code:

```
> (raise (System.InvalidOperationException("not today thank you")) : unit);;
System.InvalidOperationException: not today thank you
```

In F#, exceptions are commonly raised using the F# failwith function:

```
> if false then 3 else failwith "hit the wall";;
System.Exception: hit the wall
```

The types of some of the common functions used to raise exceptions are shown here:

```
val failwith  : string -> 'T
val raise : System.Exception -> 'T
val failwithf  : StringFormat<'T,'U> -> 'T
val invalidArg  : string -> string -> 'T
```

Note that the return types of all these are generic type variables: the functions never return normally and instead return by raising an exception. This means they can be used to form an expression of any particular type and can be handy when you're drafting your code. For example, in the following example, we've left part of the program incomplete:

```
if (System.DateTime.Now > failwith "not yet decided") then
    printfn "you've run out of time!"
```

Table 4-2 shows some of the common exceptions that are raised by failwith and other operations.

Table 4-2. Common Categories of Exceptions and F# Functions That Raise Them

Exception Type	F# Abbreviation	Description	Example
Exception	Failure	General failure	failwith "fail"
ArgumentException	InvalidArgument	Bad input	invalidArg "x" "y"
DivideByZeroException		Integer divide by 0	1 / 0
NullReferenceException		Unexpected null	(null : string).Length

Catching Exceptions

You can catch exceptions using the try ... with ... language construct and :? type-test patterns, which filter any exception value caught by the with clause. For example:

```
> try
      raise (System.InvalidOperationException ("it's just not my day"))
  with
      | :? System.InvalidOperationException -> printfn "caught!";;
caught!
```

Chapter 5 covers these patterns more closely. The following code sample shows how to use try ... with ... to catch two kinds of exceptions that may arise from the operations that make up the http method, in both cases returning the empty string "" as the incomplete result. Note that try ... with ... is just an expression, and it may return a result in both branches:

```
open System.IO

let http(url: string) =
    try
        let req = System.Net.WebRequest.Create(url)
        let resp = req.GetResponse()
        let stream = resp.GetResponseStream()
        let reader = new StreamReader(stream)
        let html = reader.ReadToEnd()
        html
    with
        | :? System.UriFormatException -> ""
        | :? System.Net.WebException -> ""
```

When an exception is thrown, a value is created that records information about the exception. This value is matched against the earlier type-test patterns. It may also be bound directly and manipulated in the with clause of the try ... with constructs. For example, all exception values support the Message property:

```
> try
      raise (new System.InvalidOperationException ("invalid operation"))
  with
      | err -> printfn "oops, msg = '%s'" err.Message;;
oops, msg = 'invalid operation'
```

Using try ... finally

Exceptions may also be processed using the try ... finally ... construct. This guarantees to run the finally clause both when an exception is thrown and when the expression evaluates normally. This allows you to ensure that resources are disposed after the completion of an operation. For example, you can ensure that the web response from the previous example is closed as follows:

```
let httpViaTryFinally(url: string) =
    let req = System.Net.WebRequest.Create(url)
    let resp = req.GetResponse()
    try
        let stream = resp.GetResponseStream()
        let reader = new StreamReader(stream)
        let html = reader.ReadToEnd()
        html
    finally
        resp.Close()
```

In practice, you can use a shorter form to close and dispose of resources, simply by using a use binding instead of a let binding. This closes the response at the end of the scope of the resp variable, a technique that is discussed in full in Chapter 8. Here is how the previous function looks using this form:

```
let httpViaUseBinding(url: string) =
    let req = System.Net.WebRequest.Create(url)
    use resp = req.GetResponse()
    let stream = resp.GetResponseStream()
    let reader = new StreamReader(stream)
    let html = reader.ReadToEnd()
    html
```

Defining New Exception Types

F# lets you define new kinds of exception objects that carry data in a conveniently accessible form. For example, here is a declaration of a new class of exceptions and a function that wraps http with a filter that catches particular cases:

```
exception BlockedURL of string

let http2 url =
    if url = "http://www.kaos.org"
    then raise(BlockedURL(url))
    else http url
```

You can extract the information from F# exception values, again using pattern matching:

```
> try
      raise(BlockedURL("http://www.kaos.org"))
  with
      | BlockedURL(url) -> printf "blocked! url = '%s'\n" url;;
blocked! url = 'http://www.kaos.org'
```

Exception values are always subtypes of the F# type exn, an abbreviation for the .NET type System.Exception. The declaration exception BlockedURL of string is shorthand for defining a new F# class type BlockedURLException, which is a subtype of System.Exception. Exception types can also be defined explicitly by defining new object types. Chapters 5 and 6 look more closely at object types and subtyping.

Table 4-3 summarizes the exception-related language and library constructs.

Table 4-3. *Exception-Related Language and Library Constructs*

Example Code	Kind	Notes
`raise expr`	F# library function	Raises the given exception
`failwith expr`	F# library function	Raises an Exception exception
`try expr with rules`	F# expression	Catches expressions matching the pattern rules
`try expr finally expr`	F# expression	Executes the finally expression both when the computation is successful and when an exception is raised
`| :? ArgumentException ->`	F# pattern rule	A rule matching the given .NET exception type
`| :? ArgumentException as e ->`	F# pattern rule	A rule matching the given .NET exception type and naming it as its stronger type
`| Failure(msg) -> expr`	F# pattern rule	A rule matching the given data-carrying F# exception
`| exn -> expr`	F# pattern rule	A rule matching any exception, binding the name exn to the exception object value
`| exn when expr -> expr`	F# pattern rule	A rule matching the exception under the given condition, binding the name exn to the exception object value

Having an Effect: Basic I/O

Imperative programming and input/output are closely related topics. The following sections show some very simple I/O techniques using F# and .NET libraries.

Very Simple I/O: Reading and Writing Files

The .NET types System.IO.File and System.IO.Directory contain a number of simple functions to make working with files easy. For example, here's a way to output lines of text to a file:

```
> open System.IO;;

> File.WriteAllLines("test.txt", [| "This is a test file.";
                                     "It is easy to read." |]);;
val it : unit = ()
```

Many simple file-processing tasks require reading all the lines of a file. You can do this by reading all the lines in one action as an array using System.IO.File.ReadAllLines:

```
> open System.IO;;

> File.ReadAllLines("test.txt");;
val it : string [] = [| "This is a test file.";   "It is easy to read." |]
```

If necessary, the entire file can be read as a single string using System.IO.File.ReadAllText:

```
> File.ReadAllText("test.txt");;
val it : string = "This is a test file.\r\nIt is easy to read\r\n"
```

You can also use the results of System.IO.File.ReadAllLines as part of a list or sequence defined using a sequence expression:

```
> [ for line in File.ReadAllLines("test.txt") do
       let words = line.Split [| ' ' |]
       if words.Length > 3 && words.[2] = "easy" then
           yield line ];;
val it : string list = [| "It is easy to read." |]
```

.NET I/O via Streams

The .NET namespace System.IO contains the primary .NET types for reading/writing bytes and text to/from data sources. The primary output constructs in this namespace are as follows:

- System.IO.BinaryWriter: Writes primitive data types as binary values. Create using new BinaryWriter(stream). You can create output streams using File.Create(filename).

- System.IO.StreamWriter: Writes textual strings and characters to a stream. The text is encoded according to a particular Unicode encoding. Create by using new StreamWriter(stream) and its variants or by using File.CreateText(filename).

- System.IO.StringWriter: Writes textual strings to a StringBuilder, which eventually can be used to generate a string.

Here is a simple example of using System.IO.File.CreateText to create a StreamWriter and write two strings:

```
> let outp = File.CreateText("playlist.txt");;
val outp : StreamWriter

> outp.WriteLine("Enchanted");;
val it : unit = ()
```

```
> outp.WriteLine("Put your records on");;
val it : unit = ()

> outp.Close();
```

These are the primary input constructs in the System.IO namespace:

- System.IO.BinaryReader: Reads primitive data types as binary values. When reading the binary data as a string, it interprets the bytes according to a particular Unicode encoding. Create using new BinaryReader(stream).

- System.IO.StreamReader: Reads a stream as textual strings and characters. The bytes are decoded to strings according to a particular Unicode encoding. Create by using new StreamReader(stream) and its variants or by using File.OpenText(filename).

- System.IO.StringReader: Reads a string as textual strings and characters.

Here is a simple example of using System.IO.File.OpenText to create a StreamReader and read two strings:

```
> let inp = File.OpenText("playlist.txt");;
val inp : StreamReader

> inp.ReadLine();;
val it : string = "Enchanted"

> inp.ReadLine();;
val it : string = "Put your records on"

> inp.Close();;
val it : unit = ()
```

■ **Tip** Whenever you create objects such as a StreamReader that have a Close or Dispose operation or that implement the IDisposable interface, you should consider how to eventually close or otherwise dispose of the resource. We discuss this later in this chapter and in Chapter 8.

Some Other I/O-Related Types

The System.IO namespace contains a number of other types, all of which are useful for corner cases of advanced I/O but that you won't need to use from day to day. For example, the following abstractions appear in the .NET documentation:

- `System.IO.TextReader`: Reads textual strings and characters from an unspecified source. This is the common functionality implemented by the `StreamReader` and `StringReader` types and the `System.Console.In` object. The latter is used to access the stdin input.

- `System.IO.TextWriter`: Writes textual strings and characters to an unspecified output. This is the common functionality implemented by the `StreamWriter` and `StringWriter` types and the `System.Console.Out` and `System.Console.Error` objects. The latter are used to access the stdout and stderr output streams.

- `System.IO.Stream`: Provides a generic view of a sequence of bytes.

Some functions that are generic over different kinds of output streams make use of these; for example, the formatting function `twprintf` discussed in the section "Using `printf` and Friends" writes to any `System.IO.TextWriter`.

Using System.Console

Some simple input/output routines are provided in the `System.Console` class. For example:

```
> System.Console.WriteLine("Hello World");;
Hello World

> System.Console.ReadLine();;
<enter "I'm still here" here>
val it : string = "I'm still here"
```

The `System.Console.Out` object can also be used as a `TextWriter`.

Using printf and Friends

Throughout this book, you've used the `printfn` function, which is one way to print strings from F# values. This is a powerful, extensible technique for type-safe formatting. A related function called `sprintf` builds strings:

```
> sprintf "Name: %s, Age: %d" "Anna" 3;;
val it : string = "Name: Anna, Age: 3"
```

The format strings accepted by `printf` and `sprintf` are recognized and parsed by the F# compiler, and their use is statically type checked to ensure the arguments given for the formatting holes are consistent with the formatting directives. For example, if you use an integer where a string is expected, you see a type error:

```
> sprintf "Name: %s, Age: %d" 3 10;;
-----------------------------^
error: FS0001: This expression was expected to have type string but here
has type int
```

Several `printf`-style formatting functions are provided in the `Microsoft.FSharp.Text.Printf` module. Table 4-4 shows the most important of these.

Table 4-4. *Formatting Functions in the* `Printf` *Module*

Function(s)	Outputs via Type	Outputs via Object	Example
`printf(n)`[a]	`TextWriter`	`Console.Out`	`printf "Result: %d" res`
`eprintf(n)`	`TextWriter`	`Console.Error`	`eprintf "Result: %d" res`
`fprintf(n)`	`TextWriter`	Any `TextWriter`	`twprintf stderr "Error: %d" res`
`sprintf`	`string`	Generates strings	`sprintf "Error: %d" res`
`bprintf(n)`	`StringBuilder`	Any `StringBuilder`	`bprintf buf "Error: %d" res`

[a] *The functions with a suffix n add a new line to the generated text.*

Table 4-5 shows the basic formatting codes for `printf`-style formatting.

Table 4-5. *Formatting Codes for* `printf`*-style String and Output Formatting*

Code	Type Accepted	Notes
`%b`	`bool`	Prints `true` or `false`
`%s`	`string`	Prints the string
`%d, %x, %X, %o, %u`	`int/int32`	Decimal/hex/octal format for any integer types
`%e, %E, %f, %g`	`float`	Floating-point formats
`%M`	`decimal`	See the .NET documentation
`%A`	Any type	Uses structured formatting, discussed in the section "Generic Structural Formatting" and in Chapter 5
`%O`	Any type	Uses `Object.ToString()`
`%a`	Any type	Takes two arguments: one is a formatting function, and one is the value to format
`%t`	Function	Runs the function given as an argument

Any value can be formatted using a %O or %A pattern; these patterns are extremely useful when you're prototyping or examining data. %O converts the object to a string using the `Object.ToString()` function supported by all values. For example:

```
> System.DateTime.Now.ToString();;
val it : string = "28/06/20.. 17:14:07 PM"

> sprintf "It is now %O" System.DateTime.Now;;
val it : string = "It is now 28/06/20... 17:14:09"
```

■ **Note** The format strings used with `printf` are scanned by the F# compiler during type checking, which means the use of the formats are type-safe; if you forget arguments, a warning is given, and if your arguments are of the wrong type, an error is given. The format strings may also include the usual range of specifiers for padding and alignment used by languages such as C, as well as some other interesting specifiers for computed widths and precisions. You can find the full details in the F# library documentation for the `Printf` module.

Generic Structural Formatting

`Object.ToString()` is a somewhat undirected way of formatting data. Structural types such as tuples, lists, records, discriminated unions, collections, arrays, and matrices are often poorly formatted by this technique. The %A pattern uses .NET reflection to format any F# value as a string based on the structure of the value. For example:

```
> printf "The result is %A\n" [1;2;3];;
"The result is [1; 2; 3]"
```

Generic structural formatting can be extended to work with any user-defined data types, a topic covered on the F# web site. This is covered in detail in the F# library documentation for the `printf` function.

Cleaning Up with IDisposable, use, and using

Many constructs in the `System.IO` namespace need to be closed after use, partly because they hold on to operating system resources such as file handles. You can ignore this issue when prototyping code in F# Interactive. However, as we touched on earlier in this chapter, in more polished code, you should use language constructs such as `use var = expr` to ensure that the resource is closed at the end of the lexical scope where a stream object is active. For example:

```
let myWriteStringToFile () =
    use outp = File.CreateText(@"playlist.txt")
    outp.WriteLine("Enchanted")
    outp.WriteLine("Put your records on")
```

This is equivalent to the following:

```
let myWriteStringToFile () =
    using (File.CreateText(@"playlist.txt")) (fun outp ->
        outp.WriteLine("Enchanted")
        outp.WriteLine("Put your records on"))
```

where the function using has the following definition in the F# library:

```
let using (ie : #System.IDisposable) f =
    try f(ie)
    finally ie.Dispose()
```

use and using ensure that the underlying stream is closed deterministically and the operating system resources are reclaimed when the lexical scope is exited. This happens regardless of whether the scope is exited because of normal termination or because of an exception. Chapter 8 covers the language construct use, the operator using, and related issues in more detail.

■ **Note** If you don't use using or otherwise explicitly close the stream, the stream is closed when the stream object is finalized by the .NET garbage collector. However, it's generally bad practice to rely on finalization to clean up resources this way, because finalization isn't guaranteed to happen in a deterministic, timely fashion.

Working with null Values

The keyword null is used in imperative programming languages as a special, distinguished value of a type that represents an uninitialized value or some other kind of special condition. In general, null isn't used in conjunction with types defined in F# code, although it's common to simulate null with a value of the option type. For example:

```
> let parents = [("Adam",None); ("Cain",Some("Adam","Eve"))];;
val parents : (string * (string * string) option) list = ...
```

However, reference types defined in other .NET languages do support null; when using .NET APIs, you may have to explicitly pass null values to the API and also, where appropriate, test return values for null. The .NET Framework documentation specifies when null may be returned from an API. It's recommended that you test for this condition using null pattern tests. For example:

```
match System.Environment.GetEnvironmentVariable("PATH") with
| null -> printf "the environment variable PATH is not defined\n"
| res -> printf "the environment variable PATH is set to %s\n" res
```

The following is a function that incorporates a pattern type test and a null-value test:

```
let switchOnType (a:obj) =
    match a with
    | null                     -> printf "null!"
    | :? System.Exception as e -> printf "An exception: %s!" e.Message
    | :? System.Int32 as i     -> printf "An integer: %d!" i
    | :? System.DateTime as d  -> printf "A date/time: %O!" d
    | _                        -> printf "Some other kind of object\n"
```

There are other important sources of null values. For example, the semisafe function
Array.zeroCreate creates an array whose values are initially null or, in the case of value types, an array
each of whose entries is the zero bit pattern. This function is included with F# primarily because there is
no other alternative technique to initialize and create the array values used as building blocks of larger,
more sophisticated data structures such as queues and hash tables. Of course, you must use this
function with care, and in general you should hide the array behind an encapsulation boundary and be
sure the values of the array aren't referenced before they're initialized.

■ **Note** Although F# generally enables you to code in a null-free style, F# isn't totally immune to the potential
existence of null values: they can come from the .NET APIs, and it's also possible to use Array.zeroCreate and
other back-door techniques to generate null values for F# types. If necessary, APIs can check for this condition by
first converting F# values to the obj type by calling box and then testing for null (see the F# Informal Language
Specification for full details). But in practice, this isn't required by the vast majority of F# programs; for most
purposes, the existence of null values can be ignored.

Some Advice: Functional Programming with Side Effects

F# stems from a tradition in programming languages where the emphasis has been on declarative and
functional approaches to programming in which state is made explicit, largely by passing extra parameters.
Many F# programmers use functional programming techniques first before turning to their imperative
alternatives, and we encourage you to do the same, for all the reasons listed at the start of this chapter.

However, F# also integrates imperative and functional programming together in a powerful way. F#
is actually an extremely succinct imperative programming language! Furthermore, in some cases, no
good functional techniques exist to solve a problem, or those that do are too experimental for
production use. This means that in practice, using imperative constructs and libraries is common in F#:
for example, many of the examples you saw in Chapters 2 and 3 used side effects to report their results or
to create GUI components.

Regardless, we still encourage you to think functionally, even about your imperative programming.
In particular, it's always helpful to be aware of the potential side effects of your overall program and the
characteristics of those side effects. The following sections describe five ways to help tame and reduce
the use of side effects in your programs.

Consider Replacing Mutable Locals and Loops with Recursion

When imperative programmers begin to use F#, they frequently use mutable local variables or reference cells heavily as they translate code fragments from their favorite imperative language into F#. The resulting code often looks very bad. Over time, they learn to avoid many uses of mutable locals. For example, consider the following (naive) implementation of factorization, transliterated from C code:

```
let factorizeImperative n =
    let mutable primefactor1 = 1
    let mutable primefactor2 = n
    let mutable i = 2
    let mutable fin = false
    while (i < n && not fin) do
        if (n % i = 0) then
            primefactor1 <- i
            primefactor2 <- n / i
            fin <- true
        i <- i + 1

    if (primefactor1 = 1) then None
    else Some (primefactor1, primefactor2)
```

This code can be replaced by the following use of an inner recursive function:

```
let factorizeRecursive n =
    let rec find i =
        if i >= n then None
        elif (n % i = 0) then Some(i,n / i)
        else find (i+1)
    find 2
```

The second code is not only shorter but also uses no mutation, which makes it easier to reuse and maintain. You can also see that the loop terminates (i is increasing toward n) and see the two exit conditions for the function (i >= n and n % i = 0). Note that the state i has become an explicit parameter.

Separate Pure Computation from Side-Effecting Computations

Where possible, separate out as much of your computation as possible using side-effect-free functional programming. For example, sprinkling printf expressions throughout your code may make for a good debugging technique but, if not used wisely, can lead to code that is difficult to understand and inherently imperative.

Separate Mutable Data Structures

A common technique of object-oriented programming is to ensure that mutable data structures are private, nonescaping, and, where possible, fully separated, which means there is no chance that distinct pieces of code can access each other's internal state in undesirable ways. Fully separated state can even be used inside the implementation of what, to the outside world, appears to be a purely functional piece of code.

For example, where necessary, you can use side effects on private data structures allocated at the start of an algorithm and then discard these data structures before returning a result; the overall result is then effectively a side-effect-free function. One example of separation from the F# library is the library's implementation of List.map, which uses mutation internally; the writes occur on an internal, separated data structure that no other code can access. Thus, as far as callers are concerned, List.map is pure and functional. The following is a second example that divides a sequence of inputs into equivalence classes (the F# library function Seq.groupBy does a similar thing):

```
open System.Collections.Generic

let divideIntoEquivalenceClasses keyf seq =

    // The dictionary to hold the equivalence classes
    let dict = new Dictionary<'key,ResizeArray<'T>>()

    // Build the groupings
    seq |> Seq.iter (fun v ->
        let key = keyf v
        let ok,prev = dict.TryGetValue(key)
        if ok then prev.Add(v)
        else let prev = new ResizeArray<'T>()
             dict.[key] <- prev
             prev.Add(v))

    // Return the sequence-of-sequences. Don't reveal the
    // internal collections: just reveal them as sequences
    dict |> Seq.map (fun group -> group.Key, Seq.readonly group.Value)
```

This uses the Dictionary and ResizeArray mutable data structures internally, but these mutable data structures aren't revealed externally. The inferred type of the overall function is as follows:

```
val divideIntoEquivalenceClasses : ('T -> 'key) -> seq<'T> -> seq<'key * seq<'T>>
```

Here is an example use:

```
> divideIntoEquivalenceClasses (fun n -> n % 3) [ 0 .. 10 ];;

val it : seq<int * seq<int>>
= seq [(0, seq [0; 3; 6; 9]); (1, seq [1; 4; 7; 10]); (2, seq [2; 5; 8])]
```

Not All Side Effects Are Equal

It's often helpful to use the weakest set of side effects necessary to achieve your programming task and at least be aware when you're using strong side effects:

- Weak side effects are effectively benign given the assumptions you're making about your application. For example, writing to a log file is very useful and is essentially benign (if the log file can't grow arbitrarily large and crash your machine!). Similarly, reading data from a stable, unchanging file store on a local disk is effectively treating the disk as an extension of read-only memory, so reading these files is a weak form of side effect that isn't difficult to incorporate into your programs.

- Strong side effects have a much more corrosive effect on the correctness and operational properties of your program. For example, blocking network I/O is a relatively strong side effect by any measure. Performing blocking network I/O in the middle of a library routine can have the effect of destroying the responsiveness of a GUI application, at least if the routine is invoked by the GUI thread of an application. Any constructs that perform synchronization between threads are also a major source of strong side effects.

Whether a particular side effect is stronger or weaker depends very much on your application and whether the consequences of the side effect are sufficiently isolated and separated from other entities. Strong side effects can and should be used freely in the outer shell of an application or when you're scripting with F# Interactive; otherwise, not much can be achieved.

When you're writing larger pieces of code, you should write your application and libraries in such a way that most of your code either doesn't use strong side effects or at least makes it obvious when these side effects are being used. Threads and concurrency are commonly used to mediate problems associated with strong side effects; Chapter 14 covers these issues in more depth.

Avoid Combining Imperative Programming and Laziness

It's generally thought to be bad style to combine delayed computations (that is, laziness) and side effects. This isn't entirely true; for example, it's reasonable to set up a read from a file system as a lazy computation using sequences. However, it's relatively easy to make mistakes in this sort of programming. For example, consider the following code:

```
open System.IO
let reader1, reader2 =
    let reader = new StreamReader(File.OpenRead("test.txt"))
    let firstReader() = reader.ReadLine()
    let secondReader() = reader.ReadLine()

    // Note: we close the stream reader here!
    // But we are returning function values which use the reader
    // This is very bad!
    reader.Close()
    firstReader, secondReader

// Note: stream reader is now closed! The next line will fail!
let firstLine = reader1()
let secondLine = reader2()
firstLine, secondLine
```

This code is wrong because the StreamReader object reader is used after the point indicated by the comment. The returned function values are then called, and they try to read from the captured variable reader. Function values are just one example of delayed computations: other examples are lazy values, sequences, and any objects that perform computations on demand. Be careful not to build delayed objects such as reader that represent handles to transient, disposable resources, unless those objects are used in a way that respects the lifetime of that resource.

The previous code can be corrected to avoid using laziness in combination with a transient resource:

```
open System.IO

let line1, line2 =
    let reader = new StreamReader(File.OpenRead("test.txt"))
    let firstLine = reader.ReadLine()
    let secondLine = reader.ReadLine()
    reader.Close()
    firstLine, secondLine
```

Another technique uses language and/or library constructs that tie the lifetime of an object to some larger object. For example, you can use a use binding within a sequence expression, which augments the sequence object with the code needed to clean up the resource when iteration is finished or terminates. This technique is discussed further in Chapter 8 and shown by example here:

```
let reader =
    seq { use reader = new StreamReader(File.OpenRead("test.txt"))
          while not reader.EndOfStream do
              yield reader.ReadLine() }
```

The general lesson is to try to keep your core application pure. Use both delayed computations (laziness) and imperative programming (side effects) where appropriate, but be careful about using them together.

Summary

In this chapter, you learned how to do imperative programming in F#, from some of the basic mutable data structures such as reference cells to working with side effects such as exceptions and I/O. You also looked at some general principles for avoiding the need for imperative programming and isolating your uses of side effects. The next chapter returns to some of the building blocks of both functional and imperative programming in F#, with a deeper look at types, type inference, and generics.

■ ■ ■

Mastering Types and Generics

F# constructs such as lists, tuples, and function values are all *generic*, which means they can be instantiated at multiple different types. For example, int list, string list, and (int * int) list are all instantiations of the generic family of F# list types. Likewise, int -> int and string -> int are both instantiations of the generic family of F# function types. The F# library and the .NET Framework have many other generic types and operations in addition to these.

Closely related to generics is the notion of *subtyping*. Generics and subtyping combine to allow you to write code that is generic over families of types. This chapter covers .NET and F# types in general and generics and subtyping in particular. You show how F# uses *automatic generalization* to automatically infer generic types for your code, and the chapter covers some of the basic generic functions in the F# libraries, such as generic comparison, hashing, and binary serialization.

Understanding Generic Type Variables

Generic constructs are always represented through the use of *type variables*, which in F# syntax are written 'T, 'U, 'a, 'Key, and so on. For example, the definition of the Set type in the F# library begins like this:

type Set<'T> = ...

Values can also be generic. A typical generic value is List.map, whose type is as follows:

```
val map : ('T -> 'U) -> 'T list -> 'U list
```

Each time you name a generic type or value, the F# type system must infer instantiations for the type variables involved. For example, in Chapter 3, you used List.map fetch over an input list, where fetch had the following type:

```
val fetch : string -> string * string
```

In this case, the type variable 'T in the signature of List.map is instantiated to string, and the type variable 'U is instantiated to string * string, giving a return type of (string * string) list.

Generic values and functions such as List.map are common in F# programming; they're so common that you usually don't even write the declarations of the type variables in the types of these values.

However, sometimes the declaration point of these variables is made explicit in output from tools and the F# compiler. For example, you may see this:

```
val map<'T,'U> : ('T -> 'U) -> 'T list -> 'U list
```

Frequently, type variables have an implicit scope, governed by the rules of automatic generalization discussed in the section "Writing Generic Functions." This means you can introduce type variables simply by writing them as part of the type annotations of a function:

```
let rec map (f : 'T -> 'U) (l : 'T list) =
    match l with
    | h :: t -> f h :: map f t
    | [] -> []
```

If you want, you can also write the type parameters explicitly on a declaration. You typically have to use each type variable at least once in a type annotation in order to relate the type parameters to the actual code:

```
let rec map<'T,'U> (f : 'T -> 'U) (l : 'T list) =
    match l with
    | h :: t -> f h :: map f t
    | [] -> []
```

■ **Note** By convention, uppercase type-variable names are used for user-declared type parameters, and lowercase names are used for inferred type parameters. In general, the style *TypeName*<'T> is preferred for F# types, although for historical reasons the style 'T *TypeName* is used for list, option, reference and array types.

Writing Generic Functions

A key feature of F# is the automatic generalization of code. The combination of automatic generalization and type inference makes many programs simpler, more succinct, and more general. It also greatly enhances code reuse. Languages without automatic generalization force programmers to compute and explicitly write down the most general type of their functions, and often this is so tedious that programmers don't take the time to abstract common patterns of data manipulation and control.

For example, type parameters are automatically introduced when you write simple functions that are independent of some of their arguments:

```
let getFirst (a,b,c) = a
```

The inferred type of getFirst is reported as follows:

```
val getFirst: 'a * 'b * 'c -> 'a
```

Here, getFirst has been *automatically inferred to be generic*. The function is generic in three type variables, where the result type is the first element of the input tuple type. Automatic generalization is applied when a let or member definition doesn't fully constrain the types of inputs or outputs. You can tell automatic generalization has been applied by the presence of type variables in an inferred type and ultimately by the fact that you can reuse a construct with multiple types.

Automatic generalization is particularly useful when taking functions as inputs. For example, the following takes two functions as input and applies them to each side of a tuple:

```
let mapPair f g (x,y) = (f x, g y)
```

The generalized, inferred type is as follows:

```
val mapPair : ('a -> 'b) -> ('c -> 'd) -> ('a * 'c) -> ('b * 'd)
```

Understanding Some Important Generic Functions

The F# and .NET libraries include definitions for some important generic functions. You saw a number of these in action in earlier chapters. It's important to have a working knowledge of these building blocks, because often your code will automatically become generic when you use these primitives.

Generic Comparison

The first primitives are all related to *generic comparison*, also often called *structural comparison*. Every time you use operators such as <, >, <=, >=, =, <>, compare, min, and max in F# code, you're using generic comparison. All of these operators are located in the Microsoft.FSharp.Core.Operators module, which is opened by default in all F# code. Some important data structures also use generic comparison internally; for example, you may also be using generic comparison when you use F# collection types such as Microsoft.FSharp.Collections.Set and Microsoft.FSharp.Collections.Map. This is discussed in the documentation for these types. The type signatures of the basic generic comparison operators are shown here:

```
val compare : 'T -> 'T -> int when 'T : comparison
val (=) : 'T -> 'T -> bool when 'T : equality
val (<) : 'T -> 'T -> bool when 'T : comparison
val (<=) : 'T -> 'T  -> bool when 'T : comparison
val (>) : 'T -> 'T  -> bool when 'T : comparison
val (>=) : 'T  -> 'T  -> bool when 'T : comparison
val (min) : 'T  -> 'T  -> 'T  when 'T : comparison
val (max) : 'T  -> 'T  -> 'T  when 'T : comparison
```

All of these routines are constrained, which means they may only be used on a subset of types that are known to support either equality (for =) or ordered comparison (for the others). It may help to think of those that implement ordered comparison as being implemented in terms of compare, which returns 0 if the arguments are equal and returns –1 and 1 for less than and greater than, respectively.

On ordinary simple types such as integers, generic comparison works by invoking the default .NET behavior for these types, giving the natural ordering for these types. For strings, culture-neutral ordinal comparison is used, which means the local culture settings on your machine don't affect string comparison (see System.Globalization for more information about local settings). Most other .NET base types implement the System.IComparable interface, such as System.DateTime values, and generic comparison uses these implementations where necessary.

You can also use the comparison operators on most structured types. For example, you can use them on F# tuple values, where a lexicographic left-to-right comparison is used:

```
> ("abc","def") < ("abc","xyz");;
val it : bool = true

> compare (10,30) (10,20);;
val it : int = 1
```

Likewise, you can use generic comparison with list and array values:

```
> compare [10;30] [10;20];;
val it : int = 1

> compare [| 10;30 |] [| 10;20 |];;
val it : int = 1

> compare [| 10;20 |] [| 10;30 |];;
val it : int = -1
```

Generic Hashing

Generic hashing is an important partner of generic comparison. The primary primitive function used to invoke generic hashing is hash, again located in the `Microsoft.FSharp.Core.Operators` module. The type signature is as follows:

```
val hash : 'T -> int when 'T : equality
```

Again, this is a constrained operation, requiring that the type support equality. Most types support some form of equality, even if it's the default reference equality of .NET.

When used with simple structural types, the function returns an integer that gives a stable hash of the input value:

```
> hash 100;;
val it : int = 100

> hash "abc";;
val it : int = 536991770

> hash (100,"abc");;
val it : int = 536990974
```

Generic hashing is implemented similarly to generic comparison. Like generic comparison, generic hashing should generally be used only with base types such as integers and structural types built using records and discriminated unions.

For the most part, generic hashing and comparison are implemented efficiently—code is autogenerated for each type definition where possible fast-path comparison techniques are used. For example, the generated code uses primitive Common IL/native instructions for integer comparisons. This means that in practice, structural comparison is typically fast when used with appropriately sized keys. However, you should consider the following before using generic comparison over complex new data types:

- When using .NET collections, consider passing the `HashIdentity.Structural` or `ComparisonIdentity.Structural` parameters to the object constructor of the collection. This helps the F# compiler optimize the performance of the hashing, equality and comparison functions for the collection instance.

- Hashing, comparison and equality on tuples can be slower than expected in some circumstances where the F# compiler can't optimize the hashing, equality and comparison functions for these types. Consider replacing uses of tuples as keys by the use of a new, named key type, often using a union type with a single case, e.g. `type Key = Key of string * int`.

- Consider customizing the behavior of generic comparison and equality for new types you define, at least when those types will be used as keys in a data structure. You can do this by implementing the `System.IComparable` interface and overriding the `System.Object.Equals` method, covered in Chapter 8. You can customize generic hashing for new types by either overriding the `GetHashCode` method or implementing the `Microsoft.FSharp.Core.IStructuralHash` interface, again covered in Chapter 8.

- Both ordered comparison and equality (in combination with hashing) can be used to build interesting indexed data structures. Collections built using these techniques are efficient over small keys. However, performance issues may arise if they're used repeatedly over large structured keys. In this case, using custom comparison may be appropriate.

Generic Pretty-Printing

Some useful generic functions do generic formatting of values. The simplest ways to access this functionality is to use the `%A` specifiers in `printf` format strings. Here is an example:

```
> sprintf "result = %A" ([1], [true]);;
val it : string = "result = ([1], [true])"
```

This code uses .NET and F# reflection to walk the structure of values to build a formatted representation of the value. You format structural types such as lists and tuples using the syntax of F# source code. Unrecognized values are formatted by calling the .NET `ToString()` method for these values. F# and .NET reflection are discussed in more depth toward the end of Chapter 9.

Generic Boxing and Unboxing

Two useful generic functions convert any F# data to and from the universal type `System.Object` (the F# type `obj`):

```
val box   : 'T -> obj
val unbox : obj -> 'T
```

Here are some simple examples of these functions in action:

```
> box 1;;
val it : obj = 1

> box "abc";;
val it : obj = "abc"

> let stringObj = box "abc";;
val stringObj: obj = "abc"

> (unbox<string> stringObj);;
val it : string = "abc"

> (unbox stringObj : string);;
val it : string = "abc"
```

Note that using unbox generally requires you to specify the target type, given either as an explicit type parameter unbox<string> or as a type constraint (unbox stringObj: string)—these forms are equivalent. A runtime check is performed on unboxing to ensure that the object can be safely converted to the target type. Values of type obj carry dynamic type information, and attempting to unbox a value to an incompatible type raises an error:

```
> (unbox stringObj: int);;
System.InvalidCastException: Specified cast is not valid.
   at <StartupCode>.FSI_0014._main()
stopped due to error
```

Boxing is important partly because many .NET libraries provide generic operations through functions that accept arguments of type obj. You see an example in the next section. Furthermore, some .NET APIs are dynamically typed, and almost all parameters are of type obj.

Generic Binary Serialization via the .NET Libraries

The .NET libraries provide an implementation of generic binary serialization that is useful as a quick and easy way of saving computed values to disk and sending values over the network. Let's use this as an example to see how you can define building-block generic operations using functionality in the .NET libraries combined with box and unbox. You first define functions with the following signatures:

```
val writeValue : System.IO.Stream -> 'T -> unit
val readValue  : System.IO.Stream -> 'T
```

The function writeValue takes an arbitrary value and writes a binary representation of its underlying object graph to the given I/O stream. The function readValue reverses this process, in much the same way that unbox reverses the process performed by box. Here are the implementations of the functions in terms of the .NET binary serializer located in the namespace System.Runtime.Serialization.Formatters.Binary:

```
open System.IO
open System.Runtime.Serialization.Formatters.Binary

let writeValue outputStream (x: 'T) =
    let formatter = new BinaryFormatter()
    formatter.Serialize(outputStream, box x)

let readValue inputStream =
    let formatter = new BinaryFormatter()
    let res = formatter.Deserialize(inputStream)
    unbox res
```

Note that box and unbox are used in the implementation, because the Serialize and Deserialize functions accept and return a value of type obj. Here is an example of how to use the functions to write a value of type Microsoft.FSharp.Collections.Map<string,string> to a FileStream and read it back in again:

```
open System.IO
let addresses = Map.ofList [ "Jeff", "123 Main Street, Redmond, WA 98052";
                             "Fred", "987 Pine Road, Phila., PA 19116";
                             "Mary", "PO Box 112233, Palo Alto, CA 94301" ]


let fsOut = new FileStream("Data.dat", FileMode.Create)
writeValue fsOut addresses
fsOut.Close()
let fsIn = new FileStream("Data.dat", FileMode.Open)
let res : Map<string,string> = readValue fsIn
fsIn.Close()
```

The final result of this code when executed interactively is as follows:

```
> res;;
val it : Map<string,string>
      = seq
          [[Fred, 987 Pine Road, Phila., PA 19116]
             {Key = "Fred";
              Value = "987 Pine Road, Phila., PA 19116";};
          [Jeff, 123 Main Street, Redmond, WA 98052]
             {Key = "Jeff";
              Value = "123 Main Street, Redmond, WA 98052";};
          [Mary, PO Box 112233, Palo Alto, CA 94301]
             {Key = "Mary";
              Value = "PO Box 112233, Palo Alto, CA 94301";}]
```

Note that values of type `Map<string,string>` are printed interactively as sequences of key/value pairs. Also, a type annotation is required when reading the data back in using `readValue`, and a runtime type error results if the types of the objects reconstructed from the binary data don't match this type annotation.

The .NET Framework provides several other generic serializers that differ in output format and operational characteristics. The most important of these are based around the notion of `DataContract` serialization:

- `System.Runtime.Serialization.Json.DataContractJsonSerializer`: Used for serializing public data objects into the popular JavaScript Object Notation (JSON) format, using formats that aren't specifically tied to particular .NET types but are rather compatible with a range of types

- `System.Runtime.Serialization.DataContractSerializer`: Used for serializing public data objects into XML, using formats that aren't specifically tied to particular .NET types but are rather compatible with a range of types

- `System.Runtime.Serialization.NetDataContractSerializer`: Used for serializing arbitrary object graphs, including private data and closures, into XML using the same idioms as the other `DataContract` serializers

In addition, you can use some older serializers with F#. For example, `System.Runtime.Serialization.XmlSerializer` is used for serializing public data into XML. However, this serializer is now used less frequently; you should generally use `NetDataContractSerializer` instead. You can also write your own generic serializer, using the techniques described in Chapter 9.

Making Things Generic

The following sections discuss how to make existing code more generic (that is, reusable) and how to systematically represent the abstract parameters of generic algorithms.

Generic Algorithms through Explicit Arguments

A common pattern in F# programming is to accept function parameters in order to make an algorithm abstract and reusable. A simple sample is the following generic implementation of Euclid's algorithm for finding the highest common factor (HCF) of two numbers:

```
let rec hcf a b =
    if   a=0 then b
    elif a<b then hcf a (b-a)
    else hcf (a-b) b
```

The type of this function is as follows:

```
val hcf : int -> int -> int
```

For example:

```
> hcf 18 12;;
val it : int = 6

> hcf 33 24;;
val it : int = 3
```

But this algorithm isn't generic, because as written it works only over integers. In particular, although the operator (-) is by default overloaded in F#, each use of the operator must be associated with at most one type decided at compile time. This restriction is discussed in more detail in the section "Understanding Generic Overloaded Operators." In addition, the constant 0 is an integer and isn't overloaded.

Despite this, this algorithm can be easily generalized to work over any type. To achieve this, you must provide an explicit zero, a subtraction function, and an ordering. Here's one way:

```
let hcfGeneric (zero,sub,lessThan) =
    let rec hcf a b =
        if    a=zero then b
        elif lessThan a b then hcf a (sub b a)
        else hcf (sub a b) b
    hcf
```

The inferred, generic type of this function is as follows:

```
val hcfGeneric :
     'a * ('a -> 'a -> 'a) * ('a -> 'a -> bool) -> ('a -> 'a -> 'a)
         when 'a : equality
```

The numeric type being manipulated has type 'a in the inferred type, and the result is a computed function. This approach uses techniques for computing functions similar to those discussed in Chapter 3. Here are some examples of using this generic function:

```
let hcfInt    = hcfGeneric (0, (-),(<))
let hcfInt64  = hcfGeneric (0L,(-),(<))
let hcfBigInt = hcfGeneric (0I,(-),(<))
```

Note that when you instantiate the generic function for these cases, you're drawing on particular instances of the default overloaded operator (-). You can check that the code is executing correctly as follows:

```
> hcfInt 18 12;;
val it : int = 6

> hcfBigInt 1810287116162232383039576I 1239028178293092830480239032I;;
val it : bigint = 33224I
```

Generic Algorithms through Abstract Object Types

The generic implementation from the previous section took three related parameters for zero, comparison, and subtraction. It's common practice to package related operations together. One way to do this is to use a concrete record type containing function values:

```
type Numeric<'T> =
    { Zero: 'T;
      Subtract: ('T -> 'T -> 'T);
      LessThan: ('T -> 'T -> bool); }

let intOps    = { Zero=0 ; Subtract=(-); LessThan=(<) }
let bigintOps = { Zero=0I; Subtract=(-); LessThan=(<) }
let int64Ops  = { Zero=0L; Subtract=(-); LessThan=(<) }

let hcfGeneric (ops : Numeric<'T>) =
    let rec hcf a b =
        if a = ops.Zero then b
        elif ops.LessThan a b then hcf a (ops.Subtract b a)
        else hcf (ops.Subtract a b) b
    hcf

let hcfInt    = hcfGeneric intOps
let hcfBigInt = hcfGeneric bigintOps
```

The inferred types are as follows:

```
val hcfGeneric : Numeric<'T> -> ('T -> 'T -> 'T) when 'T : equality
val hcfInt : (int -> int -> int)
val hcfBigInt : (bigint -> bigint -> bigint)
```

Here are some examples of the functions in action:

```
> hcfInt 18 12;;
val it : int = 6

> hcfBigInt 1810287116162232383039576I 1239028178293092830480239032I;;
val it : bigint = 33224I
```

Record types such as Numeric<'T> are often called *dictionaries of operations* and are similar to vtables from object-oriented programming and the compiled form of type classes from Haskell. As you've seen, dictionaries such as these can be represented in different ways according to your tastes, using tuples or records. For larger frameworks, a carefully constructed classification of *object interface types* is often used in place of records. Here is an interface type definition that plays the same role as the record in the previous example:

```
type INumeric<'T> =
    abstract Zero : 'T
    abstract Subtract: 'T * 'T -> 'T
    abstract LessThan: 'T * 'T -> bool
```

You can implement and use abstract object types similarly to record values:

```
let intOps =
    { new INumeric<int> with
        member ops.Zero = 0
        member ops.Subtract(x,y) = x - y
        member ops.LessThan(x,y) = x < y }
```

```
val intOps : INumeric<int>
```

The code for Euclid's algorithm using abstract object types is essentially the same as for the code based on record types:

```
let hcfGeneric (ops : INumeric<'T>) =
    let rec hcf a b =
        if a= ops.Zero then b
        elif ops.LessThan(a,b) then hcf a (ops.Subtract(b,a))
        else hcf (ops.Subtract(a,b)) b
    hcf
```

Generic Algorithms and Function Parameters

One of the remarkable features of functional programming with F# is that generic programming is practical even when the types involved aren't explicitly related. For example, the previous generic algorithm shows how you can write reusable code without resorting to relating the types involved through an inheritance hierarchy: the generic algorithm works over any type, if an appropriate set of operations is provided to manipulate values of that type. This is a form of *explicit factoring by functions*. Object-oriented programming typically uses *implicit factoring by hierarchy*, because the library designer decides the relationships that hold between various types, and these are fixed in stone.

Type inference in F# makes explicit factoring by functions convenient. Given the simplicity and flexibility of this approach, it's a useful way to write applications and to prototype frameworks. However, factoring by hierarchy still plays a role in F# programming. For example, all F# values can be implicitly converted to and from the type System.Object, something that is extremely useful when you're interoperating with many libraries. It would obviously be inconvenient to have to pass around functions to marshal (box/unbox) types to System.Object and back. Similarly, many F# values can be implicitly converted to the IDisposable interface. Hierarchical factoring requires careful design choices; in general, we recommend that you use explicit factoring first, moving toward implicit factoring only when a design pattern is truly universal and repeats itself many times, as is the case with the IDisposable idiom. The .NET and F# libraries contain definitions of many of the implicit factors you should use in practice, such as IDisposable and IEnumerable.

Some functional languages such as Haskell allow you to implicitly pass dictionaries of operations through an extension to type inference known as *type classes*. At the time of writing, this isn't supported by F#. However, the designers of F# have stated that they expect a future version of the language to support this. Either way, explicitly passing dictionaries of operations is common in all functional programming and is an important technique to master.

Arithmetic Operators and Generic Algorithms through Inlining

There is one additional way to make code generic: by marking a function as inline. You can use this technique for code that uses F# operators such as float, int, +, -, *, /, and other arithmetic operations. As discussed in the section "Understanding Generic Overloaded Operators," each use of these operators is normally statically resolved. For example, consider the following code:

```
let convertToFloat x = float x
```

In the F# type system, the type of the float function is 'T -> float (requires member op_Explicit). This means the type 'T must support an explicit conversion from 'T to float. Thus you can use it with integers, singles, doubles, decimals, and so on, but you can't use it with any old type. The 'T is constrained.

As mentioned earlier, F# operators like float are statically resolved. This means each use of float is associated with one statically inferred type. The same applies to other operators such as +, *, and so on. These operators also generally default to working over integers. For example, this shows float being used with three different statically resolved types:

```
float 3.0 + float 1 + float 3L
```

To make code like this generic, you can use inline. For example, consider this:

```
let inline convertToFloatAndAdd x y = float x + float y
```

convertToFloatAndAdd can be used with an integer and a float, or a decimal and an integer, or two decimals. You can use inline to write code and algorithms that are implicitly generic over arithmetic type while still maintaining type safety. This gives you generic, type-safe code while ensuring static resolution of basic numeric operations, making it easy to reason about the efficiency of your code.

You can also apply this technique to the earlier HCF algorithm:

```
let inline hcf a b =
    let rec loop a b =
        if   a=LanguagePrimitives.GenericZero<_> then b
        elif a<b then loop a (b-a)
        else loop (a-b) b
    loop a b
```

The type of this function is as follows:

```
val inline hcf :
    ^a ->  ^a ->  ^a
    when ^a : (static member Zero : ^a)
    and  ^a : (static member ( - ) :  ^a *  ^a ->  ^a)
    and   ^a : comparison
```

For example:

```
> hcf 18 12;;
val it : int = 6

> hcf 18I 12I;;
val it : bigint = 6I
```

The algorithm is now generic. You should use this technique sparingly, but it can be extremely powerful. Note the use of the F# library primitive GenericZero to get a zero value for an arbitrary type supporting a Zero static property.

One variation on this technique provides a simple wrapper that delegates to a non-inlined generic routine. For example, the following code delegates to the non-inlined routine hcfGeneric, defined earlier in this section:

```
let inline hcf a b =
    hcfGeneric
        { new INumeric<'T> with
              member ops.Zero = LanguagePrimitives.GenericZero<'T>
              member ops.Subtract(x,y) = x - y
              member ops.LessThan(x,y) = x < y }
        a b
```

This gives you a generic routine hcfGeneric that can be used with any explicit set of arithmetic operations, and a generic routine hcf that can be used with any type that supports an implicit set of arithmetic operations.

Understanding .NET Types

For the most part, programming in F# involves using types in a simple way: each type has some values, and types are related by using explicit functions to map from one type to another. But in reality, types in F# are more sophisticated than this statement implies. First, F# types are really .NET types, and .NET makes some distinctions between different kinds of types that are occasionally important, such as between value types and reference types. Furthermore, .NET and F# support hierarchical relationships between types through *subtyping*. The following sections first cover .NET types from the F# perspective and then cover subtyping.

Reference Types and Value Types

The .NET documentation and other .NET languages often describe types as either *reference types* or *value types*. You can use System.String and System.DateTime as a typical example of each. First note that both of these types are immutable. That is, given a value of type System.String, you can't modify the contents of the string; the same is true for System.DateTime. This is by far the most important fact you need to know about these types: for immutable types the reference/value type distinction is relatively unimportant. However, it's still useful to know the following:

- *Representation:* Values of type System.String are single pointers into the garbage-collected heap where the actual data for the string resides. Two System.String values may point to the same data. In contrast, values of type System.DateTime are somewhat larger blobs of integer data (64-bits of data, in this case), and no data lives on the garbage-collected heap. The full data for the value is copied as needed.

- *Boxing:* All .NET types can be marshaled to and from the .NET type System.Object (the F# type obj) by using F# functions such as box and unbox. All reference types are trivially marshaled to this type without any change of representation or identity, so for reference types, box is a no-op. Boxing a value type involves a heap allocation, resulting in a new object. Often this object is immediately discarded after the operation on the obj type has been performed.

If a value can be mutated, then the distinction between value types and reference types is more serious. Fortunately, essentially all mutable values in the .NET libraries are reference types, which means mutation actually mutates the heap-allocated data referred to by the reference.

Other Flavors of .NET Types

The .NET type system makes some additional distinctions between types that are occasionally significant for F# programming:

- *Delegate types:* Delegate types such as System.Windows.Forms.MouseEventHandler are a form of named function type supported by all .NET languages. They tend not to be as convenient to use as F# function types, because they don't support compositional operations such as pipelining and forward composition. However, .NET APIs use delegates extensively. To create a delegate value, you name the delegate type and pass it a function value that accepts the same arguments expected by the delegate type, such as MouseEventHandler(fun sender args -> printf "click!\n").

- *Attribute types:* Types derived from the System.Attribute class are used to add metadata to source-code declarations and typically end in the suffix Attribute. You can access these attributes via .NET and F# reflection. You can add attributes to F# declarations using the [<...>] syntax. For example, System.ObsoleteAttribute marks a function as obsolete, and the F# compiler produces a warning if the function is used.

- *Exception types:* Types derived from the System.Exception class are used to represent raised exceptions. Chapter 4 discussed exceptions in detail.

- *Enum types:* .NET enum types are simple integer-like value types associated with a particular name. They're typically used for specifying flags to APIs; for example, FileMode in the System.IO namespace is an enum type with values such as FileMode.Open and FileMode.Create. .NET enum types are easy to use from F# and can be combined using bitwise AND, OR, and XOR operations using the &&&, |||, and ^^^ operators. Most commonly, the ||| operator is used to combine multiple flags. On occasion, you may have to mask an attribute value using &&& and compare the result to enum 0. You see how to define .NET-compatible enum types in F# at the end of Chapter 6.

Understanding Subtyping

Simple types are related in simple ways; for example, values of the type int are distinct from values of the type float, and values of one record type are distinct from values of another. This approach to types is powerful and often sufficient, partly because type inference and function values make it easy to write generic code. However, .NET and F# also support hierarchical relationships between types through *subtyping*. Subtyping is a key concept of object-oriented programming and is discussed in more detail in Chapter 6. In addition, you can use subtyping in conjunction with pure functional programming, because it offers one technique to make algorithms generic over a restricted family of types.

The following sections explain how these constructs appear to the F# programmer and the role they play in F# programming. Subtyping in F# is the same as that used by the .NET Framework, so if you're familiar with another .NET language, you already know how things work.

Casting Up Statically

You can explore how subtyping works by using F# Interactive. First, let's look at how some of the F# types you've already seen relate to the type obj:

```
> let xobj = (1 :> obj);;
val xobj : obj = 1

> let sobj = ("abc" :> obj);;
val sobj : obj = "abc"
```

This example shows the subtyping relationship through the use of the built-in coercion (or *upcast*) operator, which is :>. This operator converts a value to any of its supertypes in precisely the same way as the box function.

The previous code indicates the subtyping between ordinary types and the type obj. Subtyping occurs between other kinds of types as well (Chapters 3 and 6 discuss the various kinds of type definitions, such as records, discriminated unions, classes, and interfaces):

- All types are subtypes of System.Object (called obj in F#).

- Record and discriminated union types are subtypes of the interface types they implement.

- Interfaces types are subtypes of the other interfaces they extend.

- Class types are subtypes of both the interfaces they implement and the classes they extend.

- Array types are subtypes of the .NET type System.Array.

- Value types (types such as int32 that are abbreviations of .NET value types) are subtypes of the .NET type System.ValueType. Likewise, .NET enumeration types are subtypes of System.Enum.

Casting Down Dynamically

Values that may have subtypes carry a *runtime type*, and you can use runtime-type tests to query the type of an object and convert it to one of the subtypes. You can do this in three main ways: the unbox operation, downcasts, and pattern type tests. We've already explained the unbox function. As with most object-oriented languages, the upcasts performed through subtyping are reversible through the use of downcasts—in other words, by using the :?> operator. You can see this in the following examples:

```
> let boxedObject = box "abc";;
val boxedObject : obj

> let downcastString = (boxedObject :?> string);;
val downcastString : string = "abc"
```

Downcasts are checked at runtime and are safe because all values of the obj type are implicitly annotated with the runtime type of the value. The operator :?> raises an exception if the object isn't of a suitable type:

```
> let xobj = box 1;;
val xobj : obj = 1

> let x = (xobj :?> string);;
error: InvalidCastException raised at or near stdin:(2,0)
```

Performing Type Tests via Pattern Matching

A more convenient way of performing dynamic type tests uses *type-test patterns*—in particular the :? pattern construct, which you encountered in Chapter 4 in the context of catching various .NET exception types. This example uses a pattern-type test to query the dynamic type of a value of type obj:

```
let checkObject (x: obj) =
    match x with
    | :? string -> printfn "The object is a string"
    | :? int    -> printfn "The object is an integer"
    | _         -> printfn "The input is something else"
```

```
> checkObject (box "abc");;
The object is a string
val it : unit = ()
```

Such a pattern may also bind the matched value at its more specific type:

```
let reportObject (x: obj) =
    match x with
    | :? string as s -> printfn "The input is the string '%s'" s
    | :? int as d    -> printfn "The input is the integer '%d'" d
    | _              -> printfn "the input is something else"
```

```
> reportObject (box 17);;
The input is the integer '17'
val it : unit = ()
```

Knowing When Upcasts Are Applied Automatically

Like most object-oriented languages, F# automatically applies upcasts whenever a function or method is called or wherever a value is used. If a parameter to an F# function has a named type, then the function implicitly accepts parameters that are any subtype, assuming that type supports subtyping. This is particularly common when working with .NET libraries that use subtyping heavily. For example:

```
> open System.Windows.Forms;;

> let setTextOfControl (c: Control) (s:string) = c.Text <- s;;
val setTextOfControl: Control -> string -> unit

> let form = new Form();;
val form: Form

> let textBox = new TextBox();;
val textBox : TextBox

> setTextOfControl form "Form Text";;
val it : unit = ()

> setTextOfControl textBox "Text Box Text";;
val it : unit = ()
```

Here, the function setTextOfControl is used on two different subtypes of Control. When functions have parameters that accept named types such as Control, you don't need to supply an upcast explicitly.

However, F# doesn't apply upcasts in all the situations where other object-oriented languages do. In practice, this means you sometimes have to add explicit upcasts to your code to throw away information. For example, if each branch of an if ... then ... else ... construct returns different types, then you need to upcast the results of one or both of the branches. This is shown by the type error given for the following code, which returns Console.In (a TextReader) from one branch and the results of File.OpenText (a StreamReader) from the other branch:

```
open System
open System.IO
let textReader  =
    if DateTime.Today.DayOfWeek = DayOfWeek.Monday
    then Console.In
    else File.OpenText("input.txt")
```

The error reported is as follows:

```
    else File.OpenText("input.txt")
         ^^^^^^^^^^^^^^^^^^^^^^^^^^
  error: FS0001: This expression has type
         StreamReader
but is here used with type
         TextReader
stopped due to error
```

StreamReader is a subtype of TextReader, so the code can be corrected by throwing away the information that the returned type is a StreamReader:

```
open System
open System.IO

let textReader  =
    if DateTime.Today.DayOfWeek = DayOfWeek.Monday
    then Console.In
    else (File.OpenText("input.txt") :> TextReader)
```

Upcasts are applied automatically in the following situations:

- When passing arguments to functions and all members associated with .NET and F# objects and types. This applies when parameters have named types such as TextReader, rather than variable types.

- When calling functions with flexible parameter types, such as #TextReader.

- When assigning into fields and properties.

- When accessing members using dot notation. For example, given a value of type StreamReader, all the members associated with TextReader can also be accessed without needing to apply an upcast.

Note particularly that upcasts aren't applied automatically for the result of a function. For example, an upcast is needed here, to coerce a StreamReader to a TextReader, despite the presence of an explicit type annotation for the return type:

```
let getTextReader () : TextReader = (File.OpenText("input.txt") :> TextReader)
```

Flexible Types

F# also has the notion of a *flexible type constraint*, which is shorthand for a generic function and a constraint on the type variable. You could equally write this:

```
> open System.Windows.Forms;;

> let setTextOfControl (c : 'T when 'T :> Control) (s:string) = c.Text <- s;;
val setTextOfControl: #Control -> string -> unit
```

Automatic generalization lifts the constraints implicit in types of the form #type to the nearest enclosing function or member definition. Flexible type constraints sometimes occur when you're working with sequence values. For example, consider the following two functions from the F# library:

```
module Seq =
    ...
    val concat : seq<#seq<'T>> -> seq<'T>
    ...
```

When implicit flexibility or arguments is taken into account, the signature of concat means that Seq.concat accepts a list of lists, or a list of arrays, or an array of lists, and so forth. For example:

```
Seq.concat [ [1;2;3]; [4;5;6] ]
Seq.concat [ [| 1;2;3 |]; [| 4;5;6 |] ]
```

Units of Measure

F# includes a beautiful feature in its type system called *units of measure*. It lets you annotate numeric types with annotations such as kg, m, and sec that indicate the kind of number the quantity represents—that is, its unit of measure. You can also use the feature to annotate other, user-defined types that are ultimately based on numeric quantities. This feature is simplest explained using code for physical simulations and is rooted in scalable quantities. However, it also has a wide range of surprising applications outside physical simulation, including annotating code with units for integer quantities such as pixels, currencies, or click-counts.

To define a new kind of measure annotation, you use a type definition with a Measure attribute:

```
[<Measure>]
type m

[<Measure>]
type s

[<Measure>]
type kg
```

The F# version 2.0 core library doesn't come with predefined units, although a set of definitions matching the Système International (SI) standard is included in the F# Power Pack (an open source project available at www.codeplex.com).

Once a set of measures are defined, the basic numeric types and literals can include these qualifications. For example:

```
let gravityOnEarth = 9.81<m/s^2>
let heightOfMyOfficeWindow = 3.5<m>
```

A calculation involving these quantities is shown here:

```
let speedOfImpact = sqrt (2.0 * gravityOnEarth * heightOfMyOfficeWindow)
```

The inferred type of speedOfImpact is float<m/s> (a speed). If a mismatched unit type is used in such a calculation, then a type error is normally reported.

When you define a new type, you may include measure parameters as part of the definition of the type. These parameters must be marked with the Measure attribute. For example:

```
type Vector2D<[<Measure>] 'u> =
    { DX: float<'u>; DY: float<'u> }
```

You can use units of measure in conjunction with object-oriented programming, discussed in Chapter 6. For example, here is a vector type generic over units of measure:

```
/// Two-dimensional vectors
type Vector2D<[<Measure>] 'u>(dx: float<'u>, dy: float<'u>) =

    /// Get the X component of the vector
    member v.DX = dx

    /// Get the Y component of the vector
    member v.DY = dy

    /// Get the length of the vector
    member v.Length = sqrt(dx * dx + dy * dy)

    /// Get a vector scaled by the given factor
    member v.Scale k = Vector2D(k*dx, k*dy)

    /// Return a vector shifted by the given delta in the X coordinate
    member v.ShiftX x = Vector2D(dx+x, dy)

    /// Return a vector shifted by the given delta in the Y coordinate
    member v.ShiftY y = Vector2D(dx, dy+y)

    /// Get the zero vector
    static member Zero = Vector2D<'u>(0.0<_>, 0.0<_>)

    /// Return a constant vector along the X axis
    static member ConstX dx = Vector2D<'u>(dx, 0.0<_>)

    /// Return a constant vector along the Y axis
    static member ConstY dy = Vector2D<'u>(0.0<_>, dy)

    /// Return the sum of two vectors
    static member (+) (v1: Vector2D<'u>, v2: Vector2D<'u>) =
        Vector2D(v1.DX + v2.DX, v1.DY + v2.DY)

    /// Return the difference of two vectors
    static member (-) (v1: Vector2D<'u>, v2: Vector2D<'u>) =
        Vector2D(v1.DX - v2.DX, v1.DY - v2.DY)

    /// Return the pointwise-product of two vectors
    static member (.*) (v1: Vector2D<'u>, v2: Vector2D<'u>) =
        Vector2D(v1.DX * v2.DX, v1.DY * v2.DY)
```

Note that some measure annotations are needed on zero values in this sample. In addition, a vector type like this should normally implement the IComparable interface, and the Equals and GetHashCode methods, as described in Chapter 8.

■ **Note** F# units of measure are covered only briefly in this book. For more information, see the MSDN documentation, or Andrew Kennedy's four-part introduction to the topic: search for "Andrew Kennedy Units of Measure Part One," or visit http://blogs.msdn.com/andrewkennedy.

Troubleshooting Type-Inference Problems

The following sections cover some of the techniques you can use to understand the type-inference process and to debug problems when inferred types aren't as expected.

Using a Visual Editing Environment

The best and most important technique to debug and understand type inference is to use a visual editing environment for F#. For example, Visual Studio performs interactive type-checking as you're writing code. Such tools display errors interactively and show inferred types as you move the mouse pointer over identifiers.

Using Type Annotations

Type inference in F# works through a process of type-constraint *propagation*. As a programmer, you can add further type constraints to your code in several ways. For example, you can do the following:

- Add a rigid type constraint using the : notation, such as let t : float = 5.0.

- Add a type constraint to an argument, such as let setTextOfControl (c : Control) (s:string) = c.Text <- s.

- Apply a function that accepts only a particular type of argument, such as let f x = String.length x. Here, the use of String.length generates a constraint on the type of x.

Adding type annotations to and removing them from your code is the standard technique to troubleshoot type-inference problems. For example, the following code doesn't type-check:

```
> let transformData inp =
    inp |> Seq.map (fun (x,y) -> (x,y.Length)) ;;

inp |> Seq.map (fun (x,y) -> (x,y.Length))
---------------------------------^^^^^^^^

stdin(11,36): error: Lookup on object of indeterminate type. A type annotation
may be needed prior to this program point to constrain the type of the object.
This may allow the lookup to be resolved.
```

You can easily solve this problem by adding a type annotation, such as to y:

```
let transformData inp =
    inp |> Seq.map (fun (x,y:string) -> (x,y.Length))
```

You can also use type annotations to discover why code isn't as generic as you think it should be. For example, the following code has a mistake, and the F# type checker says the code is less generic than expected:

```
let printSecondElements (inp : seq<'T * int>) =
    inp
    |> Seq.iter (fun (x,y) -> printfn "y = %d" x)
```

```
> ... enter the code above ...

    |> Seq.iter (fun (x,y) -> printfn "y = %d" x)
-------------------------------------^^^^^^^^^

stdin(21,38): warning: FS0064: This construct causes code to be less generic than
indicated by the type annotations. The type variable 'T has been constrained to
the type 'int'.
```

The mistake here is that you're printing the variable x instead of y, but it's not always so easy to spot what has caused this kind of problem. One way to track down this problem is to temporarily change the generic type parameter to some arbitrary, unrelated type. After all, if code is generic, then you should be able to use *any* type; and by changing the type variable to an unrelated type, you can track down where the inconsistency first arises. For example, let's change 'T to the type PingPong:

```
type PingPong = Ping | Pong

let printSecondElements (inp : seq<PingPong * int>) =
    inp
    |> Seq.iter (fun (x,y) -> printfn "y = %d" x)
```

You now get a different and in many ways more informative error message, localized to the first place that the value x marked with type PingPong is used in an unexpected way:

```
> ... enter the code above ...

    |> Seq.iter (fun (x,y) -> printfn "y = %d" x)
-------------------------------------------------^

stdin(27,47): error: FS0001: The type 'PingPong' is not compatible with any of
the types byte,int16,int32,int64,sbyte,uint16,uint32,uint64,nativeint,unativeint,
arising from the use of a printf-style format string
```

Understanding the Value Restriction

F# sometimes requires a little help before a definition is automatically generalized. In particular, only function definitions and simple immutable data expressions are automatically generalized; this is called the *value restriction*. For example, the following definition doesn't result in a generic type and gives an error:

```
> let empties = Array.create 100 [];;
------^^^^^^
error: FS0030: Value restriction. The value 'empties' has been inferred to
have generic type
        val empties : '_a list []
Either define 'empties' as a simple data term, make it a function
with explicit arguments or, if you do not intend for it to be generic,
add a type annotation.
```

The code attempts to create an array of empty lists. The error message indicates that type inference has given empties the type '_a list []. The underscore (_) indicates that the type variable 'a is *ungeneralized*, meaning this code isn't fully generic. It would make no sense to give empties the truly generic type 'a list [], because this would imply that you've created an array of lists somehow suitable for use with any type 'a. In reality, any particular array should have one specific type, such as int list [] or string list [], but not both. (If it were usable with both types, then you could store an integer list in the array and fetch it out as a string list!)

The value restriction ensures that declarations don't result in this kind of confusion; automatic generalization isn't applied to declarations unless they're functions or simple, immutable data constructs. One way to think of this is that you can create concrete objects only after the type-inference problem is sufficiently constrained so that every concrete object created at the top level of your program has a ground type—a type that doesn't contain any ungeneralized type variables.

The value restriction doesn't apply to simple immutable data constants or function definitions. For example, the following declarations are all automatically generalized, giving the generic types shown:

```
let emptyList = []
let initialLists = ([],[2])
let listOfEmptyLists = [[];[]]
let makeArray ()  = Array.create 100 []
```

```
val emptyList : 'a list
val initialLists : ('a list * int list)
val listOfEmptyLists : 'a list list
val makeArray : unit -> 'a list []
```

Working Around the Value Restriction

The value restriction crops up with mild regularity in F# coding—particularly when you're using F# Interactive, where the scope of type inference is at the granularity of each entry sent to the tool rather than an entire file and hence fewer constraints are placed on these code fragments. You can work around the value restriction in several ways, depending on what you're trying to do.

Technique 1: Constrain Values to Be Nongeneric

The first technique applies when you make a definition such as empties, shown earlier, but you meant to create one value. Recall that this definition was problematic because it's not clear what type of array is being created:

```
let empties = Array.create 100 []
```

If you meant to create one value with a specific type, then use an explicit type annotation:

```
let empties : int list [] = Array.create 100 []
```

The value is then not generic, and the value restriction doesn't apply.

Technique 2: Ensure Generic Functions Have Explicit Arguments

The next technique applies when you're defining generic functions. In this case, make sure you define them with explicit arguments. For example, look at the following definition of a function value:

```
let mapFirst = List.map fst
```

You may expect this to be a generic function with type ('a * 'b) list -> 'a list. However, this isn't what happens. Type variables are automatically generalized at true syntactic function definitions—that is, function definitions with *explicit* arguments. The function mapFirst has *implicit* arguments. Fortunately, it's easy to work around this by making the arguments explicit:

```
let mapFirst inp = List.map fst inp
```

This function now has the following type:

```
val mapFirst : ('a * 'b) list -> 'a list
```

When there is only one argument, our favorite way of writing the extra arguments is as follows:

```
let mapFirst inp = inp |> List.map (fun (x,y) -> x)
```

The same problem arises when you try to define functions by composition. For example:

```
let printFstElements = List.map fst >> List.iter (printf "res = %d")
```

The arguments here are implicit, which causes problems. This definition isn't automatically generalized because this isn't a syntactic function. Again, make the arguments explicit:

```
let printFstElements inp = inp |> List.map fst |> List.iter (printf "res = %d")
```

Technique 3: Add Dummy Arguments to Generic Functions When Necessary

Look at this definition again:

```
let empties = Array.create 100 []
```

It's possible that you really did intend to define a function that generates arrays of different types on demand. In this case, add a dummy argument:

```
let empties () = Array.create 100 []
let intEmpties : int list [] = empties()
let stringEmpties : string list [] = empties()
```

The dummy argument ensures that `empties` is a function with generic arguments and can be automatically generalized.

Technique 4: Add Explicit Type Arguments When Necessary

You can use one final technique to make a value generic. This one is rarely used but is very handy when it's required. It's normally used when you're defining values that are generic but that are neither functions nor simple data expressions. For example, let's define a sequence of 100 empty lists:

```
let emptyLists = Seq.init 100 (fun _ -> [])
```

The expression on the right isn't a function or simple data expression (it's a function application), so the value restriction applies. One solution is to add an extra dummy argument, as in the previous section. However, if you're designing a library, this can seem very artificial. Instead, you can use the following declaration form to make `emptyLists` generic:

```
let emptyLists<'T> : seq<'T list> = Seq.init 100 (fun _ -> [])
```

You can now use `emptyLists` as a *type function* to generate values of different types. For example:

```
> Seq.length emptyLists;;
val it : int = 100

> emptyLists<int>;;
val it : seq<int list> = seq [[]; []; []; []; ...]

> emptyLists<string>;;
val it : seq<string list> = seq [[]; []; []; []; ...]
```

Some values and functions in the F# library are defined in this way, including `typeof<_>`, `Seq.empty`, and `Set.empty`. Chapter 9 covers `typeof`.

Understanding Generic Overloaded Operators

There is one further important way in which code doesn't automatically become generic in F#: when you use overloaded operators such as +, -, *, and /, or overloaded conversion functions such as `float` and `int64`. For example, the following is *not* a generic function:

```
let twice x = (x + x)
```

In the absence of further information, the type of this function is as follows:

```
val twice : int -> int
```

This is because the overloaded operator + defaults to operating on integers. If you add type annotations or further type constraints, you can force the function to operate on any type supporting the overloaded + operator:

```
let twiceFloat (x:float) = x + x
```

```
val twiceFloat : float -> float
```

The information that resolves a use of an overloaded operator can come after the use of the operator:

```
let threeTimes x = (x + x + x)
let sixTimesInt64 (x:int64) = threeTimes x + threeTimes x
```

```
val threeTimes : int64 -> int64
val sixTimesInt64 : int64 -> int64
```

Note how the constraint in the definition of sixTimesInt64 is the only mention of int64 and affects the type of threeTimes. The technical explanation is that overloaded operators such as + give rise to *floating* constraints, which can be resolved later in the type-inference scope.

Summary

F# is a typed language, and F# programmers often use types in sophisticated ways. In this chapter, you learned about the foundations of types, focusing on how types are used in functional programming and on generics and subtyping in particular. The next chapter covers the related topics of object-oriented and modular programming in F#.

CHAPTER 6

■■■

Working with Objects and Modules

Chapters 2 through 5 dealt with the basic constructs of F# functional and imperative programming, and by now we trust you're familiar with the foundational concepts and techniques of practical, small-scale F# programming. This chapter covers language constructs related to *object-oriented (OO) programming*. We assume some familiarity with the basic concepts of OO programming, although you may notice that our discussion of objects deliberately deemphasizes techniques such as implementation inheritance.

The first part of this chapter focuses on OO programming with concrete types. You're then introduced to the notion of object interface types and some simple techniques to implement them. The chapter covers more advanced techniques to implement objects using function parameters, delegation, and implementation inheritance. Finally, it covers the related topics of modules (which are simple containers of functions and values) and extensions (in other words, how to add ad hoc dot-notation to existing modules and types). Chapter 7 covers the topic of encapsulation.

Getting Started with Objects and Members

One of the most important activities of OO programming is defining concrete types equipped with dot-notation. A concrete type has *fixed* behavior: that is, it uses the same member implementations for each concrete value of the type.

You've already met many important concrete types, such as integers, lists, strings, and records (introduced in Chapter 3). It's easy to add OO members to concrete types. Listing 6-1 shows an example.

Listing 6-1. A Vector2D Type with Object-Oriented Members

```
/// Two-dimensional vectors
type Vector2D =
    { DX: float; DY: float }

    /// Get the length of the vector
    member v.Length = sqrt(v.DX * v.DX + v.DY * v.DY)

    /// Get a vector scaled by the given factor
    member v.Scale(k) = { DX=k*v.DX; DY=k*v.DY }

    /// Return a vector shifted by the given delta in the X coordinate
    member v.ShiftX(x) = { v with DX=v.DX+x }

    /// Return a vector shifted by the given delta in the Y coordinate
    member v.ShiftY(y) = { v with DY=v.DY+y }
```

```
/// Return a vector shifted by the given distance in both coordinates
member v.ShiftXY(x,y) = { DX=v.DX+x; DY=v.DY+y }

/// Get the zero vector
static member Zero = { DX=0.0; DY=0.0 }

/// Return a constant vector along the X axis
static member ConstX(dx) = { DX=dx; DY=0.0 }

/// Return a constant vector along the Y axis
static member ConstY(dy) = { DX=0.0; DY=dy }
```

You can use the properties and methods of this type as follows:

```
> let v = {DX = 3.0; DY=4.0 };;
val v : Vector2D

> v.Length;;
val it : float = 5.0

> v.Scale(2.0).Length;;
val it : float = 10.0

> Vector2D.ConstX(3.0);;
val it : Vector2D = {DX = 3.0; DY = 0.0}
```

As usual, it's useful to look at inferred types to understand a type definition. Here are the inferred types for the Vector2D type definition of Listing 6-1.

```
type Vector2D =
    { DX: float; DY: float }
    member Length : float
    member Scale : k:float -> Vector2D
    member ShiftX : x:float -> Vector2D
    member ShiftY : y:float -> Vector2D
    member ShiftXY : x:float * y:float -> Vector2D
    static member Zero : Vector2D
    static member ConstX : dx:float -> Vector2D
    static member ConstY : dy:float -> Vector2D
```

You can see that the Vector2D type contains the following:

- A collection of record fields

- One instance property (Length)

- Four instance methods (Scale, ShiftX, ShiftY, ShiftXY)

- One static property (Zero)

- Two static methods (ConstX, ConstY)

Let's look at the implementation of the Length property:

```
member v.Length = sqrt(v.DX * v.DX + v.DY * v.DY)
```

Here, the identifier v stands for the Vector2D value on which the property is being defined. In many other languages, this is called this or self, but in F# you can name this parameter as you see fit. The implementation of a property such as Length is executed each time the property is invoked; in other words, properties are syntactic sugar for method calls. For example, let's repeat the earlier type definition with an additional property that adds a side effect:

```
member v.LengthWithSideEffect =
    printfn "Computing!"
    sqrt(v.DX * v.DX + v.DY * v.DY)
```

Each time you use this property, you see the side effect:

```
> let x = {DX = 3.0; DY=4.0 };;
val x : Vector2D

> x.LengthWithSideEffect;;
Computing!
val it : float = 5.0

> x.LengthWithSideEffect;;
Computing!
val it : float = 5.0
```

The method members for a type look similar to the properties but also take arguments. For example, let's look at the implementation of the ShiftX method member:

```
member v.ShiftX(x) = { v with DX=v.DX+x }
```

Here the object is v, and the argument is dx. The return result clones the input record value and adjusts the DX field to be v.DX+dx. Cloning records is described in Chapter 3. The ShiftXY method member takes two arguments:

```
member v.ShiftXY(x,y) = { DX=v.DX+x; DY=v.DY+y }
```

Like functions, method members can take arguments in either tupled or iterated form. For example, you could define ShiftXY as follows:

```
member v.ShiftXY x y = { DX=v.DX+x; DY=v.DY+y }
```

However, it's conventional for methods to take their arguments in tupled form. This is partly because OO programming is strongly associated with the design patterns and guidelines of the .NET Framework, and arguments always appear as tupled when using .NET methods from F#.

Discriminated unions are also a form of concrete type. In this case, the shape of the data associated with a value is drawn from a finite, fixed set of choices. Discriminated unions can also be given members. For example:

```
/// A type of binary trees, generic in the type of values carried at nodes and tips
type Tree<'T> =
    | Node of 'T * Tree<'T> * Tree<'T>
    | Tip

    /// Compute the number of values in the tree
    member t.Size =
        match t with
        | Node(_,l,r) -> 1 + l.Size + r.Size
        | Tip -> 0
```

Should You Use Members or Functions?

F# lets you define both members associated with types and objects via the dot-notation and static functions that can perform essentially the same operations. For example, the length of a string s can be computed by both the s.Length property and the String.length function. Given the choice, which should you use in your code? Although there is no fixed answer to this, here are some general rules:

- Use members (methods and properties) where they already exist, unless you have other good reasons not to do so. It's better to use s.Length than String.length, simply because it's shorter, even if it occasionally requires using an additional type annotation. That is, embrace dot-notation, but use it tastefully.

- When designing a framework or library, define members for the intrinsic, essential properties and operations associated with a type.

- When designing a framework or library, define additional functionality in new modules or by using extension members. The section "Extending Existing Types and Modules" later in this chapter covers extension members.

- Sometimes there is duplication in functionality between dot-notation members and values in associated modules. This is intended and should be accepted as part of the mixed OO/functional nature of F#.

Using Classes

Record and union types are symmetric: the values used to *construct* an object are the same as those *stored* in the object, which are a subset of those *published* by the object. This symmetry makes record and union types succinct and clear, and it helps give them other properties; for example, the F# compiler automatically derives generic equality, comparison, and hashing routines for these types.

However, more advanced OO programming often needs to break these symmetries. For example, let's say you want to precompute and store the length of a vector in each vector value. It's clear you don't want everyone who creates a vector to have to perform this computation for you. Instead, you precompute the length as part of the construction sequence for the type. You can't do this using a record, except by using a helper function, so it's convenient to switch to a more general notation for *class types*. Listing 6-2 shows the Vector2D example using a class type.

Listing 6-2. A Vector2D Type with Length Precomputation via a Class Type

```
type Vector2D(dx: float, dy: float) =

    let len = sqrt(dx * dx + dy * dy)

    /// Get the X component of the vector
    member v.DX = dx

    /// Get the Y component of the vector
    member v.DY = dy

    /// Get the length of the vector
    member v.Length = len

    /// Return a vector scaled by the given factor
    member v.Scale(k)  = Vector2D(k*dx,   k*dy)

    /// Return a vector shifted by the given delta in the Y coordinate
    member v.ShiftX(x) = Vector2D(dx=dx+x, dy=dy)

    /// Return a vector shifted by the given delta in the Y coordinate
    member v.ShiftY(y) = Vector2D(dx=dx, dy=dy+y)

    /// Return a vector that is shifted by the given deltas in each coordinate
    member v.ShiftXY(x,y) = Vector2D(dx=dx+x, dy=dy+y)

    /// Get the zero vector
    static member Zero = Vector2D(dx=0.0, dy=0.0)

    /// Get a constant vector along the X axis of length one
    static member OneX = Vector2D(dx=1.0, dy=0.0)

    /// Get a constant vector along the Y axis of length one
    static member OneY = Vector2D(dx=0.0, dy=1.0)
```

You can now use this type as follows:

```
> let v = Vector2D(3.0, 4.0);;
val v : Vector2D

> v.Length;;
val it : float = 5.0

> v.Scale(2.0).Length;;
val it : float = 10.0
```

Once again, it's helpful to look at the inferred type signature for the Vector2D type definition of Listing 6-2:

```
type Vector2D =
    new : dx:float * dy:float -> Vector2D
    member DX : float
    member DY : float
    member Length : float
    member Scale : k:float -> Vector2D
    member ShiftX : x:float -> Vector2D
    member ShiftY : y:float -> Vector2D
    member ShiftXY : x:float * y:float -> Vector2D
    static member Zero : Vector2D
    static member ConstX : dx:float -> Vector2D
    static member ConstY : dy:float -> Vector2D
```

The signature of the type is almost the same as that for Listing 6-1. The primary difference is in the construction syntax. Let's look at what's going on here. The first line says you're defining a type Vector2D with a *primary constructor*. This is sometimes called an *implicit constructor*. The constructor takes two arguments, dx and dy. The variables dx and dy are in scope throughout the (nonstatic) members of the type definition.

The second line is part of the computation performed each time an object of this type is constructed:

```
let len = sqrt(dx * dx + dy * dy)
```

Like the input values, the len value is in scope throughout the rest of the (nonstatic) members of the type. The next three lines publish both the input values and the computed length as properties:

```
member v.DX = dx
member v.DY = dy
member v.Length = len
```

The remaining lines implement the same methods and static properties as the original record type. The Scale method creates its result by calling the constructor for the type using the expression Vector2D(k*dx, k*dy). In this expression, arguments are specified by position.

Class types with primary constructors always have the following form, where elements in brackets are optional and * indicates that the element may appear zero or more times:

```
type TypeName <type-arguments>optional arguments [ as ident ] optional =
    [ inherit type [ as base ] optional ] optional
    [ let-binding | let-rec bindings ] zero-or-more
    [ do-statement ] zero-or-more
    [ abstract-binding | member-binding | interface-implementation ] zero-or-more
```

Later sections cover inheritance, abstract bindings, and interface implementations.

The Vector2D in Listing 6-2 uses a construction sequence. Construction sequences can enforce object invariants. For example, the following defines a vector type that checks that its length is close to 1.0 and refuses to construct an instance of the value if not:

```
/// Vectors whose length is checked to be close to length one.
type UnitVector2D(dx,dy) =
    let tolerance = 0.000001
```

```
let length = sqrt (dx * dx + dy * dy)

do if abs (length - 1.0) >= tolerance then failwith "not a unit vector";

member v.DX = dx

member v.DY = dy

new() = UnitVector2D (1.0,0.0)
```

This example shows something else: sometimes it's convenient for a class to have multiple constructors. You do this by adding extra *explicit constructors* using a member named new. These must ultimately construct an instance of the object via the primary constructor. The inferred signature for this type contains two constructors:

```
type UnitVector2D =
    new : unit -> UnitVector2D
    new : dx:float * dy:float -> UnitVector2D
    member DX : float
    member DY : float
```

This represents a form of method overloading, covered in more detail in the "Adding Method Overloading" section later in this chapter.

Class types can also include static bindings. For example, this can be used to ensure only one vector object is allocated for the Zero and One properties of the vector type:

```
/// A class including some static bindings
type Vector2D(dx: float, dy: float) =

    static let zero = Vector2D(0.0, 0.0)
    static let onex = Vector2D(1.0, 0.0)
    static let oney = Vector2D(0.0, 1.0)

    /// Get the zero vector
    static member Zero = zero

    /// Get a constant vector along the X axis of length one
    static member OneX = onex

    /// Get a constant vector along the Y axis of length one
    static member OneY = oney
```

Static bindings in classes are initialized once, along with other module and static bindings in the file. If the class type is generic, it's initialized once per concrete type generic instantiation.

Adding Further Object Notation to Your Types

As we mentioned, one of the most useful aspects of OO programming is the notational convenience of dot-notation. This extends to other kinds of notation, in particular expr.[expr] *indexer* notation, named arguments, optional arguments, operator overloading, and method overloading. The following sections cover how to define and use these notational conveniences.

Working with Indexer Properties

Like methods, properties can take arguments; these are called *indexer* properties. The most commonly defined indexer property is called Item, and the Item property on a value v is accessed via the special notation v.[i]. As the notation suggests, these properties are normally used to implement the lookup operation on collection types. The following example implements a sparse vector in terms of an underlying sorted dictionary:

```
open System.Collections.Generic
type SparseVector(items: seq<int * float>)=
    let elems = new SortedDictionary<_,_>()
    do items |> Seq.iter (fun (k,v) -> elems.Add(k,v))

    /// This defines an indexer property
    member t.Item
        with get(idx) =
            if elems.ContainsKey(idx) then elems.[idx]
            else 0.0
```

You can define and use the indexer property as follows:

```
> let v = SparseVector [(3,547.0)];;
val v : SparseVector

> v.[4];;
val it : float = 0.0

> v.[3];;
val it : float = 547.0
```

You can also use indexer properties as mutable setter properties with the syntax expr.[expr] <- expr. This is covered in the section "Defining Object Types with Mutable State." Indexer properties can also take multiple arguments; for example, the indexer property for the F# Power Pack type Microsoft.FSharp.Math.Matrix<'T> takes two arguments. Chapter 10 describes this type.

Adding Overloaded Operators

Types can also include the definition of overloaded operators. Typically, you do this by defining static members with the same names as the relevant operators. Here is an example:

```
type Vector2DWithOperators(dx:float,dy:float) =
    member x.DX = dx
```

```
member x.DY = dy

static member (+) (v1: Vector2DWithOperators ,v2: Vector2DWithOperators) =
    Vector2DWithOperators(v1.DX + v2.DX, v1.DY + v2.DY)

static member (-) (v1: Vector2DWithOperators ,v2: Vector2DWithOperators) =
    Vector2DWithOperators (v1.DX - v2.DX, v1.DY - v2.DY)
```

```
> let v1 = new Vector2DWithOperators (3.0,4.0);;
val v1 : Vector2DWithOperators

> v1 + v1;;
val it : Vector2DWithOperators = { DX=6.0; DY=8.0 }

> v1 - v1;;
val it : Vector2DWithOperators = { DX=0.0; DY=0.0 }
```

If you add overloaded operators to your type, you may also have to customize how generic equality, hashing, and comparison are performed. In particular, the behavior of generic operators such as hash, <, >, <=, >=, compare, min, and max isn't specified by defining new static members with these names, but rather by the techniques described in Chapter 8.

How Does Operator Overloading Work?

Operator overloading in F# works by having fixed functions that map uses of operators through to particular static members on the static types involved in the operation. These functions are usually defined in the F# library. For example, the F# library includes the following definition for the (+) operator:

```
let inline (+) x y = ((^a or ^b): (static member (+) : ^a * ^b -> ^c) (x,y))
```

This defines the infix function (+) and is implemented using a special expression that says "implement x + y by calling a static member (+) on the type of the left or right operand." The function is marked inline to ensure that F# can always check for the existence of this member and call it efficiently. When you name a static member (+), then that is really shorthand for the name op_Addition, which is the .NET standard encoded name for addition operators.

You can define your own operators if you want, but they aren't automatically overloaded in the same way as F# library definitions like the one shown previously. For example, the following defines a new infix operator that appends a single element to the end of a list:

```
let (++) x y = List.append x [y]
```

This operator isn't overloaded; it's a single fixed function. Defining non-overloaded operators can help make some implementation code more succinct, and you use this technique in the symbolic programming examples in Chapter 12.

In principle, you can define new operators that are truly overloaded in the same way as the definition of (+) in the F# library, mapping the operator across to particular static members. However, code is generally much clearer if you stick to the standard overloaded operators.

Using Named and Optional Arguments

The F# OO constructs are designed largely for use in APIs for software components. Two useful mechanisms in APIs permit callers to name arguments and let API designers make certain arguments optional.

Named arguments are simple. For example, in Listing 6-2, the implementations of some methods specify arguments by name, as in the expression Vector2D(dx=dx+x, dy=dy). You can use named arguments with all dot-notation method calls. Code written using named arguments is often much more readable and maintainable than code relying on argument position. The rest of this book frequently uses named arguments.

You declare a member argument optional by prefixing the argument name with ?. Within a function implementation, an optional argument always has an option<_> type; for example, an optional argument of type int appears as a value of type option<int> within the function body. The value is None if no argument is supplied by the caller and Some(arg) if the argument arg is given by the caller. For example:

```
open System.Drawing

type LabelInfo(?text:string, ?font:Font) =
    let text = defaultArg text ""
    let font = match font with
                | None -> new Font(FontFamily.GenericSansSerif,12.0f)
                | Some v -> v
    member x.Text = text
    member x.Font = font
```

The inferred signature for this type shows how the optional arguments have become named arguments accepting option values:

```
type LabelInfo =
    new : text:string option * font:System.Drawing.Font option -> LabelInfo
    member Font : System.Drawing.Font
    member Text : string
```

You can now create LabelInfo values using several different techniques:

```
> LabelInfo (text="Hello World");;
val it : LabelInfo =
    {Font = [Font: Name=Microsoft Sans Serif, Size=12]; Text = "Hello World"}

> LabelInfo("Goodbye Lenin");;
val it : LabelInfo =
    {Font = [Font: Name=Microsoft Sans Serif, Size=12];  Text = "Goodbye Lenin"}

> LabelInfo(font=new Font(FontFamily.GenericMonospace,36.0f),
            text="Imagine");;
val it : LabelInfo =
    {Font = [Font: Name=Courier New, Size=36]; Text = "Imagine"}
```

Optional arguments must always appear last in the set of arguments accepted by a method. They're usually used as named arguments by callers.

The implementation of LabelInfo uses the F# library function defaultArg, which is a useful way to specify simple default values for optional arguments. Its type is as follows:

```
val defaultArg : 'T option -> 'T-> 'T
```

■ **Note** The second argument given to the defaultArg function is evaluated *before* the function is called. This means you should take care that this argument isn't expensive to compute and doesn't need to be disposed. The previous example uses a match expression to specify the default for the font argument for this reason.

Using Optional Property Settings

Throughout this book, you've used a second technique to specify configuration parameters when creating objects: *initial property settings* for objects. For example, in Chapter 2, you used the following code:

```
open System.Windows.Forms
let form = new Form(Visible=true,TopMost=true,Text="Welcome to F#")
```

The constructor for the System.Windows.Forms.Form class takes no arguments, so in this case the named arguments indicate post-hoc set operations for the given properties. The code is shorthand for this:

```
open System.Windows.Forms

let form =
    let tmp = new Form()
    tmp.Visible <- true
    tmp.TopMost <- true
    tmp.Text <- "Welcome to F#"
    tmp
```

The F# compiler interprets unused named arguments as calls that set properties of the returned object. This technique is widely used for mutable objects that evolve over time, such as graphical components, because it greatly reduces the number of optional arguments that need to be plumbed around. Here's how to define a version of the LabelInfo type used earlier that is configurable by optional property settings:

```
open System.Drawing

type LabelInfoWithPropertySetting() =
    let mutable text = "" // the default
    let mutable font = new Font(FontFamily.GenericSansSerif,12.0f)
    member x.Text with get() = text and set v = text <- v
    member x.Font with get() = font and set v = font <- v
```

```
> LabelInfoWithPropertySetting(Text="Hello World");;
val it : LabelInfo =
    {Font = [Font: Name=Microsoft Sans Serif, Size=12]; Text = "Hello World"}
```

You use this technique in Chapter 11 when you learn how to define a Windows Forms control with configurable properties. The "Defining Object Types with Mutable State" section later in this chapter covers mutable objects in more detail.

Adding Method Overloading

.NET APIs and other OO design frameworks frequently use a notational device called *method overloading*. This means a type can support multiple methods with the same name, and uses of methods are distinguished by name, number of arguments, and argument types. For example, the System.Console.WriteLine method of .NET has 19 overloads!

Method overloading is used relatively rarely in F#-authored classes, partly because optional arguments and mutable property setters tend to make it less necessary. However, method overloading is permitted in F#. First, methods can easily be overloaded by the number of arguments. For example, Listing 6-3 shows a concrete type representing an interval of numbers on the number line. It includes two methods called Span, one taking a pair of intervals and the other taking an arbitrary collection of intervals. The overloading is resolved according to argument count.

Listing 6-3. An Interval Type with Overloaded Methods

```
/// Interval(lo,hi) represents the range of numbers from lo to hi,
/// but not including either lo or hi.
type Interval(lo,hi) =
    member r.Lo = lo
    member r.Hi = hi
    member r.IsEmpty = hi <= lo
    member r.Contains v = lo < v && v < hi

    static member Empty = Interval(0.0,0.0)

    /// Return the smallest interval that covers both the intervals
    /// This method is overloaded.
    static member Span (r1:Interval, r2:Interval) =
        if r1.IsEmpty then r2 else
        if r2.IsEmpty then r1 else
        Interval(min r1.Lo r2.Lo, max r1.Hi r2.Hi)

    /// Return the smallest interval that covers all the intervals
    /// This method is overloaded.
    static member Span(ranges: seq<Interval>) =
        Seq.fold (fun r1 r2 -> Interval.Span(r1,r2)) Interval.Empty ranges
```

Second, multiple methods can also have the same number of arguments and be overloaded by type. One of the most common examples is providing multiple implementations of overloaded operators on the same type. The following example shows a Point type that supports two subtraction operations, one subtracting a Point from a Point to give a Vector and one subtracting a Vector from a Point to give a Point:

```
type Vector =
    { DX:float; DY:float }
    member v.Length = sqrt(v.DX*v.DX+v.DY*v.DY)

type Point =
    { X:float; Y:float }

    static member (-) (p1:Point,p2:Point) = { DX=p1.X-p2.X; DY=p1.Y-p2.Y }

    static member (-) (p:Point,v:Vector) = { X=p.X-v.DX; Y=p.Y-v.DY }
```

Overloads must be unique by signature, and you should take care to make sure your overload set isn't too ambiguous—the more overloads you use, the more type annotations users of your types will need to add.

Defining Object Types with Mutable State

All the types you've seen so far in this chapter have been immutable. For example, the values of the Vector2D types shown in Listing 6-1 and Listing 6-2 can't be modified after they're created. Frequently, you want to define mutable objects, particularly because OO programming is a generally useful technique for encapsulating mutable and evolving state. Listing 6-4 shows the definition of a mutable representation of a 2D vector.

Listing 6-4. A Concrete Object Type with State

```
type MutableVector2D(dx:float,dy:float) =
    let mutable currDX = dx
    let mutable currDY = dy

    member vec.DX with get() = currDX and set v = currDX <- v
    member vec.DY with get() = currDY and set v = currDY <- v

    member vec.Length
        with get () = sqrt (currDX * currDX + currDY * currDY)
        and  set len =
            let theta = vec.Angle
            currDX <- cos theta * len
            currDY <- sin theta * len

    member vec.Angle
        with get () = atan2 currDY currDX
        and  set theta =
            let len = vec.Length
            currDX <- cos theta * len
            currDY <- sin theta * len
```

The mutable state is held in two mutable local let bindings for currDX and currDY. It also exposes additional settable properties, Length and Angle, that interpret and adjust the underlying currDX/currDY values. Here is the inferred signature for the type:

```
type MutableVector2D =
    new : float * float -> MutableVector2D
    member DX : float with get,set
    member DY : float with get,set
    member Angle : float with get,set
    member Length : float with get,set
```

You can use this type as follows:

```
> let v = MutableVector2D(3.0,4.0);;
val v : MutableVector2D

> (v.DX, v.DY);;
val it : float * float = (3.0, 4.0)

> (v.Length, v.Angle);;
val it : float * float = (5.0, 0.927295218)

> v.Angle <- System.Math.PI / 6.0;;      // "30 degrees"
val it : unit = ()

> (v.DX, v.DY);;
val it : float * float = (4.330127019, 2.5)

> (v.Length, v.Angle);;
val it : float * float = (5.0, 0.523598775)
```

Adjusting the Angle property rotates the vector while maintaining its overall length. This example uses the long syntax for properties, where you specify both set and get operations for the property.

If the type has an indexer (Item) property, then you write an indexed setter as follows:

```
open System.Collections.Generic
type IntegerMatrix(rows:int, cols:int)=
    let elems = Array2D.zeroCreate<int> rows cols

    /// This defines an indexer property with getter and setter
    member t.Item
        with get (idx1,idx2) = elems.[idx1, idx2]
        and set (idx1,idx2) v = elems.[idx1, idx2] <- v
```

■ **Note** Class types with a primary constructor are useful partly because they implicitly *encapsulate* internal functions and mutable state. This is because all the construction arguments and `let` bindings are private to the object instance being constructed. This is just one of the ways of encapsulating information in F# programming. Chapter 7 covers encapsulation more closely.

Objects and Mutation

OO programming is often presented primarily as a technique for controlling the complexity of mutable state. However, many of the concerns of OO programming are orthogonal to this. For example, programming constructs such as object interface types, inheritance, and higher-level design patterns such as publish/subscribe stem from the OO tradition, whereas techniques such as functions, type abstraction, and aggregate operations such as map and fold stem from the functional programming tradition. Many OO techniques have no fundamental relationship to object mutation and identity; for example, interfaces and inheritance can be used very effectively with immutable objects. Much of the expressivity of F# lies in the way it brings the techniques of OO programming and functional programming comfortably together.

Getting Started with Object Interface Types

So far in this chapter, you've seen only how to define *concrete* object types. One of the key advances in both functional and OO programming has been the move toward using *abstract* types for large portions of modern software. These values are typically accessed via *interfaces*, and you now look at defining new *object interface types*. Many .NET object interface types begin with the letter I, as in System.IDisposable.

The notion of an object interface type can sound a little daunting at first, but the concept is actually simple; object interface types are ones whose member implementations can vary from value to value. As it happens, you've already met one important family of types whose implementations also vary from value to value: F# function types!

- In Chapter 3, you saw how functions can be used to model a range of concepts such as comparison functions, aggregation functions, and transformation functions.

- In Chapter 5, you saw how records of function values can be used for the parameters needed to make an algorithm generic.

You've also already met some other important object interface types such as System.Collections.Generic.IEnumerable<'T> and System.IDisposable.

Object interface types are always *implemented*, and the type definition itself doesn't specify how this is done. Listing 6-5 shows an object interface type IShape and a number of implementations of it. This section walks through the definitions in this code piece by piece, because they illustrate the key concepts behind object interface types and how they can be implemented.

Listing 6-5. An Object Interface Type IShape and Some Implementations

```
open System.Drawing
type IShape =
    abstract Contains : Point -> bool
    abstract BoundingBox : Rectangle

let circle (center:Point, radius:int) =
    { new IShape with

        member x.Contains(p:Point) =
            let dx = float32 (p.X - center.X)
            let dy = float32 (p.Y - center.Y)
            sqrt(dx*dx+dy*dy) <= float32 radius
```

```
            member x.BoundingBox =
                Rectangle(center.X-radius,center.Y-radius,2*radius+1,2*radius+1) }

let square (center:Point, side:int) =
    { new IShape with

            member x.Contains(p:Point) =
                let dx = p.X - center.X
                let dy = p.Y - center.Y
                abs(dx) < side/2 && abs(dy) < side/2

            member x.BoundingBox =
                Rectangle(center.X-side,center.Y-side,side*2,side*2) }

type MutableCircle() =

    let mutable center = Point(x=0,y=0)
    let mutable radius = 10

    member sq.Center with get() = center and set v = center <- v

    member sq.Radius with get() = radius and set v = radius <- v

    member c.Perimeter = 2.0 * System.Math.PI * float radius

    interface IShape with

        member x.Contains(p:Point) =
            let dx = float32 (p.X - center.X)
            let dy = float32 (p.Y - center.Y)
            sqrt(dx*dx+dy*dy) <= float32 radius

        member x.BoundingBox =
            Rectangle(center.X-radius,center.Y-radius,2*radius+1,2*radius+1)
```

Defining New Object Interface Types

The key definition in Listing 6-5 is the following (it also uses Rectangle and Point, two types from the System.Drawing namespace):

```
open System.Drawing
type IShape =
    abstract Contains : Point -> bool
    abstract BoundingBox : Rectangle
```

Here you use the keyword abstract to define the member signatures for this type, indicating that the implementation of the member may vary from value to value. Also note that IShape isn't concrete; it's neither a record nor a discriminated union or class type. It doesn't have any constructors and doesn't accept any arguments. This is how F# infers that it's an object interface type.

Implementing Object Interface Types Using Object Expressions

The following code from Listing 6-5 implements the object interface type IShape using an *object expression*:

```
let circle(center:Point,radius:int) =
    { new IShape with
          member x.Contains(p:Point) =
              let dx = float32 (p.X - center.X)
              let dy = float32 (p.Y - center.Y)
              sqrt(dx*dx+dy*dy) <= float32 radius
          member x.BoundingBox =
              Rectangle(center.X-radius,center.Y-radius,2*radius+1,2*radius+1) }
```

The type of the function circle is as follows:

```
val circle : Point * int -> IShape
```

The construct in the braces, { new IShape with ... }, is the object expression. This is a new expression form that you haven't encountered previously in this book, because it's generally used only when implementing object interface types. An object expression must give implementations for all the members of an object interface type. The general form of this kind of expression is simple:

```
{ new Type optional-arguments with
      member-definitions
  optional-extra-interface-definitions }
```

The member definitions take the same form as members for type definitions described earlier in this chapter. The optional arguments are given only when object expressions inherit from a class type, and the optional interface definitions are used when implementing additional interfaces that are part of a hierarchy of object interface types.

You can use the function circle as follows:

```
> let bigCircle = circle(Point(0,0), 100);;
val bigCircle : IShape

> bigCircle.BoundingBox;;
val it : Rectangle = {X=-100,Y=-100,Width=201,Height=201}

> bigCircle.Contains(Point(70,70));;
val it : bool = true

> bigCircle.Contains(Point(71,71));;
val it : bool = false
```

Listing 6-5 also contains another function square that gives a different implementation for IShape, also using an object expression:

```
> let smallSquare = square(Point(1,1), 1);;
val smallSquare : IShape

> smallSquare.BoundingBox;;
val it : Rectangle = {X=0,Y=0,Width=2,Height=2}

> smallSquare.Contains(Point(0,0));;
val it : bool = false
```

■ **Note** In OO languages, implementing types in multiple ways is commonly called *polymorphism*, which you may call *polymorphism of implementation*. Polymorphism of this kind is present throughout F#, and not just with respect to the OO constructs. In functional programming, the word *polymorphism* is used to mean generic type parameters. These are an orthogonal concept discussed in Chapters 2 and 5.

Implementing Object Interface Types Using Concrete Types

It's common to have concrete types that both implement one or more object interface types and provide additional services of their own. Collections are a primary example, because they always implement IEnumerable<'T>. To give another example, in Listing 6-5 the type MutableCircle is defined as follows:

```
type MutableCircle() =
    let mutable center = Point(x=0,y=0)
    let mutable radius = 10
    member c.Center with get() = center and set v = center <- v
    member c.Radius with get() = radius and set v = radius <- v
    member c.Perimeter = 2.0 * System.Math.PI * float radius
    interface IShape with
        member c.Contains(p:Point) =
            let dx = float32 (p.X - center.X)
            let dy = float32 (p.Y - center.Y)
            sqrt(dx*dx+dy*dy) <= float32 radius
        member c.BoundingBox =
            Rectangle(center.X-radius,center.Y-radius,2*radius+1,2*radius+1)
```

This type implements the IShape interface, which means MutableCircle is a subtype of IShape, but it also provides three properties—Center, Radius, and Perimeter—that are specific to the MutableCircle type, two of which are settable. The type has the following signature:

```
type MutableCircle =
    interface IShape
    new : unit -> MutableCircle
    member Perimeter : float
    member Center : Point with get,set
    member Radius : int with get,set
```

You can now reveal the interface (through a type cast) and use its members. For example:

```
> let circle2 = MutableCircle();;
val circle2 : MutableCircle

> circle2.Radius;;
val it : int = 10

> (circle2 :> IShape).BoundingBox;;
val it : Rectangle = {X=-10,Y=-10,Width=21,Height=21}
```

Using Common Object Interface Types from the .NET Libraries

Like other constructs discussed in this chapter, object interface types are often encountered when using
.NET libraries. Some object interface types such as IEnumerable<'T> (called seq<'T> in F# coding) are
also used throughout F# programming. It's a .NET convention to prefix the name of all object interface
types with I. However, using object interface types is very common in F# OO programming, so this
convention isn't always followed.

Here's the essence of the definition of the System.Collections.Generic.IEnumerable<'T> type and
the related type IEnumerator using F# notation:

```
type IEnumerator<'T> =
    abstract Current : 'T
    abstract MoveNext : unit -> bool

type IEnumerable<'T> =
    abstract GetEnumerator : unit -> IEnumerator<'T>
```

The IEnumerable<'T> type is implemented by most concrete collection types. It can also be
implemented by a sequence expression or by calling a library function such as Seq.unfold, which in turn
uses an object expression as part of its implementation.

■ **Note** The IEnumerator<'T> and IEnumerable<'T> interfaces are defined in a library component that is
implemented using another .NET language. This section uses the corresponding F# syntax. In reality,
IEnumerator<'T> also inherits from the nongeneric interface System.Collections.IEnumerator and the type
System.IDisposable, and IEnumerable<'T> also inherits from the nongeneric interface
System.Collections.IEnumerable. For clarity, we've ignored this. See the F# library documentation for full
example implementations of these types.

Some other useful predefined F# and .NET object interface types are as follows:

- System.IDisposable: Represents values that may own explicitly reclaimable
  resources.

- System.IComparable and System.IComparable<'T>: Represent values that can be compared to other values. F# generic comparison is implemented via these types, as you see in Chapter 8.

- Microsoft.FSharp.Control.IEvent: Represents mutable ports into which you can plug event listeners, or *callbacks*. This technique is described in Chapter 8. Some other entity is typically responsible for raising the event and thus calling all the listener callbacks. In F#, .NET events become values of this type or the related type Microsoft.FSharp.Control.IDelegateEvent, and the module Microsoft.FSharp.Control.Event contains many useful combinators for manipulating these values. You can open this module by using open Event.

Understanding Hierarchies of Object Interface Types

Object interface types can be arranged in hierarchies using *interface inheritance*. This provides a way to classify types. To create a hierarchy, you use the inherit keyword in an object interface type definition along with each parent object interface type. For example, the .NET Framework includes a hierarchical classification of collection types: ICollection<'T> extends IEnumerable<'T>. Here are the essential definitions of these types in F# syntax, with some minor details omitted:

```
type IEnumerable<'T> =
    abstract GetEnumerator : unit -> IEnumerator<'T>

type ICollection<'T> =
    inherit IEnumerable<'T>
    abstract Count : int
    abstract IsReadOnly : bool
    abstract Add : 'T -> unit
    abstract Clear : unit -> unit
    abstract Contains  : 'T -> bool
    abstract CopyTo  : 'T[] * int -> unit
    abstract Remove  : 'T -> unit
```

When you implement an interface that inherits from another interface, you must effectively implement both interfaces.

■ **Caution** Although hierarchical modeling is useful, you must use it with care: poorly designed hierarchies often have to be abandoned late in the software development life cycle, leading to major disruptions. For many applications, it's adequate to use existing classification hierarchies in conjunction with some new nonhierarchical interface types.

More Techniques to Implement Objects

Objects can be difficult to implement from scratch; for example, a graphical user interface (GUI) component must respond to many different events, often in regular and predictable ways, and it would be tedious to have to recode all this behavior for each component. This makes it essential to support the process of creating partial implementations of objects, where the *partial implementations* can then be completed or customized. The following sections cover techniques to build partial implementations of objects.

Combining Object Expressions and Function Parameters

One of the easiest ways to build a partial implementation of an object is to qualify the implementation of the object by a number of function parameters that complete the implementation. For example, the following code defines an object interface type called ITextOutputSink, a partial implementation of that type called simpleOutputSink, and a function called simpleOutputSink that acts as a partial implementation of that type. The remainder of the implementation is provided by a function parameter called writeCharFunction:

```
/// An object interface type that consumes characters and strings
type ITextOutputSink =

    /// When implemented, writes one Unicode character to the sink
    abstract WriteChar : char -> unit

    /// When implemented, writes one Unicode string to the sink
    abstract WriteString : string -> unit

/// Returns an object that implements ITextOutputSink by using writeCharFunction
let simpleOutputSink writeCharFunction =
    { new ITextOutputSink with
          member x.WriteChar(c) = writeCharFunction c
          member x.WriteString(s) = s |> String.iter x.WriteChar }
```

This construction function uses function values to build an object of a given shape. Here the inferred type is as follows:

```
val simpleOutputSink: (char -> unit) -> ITextOutputSink
```

The following code instantiates the function parameter to output the characters to a particular System.Text.StringBuilder object, an imperative type for accumulating characters in a buffer before converting these to an immutable System.String value:

```
let stringBuilderOuputSink (buf : System.Text.StringBuilder ) =
    simpleOutputSink (fun c -> buf.Append(c) |> ignore)
```

Here is an example that uses this function interactively:

```
> let buf = new System.Text.StringBuilder();;
val buf : StringBuilder

> let c = stringBuilderOuputSink(buf);;
val c : ITextOutputSink

> ["Incy"; " "; "Wincy"; " "; "Spider"] |> List.iter c.WriteString;;
val it : unit = ()

> buf.ToString();;
val it : string = "Incy Wincy Spider"
```

Object expressions must give definitions for all unimplemented abstract members and can't add other members.

One powerful technique implements some or all abstract members in terms of function parameters. As you saw in Chapter 3, function parameters can represent a wide range of concepts. For example, here is a type CountingOutputSink that performs the same role as the earlier function simpleOutputSink, except that the number of characters written to the sink is recorded and published as a property:

```
/// A type which fully implements the ITextOutputSink object interface
type CountingOutputSink(writeCharFunction: char -> unit) =

    let mutable count = 0

    interface ITextOutputSink with
        member x.WriteChar(c) = count <- count + 1; writeCharFunction(c)
        member x.WriteString(s) = s |> String.iter (x :> ITextOutputSink).WriteChar

    member x.Count = count
```

■ **Note** Qualifying object implementations by function parameters can be seen as a simple form of the OO design pattern known as *delegation*, because parts of the implementation are delegated to the function values. Delegation is a powerful and compositional technique for reusing fragments of implementations and is commonly used in F# as a replacement for OO implementation inheritance.

Defining Partially Implemented Class Types

In this chapter, you've seen how to define concrete types, such as Vector2D in Listings 6-2 and 6-3, and you've seen how to define object interface types, such as IShape in Listing 6-5. Sometimes it's useful to define types that are halfway between these types: *partially concrete types*. Partially implemented types are class types that also have abstract members, some of which may be unimplemented and some of which may have default implementations. For example, consider the following class:

```
/// A type whose members are partially implemented
[<AbstractClass>]
type TextOutputSink() =
    abstract WriteChar : char -> unit
    abstract WriteString : string -> unit
    default x.WriteString s = s |> String.iter x.WriteChar
```

This class defines two abstract members, `WriteChar` and `WriteString`, but gives a default implementation for `WriteString` in terms of `WriteChar`. Because `WriteChar` isn't yet implemented, you can't create an instance of this type directly; unlike other concrete types, partially implemented types still need to be implemented. One way to do this is to complete the implementation via an object expression. For example:

```
{ new TextOutputSink() with
    member x.WriteChar c = System.Console.Write(c) }
```

Using Partially Implemented Types via Delegation

This section covers how you can use partially implemented types to build complete objects. One approach is to instantiate one or more partially implemented types to put together a complete concrete type. This is often done via delegation to an instantiation of the partially concrete type; for example, the following example creates a private, internal `TextOutputSink` object whose implementation of `WriteChar` counts the number of characters written through that object. You use this object to build the `HtmlWriter` object that publishes three methods specific to the process of writing a particular format:

```
/// A type which uses a TextOutputSink internally
type HtmlWriter() =
    let mutable count = 0
    let sink =
        { new TextOutputSink() with
            member x.WriteChar c =
                count <- count + 1;
                System.Console.Write c }

    member x.CharCount = count
    member x.WriteHeader() = sink.WriteString("<html>")
    member x.WriteFooter() = sink.WriteString("</html>")
    member x.WriteString(s) = sink.WriteString(s)
```

Using Partially Implemented Types via Implementation Inheritance

Another technique to use partially implemented types is called *implementation inheritance*, which is widely used in OO languages despite being a somewhat awkward technique. Implementation inheritance tends to be much less significant in F# because it comes with major drawbacks:

- Implementation inheritance takes base objects and makes them more complex. This is against the spirit of functional programming, where the aim is to build simple, composable abstractions. Functional programming, object expressions, and delegation tend to provide good alternative techniques for defining, sharing, and combining implementation fragments.

- Implementation hierarchies tend to leak across API boundaries, revealing how objects are implemented rather than how they can be used and composed.

- Implementation hierarchies are often fragile in response to minor changes in program specification.

If implementation inheritance is used, you should in many cases consider making all implementing classes private or hiding all implementing classes behind a signature. For example, the Microsoft.FSharp.Collections.Seq module provides many implementations of the seq<'T> interface but exposes no implementation inheritance.

Nevertheless, hierarchies of classes are important in domains such as GUI programming, and the technique is used heavily by .NET libraries written in other .NET languages. For example, System.Windows.Forms.Control, System.Windows.Forms.UserControl, and System.Windows.Forms.RichTextBox are part of a hierarchy of visual GUI elements. Should you want to write new controls, then you must understand this implementation hierarchy and how to extend it. Chapter 11 shows a complete example of extending UserControl. However, even in this domain, implementation inheritance is often less important than you may think, because these controls can often be configured in powerful and interesting ways by adding function callbacks to events associated with the controls.

Here is a simple example of applying the technique to instantiate and extend the partially implemented type TextOutputSink:

```
/// An implementation of TextOutputSink, counting the number of bytes written
type CountingOutputSinkByInheritance() =
    inherit TextOutputSink()

    let mutable count = 0

    member sink.Count = count

    default sink.WriteChar c =
        count <- count + 1;
        System.Console.Write c
```

The keywords override and default can be used interchangeably; both indicate that an implementation is being given for an abstract member. By convention, override is used when giving implementations for abstract members in inherited types that already have implementations, and default is used for implementations of abstract members that didn't previously have implementations.

Implementations are also free to override and modify default implementations such as the implementation of WriteString provided by TextOutputSink. Here is an example:

```
{ new TextOutputSink() with
    member sink.WriteChar c = System.Console.Write c
    member sink.WriteString s = System.Console.Write s }
```

You can also build new partially implemented types by extending existing partially implemented types. The following example takes the TextOutputSink type from the previous section and adds two abstract members called WriteByte and WriteBytes, adds a default implementation for WriteBytes, adds an initial implementation for WriteChar, and overrides the implementation of WriteString to use WriteBytes. The implementations of WriteChar and WriteString use the .NET functionality to convert the Unicode characters and strings to bytes under System.Text.UTF8Encoding, documented in the .NET Framework class libraries:

```
open System.Text

/// A component to write bytes to an output sink
[<AbstractClass>]
type ByteOutputSink() =
    inherit TextOutputSink()

    /// When implemented, writes one byte to the sink
    abstract WriteByte : byte -> unit

    /// When implemented, writes multiple bytes to the sink
    abstract WriteBytes : byte[] -> unit

    default sink.WriteChar c = sink.WriteBytes(Encoding.UTF8.GetBytes [|c|])

    override sink.WriteString s = sink.WriteBytes(Encoding.UTF8.GetBytes s)

    default sink.WriteBytes b = b |> Array.iter sink.WriteByte
```

Using Modules and Static Members

A common OO design technique is to use a class that contains only static items as a way of organizing values, global state, and type definitions. In F#, this is called a *module*. A module is a simple container for values, type definitions, and submodules. For example, here is the Vector2D example rewritten to use a module to hold the operations associated with the type:

```
type Vector2D =
    { DX: float; DY: float }

module Vector2DOps =
    let length v = sqrt (v.DX * v.DX + v.DY * v.DY)
    let scale k v = { DX=k*v.DX; DY=k*v.DY }
    let shiftX x v = { v with DX=v.DX+x }
    let shiftY y v = { v with DY=v.DY+y }
    let shiftXY (x,y) v = { DX=v.DX+x; DY=v.DY+y }
    let zero = { DX=0.0; DY=0.0 }
    let constX dx = { DX=dx; DY=0.0 }
    let constY dy = { DX=0.0; DY=dy }
```

A module is compiled as a class that contains only static values, types, and additional submodules. Some people prefer to use classes with static members for this purpose, although in practice there is little difference between the two techniques. Modules may also contain type and submodule definitions. Sometimes you want to have a module with the same name as one of your types. You can do this by adding an attribute to your code:

```
type Vector2D =
    { DX: float; DY: float }

[<CompilationRepresentation(CompilationRepresentationFlags.ModuleSuffix)>]
module Vector2D =
    let length v = sqrt(v.DX * v.DX + v.DY * v.DY)
```

Values in a module can be used via a long path, such as Vector2D.length. Alternatively, you can open the module, which makes all the contents accessible without qualification. For example, open Vector2D makes the identifier length available without qualification.

Using Modules and Types to Organize Code

You often have to choose whether to use modules or OO dot-notation to organize your code. Here are some of the rules for using these to organize your code effectively and to lay the groundwork for applying good .NET library and framework design principles to your code:

- Use modules when prototyping and to organize scripts, ad hoc algorithms, initialization code, and active patterns.

- Use concrete types (records, discriminated unions, and class types) to implement concrete data structures. In the long term, plan on completely hiding the implementation of these types. You see how to do this in Chapter 7. You can provide dot-notation operations to help users access parts of the data structure. Avoid revealing other representation details.

- Use object interface types for types that have several possible implementations.

- Implement object interface types by private concrete types or by object expressions.

- In polished libraries, most concrete types exposed in an implementation should also implement one or more object interface types. For example, collections should implement IEnumerable<'T>, and many types should implement IDisposable (see Chapter 8 for more details on IDisposable).

- Avoid relying on or revealing complex type hierarchies. In particular, avoid relying on implementation inheritance, except as an internal implementation technique or when doing GUI programming or authoring very large objects.

- Avoid nesting modules or types inside other modules or types. Nested modules and types are useful implementation details, but they're rarely made public in APIs. Deep hierarchical organization can be confusing; when you're designing a library, you should place nearly all public modules and types immediately inside a well-named namespace.

Extending Existing Types and Modules

The final topic covered in this chapter is how you can define ad hoc dot-notation extensions to existing library types and modules. This technique is used rarely but can be invaluable in certain circumstances. For example, the following definition adds the member IsPrime. You see uses of this technique in Chapter 13:

```
module NumberTheoryExtensions =
    let isPrime i =
        let lim = int (sqrt (float i))
        let rec check j =
            j > lim || (i % j <> 0 && check (j+1))
        check 2

    type System.Int32 with
        member i.IsPrime = isPrime i
```

The IsPrime property is then available for use in conjunction with int32 values whenever the
NumberTheoryExtensions module has been opened. For example:

```
> open NumberTheoryExtensions;;

> (3).IsPrime;;
val it : bool = true

> (6093711).IsPrime;;
val it : bool = false
```

Type extensions can be given in any assembly, but priority is always given to the intrinsic members
of a type when resolving dot-notation.

■ **Note** Type extensions are a good technique for equipping simple type definitions with OO functionality. However,
don't fall into the trap of adding too much functionality to an existing type via this route. Instead, it's often simpler to
use additional modules and types. For example, the module Microsoft.FSharp.Collections.List contains extra
functionality associated with the F# list type.

Modules can also be extended in a fashion. For example, say you think the List module is missing
an obvious function such as List.pairwise to return a new list of adjacent pairs. You can extend the set
of values accessed by the path List by defining a new module List:

```
module List =
    let rec pairwise l =
        match l with
        | [] | [_] -> []
        | h1::(h2::_ as t) -> (h1,h2) :: pairwise t
```

```
> List.pairwise [1;2;3;4];;
val it : (int * int) list = [ (1,2); (2,3); (3,4) ]
```

Modules can also be labeled AutoOpen, meaning they're treated as opened whenever the enclosing namespace or module is opened. This can be useful when you're defining ad hoc top-level operators and functions:

```
[<AutoOpen>]
module Utilities =
    let swap (x,y) = (y,x)

swap (3,4)
```

You can also attach an AutoOpen attribute to an assembly, with a string path. This means the path is opened as soon as the assembly is referenced, in the order in which the assemblies are given to the F# command- line compiler:

```
[<assembly: AutoOpen("Acme.Utilities")>]
```

Working with F# Objects and .NET Types

This chapter has deemphasized the use of .NET terminology for object types, such as class and interface. However, all F# types are ultimately compiled as .NET types. Here is how they relate:

- Concrete types such as record types, discriminated unions, and class types are compiled as .NET classes.

- Object interface types are by default compiled as .NET interface types.

If you want, you can delimit class types using class/end:

```
type Vector2D(dx: float, dy: float) =
    class
        let len = sqrt(dx * dx + dy * dy)
        member v.DX = dx
        member v.DY = dy
        member v.Length = len
    end
```

You see this in F# code samples on the Web and in other books. However, we have found that this tends to make types harder to understand, so we've omitted class/end throughout this book. You can also delimit object interface types by interface/end:

```
open System.Drawing

type IShape =
    interface
        abstract Contains : Point -> bool
        abstract BoundingBox : Rectangle
    end
```

Structs

It's occasionally useful to direct the F# compiler to use a .NET struct (value type) representation for small, generally immutable objects. You can do this by adding a Struct attribute to a class type and adding type annotations to all arguments of the primary constructor:

```
[<Struct>]
type Vector2DStruct(dx : float, dy: float) =
    member v.DX = dx
    member v.DY = dy
    member v.Length = sqrt (dx * dx + dy * dy)
```

Finally, you can also use a form that makes the values held in a struct explicit:

```
[<Struct>]
type Vector2DStructUsingExplicitVals =
    val dx : float
    val dy: float
    member v.DX = v.dx
    member v.DY = v.dy
    member v.Length = sqrt (v.dx * v.dx + v.dy * v.dy)
```

Structs are often more efficient, but you should use them with care because the full contents of struct values are frequently copied. The performance characteristics of structs can also change depending on whether you're running on a 32-bit or 64-bit machine.

Delegates

Occasionally, you need to define a new .NET delegate type in F#:

```
type ControlEventHandler = delegate of int -> bool
```

This is usually required only when using C code from F#, because some magic performed by the .NET Common Language Runtime lets you marshal a delegate value as a C function pointer. Chapter 17 looks at interoperating with C and COM. For example, here's how you add a new handler to the Win32 Ctrl+C–handling API:

```
open System.Runtime.InteropServices
let ctrlSignal = ref false
[<DllImport("kernel32.dll")>]
extern void SetConsoleCtrlHandler(ControlEventHandler callback,bool add)

let ctrlEventHandler = new ControlEventHandler(fun i ->  ctrlSignal := true; true)

SetConsoleCtrlHandler(ctrlEventHandler,true)
```

Enums

Occasionally, you need to define a new .NET enum type in F#. You do this using a notation similar to discriminated unions:

```
type Vowels =
    | A = 1
    | E = 5
    | I = 9
    | O = 15
    | U = 21
```

This type is compiled as a .NET enum whose underlying bit representation is a simple integer.

Summary

This chapter looked at the basic constructs of object-oriented programming in F#, including concrete object types, OO notation, and object interface types and their implementations, as well as more advanced techniques to implement object interface types. You also saw how implementation inheritance is less important as an object implementation technique in F# than in other OO languages and then learned how the F# object model relates to the .NET object model. The next chapter covers language constructs and practical techniques related to encapsulating, packaging, and deploying your code.

CHAPTER 7

■■■

Encapsulating and Packaging Your Code

Packaging code and making it available for people and programs to use is a key part of making the best use of F#. In this book, you've already seen many of the constructs to help do this: functions, objects, type definitions, modules, namespaces, and assemblies. However, in some cases you've encountered these only peripherally when using the .NET Base Class Library (BCL). This chapter covers these constructs from the perspective of code organization and packaging.

Packaging code has four distinct but related meanings:

- *Organizing* code into sensible entities using namespaces, types, and modules.

- *Encapsulating* internal data structures and implementation details by making them private.

- *Assembling* code and data as a component, which on .NET is called an assembly. An assembly is one or more DLL or EXE packaged together with supporting data as a single logical unit.

- *Deploying* one or more assemblies, such as a web application or framework, often with an installer, for use on client machines, on web servers, or for download over the Web.

The first two of these topics are associated with the F# language, and the last is more associated with the pragmatics of deploying, installing, configuring, and maintaining software. The third lies in between, because a .NET assembly can act as both a unit of encapsulation and a unit of deployment.

Knowing these techniques isn't the same as knowing how to use them effectively, or indeed when to use them. At the end of this chapter, we cover some of the different kinds of .NET software you may write with F# and how you can organize and package your code for these different cases.

Hiding Things Away

In all kinds of software, it's common to hide implementation details of data structures and algorithms behind *encapsulation boundaries*. Encapsulation is a fundamental technique when writing software and is possibly the most important idea associated with object-oriented (OO) programming.

For this book's purposes, *encapsulation* means hiding implementation details behind well-defined boundaries. This lets you enforce consistency properties and makes the structure of a program easier to manage. It also lets an implementation evolve over time. A good rule of thumb is that anything you don't want used directly by client code should be hidden.

153

Later, this chapter explains how encapsulation applies when you're building assemblies, frameworks, and applications. In the extreme, you may even be ensuring that your code is *secure* when used in partial trust mode—in other words, that it can't be inadvertently or deliberately used to achieve malicious results when used as a library by code that doesn't have full permissions. However, the most important kind of encapsulation is the day-to-day business of hiding the internal implementation details of functions, objects, types, and modules. The primary techniques used to do this are as follows:

- Local definitions
- Accessibility annotations
- Explicit signatures

We cover the first two of these techniques next, and we cover explicit signatures in the "Using Signature Types and Files" section later in this chapter.

Hiding Things with Local Definitions

The easiest way to hide definitions is to make them local to expressions or constructed class definitions using inner `let` bindings. These aren't directly accessible from outside their scope. This technique is frequently used to hide state and other computed values inside the implementations of functions and objects. Let's begin with a simple example. Here is the definition of a function that incorporates a single item of encapsulated state:

```
let generateTicket =
    let count = ref 0
    (fun () -> incr count; !count)
```

If you examine this definition, you see that the `generateTicket` function isn't defined immediately as a function but instead first declares a local element of state called `count` and then returns a function value that refers to this state. Each time the function value is called, `count` is incremented and dereferenced, but the reference cell is never published outside the function implementation and is thus encapsulated.

Encapsulation through local definitions is a particularly powerful technique in F# when used in conjunction with object expressions. For example, Listing 7-1 shows the definition of an object interface type called `IPeekPoke` and a function that implements objects of this type using an object expression.

Listing 7-1. Implementing Objects with Encapsulated State

```
type IPeekPoke =
    abstract member Peek: unit -> int
    abstract member Poke: int -> unit

let makeCounter initialState =
    let state = ref initialState
    { new IPeekPoke with
        member x.Poke(n) = state := !state + n
        member x.Peek() = !state  }
```

The type of the function `Counter` is as follows:

```
val makeCounter : int -> IPeekPoke
```

As with the earlier generateTicket function, the internal state for each object generated by the makeCounter function is hidden and accessible only via the published Peek and Poke methods.

The previous examples show how to combine let bindings with anonymous functions and object expressions. You saw in Chapter 6 how let bindings can also be used in constructed class types. For example, Listing 7-2 shows a constructed class type with private mutable state count and that publishes two methods: Next and Reset.

Listing 7-2. A Type for Objects with Encapsulated State

```
type TicketGenerator() =
    // Note: let bindings in a type definition are implicitly private to the object
    // being constructed. Members are implicitly public.
    let mutable count = 0

    member x.Next() =
        count <- count + 1;
        count

    member x.Reset () =
        count <- 0
```

The variable count is implicitly private to the object being constructed and is hence hidden from outside consumers. By default, other F# definitions are public, which means they're accessible throughout their scope.

Frequently, more than one item of state is hidden behind an encapsulation boundary. For example, the following code shows a function makeAverager that uses an object expression and two local elements of state, count and total, to implement an instance of the object interface type IStatistic:

```
type IStatistic<'T,'U> =
    abstract Record : 'T -> unit
    abstract Value : 'U

let makeAverager(toFloat: 'T -> float) =
    let count = ref 0
    let total = ref 0.0
    { new IStatistic<'a,float> with
          member stat.Record(x) = incr count; total := !total + toFloat x
          member stat.Value = (!total / float !count) }
```

The inferred types here are as follows:

```
type IStatistic<'T,'U> =
    abstract Record : 'T -> unit
    abstract Value: 'U
val makeAverager : ('T -> float) -> IStatistic<'T,float>
```

The internal state is held in values count and total and is, once again, encapsulated.

■ **Note** Most of the examples of encapsulation in this chapter show ways to hide *mutable state* behind encapsulation boundaries. However, encapsulation can be just as important for immutable constructs, especially in larger software components. For example, the implementation of the immutable System.DateTime type in the .NET BCL hides the way the date and time are stored internally but reveals the information via properties. This allows the .NET designers to adjust the implementation of this type between releases of the .NET Framework if necessary.

Hiding Things with Accessibility Annotations

Local definitions are good for hiding most implementation details. However, sometimes you may need definitions that are local to a module, an assembly, or a group of assemblies. You can change the default accessibility of an item by using an *accessibility annotation* to restrict the code locations that can use a construct. These indicate what is private or partially private to a module, file, or assembly. The primary accessibility annotations are private, internal, and public:

- private makes a construct private to the enclosing type definition/module.

- internal makes a construct private to the enclosing assembly (DLL or EXE).

- public makes a construct available globally, which is the default for most constructs.

Accessibility annotations are placed immediately prior to the name of the construct. Listing 7-3 shows how to protect an internal table of data in a module using accessibility annotations.

Listing 7-3. Protecting a Table Using Accessibility Annotations

```
open System

module public VisitorCredentials =

    /// The internal table of permitted visitors and the
    /// days they are allowed to visit.
    let private  visitorTable =
        dict [ ("Anna",   set [DayOfWeek.Tuesday; DayOfWeek.Wednesday]);
               ("Carolyn", set [DayOfWeek.Friday]) ]

    /// This is the function to check if a person is a permitted visitor.
    /// Note: this is public and can be used by external code
    let public checkVisitor(person) =
        visitorTable.ContainsKey(person) &&
        visitorTable.[person].Contains(DateTime.Today.DayOfWeek)

    /// This is the function to return all known permitted visitors.
    /// Note: this is internal and can only be used by code in this assembly.
    let internal allKnownVisitors() =
        visitorTable.Keys
```

The private table is visitorTable. Attempting to access this value from another module gives a type-checking error. The function checkVisitor is marked public and is thus available globally. The function allKnownVisitors is available only within the same assembly (or the same F# Interactive session) as the definition of the VisitorCredentials module. Note that you could drop the public annotations from checkVisitor and VisitorCredentials because these declarations are public by default.

Accessibility annotations are often used to hide state or handles to resources such as files. In Listing 7-4, you protect a single reference cell containing a value that alternates between Tick and Tock. This example uses an internal *event*, a technique covered in more detail in Chapter 8.

Listing 7-4. Protecting Internal State Using Accessibility Annotations

```
module public GlobalClock =

    type TickTock = Tick | Tock

    let private clock = ref Tick

    let private tick = new Event<TickTock>()

    let internal oneTick() =
        (clock := match !clock with Tick -> Tock | Tock -> Tick);
        tick.Trigger (!clock)

    let tickEvent = tick.Publish

module internal TickTockDriver =
    open System.Threading
    let timer = new Timer(callback=(fun _ -> GlobalClock.oneTick()),
                            state=null,dueTime=0,period=100)
```

In Listing 7-4, the private state is clock. The assembly-internal module TickTockDriver uses the System.Threading.Timer class to drive the alternation of the state via the internal function oneTick. The GlobalClock module publishes one IEvent value, tickEvent, which any client can use to add handlers to listen for the event. Note that you can give different accessibility annotations for different identifiers bound in the same pattern. The sample uses the Event type, covered in more detail in Chapter 8.

Another assembly can now contain the following code that adds a handler to TickEvent:

```
module TickTockListener =
    do GlobalClock.tickEvent.Add(function
        | GlobalClock.Tick -> printf "tick!"
        | GlobalClock.Tock -> System.Windows.Forms.MessageBox.Show "tock!" |> ignore)
```

You can add accessibility annotations quite a number of places in F# code:

- On let, and extern definitions in modules, and in individual identifiers in patterns
- On new(...) object constructor definitions
- On member definitions associated with types
- On module definitions
- On type definitions associated with types
- On primary constructors, such as type C private (...) = ...

■ **Note** You can add accessibility annotations to type abbreviations. However, the abbreviation is still just an abbreviation—only the name is hidden, not the actual equivalence. That is, if you define a type abbreviation such as `type private label = int`, then all users of the type label know that it's really just an abbreviation for `int` and not a distinct type definition of its own. This is because .NET provides no way to hide type abbreviations; the F# compiler expands type abbreviations in the underlying generated .NET IL code.

Listing 7-5 shows a type where some methods and properties are labeled `public` but the methods that mutate the underlying collection (Add and the set method associated with the `Item` property) are labeled `internal`.

Listing 7-5. Making Property Setters Internal to a Type Definition

```
open System.Collections.Generic

type public SparseVector () =

    let elems = new SortedDictionary<int,float>()

    member internal vec.Add (k,v) = elems.Add(k,v)

    member public vec.Count = elems.Keys.Count
    member vec.Item
        with public get i =
            if elems.ContainsKey(i) then elems.[i]
            else 0.0
        and internal set i v =
            elems.[i] <- v
```

■ **Note** In class types, `let` bindings in types are private to the object being constructed, and all `member` bindings are public—they have the same accessibility as the type definition. This is a useful default because it corresponds to the common situation where internal implementation details are fully private and published constructs are available widely, and because omitting accessibility annotations makes code more readable in the common case. When you start to add more specific accessibility annotations, such as by making individual members internal or private, then it's useful to explicitly mark *all* members with accessibility annotations. Doing so makes your code more readable because readers don't have to remember that unmarked members are public. You can leave the remaining `let` bindings unmarked and implicitly private. In short, we recommend that if you mark any members of a type with accessibility annotations, you should mark them all.

Using Namespaces and Modules

An important organizational technique is to give sensible qualified names to your types and values. A qualified name is, for example, `Microsoft.FSharp.Collections.List` (for the F# list type) or `System.IO.StreamReader` (for one of the types in the .NET Framework BCL). Qualified names are particularly important when you're writing frameworks to be used by other people and are also a useful way of organizing your own code.

You give types and functions qualified names by placing them in namespaces, modules, and type definitions. Table 7-1 shows these three kinds of containers and what they can contain. For completeness, the table includes type abbreviations, which are slightly different because you can't use them as a container for other constructs.

Table 7-1. Namespaces, Modules, Types, and What They Can Contain

Entity	Description	Examples
Namespace	A namespace can contain further namespaces, modules, and types. Multiple DLLs can contribute to the same namespace.	`System`, `Microsoft.FSharp`
Module	A module can contain nested modules, types, and values.	`Microsoft.FSharp.Collections.Map`, `Microsoft.FSharp.Collections.List`
Concrete type definition	A type definition can contain members and nested type definitions.	`System.String`, `System.Int32`
Type abbreviation	A type abbreviation such as `string`, for `System.String`, can't act as containers for additional members, values, or types.	`int`, `string`

Putting Your Code in a Namespace

You saw in Chapter 6 how to define type definitions with members and modules with values. Now, you look at how to place these in namespaces. Listing 7-6 shows a file that contains two type definitions, both located in the namespace `Acme.Widgets`.

Listing 7-6. A File Containing Two Type Definitions in a Namespace

```
namespace Acme.Widgets

    type Wheel    = Square | Round | Triangle

    type Widget   = { id: int; wheels: Wheel list; size: string }
```

Namespaces are *open*, which means multiple source files and assemblies can contribute to the same namespace. For example, another implementation file or assembly can contain the definitions shown in Listing 7-7.

Listing 7-7. A File Containing Two Type Definitions in Two Namespaces

```
namespace Acme.Widgets

    type Lever     = PlasticLever | WoodenLever

namespace Acme.Suppliers

    type LeverSupplier    = { name: string; leverKind: Acme.Widgets.Lever }
```

The file in Listing 7-7 contributes to two namespaces: Acme.Widgets and Acme.Suppliers. The two files can occur in the same DLL or different DLLs. Either way, when you reference the DLL(s), the namespace Acme.Widgets appears to have at least three type definitions (perhaps more, if other DLLs contribute further type definitions), and the namespace Acme.Suppliers has at least one.

Using Files as Modules

Chapter 6 introduced the notion of a module. In F#, a module is a simple container for values and type definitions. Modules are also often used to provide outer structure for fragments of F# code; many of the simple F# programs you've seen so far in this book have been in modules without your knowing. In particular:

- Code fragments typed into F# Interactive and delimited by ;; are each implicitly placed in a module of their own.

- Files compiled with the command-line compiler using Visual Studio or loaded into F# Interactive with #load have their values and types placed in a namespace or module according to the leading module or namespace declaration in the file. Declarations in files without a leading module or namespace declaration are placed in a module whose name is derived from the name of the implementation file.

Let's look at the second case in more detail. You can explicitly declare the name of the namespace/module for a file by using a leading module declaration. For example, Listing 7-8 defines the module Acme.Widgets.WidgetWheels, regardless of the name of the file containing the constructs.

Listing 7-8. An Implementation Module with an Explicit Initial module Declaration

```
module Acme.Widgets.WidgetWheels

    let wheelCornerCount = Map.of_list [(Wheel.Square,   4);
                                        (Wheel.Triangle, 3);
                                        (Wheel.Round,    0);  ]
```

Here the first line gives the name for the module defined by the file. The namespace is Acme.Widgets, the module name is WidgetWheels, and the full path to the value is Acme.Widgets.WidgetWheels.wheelCornerCount.

Creating Assemblies, DLLs, and EXEs

This book has used F# Interactive for most of the samples. F# Interactive is excellent when you're exploring a set of libraries and writing scripts or small applications that use them. But to understand how to write libraries and organize other kinds of applications, you need to learn how to use the F# command-line compiler, fsc.exe, to compile your code into DLLs and EXEs. A Dynamic Link Library (DLL) is the Windows name for library components, and .exe is the extension used for executable programs.

As you saw at the start of this chapter, all .NET code exists in an *assembly*, which is, roughly speaking, either a DLL or an EXE. Assemblies can also contain supporting code and data files. Every time you compile a set of files using fsc.exe, you create one assembly: either a DLL or an EXE. Even when you use F# Interactive (fsi.exe), you're dynamically adding code to a dynamically generated DLL. You now learn how to use the command-line compiler to create DLLs and EXEs.

Compiling EXEs

To compile code to an EXE, you call fsc.exe with the names of your source code files in dependency order. For example, if the file dolphin.fs contains the code in Listing 7-9, then you can compile the code using fsc dolphin.fs. You can also use the -o flag to name the generated EXE.

Listing 7-9. *File dolphins.fs*

```
let longBeaked = "Delphinus capensis"
let shortBeaked = "Delphinus delphis"
let dolphins = [ longBeaked; shortBeaked ]
printfn "Known Dolphins:  %A" dolphins
```

You can now compile this code to an EXE as shown here:

```
C:\fsharp> fsc dolphins.fs
C:\fsharp> dir dolphins.exe
...
05/04/2010  19:21              3,124 dolphins.exe

C:\fsharp>dolphins.exe
Known Dolphins: ["Delphinus capensis"; "Delphinus delphis"]
```

Compiling DLLs

A DLL is a library containing compiled .NET or F# code (it can also contain native code with instructions and data dependent on particular machine architectures, such as Intel x86 and AMD x64). To compile F# code into a DLL, you take one or more source files and invoke fsc.exe with the -a option. For example, let's assume the file whales.fs contains the code shown in Listing 7-10. (This sample also includes some documentation comments, referred to in the "Generating Documentation" section later in this chapter.)

Listing 7-10. File whales.fs

```
module Whales.Fictional

/// The three kinds of whales we cover in this release
type WhaleKind =
    | Blue
    | Killer
    | GreatWhale

/// The main whale
let moby = "Moby Dick, Pacific", GreatWhale

/// The backup whale
let bluey = "Blue, Southern Ocean", Blue

/// This whale is for experimental use only
let orca = "Orca, Pacific", Killer

/// The collected whales
let whales = [| moby; bluey; orca |]
```

You can now compile the code as follows:

```
C:\test> fsc -g -a whales.fs
C:\test> dir whales.dll
...
05/04/2010  19:18               6,656 whales.dll
```

Here you've added one command-line flag: -g to generate debug output. When compiling other assemblies, you need to reference your DLLs. For example, consider the code in Listing 7-11, which needs to reference whales.dll.

Listing 7-11. File whalewatcher.fs

```
open Whales
open System

let idx = Int32.Parse(Environment.GetCommandLineArgs().[1])
let spotted = Fictional.whales.[idx]

printfn "You spotted %A!" spotted
```

You can compile this file by adding an -r flag to reference the DLLs on which the code depends. You can also use the -o flag to name the generated EXE or DLL and the -I flag to list search paths:

```
C:\fsharp> fsc -g -r whales.dll -o watcher.exe whaleWatcher.fs
C:\fsharp> dir watcher.exe
...
05/04/2010  19:25                 3,584 watcher.exe

C:\fsharp> watcher.exe 1
You spotted ("Blue, Southern Ocean", Blue)!
```

■ **Note** .NET assemblies often contain a large amount of code. For example, a single assembly may contain as many as 50 or 100 F# source code files. Having many small assemblies may seem tempting, such as to improve compilation times during development, but can lead to difficulties when you're managing updates and can be confusing to end users. Large assemblies are easier to version: you have to update only one component, and you can package multiple updates into a single new version of the DLL.

Mixing Scripting and Compiled Code

Small programs are often used as both interactive scripts and as small compiled applications. Here are some useful facts to know about scripting with F# and F# Interactive:

- Small F# scripts use the extension `.fsx`.

- You can use the scripting directive `#load` from F# Interactive to load and compile one or more source code files as if they had been compiled using the command-line compiler.

- You can load one script from another script by the F# Interactive directive `#use`. This is very much like `#load` except that the file being loaded may contain further scripting directives.

- You can reference DLLs from within scripts by using the `#r` and `#I` directives, which act like the `-r` and `-I` directives of the F# command-line compiler.

- You can access command-line arguments from within scripts by using the expression `fsi.CommandLineArgs`. Within compiled code, you should use `System.Environment.GetCommandLineArgs`. Within code used in both modes, you should use conditional compilation to switch between these, as shown in the next coding example.

- You can run a script on startup by using the `--exec` command-line option for `fsi.exe` or by giving a single file name on the command line. You can find other command-line options by using `fsi.exe --help`.

Conditional compilation is a particularly useful feature for scripts—especially the predefined conditional compilation symbols `COMPILED` and `INTERACTIVE`. The former is set whenever you compile code using the command-line compiler, `fsc.exe`, and the latter is set whenever you load code interactively using F# Interactive. A common use for these flags is to start the GUI event loop for a Windows Forms or other graphical application, such as using `System.Windows.Forms.Application.Run`.

F# Interactive starts an event loop automatically, so you require a call to this function in the compiled code only:

```
open System.Windows.Forms

let form = new Form(Width=400, Height=300,
                    Visible=true, Text="F# Forms Sample")
#if COMPILED
// Run the main code
System.Windows.Forms.Application.Run(form)
#endif
```

■ **Note** You can specify additional conditional compilation directives by using the `--define` command-line compiler option.

Choosing Optimization Settings

The F# compiler comes with a simple choice of optimization levels. You nearly always want to compile your final code using `--optimize`, which applies maximum optimizations to your code. This is also the default optimization setting for `fsc.exe`.

The F# compiler is a cross-module, cross-assembly optimizing compiler, and it attaches optimization information to each assembly you create when using optimization. This information may contain some code fragments of your assembly, which may be inlined into later assemblies by the optimizing compiler. In some situations, you may not want this information included in your assembly. For example, you may expect to independently version assemblies, and in this case you may want to ensure that code is never duplicated from one assembly to another during compilation. In this case, you can use the `--nooptimizationdata` switch to prevent optimization data being recorded with the assemblies you create.

Generating Documentation

In Chapter 2, you saw that comments beginning with `///` are XML documentation comments, which are used by interactive tools such as Visual Studio. They can also be collected to generate either HTML or XML documentation. You generate HTML documentation using an auxiliary tool such as FsHtmlDoc, available in the F# Power Pack.

You can also generate a simple XML documentation file using the `--doc` command-line option. You must name the output file. For example, using `fsc -a --doc:whales.xml whales.fs` for the code in Listing 7-10 generates the file `whales.xml` containing the following:

```xml
<?xml version="1.0" encoding="utf-8"?>
<doc>
    <assembly><name>whales</name></assembly>
    <members>
      <member name="T:Whales.Fictional.WhaleKind">
        <summary> The three kinds of whales we cover in this release</summary>
      </member>
      <member name="P:Whales.Fictional.bluey">
      <summary> The backup whale</summary>
      </member>
      <member name="P:Whales.Fictional.moby">
       <summary>The main whale</summary>
      </member>

      <member name="P:Whales.Fictional.orca">
       <summary> This whale is for experimental use only</summary>
      </member>
      <member name="P:Whales.Fictional.whales">
       <summary> The collected whales</summary>
      </member>
      <member name="T:Whales.Fictional">
      </member>
    </members>
</doc>
```

Building Shared Libraries and Using the Global Assembly Cache

You commonly need to share libraries among multiple applications. You can do this by using any of the following techniques:

- Including the same library source file in multiple projects and/or compilations
- Duplicating the DLL for the library into each application directory
- Creating a strong name-shared library

This section covers the last option in more detail. A strong name-shared library has the following characteristics:

- It's a DLL.
- You install it in the .NET global assembly cache (GAC) on the target machine.
- You give it a strong name by using --keyfile.
- You package all of its supporting data files using --linkresource.
- You (optionally) give it a version number using an AssemblyVersion attribute in your code.
- You ensure that all of its dependencies are shared libraries.

The usual place to install shared libraries is the .NET GAC. The GAC is a collection of assemblies installed on the machine and available for use by any application that has sufficient privileges. Most libraries used in this book such as System.Windows.Forms.dll are installed in the GAC when you install the .NET Framework on a machine.

The remaining requirements are easy to satisfy and are conditions that must hold before you install something in the GAC. For example, assemblies must have strong names. All assemblies have names; for example, the assembly whales.dll (which you compiled in the earlier "Compiling DLLs" section using fsc -a whales.fs) has the name whales. An assembly with a strong name includes a hash using a cryptographic public/private key pair. This means only people who have access to the private key can create a strong-named assembly that matches the public key. Users of the DLL can verify that the contents of the DLL were generated by someone holding the private key. A strong name looks something like this:

```
mscorlib, Version=2.0.0.0, Culture=neutral, PublicKeyToken=b77a5c561934e089
```

It's easy to create a strong-named assembly: generate a public/private key pair using the sn.exe tool that comes with the .NET Framework SDK, and give that as your keyfile argument. You can install libraries into the GAC using the .NET Framework SDK utility gacutil.exe. The following command-line session shows how to do this for the code shown in Listing 7-10:

```
C:\Users\dsyme\Desktop> sn.exe -k whales.snk
Microsoft (R) .NET Framework Strong Name Utility  Version 2.0.50727.42
Copyright (c) Microsoft Corporation. All rights reserved.

Key pair written to whales.snk

C:\Users\dsyme\Desktop> fsc -a --keyfile:whales.snk whales.fs

C:\Users\dsyme\Desktop> gacutil /i whales.dll
Microsoft (R) .NET Global Assembly Cache Utility. Version 2.0.50727.42
Copyright (c) Microsoft Corporation. All rights reserved.

Assembly successfully added to the cache
```

Installer generators such as WiX also include directives to install libraries into the GAC. Installer generators are discussed later in this chapter.

■ **Note** If you're planning to write libraries for use by the rest of the world, we recommend that you take the time to read the .NET library design guidelines, document them using XML and HTML docs, and learn how to version your libraries. Chapter 19 takes a deeper look at guidelines for library design.

Using Static Linking

Sometimes applications use a DLL as a library; but when it comes to deploying the application on a website or as installed software, it may be easier to bundle that DLL as part of the application. You can do this in two ways: by placing the DLL alongside the EXE for the application or by statically linking the

DLL when you create the EXE. You select the DLL by using the `--staticlink` compiler option with the assembly name of the DLL.

You can also bundle the F# libraries into your application to give a zero-dependency application. You statically link all DLLs that depend on the F# libraries by using the `--standalone` compiler option.

Static linking can cause problems in some situations and should only be used for a final EXE or a DLL used as an application plug-in.

Using Signature Types and Files

Every piece of F# code you write has a *signature type*. The inferred signature type for a piece of code is shown for every code fragment you enter into F# Interactive and can also be reported by using the F# command-line compiler, `fsc.exe`, with the `-i` option. For example, consider the following code, placed in an implementation file `ticktock.fs`:

```
module Acme.TickTock

    type TickTock = Tick | Tock

    let ticker x =
        match x with
        | Tick -> Tock
        | Tock -> Tick
```

You can now invoke the command-line compiler from a command prompt:

```
C:\Users\dsyme\Desktop> fsc -i -a ticktock.fs

namespace Acme

module TickTock =
    type TickTock = Tick | Tock
    val ticker : TickTock -> TickTock
```

The inferred signature shows the results of type inference and takes into account other information such as accessibility annotations.

Using Explicit Signature Types and Signature Files

If you want, you can make the inferred types explicit by using an *explicit signature type* for each implementation file. The syntax used for explicit signature types is identical to the inferred types reported by F# Interactive or `fsc.exe`, like those shown previously. If you use explicit signatures, they're placed in a *signature file*, and they list the names and types of all values and members that are accessible in some way to the outside world. Signature files should use the same root name as the matching implementation file with the extension `.fsi`. For example, Listing 7-12 shows the implementation file `vector.fs` and the explicit signature file `vector.fsi`.

Listing 7-12. A Signature File `vector.fsi` *with Implementation File* `vector.fs`

```
namespace Acme.Collections
    type SparseVector =
        new: unit -> SparseVector
        member Add: int * float -> unit
        member Item : int -> float with get

namespace Acme.Collections
    open System.Collections.Generic
    type SparseVector() =
        let elems = new SortedDictionary<int,float>()
        member vec.Add(k,v) = elems.Add(k,v)
        member vec.Item
            with get i =
                if elems.ContainsKey(i) then elems.[i]
                else 0.0
            and  set i v =
                elems.[i] <- v
```

You can now invoke the command-line compiler from a command-line shell:

```
C:\Users\dsyme\Desktop> fsc vector.fsi vector.fs
```

Although signature files are optional, many programmers like using them, especially when writing a library framework, because the signature file gives a place to document and maintain a component's public interface. But there is a cost to this technique: signatures duplicate names and some other information found in the implementation.

■ **Note** You can use signature types to hide constructs, which can be used as an alternative to giving accessibility annotations on types, values, and members. Neither accessibility annotations nor signatures can hide type abbreviations, for the reasons discussed in the earlier "Hiding Things with Accessibility Annotations" section. Some additional restrictions apply to both hiding techniques. For example, if a type is revealed to be a constructed class type or interface type, then all its abstract members must be included in the signature. Similarly, a record type must reveal all its fields, and a discriminated union type must reveal all its cases. Also, in some languages such as OCaml, a signature may restrict the type of an implementation construct. For example, if a function is inferred to have a generic type `'a -> 'a`, then in OCaml the signature may specify a more restricted type such as `int -> int`. This isn't permitted in F#.

When Are Signature Types Checked?

Signature types are checked *after* an implementation has been fully processed. This is unlike type annotations that occur directly in an implementation file, which are applied *before* an implementation fragment is processed. This means the type information in a signature file isn't used as part of the type-inference process when processing the implementation.

■ **Note** Each signature file must appear before its corresponding implementation file in the compilation order for an F# project. In Visual Studio, this means the signature file must come before the implementation file in the project listing. This is because the signature is required in order to check the contents of the implementation file after the implementation file is fully processed.

Packaging Applications

This section covers some of the more pragmatic issues involved in in designing applications and choosing how to package both your code and data. First, however, let's talk about the sorts of things you may be building with F#.

Packaging Different Kinds of Code

Table 7-2 lists some of the kinds of software implemented with F#. These tend to be organized in slightly different ways and tend to use encapsulation to varying degrees. For example, encapsulation is used heavily in frameworks but not when you're writing 100-line scripts.

Table 7-2. Some Kinds of Software Built Using F#

Software Entity	Description
Script	A program or set of program fragments, usually in a single file and less than 1,000 lines, usually with an .fsx extension, run through F# Interactive. Sometimes also compiled. Organized using functions and occasional type definitions. Freely uses static global state. Usually has no signature file or accessibility annotations.
Application	An EXE or a web application DLL, perhaps with some supporting DLLs. Organized using namespaces, modules, functions, and some abstract types. Often uses some static global state. Some internal files and data structures may have signatures, but often these aren't needed.
Application extension (plug-in or add-on)	A component that extends an application, often compiled as a DLL containing types along with an accompanying XML file that describes the plug-in to the application. The host application loads the DLLs using .NET reflection. Generally has no static state because this lets the application instantiate multiple instances of the plug-in. Example: the DLL plug-ins for Paint.NET, a popular .NET image-manipulation program.
Framework	A collection of related type definitions, functions, and algorithms organized according to established .NET and F# library-design guidelines. Usually compiled as a DLL, strong-name signed, installed into the GAC on the target machine, and versioned as an independent entity. Generally has no static state except where it mediates essential state on the host computer or operating system.

Software Entity	Description
Framework extension	A component that extends a framework, usually by defining types that implement particular interfaces. Organized in an appropriate namespace as a simple set of classes and functions that generate objects that implement the interfaces defined in a framework. Generally has no static state. Example: the Firebird.NET API, which provides implementations of the ADO.NET Data Access framework interfaces to enable access to Firebird databases.

Using Data and Configuration Settings

So far, this book has focused on code. In reality, almost every program comes with additional data resources that form an intrinsic part of the application. Common examples of the latter include the resource strings, sounds, fonts, and images for GUI applications. Applications typically select between different data resources based on language or culture settings. Often, programs also access additional parameters, such as environment variables derived from the execution context or registry settings recording user-configuration options. It can be useful to understand the idioms used by .NET to make managing data and configuration settings more uniform. Table 7-3 shows some of the terminology used for data resources.

Table 7-3. Application Data: Terminology

Terminology	Meaning	Example
Static application data	A data resource whose name/location is always known, whose value doesn't change during execution, and that your application can generally assume always exists.	The PATH environment variable or a data file distributed with your application.
Strongly typed data	Data accessed as a named, typed .NET value through code written by you or generated by a tool you're using. The code hides the complexity of locating and decoding the resource.	An icon data resource decoded to a System.Drawing.Icon value. The ResGen.exe tool can generate strongly typed APIs for common Windows resources such as bitmaps and icons.
GUI resource	A string, a font, an icon, a bitmap, an image, a sound, or another binary resource that is attached to a Windows application or DLL using the Win32 .res format or .NET managed .resx format. Often dependent on language/culture settings.	A bitmap added as a resource to a Windows Forms application or an error message from a compiler.

You may need to access many different kinds of data resources and application settings. Table 7-4 summarizes the most common ones.

Table 7-4. Commonly Used Data and Configuration Settings

Data Resource	Notes
Source directory	The source directory containing the source file(s) at time of compilation. Often used to access further resources in F# Interactive scripts or for error reporting in compiled applications. Accessed using the `__SOURCE_DIRECTORY__` predefined identifier.
Command arguments	Arguments passed to the invocation of the program. Accessed using `System.Environment.GetCommandLineArgs` and `fsi.CommandLineArgs` when running in F# Interactive.
Installation location	Where a program EXE or DLL is installed. Accessed by using `System.Windows.Forms.Application.StartupPath` or by reading the `Assembly.Location` of any of the types defined in your assembly. For F# Interactive scripts, the installation location is usually the same as the source directory.
User directories	Paths to common logical directories such as `Program Files`, `My Documents`, and `Application Data`. Accessed using `System.Environment.GetFolderPath`.
Environment variables	User- or machine-wide settings such as `PATH` and `COMPUTERNAME`. Accessed using `System.Environment.GetEnvironmentVariable`.
Registry settings	User- or machine-wide settings used to hold the vast majority of settings on a Windows machine. Accessed using `Microsoft.Win32.Registry.GetValue` and related types and methods.
Configuration settings	Database connection strings and other configuration settings, often used for web applications. If an application is called `MyApp.exe`, then this is usually stored in a file such as `MyApp.exe.config` alongside the executable; web applications use a `Web.Config` file. Accessed using `System.Configuration.ConfigurationManager`.
Isolated storage	A special storage area accessible only to an installed application and that looks just like disk storage.
Fonts, colors, icons, and so on	Specifications of Windows-related resources. Often taken from predefined system fonts and colors using the functions in `System.Drawing`: for example, `Color.MidnightBlue` or `new Font(FontFamily.GenericMonospace, 8.0f)`. Can be added as a binary resource to an assembly and accessed using `System.Resources.ResourceManager`.

You can author GUI data resources such as fonts, images, strings, and colors by creating a `.resx` file using a tool like Visual Studio. You then compile them to binary resources by using the `resgen.exe` tool that is part of the .NET Framework SDK. Most development environments have tools for designing and creating these resources. Often, the .NET Framework contains a canonical type such as `System.Drawing.Color` for any particular kind of resource; you should avoid writing needless duplicate types to represent them.

Sometimes it's a good idea to make sure a data resource is officially part of an assembly. For example, this is required if the assembly will be installed into the GAC. You can embed resources in applications (or associate them with a DLL) by using the `--resource` compiler option.

For example, a set of samples called F# Samples101 on the Microsoft Code Gallery contains the following:

- The source files `samples.fs`, `sampleform.fs`, and `program.fs`.

- The .NET resource file `SampleForm.resx`, created and edited using the Visual Studio tools for designing icons. This file contains 57KB of XML data specifying, among other things, a default icon for the upper-left corner image on the Windows operating system and six images used by the application. These are held in an image stream under the XML key `imageList.ImageStream`.

The application is compiled using the following command line:

```
resgen SampleForm.resx
fsc.exe --resource:SampleForm.resource sample.fs sampleform.fs program.fs
```

In the application, the resources are accessed from the type `SampleForm` contained in the file `sampleform.fs`. The following code fragments occur in that file. The first creates a `ComponentResourceManager` that is ready to read resources from an assembly. The argument `typeof<SampleForm>` ensures that the resource manager reads resources from the assembly that contains the type `SampleForm` (that is, the type being defined). Chapter 9 discusses the `typeof` function in more detail:

```
open System.ComponentModel
let resources = new ComponentResourceManager(typeof<SampleForm>)
```

The following lines retrieve images from the resource stream:

```
open System.Windows.Forms
let imageList = new System.Windows.Forms.ImageList()
imageList.ImageStream <- (resources.GetObject("imageList.ImageStream")
                              :?> System.Windows.Forms.ImageListStreamer)
imageList.Images.SetKeyName(0, "Help")
imageList.Images.SetKeyName(1, "BookStack")
imageList.Images.SetKeyName(2, "BookClosed")
imageList.Images.SetKeyName(3, "BookOpen")
imageList.Images.SetKeyName(4, "Item")
imageList.Images.SetKeyName(5, "Run")
```

The images from the resource file are associated with graphical components using the `ImageKey` property of various Windows Forms controls. For example, the application's Run button is associated with the Run image stored in the resource file using the following lines:

```
let runButton = new Button(ImageAlign = ContentAlignment.MiddleRight,
                           ImageKey = "Run",
                           ImageList = imageList)
```

■ **Note** .NET uses application configuration files (for static application settings) and isolated storage for settings private to an installed application for a particular user, including for applications downloaded from the Web. You can access isolated storage using the `System.IO.IsolatedStorage` namespace and access the Windows registry using the `Microsoft.Win32.Registry` namespace.

Summary

In this chapter, you learned about a number of issues related to encapsulating, organizing, and packaging code, from the raw language devices used for accessibility and encapsulation within code to building assemblies and the related topics of packaging applications, building DLLs, and including data resources as part of your libraries and applications.

The next chapter looks at some of the foundational techniques you need to master as you progress with learning to program in F#.

CHAPTER 8

■ ■ ■

Mastering F#: Common Techniques

F# is a powerful language with relatively simple constructs. Learning the constructs of the language is easy, but learning how to use the constructs well takes a little more time. This chapter presents some of the common F# coding techniques you need as you work across multiple programming domains. These techniques are either applications of the constructs you've encountered so far or relate to the foundational libraries that ship with F# and .NET.

Equality, Hashing, and Comparison

In Chapter 5, you saw a number of predefined generic operations, including generic comparison, equality, and hashing, accessed via functions such as those shown here:

```
val compare : 'T -> 'T -> int when 'T : comparison
val (=)    : 'T -> 'T -> bool when 'T : equality
val (<)    : 'T -> 'T -> bool when 'T : comparison
val (<=)   : 'T -> 'T -> bool when 'T : comparison
val (>)    : 'T -> 'T -> bool when 'T : comparison
val (>=)   : 'T -> 'T -> bool when 'T : comparison
val min : 'T -> 'T -> 'T when 'T : comparison
val max : 'T -> 'T -> 'T when 'T : comparison
val hash  : 'T -> int when 'T : equality
```

First, note that these are *generic* operations—they can be used on objects of many different types. This can be seen by the use of 'T in the signatures of these operations. The operations take one or two parameters of the same type. For example, you can apply the = operator to two Form objects, or two System.DateTime objects, or two System.Type objects, and something reasonable happens. Some other important derived generic types such as the immutable (persistent) Set<_> and Map<_,_> types in the F# library also use generic comparison on their key type:

```
type Set<'T when 'T : comparison> = ...
type Map<'Key, 'Value when 'Key : comparison> = ...
```

These operations and types are all *constrained*, in this case by the equality and/or comparison constraints. The purpose of constraints on type parameters is to make sure the operations are only used on a particular set of types. For example, consider equality and ordered comparison on a

`System.Windows.Forms.Form` object. Equality is permitted, because the default for nearly all .NET object types is reference equality:

```
let form1 = new System.Windows.Forms.Form()
let form2 = new System.Windows.Forms.Form()
form1 = form1    // true
form1 = form2    // false
```

However, ordered comparison isn't permitted:

```
let form1 = new System.Windows.Forms.Form()
let form2 = new System.Windows.Forms.Form()
form1 <= form2
    // Error: The type 'Form' does not support the 'comparison' constraint.
    // For example, it does not support the 'System.IComparable' interface
```

That's good! There is no natural ordering for form objects, or at least no ordering is provided by the .NET libraries.

Equality and comparison can work over the structure of types. For example, you can use the equality operators on a tuple only if the constituent parts of the tuple also support equality. This means using equality on a tuple of forms is permitted:

```
let form1 = new System.Windows.Forms.Form()
let form2 = new System.Windows.Forms.Form()
(form1, form2) = (form1, form2) // true
(form1, form2) = (form2, form1) // false
```

But using ordered comparison of a tuple isn't:

```
(form1, "Data for Form1") <= (form2, " Data for Form2")
    // Error: The type 'System.Windows.Forms.Form' does not
    // support the 'comparison' constraint.
```

Again, that's good—this ordering would be a bug in your code. Now, let's take a closer look at when equality and comparison constraints are satisfied in F#.

- The equality constraint is satisfied if the type definition doesn't have the `NoEquality` attribute, and any dependencies also satisfy the equality constraint.

- The comparison constraint is satisfied if the type definition doesn't have the `NoComparison` attribute, and the type definition implements `System.IComparable`, and any dependencies also satisfy the comparison constraint.

An equality constraint is relatively weak, because nearly all CLI types satisfy it. A comparison constraint is a stronger constraint, because it usually implies that a type must implement `System.IComparable`.

Asserting Equality, Hashing, and Comparison Using Attributes

The following attributes control the comparison and equality semantics of type definitions:

- `StructuralEquality` and `StructuralComparison`: Indicate that a structural type must support equality and comparison

- NoComparison and NoEquality: Indicate that a type doesn't support equality or comparison
- CustomEquality and CustomComparison: Indicate that a structural type supports custom equality and comparison

Let's look at examples of these. Sometimes you may want to assert that a structural type must support structural equality, and you want an error at the definition of the type if it doesn't. You do this by adding the StructuralEquality or StructuralComparison attribute to the type:

```
[<StructuralEquality;StructuralComparison>]
type MiniIntegerContainer = MiniIntegerContainer of int
```

This adds extra checking. In the following example, the code gives an error at compile time—the type can't logically support automatic structural comparison because one of the element types doesn't support ordered comparison:

```
[<StructuralEquality;StructuralComparison>]
type MyData = MyData of int * string * string * System.Windows.Forms.Form
```

```
error FS1177: The struct, record or union type 'MyData' has the
'StructuralComparison' attribute but the component type
'System.Windows.Forms.Form' does not satisfy the 'comparison' constraint
```

Fully Customizing Equality, Hashing, and Comparison on a Type

Many types in the .NET libraries come with custom equality, hashing and comparison implementations. For example, System.DateTime has custom implementations of these.

F# also allows you to define custom equality, hashing, and comparison for new type definitions. For example, values of a type may carry a unique integer tag that can be used for this purpose. In such cases, we recommend that you take full control of your destiny and define custom comparison and equality operations on your type. For example, Listing 8-1 shows how to customize equality, hashing and comparison based on a unique stamp integer value. The type definition includes an implementation of System.IComparable and overrides of Object.Equals and Object.GetHashCode.

Listing 8-1. *Customizing Equality, Hashing, and Comparison for a Record Type Definition*

```
/// A type abbreviation indicating we're using integers for unique stamps
/// on objects
type stamp = int

/// A structural type containing a function that can't be compared for equality
[<CustomEquality; CustomComparison>]
type MyThing =
    { Stamp: stamp;
      Behaviour: (int -> int) }

    override x.Equals(yobj) =
        match yobj with
        | :? MyThing as y -> (x.Stamp = y.Stamp)
        | _ -> false
```

```
override x.GetHashCode() = hash x.Stamp
interface System.IComparable with
  member x.CompareTo yobj =
      match yobj with
      | :? MyThing as y -> compare x.Stamp y.Stamp
      | _ -> invalidArg "yobj" "cannot compare values of different types"
```

The System.IComparable interface is defined in the .NET libraries:

```
namespace System

  type IComparable =
      abstract CompareTo : obj -> int
```

Recursive calls to compare subexpressions are processed using the following functions:

```
val hash : 'T -> int when 'T : equality
val (=) : 'T -> 'T -> bool when 'T : equality
val compare : 'T -> 'T -> int when 'T : comparison
```

Listing 8-2 shows the same for a union type, this time using some helper functions.

Listing 8-2. Customizing Generic Hashing and Comparison on a Union Type

```
let inline equalsOn f x (yobj:obj) =
    match yobj with
    | :? 'T as y -> (f x = f y)
    | _ -> false

let inline hashOn f x =  hash (f x)

let inline compareOn f x (yobj: obj) =
    match yobj with
    | :? 'T as y -> compare (f x) (f y)
    | _ -> invalidArg "yobj" "cannot compare values of different types"

type stamp = int

[<CustomEquality; CustomComparison>]
type MyUnionType =
    | MyUnionType of stamp * (int -> int)

    static member Stamp (MyUnionType (s,_)) = s

    override x.Equals y = equalsOn MyUnionType.Stamp x y
    override x.GetHashCode() = hashOn MyUnionType.Stamp x
    interface System.IComparable with
      member x.CompareTo y = compareOn MyUnionType.Stamp x y
```

Listing 8-2 also shows how to implement the System.Object method GetHashCode. This follows the same pattern as generic equality.

Finally, you can declare that a structural type should use reference equality:

```
[<ReferenceEquality>]
type MyFormWrapper = MyFormWrapper of System.Windows.Forms.Form * (int -> int)
```

There is no such thing as reference comparison (the object pointers used by .NET move around, so the ordering would change). You can implement that by using a unique tag and custom comparison.

Suppressing Equality, Hashing, and Comparison on a Type

You can suppress equality on an F# defined type by using the NoEquality attribute on the definition of the type. This means the type isn't considered to satisfy the equality constraint. Likewise, you can suppress comparison on an F# defined type by using the NoComparison attribute on the definition of the type:

```
[<NoEquality; NoComparison>]
type MyProjections =
    | MyProjections of (int * string) * (string -> int)
```

Adding these attributes to your library types makes client code safer, because it's less likely to inadvertently rely on equality and comparison over types where these operations make no sense.

Customizing Generic Collection Types

Programmers love defining new generic collection types. This is done less often in .NET and F# programming than in other languages, because the F# and .NET built-in collections are so good, but it's still important.

Equality and comparison play a role here. For example, it's common to have collections where some of the values can be indexed using hashing, compared for equality when searching, or compared using an ordering. For example, seeing a constraint on this signature on a library type would come as no surprise:

```
type Graph<'Node when 'Node : equality>() = ...
```

The presence of the constraint is somewhat reassuring, because the requirement on node types is made clearer. Sometimes it's also desirable to be able to compare entire containers: for example, to compare one set with another, one map with another, or one graph with another. Consider the simplest generic collection type of all, which holds only one element. You can define it easily in F#:

```
type MiniContainer<'T> = MiniContainer of 'T
```

In this case, this is a structural type definition, and F# infers that there is an equality and comparison dependency on 'T. All done! You can use MiniContainer<_> with values of any type, and you can only do equality and comparison on MiniContainer values if the element type also supports equality and comparison. Perfect.

However, if MiniContainer is a class type or has customized comparison and equality logic, then you need to be more explicit about dependencies. You can declare dependencies by using the EqualityConditionalOn and ComparisonConditionalOn attributes on the type parameter. You should also use the operators Unchecked.equals, Unchecked.hash, and Unchecked.compare to process elements recursively. With these attributes, MiniContainer<A> satisfies the equality and comparison constraints if A satisfies these constraints. Here's a full example:

```
type MiniContainer<[<EqualityConditionalOn; ComparisonConditionalOn >]'T>(x : 'T) =
    member x.Value = x
    override x.Equals(yobj) =
        match yobj with
        | :? MiniContainer<'T> as y -> Unchecked.equals x.Value y.Value
        | _ -> false

    override x.GetHashCode() = Unchecked.hash x.Value

    interface System.IComparable with
      member x.CompareTo yobj =
          match yobj with
          | :? MiniContainer<'T> as y -> Unchecked.compare x.Value y.Value
          | _ -> invalidArg "yobj" "cannot compare values of different types"
```

■ **Note** Be careful about using generic equality, hashing, and comparison on mutable data. Changing the value of a field may change the value of the hash or the results of the operation. It's normally better to use the operations on immutable data or data with custom implementations.

Efficient Precomputation and Caching

All experienced programmers are familiar with the concept of *precomputation,* where computations are performed as soon as some of the inputs to a function are known. The following sections cover a number of manifestations of precomputation in F# programming and the related topics of memoization and caching.

Precomputation and Partial Application

Let's say you're given a large input list of words and you want to compute a function that checks whether a word is in this list. You can do this as follows:

```
let isWord (words: string list) =
    let wordTable = Set.ofList words
    fun w -> wordTable.Contains(w)
```

Here, isWord has the following type:

```
val isWord : string list -> (string -> bool)
```

The efficient use of this function depends crucially on the fact that useful intermediary results are computed after only one argument is applied. For example:

```
> let isCapital = isWord ["London";"Paris";"Warsaw";"Tokyo"];;
val isCapital : (string -> bool)

> isCapital "Paris";;
val it : bool = true

> isCapital "Manchester";;
val it : bool = false
```

Here, the internal table wordTable is computed as soon as isCapital is applied to one argument. It would be a mistake to write isCapital as follows:

```
let isCapitalSlow inp = isWord ["London";"Paris";"Warsaw";"Tokyo"] inp
```

This function computes the same results as isCapital. However, it does so inefficiently, because isWord is applied to both its first argument and its second argument every time you use the function isCapitalSlow. This means the internal table is rebuilt every time the function isCapitalSlow is applied, somewhat defeating the point of having an internal table in the first place. In a similar vein, the definition of isCapital shown previously is more efficient than either isCapitalSlow2 or isCapitalSlow3 in the following:

```
let isWordSlow2 (words: string list) (word:string) =
    List.exists (fun word2 -> word = word2) words

let isCapitalSlow2 inp = isWordSlow2 ["London";"Paris";"Warsaw";"Tokyo"] inp

let isWordSlow3 (words: string list) (w:string) =
    let wordTable = Set.Create(words)
    wordTable.Contains(w)

let isCapitalSlow3 inp = isWordSlow3 ["London";"Paris";"Warsaw";"Tokyo"] inp
```

The first uses an inappropriate data structure for the lookup (an F# list, which has O(n) lookup time), and the second attempts to build a better intermediate data structure (an F# set, which has O(log n) lookup time) but does so on every invocation.

There are often trade-offs between different intermediate data structures or whether to use intermediate data structures at all. For example, in the previous example, you could just as well use a HashSet as the internal data structure. This approach in general gives better lookup times (constant time), but it requires slightly more care to use because a HashSet is a mutable data structure. In this case, you don't mutate the data structure after you create it, and you don't reveal it to the outside world, so it's entirely safe:

```
#r "System.Core.dll"
let isWord (words: string list) =
    let wordTable = System.Collections.Generic.HashSet<_>(words)
    fun word -> wordTable.Contains(word)
```

Precomputation and Objects

The examples of precomputation given previously are variations on the theme of computing functions, introduced in Chapter 3. The functions computed capture the precomputed intermediate data structures. However, it's clear that precomputing via partial applications and functions can be subtle, because it matters when you apply the first argument of a function (triggering the construction of intermediate data structures) and when you apply the subsequent arguments (triggering the real computation that uses the intermediate data structures).

Luckily, functions don't just have to compute functions; they can also return more sophisticated values such as objects. This can help make it clear when precomputation is being performed. It also allows you to build richer services based on precomputed results. For example, Listing 8-3 shows how to use precomputation as part of building a name-lookup service. The returned object includes both a Contains method and a ClosestPrefixMatch method.

Listing 8-3. Precomputing a Word Table Before Creating an Object

```
open System

type NameLookupService =
    abstract Contains : string -> bool

let buildSimpleNameLookup (words: string list) =
    let wordTable = Set.ofList words
    let score (w1:string) (w2:string) =
        let lim = min w1.Length w2.Length
        let rec loop i acc =
            if i >= lim then acc
            else loop (i+1) (int w1.[i] - int w2.[i] + acc)
        loop 0 0

    { new NameLookupService with
        member t.Contains(w) = wordTable.Contains(w) }
```

The internal data structure used in Listing 8-3 is the same as before: an F# set of type Microsoft.FSharp.Collections.Set<string>. The service can now be instantiated and used as follows:

```
> let capitalLookup = buildSimpleNameLookup ["London";"Paris";"Warsaw";"Tokyo"];;
val capitalLookup : NameLookupService

> capitalLookup.Contains "Paris";;
val it : bool = true
```

In passing, note the following about this implementation:

- The table is built based on the F# default ordinal comparison for strings. This isn't always an appropriate choice when you're using natural-language text. You can specify the exact comparison function to use when building sets based on string values by creating a custom key type with a custom comparison function.

- You can extend the returned service to support a richer set of queries of the underlying information by adding further methods to the object returned.

Precomputation of the kind used previously is an essential technique for implementing many services and abstractions, from simple functions to sophisticated computation engines. You see further examples of these techniques in Chapter 9.

Memoizing Computations

Precomputation is one important way to amortize the costs of computation in F#. Another is called *memoization.* A memoizing function is one that avoids recomputing its results by keeping an internal table, often called a *lookaside table.* For example, consider the well-known Fibonacci function, whose naive, unmemoized version is as follows:

```
let rec fib n = if n <= 2 then 1 else fib (n-1) + fib (n-2)
```

Not surprisingly, a version keeping a lookaside table is much faster:

```
#nowarn "40" // do not warn on recursive computed objects and functions
let fibFast =
    let t = new System.Collections.Generic.Dictionary<int,int>()
    let rec fibCached n =
        if t.ContainsKey(n) then t.[n]
        else if n <= 2 then 1
        else let res = fibCached(n-1) + fibCached(n-2)
             t.Add(n,res)
             res
    fun n -> fibCached n
```

On one of our laptops, with n = 30, the first runs in 3.65 seconds, and the second runs in 0.015 seconds. Listing 8-4 shows how to write a generic function that encapsulates the memoization technique.

Listing 8-4. A Generic Memoization Function

```
open System.Collections.Generic
let memoize (f: 'T -> 'U) =
    let t = new Dictionary<'T,'U>(HashIdentity.Structural)
    fun n ->
        if t.ContainsKey(n) then t.[n]
        else let res = f n
             t.Add(n,res)
             res

let rec fibFast =
    memoize (fun n -> if n <= 2 then 1 else fibFast (n-1) + fibFast (n-2))
```

Here, the functions have the following types:

```
val memoize : ('T -> 'U) -> ('T -> 'U) when 'T : equality
val fibFast : (int -> int)
```

In the definition of fibFast, you use let rec because fibFast is self-referential—that is, used as part of its own definition. You can think of fibFast as a *computed, recursive* function. Such a function generates an informational warning when used in F# code, because it's important to understand when this feature of F# is being used; you then suppress the warning with #nowarn "40". As with the examples of computed functions from the previous section, it's important not to include the extra argument in the application of memoize, because it would lead to a fresh memoization table being allocated each time the function fibNotFast was called:

```
let rec fibNotFast n =
    memoize (fun n -> if n <= 2 then 1 else fibNotFast (n-1) + fibNotFast (n-2)) n
```

Due to this subtlety, it's often a good idea to define your memoization strategies to generate objects other than functions (note that you can think of functions as very simple kinds of objects). For example, Listing 8-5 shows how to define a new variation on memoize that returns a Table object that supports both a lookup and a Discard method.

Listing 8-5. A Generic Memoization Service

```
open System.Collections.Generic
type Table<'T,'U> =
    abstract Item : 'T -> 'U with get
    abstract Discard : unit -> unit

let memoizeAndPermitDiscard f =
    let lookasideTable = new Dictionary<_,_>(HashIdentity.Structural)
    { new Table<'T,'U> with
        member t.Item
            with get(n) =
                if lookasideTable.ContainsKey(n)
                then lookasideTable.[n]
                else let res = f n
                     lookasideTable.Add(n,res)
                     res
        member t.Discard() =
            lookasideTable.Clear() }


#nowarn "40" // do not warn on recursive computed objects and functions

let rec fibFast =
    memoizeAndPermitDiscard
        (fun n ->
            printfn "computing fibFast %d" n
            if n <= 2 then 1 else fibFast.[n-1] + fibFast.[n-2])
```

In Listing 8-5, lookup uses the a.[b] associative Item lookup property syntax, and the Discard method discards any internal partial results. The functions have the following types:

```
val memoizeAndPermitDiscard : ('T -> 'U) -> Table<'T, 'U> when 'T : equality
val fibFast : Table<int,int>
```

Here's an example showing how fibFast caches results but recomputes them after a Discard:

```
> fibFast.[3];;
computing fibFast 3
computing fibFast 2
computing fibFast 1
val it : int = 2

> fibFast.[5];;
computing fibFast 5
computing fibFast 4
val it : int = 5

> fibFast.Discard();;
val it : unit = ()

> fibFast.[5];;
computing fibFast 5
computing fibFast 4
computing fibFast 3
computing fibFast 2
computing fibFast 1
val it : int = 5
```

■ **Note** Memoization relies on the memoized function being stable and idempotent. In other words, it always returns the same results, and no additional interesting side effects are caused by further invocations of the function. In addition, memoization strategies rely on mutable internal tables. The implementation of memoize shown in this chapter isn't thread safe, because it doesn't lock this table during reading or writing. This is fine if the computed function is used only from at most one thread at a time; but in a multithreaded application, you should use memoization strategies that use internal tables protected by locks such as a .NET ReaderWriterLock. Chapter 13 discusses thread synchronization and mutable state further.

Lazy Values

Memoization is a form of *caching*. Another important variation on caching is a simple *lazy* value. A lazy value is a delayed computation of type Microsoft.FSharp.Control.Lazy<'T> for some type 'T. Lazy values are usually formed by using the special keyword lazy (you can also make them explicitly using the functions in the Microsoft.FSharp.Core.Lazy module). For example:

```
> let sixty = lazy (30+30);;
val sixty : Lazy<int>

> sixty.Force();;
val it : int = 60
```

Lazy values of this kind are implemented as thunks holding either a function value that computes the result or the actual computed result. The lazy value is computed only once, and thus its effects are executed only once. For example, in the following code fragment, "Hello world" is printed only once:

```
> let sixtyWithSideEffect = lazy (printfn "Hello world"; 30+30);;
val sixtyWithSideEffect: Lazy<int>

> sixtyWithSideEffect.Force();;
Hello world
val it : int = 60

> sixtyWithSideEffect.Force();;
val it : int = 60
```

Lazy values are implemented by a simple data structure containing a mutable reference cell. You can find the definition of this data structure in the F# library source code.

Other Variations on Caching and Memoization

You can apply many different caching and memoization techniques in advanced programming, and this chapter can't cover them all. Here are some common variations:

- Using an internal data structure that records only the last invocation of a function and basing the lookup on a very cheap test on the input.

- Using an internal data structure that contains both a fixed-size queue of input keys and a dictionary of results. Entries are added to both the table and the queue as they're computed. When the queue is full, the input keys for the oldest computed results are dequeued, and the computed results are discarded from the dictionary.

Cleaning Up Resources

All programming involves the use of real resources on the host machine(s) and operating system. For example:

- *Stack:* Implicitly allocated and deallocated as functions are called

- *Heap allocated memory:* Used by all reference-typed objects

- *File handles:* Such as operating system file handles represented by System.IO.FileStream objects and its subtypes

- *Network connections:* Such as operating system I/O completion ports represented by System.Net.WebResponse and its subtypes

- *Threads:* Such as operating system threads represented by System.Threading.Thread objects and also worker threads in the .NET thread pool

- *Graphics objects:* Such as drawing objects represented by various constructs under the System.Drawing namespace

- *Concurrency objects:* Such as operating system synchronization objects represented by System.Threading.WaitHandle objects and its subtypes

All resources are necessarily finite. In .NET programming, some resources such as memory are fully *managed*, in the sense that you almost never need to consider when to clean up memory. This is done automatically through a process called *garbage collection*. Chapter 17 looks at garbage collection in a little more detail. Other resources must be *reclaimed* and/or *recycled*.

When prototyping, you can generally assume that resources are unbounded, although it's good practice when you're using a resource to be aware of how much of the resource you're using and roughly what your budget for the resource is. For example:

- On a modern 32-bit desktop machine, 10,000 tuple values occupy only a small fragment of a machine's memory, roughly 160KB. However, 10,000 open file handles is an extreme number and will stress the operating system. 10,000 simultaneous web requests may stress your network administrator!

- In some cases, even memory should be explicitly and carefully reclaimed. For example, on a modern 64-bit machine, the largest single array you can allocate in a .NET 2.0 program is 2GB. If your machine has, say, 4GB of real memory, you may be able to have only a handful of these objects and should strongly consider moving to a regime where you explicitly recycle these objects and think carefully before allocating them.

Cleaning Up with use

With the exception of stack and memory, all objects that own resources should be subtypes of the .NET type System.IDisposable. This is the primary way you can recognize primitive resources and objects that wrap resources. The System.IDisposable interface has a single method; in F# syntax, it can be defined as follows:

```
namespace System
    type IDisposable =
        abstract Dispose: unit -> unit
```

One of the simplest approaches to managing IDisposable objects is to give each resource a *lifetime*: that is, some well-defined portion of the program execution for which the object is active. This is even easier when the lifetime of a resource is lexically scoped, such as when a resource is allocated on entry to a function and deallocated on exit. In this case, the resource can be tied to the scope of a particular variable, and you can protect and dispose of a value that implements IDisposable by using a use binding instead of a let binding. For example, in the following code, three values implement IDisposable, all of which are bound using use:

```
/// Fetch a web page
let http (url: string) =
    let req = System.Net.WebRequest.Create url
    use resp = req.GetResponse()
    use stream = resp.GetResponseStream()
    use reader = new System.IO.StreamReader(stream)
    let html = reader.ReadToEnd()
    html
```

In all three cases, the objects (a WebResponse, a Stream, and a StreamReader) are automatically closed and disposed at the end of an execution of the function. To see what's going on, notice that a use binding is syntactic sugar. For example, the following

```
use var = expr in body
```

is shorthand for this:

```
let var = expr
try body
finally
    match var with
    | null -> ()
    | _ -> var.Dispose()
```

A number of important types implement IDisposable; Table 8-1 shows some of them. You can use tables such as this to chart the portions of the .NET Framework that reveal operating system functionality to .NET applications.

Table 8-1. *A Selection of the Types That Implement IDisposable*

Namespace	Some Types Implementing IDisposable
System.IO	BinaryReader, BinaryWriter, FileSystemWatcher, IsolatedFileStorage, Stream, TextReader, TextWriter, ...
System.Drawing	Brush, BufferedGraphics, Font, FontFamily, Graphics, Icon, Image, Pen, Region, TextureBrush, ...
System.Drawing.Text	FontCollection, ...
System.Drawing.Drawing2D	CustomLineCap, GraphicsPath, GraphicsPathIterator, Matrix, ...
System.Drawing.Imaging	EncoderParameter, ImageAttributes, ...
System.Net	WebResponse, ...
System.Net.Sockets	Socket, TcpClient, ...
System.Data.SqlClient	SqlBulkCopy, SqlCommand, SqlConnection, SqlTransaction, ...
System.Threading	Timer, WaitHandle, AutoResetEvent, ManualResetEvent, Mutex, Semaphore, ...
System.Web.UI	Control, HttpApplication, ...
System.Web.UI.WebControls	Button, CheckBox, DataGrid, ...
System.Windows.Forms	Button, CheckBox, Cursor, Control, DataGrid, Form, ...
Microsoft.Win32	RegistryKey, ...

■ **Tip** A tool such as Visual Studio can help you determine when a type has implemented IDisposable. When you rest your mouse pointer over a value, you normally see this noted on the information displayed for a value.

When Will the Runtime Clean Up for You?

People often ask if the .NET Common Language Runtime automatically cleans up resources such as file handles the same way it cleans up memory. It's true that when an object gets garbage collected, it may be *finalized*; if the object is well-implemented, this results in it deallocating any unmanaged resources, closing any outstanding file connections, and releasing any operating system resources. However, although it's appropriate to rely on finalization when prototyping, you should never rely on finalization in code where you're hitting resource limits.

For example, let's say you have a loop where you open files using System.IO.File.OpenRead. If you forget to close the file handles, you may quickly allocate thousands of file handles. If you're lucky, the garbage collector may finalize these before you run out of OS resources; but if not, one of your File.OpenRead calls will fail with an exception, even if the file exists on disk.

You should also be aware of the potential for memory stickiness. Memory stickiness occurs when the .NET Common Language Runtime is unable to garbage-collect memory even though objects have become unreachable. This happens especially when long-running computations and inactive callbacks hold on to object handles related to the earlier phases of execution of a program. Memory stickiness can also lead to objects never being finalized, reinforcing that you shouldn't rely on finalization to release nonmemory resources. Memory profiling tools such as CLRProfiler are indispensable when you're tracking down memory leaks in production code or long-running applications.

Managing Resources with More Complex Lifetimes

Sometimes, the lifetime of a resource isn't simple in the sense that it doesn't follow a stack discipline. In these cases, you should almost always adopt one of two techniques:

- Design objects that can own one or more resources and that are responsible for cleaning them up. Make sure these objects implement System.IDisposable.

- Use control constructs that help you capture the kind of computation you're performing. For example, when generating sequences of data (such as from a database connection), you should strongly consider using sequence expressions, discussed in Chapter 3. These may have internal *use* bindings, and the resources are disposed when each sequence iteration finishes. Likewise, when using asynchronous I/O, it may be helpful to write your computation as an asynchronous workflow. Chapter 13 and the following sections provide examples.

You should consider implementing the IDisposable interface on objects and types in the following situations:

- When you build an object that uses one or more IDisposable objects internally.

- When you're writing a wrapper for an operating system resource or some resource allocated and managed in a native (C or C++) DLL. In this case, you should also implement a finalizer by overriding the Object.Finalize method.

- When you implement the System.Collections.Generic.IEnumerable<'T> (that is, sequence) interface on a collection. The IEnumerable interface isn't IDisposable, but it must generate System.Collection.Generic.IEnumerator<'T> values, and this interface inherits from IDisposable. For nearly all collection types, the disposal action returns without doing anything.

The following sections give some examples of these.

Cleaning Up Internal Objects

Listing 8-6 shows an example that implements an object that reads lines from a pair of text files, choosing the file at random. You must implement the type IDisposable because the object owns two internal System.IO.StreamReader objects, which are IDisposable. Note that you explicitly check to see whether the object has already been disposed.

Listing 8-6. Implementing IDisposable to Clean Up Internal Objects

```
open System
open System.IO

type LineChooser(fileName1, fileName2) =
    let file1 = File.OpenText(fileName1)
    let file2 = File.OpenText(fileName2)
    let rnd = new System.Random()

    let mutable disposed = false

    let cleanup() =
        if not disposed then
            disposed <- true;
            file1.Dispose();
            file2.Dispose();

    interface System.IDisposable with
        member x.Dispose() = cleanup()

    member obj.CloseAll() = cleanup()

    member obj.GetLine() =
        if not file1.EndOfStream &&
           (file2.EndOfStream  || rnd.Next() % 2 = 0) then file1.ReadLine()
        elif not file2.EndOfStream then file2.ReadLine()
        else raise (new EndOfStreamException())
```

You can now instantiate, use, and dispose of this object as follows:

```
> open System.IO;;

> File.WriteAllLines("test1.txt", [| "Daisy, Daisy"; "Give me your hand oh do" |]);;
val it : unit = ()

> File.WriteAllLines("test2.txt", [| "I'm a little teapot"; "Short and stout" |]);;
val it : unit = ()

> let chooser = new LineChooser ("test1.txt", "test2.txt");;
val chooser : LineChooser

> chooser.GetLine();;
val it : string = "Daisy, Daisy"

> chooser.GetLine();;
val it : string = "I'm a little teapot"

> (chooser :> IDisposable).Dispose();;
val it : unit = ()

> chooser.GetLine();;
System.ObjectDisposedException: Cannot read from a closed TextReader.
```

Disposal should leave an object in an unusable state, as shown in the last line of the previous example. It's also common for objects to implement a member with a more intuitive name that does precisely the same thing as its implementation of IDisposable.Dispose, which is CloseAll in Listing 8-6.

Cleaning Up Unmanaged Objects

If you're writing a component that explicitly wraps some kind of unmanaged resource, then implementing IDisposable is a little trickier. Listing 8-7 shows the pattern that is used for this cleanup. Here, you mimic an external resource via a data structure that generates fresh, reclaimable integer tickets. The idea is that customers are each given an integer ticket, but this is kept internal to the customer, and customers return their ticket to the pool when they leave (that is, are disposed).

Listing 8-7. Reclaiming Unmanaged Tickets with IDisposable

```
open System

type TicketGenerator() =
    let mutable free = []
    let mutable max = 0
    member h.Alloc() =
        match free with
        | [] -> max <- max + 1; max
        | h::t -> free <- t; h
    member h.Dealloc(n:int) =
        printfn "returning ticket %d" n
        free <- n :: free
```

```
let ticketGenerator = new TicketGenerator()

type Customer() =
    let myTicket = ticketGenerator.Alloc()
    let mutable disposed = false
    let cleanup() =
            if not disposed then
                disposed <- true
                ticketGenerator.Dealloc(myTicket)
    member x.Ticket = myTicket
    interface IDisposable with
        member x.Dispose() = cleanup(); GC.SuppressFinalize(x)
    override x.Finalize() = cleanup()
```

Note that you override the `Object.Finalize` method. This makes sure cleanup occurs if the object isn't disposed but is still garbage-collected. If the object is explicitly disposed, you call `GC.SuppressFinalize()` to ensure that the object isn't later finalized. The finalizer shouldn't call the `Dispose()` of other managed objects, because they have their own finalizers if needed. The following example session generates some customers, and tickets used by some of the customers are automatically reclaimed as they exit their scopes:

```
> let bill = new Customer();;
val bill : Customer

> bill.Ticket;;
val it : int = 1

> begin
      use joe = new Customer()
      printfn "joe.Ticket = %d" joe.Ticket
  end;;
joe.Ticket = 2
returning ticket 2

> begin
      use jane = new Customer()
      printfn "jane.Ticket = %d" jane.Ticket
  end;;
jane.Ticket = 2
returning ticket 2
val it : unit = ()
```

In the example, Joe and Jane get the same ticket. Joe's ticket is returned at the end of the scope where the `joe` variable is declared because of the `IDisposable` cleanup implicit in the use binding.

Cleaning Up in Sequence Expressions

It's common to implement computations that access external resources such as databases but that return their results on demand. But this raises a difficulty: how do you manage the lifetime of the resources for the underlying operating system connections? One solution to this is captured by use bindings in sequence expressions:

- When a use binding occurs in a sequence expression, the resource is initialized each time a client enumerates the sequence.

- The connection is closed when the client disposes of the enumerator.

For example, consider the following function that creates a sequence expression that reads the first two lines of a file on demand:

```
open System.IO

let firstTwoLines(file) =
    seq { use s = File.OpenText(file)
          yield s.ReadLine()
          yield s.ReadLine() }
```

Let's now create a file and a sequence that reads the first two lines of the file on demand:

```
> File.WriteAllLines("test1.txt", [| "Es kommt ein Schiff";
                                      "A ship is coming" |]);;
val it : unit = ()

> let seq = firstTwoLines("test1.txt");;
val seq : seq<string>
```

At this point, the file hasn't yet been opened, and no lines have been read from the file. If you now iterate the sequence expression, the file is opened, the first two lines are read, and the results are consumed from the sequence and printed. Most important, the file has now also been closed, because the Seq.iter aggregate operator is careful to dispose of the underlying enumerator it uses for the sequence, which in turn disposes of the file handle generated by File.OpenText:

```
> seq |> Seq.iter (printfn "line = '%s'");;
line = 'Es kommt ein Schiff'
line = A ship is coming'
```

Chapter 9 covers sequence expressions and the more general mechanism of workflows in more detail.

Using using

In some older F# code, you may see the function using. For example:

```
using (new Customer()) (fun jane ->
    printfn "jane.Ticket = %d" jane.Ticket
)
```

The definition of using is as follows:

```
let using (ie : #System.IDisposable) f =
    try f(ie)
    finally ie.Dispose()
```

This is more explicit than writing use bindings but can be useful if you like to know what's going on under the hood.

Stack as a Resource: Tail Calls and Recursion

In the previous section, you saw a range of resources that are best managed explicitly, preferably by automatically cleaning up the construct at the end of its lifetime using constructs such as use x = expr and idioms such as System.IDisposable. You also saw that two resources are managed automatically, *stack* and *heap-allocated* memory, with the latter allocated on the garbage-collected heap.

Stack space is needed every time you call an F# function and is reclaimed when the function returns or when it performs a *tail call*, which is discussed in a moment. It's perhaps surprising that stack space is more limited than space in the garbage-collected heap. For example, on a 32-bit Windows machine, the default settings are such that each thread of a program can use up to 1MB of stack space. Because stack is allocated every time a function call is made, a very deep series of nested function calls causes a StackOverflowException to be raised. For example, on a 32-bit Windows machine, the following program causes a stack overflow when n reaches about 79000:

```
let rec deepRecursion n =
    if n = 1000000 then () else
    if n % 100 = 0 then
        printfn "--> deepRecursion, n = %d" n
    deepRecursion (n+1)
    printfn "<-- deepRecursion, n = %d" n
```

You can see this in F# Interactive:

```
> deepRecursion 0;;
--> deepRecursion, n = 0
...
--> deepRecursion, n = 79100
--> deepRecursion, n = 79200
--> deepRecursion, n = 79300
Process is terminated due to StackOverflowException
Session termination detected. Press Enter to restart.
```

Stack overflows are extreme exceptions, because it's often difficult to recover correctly from them. For this reason, it's important to ensure that the amount of stack used by your program doesn't grow in an unbounded fashion as your program proceeds, especially as you process large inputs. Furthermore, deep stacks can hurt in other ways; for example, the .NET garbage collector traverses the entire stack on every garbage collection. This can be expensive if your stacks are very deep.

Because recursive functions are common in F# functional programming, this may seem to be a major problem. However, there is one important case in which a function call recycles stack space eagerly: a *tail call*. A tail call is any call that is the last piece of work done by a function. For example, Listing 8-8 shows the same program with the last line deleted.

Listing 8-8. A Simple Tail-Recursive Function

```
let rec tailCallRecursion n : unit =
    if n = 1000000 then () else
    if n % 100 = 0 then
        printfn "--> tailCallRecursion, n = %d" n
    tailCallRecursion (n+1)
```

The code now runs to completion without a problem:

```
> tailCallRecursion 0;;
...
--> tailCallRecursion, n = 999600
--> tailCallRecursion, n = 999700
--> tailCallRecursion, n = 999800
--> tailCallRecursion, n = 999900
val it : unit = ()
```

When a tail call is made, the .NET Common Language Runtime can drop the current stack frame before executing the target function, rather than waiting for the call to complete. Sometimes this optimization is performed by the F# compiler. If the n = 1000000 check were removed in the previous program, then the program would run indefinitely. (Note that n would cycle around to the negative numbers, because arithmetic is unchecked for overflow unless you open the module Microsoft.FSharp.Core.Operators.Checked.)

Functions such as tailCallRecursion are known as *tail-recursive* functions. When you write recursive functions, you should check either that they're tail recursive or that they won't be used with inputs that cause them to recurse to an excessive depth. The following sections, give some examples of techniques you can use to make your functions tail recursive.

Tail Recursion and List Processing

Tail recursion is particularly important when you're processing F# lists, because lists can be long and recursion is the natural way to implement many list-processing functions. For example, here is a function to find the last element of a list (this must traverse the entire list, because F# lists are pointers to the head of the list):

```
let rec last l =
    match l with
    | [] -> invalidArg "l" "the input list should not be empty"
    | [h] -> h
    | h::t -> last t
```

This function is tail recursive because no work happens after the recursive call last t. However, many list functions are written most naturally in non-tail-recursive ways. Although it can be a little annoying to write these functions using tail recursion, it's often better to use tail recursion than to leave the potential for stack overflow lying around your code. For example, the following function creates a list of length n where every entry in the list is the value x:

```
let rec replicateNotTailRecursiveA n x =
    if n <= 0 then []
    else x :: replicateNotTailRecursiveA (n-1) x
```

The problem with this function is that work is done after the recursive call. This becomes obvious when you write the function in the following fashion:

```
let rec replicateNotTailRecursiveB n x =
    if n <= 0 then []
    else
        let recursiveResult = replicateNotTailRecursiveB (n-1) x
        x :: recursiveResult
```

Clearly, a value is being constructed by the expression x :: recursiveResult after the recursive call replicateNotTailRecursiveB (n-1) x. This means the function isn't tail recursive. The solution is to write the function using an *accumulating parameter*. This is often done by using an auxiliary function that accepts the accumulating parameter:

```
let rec replicateAux n x acc =
    if n <= 0 then acc
    else replicateAux (n-1) x (x::acc)

let replicate n x = replicateAux n x []
```

Here, the recursive call to replicateAux is tail recursive. Sometimes the auxiliary functions are written as inner recursive functions:

```
let replicate n x =
    let rec loop i acc =
        if i >= n then acc
        else loop (i+1) (x::acc)
    loop 0 []
```

The F# compiler optimizes inner recursive functions such as these to produce an efficient pair of functions that pass extra arguments as necessary.

When you're processing lists, accumulating parameters often accumulate a list in reverse order. This means a call to List.rev may be required at the end of the recursion. For example, consider the following implementation of List.map, which isn't tail recursive:

```
let rec mapNotTailRecursive f inputList =
    match inputList with
    | [] -> []
    | h::t -> (f h) :: mapNotTailRecursive f t
```

Here is an implementation that neglects to reverse the accumulating parameter:

```
let rec mapIncorrectAcc f inputList acc =
    match inputList with
    | [] -> acc                // whoops! Forgot to reverse the accumulator here!
    | h::t -> mapIncorrectAcc f t (f h :: acc)

let mapIncorrect f inputList = mapIncorrectAcc f inputList []
```

```
> mapIncorrect (fun x -> x * x) [1;2;3;4];;
val it : int list = [ 16; 9; 4; 1]
```

Here is a correct implementation:

```
let rec mapAcc f inputList acc =
    match inputList with
    | [] -> List.rev acc
    | h::t -> mapAcc f t (f h :: acc)

let map f inputList = mapAcc f inputList []
```

```
> map (fun x -> x * x) [1;2;3;4];;
val it : int list = [ 1; 4; 9; 16]
```

Tail Recursion and Object-Oriented Programming

You often need to implement object members with a tail-recursive implementation. For example, consider the following list-like data structure:

```
type Chain =
    | ChainNode of int * string * Chain
    | ChainEnd of string

    member chain.LengthNotTailRecursive =
        match chain with
        | ChainNode(_,_,subChain) -> 1 + subChain.LengthNotTailRecursive
        | ChainEnd _ -> 0
```

The implementation of LengthNotTailRecursive is *not* tail recursive, because the addition 1 + applies to the result of the recursive property invocation. One obvious tail-recursive implementation uses a local recursive function with an accumulating parameter, as shown in Listing 8-9.

Listing 8-9. Making an Object Member Tail Recursive

```
type Chain =
    | ChainNode of int * string * Chain
    | ChainEnd of string

    // The implementation of this property is tail recursive.
    member chain.Length =
```

```
let rec loop c acc =
    match c with
    | ChainNode(_,_,subChain) -> loop subChain (acc+1)
    | ChainEnd _ -> acc
loop chain 0
```

■ **Note** The list-processing functions in the F# library module `Microsoft.FSharp.Collections.List` are tail recursive, except where noted in the documentation. Some of them have implementations that are specially optimized to take advantage of the implementation of the `list` data structure.

Tail Recursion and Processing Unbalanced Trees

This section considers tail-recursion problems that are much less common in practice but for which it's important to know the techniques to apply if required. The techniques also illustrate some important aspects of functional programming, in particular an advanced technique called *continuation passing*.

Tree-structured data is generally more difficult to process in a tail-recursive way than list-structured data. For example, consider the following tree structure:

```
type Tree =
    | Node of string * Tree * Tree
    | Tip of string

let rec sizeNotTailRecursive tree =
    match tree with
    | Tip _ -> 1
    | Node(_,treeLeft,treeRight) ->
        sizeNotTailRecursive treeLeft + sizeNotTailRecursive treeRight
```

The implementation of this function isn't tail recursive. Luckily, this is rarely a problem, especially if you can assume that the trees are *balanced*. A tree is balanced when the depth of each subtree is roughly the same. In that case, a tree of depth 1,000 will have about 21000 entries. Even for a balanced tree of this size, the recursive calls to compute the overall size of the tree won't recurse to a depth greater than 1,000—not deep enough to cause stack overflow except when the routine is being called by some other function already consuming inordinate amounts of stack. Many data structures based on trees are balanced by design; for example, the Set and Map data structures implemented in the F# library are based on balanced binary trees.

However, some trees can be unbalanced; for example, you can explicitly make a highly unbalanced tree:

```
let rec mkBigUnbalancedTree n tree =
    if n = 0 then tree
    else Node("node",Tip("tip"),mkBigUnbalancedTree (n-1) tree)

let tree1 = Tip("tip")
let tree2 = mkBigUnbalancedTree 10000 tree1
let tree3 = mkBigUnbalancedTree 10000 tree2
let tree4 = mkBigUnbalancedTree 10000 tree3
let tree5 = mkBigUnbalancedTree 10000 tree4
let tree6 = mkBigUnbalancedTree 10000 tree5
```

Calling tree6.Size now risks a stack overflow. You can solve this in part by trying to predict whether the tree will be unbalanced to the left or right and by using an accumulating parameter:

```
let rec sizeAcc acc tree =
    match tree with
    | Tip _ -> 1+acc
    | Node(_,treeLeft,treeRight) ->
        let acc = sizeAcc acc treeLeft
        sizeAcc acc treeRight

let size tree = sizeAcc 0 tree
```

This algorithm works for tree6, because it's biased toward accepting trees that are skewed to the right. The recursive call that processes the right branch is a tail call, which the call that processes the left branch isn't. This may be OK if you have prior knowledge of the shape of your trees. However, this algorithm still risks a stack overflow, and if necessary, you may have to change techniques. One way to do this is to use a much more general and important technique known as continuation passing.

Using Continuations to Avoid Stack Overflows

A continuation is a function that receives the result of an expression after it's been computed. Listing 8-10 shows an example implementation of the previous algorithm that handles trees of arbitrary size.

Listing 8-10. Making a Function Tail Recursive via an Explicit Continuation

```
let rec sizeCont tree cont =
    match tree with
    | Tip _ -> cont 1
    | Node(_,treeLeft,treeRight) ->
        sizeCont treeLeft (fun leftSize ->
          sizeCont treeRight (fun rightSize ->
            cont (leftSize + rightSize)))

let size tree = sizeCont tree (fun x -> x)
```

What's going on here? Let's look at the type of sizeCont and size:

```
val sizeCont : Tree -> (int -> 'a) -> 'a
val size : Tree -> int
```

The type of sizeCont tree cont can be read as "compute the size of the tree and call cont with that size." If you look at the type of sizeCont, you can see that it will call the second parameter of type int -> 'T at some point—how else could the function produce the final result of type 'T? And when you look at the implementation of sizeCont, you can see that it does call cont on both branches of the match.

Now, if you look at recursive calls in sizeCont, you can see that they're both tail calls:

```
sizeCont treeLeft (fun leftSize ->
  sizeCont treeRight (fun rightSize ->
    cont (leftSize + rightSize)))
```

That is, the first call to sizeCont is a tail call with a new continuation, as is the second. The first continuation is called with the size of the left tree, and the second is called with the size of the right tree. Finally, you add the results and call the original continuation cont. Calling size on an unbalanced tree such as tree6 now succeeds:

```
> size tree6;;
val it : int = 50001
```

How did you turn a tree walk into a tail-recursive algorithm? The answer lies in the fact that continuations are function objects, which are allocated on the garbage-collected heap. Effectively, you've generated a work list represented by objects, rather than keeping a work list via a stack of function invocations.

As it happens, using a continuation for both the right and left trees is overkill, and you can use an accumulating parameter for one side. This leads to a more efficient implementation because each continuation function object is likely to involve one allocation (short-lived allocations such as continuation objects are very cheap but not as cheap as not allocating at all!). For example, Listing 8-11 shows a more efficient implementation.

Listing 8-11. Combining an Accumulator with an Explicit Continuation

```
let rec sizeContAcc acc tree cont =
    match tree with
    | Tip _ -> cont (1+acc)
    | Node (_, treeLeft, treeRight) ->
        sizeContAcc acc treeLeft (fun accLeftSize ->
        sizeContAcc accLeftSize treeRight cont)

let size tree = sizeContAcc 0 tree (fun x -> x)
```

The behavior of this version of the algorithm is as follows:

1. You start with an accumulator acc of 0.

2. You traverse the left spine of the tree until a Tip is found, building up a continuation for each Node along the way.

3. When a Tip is encountered, the continuation from the previous Node is called with accLeftSize increased by 1. The continuation makes a recursive call to sizeContAcc for its right tree, passing the continuation for the second-to-last node along the way.

4. When all is done, all the left and right trees have been explored, and the final result is delivered to the (fun x -> x) continuation.

As you can see from this example, continuation passing is a powerful control construct, although it's used only occasionally in F# programming.

Another Example: Processing Syntax Trees

One real-world example where trees may become unbalanced is syntax trees for parsed languages when the inputs are very large and machine generated. In this case, some language constructs may be repeated very large numbers of times in an unbalanced way. For example, consider the following data structure:

```
type Expr =
    | Add  of Expr * Expr
    | Bind of string * Expr * Expr
    | Var  of string
    | Num  of int
```

This data structure would be suitable for representing arithmetic expressions of the forms *var*, *expr + expr*, and *bind var = expr in expr*. Chapters 9 and 11 are dedicated to techniques for representing and processing languages of this kind. As with all tree structures, most traversal algorithms over this type of abstract syntax trees aren't naturally tail recursive. For example, here is a simple evaluator:

```
type env = Map<string,int>

let rec eval (env: env) expr =
    match expr with
    | Add (e1,e2)          -> eval env e1 + eval env e2
    | Bind (var,rhs,body) -> eval (env.Add(var, eval env rhs)) body
    | Var var              -> env.[var]
    | Num n                -> n
```

The recursive call eval env rhs isn't tail recursive. For the vast majority of applications, you never need to worry about making this algorithm tail recursive. However, stack overflow may be a problem if bindings are nested to great depth, such as in *bind v1 = (bind v2 = . . . (bind v1000000 = 1. . .)) in v1+v1*. If the syntax trees come from human-written programs, you can safely assume this won't be the case. But if you need to make the implementation tail recursive, you can use continuations, as shown in Listing 8-12.

Listing 8-12. A Tail-Recursive Expression Evaluator Using Continuations

```
let rec evalCont (env: env) expr cont =
    match expr with
    | Add (e1,e2)         ->
        evalCont env e1 (fun v1 ->
        evalCont env e2 (fun v2 ->
        cont (v1+v2)))
    | Bind (var,rhs,body) ->
        evalCont env rhs (fun v1 ->
        evalCont (env.Add(var,v1)) body cont)
    | Num n               ->
        cont n
    | Var var             ->
        cont (env.[var])

let eval env expr = evalCont env expr (fun x -> x)
```

■ **Note** Programming with continuations can be tricky, and you should use them only when necessary, or use the F# async type as a way of managing continuation-based code. Where possible, abstract the kind of transformation you're doing on your tree structure (for example, a map, fold, or bottom-up reduction) so you can concentrate on getting the traversal right. In the previous examples, the continuations all effectively play the role of a *work list*. You can also reprogram your algorithms to use work lists explicitly and to use accumulating parameters for special cases. Sometimes this is necessary to gain maximum efficiency, because an array or a queue can be an optimal representation of a work list. When you make a work list explicit, then the implementation of an algorithm becomes more verbose; but in some cases, debugging can become simpler.

Events

One recurring idiom in .NET programming (and, for example, JavaScript) is that of *events*. An event is something you can listen to by registering a callback with the event. For example, here's how you can create a WinForms form and listen to mouse clicks on the form:

```
> open System.Windows.Forms;;
> let form = new Form(Text="Click Form",Visible=true,TopMost=true);;
val form : Form

> form.Click.Add(fun evArgs -> printfn "Clicked!");;
val it : unit = ()
```

When you run this code in F# Interactive, a window appears; and each time you click the window with the mouse, you see "Clicked!" printed to the console. In .NET terminology, form.Click is an event, and form.Click.Add registers a callback with the event. You can register multiple callbacks with the same event, and many objects publish many events. For example, when you add the following, you see a stream of output when you move the mouse over the form:

```
> form.MouseMove.Add(fun args -> printfn "Mouse, (X,Y) = (%A,%A)" args.X args.Y);;
val it : unit = ()
```

If necessary, you can also remove event handlers by first adding them using the AddHandler method and removing them by using RemoveHandler.

The process of clicking the form *triggers* (or fires) the event, which means the callbacks are called in the order they were registered. Events can't be triggered from the outside. In other words, you can't trigger the Click event on a form; you can only handle it. Events also have *event arguments*. In the first example shown previously, the event arguments are called evArgs and are ignored. .NET events usually pass arguments of type System.EventArgs or some related type such as System.Windows.Forms.MouseEventArgs or System.Windows.Forms.PaintEventArgs. These arguments generally carry pieces of information; for example, a value of type MouseEventArgs has the properties Button, Clicks, Delta, Location, X, and Y.

Events occur throughout the design of the .NET class libraries. Table 8-2 shows some of the more important events.

Table 8-2. A Selection of Events from the .NET Libraries

Type	Some Sample Events
System.AppDomain	AssemblyLoad, AssemblyResolve, DomainUnload, ProcessExit, UnhandledException (and others)
System.Diagnostics.Process	ErrorDataReceived, Exited, OutputDataReceived (and others)
System.IO.FileSystemWatcher	Changed, Created, Deleted, Error, Renamed (and others)
System.Windows.Forms.Control	BackgroundImageChanged, Click, Disposed, DragDrop, KeyPress, KeyUp, KeyDown, Layout, LostFocus, MouseClick, MouseDown, MouseEnter, MouseHover, MouseLeave, MouseUp, Paint, Resize, TextChanged, Validated, Validating (and others)
System.Windows.Forms.Timer	Tick
System.Timers.Timer	Elapsed

Events as First-Class Values

In F#, an event such as form.Click is a *first-class value*, which means you can pass it around like any other value. The main advantage this brings is that you can use the combinators in the F# library module Microsoft.FSharp.Control.Event to map, filter, and otherwise transform the event stream in compositional ways. For example, the following code filters the event stream from form.MouseMove so that only events with X > 100 result in output to the console:

```
form.MouseMove
    |> Event.filter (fun args -> args.X > 100)
    |> Event.listen (fun args -> printfn "Mouse, (X,Y) = (%A,%A)" args.X args.Y)
```

If you work with events a lot, you find yourself factoring out useful portions of code into functions that preprocess event streams. Table 8-3 shows some of the functions from the F# Event module. One interesting combinator is Event.partition, which splits an event into two events based on a predicate.

Table 8-3. Some Functions from the Event Module

Function	Type
Event.choose	: ('T -> 'U option) -> IEvent<'T> -> IEvent<'U>
Event.create	: unit -> ('T -> unit) * IEvent<'T>
Event.filter	: ('T -> bool) -> IEvent<'T> -> IEvent<'T>
Event.scan	: ('U -> 'T -> 'U) -> 'U -> IEvent<'T> -> IEvent<'U>
Event.listen	: ('T -> unit) -> IEvent<'T> -> unit
Event.map	: ('T -> 'U) -> IEvent<'T> -> IEvent<'U>
Event.partition	: ('T -> bool) -> IEvent<'T> -> IEvent<'T> * IEvent<'T>

Creating and Publishing Events

As you write code in F#, particularly object-oriented code, you need to implement, publish, and trigger events. The normal idiom for doing this is to call new Event<_>(). Listing 8-13 shows how to define an event object that is triggered at random intervals.

Listing 8-13. Creating a RandomTicker That Defines, Publishes, and Triggers an Event

```
open System
open System.Windows.Forms

type RandomTicker(approxInterval) =
    let timer = new Timer()
    let rnd = new System.Random(99)
    let tickEvent = new Event<int> ()

    let chooseInterval() :int =
        approxInterval + approxInterval/4 - rnd.Next(approxInterval/2)

    do timer.Interval <- chooseInterval()

    do timer.Tick.Add(fun args ->
        let interval = chooseInterval()
        tickEvent.Trigger interval;
        timer.Interval <- interval)

    member x.RandomTick = tickEvent.Publish
    member x.Start() = timer.Start()
    member x.Stop() = timer.Stop()
    interface IDisposable with
        member x.Dispose() = timer.Dispose()
```

Here's how you can instantiate and use this type:

```
> let rt = new RandomTicker(1000);;
val rt : RandomTicker

> rt.RandomTick.Add(fun nextInterval -> printfn "Tick, next = %A" nextInterval);;
val it : unit = ()

> rt.Start();;
Tick, next = 1072
Tick, next = 927
Tick, next = 765
...
val it : unit = ()

> rt.Stop();;
val it : unit = ()
```

Events are an idiom understood by all .NET languages. F# event values are immediately compiled in the idiomatic .NET form. This is because F# allows you to go one step further and use events as first-class values. If you need to ensure that your events can be used by other .NET languages, then you should do both of the following:

- Create the events using new Event<*DelegateType, Args*> instead of new Event<*Args*>.

- Publish the event as a property of a type with the [<CLIEvent>] attribute.

Events are used in most of the later chapters of this book, and you can find many examples there.

■ **Note** Because events allow you to register callbacks, it's sometimes important to be careful about the thread on which an event is being raised. This is particularly true when you're programming with multiple threads or the .NET thread pool. Events are usually fired on the GUI thread of an application. See Chapter 13 for more details about concurrent and multithreaded programming.

Summary

This chapter covered some of the techniques you're likely to use in your day-to-day F# programming, including an in-depth look at hashing, equality, comparison, resource management, tail calls, caching, memoization, and the basics of how F# reveals the wiring for first-class events. The next chapter introduces a final set of language constructs and techniques related to language-oriented programming tasks.

CHAPTER 9

■■■

Introducing Language-Oriented Programming

Chapters 3, 4, and 6 covered three well-known programming paradigms in F#: *functional*, *imperative*, and *object-oriented* programming. This chapter covers techniques and constructs related to what is essentially a fourth programming paradigm: *language-oriented programming*. The word *language* can have a number of meanings in this context. For example, take the simple language of arithmetic expressions and algebra that you learned in high-school mathematics, made up of named variables such as x and y and composite expressions such as $x+y$, xy, $-x$, and x^2. For the purposes of this chapter, this language can have a number of manifestations:

- One or more *concrete representations*: for example, using an ASCII text format or an XML representation of arithmetic expressions.

- One or more *abstract representations*: for example, as F# values representing the normalized form of an arithmetic expression tree.

- One or more *computational representations*, either by functions that compute the values of arithmetic expressions or via other engines that perform analysis, interpretation, compilation, execution, or transformation on language fragments. These can be implemented in F#, in another .NET language, or in external engines.

This and later chapters cover many of the tasks associated with language-oriented programming. The techniques covered in this book are as follows:

- Manipulating formats such as XML, which are often used for concrete representations of languages (Chapters 9 and 11)

- Writing parsers and lexers for other text formats, also often used as concrete representations of languages (Chapter 16)

- Using F# types for abstract representations of languages (Chapters 9 and 11)

- Using three techniques related to computational representations of languages: *active patterns*, *quotations*, and *workflows* (Chapters 9 and 13)

- Interfacing with existing language execution components (SQL via LINQ in Chapter 15)

Language-oriented programming isn't a single technique; sometimes you work with fully concrete representations (for example, reading bits on a magnetic disk) and sometimes with fully computational representations (for example, defining and using functions that compute the value of arithmetic expressions). Most often, you work somewhere in between (for example, manipulating abstract syntax trees). These tasks require different techniques, and there are trade-offs between choosing to work with different kinds of representations. For example, if you're generating human-readable formulae, then you may need to store more concrete information; but if you're interested just in evaluating arithmetic expressions, then a purely computational encoding may be more effective. You see some of those trade-offs in this chapter.

■ **Note** The term *language-oriented programming* was originally applied to F# by Robert Pickering in the Apress book *Beginning F#*, and it really captures a key facet of F# programming. Thanks, Robert!

Using XML as a Concrete Language Format

To get started with language-oriented programming, it's helpful to begin with the standard structured data format Extensible Markup Language (XML). .NET comes with well-engineered libraries for reading and generating XML, so you can initially skirt many of the issues associated with concrete language formats. Chapter 15 also covers XML as a data format, and Chapter 16 discusses techniques to tokenize and parse other textual formats. Chapter 16 also briefly covers binary formats.

Using the System.Xml Namespace

XML is a general-purpose markup language and is extensible because it allows its users to define their own tags. Its primary purpose is to facilitate the sharing of data across different information systems, particularly via the Internet. Here is a sample fragment of XML, defined as a string directly in F#:

```
let inp = "<?xml version=\"1.0\" encoding=\"utf-8\" ?>
        <Scene>
          <Composite>
            <Circle radius='2' x='1' y='0'/>
            <Composite>
              <Circle radius='2' x='4' y='0'/>
              <Square side='2' left='-3' top='0'/>
            </Composite>
            <Ellipse top='2' left='-2' width='3' height='4'/>
          </Composite>
        </Scene>"
```

The backbone of an XML document is a hierarchical structure, and each node is decorated with attributes keyed by name. You can parse XML using the types and methods in the System.Xml namespace provided by the .NET libraries and then examine the structure of the XML interactively:

```
> open System.Xml;;
> let doc = new XmlDocument();;
val doc : XmlDocument

> doc.LoadXml(inp);;
val it : unit = ()

> doc.ChildNodes;;
val it : XmlNodeList
    = seq [seq []; seq [seq [seq []; seq [seq []; seq []]]; seq []]]]
```

The default F# Interactive display for the XmlNode type isn't particularly useful. Luckily, you can add an interactive printer to the fsi.exe session using the AddPrinter method on the fsi object:

```
> fsi.AddPrinter(fun (x:XmlNode) -> x.OuterXml);;

> doc.ChildNodes;;
val it : XmlNodeList
seq
    [<?xml version="1.0" encoding="utf-8"?>;
     <Scene><Composite><Circle radius="2" x="1" y="0" /><Composite>...</Scene>]

> doc.ChildNodes.Item(1);;
val it : XmlNode
  = <Scene><Composite><Circle radius="2" x="1" y="0" /><Composite>...</Scene>

> doc.ChildNodes.Item(1).ChildNodes.Item(0);;
val it : XmlNode
  = <Composite><Circle radius="2" x="1" y="0" /><Composite>...</Composite>

> doc.ChildNodes.Item(1).ChildNodes.Item(0).ChildNodes.Item(0);;
val it : XmlNode = <Circle radius="2" x="1" y="0" />

> doc.ChildNodes.Item(1).ChildNodes.Item(0).ChildNodes.Item(0).Attributes;;
val it : val it : XmlAttributeCollection = seq [radius="2"; x="1"; y="0"]
```

Table 9-1 shows the most commonly used types and members from the System.Xml namespace.

Table 9-1. Commonly Used Types and Members from the System.Xml Namespace

Type/Member	Description
type XmlNode	Represents a single node in an XML document
member ChildNodes	Gets all the child nodes of an XmlNode
member Attributes	Gets all the attributes of an XmlNode
member OuterXml	Gets the XML text representing the node and all its children
member InnerText	Gets the concatenated values of the node and all its children
member SelectNodes	Selects child nodes using an XPath query

Type/Member	Description
type XmlAttribute member Value	Represents one attribute for an XmlNode; also an XmlNode Gets the string value for the attribute

type XmlDocument
    member Load
    member LoadXml
	Represents an entire XML document; also an XmlNode
	Populates the document from the given XmlReader, stream, or file name
	Populates the document object from the given XML string

type XmlReader	Represents a reader for an XML document or source
type XmlWriter	Represents a writer for an XML document

■ **Note** .NET provides tools to generate a typed .NET object model view of an XML schema, in particular xsd.exe from the .NET Framework SDK. This tool has some limitations, and sometimes it's worth exploring your own techniques for interoperating with external data schemas, whether they're in XML or otherwise, as discussed later in this chapter. Tools like xsd.exe can be configured to generate F# code through the use of the F# CodeDOM implementation that comes with the F# distribution. However, this chapter doesn't show how to use these tools. An alternative technique for querying XML is the XLinq API that is part of the LINQ framework, covered briefly in Chapter 15. You can also use F# active patterns to define decomposition and query techniques for XML (we cover F# active patterns later in this chapter).

From Concrete XML to Abstract Syntax

Often, your first task in processing a concrete language is to bring the language fragments under the type discipline of F#. This section shows how to transform the data contained in the XML from the previous section into an instance of the recursive type shown here. This kind of type is usually called an *abstract syntax tree* (AST):

```
open System.Drawing
type Scene =
    | Ellipse   of RectangleF
    | Rect      of RectangleF
    | Composite of Scene list
```

This example uses the types PointF and RectangleF from the System.Drawing namespace, although you can equally define your own types to capture the information carried by the leaves of the tree. Listing 9-1 shows a recursive transformation to convert XML documents like the one used in the previous section into the type Scene.

Listing 9-1. Converting XML into a Typed Format Using the System.Xml Namespace

```
open System.Xml
open System.Drawing
type Scene =
    | Ellipse of RectangleF
    | Rect    of RectangleF
    | Composite   of Scene list

    /// A derived constructor
    static member Circle(center:PointF,radius) =
        Ellipse(RectangleF(center.X-radius,center.Y-radius,
                           radius*2.0f,radius*2.0f))

    /// A derived constructor
    static member Square(left,top,side) =
        Rect(RectangleF(left,top,side,side))

let extractFloat32 attrName (attribs: XmlAttributeCollection) =
    float32 (attribs.GetNamedItem(attrName).Value)

let extractPointF (attribs: XmlAttributeCollection) =
    PointF(extractFloat32 "x" attribs,extractFloat32 "y" attribs)

let extractRectangleF (attribs: XmlAttributeCollection) =
    RectangleF(extractFloat32 "left" attribs,extractFloat32 "top" attribs,
               extractFloat32 "width" attribs,extractFloat32 "height" attribs)

let rec extractScene (node: XmlNode) =
    let attribs = node.Attributes
    let childNodes = node.ChildNodes
    match node.Name with
    | "Circle" ->
        Scene.Circle(extractPointF(attribs), extractFloat32 "radius" attribs)
    | "Ellipse"  ->
        Scene.Ellipse(extractRectangleF(attribs))
    | "Rectangle"  ->
        Scene.Rect(extractRectangleF(attribs))
    | "Square"  ->
        Scene.Square(extractFloat32 "left" attribs,extractFloat32 "top" attribs,
                     extractFloat32 "side" attribs)

    | "Composite"   ->
        Scene.Composite [ for child in childNodes -> extractScene(child) ]
    | _ -> failwithf "unable to convert XML '%s'" node.OuterXml

let extractScenes (doc: XmlDocument) =
    [ for node in doc.ChildNodes do
        if node.Name = "Scene" then
            yield (Composite
                      [ for child in node.ChildNodes -> extractScene(child) ]) ]
```

The inferred types of these functions are as follows:

```
type Scene =
    | Ellipse of RectangleF
    | Rect of RectangleF
    | Composite of Scene list
    static member Circle : PointF * float32 -> Scene
    static member Square : float32 * float32 * float32 -> Scene

val extractFloat32 : string -> XmlAttributeCollection -> float32
val extractPointF : XmlAttributeCollection -> PointF
val extractRectangleF :  XmlAttributeCollection -> RectangleF
val extractScene : XmlNode -> Scene
val extractScenes : XmlDocument -> Scene list
```

The definition of extractScenes in Listing 9-1 generates lists using sequence expressions, covered in Chapter 3. You can now apply the extractScenes function to the original XML. (You first add a pretty-printer to the F# Interactive session for the RectangleF type using the AddPrinter function on the fsi object, described in Chapter 10.)

```
> fsi.AddPrinter(fun (r:RectangleF) ->
      sprintf "[%A,%A,%A,%A]" r.Left r.Top r.Width r.Height);;
val it : unit = ()

> extractScenes doc;;
val it : Scene list
= [Composite
    [Composite
      [Ellipse [-1.0f,-2.0f,4.0f,4.0f];
        Composite [Ellipse [2.0f,-2.0f,4.0f,4.0f]; Rect [-3.0f,0.0f,2.0f,2.0f]];
        Ellipse [-2.0f,2.0f,3.0f,4.0f]]]]
```

The following sections more closely explain some of the choices we've made in the abstract syntax design for the type Scene.

■ **Tip** Translating to a typed representation isn't always necessary: some manipulations and analyses are better performed directly on heterogeneous, general-purpose formats such as XML or even on strings. For example, XML libraries support XPath, accessed via the SelectNodes method on the XmlNode type. If you need to query a large semistructured document whose schema is frequently changing in minor ways, then XPath is the right way to do it. Likewise, if you need to write significant amounts of code that interprets or analyzes a tree structure, then converting to a typed abstract syntax tree is usually better.

Working with Abstract Syntax Representations

In the previous section, you saw how to move from one particular concrete language format to an abstract syntax format. You now learn about some important recurring techniques in designing and working with abstract syntax representations.

Abstract Syntax Representations: Less Is More

Let's look at the design of the abstract syntax type Scene from Listing 9-1. The type Scene uses fewer kinds of nodes than the concrete XML representation: the concrete XML has node kinds Circle, Square, Composite, and Ellipse, whereas Scene has just three (Rect, Ellipse, and Composite), with two derived constructors Circle and Square, defined as static members of the Scene:

```
static member Circle(center:PointF,radius) =
    Ellipse(RectangleF(center.X-radius,center.Y-radius,
                       radius*2.0f,radius*2.0f))

/// A derived constructor
static member Square(left,top,side) =
    Rect(RectangleF(left,top,side,side))
```

This is a common step when abstracting from a concrete syntax; details are dropped and unified to make the abstract representation simpler and more general. Extra functions are then added that compute specific instances of the abstract representation. This approach has pros and cons:

- Transformational and analytical manipulations are almost always easier to program if you have fewer constructs in your abstract syntax representation.

- You must be careful not to eliminate truly valuable information from an abstract representation. For some applications, it may really matter if the user specified a Square or a Rectangle in the original input; for example, an editor for this data may provide different options for editing these objects.

The AST uses the types PointF and RectangleF from the System.Drawing namespace. This simplification is also a design decision that should be assessed: PointF and RectangleF use 32-bit low-precision floating-point numbers, which may not be appropriate if you're eventually rendering on high-precision display devices. You should be wary of deciding on abstract representations on the basis of convenience alone, although of course this is useful during prototyping.

The lesson here is that you should look carefully at your abstract syntax representations, trimming out unnecessary nodes and unifying nodes where possible, but only as long as doing so helps you achieve your ultimate goals.

Processing Abstract Syntax Representations

Common operations on abstract syntax trees include traversals that collect information and transformations that generate new trees from old. For example, the abstract representation from Listing 9-1 has the property that for nearly all purposes, the Composite nodes are irrelevant (this wouldn't be the case if you added an extra construct such as an Intersect node). This means you can flatten to a sequence of Ellipse and Rectangle nodes as follows:

```
let rec flatten scene =
    seq { match scene with
            | Composite scenes -> for x in scenes do yield! flatten x
            | Ellipse _ | Rect _ -> yield scene }
```

Here, flatten is defined using sequence expressions, introduced in Chapter 3. Its type is as follows:

```
val flatten : Scene -> seq<Scene>
```

Let's look at this more closely. Recall from Chapter 3 that sequences are on-demand (lazy) computations. Using functions that recursively generate seq<'T> objects can lead to inefficiencies in your code if your abstract syntax trees are deep. It's often better to traverse the entire tree in an *eager* way (eager traversals run to completion immediately). For example, it's typically faster to use an accumulating parameter to collect a list of results. Here's an example:

```
let rec flattenAux scene acc =
    match scene with
    | Composite(scenes) -> List.foldBack flattenAux scenes acc
    | Ellipse _
    | Rect _ -> scene :: acc

let flatten2 scene = flattenAux scene [] |> Seq.ofList
```

The following does an eager traversal using a local mutable instance of a ResizeArray as the accumulator and then returns the result as a sequence. This example uses a local function and ensures that the mutable state is locally encapsulated:

```
let flatten3 scene =
    let acc = new ResizeArray<_>()
    let rec flattenAux s =
        match s with
        | Composite(scenes) -> scenes |> List.iter flattenAux
        | Ellipse _ | Rect _ -> acc.Add s
    flattenAux scene;
    Seq.readonly acc
```

The types of these are as follows:

```
val flatten2 : Scene -> seq<Scene>
val flatten3 : Scene -> seq<Scene>
```

There is no hard and fast rule about which of these is best. For prototyping, the second option—doing an efficient, eager traversal with an accumulating parameter—is often the most effective. However, even if you implement an accumulation using an eager traversal, returning the result as an on-demand sequence can still give you added flexibility later in the design process.

Transformational Traversals of Abstract Syntax Representations

In the previous section, you saw examples of accumulating traversals of a syntax representation. It's common to traverse abstract syntax in other ways:

Leaf rewriting (mapping): Translating some leaf nodes of the representation but leaving the overall shape of the tree unchanged

Bottom-up rewriting: Traversing a tree but making local transformations on the way up

Top-down rewriting: Traversing a tree but before traversing each subtree, attempting to locally rewrite the tree according to some particular set of rules

Accumulating and rewriting transformations: For example, transforming the tree left to right but accumulating a parameter along the way

For example, the following mapping transformation rewrites all leaf ellipses to rectangles:

```
let rec rectanglesOnly scene =
    match scene with
    | Composite scenes -> Composite (scenes |> List.map rectanglesOnly)
    | Ellipse rect | Rect rect -> Rect rect
```

Often, whole classes of transformations are abstracted into aggregate transformation operations, taking functions as parameters. For example, here is a function that applies one function to each leaf rectangle:

```
let rec mapRects f scene =
    match scene with
    | Composite scenes -> Composite (scenes |> List.map (mapRects f))
    | Ellipse rect -> Ellipse (f rect)
    | Rect rect -> Rect (f rect)
```

The types of these functions are as follows:

```
val rectanglesOnly : Scene -> Scene
val mapRects: (RectangleF -> RectangleF) -> Scene -> Scene
```

Here is a use of the mapRects function to adjust the aspect ratio of all the RectangleF values in the scene (RectangleF values support an Inflate method):

```
let adjustAspectRatio scene =
    scene |> mapRects (fun r -> RectangleF.Inflate(r, 1.1f, 1.0f/1.1f))
```

Using On-Demand Computation with Abstract Syntax Trees

Sometimes it's feasible to delay the loading or processing of some portions of an abstract syntax tree. For example, imagine if the XML for the small geometric language from the previous section included a construct such as the following, where the File nodes represent entire subtrees defined in external files:

```
<Composite>
    <File file='spots.xml'/>
    <File file='dots.xml'/>
</Composite>
```

It may be useful to delay the loading of these files. One general way to do this is to add a `Delay` node to the `Scene` type:

```
type Scene =
    | Ellipse   of RectangleF
    | Rect      of RectangleF
    | Composite of Scene list
    | Delay     of Lazy<Scene>
```

You can then extend the `extractScene` function of Listing 9-1 with the following case to handle this node:

```
let rec extractScene (node: XmlNode) =
    let attribs = node.Attributes
    let childNodes = node.ChildNodes
    match node.Name with
    | "Circle"  ->
        ...
    | "File"    ->
        let file = attribs.GetNamedItem("file").Value
        let scene = lazy (let d = XmlDocument()
                          d.Load(file)
                          extractScene(d :> XmlNode))
        Scene.Delay scene
```

Code that analyzes trees (for example, via pattern matching) must typically be adjusted to force the computation of delayed values. One way to handle this is to first call a function to eliminate immediately delayed values:

```
let rec getScene scene =
    match scene with
    | Delay d -> getScene (d.Force())
    | _ -> scene
```

Here is the function `flatten2` from the "Processing Abstract Syntax Representations" section, but redefined to first eliminate delayed nodes:

```
let rec flattenAux scene acc =
    match getScene(scene) with
    | Composite   scenes -> List.foldBack flattenAux scenes acc
    | Ellipse _ | Rect _ -> scene :: acc
    | Delay _ -> failwith "this lazy value should have been eliminated by getScene"

let flatten2 scene = flattenAux scene []
```

It's generally advisable to have a single representation of laziness within a single syntax tree design. For example, the following abstract syntax design uses laziness in too many ways:

```
type SceneVeryLazy =
    | Ellipse   of Lazy<RectangleF>
    | Rect      of Lazy<RectangleF>
    | Composite of seq<SceneVeryLazy>
    | LoadFile  of string
```

The shapes of ellipses and rectangles are lazy computations; each Composite node carries a seq<SceneVeryLazy> value to compute subnodes on demand, and a LoadFile node is used for delayed file loading. This is a bit of a mess, because a single Delay node would in practice cover all these cases.

■ **Note** The Lazy<'T> type is defined in System and represents delayed computations. You access a lazy value via the Value property. F# includes the special keyword lazy for constructing values of this type. Chapter 8 also covered lazy computations.

Caching Properties in Abstract Syntax Trees

For high-performance applications of abstract syntax trees, it can occasionally be useful to cache computations of some derived attributes within the syntax tree itself. For example, let's say you want to compute bounding boxes for the geometric language described in Listing 9-1. It's potentially valuable to cache this computation at Composite nodes. You can use a type such as the following to hold a cache:

```
type SceneWithCachedBoundingBox =
    | Ellipse of RectangleF
    | Rect    of RectangleF
    | CompositeRepr  of SceneWithCachedBoundingBox list * RectangleF option ref
```

This is useful for prototyping, although you should be careful to encapsulate the code that is responsible for maintaining this information. Listing 9-2 shows the full code for doing this.

Listing 9-2. Adding the Cached Computation of a Local Attribute to an Abstract Syntax Tree

```
type SceneWithCachedBoundingBox =
    | Ellipse of RectangleF
    | Rect    of RectangleF
    | CompositeRepr   of SceneWithCachedBoundingBox list * RectangleF option ref

    member x.BoundingBox =
        match x with
        | Ellipse rect | Rect rect -> rect
        | CompositeRepr (scenes,cache) ->
            match !cache with
            | Some v -> v
            | None ->
                let bbox =
                    scenes
                    |> List.map (fun s -> s.BoundingBox)
                    |> List.reduce (fun r1 r2 -> RectangleF.Union(r1,r2))
```

```
            cache := Some bbox
            bbox

    /// Create a Composite node with an initially empty cache
    static member Composite(scenes)  = CompositeRepr(scenes,ref None)
```

Other attributes that are sometimes cached include the hash values of tree-structured terms and the computation of all the identifiers in a subexpression. The use of caches makes it more awkward to pattern-match on terms. This issue can be largely solved by using active patterns, covered later in this chapter.

Memoizing Construction of Syntax Tree Nodes

In some cases, abstract syntax tree nodes can end up consuming significant portions of the application's memory budget. In this situation, it can be worth memoizing some or all of the nodes constructed in the tree. You can even go as far as memoizing *all* equivalent nodes, ensuring that equivalence between nodes can be implemented by pointer equality, a technique often called *hash-consing*. Listing 9-3 shows an abstract representation of propositional logic terms that ensures that any two nodes that are syntactically identical are shared via a memoizing table. Propositional logic terms are terms constructed using *P* AND *Q*, *P* OR *Q*, NOT *P*, and variables *a*, *b*, and so on. A non-cached version of the expressions is as follows:

```
type Prop =
    | And of Prop * Prop
    | Or  of Prop * Prop
    | Not of Prop
    | Var of string
    | True
```

Listing 9-3. Memoizing the Construction of Abstract Syntax Tree Nodes

```
type Prop =
    | Prop of int

and internal PropRepr =
    | AndRepr of Prop * Prop
    | OrRepr  of Prop * Prop
    | NotRepr of Prop
    | VarRepr of string
    | TrueRepr

open System.Collections.Generic

module PropOps =

    let internal uniqStamp = ref 0
    type internal PropTable() =
        let fwdTable = new Dictionary<PropRepr,Prop>(HashIdentity.Structural)
        let bwdTable = new Dictionary<int,PropRepr>(HashIdentity.Structural)
        member t.ToUnique repr =
            if fwdTable.ContainsKey repr then fwdTable.[repr]
            else let stamp = incr uniqStamp; !uniqStamp
                let prop = Prop stamp
```

```
                fwdTable.Add (repr, prop)
                bwdTable.Add (stamp, repr)
                prop
        member t.FromUnique (Prop stamp) =
            bwdTable.[stamp]

    let internal table = PropTable ()

    // Public construction functions
    let And (p1,p2) = table.ToUnique (AndRepr (p1, p2))
    let Not p       = table.ToUnique (NotRepr p)
    let Or (p1,p2)  = table.ToUnique (OrRepr (p1, p2))
    let Var p       = table.ToUnique (VarRepr p)
    let True        = table.ToUnique TrueRepr
    let False       = Not True

    // Deconstruction function
    let internal getRepr p = table.FromUnique p
```

You can construct terms using the operations in PropOps much as you would construct terms using the nonmemoized representation:

```
> open PropOps;;
> True;;
val it : Prop = Prop 1

> And (Var "x",Var "y");;
val it : Prop = Prop 5

> getRepr it;;
val it : PropRepr = AndRepr(Prop 3, Prop 4)

> And(Var "x",Var "y");;
val it : Prop = Prop 5
```

In this example, when you create two syntax trees using the same specification, And (Var "x", Var "y"), you get back the same Prop object with the same stamp 5. You can also use memoization techniques to implement interesting algorithms; in Chapter 12, you see an important representation of propositional logic called a *binary decision diagram* (BDD) based on a memoization table similar to the previous example.

The use of unique integer stamps and a lookaside table in the previous representation also has some drawbacks; it's harder to pattern-match on abstract syntax representations, and you may need to reclaim and recycle stamps and remove entries from the lookaside table if a large number of terms is created or if the overall set of stamps must remain compact. You can solve the first problem by using active patterns, covered next in this chapter. If necessary, you can solve the second problem by scoping stamps in an object that encloses the uniqStamp state, the lookaside table, and the construction functions. Alternatively, you can explicitly reclaim the stamps by using the IDisposable idiom described in Chapter 8, although this approach can be intrusive to your application.

Introducing Active Patterns

Pattern matching is one of the key techniques provided in F# for decomposing abstract syntax trees and other abstract representations of languages. So far in this book, all the examples of pattern matching have been directly over the core representations of data structures: for example, directly matching on the structure of lists, options, records, and discriminated unions. But pattern matching in F# is also *extensible*—that is, you can define new ways of matching over existing types. You do this through a mechanism called *active patterns*.

This book covers only the basics of active patterns. However, they can be indispensable, because they can let you continue to use pattern matching with your types even after you hide their representations. Active patterns also let you use pattern matching with .NET object types. The following section covers active patterns and how they work.

Converting the Same Data to Many Views

In high-school math courses, you were probably taught that you can view complex numbers in two ways: as rectangular coordinates $x + yi$ or as polar coordinates of a phase r and magnitude ▮. In most computer systems, complex numbers are stored in the first format, although often the second format is more useful.

Wouldn't it be nice if you could look at complex numbers through either lens? You could do this by explicitly converting from one form to another when needed, but it would be better to have your programming language look after the transformations needed to do this for you. Active patterns let you do exactly that. First, here is a standard definition of complex numbers:

```
[<Struct>]
type Complex(r: float, i: float) =
    static member Polar(mag,phase) = Complex(mag * cos phase, mag * sin phase)
    member x.Magnitude = sqrt(r*r + i*i)
    member x.Phase = atan2 i r
    member x.RealPart = r
    member x.ImaginaryPart = i
```

Here is a pattern that lets you view complex numbers as rectangular coordinates:

```
let (|Rect|) (x:Complex) = (x.RealPart, x.ImaginaryPart)
```

And here is an active pattern to help you view complex numbers in polar coordinates:

```
let (|Polar|) (x:Complex) = (x.Magnitude, x.Phase)
```

The key thing to note is that these definitions let you use Rect and Polar as tags in pattern matching. For example, you can now write the following to define addition and multiplication over complex numbers:

```
let addViaRect a b =
    match a, b with
    | Rect (ar, ai), Rect (br, bi) -> Complex (ar+br, ai+bi)

let mulViaRect a b =
    match a, b with
    | Rect (ar, ai), Rect (br, bi) -> Complex (ar*br - ai*bi, ai*br + bi*ar)
```

As it happens, multiplication on complex numbers is easier to express using polar coordinates, implemented as follows:

```
let mulViaPolar a b =
    match a, b with
    | Polar (m, p), Polar (n, q) -> Complex.Polar (m*n, p+q)
```

Here is an example of using the (|Rect|) and (|Polar|) active patterns directly on some complex numbers via the pattern tags Rect and Polar. You first make the complex number 3+4*i*:

```
> let c = Complex (3.0, 4.0);;
val c : complex

> c;;
val it : complex = 3.0r+4.0i

> match c with
    | Rect (x, y) -> printfn "x = %g, y = %g" x y;;
x = 3, y = 4
val it : unit = ()

> match c with
    | Polar (x, y) -> printfn "x = %g, y = %g" x y;;
x = 5.0, y = 0.927295
val it : unit = ()

> addViaRect c c;;
val it : complex = 6.0r+8.0i

> mulViaRect c c;;
val it : complex = -7.0r+24.0i

> mulViaPolar c c;;
val it : complex = -7.0r+24.0i
```

As you may expect, you get the same results if you multiply via rectangular or polar coordinates. However, the execution paths are quite different. Let's look closely at the definition of mulViaRect. The important lines are in bold here:

```
let mulViaRect a b =
    match a, b with
    | Rect (ar, ai), Rect (br, bi) ->
        Complex (ar*br - ai*bi, ai*br + bi*ar)
```

When F# needs to match the values a and b against the patterns Rect (ar, ai) and Rect (br, bi), it doesn't look at the contents of a and b directly. Instead, *it runs a function as part of pattern matching* (which is why they're called *active* patterns). In this case, the function executed is (|Rect|), which produces a pair as its result. The elements of the pair are then bound to the variables ar and ai. Likewise, in the definition of mulViaPolar, the matching is performed partly by running the function (|Polar|).

The functions (|Rect|) and (|Polar|) are allowed to do anything, as long as each ultimately produces a pair of results. Here are the types of (|Rect|) and (|Polar|):

```
val (|Rect|) : complex -> float * float
val (|Polar|) : complex -> float * float
```

These types are identical, but they implement completely different views of the same data.

The definitions of addViaRect and mulViaPolar can also be written using pattern matching in argument position:

```
let add2 (Rect (ar, ai)) (Rect (br, bi))   = Complex (ar+br, ai+bi)
let mul2 (Polar (r1, th1)) (Polar (r2, th2)) = Complex (r1*r2, th1+th2)
```

Matching on .NET Object Types

One of the useful things about active patterns is that they let you use pattern matching with existing .NET object types. For example, the .NET object type System.Type is a runtime representation of types in .NET and F#. Here are the members found on this type:

```
type System.Type with
    member IsGenericType : bool
    member GetGenericTypeDefinition : unit -> Type
    member GetGenericArguments : unit -> Type[]
    member HasElementType : bool
    member GetElementType : unit -> Type
    member IsByRef : bool
    member IsPointer : bool
    member IsGenericParameter : bool
    member GenericParameterPosition : int
```

This type looks very much like one you'd like to pattern-match against. There are clearly three or four distinct cases here, and pattern matching helps you isolate them. You can define an active pattern to achieve this, as shown in Listing 9-4.

Listing 9-4. Defining an Active Pattern for Matching on System.Type Values

```
let (|Named|Array|Ptr|Param|) (typ : System.Type) =
    if typ.IsGenericType
    then Named(typ.GetGenericTypeDefinition(),typ.GetGenericArguments())
    elif typ.IsGenericParameter then Param(typ.GenericParameterPosition)
    elif not typ.HasElementType then Named(typ, [| |])
    elif typ.IsArray then Array(typ.GetElementType(),typ.GetArrayRank())
    elif typ.IsByRef then Ptr(true,typ.GetElementType())
    elif typ.IsPointer then Ptr(false,typ.GetElementType())
    else failwith "MSDN says this can't happen"
```

This then lets you use pattern matching against a value of this type:

```
open System

let rec formatType typ =
    match typ with
    | Named (con, [| |]) -> sprintf "%s" con.Name
    | Named (con, args) -> sprintf "%s<%s>" con.Name (formatTypes args)
    | Array (arg, rank) -> sprintf "Array(%d,%s)" rank (formatType arg)
    | Ptr(true,arg) -> sprintf "%s&" (formatType arg)
    | Ptr(false,arg) -> sprintf "%s*" (formatType arg)
    | Param(pos) -> sprintf "!%d" pos

and formatTypes typs =
    String.Join(",", Array.map formatType typs)
```

or collect the free generic type variables:

```
let rec freeVarsAcc typ acc =
    match typ with
    | Array (arg, rank) -> freeVarsAcc arg acc
    | Ptr (_,arg) -> freeVarsAcc arg acc
    | Param _ -> (typ :: acc)
    | Named (con, args) -> Array.foldBack freeVarsAcc args acc
let freeVars typ = freeVarsAcc typ []
```

Defining Partial and Parameterized Active Patterns

Active patterns can also be *partial*. You can recognize a partial pattern by a name such as
(|MulThree|_|) and by the fact that it returns a value of type 'T option for some 'T. For example:

```
let (|MulThree|_|) inp = if inp % 3 = 0 then Some(inp/3) else None
let (|MulSeven|_|) inp = if inp % 7 = 0 then Some(inp/7) else None
```

Finally, active patterns can also be *parameterized*. You can recognize a parameterized active
pattern by the fact that it takes several arguments. For example:

```
let (|MulN|_|) n inp = if inp % n = 0 then Some(inp/n) else None
```

The F# quotation API Microsoft.FSharp.Quotations uses both parameterized and partial patterns
extensively.

Hiding Abstract Syntax Implementations with Active Patterns

Earlier in this chapter, you saw the following type that defines an optimized representation of
propositional logic terms using a unique stamp for each syntactically unique term:

```
type Prop = Prop of int
and internal PropRepr =
    | AndRepr of Prop * Prop
    | OrRepr  of Prop * Prop
    | NotRepr of Prop
    | VarRepr of string
    | TrueRepr
```

However, what happens if you want to pattern-match against values of type Prop? Even if you exposed the representation, all you would get is an integer, which you would have to look up in an internal table. You can define an active pattern for restoring matching on that data structure, as shown in Listing 9-5.

Listing 9-5. Extending Listing 9-3 with an Active Pattern for the Optimized Representation

```
module PropOps =
    ...
    let (|And|Or|Not|Var|True|) prop =
        match table.FromUnique prop with
        | AndRepr (x, y) -> And (x, y)
        | OrRepr (x, y) -> Or (x, y)
        | NotRepr x -> Not x
        | VarRepr v -> Var v
        | TrueRepr -> True
```

This code defines an active pattern in the auxiliary module PropOps that lets you pattern-match against Prop values, despite the fact that they're using optimized unique-integer references under the hood. For example, you can define a pretty-printer for Prop terms as follows, even though they're using optimized representations:

```
open PropOps

let rec showProp prec prop =
    let parenIfPrec lim s = if prec < lim then "(" + s + ")" else s
    match prop with
    | Or (p1, p2)  -> parenIfPrec 4 (showProp 4 p1 + " || " + showProp 4 p2)
    | And (p1, p2) -> parenIfPrec 3 (showProp 3 p1 + " && " + showProp 3 p2)
    | Not p        -> parenIfPrec 2 ("not " + showProp 1 p)
    | Var v        -> v
    | True         -> "T"
```

Likewise, you can define functions to place the representation in various normal forms. For example, the following function computes *negation normal form* (NNF), where all instances of NOT nodes have been pushed to the leaves of the representation:

```
let rec nnf sign prop =
    match prop with
    | And (p1, p2) -> if sign then And (nnf sign p1, nnf sign p2)
                      else Or (nnf sign p1, nnf sign p2)
    | Or (p1, p2)  -> if sign then Or (nnf sign p1, nnf sign p2)
                      else And (nnf sign p1, nnf sign p2)
    | Not p        -> nnf (not sign) p
    | Var _ | True -> if sign then prop else Not prop

let NNF prop = nnf true prop
```

The following demonstrates that two terms have equivalent NNF normal forms:

```
> let t1 = Not(And(Not(Var("x")),Not(Var("y"))));;
val t1 : Prop

> fsi.AddPrinter(showProp);;
> t1;;
val it : Prop = not (not x && not y)

> let t2 = Or(Not(Not(Var("x"))),Var("y"));;
val t2 : Prop

> t2;;
val it : Prop = not (not x) || y

> (t1 = t2);;
val it : bool = false

> NNF t1;;
val it : Prop = x || y

> NNF t2;;
val it : Prop = x || y

> NNF t1 = NNF t2;;
val it : bool = true
```

Embedded Computational Languages with Workflows

Chapter 3 introduced a useful notation for generating sequences of data, called *sequence expressions*. For example:

```
> seq { for i in 0 .. 3 -> (i,i*i) };;
val it : seq<int * int> = seq [ (0,0); (1,1); (2,4); (3,9) ]
```

Sequence expressions are used extensively throughout this book. For example, Chapter 15 uses sequence expressions for queries that are executed on a database. It turns out that sequence expressions are just one instance of a more general construct called *computation expressions*. These are also called *workflows*, although they bear only a passing similarity to the workflows used to model business processes. The general form of a computation expression is builder { comp-expr }. Table 9-2 shows the primary constructs that can be used within the braces of a computation expression and how these constructs are de-sugared by the F# compiler given a computation expression builder builder.

The three most important applications of computation expressions in F# programming are as follows:

- General-purpose programming with sequences, lists, and arrays

- Parallel, asynchronous, and concurrent programming using asynchronous workflows, discussed in detail in Chapter 13

- Database queries, by quoting a workflow and translating it to SQL via the .NET LINQ libraries, a technique demonstrated in Chapter 15

This section covers briefly how computation expressions work through some simple examples.

Table 9-2. Main Constructs in Computation Expressions and Their De-sugaring

Construct	De-sugared Form
let! pat = expr in cexpr	b.Bind (expr, (fun pat -> «cexpr»))
let pat = expr in cexpr	b.Let (expr, (fun pat -> «cexpr»))
use pat = expr in cexpr	b.Using (expr, (fun pat -> «cexpr»))
use! pat = expr in cexpr	b.Bind (*expr*, (fun x -> b.Using (x, fun *pat* -> «*cexpr*»)))
do! expr in cexpr	b.Bind (expr, (fun () -> «cexpr»))
do expr in cexpr	b.Let (expr, (fun () -> «cexpr»))
for pat in expr do cexpr	b.For (expr, (fun pat -> «cexpr»))
while expr do cexpr	b.While ((fun () -> expr), b.Delay (fun () -> «cexpr»))
if expr then cexpr1 else cexpr2	if expr then «cexpr1» else «cexpr2»
if expr then cexpr	if expr then «cexpr» else b.Zero()
cexpr1cexpr2	v.Combine («cexpr1», b.Delay(fun () -> «cexpr2»))
yield expr	b.Yield expr
yield! expr	b.YieldFrom expr
return expr	b.Return expr
return! expr	b.ReturnFrom expr

■ **Note** If you've never seen F# workflows or Haskell monads before, then you may find that workflows take a bit of getting used to. They give you a way to write computations that may behave and execute quite differently than normal programs.

F# Workflows and Haskell Monads

Computation expressions are the F# equivalent of monadic syntax in the programming language Haskell. Monads are a powerful and expressive design pattern and are characterized by a generic type M<'T> combined with at least two operations:

```
bind : M<'T> -> ('T -> M<'U>) -> M<'U>
return : 'T -> M<'T>
```

These correspond to the primitives let! and return in the F# computation expression syntax. Several other elements of the computation expression syntax can be implemented in terms of these primitives; but the F# de-sugaring process leaves this up to the implementer of the workflow, because sometimes derived operations can have more efficient implementations. Well-behaved monads should satisfy three important rules called the *monad laws*.

F# uses the terms *computation expression* and *workflow* for four reasons:

- When the designers of F# talked with the designers of Haskell about this, they agreed that the word *monad* is obscure and sounds a little daunting and that using other names might be wise.

- There are some technical differences: for example, some F# workflows can be combined with imperative programming, utilizing the fact that workflows can have side effects that aren't tracked by the F# type system. In Haskell, all side-effecting operations must be lifted into the corresponding monad. The Haskell approach has some important advantages: you can know for sure what side effects a function can have by looking at its type. However, it also makes it more difficult to use external libraries from within a computation expression.

- F# workflows can be reified using F# quotations, providing a way to execute the workflow by alternative means—for example, by translation to SQL. This gives them a different role in practice, because they can be used to model both concrete languages and computational languages.

- F# workflows can also be used to embed computations that generate multiple results (called *monoids*) such as sequence expressions (also known as *comprehension syntax*). These generally use yield and yield! instead of return and return! and often have no let!.

An Example: Success/Failure Workflows

Perhaps the simplest kind of workflow is one where failure of a computation is made explicit: for example, where each step of the workflow may either *succeed*, by returning a result Some(v), or *fail*, by returning the value None. You can model such a workflow using functions of type unit -> 'T option—that is, functions that may compute a result or may not. In this section, you can assume that these functions are pure and terminating: they have no side effects, raise no exceptions, and always terminate.

Whenever you define a new kind of workflow, it's useful to give a name to the type of values/objects generated by the workflow. In this case, let's call them Attempt objects:

```
type Attempt<'T> = (unit -> 'T option)
```

Of course, you can use regular functional programming to start to build Attempt<'T> objects:

```
let succeed x = (fun () -> Some(x)) : Attempt<'T>
let fail      = (fun () -> None) : Attempt<'T>
let runAttempt (a:Attempt<'T>) = a()
```

These conform to the following types:

```
val succeed : 'T -> Attempt<'T>
val fail : Attempt<'T>
val runAttempt : Attempt<'T> -> 'T option
```

However, using only normal F# expressions to build Attempt values can be a little tedious and lead to a proliferation of many different functions that stitch together Attempt values in straightforward ways. Luckily, as you've seen with sequence expressions, F# comes with predefined syntax for building objects such as Attempt values. You can use this syntax with a new type by defining a *builder* object that helps stitch together the fragments that make up the computation expression. Here's an example of the signature of an object you have to define in order to use workflow syntax with a new type (note that this is a type signature for an object, not actual code—we show how to define the AttemptBuilder type and its members later in this section):

```
type AttemptBuilder =
    member Bind : Attempt<'T> * ('T -> Attempt<'U>) -> Attempt<'U>
    member Delay : (unit -> Attempt<'T>) -> Attempt<'T>
    member Let : 'T * ('T -> Attempt<'T>) -> Attempt<'T>
    member Return : 'T -> Attempt<'T>
```

Typically, there is one global instance of each such builder object. For example:

```
let attempt = new AttemptBuilder()
```

```
val attempt : AttemptBuilder
```

First, let's see how you can use the F# syntax for workflows to build Attempt objects. You can build Attempt values that always succeed:

```
> let alwaysOne = attempt { return 1 };;
val alwaysOne: Attempt<int>

> let alwaysPair = attempt { return (1,"two") };;
val alwaysPair: Attempt<int * string>

> runAttempt alwaysOne;;
val it : int option = Some 1

> runAttempt alwaysPair;;
val it : (int * string) option = Some(1,"two")
```

Note that Attempt values such as alwaysOne are just functions; to run an Attempt value, you just apply it. These correspond to uses of the succeed function, as you see shortly.

You can also build more interesting Attempt values that check a condition and return different Attempt values on each branch, as shown in the next example:

```
> let failIfBig n = attempt { if n > 1000 then return! fail else return n };;
val failIfBig: int -> Attempt<int>

> runAttempt (failIfBig 999);;
val it : int option = Some 999

> runAttempt (failIfBig 1001);;
val it : int option = None
```

Here, one branch uses return! to return the result of running another Attempt value, and the other uses return to give a single result. These correspond to yield! and yield in sequence expressions.

Next, you can build Attempt values that sequence together two Attempt values by running one, getting its result, binding it to a variable, and running the second. You do this by using the syntax form let! pat = expr, which is unique to computation expressions:

```
> let failIfEitherBig (inp1,inp2) =
        attempt { let! n1 = failIfBig inp1
                  let! n2 = failIfBig inp2
                  return (n1,n2) };;
val failIfEitherBig: int * int -> Attempt<int * int>

> runAttempt (failIfEitherBig (999,998));;
val it : (int * int) option = Some(999,998)

> runAttempt (failIfEitherBig (1003,998));;
val it : (int * int) option = None

> runAttempt (failIfEitherBig (999,1001));;
val it : (int * int) option = None
```

Let's look at this more closely. First, what does the first let! do? It runs the Attempt value failIfBig inp1; and if this returns None, the whole computation returns None. If the computation on the right delivers a value (that is, returns Some), then it binds the result to the variable n1 and continues. It's important to note the following for the expression let! n1 = failIfBig inp1:

- The expression on the right (failIfBig inp1) has type Attempt<int>.

- The variable on the left (n1) is of type int.

This is somewhat similar to a sequence of normal let binding. However, let! also controls whether the rest of the computation is executed; in the case of the Attempt type, it executes the rest of the computation only when it receives a Some value. Otherwise, it returns None, and the rest of the code is never executed.

You can use normal let bindings in computation expressions. For example:

```
let sumIfBothSmall (inp1,inp2) =
     attempt { let! n1 = failIfBig inp1
               let! n2 = failIfBig inp2
               let sum = n1 + n2
               return sum }
```

In this case, the let binding executes exactly as you would expect; it takes the expression n1+n2 and binds its result to the value sum. To summarize, you've seen that computation expressions let you do the following:

- Use an expression-like syntax to build Attempt computations

- Sequence these computations together using the let! construct

- Return results from these computations using return and return!

- Compute intermediate results using let

Workflows let you do a good deal more than this, as you see in the sections that follow.

Defining a Workflow Builder

Listing 9-6 shows the implementation of the workflow builder for Attempt workflows; this is the simplest definition for AttemptBuilder.

Listing 9-6. Defining a Workflow Builder

```
let succeed x = (fun () -> Some(x))
let fail       = (fun () -> None)
let runAttempt (a:Attempt<'T>) = a()
let bind p rest = match runAttempt p with None -> fail | Some r -> (rest r)
let delay f = (fun () -> runAttempt (f ()))

type AttemptBuilder() =
    /// Wraps an ordinary value into an Attempt value.
    /// Used to de-sugar uses of 'return' inside computation expressions.
    member b.Return(x) = succeed x

    /// Composes two attempt values. If the first returns Some(x) then the result
    /// is the result of running rest(x).
    /// Used to de-sugar uses of 'let!' inside computation expressions.
    member b.Bind(p,rest) = bind p rest


    /// Delays the construction of an attempt until just before it is executed
    member b.Delay(f) = delay f

    /// Used to de-sugar uses of 'let' inside computation expressions.
    member b.Let(p,rest) : Attempt<'T> = rest p

let attempt = new AttemptBuilder()
```

The inferred types here are as follows:

```
type AttemptBuilder =
    new : unit -> AttemptBuilder
    member Bind    : Attempt<'T> * ('T -> Attempt<'U>) -> Attempt<'U>
    member Delay   : (unit -> Attempt<'T>) -> Attempt<'T>
    member Let     : 'T * ('T -> Attempt<'U>) -> Attempt<'U>
    member Return  : 'T -> Attempt<'T>

val attempt : AttemptBuilder
```

F# implements workflows by de-sugaring computation expressions using a builder. For example, given the previous AttemptBuilder, the following workflow

```
attempt { let! n1 = failIfBig inp1
          let! n2 = failIfBig inp2
          let sum = n1 + n2
          return sum };;
```

de-sugars to this:

```
attempt.Bind( failIfBig inp1,(fun n1 ->
   attempt.Bind(failIfBig inp2,(fun n2 ->
      attempt.Return sum)))))
```

One purpose of the F# workflow syntax is to make sure you don't have to write this sort of thing by hand.

The de-sugaring of the workflow syntax is implemented by the F# compiler. Table 9-3 shows some of the typical signatures that a workflow builder needs to implement.

Table 9-3. Some Typical Workflow Builder Members as Required by the F# Compiler

Member	Description
member Bind : M<'T> * ('T -> M<'U>) -> M<'U>	Used to de-sugar let! and do! within computation expressions.
member Return : 'T -> M<'T>	Used to de-sugar return within computation expressions.
member ReturnFrom : M<'T> -> M<'T>	Used to de-sugar return! within computation expressions.
member Delay : (unit -> M<'T>) -> M<'T>	Used to ensure that side effects within a computation expression are performed when expected.
member For : seq<'T> * ('T -> M<'U>) -> M<'U>	Used to de-sugar for ... do ... within computation expressions. M<'U> can optionally be M<unit>.

Member	Description
`member While : (unit -> bool) * M<'T> -> M<'T>`	Used to de-sugar while ... do ... within computation expressions. M<'T> may optionally be M<unit>.
`member Using : 'T * ('T -> M<'T>) -> M<'T> when 'T :> IDisposable`	Used to de-sugar use bindings within computation expressions.
`member Combine : M<'T> * M<'T> -> M<'T>`	Used to de-sugar sequencing within computation expressions. The first M<'T> may optionally be M<unit>.
`member Zero : unit -> M<'T>`	Used to de-sugar empty else branches of if/then constructs within computation expressions.

Most of the elements of a workflow builder are usually implemented in terms of simpler primitives. For example, let's assume you're defining a workflow builder for some type M<'T> and you already have implementations of functions bindM and returnM with the following types:

```
val bindM : M<'T> -> ('T -> M<'U>) -> M<'U>
val returnM : 'T -> M<'T>
```

Then you can implement Delay using the following functions:

```
let delayM f = bindM (returnM ()) f
```

You can now define an overall builder in terms of all four functions:

```
type MBuilder() =
    member b.Return(x)   = returnM x
    member b.Bind(v,f)   = bindM v f
    member b.Delay(f)    = delayM f
```

However, Let and Delay may also have more efficient direct implementations, which is why F# doesn't insert the previous implementations automatically.

Workflows and Untamed Side Effects

It's possible, and in some cases even common, to define workflows that cause side effects. For example, you can use printfn in the middle of an Attempt workflow:

```
let sumIfBothSmall (inp1,inp2) =
    attempt { let! n1 = failIfBig inp1
              printfn "Hey, n1 was small!"
              let! n2 = failIfBig inp2
              printfn "n2 was also small!"
              let sum = n1 + n2
              return sum }
```

Here's what happens when you call this function:

```
> runAttempt(sumIfBothSmall (999,999));;
Hey, n1 was small!
n2 was also small!
val it : int option = Some 1998

> runAttempt(sumIfBothSmall (999,1003));;
Hey, n1 was small!
val it : int option = None
```

Side effects in workflows must be used with care, particularly because workflows are typically used to construct delayed or on-demand computations. In the previous example, printing is a fairly benign side effect. More significant side effects such as mutable state can also be sensibly combined with some kinds of workflows, but be sure you understand how the side effect will interact with the particular kind of workflow you're using. For example, this example allocates a piece of mutable state that is local to the Attempt workflow, and this is used to accumulate the sum:

```
let sumIfBothSmall (inp1,inp2) =
    attempt { let sum = ref 0
              let! n1 = failIfBig inp1
              sum := sum.Value + n1
              let! n2 = failIfBig inp2
              sum := sum.Value + n2
              return sum.Value }
```

We leave it as an exercise for you to examine the de-sugaring of this workflow to see that the mutable reference is indeed local, in the sense that it doesn't escape the overall computation, and that different executions of the same workflow use different reference cells.

As mentioned, workflows are nearly always delayed computations. As you saw in Chapter 4, delayed computations and side effects can interact. For this reason, the de-sugaring of workflow syntax inserts a Delay operation around the entire workflow. The following

```
let printThenSeven =
        attempt { printf "starting..."
                  return 3 + 4 }
```

de-sugars to

```
        attempt.Delay(fun () ->
            printf "starting..."
            attempt.Return(3+4))
```

This means that "starting ..." is printed each time the printThenSeven attempt object is executed.

Example: Probabilistic Workflows

Workflows provide a fascinating way to embed a range of nontrivial, nonstandard computations into F#. To give you a feel for this, this section defines a *probabilistic* workflow. That is, instead of writing expressions to compute, say, integers, you instead write expressions that compute *distributions* of integers. This case study is based on a paper by Ramsey and Pfeffer from 2002.

For the purposes of this section, you're interested in distributions over discrete domains characterized by three things:

- You want to be able to sample from a distribution (for example, sample an integer or a coin flip).

- You want to compute the support of a distribution: that is, a set of values where all elements outside the set have zero chance of being sampled.

- You want to compute the expectation of a function over the distribution. For example, you can compute the probability of selecting element A by evaluating the expectation of the function (fun x -> if x = A then 1.0 else 0.0).

You can model this notion of a distribution with abstract objects. Listing 9-7 shows the definition of a type of distribution values and an implementation of the basic primitives always and coinFlip, which help build distributions.

Listing 9-7. Implementing Probabilistic Modeling Using Computation Expressions

```
type Distribution<'T when 'T : comparison> =
    abstract Sample : 'T
    abstract Support : Set<'T>
    abstract Expectation: ('T -> float) -> float

let always x =
    { new Distribution<'T> with
        member d.Sample = x
        member d.Support = Set.singleton x
        member d.Expectation(H) = H(x) }

let rnd = System.Random()

let coinFlip (p:float) (d1:Distribution<'T>) (d2:Distribution<'T>) =
    if p < 0.0 || p > 1.0 then failwith "invalid probability in coinFlip"
    { new Distribution<'T> with
        member d.Sample =
            if rnd.NextDouble() < p then d1.Sample else d2.Sample
        member d.Support = Set.union d1.Support d2.Support
        member d.Expectation(H) =
            p * d1.Expectation(H) + (1.0-p) * d2.Expectation(H) }
```

The types of these primitives are as follows:

```
type Distribution<'T> =
    abstract Expectation: ('T -> float) -> float
    abstract Sample : 'T
    abstract Support : Set<'T>

val always: 'T -> Distribution<'T>
val coinFlip : float -> Distribution<'T> -> Distribution<'T> -> Distribution<'T>
```

The simplest distribution is always x; this is a distribution that always samples to the same value. Its expectation and support are easy to calculate. The expectation of a function H is just H applied to the value, and the support is a set containing the single value x. The next distribution defined is coinFlip, which is a distribution that models the ability to choose between two outcomes.

Listing 9-8 shows how you can define a workflow builder for distribution objects.

Listing 9-8. Defining a Builder for Probabilistic Modeling Using Computation Expressions

```
let bind (dist:Distribution<'T>) (k: 'T -> Distribution<'U>) =
    { new Distribution<'U> with
        member d.Sample =
            (k dist.Sample).Sample
        member d.Support =
            Set.unionMany (dist.Support |> Set.map (fun d -> (k d).Support))
        member d.Expectation H =
            dist.Expectation(fun x -> (k x).Expectation H) }

type DistributionBuilder() =
    member x.Delay f = bind (always ()) f
    member x.Bind (d, f) = bind d f
    member x.Return v = always v
    member x.ReturnFrom vs = vs

let dist = new DistributionBuilder()
```

The types of these primitives are as follows:

```
val bind: Distribution<'T> -> ('T -> Distribution<'U>) -> Distribution<'U>
val dist: DistributionBuilder
```

Listing 9-8 shows the all-important bind primitive; it combines two distributions, using the sample from the first to guide the sample from the second. The support and expectation are calculated by taking the support from the first and splaying it over the support of the second. The expectation is computed by using the first distribution to compute the expectation of a function derived from the second. These are standard results in probability theory and are the basic machinery you need to get going with some interesting modeling.

Before you begin using workflow syntax, you define two derived functions to compute distributions. Listing 9-9 shows the additional derived operations for distribution objects that you use later in this example.

Listing 9-9. Defining the Derived Operations for Probabilistic Modeling Using Computation Expressions

```
let weightedCases (inp: ('T * float) list) =
    let rec coinFlips w l =
        match l with
        | []          -> failwith "no coinFlips"
        | [(d,_)]     -> always d
        | (d,p)::rest -> coinFlip (p/(1.0-w)) (always d) (coinFlips (w+p) rest)
    coinFlips 0.0 inp

let countedCases inp =
    let total = Seq.sumBy (fun (_,v) -> v) inp
    weightedCases (inp |> List.map (fun (x,v) -> (x, float v / float total)))
```

The two functions weightedCases and countedCases build distributions from the weighted selection of a finite number of cases. The types are as follows:

```
val weightedCases : ('T * float) list -> Distribution<'T>
val countedCases : ('T * int) list -> Distribution<'T>
```

For example, here is the distribution of outcomes on a fair European roulette wheel:

```
type Outcome = Even | Odd | Zero
let roulette = countedCases [ Even,18; Odd,18; Zero,1]
```

You can now use sampling to draw from this distribution:

```
> roulette.Sample;;
val it:  Outcome = Even

> roulette.Sample;;
val it:  Outcome = Odd
```

And you can compute the expected payout of a $5 bet on Even, where you would get a $10 return:

```
> roulette.Expectation (function Even -> 10.0 | Odd -> 0.0 | Zero -> 0.0);;
val it:  float = 4.864864865
```

Now, let's model another scenario. Let's say you have a traffic light with the following probability distribution for showing red/yellow/green:

```
type Light =
    | Red
    | Green
    | Yellow
```

```
let trafficLightD = weightedCases [ Red,0.50; Yellow,0.10; Green, 0.40 ]
```

Drivers are defined by their behavior with respect to a traffic light. For example, a cautious driver is highly likely to brake on a yellow light and always stops on a red:

```
type Action = Stop | Drive
```

```
let cautiousDriver light =
    dist { match light with
            | Red -> return Stop
            | Yellow -> return! weightedCases [ Stop, 0.9; Drive, 0.1 ]
            | Green -> return Drive }
```

An aggressive driver is unlikely to brake on yellow and may even go through a red light:

```
let aggressiveDriver light =
    dist { match light with
           | Red    -> return! weightedCases [ Stop, 0.9; Drive, 0.1 ]
           | Yellow -> return! weightedCases [ Stop, 0.1; Drive, 0.9 ]
           | Green  -> return Drive }
```

The following gives the value of the light showing in the other direction:

```
let otherLight light =
    match light with
    | Red -> Green
    | Yellow -> Red
    | Green -> Red
```

You can now model the probability of a crash between two drivers given a traffic light. Assume there is a 10 percent chance that two drivers going through the intersection will avoid a crash:

```
type CrashResult = Crash | NoCrash

let crash (driverOneD, driverTwoD, lightD) =
    dist { // Sample from the traffic light
           let! light = lightD

           // Sample the first driver's behavior given the traffic light
           let! driverOne = driverOneD light

           // Sample the second driver's behavior given the traffic light
           let! driverTwo = driverTwoD (otherLight light)

           // Work out the probability of a crash
           match driverOne, driverTwo with
           | Drive,Drive -> return! weightedCases [ Crash, 0.9; NoCrash, 0.1 ]
           | _ -> return NoCrash }
```

You can now instantiate the model to a cautious/aggressive driver pair, sample the overall model, and compute the overall expectation of a crash as approximately 3.7 percent:

```
> let model = crash (cautiousDriver, aggressiveDriver, trafficLightD);;
val model : Distribution<CrashResult>

> model.Sample;;
val it : CrashResult = NoCrash
...
> model.Sample;;
val it : CrashResult = Crash

> model.Expectation (function Crash -> 1.0 | NoCrash -> 0.0);;
val it : float = 0.0369
```

■ **Note** This section showed how to define a simplistic embedded *computational probabilistic modeling language*. There are many more efficient and sophisticated techniques to apply to the description, evaluation, and analysis of probabilistic models than those shown here, and you can make the implementation of the primitives shown here more efficient by being more careful about the underlying computational representations.

Combining Workflows and Resources

In some situations, workflows can sensibly make use of transient resources such as files. The tricky thing is that you still want to be careful about closing and disposing of resources when the workflow is complete or when it's no longer being used. For this reason, the workflow type must be carefully designed to correctly dispose of resources halfway through a computation if necessary. Sequence expressions are a great example where this is useful. For example, the following sequence expression opens a file and reads lines on demand:

```
let linesOfFile(fileName) =
    seq { use textReader = System.IO.File.OpenText(fileName)
          while not textReader.EndOfStream do
              yield textReader.ReadLine() }
```

Chapter 8 discussed the construct use pat = expr. As shown in Table 9-2, you can also use this construct within workflows. In this case, the use pat = expr construct de-sugars into a call to seq.Using. In the case of sequence expressions, this function is carefully implemented to ensure that textReader is kept open for the duration of the process of reading from the file. Furthermore, the Dispose function on each generated IEnumerator object for a sequence calls the textReader.Dispose() method. This ensures that the file is closed even if you enumerate only half of the lines in the file. Workflows thus allow you to scope the lifetime of a resource over a delayed computation.

Recursive Workflow Expressions

Like functions, workflow expressions can be defined recursively. Many of the best examples are generative sequences. For example:

```
let rnd = System.Random()

let rec randomWalk k =
    seq { yield k
          yield! randomWalk (k + rnd.NextDouble() - 0.5) }
```

```
> randomWalk 10.0;;
val it: seq<float> = seq [10.0; 10.23817784; 9.956430122; 10.18110362; ...]

> randomWalk 10.0;;
val it : seq<float> = seq [10.0; 10.19761089; 10.26774703; 9.888072922; ...]
```

Using F# Reflection

The final topics in this chapter are *F# quotations*, which provide a way to get at a representation of F# expressions as abstract syntax trees, and *reflection*, which lets you get at representations of assemblies, type definitions, and member signatures. Let's look at reflection first.

Reflecting on Types

One of the simplest uses of reflection is to access the representation of types and generic type variables using the typeof operator. For example, typeof<int> and typeof<'T> are both expressions that generate values of type System.Type. Given a System.Type value, you can use the .NET APIs to access the System.Reflection.Assembly value that represents the .NET assembly that contains the definition of the type (.NET assemblies are described in Chapter 7). You can also access other types in the System.Reflection namespace, such as MethodInfo, PropertyInfo, MemberInfo, and ConstructorInfo. The following example examines the names associated with some common types:

```
> let intType = typeof<int>;;
val intType : System.Type

> intType.FullName;;
val it : string = "System.Int32"

> intType.AssemblyQualifiedName;;
val it : string = "System.Int32, mscorlib, Version=2.0.0.0, Culture=neutral,
PublicKeyToken=b77a5c561934e089"

> let intListType = typeof<int list>;;
val intListType : System.Type

> intListType.FullName;;
val it : string = "Microsoft.FSharp.Collections.List`1[[System.Int32, mscorlib,
Version=2.0.0.0, Culture=neutral, PublicKeyToken=b77a5c561934e089]]"
```

Schema Compilation by Reflecting on Types

The F# library includes the namespace Microsoft.FSharp.Reflection, which contains types and functions that extend the functionality of the System.Reflection namespace of .NET. Chapter 10 describes these types and functions.

You can use the combination of .NET and F# reflection to provide generic implementations of language-related transformations. This section gives one example of this powerful technique. Listing 9-10 shows the definition of a *generic schema reader compiler*, where a data schema is described using F# types and the schema compiler helps convert untyped data from text files into this data schema.

Listing 9-10. Using Types and Attributes to Guide Dynamic Schema Compilation

```
open System
open System.IO
open System.Globalization
open Microsoft.FSharp.Reflection

/// An attribute to be added to fields of a schema record type to indicate the
/// column used in the data format for the schema.
type ColumnAttribute(col:int) =
    inherit Attribute()
    member x.Column = col

/// SchemaReader builds an object that automatically transforms lines of text
/// files in comma-separated form into instances of the given type 'Schema.
/// 'Schema must be an F# record type where each field is attributed with a
/// ColumnAttribute attribute, indicating which column of the data the record
/// field is drawn from. This simple version of the reader understands
/// integer, string and DateTime values in the CSV format.
type SchemaReader<'Schema>() =

    // Grab the object for the type that describes the schema
    let schemaType = typeof<'Schema>

    // Grab the fields from that type
    let fields = FSharpType.GetRecordFields(schemaType)

    // For each field find the ColumnAttribute and compute a function
    // to build a value for the field
    let schema =
        fields |> Array.mapi (fun fldIdx fld ->
            let fieldInfo = schemaType.GetProperty(fld.Name)
            let fieldConverter =
                match fld.PropertyType with
                | ty when ty = typeof<string>   -> (fun (s:string) -> box s)
                | ty when ty = typeof<int>      -> (System.Int32.Parse >> box)
                | ty when ty = typeof<DateTime> ->
                    (fun s -> box (DateTime.Parse(s,CultureInfo.InvariantCulture)))
                | ty -> failwithf "Unknown primitive type %A" ty

            let attrib =
                match fieldInfo.GetCustomAttributes(typeof<ColumnAttribute>,
                                                    false) with
                | [| (:? ColumnAttribute as attrib) |] ->   attrib
                | _ -> failwithf "No column attribute found on field %s" fld.Name
            (fldIdx, fld.Name, attrib.Column, fieldConverter))

    // Compute the permutation defined by the ColumnAttribute indexes
    let columnToFldIdxPermutation c =
      schema |> Array.pick (fun (fldIdx,_,colIdx,_) ->
          if colIdx = c then Some fldIdx else None)

    // Drop the parts of the schema we don't need
```

```
let schema =
    schema |> Array.map (fun (_,fldName,_,fldConv) -> (fldName,fldConv))

// Compute a function to build instances of the schema type. This uses an
// F# library function.
let objectBuilder = FSharpValue.PreComputeRecordConstructor(schemaType)

// OK, now we're ready to implement a line reader
member reader.ReadLine(textReader: TextReader) =
    let line = textReader.ReadLine()
    let words = line.Split([|',','|]) |> Array.map(fun s -> s.Trim())
    if words.Length <> schema.Length then
        failwith "unexpected number of columns in line %s" line
    let words = words |> Array.permute columnToFldIdxPermutation

    let convertColumn colText (fieldName, fieldConverter) =
        try fieldConverter colText
        with e ->
            failwithf "error converting '%s' to field '%s'" colText fieldName

    let obj = objectBuilder (Array.map2 convertColumn words schema)

    // OK, now we know we've dynamically built an object of the right type
    unbox<'Schema>(obj)

/// This reads an entire file
member reader.ReadFile(file) =
    seq { use textReader = File.OpenText(file)
          while not textReader.EndOfStream do
              yield reader.ReadLine(textReader) }
```

The type of the SchemaReader is simple:

```
type SchemaReader<'Schema> =
    new : unit -> SchemaReader<'Schema>
    member ReadFile : string -> seq<'Schema>
    member ReadLine : System.IO.TextReader -> 'Schema
```

First you see how the SchemaReader is used in practice. Let's say you have a text file containing lines such as this:

```
Steve, 12 March 2010, Cheddar
Sally, 18 Feb 2010, Brie
...
```

It's reasonable to want to convert this data to a typed data representation. You can do this by defining an appropriate record type along with enough information to indicate how the data in the file maps into this type. This information is expressed using *custom attributes*, which are a way to add extra meta-information to assembly, type, member, property, and parameter definitions. Each custom attribute is specified as an instance of a typed object, here ColumnAttribute, defined in Listing 9-10. The suffix Attribute can be dropped when using the custom attribute:

```
type CheeseClub =
    { [<Column(0)>] Name             : string
      [<Column(2)>] FavouriteCheese : string
      [<Column(1)>] LastAttendance  : System.DateTime }
```

You can now instantiate the SchemaReader type and use it to read the data from the file into this typed format:

```
> let reader = new SchemaReader<CheeseClub>();;
val reader : SchemaReader<CheeseClub>

> fsi.AddPrinter(fun (c:System.DateTime) -> c.ToString());;
val it : unit = ()

> System.IO.File.WriteAllLines("data.txt", [| "Steve, 12 March 2010, Cheddar";
                                              "Sally, 18 Feb 2010, Brie"; |]);;
val it : unit = ()

> reader.ReadFile("data.txt");;
val it : seq<CheeseClub>
 = seq
    [{Name = "Steve";
      FavouriteCheese = "Cheddar";
      LastAttendance = 12/03/2010 00:00:00;};
     {Name = "Sally";
      FavouriteCheese = "Brie";
      LastAttendance = 18/02/2010 00:00:00;}]
```

There is something somewhat magical about this; you've built a layer that automatically does the impedance matching between the untyped world of a text-file format into the typed world of F# programming. Amazingly, the SchemaReader type itself is only about 50 lines of code. The comments in Listing 9-10 show the basic steps being performed. The essential features of this technique are as follows:

1. The schema information is passed to the SchemaReader as a type variable. The SchemaReader then uses the typeof operator to extract a System.Type representation of the schema type.

2. The information needed to drive the transformation process comes from custom attributes. Extra information can also be supplied to the constructor of the SchemaReader type if necessary.

3. The let bindings of the SchemaReader type are effectively a form of precomputation (they can also be seen as a form of compilation). They precompute as much information as possible given the schema. For example, the section analyzes the fields of the schema type and computes functions for creating objects of the field types. It also computes the permutation from the text file columns to the record fields.

4. The data objects are ultimately constructed using reflection functions, in this case a function computed by Microsoft.FSharp.Reflection.Value. GetRecordConstructor or primitive values parsed using System.Int32.Parse and similar functions. This and other functions for creating F# objects dynamically

are in the `Microsoft.FSharp.Reflection` library. Other functions for creating other .NET objects dynamically are in the `System.Reflection` library.

5. The member bindings of `SchemaReader` interpret the residue of the precomputation stage, in this case using the information and computed functions to process the results of splitting the text of a line.

This technique has many potential applications and has been used for CSV file reading, building F#-centric serializers/deserializers, and building generic strongly typed database schema access.

Using the F# Dynamic Reflection Operators

F# lets you define two special operators, (?) and (?<-), to perform dynamic lookups of objects. These are conceptually very simple operators, but they add interesting new opportunities for interoperability between dynamic data and static data in F# programming.

These operators implicitly translate their second argument to a string, if it's a simple identifier. That is, a use of these operators is translated as follows:

```
expr ? nm                 →    (?) expr "nm"
expr1 ? nm <- expr2   →    (?<-) expr1 "nm" expr2
```

This means the operators can be used to simulate a dynamic lookup of a property or a method on an object. This dynamic lookup can use any dynamic/reflective technique available to you. One such technique is to use .NET reflection to look up and/or set the properties of an object:

```
open System.Reflection

let (?) (obj:obj) (nm:string) : 'T =
    obj.GetType().InvokeMember(nm, BindingFlags.GetProperty, null, obj, [| |])
    |> unbox<'T>

let (?<-) (obj:obj) (nm:string) (v:obj) : unit =
    obj.GetType().InvokeMember(nm, BindingFlags.SetProperty, null, obj, [| v |])
    |> ignore
```

Now, you can use the operators to dynamically query data as follows:

```
type Record1 = { Length : int; mutable Values : int list }

let obj1 = box [1;2;3]
let obj2 = box { Length = 4; Values = [3;4;5;7] }

let n1 : int = obj1?Length
let n2 : int = obj2?Length
let valuesOld : int list = obj2?Values
```

Here, both `obj1` and `obj2` have type `obj`, but you can do dynamic lookups of the properties `Length` and `Values` using the `?` operator. Of course, these uses aren't strongly statically typed—this is why you need the type annotations `: int` and `: int list` to indicate the return type of the operation. Given the earlier definition of the (?<-) operator, you can also set a property dynamically as follows:

```
obj2?Values <- [7;8;9]

let valuesNew : int list = obj2?Values
```

Using the (?) and (?<-) operators obviously comes with strong drawbacks: you lose considerable type safety, and performance may be affected by the use of dynamic techniques. Their use is recommended only when you're consistently interoperating with weakly typed objects, or when you continually find yourself doing string-based lookup of elements of an object.

Using F# Quotations

The other side to reflective meta-programming in F# is *quotations*. These allow you to reflect over expressions in much the same way you've reflected over types in the previous section. It's simple to get going with F# quotations; you open the appropriate modules and surround an expression with <@ ... @> symbols:

```
> open Microsoft.FSharp.Quotations;;

> let oneExpr = <@ 1 @>;;
val oneExpr : Expr<int>

> oneExpr;;
val it : Expr<int> = <@ (Int32 1) @>

> let plusExpr = <@ 1 + 1 @>;;
val plusExpr : Expr<int>

> plusExpr;;
val it : Expr<int>
  = <@ Microsoft.FSharp.Core.Operators.op_Addition (Int32 1) (Int32 1) @>
```

You can see here that the act of quoting an expression gives you back the expression as data. Those familiar with Lisp or Scheme know a sophisticated version of this in the form of Lisp quotations; and those familiar with C# 3.0 will find it familiar because C# uses similar mechanisms for its lambda expressions. F# quotations are distinctive partly because they're *typed* (like C# lambda expressions) and because the functional, expression-based nature of F# means that so much of the language can be quoted and manipulated relatively easily.

This book uses quotations in only a few places. Chapter 15 uses an F# library that converts F# quotations to SQL via the .NET LINQ library. The essence of the way this converter works is summarized by the following type:

```
val SQL : Expr<'T> -> 'T
```

This function effectively acts as an evaluator for quotations. It successfully evaluates only a limited range of quotations (a runtime error may occur if the expression can't be converted to SQL).

Another application of quotations is to convert F# code to JavaScript to let you run it in web browsers. This technique is used by WebSharper, described in Chapter 14. This may be implemented by a function with a type such as the following:

```
val CompileToJavaScript : Expr<'T> -> string
```

What Are F# Quotations For?

The primary rationale for F# quotations is to allow fragments of F# syntax to be executed by alternative means: for example, as an SQL query via LINQ or by running on another device such as a GPU or as JavaScript in a client-side web browser. F# aims to leverage heavy-hitting external components that map subsets of functional programs to other execution machinery. Another example use involves executing a subset of F# array code by dynamic generation of Fortran code and invoking a high-performance vectorizing Fortran compiler. The generated DLL is loaded and invoked dynamically.

This effectively means you can convert from a computational representation of a language (for example, regular F# functions and F# workflow expressions) to an abstract syntax representation of the same language. This is a powerful technique, because it lets you prototype using a computational model of the language (for example, sampling from a distribution or running queries against local data) and then switch to a more concrete abstract syntax representation of the same programs in order to analyze, execute, print, or compile those programs in other ways.

Example: Using F# Quotations for Error Estimation

Listing 9-11 shows a prototypical use of quotations, in this case to perform error estimation on F# arithmetic expressions.

Listing 9-11. Error Analysis on F# Expressions Implemented with F# Quotations

```
open Microsoft.FSharp.Quotations
open Microsoft.FSharp.Quotations.Patterns
open Microsoft.FSharp.Quotations.DerivedPatterns

type Error = Err of float

let rec errorEstimateAux (e:Expr) (env : Map<Var,_>) =
    match e with
    | SpecificCall <@@ (+) @@> (tyargs,_,[xt;yt]) ->
        let x,Err(xerr) = errorEstimateAux xt env
        let y,Err(yerr) = errorEstimateAux yt env
        (x+y,Err(xerr+yerr))

    | SpecificCall <@@ (-) @@> (tyargs,_,[xt;yt]) ->
        let x,Err(xerr) = errorEstimateAux xt env
        let y,Err(yerr) = errorEstimateAux yt env
        (x-y,Err(xerr+yerr))

    | SpecificCall <@@ ( * ) @@> (tyargs,_,[xt;yt]) ->
        let x,Err(xerr) = errorEstimateAux xt env
        let y,Err(yerr) = errorEstimateAux yt env
        (x*y,Err(xerr*abs(y)+yerr*abs(x)+xerr*yerr))
```

```
    | SpecificCall <@@ abs @@> (tyargs,_,[xt]) ->
        let x,Err(xerr) = errorEstimateAux xt env
        (abs(x),Err(xerr))

    | Let(var,vet, bodyt) ->
        let varv,verr = errorEstimateAux vet env
        errorEstimateAux bodyt (env.Add(var,(varv,verr)))

    | Call(None,MethodWithReflectedDefinition(Lambda(v,body)),[arg]) ->
        errorEstimateAux  (Expr.Let(v,arg,body)) env

    | Var(x) -> env.[x]

    | Double(n) -> (n,Err(0.0))

    | _ -> failwithf "unrecognized term: %A" e
let rec errorEstimateRaw (t : Expr) =
    match t with
    | Lambda(x,t) ->
        (fun xv -> errorEstimateAux t (Map.ofSeq [(x,xv)]))
    | PropertyGet(None,PropertyGetterWithReflectedDefinition(body),[]) ->
        errorEstimateRaw body
    | _ -> failwithf "unrecognized term: %A - expected a lambda" t

let errorEstimate (t : Expr<float -> float>) = errorEstimateRaw t
```

The inferred types of the functions are as follows:

```
val errorEstimateAux : Expr -> Map<ExprVarName,(float * Error)> -> float * Error
val errorEstimateRaw : Expr -> (float * Error -> float * Error)
val errorEstimate : Expr<(float -> float)> -> (float * Error -> float * Error)
```

That is, errorEstimate is a function that takes an expression for a float -> float function and returns a function value of type float * Error -> float * Error.

Let's see it in action. First, you define the function err and a pretty-printer for float * Error pairs, here using the Unicode symbol for error bounds on a value:

```
> let err x = Err x;;
val err : float -> Error

> fsi.AddPrinter (fun (x:float,Err v) -> sprintf "%g±%g" x v);;
val it : unit = ()

> errorEstimate <@ fun x -> x+2.0*x+3.0*x*x @> (1.0,err 0.1);;
val it : float * Error = 6±0.61

> errorEstimate <@ fun x -> let y = x + x in y*y + 2.0 @> (1.0,err 0.1);;
val it : float * Error = 6±0.84
```

The key aspects of the implementation of errorEstimate are as follows:

- The errorEstimate function converts the input expression to a raw expression, which is an untyped abstract syntax representation of the expression designed for further processing. It then calls errorEstimateRaw. Traversals are generally much easier to perform using raw terms.

- The errorEstimateRaw function then checks that the expression given is a lambda expression, using the active pattern Lambda provided by the Microsoft.FSharp.Quotations.Patterns module.

- The errorEstimateRaw function then calls the auxiliary function errorEstimateAux. This function keeps track of a mapping from variables to value/error estimate pairs. It recursively analyzes the expression looking for +, -, * and abs operations. These are all overloaded operators and hence are called *generic functions* in F# terminology, so the function uses the active pattern SpecificCall to detect applications of these operators. At each point, it performs the appropriate error estimation.

- For variables, the environment map env is consulted. For constants, the error is zero.

- Two additional cases are covered in errorEstimateAux and errorEstimateRaw. The Let pattern allows you to include expressions of the form let x = e1 in e2 in the subset accepted by the quotation analyzer. The MethodWithReflectedDefinition case allows you to perform analyses on some function calls, as you see next.

Resolving Top Definitions

One of the problems with meta-programming with explicit <@ ... @> quotation marks alone is that you can't analyze very large programs because the entire expression to be analyzed must be delimited by these markers. This is solved in F# by allowing you to tag top-level member and let bindings as reflected. This ensures that their definition is persisted to a table attached to their compiled DLL or EXE. These functions can also be executed as normal F# code. For example, here is a function whose definition is persisted:

```
[<ReflectedDefinition>]
let poly x = x+2.0*x+3.0/(x*x)
```

You can retrieve definitions like this using the MethodWithReflectedDefinition and PropertyGetterWithReflectedDefinition active patterns, as shown in Listing 9-11. You can now use this function in a regular <@ ... @> quotation and thus analyze it for errors:

```
> errorEstimate <@ poly @> (3.0, err 0.1);;
val it : float * Error = 9.33333±0.582149

> errorEstimate <@ poly @> (30271.3, err 0.0001);;
val it : float * Error = 90813.9±3.02723
```

Summary

This chapter covered key topics in a programming paradigm that is central to F#, called *language-oriented programming*. We covered one particular concrete language format, XML, and then looked at abstracted representations of languages using abstract syntax trees. You also saw some techniques to traverse abstract syntax trees. These language representation techniques give you powerful ways to manipulate concrete and abstract syntax fragments, which form a key part of modern programming.

You then saw two language representation techniques that are more tightly coupled to F#: the F# workflow syntax, which is useful for embedded computational languages involving sequencing, and quotations, which let you give an alternative meaning to existing F# program fragments. Along the way, the chapter touched on reflection and its use to mediate between typed and untyped representations.

That completes your look at F# as a language and the major programming paradigms it covers. The following chapters look at the libraries that come with F# and the .NET Framework and then move on to more applied topics, beginning with GUI programming using the .NET Windows Forms library.

CHAPTER 10

■ ■ ■

Using the F# and .NET Libraries

F# and the .NET Framework offer a rich set of libraries for functional and imperative programming. This chapter steps back and gives you a broader overview of the .NET and F# libraries.

Many of the types and namespaces described here are also covered elsewhere in this book. In these cases, we reference the relevant chapter.

A High-Level Overview

One way to get a quick overview of the .NET Framework and the F# library is to look at the primary DLLs and namespaces contained in them. Recall from Chapters 2 and 7 that DLLs correspond to the *physical* organization of libraries and that namespaces and types give the *logical* organization of a naming hierarchy. Let's look at the physical organization first. The types and functions covered in this chapter are drawn from the DLLs in Table 10-1.

Table 10-1. DLLs Containing the Library Constructs Referred to in This Chapter

DLL Name	Notes
mscorlib.dll	Minimal system constructs, including the types in the System namespace.
System.dll	Additional commonly used constructs in namespaces such as System and System.Text.
System.Xml.dll	See the corresponding namespace in Table 10-2.
System.Data.dll	See the corresponding namespace in Table 10-2.
System.Drawing.dll	See the corresponding namespace in Table 10-2.
System.Web.dll	See the corresponding namespace in Table 10-2.
System.Windows.Forms.dll	See the corresponding namespace in Table 10-2.
System.Core.dll	The foundation types for LINQ and some other useful types. From .NET 3.5 onward.

DLL Name	Notes
WindowsBase.dll	Core functionality for Windows Presentation Foundation.
PresentationCore.dll	Core functionality for Windows Presentation Foundation.
PresentationFramework.dll	Core functionality for Windows Presentation Foundation.
FSharp.Core.dll	Minimal constructs for F# assemblies.

To reference additional DLLs, you can embed a reference directly into your source code. For example:

```
#I @"C:\Program Files\Reference Assemblies\Microsoft\Framework\v3.5";;
#r "System.Core.dll";;
```

The first line specifies an include path, the equivalent of the -I command-line option for the F# compiler. The second line specifies a DLL reference, the equivalent of the -r command-line option. Chapter 7 described these. If you're using Visual Studio, you can adjust the project property settings for your project.

■ **Note** Hundreds of high-quality frameworks and libraries are available for .NET, and more are appearing all the time. For space reasons, this chapter covers only the .NET libraries and frameworks listed in Table 10-1. The "Some Other .NET Libraries" section of this chapter lists some libraries you may find interesting.

Namespaces from the .NET Framework

Table 10-2 shows the primary namespaces in .NET Framework DLLs from Table 10-1. In some cases, parts of these libraries are covered elsewhere in this book; the table notes these cases. For example, Chapter 4 introduced portions of the .NET I/O library from the System.IO namespace.

Table 10-2. Namespaces in the DLLs from Table 10-1, with MSDN Descriptions

Namespace	Description
System	Types and methods that define commonly used value and reference data types, events and event handlers, interfaces, attributes, and processing exceptions, supporting data-type conversions, mathematics, application environment management, and runtime supervision of managed and unmanaged applications. See Chapter 3 for many of the basic types in this namespace.
System.CodeDom	Types that can be used to represent the elements and structure of a source code document. Not covered in this book.

Namespace	Description
System.Collections	Types that define various nongeneric collections of objects, such as lists, queues, and bit arrays. Partially covered in the section "Using Further F# and .NET Data Structures" later in this chapter.
System.Collections.Generic	Types that define generic collections. See Chapter 4 and the section "Using Further F# and .NET Data Structures" later in this chapter.
System.ComponentModel	Types that are used to implement the runtime and design-time behavior of components and controls. See Chapter 11.
System.Configuration	Types that provide the programming model for handling configuration data. See Chapter 15.
System.Data	Types that represent the ADO.NET database access architecture. See Chapter 15.
System.Diagnostics	Types that allow you to interact with system processes, event logs, and performance counters. See Chapter 18.
System.Drawing	Types that allow access to GDI+ basic graphics functionality. More advanced functionality is provided in the System.Drawing.Drawing2D, System.Drawing.Imaging, and System.Drawing.Text namespaces. See Chapter 11.
System.Globalization	Types that define culture-related information, including the language, the country/region, the calendars in use, the format patterns for dates, the currency, the numbers, and the sort order for strings. Not covered in this book.
System.IO	Types that allow reading and writing files and data streams, as well as types that provide basic file and directory support. See Chapter 4 for a basic overview.
System.Media	Types for playing and accessing sounds and other media formats. Not covered in this book. .NET 3.0 and later.
System.Net	Types to programmatically access many of the protocols used on modern networks. See Chapters 2 and 14 for examples and a basic overview.
System.Reflection	Types that retrieve information about assemblies, modules, members, parameters, and other entities in managed code. See Chapter 9 for a brief overview.
System.Reflection.Emit	Types for generating .NET code dynamically at runtime.
System.Resources	Types that let you create, store, and manage various culture-specific resources used in an application. See Chapters 7 and 11 for a brief overview.

Namespace	Description
System.Security	Types to interface with the underlying structure of the CLR security system, including base classes for permissions. Not covered in this book.
System.Text	Types representing ASCII, Unicode, UTF-8, and other character encodings. Also abstract types for converting blocks of characters to and from blocks of bytes. See Chapters 3 and the section "Using Regular Expressions and Formatting" later in this chapter.
System.Threading	Types for creating and synchronizing threads and, in .NET 4.0, tasks. Also parallel operations and some functionality related to cancellation. See Chapter 13.
System.Web	Types that enable web applications. See Chapter 14.
System.Windows.Forms	Types for creating windowed applications. See Chapter 11.
System.Xml	Types that implement standards-based support for processing XML. See Chapters 9 and 15.
Microsoft.Win32	Types that wrap Win32 API common dialog boxes and components. Not covered in this book.

Namespaces from the F# Libraries

Table 10-3 shows the primary namespaces in F# library DLLs from Table 10-1. The following are opened by default in F# code:

```
Microsoft.FSharp.Core
Microsoft.FSharp.Collections
Microsoft.FSharp.Control
Microsoft.FSharp.Text
```

Table 10-3. Namespaces in the DLLs from Table 10-1

Namespace	Description
Microsoft.FSharp.Core	Provides primitive constructs related to the F# language, such as tuples. See Chapter 3.
Microsoft.FSharp.Collections	Provides functional programming collections, such as sets and maps implemented using binary trees. See Chapter 3 and the section "Using Further F# and .NET Data Structures" later in this chapter.

Namespace	Description
Microsoft.FSharp.Control	Provides functional programming control structures, including asynchronous and lazy programming. Chapter 8 covers programming with the IEvent<'T> type and the IEvent module, and Chapter 13 covers the Async<'T> type.
Microsoft.FSharp.Text	Provides types for structured and printf-style textual formatting of data. See Chapter 4 for an introduction to printf formatting.
Microsoft.FSharp.Reflection	Provides extensions to the System.Reflection functionality that deal particularly with F# record and discriminated union values. See Chapter 9 for a brief introduction, and see the section "Further Libraries for Reflective Techniques" section later in this chapter for more details.
Microsoft.FSharp.Quotations	Provides access to F# expressions as abstract syntax trees. See Chapter 9.

Using the System Types

Table 10-4 shows some of the most useful core types from the System namespace. These types are particularly useful because they take real care to define correctly.

Table 10-4. Useful Core Types from the System Namespace

Function	Description
System.DateTime	A type representing a date and time
System.DayOfWeek	An enumeration type representing a day of the week
System.Decimal	A numeric type suitable for financial calculations requiring large numbers of significant integral and fractional digits and no round-off errors
System.Guid	A type representing a 128-bit globally unique ID
System.Nullable<'T>	A type with an underlying value type 'T but that can be assigned null like a reference type
System.TimeSpan	A type representing a time interval
System.Uri	A type representing a uniform resource identifier (URI), such as an Internet URL

The following session shows some sample uses of the `DateTime` type:

```
> open System;;
> DateTime.Parse("13 July 1968");;
val it : DateTime = 13/07/1968 00:00:00 {Day = 13;
                                         DayOfWeek = Saturday;
                                         DayOfYear = 195;
                                         Hour = 0;
                                         Millisecond = 0;
                                         Minute = 0;
                                         Month = 7;
                                         Second = 0;
                                         Ticks = 620892000000000000L;
                                         TimeOfDay = 00:00:00;
                                         Year = 1968;}

> let date x = DateTime.Parse(x);;
val date : string -> DateTime

> printfn "date = %A" (date "13 July 1968");;
date = 13/07/1968 00:00:00
val it : unit = ()

> printfn "birth = %A" (date "18 March 2003, 6:21:01pm");;
birth = 18/03/2003 18:21:01
val it : unit = ()
```

Note that formatting dates depends on the user's localization settings; you can achieve more explicit formatting by using the `System.DateTime.ToString` overload that accepts explicit format information.

Here you use the `System.Uri` type to parse a URL:

```
> open System;;
> System.Uri.TryCreate("http://www.thebritishmuseum.ac.uk/", UriKind.Absolute);;

val it : bool * System.Uri
= (true,
   http://www.thebritishmuseum.ac.uk/
      { AbsolutePath = "/"; ...
        DnsSafeHost = "www.thebritishmuseum.ac.uk"; ...
        Port = 80; ...
        Scheme = "http"; })

> Uri.TryCreate("e3£%//ww.gibberish.com", UriKind.Absolute);;
val it : bool * Uri = (false, null)
```

Many .NET types are used to hold static functions, such as those for converting data from one format to another. Types such as System.Random play a similar role via objects with a small amount of state. Table 10-5 shows some of the most useful of these types.

Table 10-5. *Useful Services from the System Namespace*

Function	Description
System.BitConverter	Contains functions to convert numeric representations to and from bit representations
System.Convert	Contains functions to convert between various numeric representations
System.Math	Contains constants and static methods for trigonometric, logarithmic, and other common mathematical functions
System.Random	Provides objects to act as random-number generators
System.StringComparer	Provides objects implementing various types of comparisons on strings (case insensitive, and so on)

Using Regular Expressions and Formatting

In Chapter 3, you saw the different forms of string literals (strings with escape characters, verbatim strings, and byte arrays) and the most typical operations, such as concatenation using string builders. You may also remember that string values are *immutable* and that string operations that seem to change their input actually return a new string that represents the result. The following sections cover further ways to work with strings and text.

Matching with System.Text.RegularExpressions

One of the most popular ways of working with strings as data is through the use of *regular expressions*. You do this using the functionality from the .NET System.Text.RegularExpressions namespace. To get started, first note that the F# library includes the following definition:

```
open System.Text.RegularExpressions
let regex s = new Regex(s)
```

To this, you can add the following Perl-like operators:

```
let (=~) s (re:Regex) = re.IsMatch(s)
let (<>~) s (re:Regex) = not (s =~ re)
```

Here, the inferred types are as follows:

```
val regex : string -> Regex
val ( =~ ) : string -> Regex -> bool
val ( <>~ ) : string -> Regex -> bool
```

The infix operators allow you to test for matches:

```
> let samplestring = "This is a string";;
val samplestring : string

> if samplestring =~ regex "his" then
        printfn "A Match! ";;
A Match!
val it : unit = ()
```

Regular expressions can include *, +, and ? symbols for zero or more occurrences, one or more occurrences, and zero or one occurrences of the immediately preceding regular expression, respectively, and can include parentheses to group regular expressions. For example:

```
> "This is a string" =~ regex "(is )+";;
val it : bool = true
```

Regular expressions can also be used to split strings:

```
> (regex " ").Split("This is a string");;
val it : string [] = [|"This"; "is"; "a"; "string"|]
```

Here, you use the regular expression " " for whitespace. In reality, you probably want to use the regular expression " +" to match multiple spaces. Better still, you can match any Unicode whitespace character using \s, including end-of-line markers; however, when using escape characters, you should use verbatim strings to specify the regular expression, such as @"\s+". Chapter 3 discussed verbatim strings. Let's try this:

```
> (regex @"\s+").Split("I'm a little       teapot");;
val it : string [] = [|"I'm"; "a"; "little"; "teapot"|]

> (regex @"\s+").Split("I'm a little  \t\t\n\t\n\t teapot");;
val it : string [] = [|"I'm"; "a"; "little"; "teapot"|]
```

Here's how to match by using the method Match instead of using =~ and IsMatch. This lets you examine the positions of a match:

```
> let m = (regex @"joe").Match("maryjoewashere");;
val m : Match

> if m.Success then
    printfn "Matched at position %d" m.Index;;

Matched at position 4
val it : unit = ()
```

Replacing text is also easy:

```
> let text = "was a dark and stormy night";;
val text: string

> let t2 = (regex @"\w+").Replace(text, "WORD");;
val t2: string  = "WORD WORD WORD WORD WORD WORD"
```

Here, you use the regular expression "\w+" for a sequence of word characters.
Table 10-6 shows the broad range of specifiers you can use with .NET regular expressions.

Table 10-6. Regular Expression Escape Characters

Characters	Description
Ordinary characters	Characters other than . $ ^ { [(	) * + ? \ match themselves.
.	Matches any character except \n. If RegexOptions.SingleLine is specified, then it matches every character.
[aeiou0-9]	Matches any of the given characters or character ranges.
[^aeiou0-9]	Matches any character other than the given characters or character ranges.
\p{name}	Matches any character in the named character class specified by {name}. See the .NET documentation for full details.
\P{name}	Matches text not included in groups and block ranges specified in {name}.
\w	Matches any word character.
\W	Matches any nonword character.
\s	Matches any whitespace character.
\S	Matches any nonwhitespace character.

Characters	Description
\d	Matches any decimal digit.
\D	Matches any nondigit.
\a	Matches a bell (alarm) \u0007.
\b	Matches a backspace \u0008 if in a [ ] character class; otherwise, in a regular expression, \b denotes a word boundary (between \w and \W characters). In a replacement pattern, \b always denotes a backspace.
\t	Matches a tab \u0009.
\r	Matches a carriage return \u000D.
\v	Matches a vertical tab \u000B.
\f	Matches a form feed \u000C.
\n	Matches a new line \u000A.
\e	Matches an escape \u001B.
\digit	Matches a back reference.
\040	Matches an ASCII character as octal.
\x20	Matches an ASCII character using hexadecimal representation (exactly two digits).
\cC	Matches an ASCII control character; for example, \cC is Ctrl+C.
\u0020	Matches a Unicode character using hexadecimal representation (exactly four digits).
\	When followed by a character that isn't recognized as an escaped character, matches that character. For example, * is the same as \x2A.

You can specify case-insensitive matches by using (?i) at the start of a regular expression:

```
> samplestring =~ regex "(?i)HIS";;
val it : bool = true

> samplestring =~ regex "HIS";;
val it : bool = false
```

Here is a final example, showing the use of named groups:

```
let entry = @"
Jolly Jethro
13 Kings Parade
Cambridge, Cambs CB2 1TJ
"

let re =
 regex @"(?<=\n)\s*(?<city>[^\n]+)\s*,\s*(?<county>\w+)\s+(?<pcode>.{3}\s*.{3}).*$"
```

You can now use this regular expression to match the text and examine the named elements of the match:

```
> let r = re.Match(entry);;
val r : Match

> r.Groups.["city"].Value;;
val it : string = "Cambridge"

> r.Groups.["county"].Value;;
val it : string = "Cambs"

> r.Groups.["pcode"].Value;;
val it : string = "CB2 1TJ"
```

You can also combine regular expression matching with active patterns, described in Chapter 9. For example:

```
let (|IsMatch|_|) (re: string) (inp:string) =
    if Regex(re).IsMatch(inp)  then Some() else None

let (|MatchGroups|_|) (re: string) (inp:string) =
    let results = Regex(re).Match(inp)
    if results.Success then Some results.Groups else None
```

These active patterns can now be used as follows:

```
> match "This is a string" with
| IsMatch "(?i)HIS" -> "yes, it matched"
| IsMatch "ABC" -> "this would not match"
| _ -> "nothing matched"

val it : string = "yes, it matched "

> match "This is a super string" with
  | MatchGroups "(?<word1>T\w+).*(?<word2>s\w+)" groups ->
     (groups.["word1"].Value, groups.["word2"].Value)
  | _ -> failwith "nothing matched"

val it : string * string = ("This", "string")
```

Finally, you can use the dynamic operator, also defined in Chapter 9, to make the lookups slightly more natural:

```
> match "This is a string is super" with
  | MatchGroups "(?<word1>T\w+).*(?<word2>s\w+)" groups -> (groups?word1, groups?word2)
  | _ -> failwith "nothing matched"

val it : string * string = ("This", "super")
```

■ **Note** .NET regular expressions have many more features than those described here. For example, you can compile regular expressions to make them match very efficiently. You can also use regular expressions to define sophisticated text substitutions.

Formatting Strings Using .NET Formatting

Throughout this book, you've used F# printf format strings to format text and output; Chapter 4 introduced the basic format specifiers for this kind of text formatting. Functions such as printf and printfn are located in the Microsoft.FSharp.Text.Printf module.

Another way to format strings is to use the System.String.Format static method or the other .NET composite formatting functions such as System.Console.WriteLine and TextWriter.WriteLine. This is a distinct set of formatting functions and directives redesigned and implemented from the ground up for the .NET platform. Like printf, these methods take a format specifier and the objects to be formatted. The format specifier is a string with any number of format items acting as placeholders and designating which object is to be formatted and how. Consider the following simple example:

```
> System.String.Format("{0} {1} {2}", 12, "a", 1.23);;
val it : string = "12 a 1.23"
```

Each format item is enclosed in braces giving the index of the object to be formatted, and each can include an optional alignment specification (always preceded by a comma after the index, giving the width of the region in which the object is to be inserted, as in {0, 10}) and a format type that guides how the given object is formatted (as in {0:C}, where C formats as a system currency). The general syntax of the format item is as follows:

{index[,alignment][:formatType]}

You can use the alignment value to pad the formatted object with spaces; text alignment is left if its value is negative and right if positive. Table 10-7 summarizes the most often used format types.

Table 10-7. The .NET Format Specifiers

Specifier	Type
C	Currency
D	Decimal/long date
E	Scientific
F	Fixed-point
G	General
N	Number
P	Percent
X	Hexadecimal
d/D	Short/long date
t/T	Short/long time
M	Month
Y	Year

You can find more information about .NET composite formatting at `www.expert-fsharp.com/Topics/TextFormatting`.

Encoding and Decoding Unicode Strings

It's often necessary to convert string data between different formats. For example, files read using the `ReadLine` method on the `System.IO.StreamReader` type are read with respect to a Unicode encoding. You can specify this when creating the `StreamReader`; if left unspecified, the .NET libraries attempt to determine the encoding for you.

One common requirement is to convert strings to and from ASCII representations, assuming that all the characters in the strings are in the ASCII range 0 to 127. You can do this using `System.Text.Encoding.ASCII.GetString` and `System.Text.Encoding.ASCII.GetBytes`. Table 10-8 shows the predefined encodings and commonly used members in the `System.Text.Encoding` type.

Table 10-8. Types and Members Related to Unicode Encodings

Type/Member	Description
`System.Text.Encoding`	Represents a character encoding
`UTF8 : Encoding`	The encoding for the UTF-8 Unicode format
`ASCII : Encoding`	The encoding for the ASCII 7-bit character set
`Unicode : Encoding`	The encoding for the UTF-16 Unicode format
`UTF32 : Encoding`	The encoding for the UTF-32 Unicode format
`GetEncoding : string -> Encoding`	Fetches an encoding by name
`member GetBytes : string -> byte[]`	Encodes a string to bytes
`member GetChars: byte[] -> char[]`	Decodes a sequence of bytes
`member GetString : byte[] -> string`	Decodes a sequence of bytes

Encoding and Decoding Binary Data

Another common requirement is to convert binary data to and from the standard 64-character string-encoded representation of binary data used in XML, e-mail, and other formats. You can do this using `System.Convert.FromBase64String` and `System.Convert.ToBase64String`.

Using Further F# and .NET Data Structures

As you saw in Chapter 2, F# comes with a useful implementation of some functional programming data structures. Recall that functional data structures are *persistent*: you can't mutate them, and if you add an element or otherwise modify the collection, you generate a new collection value, perhaps sharing some internal nodes but from the outside appearing to be a new value.

Table 10-9 summarizes the most important persistent functional data structures that are included in `FSharp.Core.dll`. It's likely that additional functional data structures will be added in future F# releases.

Table 10-9. The F# Functional Data Structures from `Microsoft.FSharp.Collections`

Type	Description
List<'T>	Immutable lists implemented using linked lists
Set<'T>	Immutable sets implemented using trees
Map<'Key,'Value>	Immutable maps (dictionaries) implemented using trees
LazyList<'T>	Lists generated on demand, with each element computed only once

System.Collections.Generic and Other .NET Collections

Table 10-10 summarizes the imperative collections available in the `System.Collections.Generic` namespace.

Table 10-10. The .NET and F# Imperative Data Structures from `System.Collections.Generic`

Type	Description
List<'T>	Mutable, resizable integer-indexed arrays, usually called ResizeArray<'T> in F#.
SortedList<'T>	Mutable, resizable lists implemented using sorted arrays.
Dictionary<'Key,'Value>	Mutable, resizable dictionaries implemented using hash tables.
SortedDictionary<'Key,'Value>	Mutable, resizable dictionaries implemented using sorted arrays.
Queue<'T>	Mutable, first-in, first-out queues of unbounded size.

Type	Description
Stack<'T>	Mutable, first-in, last-out stacks of unbounded size.
HashSet<'T>	Mutable, resizable sets implemented using hash tables. New in .NET 3.5. The F# library also defines a Microsoft.FSharp.Collections.HashSet type usable in conjunction with earlier versions of .NET.

Some Other Collection Libraries

Two additional libraries of .NET collections deserve particular attention. The first is PowerCollections, currently provided by Wintellect. It provides additional generic types such as Bag<'T>, MultiDictionary<'Key,'Value>, OrderedDictionary<'Key,'Value>, OrderedMultiDictionary<'T>, and OrderedSet<'T>. The second is the C5 collection library, provided by ITU in Denmark. It includes implementations of some persistent/functional data structures such as persistent trees and thus may be of particular interest for use from F#.

Introducing Microsoft.FSharp.Math

The F# Power Pack is an open source library found on www.codeplex.com. It includes a namespace Microsoft.FSharp.Math that defines a number of mathematical-related constructs, including matrix and vector types, double-precision complex numbers (type Complex, abbreviated complex), and arbitrary-precision rationals (type BigNum, abbreviated bignum).

Using Matrices and Vectors

The F# Power Pack includes matrix and column vector types, which are generic and called Matrix<'T> and Vector<'T>, respectively. For symmetry, a type of row vectors, RowVector<'T>, is also included. Most commonly, the element types are instantiated to be double (that is, float), so the following abbreviations are used:

```
type vector = Vector<float>
type matrix = Matrix<float>
type rowvec = RowVector<float>
```

The modules Matrix, Vector, and RowVector in the Microsoft.FSharp.Math namespace have many additional functions for creating and working with these types. The functions are specialized for use with floating-point matrices, but versions to work with generic types are available at Microsoft.FSharp.Math.Matrix.Generic and Microsoft.FSharp.Math.Vector.Generic. The functions vector and matrix are also available for creating literal values. Here are some examples that use these types and functions:

```
> #r "FSharp.PowerPack.dll";;

> open Microsoft.FSharp.Math;;

> vector [ 1.0; 2.0 ; 3.0 ] + vector [ 1.0; 2.0 ; 3.0 ];;
val it : Vector<float> = vector [2.0; 4.0; 6.0]

> matrix [ [ 1.0; 2.0 ];
          [ 1.0; 3.0 ] ]
  *
  matrix [ [ 1.0; -2.0 ];
          [ 0.5; 3.0 ] ];;
val it : Math.matrix = matrix [[2.0; 4.0];
                              [2.5; 7.0];]
```

Table 10-11 summarizes the primary properties of these types.

Table 10-11. *The Microsoft.FSharp.Math Matrix and Vector Types*

Type/Member	Member Type	Description
type Matrix<'T>		
.[]	: int * int -> 'T with set, get	Gets or sets the item at the given position in the matrix.
Dimensions	: int * int	Gets the number of (rows, columns) in the matrix.
NumCols	: int	Gets the number of columns in the matrix.
NumRows	: int	Gets the number of rows in the matrix.
GetSlice2D	: ?int * ?int * ?int * ?int -> Matrix<'T>	Gets a submatrix. See the slice syntax for arrays, also usable for matrices, in Chapter 4.
Transpose	: Matrix<'T>	Gets the transpose of the matrix.
type Vector<'T>		
.[]	: int -> 'T with set, get	Gets or sets the item at the given position in the vector.
NumRows	: int	Gets the number of rows in the vector.
GetSlice	: ?int * ?int -> Vector<'T>	Gets a subvector.
Transpose	: RowVector<'T>	Gets the transpose of the vector.

Using Operator Overloads on Matrices and Vectors

The F# matrix, vector, and row vector types support the use of operators such as +, -, and *. Table 10-12 shows some of the overloads supported.

Table 10-12. Primary Operator Overloads Supported by the F# Matrix and Vector Types

Operator	Overload	Description
(*)	: Matrix<'T> * 'T -> Matrix<'T>	Scalar-matrix multiplication, and so on
(*)	: 'T * Matrix<'T> -> Matrix<'T>	Scalar-matrix multiplication, and so on
(*)	: RowVector<'T> * Matrix<'T> -> RowVector<'T>	Vector-matrix multiplication
(*)	: Matrix<'T> * Vector<'T> -> Vector<'T>	Matrix-vector multiplication
(*)	: Matrix<'T> * Matrix<'T> -> Matrix<'T>	Matrix multiplication
(.*)	: Vector<'T> * Vector<'T> -> Vector<'T>	Pointwise multiplication
(.*)	: Matrix<'T> * Matrix<'T> -> Matrix<'T>	Pointwise multiplication
(+)	: Vector<'T> * Vector<'T> -> Vector<'T>	Pointwise addition
(+)	: Matrix<'T> * Matrix<'T> -> Matrix<'T>	Pointwise addition

Supervising and Isolating Execution

The .NET System namespace includes a number of useful types that provide functionality related to the execution of running programs in the .NET Common Language Runtime. Table 10-13 summarizes them.

Table 10-13. Types Related to Runtime Supervision of Applications

Function	Description
System.Runtime	Contains advanced types that support compilation and native interoperability.
System.Environment	Provides information about, and the means to manipulate, the current environment and platform.
System.GC	Controls the system garbage collector. Chapter 17 discusses garbage collection in more detail.

Function	Description
System.WeakReference	Represents a weak reference, which references an object while still allowing that object to be reclaimed by garbage collection.
System.AppDomain	Represents an application domain, which is a software-isolated environment where applications execute. Application domains can hold code generated at runtime and can be unloaded.

Further Libraries for Reflective Techniques

As discussed in Chapter 9, .NET and F# programming frequently uses reflective techniques to analyze the types of objects, create objects at runtime, and use type information to drive generic functions in general ways. For example, in Chapter 9, you saw an example of a technique called *schema compilation*, which was based on .NET attributes, F# data types, and a compiler to take these and use reflective techniques to generate an efficient text file reader and translator. The combination of reflective techniques and .NET generics allows programs to operate at the boundary between statically typed code and dynamically typed data.

Using General Types

There are a number of facets to reflective programming with .NET. In one simple kind of reflective programming, a range of data structures are accessed in a general way. For example, .NET includes a type System.Array that is a parent type of all array types. The existence of this type allows you to write code that is generic over *all* array types, even one-dimensional and multidimensional arrays. This is occasionally useful, such as when you're writing a generic array printer.

Table 10-14 summarizes the primary general types defined in the .NET Framework.

Table 10-14. General Types in the .NET Framework

Function	Description
System.Array	General type of all array values.
System.Delegate	General type of all delegates.
System.Enum	General type of all enum values.
System.Exception	General type of all exception values.
System.Collections.IEnumerable	General type of all sequence values. This is the nongeneric version of the F# type seq<'T>, and all sequence and collection values are compatible with this type.
System.IComparable	General type of all comparable types.

Function	Description
System.IDisposable	General type of all explicitly reclaimable resources.
System.IFormattable	General type of all types supporting .NET formatting.
System.Object	General type of all values.
System.Type	Runtime representation of .NET types.
System.ValueType	General type of all value types.

Using Microsoft.FSharp.Reflection

In Chapter 9, the schema compiler used functions from the Microsoft.FSharp.Reflection namespace. This namespace is a relatively thin extension of the System.Reflection namespace. It offers an interesting set of techniques to create and analyze F# values and types in ways that are somewhat simpler than those offered by the System.Reflection namespace. These operations are also designed to be used in precompilation phases to amortize costs associated with reflective programming.

Table 10-15 summarizes the two types in this namespace

Table 10-15. Some Operations in the Microsoft.FSharp.Reflection Namespace

Class and Static Members	Description
Microsoft.FSharp.Reflection.FSharpType	Operations to analyze F# types
Microsoft.FSharp.Reflection.FSharpValue	Operations to analyze F# values

Some Other .NET Types You May Encounter

When .NET was first designed, the .NET type system didn't include generics or a general notion of a function type as used by F#. Instead of functions, .NET uses delegates, which you can think of as named function types (that is, each kind of function type is given a different name).

This means you often encounter delegate types when using .NET libraries from F#. Since .NET 2.0, some of these are even generic, giving an approximation to the simple and unified view of function types used by F#. Every .NET delegate type has a corresponding F# function type. For example, the F# function type for the .NET delegate type System.Windows.Forms.PaintEventHandler is obj -> System.Windows.Forms.PaintEventArgs -> unit. You can figure out this type by looking at the signature for the Invoke method of the given delegate type.

.NET also comes with definitions for some generic delegate types. F# tends to use function types instead of these, so you don't see them often in your coding. However, Table 10-16 shows these delegate types just in case you meet them.

Table 10-16. Delegate Types Encountered Occasionally in F# Coding

Function	F# Function Type	Description
System.Action<'T>	'T -> unit	Used for imperative actions.
System.AsyncCallback	System.IAsyncResult -> unit	Used for callbacks when asynchronous actions complete.
System.Converter<'T,'U>	'T -> 'U	Used to convert between values.
System.Comparison<'T>	'T -> 'T -> int	Used to compare values.
System.EventHandler<'T>	obj -> 'T -> unit	Used as a generic event-handler type.
System.Func<'T,'U>	'T -> 'U	A .NET 3.5 LINQ function delegate. Further arity-overloaded types exist accepting additional arguments: for example, System.Func<'T,'U,'V>, System.Func<'T,'U,'V,'W>.
System.Predicate<'T>	'T -> bool	Used to test a condition.

Some Other .NET Libraries

Any review of the libraries that are usable with F# and .NET is necessarily incomplete; too many high-quality .NET libraries are available, and more are appearing all the time. However, people often ask us which libraries we recommend. Table 10-17 shows some of the frameworks and libraries available at the time of writing that we think may be of interest to you.

Table 10-17. Some Frameworks and Libraries Not Covered in This Chapter

Framework/Library Name	Description
CSLA	A .NET-based framework for defining business objects
Extreme Optimization	A commercial math, vector, statistics, and matrix library for .NET.
GTK#	A set of .NET bindings for the GTK+ GUI toolkit, primarily used on Mono to enable windowed applications on Linux and other platforms.
Irrlicht	An open-source, high-performance, real-time 3D engine.
LINQ	Language Integrated Queries, contained in .NET 3.5. See Chapter 15.
Microsoft Robotics Studio	A .NET environment for creating robotics applications that run across a variety of hardware.

Framework/Library Name	Description
Microsoft XNA	A .NET environment for games for Microsoft gaming platforms such as Xbox 360 and Microsoft Windows.
Windows Presentation Foundation (WPF)	The graphical subsystem of .NET 3.0. See Chapter 11.
Windows Communication Foundation (WCF)	A unified framework for building connected systems. Not covered in this book.

Summary

This chapter gave an overview of the primary libraries available for use with a vanilla installation of F# and .NET. Many, many other libraries are available for .NET, and we couldn't possibly cover them in a single book. Many of the design patterns you've seen here recur in those libraries; after you get to know the libraries discussed here, you'll find that other libraries are easy to use.

The chapters that follow dig into applications of F# and the .NET Framework more deeply, looking at some of the libraries discussed in this chapter in more detail.

CHAPTER 11

■ ■ ■

Building Graphical User Interfaces

GUI applications revolve around events, and F# provides a natural way to process events with functions. Graphical interfaces are often developed using visual editors, in particular to build GUIs by assembling *controls*. Applications, however, often need drawing capabilities for displaying and manipulating data, which requires custom programming to augment available controls. This chapter discusses how to develop graphical applications with F# and why the functional traits of the language suit the event-driven programming paradigm typical of GUIs.

In this chapter, you use the Windows Forms library, the graphic toolkit designed by Microsoft on top of GDI+ and Win32 that is the former Windows presentation system. The Windows Presentation Foundation (WPF) is the new presentation framework for the Windows platform; it's discussed later in this chapter.

You may wonder why it's useful to know about the old-fashioned Windows Forms toolkit. The answer is twofold: on one hand, the framework structure is shaped after a consolidated model that dominated graphical programming for decades and is still used in many other frameworks for programming GUIs such as GTK#, a .NET managed library for writing applications based on the GTK toolkit; on the other hand, Windows Forms is still the GUI toolkit for programming managed applications for mobile devices based on Windows Mobile.

Writing "Hello, World!" in a Click

It's traditional to start with a "Hello, World!" application, so let's honor that and begin with a simple program that provides a button to display the magic phrase when clicked:

```
open System.Windows.Forms

let form = new Form(Text="Hello World WinForms")
let button = new Button(Text="Click Me!", Dock=DockStyle.Fill)

button.Click.Add(fun _ -> MessageBox.Show("Hello, World!", "Hey!") |> ignore)
form.Controls.Add(button)
form.Show()
```

Even in its simplicity, the application captures many traits typical of GUI applications. After opening the namespace associated with Windows Forms, you create the form `form` that contains the button `button`, set the form and button captions by assigning their `Text` properties, and tell the button that it should fill the entire form.

Most of GUI programming is devoted to handling events through callbacks from the graphical interface. Events are described in Chapter 8. To display a message box containing the "Hello, World!" string, you have to configure the button so that when its Click event is fired, a function is called. In the example, you pass a function to the Add method for the button's Click event, which adds an event handler to an event source. You then add the button to the form and call the form's Show method to display it.

Note that this code should be executed using fsi.exe. It won't run as a stand-alone application unless you add the following line at the end:

```
Application.Run(form)
```

This line relates to the *event loop* of a GUI application, and it's required to handle events such as button clicks. Moreover, if you execute the compiled program, notice that the window uses the classic Windows look and feel rather than the more fashionable look and feels featured by recent versions of Windows. This can be easily addressed by adding the following call to the EnableVisualStyles static method, right after the open statement:

```
Application.EnableVisualStyles()
```

If you use fsi.exe, both visual styles and the event loop are handled by F# Interactive.

Understanding the Anatomy of a Graphical Application

Graphical applications are built on the abstractions provided by the graphical environment hosting them. The application must interact with its environment and process input in an unstructured way. User input isn't the only kind of input received from a windowing system. Window management often involves requests to or from the application itself, such as painting or erasing a form.

Windowing systems provide a common and abstract way to interact with a graphical application: the notion of an *event*. When an event occurs, the application receives a message in the *message queue* with information about the event.

The graphical application is responsible for delivering messages from the message queue to the control for which they're meant. A set of functions provided by the API of the windowing system supports this. This activity of reading messages from the message queue and dispatching them is known as the *event loop* of the application. If the loop fails for any reason, the GUI components cease to work, the application hangs, and Windows may eventually inform you that the application isn't responding.

It's rare for an application to program the event loop explicitly. Programming toolkits encapsulate this functionality because it's basically always the same. The Run method of the Application class is responsible for handling the event loop, and it ensures that messages related to events are delivered to targets within the application.

GUI programs often involve multiple *threads* of execution. Chapter 13 discusses threading and concurrency in more detail; for this chapter, it's important to remember that event dispatching is a single-threaded activity, even if it may seem the opposite. The thread executing the event loop calls the functions and methods registered for handling the various events. In the "Hello, World!" example, for instance, you told the button to call back the function to show the message box when clicked.

An Explicit Event Loop

A Windows Forms event loop can also be explicitly defined by the application using the
`Application.DoEvents` method; in this case, each invocation performs a step in event handling and
returns the control to the caller. Some programs can benefit from this control because they can interleave
event processing and computation using a single thread. Computer games, for instance, tend to use this
approach because event-based timers provided by the framework aren't reliable for producing the frames
of the game at the required pace. The following is a typical explicit event loop:

```
let form = new Form(Text="Explicit Event Loop")
form.Show()
while form.Created do
    // Perform some task
    Application.DoEvents()
```

When events are handled explicitly, a program must call the `DoEvents` method frequently: if events
aren't processed, the graphical interface may become unresponsive, which provides the wrong
feedback to the user.

Software reuse has always been a priority in the world of graphical applications, because of the
many details involved in realizing even simple behaviors. It's not surprising that programming
techniques favoring software reuse have always flourished in this context. You can develop a GUI
application without writing a single line of code by combining existing controls into a new interface.

Articulated frameworks, such as Windows Forms, provide a significant number of reusable
controls so that you can develop entire applications without needing to use drawing facilities provided
by the interface. For this reason, frameworks have started to support two kinds of customers: those
composing interfaces with controls and those who need to develop new controls or explicitly use
drawing primitives. The rest of this chapter explores the Windows Forms framework from both
perspectives: the functional nature of F# is very effective for using controls, and the ability to define
objects helps you develop new ones.

Composing User Interfaces

A control is represented by an object inheriting, either directly or indirectly, from the `Control` class in
the `System.Windows.Forms` namespace. Building interfaces using controls involves two tasks: placing
controls into containers (that are themselves a particular type of control) such as panels or forms, and
registering controls with event handlers to be notified of relevant events.

As an example, let's develop a simple web browser based on the Internet Explorer control, which is
a control that allows wrapping the HTML renderer (the interior of an Internet Explorer window) into
an application. This example shows how to develop the application interactively using `fsi.exe`. Start
by opening the libraries required for using Windows Forms:

```
open System
open System.Drawing
open System.Windows.Forms
```

Then, enable the Windows XP/Vista visual styles, declaring through the custom attribute
`STAThread` that the application adopts the *single thread apartment model*, which is a COM legacy often
required for Windows Forms applications to interact with COM components:

```
[<STAThread>]
do Application.EnableVisualStyles()
```

You need this in the example because Internet Explorer is a COM component accessible through a .NET wrapped type named WebBrowser in the System.Windows.Forms namespace, as are all the base controls offered by Windows Forms (assume that types are from this namespace unless otherwise specified).

Now you have to decide what the browser application should look like (see Figure 11-1). The bare minimum is a toolbar featuring the address bar and the classic Go button, a status bar with a progress bar shown during page loading, and the browser control in the middle of the form.

Figure 11-1. A simple web browser application

You next configure the elements, starting from the status bar, as shown in the following code. You add the progress bar to the status bar and configure both. The Dock property of the status bar is set to Bottom, meaning that the status bar should fill the bottom part of the form. The progress bar is resized, and then its Style property is set to Marquee, meaning that you don't want to show any specific progress but just something moving during download:

```
let statusProgress =
  new ToolStripProgressBar(Size=new Size(200, 16),
                           Style= ProgressBarStyle.Marquee,
                           Visible=false)
let status = new StatusStrip(Dock=DockStyle.Bottom)
status.Items.Add(statusProgress) |> ignore
```

You can now set up the browser's toolbar, as shown in the following code. The toolbar should be in the top area of the form, so set its `Dock` property to `Top`. First add a label, the text box for typing the URL, and the button. Then, stretch the `address` text box and associate an event handler with its `KeyPress` event. This way, you can catch the Enter key and start browsing the typed URL without having to wait for the Go button. Finally, configure the Go button by setting its label and associating an event handler with the `Click` event:

```
let toolbar = new ToolStrip(Dock=DockStyle.Top)
let address = new ToolStripTextBox(Size=new Size(400, 25))
let browser = new WebBrowser(Dock=DockStyle.Fill)
let go = new ToolStripButton(DisplayStyle=ToolStripItemDisplayStyle.Text,
                            Text="Go")
address.KeyPress.Add(fun arg ->
    if (arg.KeyChar = '\r') then browser.Url <- new Uri(address.Text))
go.Click.Add(fun arg -> browser.Url <- new Uri(address.Text))
toolbar.Items.Add(new ToolStripLabel("Address:")) |> ignore
toolbar.Items.Add(address) |> ignore
toolbar.Items.Add(go) |>ignore
```

Both event handlers set the `Url` property of the `browser` object, causing the `WebBrowser` control to load the given `Uri`. Notice how nicely and compactly F# lets you specify event handlers. This is possible because F# lets you use functions directly as arguments to `Add`.

You can now take care of the browser control and set its properties. Here, you tell the browser to occupy all of the area in the form left by the toolbar and the status bar, by setting the `Dock` property to `Fill`. You then subscribe to two events, `Navigating` and `DocumentCompleted`, in order to be notified by the browser when document loading starts and completes. When the browser begins fetching a URL, you show the progress bar in the status bar, setting its `Visible` property to `true`. After the document is loaded, you hide the progress bar, and you update the address bar so that if the user followed a link, the address shown remains consistent with the current document:

```
browser.Navigating.Add(fun args ->
    statusProgress.Visible <- true)
browser.DocumentCompleted.Add(fun args ->
    statusProgress.Visible <- false;
    address.Text <- browser.Url.AbsoluteUri)
```

You're almost finished with the interface. You have to tell Windows Forms that the controls are contained in the form `form`. Then, configure the form by setting its caption with the `Text` property and its size with the `Size` property. You call `PerformLayout` to update the current layout of the form, and then you can call `Show` to display the browser:

```
let form = new Form(Text="Web Browser", Size=new Size(800, 600))
form.Controls.Add(browser)
form.Controls.Add(toolbar)
form.Controls.Add(status)
form.PerformLayout()
form.Show()
```

To compile the application rather than execute it interactively, add the following at the end, as mentioned previously:

```
Application.Run(form)
```

Watch the Application Grow

You can see the form growing interactively using `fsi.exe`. Usually, applications first configure forms and controls and then call `Show` to present the user with a form that's ready to use. It's also useful to set the properties `TopMost=true` and `Visible=true`. The properties of a form can also be set after the form is visible, allowing you to see the effects of each operation on it. F# Interactive offers the unique opportunity to watch the form growing interactively; you can, for instance, build the interface of the simple web browser by showing the form immediately and then proceed to add controls and set their properties. Thus, you can experiment with the various properties of controls and see how they affect the interface.

What have you learned by developing this application? It's clear that building interfaces based on controls requires a significant amount of code to configure controls by setting their properties. The form's layout is also set by defining properties of controls, as you did in the browser. Moreover, an ever-increasing list of controls is available, and each provides a large number of properties. F# syntax supports this process by letting you set initial values for control properties within the call to the control constructor, and adding functions as event handlers, leading to very compact programs that are easier to understand.

Control Layout

The layout of controls, done either by hand or through a visual editor, defines how a form looks when opened. Users expect that the layout will adapt gracefully to form resizing. One simple approach to the problem is to forbid the operation, as is done in many dialog boxes; a better solution is to define how controls must adapt their positions and sizes as the form changes size.

Windows Forms has two ways to indicate how a control should adapt when the size of its container changes. You can use the property `Dock` to *dock* the control to one of the four edges or to the center of the container (as shown in Figure 11-2). Docking to the edges constrains the control to be always attached to one of them, and either its width or its height should change in order to ensure that the whole edge is filled with it (as shown in Figure 11-2, horizontal edges have precedence over vertical ones). When docked to the middle, a control is resized to fill the area of the container left by the control docked to the edges. Docking is a flexible way to define layouts that adapt to size changes of the interface. If the five areas defined by this strategy aren't enough, you can rely on logical containers such as panels: a panel represents a group of controls with a given layout. Using panels, you can nest layouts and use docking on a panel docked in the surrounding container.

An alternative to docking is *anchoring*. Through the property `Anchor`, you can dictate that the distance between an edge of the control and the corresponding edge of the container should be constant. This gives you finer control over how the component should be resized or moved. When a control is anchored only to a horizontal and vertical edge (for instance `Top` and `Left`), its size doesn't change: only the position is preserved.

Although docking and anchoring are useful for controlling how the control must be adapted to the interface, sometimes these strategies aren't enough to address the needs of a complex layout. The WPF adopts a more articulated notion of extensible layout management based on the notion of a layout manager (a similar notion has always been present in the Java AWT and in HTML).

Visual designers are graphical applications that allow you to design interfaces using a visual metaphor. Controls are dragged and dropped onto forms and then configured through a property window. Visual Studio provides a visual designer, although it isn't available for all programming languages. The F# project system doesn't feature visual design of GUIs within Visual Studio for Windows Forms or for WPF frameworks. However, using the Visual Studio designer is still a useful way to explore controls and to play with their properties, and the generated C# fragments can be examined and used in F# code. To understand how the Visual Studio designer works, let's design the same browser application in C#, as shown in Figure 11-2. The Visual Studio designer generates, for the form `Browser`, a C# file named `Browser.Designer.cs` containing all the C# code required to set up the interface. If you look at that file, you can see that it contains mainly the assignments of control properties similar to those you manually used to prepare the browser form.

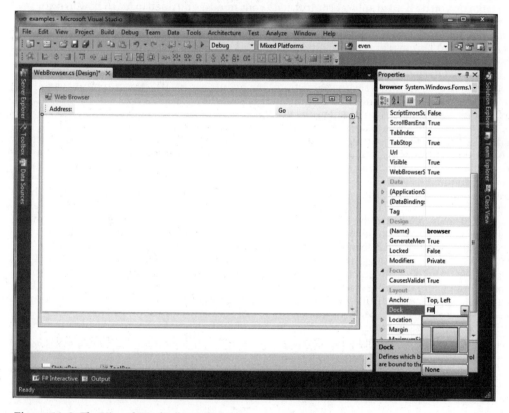

Figure 11-2. The Visual Studio form designer

Until the Windows Forms designer or another visual designer is available for F#, you have essentially four options for building graphical interfaces in the language:

- Write the interface code by hand, as you did for the browser sample.
- Develop a visual designer that outputs F# code (although it's a hard job), and use it.
- Use the C# visual designer, and then convert the assignments in *file*.Designer.cs into F#.

- Exploit the interoperability of the .NET platform by designing the interface with the designer, generating C# or another supported language and using the F# code as a library.

You can easily define simple interfaces with F# code, and the rest of this chapter shows you how. You now focus on the more important part of designing graphical applications: drawing and control development.

Drawing Applications

So far, you've developed graphical applications based on the composition of predeveloped graphical controls; but what do you do if no graphical control suits your needs? You need to learn how to draw using the drawing primitives provided by the graphical system.

To understand how drawing works, you need to review the model behind the rendering process of a graphical application. This model really distinguishes Windows Forms from WPF; later, this chapter reviews the traditional paint-based model that still dominates the presentation systems panorama. You know already that the event-driven programming paradigm best suits graphical applications; so far, you've associated event handlers with user actions, but events are used by the graphical system as a general mechanism to communicate with the graphical application.

An application uses resources provided by the graphical system, and these resources are mostly windows. A *window* is a rectangular area on the screen, not necessarily a top-level window with buttons, a title bar, and all the amenities you usually associate with it. Windows can be nested and are the unit of traditional windowing systems. Windows can contain other windows, and the windowing system is responsible for ensuring that events are routed to the callbacks registered for handling the events for each window.

Windows are allowed to draw in their own client area, and the drawing is performed through the *device context*, an object provided by the graphical system and used to perform the *graphic primitives* to draw the content. The graphic primitives issued to the graphics system aren't retained by it; therefore, when the window is covered for some reason, the portion that becomes hidden must be repainted when it's uncovered. Because the information required to redraw the hidden portion is held by the application owning the window, the graphical system sends a *paint* message to the window.

To better understand the drawing model, consider a simple graphical application that shows how to draw a curved line using the Bézier curve and canonical splines, given four control points. Start by opening your namespaces and telling Windows Forms that your form can use the XP/Vista look rather than the classic Windows 95 style; also set a global flag to tell standard controls to use the new GDI+ text-rendering primitives rather than those of the traditional GDI (this code is omitted from now on, but remember to use it later; also remember that this must be done before windows are created—otherwise, an exception is thrown):

```
open System
open System.Drawing
open System.Windows.Forms

Application.EnableVisualStyles()
Application.SetCompatibleTextRenderingDefault(false)
```

You next create the form and define the initial values of the control points. The movingPoint variable keeps track of the point the user is dragging, to adjust the curve:

```
let form = new Form(Text="Curves")
let cpt = [| Point(20, 60); Point(40, 50); Point(130, 60); Point(200, 200) |]
let mutable movingPoint = -1
```

Let's introduce three menus to configure the application. They're used to check features to be drawn:

```
let newMenu (s:string) = new ToolStripMenuItem(s,Checked=true,CheckOnClick=true)
let menuBezier = newMenu "Show &Bézier"
let menuCanonical = newMenu "Show &Canonical spline"
let menuControlPoints = newMenu "Show control &points"
```

You use a scrollbar to define different values for the tension parameter of the canonical spline curve:

```
let scrollbar = new VScrollBar(Dock=DockStyle.Right, LargeChange=2, Maximum=10)
```

Control points are drawn if required, and an ellipse is used to mark them. The function receives the device context in the form of a Graphics object; you draw the ellipse by invoking the DrawEllipse primitive on it. You use a Pen to draw the ellipse—in this case, a red pen:

```
let drawPoint (g:Graphics) (p:Point) =
    g.DrawEllipse(Pens.Red, p.X - 2, p.Y - 2, 4, 4)
```

Brushes and Pens

Windows Forms uses two kinds of objects to define colored primitives: brushes and pens. A *brush* is used to fill an area with a given pattern. A number of different patterns are available; solid colors are provided by the SolidBrush class, hatched patterns are provided by HatchBrush, gradients are provided by LinearGradientBrush and PathGradientBrush, and textured gradients are provided by TextureBrush. The Brushes class provides a number of static brush objects describing solid colors.

Pens are brushes with a contour. The line drawn by a pen has a filling (the brush part) but also a width and different styles (dashed or not, with different caps at the beginning and at the end). The Pens class provides a number of static pen objects with the basic solid colors.

Both pen and brush objects contain resources of the graphical system; it's important to dispose of them as soon as they aren't required anymore. A use binding or the using function discussed in Chapters 4 and 8 helps ensure that you don't forget to call the Dispose method that all these objects provide from the IDisposable interface that otherwise should be called explicitly.

You're now ready to define the function responsible for drawing in your window. You can't assume anything about the current state of the window; thus, the paint function always draws the visible primitives[1] depending on the state of menu entries:

```
let paint (g:Graphics) =
    if (menuBezier.Checked) then
        g.DrawLine(Pens.Red, cpt.[0], cpt.[1])
        g.DrawLine(Pens.Red, cpt.[2], cpt.[3])
        g.DrawBeziers(Pens.Black, cpt)
    if (menuCanonical.Checked) then
```

---

[1]   If primitives fall out of the area allowed for drawing, they're clipped in part or entirely.

```
        g.DrawCurve(Pens.Blue, cpt, float32 scrollbar.Value)
    if (menuControlPoints.Checked) then
        for i = 0 to cpt.Length - 1 do
            drawPoint g cpt.[i]
```

Figure 11-3 shows the result of the drawing all the elements. The Bézier curve, widely used in image-processing and vector applications, uses the four control points to define the start and end points of the curve and the two segments tangent to the curve at its ends. The cubic parametric curve is calculated from these points and produces the lines shown in Figure 11-3. The canonical spline, on the other hand, is a curve that traverses all the control points; the tension parameter controls how curvy the curve is.

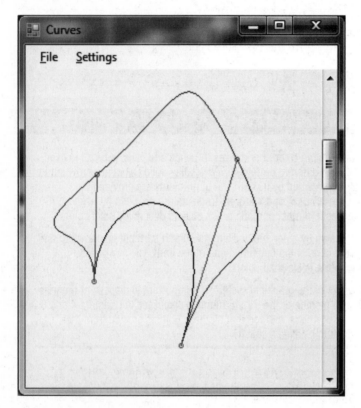

Figure 11-3. Output of the Curves application

You now want to allow users to move control points by dragging and dropping. You're interested in mouse events, in particular when the mouse button is pressed, when it moves, and when the button is released. Thanks to the well-defined model for rendering the application, you can update the state of your variables and ask the graphical system to issue a paint message that causes the window to receive a paint message and update the current frame.

Background Painting

In the Curves application, you draw assuming that the window is clean—but who is responsible for clearing the previous drawing in the window? Windows Forms calls the OnPaintBackground method before calling the paint handler, and this method by default clears the area with the color returned by the BackColor property. When the function responsible for painting draws the area entirely, painting the background could be useless and even problematic: the quick repaint may flicker because the eye can perceive the background clear and then the drawing of the current frame. You can use the SetStyle method of the Form class to configure the application to do all the paint operations in the handler of the paint event, and you can override OnPaintBackground to an empty method to avoid this effect.

You define a helper function to define a circular area around a point that is sensible to your interaction. This is required in order to not require the user to pick the exact pixel corresponding to the control point:

```
let isClose (p:Point) (l:Point) =
    let dx = p.X - l.X
    let dy = p.Y - l.Y
    (dx * dx + dy * dy) < 6
```

When the mouse button is pressed, you check whether the click is over any control point. In this case, you store its index in the movingPoint variable; otherwise, the event is ignored:

```
let mouseDown (p:Point) =
    try
      let idx = cpt |> Array.findIndex (isClose p)
      movingPoint <- idx
    with _ -> ()
```

When the mouse moves over the client area of the window, the mouse move event is generated. If the movingPoint member has a value other than –1, you have to update the corresponding control point with the current position of the mouse defined by the variable p:

```
let mouseMove (p:Point) =
    if (movingPoint <> -1) then
        cpt.[movingPoint] <- p
        form.Invalidate()
```

You next define for the window a File menu and a Settings submenu. The first features the classic Exit option, and the second shows the three checked menu items that control what the paint method should draw. You define menus by composing objects that correspond to the various menu entries. You also define the event handlers associated with each menu item. When Exit is clicked, the form is disposed. In all the other cases, you rely on the menu item's ability to change its checked state, and you invalidate the form content to force the redraw of the window:

```
let setupMenu () =
    let menu = new MenuStrip()
    let fileMenuItem = new ToolStripMenuItem("&File")
    let settMenuItem = new ToolStripMenuItem("&Settings")
    let exitMenuItem = new ToolStripMenuItem("&Exit")
```

```
menu.Items.Add(fileMenuItem) |> ignore
menu.Items.Add(settMenuItem) |> ignore
fileMenuItem.DropDownItems.Add(exitMenuItem) |> ignore
settMenuItem.DropDownItems.Add(menuBezier) |> ignore
settMenuItem.DropDownItems.Add(menuCanonical) |> ignore
settMenuItem.DropDownItems.Add(menuControlPoints) |> ignore
exitMenuItem.Click.Add(fun _ -> form.Close ())
menuBezier.Click.Add(fun _ -> form.Invalidate())
menuCanonical.Click.Add(fun _ -> form.Invalidate())
menuControlPoints.Click.Add(fun _ -> form.Invalidate())
menu
```

You're now ready to use the functions you defined to configure the controls. You set up the scrollbar and register the controls in the form and the event handlers for the various events. Finally, you start the application's event loop and play with it:

```
scrollbar.ValueChanged.Add(fun _ -> form.Invalidate())
form.Controls.Add(scrollbar)
form.MainMenuStrip <- setupMenu()
form.Controls.Add(form.MainMenuStrip)
form.Paint.Add(fun e -> paint(e.Graphics))
form.MouseDown.Add(fun e -> mouseDown(e.Location))
form.MouseMove.Add(fun e -> mouseMove(e.Location))
form.MouseUp.Add(fun e -> movingPoint <- -1)
form.Show()
```

If you're not using F# Interactive, don't forget to add the following:

```
[<STAThread>]
do Application.Run(form)
```

Writing Your Own Controls

The Curves example from the previous section draws inside a form by handling events. This is a rare way to draw things in graphical applications, because the resulting code is scarcely reusable, and drawing on the surface of a form raises issues when additional controls have to be placed in its client area.

User controls are the abstraction provided by the Windows Forms framework to program custom controls. If delegation is used to handle events generated from controls, inheritance and method overriding are the tools used to handle them in controls.

Developing a Custom Control

To make this discussion concrete, consider a control that implements a simple button. You can use the control from C# inside the Visual Studio designer like the native button, as shown in Figure 11-4.

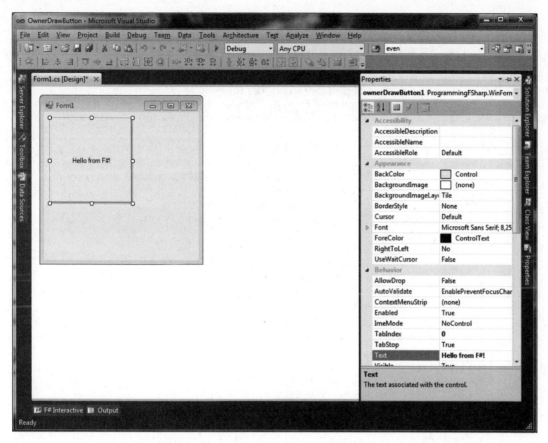

Figure 11-4. The F# button control used in a C# application and the Visual Studio designer

You start your control by inheriting from the UserControl class:[2]

```
open System
open System.Drawing
open System.Windows.Forms
open System.ComponentModel

type OwnerDrawButton() =
        inherit UserControl()
```

You then define the state of the control in terms of the class's fields:

```
        let mutable text = ""
        let mutable pressed = false
```

---

[2] Note that this example hasn't been designed to be entered using F# Interactive.

The text field contains the button's label. As you did for the movingPoint variable in the Curves example, the pressed field is responsible for remembering whether the button is currently pressed, allowing the paint handler to behave appropriately. You override the OnPaint method to handle the paint event. You allocate the pens and the brush required to draw and invert the role of the border colors in order to achieve the raised effect when the button isn't pressed and the depressed look otherwise. You also measure the size of the label string, because you're interested in drawing the string in the center of the button. You can then draw the lines on the borders, playing with colors to obtain a 3D effect. The pens and brushes are disposed at the end of the function:

```
override x.OnPaint (e:PaintEventArgs) =
    let g = e.Graphics
    use pll = new Pen(SystemColors.ControlLightLight)
    use pl = new Pen(SystemColors.ControlLight)
    use pd = new Pen(SystemColors.ControlDark)
    use pdd = new Pen(SystemColors.ControlDarkDark)
    use bfg = new SolidBrush(x.ForeColor)
    let szf = g.MeasureString(text, x.Font)
    let spt = PointF((float32(x.Width) - szf.Width) / 2.0f,
                     (float32(x.Height) - szf.Height) / 2.0f)
    let ptt = if pressed then pdd else pll
    let pt = if pressed then pd else pl
    let pb = if pressed then pl else pd
    let pbb = if pressed then pll else pdd

    g.Clear(SystemColors.Control)
    g.DrawLine(ptt, 0, 0, x.Width - 1, 0)
    g.DrawLine(ptt, 0, 0, 0, x.Height - 1)
    g.DrawLine(pt, 1, 1, x.Width - 2, 1)
    g.DrawLine(pt, 1, 1, 1, x.Height - 2)
    g.DrawLine(pbb, 0, x.Height - 1, x.Width - 1, x.Height - 1)
    g.DrawLine(pbb, x.Width - 1, 0, x.Width - 1, x.Height - 1)
    g.DrawLine(pb, 1, x.Height - 2, x.Width - 2, x.Height - 2)
    g.DrawLine(pb, x.Width - 2, 1, x.Width - 2, x.Height - 2)
    g.DrawString(text, x.Font, bfg, spt)
```

It's important to note the use of the colors defined in the SystemColors class: you use the system definition of colors so that the button uses the colors set by the user as display settings. Configuration is an important aspect of a user control, because it's normally performed through a visual editor such as Visual Studio. Well-defined controls are those that can be highly customized without having to extend the control programmatically or, even worse, to change its source code.

Now that you've defined the drawing procedure, you can define the behavior of the control by handling mouse events. You restrict the implementation to mouse events, although a key event handler should be provided in order to react to a press of the Enter key:

```
override x.OnMouseUp (e:MouseEventArgs) =
    pressed <- false
    x.Invalidate()
    fireClick()
```

```
override x.OnMouseDown (e:MouseEventArgs) =
    pressed <- true
    x.Invalidate()
```

The OnMouseDown event sets the pressed member and asks the control to repaint by invalidating its content. When the mouse is released, the OnMouseUp is called, and you reset the flag and ask for repaint.

Controls are usually configured through the assignment of properties. If you annotate a property with an attribute of type Category and one of type Browsable, the property is displayed by Visual Studio in the control property box. To show this, you define the Text property, which exposes the button's label to users of the control:

```
[<Category("Behavior")>]
[<Browsable(true)>]
override x.Text
    with get() = text
    and  set(t:string) = text <- t; x.Invalidate()
```

You're now ready to test your new control by writing a few lines of F# code as follows:

```
let form = new Form(Visible=true)
let c = new OwnerDrawButton(Text="Hello button")

c.Click.Add(fun _ -> MessageBox.Show("Clicked!") |> ignore)
form.Controls.Add(c)
```

To see your control at work in the Visual Studio designer, you must create a Windows Forms application C# project. With the default form created by the application wizard opened, right-click the Toolbox window and select the Choose Items option; then, browse for the OwnerDrawButton.dll file obtained by compiling the F# control. Now you can visually drag your F# control into the form and configure its properties using the Properties window.

Custom controls are seen as black-box objects by applications hosting them. Several hacks are possible to handle the behavior of controls from outside (subclassing is often used on Windows), but none of them are really satisfactory. Later, this chapter discusses how this constraint is overcome by the retention-based rendering process featured by the WPF.

Anatomy of a Control

As illustrated by the OwnerDrawButton control example, the structure of a graphic control tends to assume the form of a finite state automaton. Events received by the control make the automaton change its internal state, usually causing an update of its actual display.

A well-known model that describes this structure is the Model-View-Controller design pattern. As shown in Figure 11-5, the model organizes a graphical element (either an application or a single control) into three parts: the model, the view, and the controller.

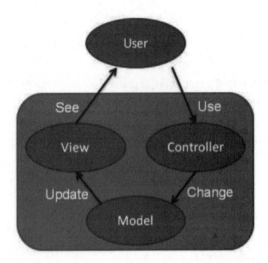

Figure 11-5. The structure of the Model-View-Controller design pattern

The model constitutes the internal representation of the information displayed by the control. A word processor, for instance, stores a document in memory as part of the model, even though the entire text doesn't fit the current visible area. In your simple button, the model is defined by the pressed and text values.

When the model changes, the view must be updated, and a rendering of the information kept in memory should be performed. Usually, the paint method corresponds to the view portion of the control. Event handlers triggered by the user form the controller of the control. The controller defines how these elements affect the model.

The Model-View-Controller pattern isn't the only model developed to describe graphical interfaces. However, it captures the intrinsic nature of the problem, providing a good framework for classifying the elements of an interface or a control. The rest of this chapter refers to this pattern to indicate the various elements of the applications you learn how to develop.

Displaying Samples from Sensors

Now that you have reviewed the essential concepts behind programming graphical interfaces, you're ready to work on some applications. They're full of details typical of real graphical applications. This section presents a graphic control whose purpose is to plot samples acquired over time—for instance, from a sensor. The control has been designed to be reusable and highly configurable, providing a rich set of properties that can be set even at runtime by the application hosting it, as shown in Figure 11-6.

Figure 11-6. *The* GraphControl *used in a test application that lets the user to change its appearance at runtime*

The basic function of the control is to receive and store samples labeled with time. If c is the variable that refers to an instance of the control, the application feeds data through an AddSample method that adds a new sample to the data set, causing the control to update the displayed chart:

```
c.AddSample(t, v)
```

The next section shows how to define the control and the AddSample method.

Despite the simple interface provided by GraphControl to update the data set, the control isn't easy to implement, because it must hold a large number of samples and provide a means to navigate through a view that doesn't fit all the samples. Another area important to controls is *configuration*: users of the control want to customize its appearance to fit the needs of their application. To support these needs, you must adopt the coding conventions required to integrate the control in the Windows Forms framework so that it integrates with all the tools used to design applications.

Building the GraphControl: The Model

According to the Model-View-Controller paradigm, you first define the control's model, which should contain all the information needed to draw the control when required. You first define the type of a sample:

```
type Sample = { Time : int64; Value : float32 }
```

Samples are pairs (t, v), with t being the time at which the sample v has been read. Samples are collected in a data structure named DataSamples, whose purpose is to provide a uniform view of data; the class definition is reported in Listing 11-1. You assume that the data set is always small enough to stay in memory; this limitation can be overcome in the future by changing this class. Samples are collected into a ResizeArray and kept in the field named data. You also use a form of run-length-encoding (RLE) compression to optimize memory usage, and you use linear interpolation to make data appear continuous in order to simplify the implementation of the zoom feature. Because not all the samples are recorded, the count field is used to keep track of the number of added samples.

The AddSample method is used to add a new sample to the data set. It assumes that data comes sorted with respect to time; if a sample preceding the last added is detected, it's discarded. The Last property returns the last-added sample; you may have discarded it because it's equal to the previous, so you rebuild the sample using the lastTime field that records the time value of the last sample added.

Interpolation is done by the GetValue method, which given a time value calculates the corresponding value. The list of samples is searched using a binary search. If a sample matches the given time, it's returned; otherwise, the interpolation is performed.

The last operation implemented by DataSamples is FindMinMax, which is a method that computes the minimum and maximum values of the data in a given interval. You can initialize the values for minimum and maximum, as well as a stride to use to do the search. The stride is useful in conjunction with zoom, because the number of samples that can be displayed is finite and the rendering procedure must subsample when zooming out.

Listing 11-1. The DataSamples Class Definition

```
open System

type Sample = { Time : int64; Value : float32 }

type DataSamples() =
    let data = new ResizeArray<Sample>()
    let mutable count = 0
    let mutable lastTime = 0L

    member x.Last = { Time=lastTime; Value=data.[data.Count - 1].Value }

    member x.AddSample(t,v) =
        let s = { Time=t; Value=v }
        let last = if (data.Count = 0) then s else x.Last

        count <- count + 1
        lastTime <- max last.Time s.Time
        if data.Count = 0 then data.Add(s)

        elif last.Time < s.Time && last.Value <> s.Value then
            if data.[data.Count-1].Time <> last.Time then data.Add(last)
```

```
        data.Add(s)

member x.Count = count

// The model is continuous: missing samples are obtained by interpolation
member x.GetValue(time:int64) =

    // Find the relevant point via a binary search
    let rec search (lo, hi) =
        let mid = (lo + hi) / 2
        if hi - lo <= 1 then (lo, hi)
        elif data.[mid].Time = time then (mid, mid)
        elif data.[mid].Time < time then search (mid, hi)
        else search (lo, mid)

    if (data.Count = 0) then failwith "No data samples"

    if (lastTime < time) then failwith "Wrong time!"

    let lo,hi = search (0, data.Count - 1)

    if (data.[lo].Time = time || hi = lo) then data.[lo].Value
    elif (data.[hi].Time = time) then data.[hi].Value
    else
        // interpolate
        let p = if data.[hi].Time < time then hi else lo
        let next = data.[min (p+1) (data.Count-1)]
        let curr = data.[p]
        let spant = next.Time - curr.Time
        let spanv = next.Value - curr.Value
        curr.Value + float32(time-curr.Time) *(spanv/float32 spant)

// This method finds the minimum and the maximum values given
// a sampling frequency and an interval of time
member x.FindMinMax(sampleFreq:int64, start:int64, finish:int64,
                    minval:float32, maxval:float32) =


    if (data.Count = 0) then (minval, maxval) else
    let start = max start 0L
    let finish = min finish lastTime

    let minv,maxv =
        seq { start .. sampleFreq .. finish }
        |> Seq.map x.GetValue
        |> Seq.fold (fun (minv,maxv) v -> (min v minv,max v maxv))
                    (minval,maxval)

    if (minv = maxv) then
        let delta = if (minv = 0.0f) then 0.01f else 0.01f * abs minv
        (minv - delta, maxv + delta)
    else (minv, maxv)
```

Building the GraphControl: Style Properties and Controller

Listing 11-2 shows the code for the GraphControl class except the OnPaint drawing method, shown in the next section. This control exhibits the typical structure of a graphic control; it features a large number of constants and fields that serve configuration purposes. The class inherits from UserControl, which is the base class of Windows Forms controls, and it contains a field named data of type DataSamples that represents the data shown by the control. The appearance is controlled through properties, fields, and constant values; for instance, the axis color is controlled by the following pattern:

```
let mutable axisColor:Color = Color.White
[<Category("Graph Style"); Browsable(true)>]
member x.AxisColor
    with get() = x.axisColor
    and set(v:Color) = x.axisColor <- v; x.Invalidate()
```

The AxisColor property lets the control's host change the color of the axis color displayed by the control, because properties are part of the controller of the control; thus, when the setter is invoked, you call the Invalidate method to ensure that a paint message is sent to the control so the view is updated. Note that a fully fledged control might read defaults from a store of user-specific configuration properties.

Listing 11-2. The GraphControl Class

```
open System
open System.Drawing
open System.Drawing.Drawing2D
open System.Windows.Forms
open System.ComponentModel

type GraphControl() as x  =
    inherit UserControl()

    let data = new DataSamples()
    let mutable minVisibleValue = Single.MaxValue
    let mutable maxVisibleValue = Single.MinValue
    let mutable absMax         = Single.MinValue
    let mutable absMin         = Single.MaxValue
    let mutable lastMin        = minVisibleValue
    let mutable lastMax        = maxVisibleValue
    let mutable axisColor      = Color.White
    let mutable beginColor     = Color.Red
    let mutable verticalLabelFormat = "{0:F2}"
    let mutable startTime       = 0L
    let mutable visibleSamples  = 10
    let mutable initView = startTime - int64(visibleSamples)
    let mutable verticalLines     = 0
    let mutable timeScale = 10000000 // In 100-nanoseconds
    let mutable timeFormat = "{0:T}"

    let rightBottomMargin = Size(10, 10)
    let leftTopMargin     = Size(10, 10)

    do
        x.SetStyle(ControlStyles.AllPaintingInWmPaint, true)
```

```
    x.SetStyle(ControlStyles.OptimizedDoubleBuffer, true)
    base.BackColor <- Color.DarkBlue

[<Category("Graph Style"); Browsable(true)>]
member x.AxisColor
    with get() = axisColor
    and set(v:Color) = axisColor <- v; x.Invalidate()

[<Category("Graph Style"); Browsable(true)>]
member x.BeginColor
    with get() = beginColor
    and set(v:Color) = beginColor <- v; x.Invalidate()

[<Category("Graph Style"); Browsable(true)>]
member x.MinVisibleValue
    with get() = minVisibleValue
    and set(v:float32) = minVisibleValue <- v; lastMin <- v; x.Invalidate()

[<Category("Graph Style"); Browsable(true)>]
member x.MaxVisibleValue
    with get() = maxVisibleValue
    and set(v:float32) = maxVisibleValue <- v; lastMax <- v; x.Invalidate()

[<Category("Graph Style"); Browsable(true)>]
member x.VerticalLines
    with get() = verticalLines
    and set(v:int) = verticalLines <- v; x.Invalidate()

[<Category("Graph Style"); Browsable(true)>]
member x.GraphBackColor
    with get() = x.BackColor
    and set(v:Color) = x.BackColor <- v

[<Category("Graph Style"); Browsable(true)>]
member x.LineColor
    with get() = x.ForeColor
    and set(v:Color) = x.ForeColor <- v

[<Category("Graph Style"); Browsable(true)>]
member x.VerticalLabelFormat
    with get() = verticalLabelFormat
    and set(v:string) = verticalLabelFormat <- v; x.Invalidate()

[<Category("Graph Style"); Browsable(true)>]
member x.StartTime
    with get() = startTime
    and set(v:int64) = startTime <- v; x.Invalidate()

[<Category("Graph Style"); Browsable(true)>]
member x.Title
    with get() = x.Text
    and set(v:string) = x.Text <- v; x.Invalidate()
```

```
[<Category("Graph Style"); Browsable(true)>]
member x.VisibleSamples
    with get() = visibleSamples
    and set(v:int) =
        visibleSamples <- v;
        initView <- startTime - int64(visibleSamples);
        x.Invalidate()

[<Category("Graph Style"); Browsable(true)>]
member x.TimeScale
    with get() = timeScale
    and set(v:int) = timeScale <- v; x.Invalidate()

[<Category("Graph Style"); Browsable(true)>]
member x.TimeFormat
    with get() = timeFormat
    and set(v:string) = timeFormat <- v; x.Invalidate()

// ... Further portions of this class shown further below
```

Listing 11-3 includes the remaining portions of the GraphControl class corresponding to the controller part of the Model-View-Controller paradigm. Samples are added through the AddSample method (AddSampleData generates random samples to display inside the control). This method adds the sample to the inner DataSamples object and updates the values of two fields meant to store the minimum and maximum values recorded for samples; both of these values are used in the display process. Because the model of the control changes, you need to update the view, and you invalidate the control as you did for properties.

Overriding vs. Delegation

Event handling can be performed by both subscribing delegates and overriding methods. The former approach is more typical of applications; the latter is more common in control development. Method overriding guarantees more control over event handling because it allows a complete redefinition of the inherited behavior, whereas with delegation you can only add behavior.

When an overridden method starts with a call to the method to be overridden in the base class, it's functionally equivalent to using delegation rather than method overriding. It's traditional, however, to use method overriding in the case of control development, to have a uniform notation for event handling.

Be careful during method overriding, because if the call to the overridden method is omitted, the corresponding delegate event isn't fired: delegate events are invoked by the event handlers of the base classes.

Let's look at how you handle the mouse-move events and the use of the mouse wheel. When the wheel of the mouse is scrolled, the control adjusts the scale factor to zoom in or out of the current view. To understand how this method works, you need to know how to decide which portion of the data is made available through the view of the control. You use two fields called initView and visibleSamples. Because you can't assume that all the samples fit in the control's display, the former indicates the time (in the time scale of the samples) corresponding to the leftmost visible value, and the latter indicates the number of time units in the unit scale of samples that should be visible. Zooming is performed by changing the density of time units to be displayed inside the viewport.

The last method of Listing 11-3 is GetTime: it converts the time unit of samples in microseconds using a scale factor that is one of the configuration properties made available by the control.

Listing 11-3. Extract of the Controller of the GraphControl Class

```
override x.OnMouseWheel (e:MouseEventArgs) =
    base.OnMouseWheel(e)
    x.Zoom(e.Delta)

override x.OnSizeChanged (e:EventArgs) =
    base.OnSizeChanged(e)
    x.Invalidate()

member x.Zoom (amount:int) =
    let newVisibleSamples = max 5 (visibleSamples + amount)
    if (initView - startTime < 0L) then
        let e = initView + int64(visibleSamples)
        initView <- startTime - int64(newVisibleSamples) + e
        visibleSamples <- newVisibleSamples
        x.Invalidate()

member x.AddSample (time:int64, value:float32) =
    if (value < absMin) then absMin <- value
    if (value > absMax) then absMax <- value
    if (data.Count > 0) then
        initView <- initView + time - data.Last.Time
    data.AddSample(time, value)
    x.Invalidate()

member x.GetTime (time:int64) =
    DateTime(max 0L time * int64(timeScale))
```

Building the GraphControl: The View

The view of the GraphControl is entirely contained within the OnPaint method, which is invoked when the GUI needs to repaint the content of the control or when an invocation of the Invalidate method occurs. Listing 11-4 shows the full code for this method. Programming graphical controls can get complicated, and often the code is factorized further using functions.

The OnPaint method begins computing some information such as the rectangles containing the string with the values to be displayed. The dimension of a string depends on the font used for display and the particular device context used to render it. You rely on the MeasureString method of the Graphics object you received from the GUI. You compute the plotBox rectangle, which represents the area where you draw the data; it's obtained by removing from the dimension of the control the margins specified in the configuration and the space required by the labels if visible. You later set an appropriate coordinate system on the device context so that the drawing primitives render in this new system:

```
g.TranslateTransform(float32(plotBox.Left), float32(x.Height - plotBox.Top))
g.ScaleTransform(1.0f, -1.0f)
```

You translate the origin of the coordinate system in the lower-left vertex of the margins rectangle. You also flip the y axis by setting a scale transform that inverts the direction, multiplying y coordinates by –1.0f; in this way, you obtain a coordinate system oriented as in mathematics. Coordinate transformation is supported by Windows Forms on the `Graphics` object: all the coordinates specified in the drawing primitives are affected by a transformation matrix stored in the device context. Once set, a transformation of the library takes care of the calculations necessary to rotate, translate, and scale all the objects.

After clearing the background using the `Background` color property, you draw the various lines such as the axes and the labels depending on the configuration settings specified by setting the control's properties. This is the typical structure of a paint method, where the model is tested to decide what should be drawn and the style to be used.

The drawing of the data samples is controlled by the `timePerUnit` and `pixelsPerUnit` variables, and then the inner recursive function `drawSamples` selects the visible samples and uses the `DataSamples` object to compute results. You rely on the ability of the `DataSamples` class to interpolate data and not have to deal with discrete samples.

The core business of the paint method is often simple (having paid attention when you defined the model and the controller of the control); it quickly becomes entangled in testing all the configuration properties to determine how the control should be rendered.

Listing 11-4. Drawing the Control

```
override x.OnPaint (e:PaintEventArgs) =
    let g = e.Graphics

    // A helper function to size up strings
    let measurestring s = g.MeasureString(s, x.Font)

    // Work out the size of the box to show the values
    let valBox =
        let minbox = measurestring (String.Format(verticalLabelFormat, lastMin))
        let maxbox = measurestring (String.Format(verticalLabelFormat, lastMax))
        let vbw = max minbox.Width maxbox.Width
        let vbh = max minbox.Height maxbox.Height
        SizeF(vbw, vbh)

    // Work out the size of the box to show the times
    let timeBox =
        let lasttime = x.GetTime(initView + int64(visibleSamples))
        let timelbl = String.Format(timeFormat, lasttime)
        measurestring timelbl

    // Work out the plot area for the graph
    let plotBox =
        let ltm = leftTopMargin
        let rbm = rightBottomMargin

        let ltm,rbm =
            let ltm = Size(width=max ltm.Width (int(valBox.Width)+5),
                           height=max ltm.Height (int(valBox.Height/2.0f) + 2))
            let rbm = Size(width=rightBottomMargin.Width,
                           height=max rbm.Height (int(timeBox.Height) + 5))
            ltm,rbm

        // Since we invert y axis use Top instead of Bottom and vice versa
        Rectangle(ltm.Width, rbm.Height,
                  x.Width - ltm.Width - rbm.Width,
                  x.Height - ltm.Height - rbm.Height)
```

```
// The time interval per visible sample
let timePerUnit =
    let samplew = float32(visibleSamples) / float32(plotBox.Width)
    max 1.0f samplew

// The pixel interval per visible sample
let pixelsPerUnit =
    let pixelspan = float32(plotBox.Width) / float32(visibleSamples)
    max 1.0f pixelspan

// Compute the range we need to plot
let (lo, hi) = data.FindMinMax(int64(timePerUnit),
                               initView,
                               initView + int64(visibleSamples),
                               minVisibleValue,
                               maxVisibleValue)

// Save the range to help with computing sizes next time around
lastMin <- lo; lastMax <- hi

// We use these graphical resources during plotting
use linePen  = new Pen(x.ForeColor)
use axisPen  = new Pen(axisColor)
use beginPen = new Pen(beginColor)
use gridPen  = new Pen(Color.FromArgb(127, axisColor),
                       DashStyle=DashStyle.Dash)
use fontColor = new SolidBrush(axisColor)

// Draw the title
if (x.Text <> null && x.Text <> string.Empty) then

    let sz = measurestring x.Text
    let mw = (float32(plotBox.Width) - sz.Width) / 2.0f
    let tm = float32(plotBox.Bottom - plotBox.Height)

    let p = PointF(float32(plotBox.Left) + mw, tm)
    g.DrawString(x.Text, x.Font, new SolidBrush(x.ForeColor), p)

// Draw the labels
let nly = int((float32(plotBox.Height) /valBox.Height) / 3.0f)
let nlx = int((float32(plotBox.Width) / timeBox.Width) / 3.0f)
let pxly = plotBox.Height / max nly 1
let pxlx = plotBox.Width / max nlx 1
let dvy = (hi - lo) / float32(nly)
let dvx = float32(visibleSamples) / float32(nlx)
let drawString (s:string) (xp:float32) (yp:float32) =
    g.DrawString(s,x.Font,fontColor,xp,yp)

// Draw the value (y) labels
for i = 0 to nly do
  let liney = i * pxly + int(valBox.Height / 2.0f) + 2
  let lblfmt = verticalLabelFormat
  let posy = float32(x.Height - plotBox.Top - i * pxly)
```

```
    let label = String.Format(lblfmt, float32(i) * dvy + lo)
    drawString label (float32(plotBox.Left) - valBox.Width)
                     (posy - valBox.Height / 2.0f)

    if (i = 0 ||((i > 0) && (i < nly))) then
       g.DrawLine(gridPen, plotBox.Left,liney,plotBox.Right, liney)

// Draw the time (x) labels
for i = 0 to nlx do
   let linex = i * pxlx + int(timeBox.Width / 2.0f) + 2
   let time = int64(float32(i) * dvx + float32(initView))
   let label = String.Format(timeFormat, x.GetTime(time))

   if (time > 0L) then
      drawString label
            (float32(plotBox.Left + i * pxlx) + timeBox.Width / 2.0f)
            (float32(x.Height - plotBox.Top + 2))

// Set a transform on the graphics state to make drawing in the
// plotBox simpler
g.TranslateTransform(float32(plotBox.Left),
                        float32(x.Height - plotBox.Top));
g.ScaleTransform(1.0f, -1.0f);

// Draw the plotBox of the plot area
g.DrawLine(axisPen, 0, 0, 0, plotBox.Height)
g.DrawLine(axisPen, 0, 0, plotBox.Width, 0)
g.DrawLine(axisPen, plotBox.Width, 0, plotBox.Width, plotBox.Height)
g.DrawLine(axisPen, 0, plotBox.Height, plotBox.Width, plotBox.Height)


// Draw the vertical lines in the plotBox
let px = plotBox.Width / (verticalLines + 1)
for i = 1 to verticalLines do
    g.DrawLine(gridPen, i*px, 0, i*px, plotBox.Height)

// Draw the 'begin' marker that shows where data begins
if (initView - startTime <= 0L) then
    let off = float32(Math.Abs(x.StartTime - initView))
    let sx = int((off/timePerUnit) * pixelsPerUnit)
    g.DrawLine(beginPen, sx, 0, sx, plotBox.Height)

// Draw the 'zero' horizontal line if it's visible
if (hi <> lo && lo < 0.0f) then
    let sy = int((float32(plotBox.Height)/(hi - lo))*(0.0f - lo))
    g.DrawLine(axisPen, 0, sy, plotBox.Width, sy)

// Draw the visible data samples
let rec drawSamples i pos =
    if (i < (float32(plotBox.Width) / pixelsPerUnit) &&
        pos <= (initView + int64 visibleSamples - int64 timePerUnit)) then

        if (pos >= 0L) then
```

```
            let dh = float32(plotBox.Height) / (hi - lo)
            let sx = int(pixelsPerUnit * i)
            let dx = int(pixelsPerUnit * (i + 1.0f))
            let sy = int(dh * (data.GetValue(pos) - lo))
            let dy = int(dh * (data.GetValue(pos + int64 timePerUnit) - lo))
            g.DrawLine(linePen, sx, sy, dx, dy);

        drawSamples (i + 1.0f) (pos + int64 timePerUnit)

    drawSamples 0.0f initView
```

Double Buffering

Flickering is a very annoying phenomenon of graphical applications. It happens when two updates of a graphical element are interleaved by a refresh of its background. The graphic adapter sends the video signal to the display, reading bytes from video memory at a given frequency that is different than the update frequency of the paint message.

Flickering happens during animations when a pixel is cleared with the background color and then with the desired one. The graphic adapter may display the pixel before the update, making it blink. A standard technique to avoid this phenomenon is known as *double buffering*: it consists of performing the drawing primitives into a bitmap offscreen; then, when the entire drawing is finished, the bitmap is drawn.

You can easily implement double buffering explicitly, although modern frameworks provide support for it. The example uses the SetStyle method inherited from UserControl to enable implicit support for double buffering. If you comment the two invocations to that method, you see flickering in action.

Putting It Together

The following code uses the control that defines the application shown in Figure 11-6:

```
let form = new Form(Text="Chart test",Size=Size(800, 600),Visible=true,TopMost=true)
let graph = new GraphControl(VisibleSamples=60, Dock=DockStyle.Fill)
let properties = new PropertyGrid(Dock=DockStyle.Fill)
let timer = new Timer(Interval=200)
let container = new SplitContainer(Dock=DockStyle.Fill, SplitterDistance=350)

// We use a split container to divide the area into two parts
container.Panel1.Controls.Add(graph)
container.Panel2.Controls.Add(properties)


// Configure the property grid to display only properties in the
// category "Graph Style"
properties.SelectedObject <- graph
let graphStyleCat = (CategoryAttribute("Graph Style") :> Attribute)
properties.BrowsableAttributes <- AttributeCollection([| graphStyleCat |])
form.Controls.Add(container)
let rnd = new Random()
```

```
let time = ref 0
// A timer is used to simulate incoming data
timer.Tick.Add(fun _ ->
    incr time
    let v = 48.0 + 2.0 * rnd.NextDouble()
    graph.AddSample(int64(!time),float32(v)))
timer.Start()
form.Disposed.Add(fun _ -> timer.Stop())
```

The form uses a SplitContainer control to define two areas, one for GraphControl and the other for a PropertyGrid control. A timer object is used to add samples periodically, and you use the AddSample method to add random samples to the control.

The PropertyGrid Control

PropertyGrid is a graphic control that lets you inspect object properties at runtime and change them, as shown in the right side of the window in Figure 11-6. You set the SelectedObject property to indicate the control to display, in this case the GraphControl.

PropertyGrid uses the reflection abilities of the Common Language Runtime to dynamically inspect the object and generate the visual grid. By default, the control displays the properties of the given object annotated using the BrowsableAttribute custom attribute. You set the BrowsableAttributes property to indicate you're interested in displaying only the properties annotated as [<Category("Graph Style")>].

Not all types can be edited from the PropertyGrid, although the control can deal with many. A property of type Color, for instance, causes the grid to display the preview of the color and lets you define the value several ways, including the Color Chooser dialog box.

Creating a Mandelbrot Viewer

Fractals are one of the diamonds of mathematics. They show the beauty of mathematical structures visually, which allows non-experts to see something that is often hidden by formulas that few really appreciate. The Mandelbrot set is one of the most famous fractals. This section shows how to develop an application to browse this set. The result is shown in Figure 11-7.

This application adopts the *delegation* programming style, subscribing to events rather than using inheritance to override the behavior of a component. This allows you to develop the application interactively using fsi.exe. This is a good example of how effectively you can use F# to develop an application interactively while retaining the performance of a compiled language, which is extremely important in such CPU-intensive tasks as computing the points of the Mandelbrot set.

Figure 11-7. The Mandelbrot viewer in action

Computing Mandelbrot

First you need to be familiar with the math required to generate the Mandelbrot set. The set is defined over the set of complex numbers, which is an extension of the real numbers, allowing computation of square roots over negative numbers. A complex number has the following form, where a and b are real numbers and i is the imaginary unit (by definition, $i^2 = -1$):

```
c = a + bi
```

Using standard algebraic calculations, you can define the sum and product of these numbers:

```
c₁+c₂ = (a₁+a₂) + i(b₁+b₂)
c₁·c₂ = (a₁·a₂ - b₁·b₂) + i(a₁·b₂ + a₂·b₁)
```

Because you have two components in the definition of the number, you can graphically represent complex numbers using a plane.

This Mandelbrot viewer shows a portion of the complex plane, where each point in the plane is colored according to a relation that defines the Mandelbrot set. The relation is based on the following iterative definition:

$$M(c) = \begin{cases} z_0 = c \\ z_{i+1} = z_i^2 + c \end{cases}$$

A complex number belongs to the Mandelbrot set if z_n converges for n. You can test each number c in the complex plane and decide whether the number belongs to the Mandelbrot set. Because it's not practical to perform an infinite computation to test each number of the complex plane, there is an approximation of the test based on a theorem that if the distance of z_i from the origin passes 2, then the sequence will diverge and the corresponding z_0 won't belong to the set.

The code to compute membership of the Mandelbrot set is as follows:

```
open System.Numerics

let sqrMod (x:Complex) = x.Real * x.Real + x.Imaginary * x.Imaginary
let rec mandel maxit (z:Complex) (c: Complex) count =
    if (sqrMod(z) < 4.0) &&  (count < maxit) then
        mandel maxit ((z * z) + c) c (count + 1)
    else count
```

You can create a simple visual representation of the Mandelbrot set by coloring all the points belonging to the set. In this way, you obtain the black portion of Figure 11-7. How can you obtain the richness of color? The trick is to color points depending on how fast the sequence reaches the distance of 2 from the origin. You use 250 colors and map the [0, maxit] interval to the [0, 250] discrete color interval.

Setting Colors

In order for the Mandelbrot viewer application to have appealing coloring, you need to produce some form of continuity in the color variation in the chosen range. You use an array of colors to store these values, but you need a procedure to fill this array so that colors change continuously.

Colors in the Red Green Blue (RGB) space used in the graphics libraries are known to define a color space that isn't perceived as continuous by human vision. A color space known to be more effective in this respect is the Hue Saturation Value (HSV), where a color is defined in terms of hue, color saturation, and the value of luminance (see Figure 11-8). This model was inspired by the method used by painters to create colors in oil painting.

Figure 11-8. The RGB (left) and HSV (right) color spaces and their geometric representation

Figure 11-8 shows a typical geometric representation of the two color spaces. In the RGB color model, the three axes represent the three base colors varying from black to the full color; in the HSV space, the angle is used to indicate the hue, the distance from the axis of the cone represents the saturation, and the value corresponds to the height of the point inside the cone.

You can define a conversion from RGB color space to HSV, and vice versa. Listing 11-5 shows the F# functions performing the conversions between the two models. These functions assume the three components R, G, and B are in the interval [0, 1] rather than integers between 0 and 255.

Listing 11-5. Conversion from RGB to HSV, and Vice Versa

```
let RGBtoHSV (r, g, b) =
    let (m:float) = min r (min g b)
    let (M:float) = max r (max g b)
    let delta = M - m
    let posh (h:float) = if h < 0.0 then h + 360.0 else h
    let deltaf (f:float) (s:float) = (f - s) / delta
    if M = 0.0 then (-1.0, 0.0, M) else
        let s = (M - m) / M
        if r = M then (posh(60.0 * (deltaf g b)), s, M)
        elif g = M then (posh(60.0 * (2.0 + (deltaf b r))), s, M)
        else (posh(60.0 * (4.0 + (deltaf r g))), s, M)

let HSVtoRGB (h, s, v) =
    if s = 0.0 then (v, v, v) else
    let hs = h / 60.0
    let i = floor (hs)
    let f = hs - i
    let p = v * ( 1.0 - s )
    let q = v * ( 1.0 - s * f )
```

```
let t = v * ( 1.0 - s * ( 1.0 - f ))
match int i with
    | 0 -> (v, t, p)
    | 1 -> (q, v, p)
    | 2 -> (p, v, t)
    | 3 -> (p, q, v)
    | 4 -> (t, p, v)
    | _ -> (v, p, q)
```

To let users choose the coloring of the set, you create an array of 10 functions, given an integer between 0 and 250, for a corresponding color. The default color function is based on the HSV color model; it uses the input parameter to set the hue of the color, leaving the saturation and luminance at the maximum values. The other functions use the RGB color space, following directions in the color cube. You use the createPalette function to generate the color palette that is used while drawing fractal points; the palette mutable variable holds this palette. Listing 11-6 shows the code that deals with colors. The pickColor function is responsible for mapping the iteration, it, at which the computation of the Mandelbrot set terminates given the maximum number of iterations allowed, maxit.

Listing 11-6. Color Palette Definition

```
let makeColor (r, g, b) =
    Color.FromArgb(int32(r * 255.0), int32(g * 255.0), int32(b * 255.0))

let defaultColor i = makeColor(HSVtoRGB(360.0 * (float i / 250.0), 1.0, 1.0))

let coloring =
    [| defaultColor;
        (fun i -> Color.FromArgb(i, i, i));
        (fun i -> Color.FromArgb(i, 0, 0));
        (fun i -> Color.FromArgb(0, i, 0));
        (fun i -> Color.FromArgb(0, 0, i));
        (fun i -> Color.FromArgb(i, i, 0));
        (fun i -> Color.FromArgb(i, 250 - i, 0));
        (fun i -> Color.FromArgb(250 - i, i, i));
        (fun i -> if i % 2 = 0 then Color.White else Color.Black);
        (fun i -> Color.FromArgb(250 - i, 250 - i, 250 - i))
    |]

let createPalette c =
    Array.init 253 (function
            | 250 -> Color.Black
            | 251 -> Color.White
            | 252 -> Color.LightGray
            | i ->   c i)


let mutable palette = createPalette coloring.[0]

let pickColor maxit it =
    palette.[int(250.0 * float it / float maxit)]
```

Creating the Visualization Application

You're now ready to implement the graphical application. The basic idea is to map a rectangle of the complex plane in the client area of your form. Each point of your window corresponds to a complex number and is colored according to the value computed by the mandel function.

A typical value for maxit is 150 for the initial rendering of the Mandelbrot set, although it should be incremented when zooming into the fractal. The total computation required to generate an entire image is significant; therefore, you can't rely on the main thread to perform the computation of the various points. It's important to recall that event handlers are invoked by the graphical interface's thread, and if this thread is used to perform heavy computations, the application windows won't respond to other events.

You introduce a thread responsible for performing the computations required by the Mandelbrot set so that the GUI thread can continue to handle events. (Chapter 13 discusses threads in more detail.) Here, you use shared memory to communicate the results between the threads by using a bitmap image in memory, referenced by the bitmap variable, which is updated by the thread performing the computation task and read by the GUI thread when the form must be painted. The bitmap is convenient because you need a matrix of points to be colored, and the device context is designed to avoid pixel coloring to be device independent (it doesn't provide a SetColor(x, y) operation). To avoid race conditions, you use the lock function to guarantee exclusive access to the bitmap shared between the two threads. Chapter 13 looks at this in more detail. The thread responsible for the set computation executes the following function:

```
let run filler (form:#Form) (bitmap:Bitmap) (tlx, tly) (brx, bry) =
    let dx = (brx - tlx) / float bmpw
    let dy = (tly - bry) / float bmph
    let maxit = iterations (tlx, tly) (brx, bry)
    let x = 0
    let y = 0
    let transform x y = new Complex(tlx + (float x) * dx, tly - (float y) * dy )
    form.Invoke(new MethodInvoker(fun () ->
        form.Text <- sprintf "Mandelbrot set [it: %d] (%f, %f) -> (%f, %f)"
                        maxit tlx tly brx bry
    )) |> ignore
    filler maxit transform
    timer.Enabled <- false
```

You use dx and dy variables to map the x and y coordinates of the bitmap into the complex plane. You then invoke the filler function responsible for performing the calculation. There are different possible filling strategies to compute the colors of the set; the straightforward approach is left to right and top to bottom, implemented by the linearFill function:

```
let linearFill (bw:int) (bh:int) maxit map =
    for y = 0 to bh - 1 do
        for x = 0 to bw - 1 do
            let c = mandel maxit Complex.Zero (map x y) 0
            lock bitmap (fun () -> bitmap.SetPixel(x, y, pickColor maxit c))
```

Another typical filling strategy is to gradually refine the set by computing points in blocks and filling the blocks of the appropriate color; then, the missing points are computed by refining the block size. Using this strategy, you can provide a quick preview of the fractal without having to wait for the entire computation. The blockFill function implements this strategy:

```
let blockFill (bw:int) (bh:int) maxit map =
    let rec fillBlock first sz x y =
```

```
        if x < bw then
            let c = mandel maxit Complex.Zero (map x y) 0
            lock bitmap (fun () ->
                let g = Graphics.FromImage(bitmap)
                g.FillRectangle(new SolidBrush(pickColor maxit c), x, y, sz, sz)
                g.Dispose()
            )
            fillBlock first sz (if first || ((y / sz) % 2 = 1) then x + sz
                                else x + 2 * sz) y
        elif y < bh then
            fillBlock first sz (if first || ((y / sz) % 2 = 0) then 0 else sz)
                      (y + sz)
        elif sz > 1 then
            fillBlock false (sz / 2) (sz / 2) 0

    fillBlock true 64 0 0
```

The variable fillFun is used to store the current filling function:

```
let mutable fillFun = blockFill
```

You clear the bitmap by obtaining a device context to the bitmap and clearing it. The global variable bitmap is used to access the image from the code; this is an effective choice to speed up the development of the application. However, this technique can be a problem from a software engineering standpoint because the program is less modular and the mutable state isn't encapsulated:

```
let clearOffScreen (b : Bitmap) =
    use g = Graphics.FromImage(b)
    g.Clear(Color.White)

let mutable bitmap = new Bitmap(form.Width, form.Height)
let mutable bmpw = form.Width
let mutable bmph = form.Height
```

To refresh the application form while the fractal computation is ongoing, you use a timer that triggers a refresh of the form every tenth of a second. The paint function draws the bitmap that is updated by the worker thread:

```
let paint (g: Graphics) =
    lock bitmap (fun () -> g.DrawImage(bitmap, 0, 0))
    g.DrawRectangle(Pens.Black, rect)
    g.FillRectangle(new SolidBrush(Color.FromArgb(128, Color.White)), rect)

let timer = new Timer(Interval=100)
timer.Tick.Add(fun _ -> form.Invalidate() )

let stopWorker () =
    if worker <> Thread.CurrentThread then
        worker.Abort()
        worker <- Thread.CurrentThread
```

The drawMandel function is responsible for starting the rendering process:

```
let drawMandel () =
    let bf = fillFun bmpw bmph
    stopWorker();
    timer.Enabled <- true
    worker <- new Thread(fun () -> run bf form bitmap tl br)
    worker.IsBackground <- true
    worker.Priority <- ThreadPriority.Lowest
    worker.Start()
```

Creating the Application Plumbing

Now that you've defined the architecture of the application, you can define the graphical aspects, the form, and the menus, as well as how users interact with the application. The code is similar to the previous applications, as shown in Listing 11-7. Note two aspects: the `rect` variable contains the current selection, and it's drawn as a rectangle filled with transparent white; the application uses the clipboard to store and retrieve the coordinates of a particular fractal view or save the current state of the drawn bitmap. When Ctrl+C is pressed, a small XML document similar to the following is saved to the clipboard:

```
<Mandel iter="1000">
  <topleft>
    <re>-7.474213339220139e-001</re>
    <im>1.64667039391667e-001</im>
  </topleft>
  <bottomright>
    <re>-7.47082959511805e-001</re>
    <im>1.64413254610417e-001</im>
  </bottomright>
</Mandel>
```

The saved parameters are the most compact representation of the current view and are loaded back if Ctrl+V is pressed; this way, you can save the state of navigation. You save and read text from the clipboard using the `Clipboard` class's `SetText` and `GetText` methods. When the Ctrl+Shift+C key sequence is pressed, the current bitmap is copied to the clipboard using the `SetDataObject` method; the bitmap can be pasted in any program capable of pasting images.

The selection rectangle is updated by the mouse event handlers. You obtain the zoom facility by setting the bounds of the complex plane defined by the variables `tl` and `br`.

Listing 11-7. Setup of the Application Form and Event Handling

```
type CanvasForm() as x =
    inherit Form()
    do x.SetStyle(ControlStyles.OptimizedDoubleBuffer, true)
    override x.OnPaintBackground(args) = ()

// Creates the Form
let form = new CanvasForm(Width=800, Height=600,Text="Mandelbrot set")

let mutable worker = Thread.CurrentThread


let mutable startsel = Point.Empty
let mutable rect = Rectangle.Empty
```

```
let mutable tl = (-3.0, 2.0)
let mutable br = (2.0, -2.0)

let mutable menuIterations = 150

let iterations (tlx, tly) (brx, bry) =
    menuIterations

let setCoord (tlx:float, tly:float) (brx:float, bry:float)  =
    let dx = (brx - tlx) / float bmpw
    let dy = (tly - bry) / float bmph
    let mapx x = tlx + float x * dx
    let mapy y = tly - float y * dy
    tl <- (mapx rect.Left, mapy rect.Top)
    br <- (mapx rect.Right, mapy rect.Bottom)

let ensureAspectRatio (tlx:float, tly:float) (brx:float, bry:float) =
    let ratio = (float bmpw / float bmph)
    let w, h = abs(brx - tlx), abs(tly - bry)
    if ratio * h > w then
        br <- (tlx + h * ratio, bry)
    else
        br <- (brx,tly - w / ratio)

let updateView () =
    if rect <> Rectangle.Empty then setCoord tl br
    ensureAspectRatio tl br
    rect <- Rectangle.Empty
    stopWorker()
    clearOffScreen bitmap
    drawMandel()
let click (arg:MouseEventArgs) =
    if rect.Contains(arg.Location) then
        updateView()
    else
        form.Invalidate()
        rect <- Rectangle.Empty
        startsel <- arg.Location

let mouseMove (arg:MouseEventArgs) =
    if arg.Button = MouseButtons.Left then
        let tlx = min startsel.X arg.X
        let tly = min startsel.Y arg.Y
        let brx = max startsel.X arg.X
        let bry = max startsel.Y arg.Y
        rect <- new Rectangle(tlx, tly, brx - tlx, bry - tly)
        form.Invalidate()

let resize () =
    if bmpw <> form.ClientSize.Width ||
       bmph <> form.ClientSize.Height then
         stopWorker()
         rect <- form.ClientRectangle
```

```
            bitmap <- new Bitmap(form.ClientSize.Width, form.ClientSize.Height)
            bmpw <- form.ClientSize.Width
            bmph <- form.ClientSize.Height

            updateView()
let zoom amount (tlx, tly) (brx, bry) =
    let w, h = abs(brx - tlx), abs(tly - bry)
    let nw, nh = amount * w, amount * h
    tl <- (tlx + (w - nw) / 2., tly - (h - nh) / 2.)
    br <- (brx - (w - nw) / 2., bry + (h - nh) / 2.)
    rect <- Rectangle.Empty
    updateView()

let selectDropDownItem (l:ToolStripMenuItem) (o:ToolStripMenuItem) =
    for el in l.DropDownItems do
      let item = (el :?> ToolStripMenuItem)
      item.Checked <- (o = item)
let setFillMode (p:ToolStripMenuItem) (m:ToolStripMenuItem) filler _ =
    if (not m.Checked) then
        selectDropDownItem p m
        fillFun <- filler
        drawMandel()

let setupMenu () =
  let m = new MenuStrip()
  let f = new ToolStripMenuItem("&File")
  let c = new ToolStripMenuItem("&Settings")
  let e = new ToolStripMenuItem("&Edit")
  let ext = new ToolStripMenuItem("E&xit")
  let cols = new ToolStripComboBox("ColorScheme")
  let its = new ToolStripComboBox("Iterations")
  let copybmp = new ToolStripMenuItem("Copy &bitmap")
  let copy = new ToolStripMenuItem("&Copy")
  let paste = new ToolStripMenuItem("&Paste")
  let zoomin = new ToolStripMenuItem("Zoom &In")
  let zoomout = new ToolStripMenuItem("Zoom &Out")
  let fillMode = new ToolStripMenuItem("Fill mode")
  let fillModeLinear = new ToolStripMenuItem("Line")
  let fillModeBlock = new ToolStripMenuItem("Block")

  let itchg = fun _ ->
    menuIterations <- System.Int32.Parse(its.Text)
    stopWorker()
    drawMandel()
    c.HideDropDown()
  ext.Click.Add(fun _ -> form.Dispose()) |> ignore

  copybmp.Click.Add(fun _ -> Clipboard.SetDataObject(bitmap))|> ignore
  copybmp.ShortcutKeyDisplayString <- "Ctrl+Shift+C"
  copybmp.ShortcutKeys <- Keys.Control ||| Keys.Shift ||| Keys.C

  copy.Click.Add(fun _ ->
```

```fsharp
        let maxit = (iterations tl br)
        let tlx, tly = tl
        let brx, bry = br
        Clipboard.SetText
            (sprintf "<Mandel iter=\"%d\">
                            <topleft><re>%.14e</re><im>%.14e</im></topleft>
                            <bottomright><re>%.14e</re><im>%.14e</im></bottomright>
                      </Mandel>" maxit tlx tly brx bry)
) |> ignore
copy.ShortcutKeyDisplayString <- "Ctrl+C"
copy.ShortcutKeys <- Keys.Control ||| Keys.C

paste.Click.Add(fun _ ->
    if Clipboard.ContainsText() then
        let doc = new XmlDocument()
        try
          doc.LoadXml(Clipboard.GetText())
          menuIterations <-
              int (doc.SelectSingleNode("/Mandel").Attributes.["iter"].Value)
          tl <- (float (doc.SelectSingleNode("//topleft/re").InnerText),
                 float (doc.SelectSingleNode("//topleft/im").InnerText))
          br <- (float (doc.SelectSingleNode("//bottomright/re").InnerText),
                 float (doc.SelectSingleNode("//bottomright/im").InnerText))
          rect <- Rectangle.Empty
          updateView()
        with _ -> ()
) |> ignore
paste.ShortcutKeyDisplayString <- "Ctrl+V"
paste.ShortcutKeys <- Keys.Control ||| Keys.V
zoomin.Click.Add(fun _ -> zoom 0.9 tl br) |> ignore
zoomin.ShortcutKeyDisplayString <- "Ctrl+T"
zoomin.ShortcutKeys <- Keys.Control ||| Keys.T
zoomout.Click.Add(fun _ -> zoom 1.25 tl br) |> ignore
zoomout.ShortcutKeyDisplayString <- "Ctrl+W"
zoomout.ShortcutKeys <- Keys.Control ||| Keys.W

for x in [ f;e;c ] do m.Items.Add(x) |> ignore
f.DropDownItems.Add(ext) |> ignore
let tsi x = (x :> ToolStripItem)
for x in [ tsi cols; tsi its; tsi fillMode] do c.DropDownItems.Add(x) |> ignore
for x in [ tsi copy; tsi zoomin; tsi zoomout ] do e.DropDownItems.Add(x) |> ignore
for x in ["HSL Color"; "Gray"; "Red"; "Green"] do cols.Items.Add(x) |> ignore
fillMode.DropDownItems.Add(fillModeLinear) |> ignore
fillMode.DropDownItems.Add(fillModeBlock) |> ignore
cols.SelectedIndex <- 0
cols.DropDownStyle <- ComboBoxStyle.DropDownList

cols.SelectedIndexChanged.Add(fun _ ->
  palette <- createPalette coloring.[cols.SelectedIndex]
  stopWorker()
  drawMandel()
  c.HideDropDown()
)
```

```
    its.Text <- string_of_int menuIterations
    its.DropDownStyle <- ComboBoxStyle.DropDown
    for x in [ "150"; "250"; "500"; "1000" ] do its.Items.Add(x) |> ignore
    its.LostFocus.Add(itchg)
    its.SelectedIndexChanged.Add(itchg)
    fillModeBlock.Checked <- true
    fillModeLinear.Click.Add(setFillMode fillMode fillModeLinear linearFill)
    fillModeBlock.Click.Add(setFillMode fillMode fillModeBlock blockFill)
    m

clearOffScreen bitmap
form.MainMenuStrip <- setupMenu()
form.Controls.Add(form.MainMenuStrip)
form.MainMenuStrip.RenderMode <- ToolStripRenderMode.System
form.Paint.Add(fun arg ->  paint arg.Graphics)
form.MouseDown.Add(click)
form.MouseMove.Add(mouseMove)
form.ResizeEnd.Add(fun _ -> resize())
form.Show()

Application.DoEvents()

drawMandel()

[<STAThread>]
do Application.Run(form)
```

You should use the program's last statement only if the application is compiled; with fsi.exe, it must be omitted. As already noted, the plumbing code is dominated by setting up menus and configuring the application form; the rest contains the event handlers that are registered with the various controls.

Windows Presentation Foundation

Microsoft introduced a new presentation framework called Windows Presentation Foundation (WPF) for programming graphical applications on the Windows platform with Windows Vista. It's not merely a new framework such as Windows Forms; rather than another layer on top of the traditional Win32 presentation system, it's a complete new rendering system that coexists with the traditional one.

■ **Note** WPF is a .NET framework and thus accessible to F# applications. In Visual Studio 2010, the tight integration with XAML markup language used by WPF isn't supported by the F# project system, and you should instead add your XAML files to your Visual Studio solution. You can use F# to develop Silverlight code, because Silverlight is a web plug-in featuring a subset of WPF capabilities.

At first sight, a WPF application doesn't differ much from a Windows Forms application. Here are few lines of code to open a window from F# Interactive:

```
#r "WindowsBase"
#r "PresentationCore"
#r "PresentationFramework"
#r "System.Xaml"

open System.Windows
open System.Windows.Controls

let w = new Window()

let b = new Button(Content="Hello from WPF!")
b.Click.Add(fun _ -> w.Close())

w.Content <- b
w.Show()
```

The application has an event loop (see the sidebar "WPF Event Loop") hosted by F# Interactive. With a few (very important) differences, you've created a window hosting a huge button that closes it when clicked.

WPF Event Loop

WPF applications have an event loop because events are still one of the foundations of this new presentation system; this event loop, however, differs from that used by Windows Forms applications. It's started through an instance of the `System.Windows.Application` class (note that in Windows Forms, the `System.Windows.Forms.Application` class is used as a singleton without the need to create instances).

To run the button example as a standalone application, you must add the same references to the F# project. And instead of the `w.Show()` method invocation, you can add the following lines:

```
let a = new Application()

[<STAThread>]
do a.Run(w) |> ignore
```

F# Interactive can host both Windows Forms and WPF event loops, so you can create windows using both frameworks, even at the same time. F# Interactive, however, uses Windows Forms by default. At the time of writing, the F# Power Pack includes a script `load_wpf.fsx` that you should load into F# Interactive using `#load "load_wpf.fsx"` to enable full WPF support. You must also explicitly refer to WPF assemblies before creating WPF objects.

It's reassuring that events are still there, even within a framework based on a different programming paradigm. Moreover, you still obtain interfaces by composing graphical controls and attaching to their event handlers. The button is the only control hosted by the window! You don't access a `Controls` property of the window to add the button to a list of children controls. Instead, you set all of the window content with a button, resulting in a huge button that occupies the window's entire client area.

WPF's layout model is completely different from that you've grown accustomed to using Windows Forms: objects are positioned by the container and don't have `Top` and `Left` properties to explicitly set a control position.

Layout is only one of many aspects of WPF that diverge from the traditional structure of graphic toolkits; this section introduces the most relevant. You're encouraged to look for more information about the framework in dedicated publications. The most important changes introduced by WPF are as follows:

- Retention-based device-independent rendering

- XML-based composition language

- Dependency properties and animations

When GUIs Meet the Web

The long-established model of GUI toolkits has its roots in a world very different from nowadays. Several of the assumptions made by these programming models are still true, but others no longer hold. There's an important point that you must always consider when working with WPF after any other graphical toolkit.

One of the authors was introduced to graphical programming during the 1980s, using Turbo Pascal, and was surprised that drawing primitives weren't retained by the system like console characters. But the situation was better than it was a few years later, on a MS-DOS PC with graphics: the screen buffer was owned by a single application, so redrawing was needed to remove a primitive and restore its background. With windowing systems, the user experience improved significantly for the user, but the situation worsened for the application programmer: the application's main control must be delegated to the graphical toolkit, and everything becomes an event. Events significantly optimize resource usage because applications are notified only when needed, so that a user can execute multiple applications simultaneously; but events are also used to optimize drawing resources through the paint architecture discussed previously. As you've seen, the GUI system sends the paint message to a window whenever its content needs to be updated; therefore, primitives aren't *retained* by the windowing system. It's up to you to issue them as necessary.

In essence, the familiar paint-event based paradigm you're used to exists because of the need to save memory when it's scarce; this is a form of Kolmogorov-style compression, where a program generates information instead of storing it. As illustrated by web browsers, today's computers have enough memory to change this underlying assumption and revise the original decision of who is responsible for retaining graphics primitives. With WPF, Microsoft decided to radically change the toolkit model and define a foundation based on the notion of graphics-primitive retention.

The following example shows how a typical drawing is performed by a WPF application:

```
#r "WindowsBase"
#r "PresentationCore"
#r "PresentationFramework"
#r "System.Xaml"

open System.Windows
open System.Windows.Controls
open System.Windows.Shapes
open System.Windows.Media

let w = new Window(Topmost=true)
w.Show()
let c = new Canvas()
w.Content <- c

let r = new Rectangle(Width=100.,Height=100.,RadiusX=5.,
                      RadiusY=5.,Stroke=Brushes.Black)
```

```
c.Children.Add(r)

let e = new Ellipse(Width=150.,Height=150.,Stroke=Brushes.Black)
c.Children.Add(e)
Canvas.SetLeft(e, 100.)
Canvas.SetTop(e, 100.)

e.MouseLeftButtonUp.Add(fun _ ->
  e.Fill <-
    if e.Fill = (Brushes.Yellow :> Brush) then Brushes.Red
    else Brushes.Yellow
)
```

At first, this example doesn't differ much from the one showing a button in a window: you create a
Canvas object, which is a container for multiple UI elements, and add two graphic objects. In the
Windows Form world, you'd think of two graphic controls used for drawing, although they wouldn't
blend because each traditional window is opaque. In fact, these two graphics primitives are
represented by two objects and are retained by the presentation system; pick correlation and event
dispatching are guaranteed by the graphical toolkit.

Note that the ellipse is an outline, so the click event is raised only by clicking the outline; when
the fill brush is specified, you can change the fill color by clicking inside the ellipse. Another relevant
aspect is the positioning of an element: there is no Left or Top property because it's the responsibility
of the container (in this case, the canvas) to lay out contained objects.

Drawing

An application can draw any shape by adding graphics primitives to a WPF window's *visual tree*.[3]
Because the system retains these primitives, you don't need to implement an event handler for the
paint message: it's up to the graphical toolkit to render the tree in the appropriate way whenever
needed. Problems such as visible primitives and efficient drawing fade away quickly and are dealt
with by the system; nevertheless, you're still responsible for using the visual tree.

Because graphics primitives are organized in a tree structure, it's natural to use an XML-based
language to initialize this tree with the window's initial state. WPF introduced the XAML language for this
purpose; it recalls HTML, though it was designed for defining rich UIs instead of hypertext. The drawing
example shown in the previous section can be expressed using the XAML markup in Listing 11-8.

Listing 11-8. *Example of a Window Definition Using XAML.*

```
<Window xmlns="http://schemas.microsoft.com/winfx/2006/xaml/presentation"
        xmlns:x="http://schemas.microsoft.com/winfx/2006/xaml"
        Title="MainWindow" Height="350" Width="525">
    <Canvas>
        <Rectangle Width="100" Height="100" Stroke="Black"
                   RadiusX="5" RadiusY="10"/>
        <Ellipse Name="Circle"
                 Canvas.Left="100" Canvas.Top="100"
                 Width="150" Height="150" Stroke="Black"/>
    </Canvas>
</Window>
```

---

[3] The visual tree plays a similar role to the DOM tree in Dynamic HTML applications.

The markup syntax is a wonderful tool for compacting several programming-language statements into a single line, because properties can be set as attributes. XAML adopts a well-defined bridge between the XML elements and the corresponding .NET classes and objects. Tag names are mapped onto classes and implicitly define instances, attributes are used to assign objects' properties, and attributes containing a dot are interpreted as static properties (for example, Canvas.Left and Canvas.Top). Each node may have a *name*, which is useful for retrieving a reference to the node; in this case, the ellipse element is named Circle.

Loading XAML into F# Applications

At the time of writing, the F# project system in Visual Studio 2010 doesn't include full XAML support. This means there is no WPF Visual Studio Wizard for the F# language. For C#, the compilation process for WPF applications involves a precompilation of XAML files in C# source files and an optimized representation of XAML called Binary XAML (BAML). The source-code generation has the goal of making it easier to interact with graphical objects defined within the XAML file using a mechanism successfully employed for ASP.NET files: *code behind*. Using the special attribute x:Class, you can indicate a class in which to inject the definition of graphical elements of the XAML file, so that C# methods can be referred to through XML attributes (to indicate event handlers) and XAML objects are exposed as fields. It's possible, however, to load XAML at runtime, letting F# applications benefit from the ability to use XAML UI definitions instead of having to manipulate WPF objects explicitly. The following is a simple example of a function that loads XAML markup from a file and, assuming it contains the definition of a window, converts the reference into an instance of the Window class:

```
open System.Windows
open System.Windows.Controls
open System.Windows.Markup
open System.Windows.Media
open System.Xml

let loadXamlWindow (filename:string) =
    let reader = XmlReader.Create(filename)
    XamlReader.Load(reader) :?> Window

let app = new Application()
let wnd = loadXamlWindow("Window.xaml")
```

You can use a WYSIWYG editor for XAML to visually author UIs. To load it in an F# application, you must ensure that the x:Class attribute is removed; otherwise, the Load method will raise an exception. Don't associate event handlers through the UI: they should be explicitly associated inside the F# code.

Using these functions, you can load any XAML fragment; in F#, the most common case is to load the definition of a window. Note that it's also possible to parse XAML code embedded in strings: for instance, in the resources embedded in the application or embedded as a string within the program. The rest of this chapter refers to this function without including its definition.

XAML has been rightly touted as separating the world of business logic from that of UI design, offering direct control to graphic designers through XAML and allowing programmers to rely on names to instrument graphical controls. The XAML and the names of graphical elements are the contract between programmers and designers, allowing for concurrent work on GUI application development. This approach has proven successful for the Web and shows that hardware is powerful enough to shift toward a more programmer-friendly paradigm.

XAML can be generated and manipulated from a number of graphical editors, including Visual Studio and Microsoft Expression Blend. Even though full support isn't yet available for developing WPF applications using F#, it's easy to load XAML-based UIs into F# applications; this largely addresses the lack of graphical environments for developing GUIs (see the sidebar "Loading XAML into F# Applications"). Assuming that the XAML in Listing 11-8 is saved in a file named window.xaml, you can use it from F# as follows (assuming the appropriate references and the loadXamlWindow function are defined):

```
let w = loadXamlWindow(@"window.xaml")
w.Show()

let e = w.FindName("Circle") :?> Ellipse

e.MouseLeftButtonUp.Add(fun _ ->
  e.Fill <-
    if e.Fill = (Brushes.Yellow :> Brush) then Brushes.Red
    else Brushes.Yellow
)
```

Note that you use the FindName method to find a reference to the ellipse object; this is how you can refer from F# code to elements defined in the XAML markup. Because you can define animations in markup and connect to user actions (for example, sliding or collapsing menus can be defined entirely in XAML), the number of statements needed to connect the F# state to the visual tree is small— drastically smaller than the amount of code needed to do GUIs in Windows Forms. Sometimes it may be useful to navigate the entire visual tree in which WPF stores the graphics primitives; the VisualTreeHelper class features navigation methods useful for doing so.

Drawing primitives refer to the coordinates of some coordinate space. Traditionally, computer programs relied on pixels, even though Win32 API supported different coordinate systems from the beginning. WPF features vector graphics, supporting affine transformations of the coordinate system (translation, rotation, scaling, and skew); the use of a pixel-based system seemed obsolete in a world where the dots per inch (dpi) of display devices changes significantly. The adopted unit is $1/96^{th}$ of an inch (in honor of the standard monitor resolution), whatever the target display device, including printers.

You can apply transformations to any subtree of the visual tree, transforming all the primitives, including those issued by contained controls.

Let's consider the XAML example shown in Listing 11-9. It uses a container that stacks graphical elements horizontally to lay out three elements: a block of text, a text box, and a line. Nodes may also have explicit names, like the TextBox node here. The application's output is shown in Figure 11-9, where the elements are rotated according to the indicated transformations: the container is laid out rotated 45 degrees counterclockwise, and the text box is rotated 90 degrees clockwise.

Listing 11-9. XAML Defining the Composition of Transformed Elements

```
<Window xmlns="http://schemas.microsoft.com/winfx/2006/xaml/presentation"
        xmlns:x="http://schemas.microsoft.com/winfx/2006/xaml"
        Title="MainWindow" Height="350" Width="525">
    <Canvas>
            <StackPanel Orientation="Horizontal" VerticalAlignment="Center">
                <StackPanel.LayoutTransform>
                    <RotateTransform Angle="-45"/>
                </StackPanel.LayoutTransform>
```

```
            <TextBlock>This is a test</TextBlock>
            <TextBox Name="Input">
                <TextBox.LayoutTransform>
                    <RotateTransform Angle="90"/>
                </TextBox.LayoutTransform>
                    Input here
            </TextBox>
            <Line X1="0" X2="50" Y1="0" Y2="50" Stroke="Black"/>
        </StackPanel>
    </Canvas>
</Window>
```

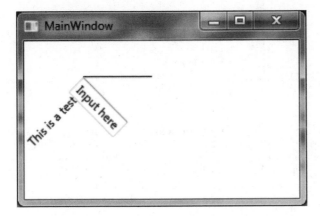

Figure 11-9. *F# application demonstrating the XAML*

Transformations are implemented using matrices, as already discussed for Windows Forms; you can use them to obtain nontrivial transformations of the coordinate space. These transformations affect the subtree rooted in the node to which they're applied and can be programmatically accessed through the LayoutTransform and RenderTransform properties; the former affects the layout computation, and the latter affects the final rendering, possibly overflowing the container node.

Drawing involves brushes and pens, which are similar to their Windows Forms counterparts.

Controls

The ability to instantiate and use existing controls is one of the pillars of user interfaces. In the earlier discussion of the difference between writing components and combining them, it was evident that a control in a traditional framework is *opaque*: the container allocates a rectangle and delegates event-handling and drawing to the window procedure coordinated by the event loop.

In WPF, things are less clear cut, which opens new horizons to graphical developers who appreciate the visual tree and the different role played by controls. To appreciate the extent of this statement, let's modify the example from Listing 11-9 by enclosing the StackPanel element in a Button element (add a <Button> tag immediately after <Canvas> and </Button> immediately before </Canvas>). The resulting window looks like the one shown in Figure 11-10: you've nested two controls, which is an almost impossible task in traditional graphical toolkits.

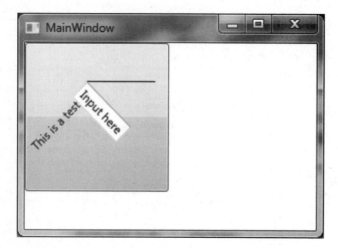

Figure 11-10. Nested controls in WPF

The designers of the WPF framework must have considered problems that never came up with traditional toolkits, given the system's ability to retain graphics primitives in the form of a tree. You can think of a button as a background shaped like a button, with the label in the middle; it can be defined as a subtree of the primitives needed to draw its borders and a placeholder in the middle to insert the label. In an opaque system, the content could be another rectangle but nothing more; in a retention-based system, you can replace the label node in the tree with an arbitrary complicated subtree.

You can display the visual tree of any WPF element using the static methods of the VisualTreeHelper class. The following F# function prints to the console (or in the F# Interactive tool window) the visual tree associated with a WPF element:

```
let ShowVisualTree(obj:DependencyObject) =
  let rec browse indentlvl node =
    let indent n = for i = 0 to (n - 1) do printf "  "
    let n = VisualTreeHelper.GetChildrenCount(node)

    indent indentlvl
    printfn "<%s%s>" (node.GetType().Name) (if n = 0 then "/" else "")
    for i = 0 to (n - 1) do
      browse (indentlvl + 1) (VisualTreeHelper.GetChild(node, i))
    if n > 0 then
      indent indentlvl
      printfn "</%s>" (node.GetType().Name)

  browse 0 obj
```

■ **Note** WPF also defines the *logical tree*, which is a simplified version of the visual tree that hides formatting nodes. The logical tree makes it easier to find relevant controls without having to deal with unneeded nodes.

The function implements a recursive visit to the visual tree rooted in the given element. If you pass the instance returned by loadXamlWindow, you get an idea of how many primitives are issued by the various controls you're using in the window. If you pass the instance of a button, perhaps found using the FindName method as you did earlier, you obtain output similar to the following:

```
<Button>
  <ButtonChrome>
    <ContentPresenter>
      <TextBlock/>
    </ContentPresenter>
  </ButtonChrome>
</Button>
```

ContentPresenter is the root of the subtree dedicated to the button content; the rest defines the graphics primitives surrounding the node. The ButtonChrome node refers to a class used to implement a specific theme; it's even possible to change the definition of the button without affecting its logic or its content. You can find more information about this ability of WPF in textbooks or online.

What are the consequences of a model in which controls are no longer black boxes? The most important is the notion of pick correlation: in the example, if you click the text block or line, you get the container button that has been pressed; but if the click is directed to the text box, the button doesn't receive it. Event routing in WPF is more complicated than in toolkits, because events are tunneled to tree nodes from the root toward the control and then bubbled up backward. In this way, the button may know that it's clicked in the first phase but may ignore the click event in the second phase. In addition, transparency may cause the same event to be triggered to more than one control at the same time. All these possibilities require further study of WPF that is beyond the scope of this book.

The type expected by the ShowVisualTree function is DependencyObject, which returns to the notion of *dependency*—a pervasive concept deeply entrenched within the framework. Dependency is a relation among two or more elements; in its asymmetry, it expresses something whose nature depends on something else. Dependency properties are a programming pattern used across WPF to define properties that you can listen to for change. If w is a Window object obtained from parsing the XAML contained in Listing 11-9, you can read and set the Text property of the TextBox object from F# as follows:

```
let t = w.FindName("Input")
MessageBox.Show(sprint "Input value is %s " t.Text) |> ignore
t.Text <- "Hello"
MessageBox.Show(sprint "Input value now is %s " t.Text) |> ignore
```

The Text property behaves as a standard property, and you can use it programmatically as you're used to doing with all properties. Text is a dependency property, and any observer in the code can listen for changes. You can detect its change as follows:

```
open System.ComponentModel

let desc =
    DependencyPropertyDescriptor.FromProperty(TextBox.TextProperty, typeof<TextBox>)
desc.AddValueChanged(t, fun _ _ -> MessageBox.Show("Text changed!") |> ignore)
```

You use the conventions used by `TextBox` implementers to access the descriptor of the `Text` dependency property called `TextProperty` and rely on appropriate data structures to register your callback. Whenever the text-box value changes, a message box is displayed.

Implementing a dependency property is easy: in the class, you define a static field describing the property; then, the property must be registered in a global structure hosted by the `DependencyProperty` class. You then add a standard .NET property using the `GetValue` and `SetValue` methods—inherited from the `DependencyObject` class, which must be an ancestor of the class defining the property—hiding the implementation details. Supported callbacks are registered to inform the framework about the observable events on the property (such as the property-value change).

At first, this may seem unnecessarily verbose: why is it useful to be able to observe when a property changes its value? The answer lies in WPF's ability to support the animation of virtually any element property, and the fact that dependency properties are the building blocks of the animation engine. Animations often correlate properties of different visual objects. For instance, think of an object and its shadow: whenever the object's position changes, its shadow must follow. Dependency properties provide a pervasive infrastructure to propagate property changes across visual tree nodes in a consistent way. To exemplify this idea, let's change Listing 11-9 again by replacing the `TextBox` element definition with the following:

```
<TextBlock Text="{Binding Path=Text, ElementName=Input}"></TextBlock>
```

The expression in curly braces is a *data-binding* expression, which is an expression evaluated by WPF engine to set the `Text` property of the `TextBlock` node. If you run the example, the text block updates its content when the text box changes its value. WPF defines several forms of data binding to declare how dependency properties must be updated without explicit coding; you can define several automatic actions using these mechanisms.

In WPF, controls are a way to instantiate subtrees and attach predefined behaviors to nodes and properties. They're less opaque in WPF than it before; nevertheless, if a change in the visual tree disrupts the assumptions made by a control's logic, a control may fail. For this reason, controls in WPF offer placeholders for inserting content, as you've seen with buttons, as well as a means to change the control's appearance while preserving the essential traits of the visual subtree that make its inner code work.

Bitmaps and Images

Vector graphics, after being abandoned in favor of raster graphics, have again become popular because they let you define graphics that can be scaled without the annoying pixelated effects typical of raster graphics. Vector primitives are exact, and the rendering engine can compute the value of any number of pixels affected by the primitive. If you zoom a line, you can compute all the pixels of the line without any loss in detail. If the line is contained in a bitmap, this isn't possible: the zoomed line contains artifacts introduced by the algorithm that resized the image.

It's impossible to imagine a user interface without images. But what does it means to work with pixels in a world of abstract coordinates where points are considered sizeless entities as in geometry? An image's size is defined in the application space, and WPF is responsible for the rastering process and for generating enough pixels at a given resolution. A 100×100 image at 96dpi uses the same number of pixels on a standard monitor, or more pixels if the device has a higher dpi resolution. This concept isn't unfamiliar: in the Mandelbrot example, you used a bitmap to set pixel colors, because of the lack of a `SetPixel` method on the `Graphics` object representing the device context for drawing. But WPF defines its own set of classes to deal with images, featuring a slightly different set of properties and capabilities.

To exemplify the use of images with WPF, let's consider a simple but useful application: a batch-size conversion for JPEG images. The application is a command-line tool that converts a directory containing hi-res pictures into a mirrored version containing resized versions of the same pictures for a specific resolution. With this tool, it's easy to convert thousands of photos into versions suitable for a photo frame, thus saving space. The conversion process preserves JPEG metadata information such as tags, which may be useful after conversion.

The two main functions are shown in Listing 11-10. transformFile is responsible for transforming a single JPEG image and saving it into a new file; transformDir performs a recursive visit to a directory tree and builds a mirror tree in the destination directory, relying on the first function to convert the image files.

The image transformation relies on JpegBitmapDecoder and JpegBitmapEncoder, two classes dealing with the JPEG format. These classes support a streaming model for decoding and encoding images, so you read information about the first frame (an image may contain more than a single frame) to ensure that all the metadata is read from the source image. The desired output size is passed in the form of a screen resolution through the width and height arguments, and a best-fit policy is used to define the size of an in-memory bitmap instance of the class BitmapImage. The image resize is performed by asking the in-memory image to load data from the source file and fit the desired size; this way, you avoid allocating the full image in memory and performing the resize operation while reading pixels from disk. You then use the encoder to save the image, with the desired quality, in the new file, along with the metadata and the creation-time and change-time information.

Listing 11-10. A Function to Resize All the Images in a Directory

```
open System
open System.IO
open System.Windows.Media.Imaging

let transformFile quality width height srcFileName outFileName =
    let dec = new JpegBitmapDecoder(
                Uri(srcFileName),
                BitmapCreateOptions.PreservePixelFormat,
                BitmapCacheOption.Default)
    let w = dec.Frames.[0].Width
    let h = dec.Frames.[0].Height

    let b = new BitmapImage()
    b.BeginInit()
    b.UriSource <- new Uri(srcFileName)
    if width > 0 then
        if w >= h then b.DecodePixelWidth <- width
        else b.DecodePixelHeight <- height
    b.EndInit()

    let metadata = dec.Frames.[0].Metadata

    let enc = new JpegBitmapEncoder()
    enc.Frames.Add(BitmapFrame.Create(b,null, metadata :?> BitmapMetadata, null))
    let fs = new FileStream(outFileName, FileMode.OpenOrCreate)
    enc.QualityLevel <- quality
    enc.Save(fs)
    fs.Close()
    let fin = new FileInfo(srcFileName)
    let fout = new FileInfo(outFileName)
    fout.CreationTime <- fin.CreationTime
    fout.LastWriteTime <- fin.LastWriteTime

let transformDir quality width height src dest =
```

```
let rec visit (dirin:DirectoryInfo) (dirout:DirectoryInfo) =
    for f in dirin.EnumerateFiles() do
        if f.Extension.ToUpper() = ".JPG" then
            printfn "Processing file %s..." f.FullName
            transformFile
                quality width height f.FullName
                (dirout.FullName + "\\" + f.Name)

    for d in dirin.EnumerateDirectories() do
        visit d (dirout.CreateSubdirectory(d.Name))

let dirin = new DirectoryInfo(src)
let dirout =
    if not(Directory.Exists(dest)) then Directory.CreateDirectory dest
    else new DirectoryInfo(dest)
visit dirin dirout
```

You start the transformation process by invoking the `transformDir` function with the JPEG compression quality, the target screen size, and the input and output folders. The following lines assume that you're converting summer photos for a frame supporting 1024×768 resolution:

```
let dn = @"C:\Users\SomeUser\Pictures\Summer 2010"
let dno = @"e:\Summer PhotoFrame 2010"

transformDir 75 1027 768 dn dno
```

Bitmap manipulation can be very tricky using WPF, and some tasks are more difficult than they are using Windows Forms. In particular, it's easy to obtain a device context to a bitmap and draw using GDI functions. You can raster WPF primitives into a bitmap, but many programmers prefer to refer to both libraries and convert images from one framework to the other, in an attempt to benefit from both worlds.

Final Considerations

WPF isn't just another framework built on top of the traditional Win32 and GDI rastering engine: it's a new presentation system designed with a different programming paradigm in mind. This section introduced some of the important ideas behind this new presentation system and how you can use it from F# applications. The content is far from exhaustive, and several topics have been left out or only mentioned in an attempt to convey the core ideas as a starting point for further investigation. The literature about WPF is very rich, and we encourage you to read more specific material.

Summary

Event-driven programming is the dominant paradigm of graphical applications. Although object-oriented programming is used to build the infrastructure for graphical frameworks, events are naturally expressed in terms of calling back a given function. F# is effective in GUI programming because it supports both paradigms and provides access to full-featured frameworks such as Windows Forms.

This chapter covered the basics of GUI programming. It introduced controls and applications, including details typical of real-world applications. The presentation was based on the Windows Forms framework, but many of the ideas discussed can be easily transposed to other graphical frameworks: the fundamental structure of this class of applications is mostly unchanged. Finally, we introduced WPF and discussed differences between it and Windows Forms.

CHAPTER 12

■ ■ ■

Working with Symbolic Representations

Symbols are everywhere. Numbers are symbols that stand for quantities, and you can add, multiply, or take square roots of numbers that are so small or large that it's hard to imagine the quantity they represent. You can solve equations, multiply polynomials, approximate functions using series, and differentiate or integrate numerically or symbolically—these are just a few everyday examples of using symbols in mathematics.

It would be a mistake to think symbols are useful only in mathematics and related fields. General problem-solving can't do without symbols; they provide the ability to abstract away details to make the larger picture clearer and help you understand relationships that may not appear obvious otherwise. Symbols always stand for something and have an attached meaning; they're created to bind this additional content to an existing object. This gives you an extraordinary tool to solve problems, describe behavior, make strategic decisions, create new words, and write poetry—the list could go on forever.

F# is well suited for symbolic computations. This chapter covers in depth two symbolic manipulation problems. First, it presents an implementation of a symbolic differentiation application, including expression rendering using techniques based on Windows Forms programming (discussed in Chapter 11). The second example shows how you can use symbolic programming to model hardware circuits and presents the core of a symbolic hardware-verification engine based on binary decision diagrams. (We could have chosen other examples of symbolic programming, but we found these two particularly enjoyable to code in F#.)

Chapter 9 already covered many of the foundational techniques for symbolic programming. One technique that is particularly important in this chapter is the use of discriminated unions to capture the shape of the abstract syntax trees for symbolic languages. Using functions as first-class values and applying recursive problem decomposition also leads to a natural and clean approach to computations on symbolic entities. These and other features of F# combine to make symbolic programming concise and painless, allowing you to focus on the really interesting parts of your application domain.

Symbolic Differentiation and Expression Rendering

You've probably come across the need to perform symbolic differentiation one way or another; and unless you had access to a full-fledged mathematics application such as Matlab or Mathematica, you had to resort to working out the math yourself on paper. This no longer has to be the case, because you can develop your own symbolic differentiation tool in almost no time and with surprising brevity and clarity. Figure 12-1 shows the symbolic differentiation application that you implement in this chapter.

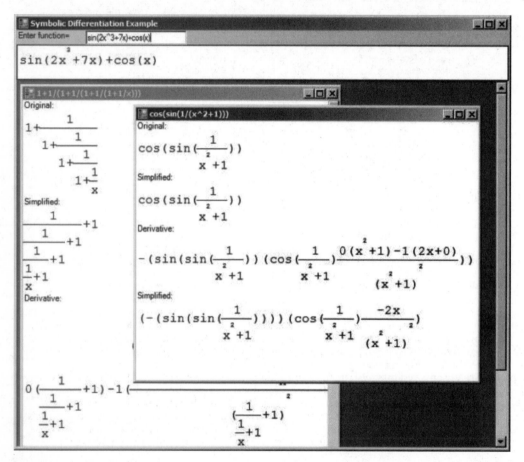

Figure 12-1. The visual symbolic differentiation application

Modeling Simple Algebraic Expressions

Let's take it easy at first and assume you're dealing with simple algebraic expressions that can consist only of numbers, a single variable (it doesn't matter what it is, but let's assume it's x), sums, and products. Listing 12-1 shows the implementation of symbolic differentiation over this simple expression type.

Listing 12-1. Symbolic Differentiation Over a Simple Expression Type

```
open System
type Expr =
    | Var
    | Num of int
    | Sum of Expr * Expr
    | Prod of Expr * Expr

let rec deriv expr =
    match expr with
    | Var           -> Num 1
    | Num _         -> Num 0
    | Sum (e1, e2)  -> Sum (deriv e1, deriv e2)
    | Prod (e1, e2) -> Sum (Prod (e1, deriv e2), Prod (e2, deriv e1))
```

The type of the deriv function is as follows:

```
val deriv : Expr -> Expr
```

Now, let's find the derivative of a simple expression, say 1+2*x*:

```
> let e1 = Sum (Num 1, Prod (Num 2, Var));;
val e1 : Expr = Sum (Num 1,Prod (Num 2,Var))

> deriv e1;;
val it : Expr = Sum (Num 0,Sum (Prod (Num 2,Num 1),Prod (Var,Num 0)))
```

The resulting expression is a symbolic representation of $0+(2*1+x*0)$, which indeed is 2— so it's right. You should do a couple of things next. First, install a custom printer so that F# Interactive responds using expressions that you're more used to using. Before you apply brute force and put parentheses around the expressions in each sum and product, let's contemplate it a bit. Parentheses are usually needed to give precedence to operations that would otherwise be applied later in the sequence of calculations. For instance, 2+3*4 is calculated as 2+(3*4) because the product has a higher precedence; if you were to find (2+3)*4, you would need to use parentheses to designate the new order of calculation. Taking this argument further, you can formulate the rule for using parentheses: they're needed in places where an operator has lower precedence than the one surrounding it. You can apply this reasoning to the expression printer by passing a context precedence parameter:

```
let precSum = 10
let precProd = 20

let rec stringOfExpr prec expr =
    match expr with
    | Var    -> "x"
    | Num i -> i.ToString()
    | Sum (e1, e2) ->
        if prec > precSum
        then "(" + stringOfExpr precSum e1 + "+" + stringOfExpr precSum e2 + ")"
        else     stringOfExpr precSum e1 + "+" + stringOfExpr precSum e2
```

```
  | Prod (e1, e2) ->
      stringOfExpr precProd e1 + "*" + stringOfExpr precProd e2
```

You can add this as a custom printer for this expression type:

```
> fsi.AddPrinter (fun expr -> stringOfExpr 0 expr);;
val it : unit = ()

> let e3 = Prod (Var, Prod (Var, Num 2));;
val e3 : Expr = x*x*2

> deriv e3;;
val it : Expr = x*(x*0+2*1)+x*2*1
```

Parentheses are omitted only when a sum is participating in an expression that has a higher precedence, which in this simplified example means products. If you didn't add precedence to the pretty-printer, you'd get $x*x*0+2*1+x*2*1$ for the last expression, which is incorrect.

Implementing Local Simplifications

The next thing to do is to get your symbolic manipulator to simplify expressions so you don't have to do so. One easy modification is to replace the use of the Sum and Prod constructors in deriv with local functions that perform local simplifications such as removing identity operations, performing arithmetic, bringing forward constants, and simplifying across two operations. Listing 12-2 shows how to do this.

Listing 12-2. Symbolic Differentiation with Local Simplifications

```
let simpSum = function
    | Num n, Num m -> Num (n+m)        // constants!
    | Num 0, e | e, Num 0 -> e         // 0+e = e+0 = e
    | e1, e2 -> Sum(e1,e2)

let simpProd = function
    | Num n, Num m -> Num (n*m)        // constants!
    | Num 0, e | e, Num 0 -> Num 0     // 0*e=0
    | Num 1, e | e, Num 1 -> e         // 1*e = e*1 = e
    | e1, e2 -> Prod(e1,e2)

let rec simpDeriv = function
    | Var            -> Num 1
    | Num            -> Num 0
    | Sum (e1, e2)   -> simpSum (simpDeriv e1, simpDeriv e2)
    | Prod (e1, e2)  -> simpSum (simpProd (e1, simpDeriv e2),
                                 simpProd (e2, simpDeriv e1))
```

These measures produce significant improvement over the previous naive approach, but they don't place the result in a normal form, as the following shows:

```
> simpDeriv e3;;
val it : Expr = x*2+x*2
```

However, you can't implement all simplifications using local rules; for example, collecting like terms across a polynomial involves looking at every term of the polynomial.

■ **Note** Listing 12-2 uses the expression form `function pattern-rules -> expression`. This is equivalent to `(fun x -> match x with pattern-rules -> expression)` and is especially convenient as a way to define functions working directly over discriminated unions.

A Richer Language of Algebraic Expressions

This section goes beyond the approach presented so far and shows how to develop a UI application that can accept algebraic expressions as input and simplify, differentiate, and render them graphically. Figure 12-2 shows the project structure. Note in particular that you need to add library references to `FSharp.PowerPack` and `System.Windows.Forms`. Furthermore, you add the lexer `ExprLexer.fsl` and the parser `ExprParser.fsy` to the project so you can quickly edit them if necessary. You can manually include a reference to the `PowerPack` targets in the project file to automatically generate code for the parser and lexer definitions, or you can manually generate these files. You do the latter for this example, but in both cases you need to add the generated files (`ExprParser.fs` and `ExprLexer.fs`) to the project.

The main `Expr` type that represents algebraic expressions is contained in `Expr.fs`. Although you can use the expression constructors defined in this type to create expression values on the fly, the most convenient method for embedding complex expressions into this representation is by parsing them.

Figure 12-2. The SymbolicDifferentiation project in Visual Studio 2010

Armed with the ability to encode and parse algebraic expressions, you place the derivation and simplification logic in its own module and file (`ExprUtil.fs`). The last piece is rendering (in `VisualExpr.fs`). Finally, a simple UI client in `Main.fs` completes the application.

Listing 12-3 shows the definition of the abstract syntax representation of expressions using a single Expr type. Expressions contain numbers, variables, negation, sums, differences, products, fractions, exponents, basic trigonometric functions (sin x, cos x), and e^x.

Let's look at this abstract syntax design more closely. In Chapter 9, you saw that choosing an abstract syntax often involves design choices, and that these choices often relate to the roles the abstract syntax representation should serve. In this case, you use the abstract syntax to compute symbolic derivatives and simplifications (using techniques similar to those earlier in this chapter) and also to graphically visualize the resulting expressions in a way that is pleasant for the human user. For this reason, you don't use an entirely minimalistic abstract syntax (for example, by replacing quotients with an inverse node), because it's helpful to maintain some additional structure in the input.

Here, you represent sums and differences not as binary terms (as you do for products and quotients) but instead as a list of expression terms. The Sub term also carries the *minuend*, the term that is to be reduced, separately. As a result, you have to apply different strategies when simplifying them.

Listing 12-3. Expr.fs: The Core Expression Type for the Visual Symbolic Differentiation Application

```
namespace Symbolic.Expressions

type Expr =
    | Num   of decimal
    | Var   of string
    | Neg   of Expr
    | Add   of Expr list
    | Sub   of Expr * Expr list
    | Prod of Expr * Expr
    | Frac of Expr * Expr
    | Pow   of Expr * decimal
    | Sin   of Expr
    | Cos   of Expr
    | Exp   of Expr

    static member StarNeeded e1 e2 =
        match e1, e2 with
        | Num _, Neg _ | _, Num _ -> true
        | _ -> false

    member self.IsNumber =
        match self with
        | Num _ -> true | _ -> false

    member self.NumOf =
        match self with
        | Num num -> num | _ -> failwith "NumOf: Not a Num"

    member self.IsNegative =
        match self with
        | Num num | Prod (Num num, _) -> num < 0M
        | Neg e -> true | _ -> false

    member self.Negate =
        match self with
        | Num num -> Num (-num)
        | Neg e -> e
        | exp -> Neg exp
```

Listing 12-3 also shows the definition of some miscellaneous augmentations on the expression type, mostly related to visual layout and presentation. The StarNeeded member is used internally to determine whether the multiplication operator (the star symbol, or asterisk) is needed in the product of two expressions, e1 and e2. You may want to extend this simple rule: any product whose right side is a number requires the explicit operator, and all other cases don't. Thus, expressions such as $2(x+1)$ and $2x$ are rendered without the asterisk.

The IsNumber member returns true if the expression at hand is numeric and is used in conjunction with NumOf, which returns this numeric component. Similarly, the IsNegative and Negate members determine whether you have an expression that starts with a negative sign, and they negate it on demand.

Parsing Algebraic Expressions

This sample uses a lexer and a parser generated by the F# tools fsyacc.exe and fslex.exe. Chapter 16 describes these tools in more detail; this chapter skips over the details of how the tools work. Listings 12-4 and 12-5 show the code for the lexer and parser. You need to manually build the lexer (generating ExprLexer.fs) and parser (generating ExprParser.fs) from the Windows command line as follows:

```
C:\samples> fsyacc ExprParser.fsy --module ExprParser
C:\samples> fslex ExprLexer.fsl --unicode
```

Listing 12-4. ExprLexer.fsl: Tokenizing the Concrete Syntax for Algebraic Expressions

```
{
module ExprLexer

open System
open Microsoft.FSharp.Text.Lexing
open ExprParser

let lexeme = LexBuffer<_>.LexemeString

let special lexbuf = function
    | "+" -> PLUS    | "-" -> MINUS
    | "*" -> TIMES   | "/" -> DIV
    | "(" -> LPAREN  | ")" -> RPAREN  | "^" -> HAT
    | _   -> failwith "Invalid operator"

let id lexbuf = function
    | "sin" -> SIN   | "cos" -> COS
    | "e"   -> E     | id    -> ID id
}

let digit     = ['0'-'9']
let int       = digit+
let float     = int ('.' int)? (['e' 'E'] int)?
let alpha     = ['a'-'z' 'A'-'Z']
let id        = alpha+ (alpha | digit | ['_' '$'])*
let ws        = ' ' | '\t'
let nl        = '\n' | '\r' '\n'
let special   = '+' | '-' | '*' | '/' | '(' | ')' | '^'
```

```
rule main = parse
    | int        { INT     (Convert.ToInt32(lexeme lexbuf)) }
    | float      { FLOAT   (Convert.ToDouble(lexeme lexbuf)) }
    | id         { id      lexbuf (lexeme lexbuf) }
    | special    { special lexbuf (lexeme lexbuf) }
    | ws | nl    { main    lexbuf }
    | eof        { EOF }
    | _          { failwith (lexeme lexbuf) }
```

The parser has some syntactic sugar for polynomial terms, so it can parse 2x, 2x^3, or x^4 without requiring you to add an explicit multiplication after the coefficient.

Listing 12-5. ExprParser.fsy: *Parsing the Concrete Syntax for Algebraic Expressions*

```
%{
open System
open Symbolic.Expressions
%}

%token <int> INT
%token <float> FLOAT
%token <string> ID

%token EOF LPAREN RPAREN PLUS MINUS TIMES DIV HAT SIN COS E

%left ID
%left prec_negate
%left LPAREN
%left PLUS MINUS
%left TIMES DIV
%left HAT


%start expr
%type <Expr> expr
%%

expr:
    | exp EOF { $1 }

number:
    | INT                           { BigNum.of_int $1 }
    | FLOAT                         { BigNum.of_string (Float.to_string $1) }
    | MINUS INT %prec prec_negate   { BigNum.of_int (-$2) }
    | MINUS FLOAT %prec prec_negate { BigNum.of_string (Float.to_string (-$2)) }

exp:
    | number             { Num $1 }
    | ID                 { Var $1 }
    | exp PLUS exp       { Add [$1; $3] }
    | exp MINUS exp      { Sub ($1, [$3]) }
    | exp TIMES exp      { Prod ($1, $3) }
    | exp DIV exp        { Frac ($1, $3) }
    | SIN LPAREN exp RPAREN { Sin $3 }
```

```
    | COS LPAREN exp RPAREN    { Cos $3 }
    | E HAT exp                { Exp $3 }
    | term                     { $1 }
    | exp HAT number           { Pow ($1, $3) }
    | LPAREN exp RPAREN        { $2 }
    | MINUS LPAREN exp RPAREN  { Neg $3 }

term:
    | number ID                { Prod (Num $1, Var $2) }
    | number ID HAT number     { Prod (Num $1, Pow (Var $2, $4)) }
    | ID HAT number            { Prod (Num 1M, Pow (Var $1, $3)) }
```

Simplifying Algebraic Expressions

At the start of this chapter, you simplified expressions using local techniques, but you also saw the limitations of this approach. Listing 12-6 shows a more complete implementation of a separate function (Simplify) that performs some nonlocal simplifications as well. Both this function and the one for derivation shown in the subsequent section are placed in a separate file (ExprUtil.fs).

Simplify uses two helper functions (collect and negate). The former collects constants from products using a bottom-up strategy that reduces constant subproducts and factors out constants by bringing them outward (to the left). Recall that product terms are binary.

Listing 12-6. ExprUtils.fs: *Simplifying Algebraic Expressions*

```
module Symbolic.Expressions.Utils

open Symbolic.Expressions

/// A helper function to map/select across a list while threading state
/// through the computation
let selectFold f l s =
    let l,s' = List.fold
                  (fun (l',s') x ->
                      let x',s'' = f x s'
                      (List.rev x') @ l',s'')
                  ([],s) l
    List.rev l,s'

/// Collect constants
let rec collect = function
    | Prod (e1, e2) ->
        match collect e1, collect e2 with
        | Num num1, Num num2       -> Num (num1 * num2)
        | Num n1, Prod (Num n2, e)
        | Prod (Num n2, e), Num n1 -> Prod (Num (n1 * n2), e)
        | Num n, e | e, Num n      -> Prod (Num n, e)
        | Prod (Num n1, e1), Prod (Num n2, e2) ->
            Prod (Num (n1 * n2), Prod (e1, e2))
        | e1', e2'                 -> Prod (e1', e2')
    | Num _ | Var _ as e  -> e
    | Neg e               -> Neg (collect e)
    | Add exprs           -> Add (List.map collect exprs)
    | Sub (e1, exprs)     -> Sub (collect e1, List.map collect exprs)
```

```
    | Frac (e1, e2)        -> Frac (collect e1, collect e2)
    | Pow (e1, num)        -> Pow (collect e1, num)
    | Sin e                -> Sin (collect e)
    | Cos e                -> Cos (collect e)
    | Exp _ as e           -> e

/// Push negations through an expression
let rec negate = function
    | Num num              -> Num (-num)
    | Var v as exp         -> Neg exp
    | Neg e                -> e
    | Add exprs            -> Add (List.map negate exprs)
    | Sub _                -> failwith "unexpected Sub"
    | Prod (e1, e2)        -> Prod (negate e1, e2)
    | Frac (e1, e2)        -> Frac (negate e1, e2)
    | exp                  -> Neg exp

/// Simplify an expression
let rec simp = function
    | Num num              -> Num num
    | Var v                -> Var v
    | Neg e                -> negate (simp e)
    | Add exprs ->
        let filterNums (e:Expr) n =
            if e.IsNumber
            then [], n + e.NumOf
            else [e], n
        let summands = function | Add es -> es | e -> [e]
        let exprs', num =
            selectFold (simp >> summands >> selectFold filterNums) exprs 0N
        match exprs' with
        | [Num _ as n] when num = 0M -> n
        | []                         -> Num num
        | [e] when num = 0M          -> e
        | _ when num = 0M            -> Add exprs'
        | _                          -> Add (exprs' @ [Num num])
    | Sub (e1, exprs) ->
        simp (Add (e1 :: List.map Neg exprs))
    | Prod (e1, e2) ->
        match simp e1, simp e2 with
        | Num num, _ | _, Num num when num = 0M -> Num 0M
        | Num num, e | e, Num num when num = 1M -> e
        | Num num1, Num num2                    -> Num (num1 * num2)
        | e1, e2                                -> Prod (e1, e2)
    | Frac (e1, e2) ->
        match simp e1, simp e2 with
        | Num num, _ when num = 0M  -> Num num
        | e1, Num num when num = 1M -> e1
        | Num (_ as num), Frac (Num (_ as num2), e) ->
            Prod (Frac (Num num, Num num2), e)
        | Num (_ as num), Frac (e, Num (_ as num2)) ->
            Frac (Prod (Num num, Num num2), e)
        | e1, e2                    -> Frac (e1, e2)
    | Pow (e, n) when n=1M -> simp e
```

```
    | Pow (e, n)              -> Pow (simp e, n)
    | Sin e                   -> Sin (simp e)
    | Cos e                   -> Cos (simp e)
    | Exp e                   -> Exp (simp e)

let Simplify e = e |> simp |> simp |> collect
```

The main simplification algorithm works as follows:

- Constants and variables are passed through verbatim. You use negate when simplifying a negation, which assumes the expression at hand no longer contains differences and that sums were flattened (see the next item in this list).

- Sums are traversed and nested sums are flattened, at the same time all constants are collected and added up. This reduces the complexity of further simplification considerably.

- Differences are converted to sums: for instance, *A-B-C* is converted to *A+(-B)+(-C)*. Thus, the first element is preserved without negation.

- When simplifying a product, you first simplify its factors, and then you remove identity operations (multiplying by zero or one) and reduce products of constants.

- Fractions are handled similarly. Zero divided by anything is 0, anything divided by 1 is itself, and multiline fractions can be collapsed if you find numeric denominators or numerators.

- The rest of the match cases deal with simplifying subexpressions.

Symbolic Differentiation of Algebraic Expressions

Applying symbolic differentiation is a straightforward translation of the mathematical rules of differentiation into code. You could use local functions that act as constructors and perform local simplifications, but with the simplification function described earlier, this isn't needed. Listing 12-7 shows the implementation of symbolic differentiation for the Expr type. Note how beautifully and succinctly the code follows the math behind it: the essence of the symbolic processing is merely 20 lines of code!

Listing 12-7. ExprUtil.fs *(continued): Symbolic Differentiation for Algebraic Expressions*

```
let Differentiate v e =
    let rec diff v = function
        | Num num                -> Num 0M
        | Var v' when v'=v        -> Num 1M
        | Var v'                  -> Num 0M
        | Neg e                   -> diff v (Prod ((Num -1M), e))
        | Add exprs               -> Add (List.map (diff v) exprs)
        | Sub (e1, exprs)         -> Sub (diff v e1, List.map (diff v) exprs)
        | Prod (e1, e2)           -> Add [Prod (diff v e1, e2); Prod (e1, diff v e2)]
        | Frac (e1, e2) ->
            Frac (Sub (Prod (diff v e1, e2), [Prod (e1, diff v e2)]), Pow (e2, 2N))
        | Pow (e1, num) ->
            Prod (Prod(Num num, Pow (e1, num - 1M)), diff v e1)
        | Sin e                   -> Prod (Cos e, diff v e)
```

```
        | Cos e                    -> Neg (Prod (Sin e, diff v e))
        | Exp (Var v') as e when v'=v  -> e
        | Exp (Var v') as e when v'<>v -> Num OM
        | Exp e                   -> Prod (Exp e, diff v e)
    diff v e
```

Rendering Expressions

Now that you have the basic machinery to easily parse, simplify, and differentiate expressions, you can start looking into how to visualize them to really enjoy the benefits of the application. The rendering engine (placed in VisualExpr.fs) has two main parts: converting expressions to VisualExpr values and then rendering them directly. Ideally, you should hide the representation of the VisualExpr (and its related VisualElement) type with a signature (not shown here) so that it isn't possible to construct these values directly.

Before you get to the conversion and rendering functions, you need to do a bit of setup. To control how the different parts of an expression are rendered on the screen, you introduce the RenderOptions type containing the fonts and pen (which determines the color used to draw) that are applied during rendering. Listing 12-8 shows the code that defines the rendering options used in the remainder of this example.

Listing 12-8. VisualExpr.fs: Rendering Options for the Visual Symbolic Differentiation Application

```
namespace Symbolic.Expressions.Visual

open Symbolic.Expressions
open System.Drawing
open System.Drawing.Imaging

type RenderOptions =
    { NormalFont: Font;  SmallFont: Font;  IsSuper: bool;  Pen: Pen; }

    static member Default =
        { NormalFont = new Font("Courier New",18.0f,FontStyle.Regular);
          SmallFont = new Font("Courier New", 12.0f, FontStyle.Regular);
          IsSuper = false;
          Pen = new Pen(Color.Black, 1.0f); }

    member self.Brush =
        (new SolidBrush(Color.FromArgb(255, self.Pen.Color)) :> Brush)
```

Each algebraic expression is converted to a VisualExpr value as part of the rendering process. This ensures that you don't have to deal with the variety of expression forms but only with a small set of simple shapes that can be rendered according to a few simple rules. These simpler building blocks are defined in the VisualElement type and shown in Listing 12-9. For instance, there are no sums or products; these and similar expressions are broken down into sequences of symbols (such as 1, x, and +). The two other visual elements are exponentiation and fractions, which are used to guide the display logic later during the rendering phase. Each visual element carries a size value that is calculated using a given set of rendering options.

Listing 12-9. `VisualExpr.fs` *(continued): Visual Elements and Sizes for the Visual Symbolic Differentiation Application*

```
type VisualElement =
    | Symbol   of string * ExprSize
    | Power    of VisualElement * VisualElement * ExprSize
    | Sequence of VisualElement list * ExprSize
    | Fraction of VisualElement * VisualElement * ExprSize
    member self.Size =
        match self with
        | Symbol (_, size)   | Power (_, _, size)
        | Sequence (_, size) | Fraction (_, _, size) -> size

    member self.Height = self.Size.height
    member self.Width = self.Size.width
    member self.Midline = self.Size.midline

and ExprSize =
    { width: int;  height: int;  midline: int; }

    member self.CenterOnMidline size x y =
        x + (size.width-self.width)/2, y + (size.midline-self.midline)

    member self.Frac size opt =
        { width = max self.width size.width;
          height = self.height + size.height + self.FracSepHeight opt;
          midline = self.height + (self.FracSepHeight opt)/2; }

    member self.FracSepHeight (opt: RenderOptions) =
        max (int (opt.Pen.Width*5.0f)) 4

    member self.AddPower (e: VisualElement) =
        { width = self.width + e.Width;
          height = self.height + e.Height;
          midline = self.midline + e.Height; }

    static member ExpandOne (size: ExprSize) (e: VisualElement) =
        { width   = size.width + e.Width;
          height  = max size.height e.Height;
          midline = max size.midline e.Midline; }

    member self.Expand (exprs: VisualElement list) =
        List.fold ExprSize.ExpandOne self exprs

    static member Seq (exprs: VisualElement list) =
        List.fold ExprSize.ExpandOne ExprSize.Zero exprs

    static member Zero =
        { width=0; height=0; midline=0; }
```

The `size` value encodes the dimensions (width and height in pixels) of the related visual expression and is managed through the `ExprSize` type, which provides various members to compute precise dimensions. Basically, this type handles the gory details of putting together small visuals to compose a large expression and manages how and where these small visuals should be placed. The main guideline is to align these visuals on a line (measured from the top of the expression in pixels and stored in the `midline` field), as depicted in Figure 12-3.

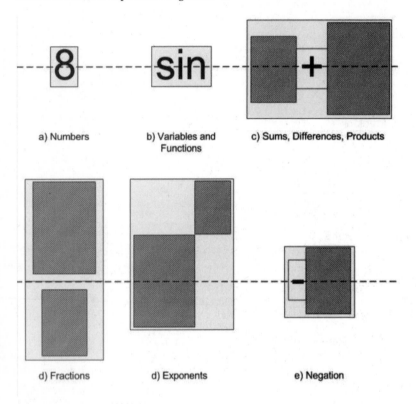

Figure 12-3. Expressions and their sizes

The darker rectangles in this figure denote arbitrary expressions, whereas the lighter rectangles mark the dimensions of the parent expression aligned on the midline.

Converting to VisualExpr

Listing 12-10 shows the type `VisualExpr` that carries the main visual element and the rendering options that were used to produce it. This type also provides the method `OfExpr` to build a `VisualExpr` from an `Expr`.

Listing 12-10. `VisualExpr.fs` (continued): Visual Expressions for the Visual Symbolic Differentiation Application

```
type VisualExpr =
    {  Expression : VisualElement;  RenderOptions: RenderOptions; }

    static member OfExpr (opt: RenderOptions) e =
        use bmp = new Bitmap(100, 100, PixelFormat.Format32bppArgb)
```

```
use gra = Graphics.FromImage(bmp)
let sizeOf (opt: RenderOptions) s =
    use sFormat = new StringFormat(StringFormat.GenericTypographic)
    let font = if opt.IsSuper then opt.SmallFont else opt.NormalFont
    let size = gra.MeasureString(s, font, PointF(0.0f, 0.0f), sFormat)
    let height = int size.Height
    { width = int size.Width + 2;
      height = height;
      midline = height/2; }
let precPow = 70
let precProd1, precProd2 = 30, 40
let precAdd1, precAdd2 = 10, 11
let precStart = 5
let precNeg1, precNeg2 = 1, 20
let sym opt s = Symbol (s, sizeOf opt s)

let applyPrec opt pprec prec exprs (size: ExprSize) =
    if pprec > prec then
        sym opt "(" :: exprs @ [sym opt ")"],
        size.Expand [sym opt "("; sym opt ")"]
    else
        exprs, size

let mkSequence opt pprec prec exprs =
    let size = ExprSize.Seq exprs
    let exprs, size = applyPrec opt pprec prec exprs size
    Sequence (exprs, size)

let rec expFunc opt f par =
    let f' = sym opt f
    let exprs' = [sym opt "("; exp opt precStart par; sym opt ")"]
    Sequence (f' :: exprs', f'.Size.Expand exprs')

and exp (opt: RenderOptions) prec = function
    | Num n ->
        let s = n.ToString() in Symbol (s, sizeOf opt s)
    | Var v ->
        Symbol (v, sizeOf opt v)
    | Neg e ->
        let e' = exp opt precNeg1 e
        let exprs, size = applyPrec opt prec precNeg1 [e'] e'.Size
        let exprs' = [sym opt "-"] @ exprs
        mkSequence opt prec precNeg2 exprs'
    | Add exprs ->
        let exprs' =
            [ for i,e in Seq.mapi (fun i x -> (i,x)) exprs do
                  let first = (i=0)
                  let e' = exp opt (if first then precAdd1 else precAdd2) e
                  if first || e.IsNegative
                  then yield! [e']
                  else yield! [sym opt "+"; e'] ]
        mkSequence opt prec precAdd1 exprs'
    | Sub (e1, exprs) ->
        let e1' = exp opt prec e1
```

```
                    let exprs' =
                        [ for e in exprs do
                                if e.IsNegative then
                                    let e' = exp opt precAdd2 e.Negate
                                    yield! [sym opt "+"; e']
                                else
                                    let e' = exp opt precAdd2 e
                                    yield! [sym opt "-"; e'] ]
                    mkSequence opt prec precAdd1 (e1'::exprs')
            | Prod (e1, e2) ->
                let e1' = exp opt precProd1 e1
                let e2' = exp opt precProd2 e2
                let exprs' =
                    if Expr.StarNeeded e1 e2
                    then [e1'; sym opt "*"; e2']
                    else [e1'; e2']
                mkSequence opt prec precProd1 exprs'
            | Pow (e1, e2) ->
                let e1' = exp opt precPow e1
                let e2' = exp { opt with IsSuper=true } precPow (Num e2)
                Power (e1', e2', e1'.Size.AddPower e2')
            | Sin e ->
                expFunc opt "sin" e
            | Cos e ->
                expFunc opt "cos" e
            | Exp expo ->
                let e' = sym opt "e"
                let expo' = exp { opt with IsSuper=true } precPow expo
                Power (e', expo', e'.Size.AddPower expo')

            | Frac (e1, e2) ->
                let e1' = exp opt precStart e1
                let e2' = exp opt precStart e2
                Fraction (e1', e2', e1'.Size.Frac e2'.Size opt)
        let exp = exp opt precStart e
        { Expression=exp; RenderOptions=opt; }
```

The conversion implemented in Listing 12-10 is relatively straightforward. It uses various local helper functions to break each expression into smaller visual elements, carefully keeping track of the bounding-box calculation. There are a number of things to consider: precedence is enforced, and expressions are parenthesized as necessary. For example, consider how you convert a product:

```
| Prod (e1, e2) ->
    let e1' = exp opt precProd1 e1
    let e2' = exp opt precProd2 e2
    let exprs' =
        if Expr.StarNeeded e1 e2
        then [e1'; sym opt "*"; e2']
        else [e1'; e2']
    mkSequence opt prec precProd1 exprs'
```

This code converts the two interior expressions and decides on a list of display symbols by first checking whether a multiplication symbol is required. The function mkSequence then calculates the size of this new list of expressions, applies precedence rules to determine whether parentheses are required, and produces a final visual element as a result.

Other cases are handled similarly; for sums, you iterate through the elements exprs in the sum using sequence expression notation. If you find a negative term, you omit the plus sign (so 1+(-2) is rendered as 1-2). Differences are treated similarly, but here you change negative terms to positive, so 3-2-(-1) becomes 3-2+1. When converting products, you omit the multiplication operator if you can.

Rendering

Listing 12-11 shows the code for rendering visual expressions. You may have noticed in the definition of the VisualElement type that the only directly drawable visual element is Symbol. The other constructors carry one or more visual elements that must be drawn recursively and according to a well-defined logic. The key observation in the rendering function in Listing 12-11 is that, when drawing each element, you pass in the x and y coordinates of the bounding box in which it's to be drawn. You also pass in the size of the parent box in which the element is to be aligned (as guided by the midline property).

Listing 12-11. VisualExpr.fs *(continued): Rendering Visual Expressions*

```
type VisualExpr =
    ...
    member self.Render =
        let pt x y = PointF(float32 x, float32 y)
        let rec draw (gra: Graphics) opt x y psize = function
            | Symbol (s, size) ->
                let font = if opt.IsSuper then opt.SmallFont else opt.NormalFont
                let x', y' = size.CenterOnMidline psize x y
                gra.DrawString(s, font, opt.Brush, pt x' y')
            | Power (e1, e2, size) ->
                let x', y' = size.CenterOnMidline psize x y
                draw gra opt x' (y'+e2.Height) e1.Size e1
                draw gra { opt with IsSuper=true } (x'+e1.Width) y' e2.Size e2
            | Sequence (exps, size) ->
                let x', y' = size.CenterOnMidline psize x y
                List.fold (fun (x, y) (e: VisualElement) ->
                    let psize' = { width = e.Width; height = psize.height;
                                   midline=size.midline; }
                    draw gra opt x y psize' e
                    x+e.Width, y) (x', y') exps |> ignore
            | Fraction (e1, e2, size) as e ->
                let psize1 = { psize with height=e1.Height; midline=e1.Midline }
                let psize2 = { psize with height=e2.Height; midline=e2.Midline }
                draw gra opt x y psize1 e1
                gra.DrawLine(self.RenderOptions.Pen, x, y+size.midline,
                             x+psize.width, y+size.midline);
                draw gra opt x (y+e1.Height+size.FracSepHeight opt) psize2 e2
        let bmp = new Bitmap(self.Expression.Width, self.Expression.Height,
                     PixelFormat.Format32bppArgb)
        let gra = Graphics.FromImage(bmp)
        gra.FillRectangle(new SolidBrush(Color.White), 0, 0,
                     self.Expression.Width+1, self.Expression.Height+1)
        draw gra self.RenderOptions 0 0 self.Expression.Size self.Expression
        bmp
```

Building the User Interface

Listing 12-12 is the final piece: the UI client (`Main.fs`). It's simple yet powerful. The main form contains an input field and a preview panel where the expressions are rendered on the fly as typed in. When the user presses the Enter key, a new MDI child window is created, and the original, simplified, derived, and final expressions are rendered on it. A bit of extra work is involved in creating the child windows to make them scrollable.

Listing 12-12. `Main.fs`: The User Interface Client for the Visual Symbolic Differentiation Application

```
module Symbolic.Expressions.UI

open Symbolic.Expressions
open Symbolic.Expressions.Visual
open System.Windows.Forms
open System.Drawing

let CreateScrollableChildWindow parent =
    let scroll = new ScrollableControl(Dock=DockStyle.Fill, AutoScroll=true)
    let form2 = new Form(MdiParent=parent, BackColor=Color.White)
    form2.Controls.Add scroll
    form2, scroll

let NewExpression parent s es =
    let form, scroll = CreateScrollableChildWindow parent
    let AddLabel (top, maxw) (parent: Control) s =
        let l = new Label(Text=s, AutoSize=true, Top=top)
        parent.Controls.Add l
        (top+l.Height), max maxw l.Width
    let AddPic (top, maxw) (parent: Control) (e: Expr) =
        let e' = VisualExpr.OfExpr RenderOptions.Default e
        let bmp = e'.Render
        let pic = new PictureBox(Image=bmp, Height=bmp.Height,
                                 Width=bmp.Width, Top=top)
        parent.Controls.Add pic
        (top+bmp.Height), max maxw bmp.Width
    let height, width = List.fold (fun top (lab, e) ->
        AddPic (AddLabel top scroll lab) scroll e) (0, 0) es
    form.Text <- s
    form.Height <- min 640 (height+40)
    form.Width <- min 480 (width+40)
    form.Show()

let UpdatePreview (scroll: Control) e =
    let e' = VisualExpr.OfExpr RenderOptions.Default e
    let bmp = e'.Render
    let pic = new PictureBox(Image=bmp, Height=bmp.Height, Width=bmp.Width)
    scroll.Controls.Clear()
    scroll.Controls.Add pic

let NewExpressionError form s =
    let cform, scroll = CreateScrollableChildWindow form
    let label = new Label(Text=s, Font=new Font("Courier New", 10.f), AutoSize=true)
```

```
    scroll.Controls.Add label
    cform.Show()

exception SyntaxError

let Parse s =
    let lex = Lexing.LexBuffer<char>.FromString s
    try ExprParser.expr ExprLexer.main lex
    with _ -> raise SyntaxError

let NewStringExpression form s =
    try
        let e1 = Parse s
        let e2 = Utils.Simplify e1
        let e3 = Utils.Differentiate "x" e2
        let e4 = Utils.Simplify e3
        NewExpression form s ["Original:", e1; "Simplified:", e2;
                              "Derivative:", e3; "Simplified:", e4]
    with
      | SyntaxError ->
         let msg = Printf.sprintf "Syntax error in:\n%s" s
         NewExpressionError form msg
      | Failure msg ->
         NewExpressionError form msg

let ConstructMainForm () =
    let form    = new Form(Text="Symbolic Differentiation Example",
                           IsMdiContainer=true,
                           Visible=true, Height=600, Width=700)
    let label   = new Label(Text="Enter function=", Width=100, Height=20)
    let tb      = new TextBox(Width=150, Left=100)
    let panel   = new Panel(Dock=DockStyle.Top, Height=tb.Height+50)
    let preview = new Panel(Dock=DockStyle.Bottom, BackColor=Color.White,
                            Height=50, BorderStyle=BorderStyle.FixedSingle)
    panel.Controls.AddRange([|label; preview; tb |])
    form.Controls.Add(panel)
    tb.KeyUp.Add (fun arg ->
       if arg.KeyCode = Keys.Enter then
           NewStringExpression form tb.Text
           tb.Text <- ""
           tb.Focus() |> ignore
       else
           try
               let e = Parse tb.Text
               UpdatePreview preview e
           with
           | _ -> ())
    form

let form = ConstructMainForm ()
NewStringExpression form "cos(sin(1/(x^2+1)))"
Application.Run(form)
```

To recap, in this example you've seen the following:

- Two abstract syntax representations for different classes of algebraic expressions: one simple, and one much more realistic

- How to implement simplification and symbolic differentiation routines on these representations of algebraic expressions

- How to implement parsing and lexing for concrete representations of algebraic expressions

- How to perform size estimation and visual layout for abstract syntax representations of algebraic expressions, here using Windows Forms

- How to put this together into a final application

Verifying Circuits with Propositional Logic

The next example turns to a traditional application area for functional programming: describing digital hardware circuits and symbolically verifying their properties. We assume a passing familiarity with hardware design, but if you haven't looked inside a microprocessor chip for some time, a brief recap is included in the "About Hardware Design" sidebar.

In this example, you model circuits by *propositional logic*, a simple and familiar symbolic language made up of constructs such as AND, OR, NOT, and TRUE/FALSE values. You then implement an analysis that converts propositional logic formulae into a canonical form called *binary decision diagrams* (BDDs). Converting to a canonical form allows you to check conditions and properties associated with the digital circuits.

About Hardware Design

Digital hardware circuits such as microprocessors almost universally manipulate *bits*—that is, signals that are either low or high, represented by 0/1 or false/true values, respectively. The building blocks of interesting hardware circuits are primitives such as *gates* and *registers*. Gates are logical components that relate their inputs to their outputs; for example, an AND gate takes two input signals, and if both are high, it gives a high signal on its output. Registers are stateful components associated with a clock. This chapter doesn't consider registers and stateful circuits, although they can be tackled using techniques similar to those described here.

Hardware design is largely about building interesting behavior out of these primitives. For example, you can build arithmetic circuits that compute the sum or product of integers by using logical gates alone. These combinatorial circuits can be massive, and a key concern is to both verify their correctness and minimize the overall electrical delay through the circuit.

■ **Note** The examples in this section are inspired by the tutorials for the HOL88 system, a symbolic theorem prover implemented using an F#-like language that has been used for many purposes, including hardware verification. The carry/select adder and the BDD implementation follow those given by John Harrison in his HOL Light version of the same system. You can find out more about these and other systems, as well as delve into theorem proving, in *Handbook of Practical Logic and Automated Reasoning* by John Harrison (Cambridge University Press, 2009).

Representing Propositional Logic

You begin by using language-oriented programming techniques to implement a little logic of Boolean expressions, of the kind that might be used to describe part of a hardware circuit or a constraint. Let's assume these have forms like the following:

```
P1 AND P2
P1 OR P2
P1 IMPLIES P2
NOT(P1)
v                       -- variable, ranging over true/false
TRUE
FALSE
Exists v. P[v]          -- v ranges over true/false, P may use v
Forall v. P[v]          -- v ranges over true/false, P may use v
```

This is known as *quantified Boolean formulae* (QBF) and is an expressive way of modeling many interesting problems and artifacts that work over finite data domains. Listing 12-13 shows how you model this language in F#.

Listing 12-13. A Minimalistic Representation of Propositional Logic

```
type Var = string

type Prop =
    | And of Prop * Prop
    | Var of Var
    | Not of Prop
    | Exists of Var * Prop
    | False

let True = Not(False)
let Or(p,q)      = Not(And(Not(p),Not(q)))
let Iff(p,q)     = Or(And(p,q),And(Not(p),Not(q)))
let Implies(p,q) = Or(Not(p),q)
let Forall(v,p)  = Not(Exists(v,Not(p)))

let (&&&) p q = And(p,q)
let (|||) p q = Or(p,q)
let (~~~) p   = Not (p)
```

341

```
let (<=>) p q = Iff(p,q)
let (===) p q = (p <=> q)
let (==>) p q = Implies(p,q)
let (^^^) p q = Not (p <=> q)

let var (nm:Var) = Var(nm)

let fresh =
    let count = ref 0
    fun nm -> incr count; (sprintf "_%s%d" nm !count : Var)
```

Listing 12-13 uses a *minimalistic* encoding of propositional logic terms, where True, Or, Iff, Implies, and Forall are *derived* constructs, defined using their standard classical definitions in terms of the primitives Var, And, Not, Exists, and False. This is adequate for your purposes because you aren't so interested in preserving the original structure of formulae; if you do need to display a symbolic propositional formula, you're happy to display a form different than the original input.

Variables in formulae of type Prop are *primitive propositions*. A primitive proposition is often used to model some real-world possibility. For example, "it is raining," "it is cold," and "it is snowing" can be represented by Var("raining"), Var("cold"), and Var("snowing"). A Prop formula may be a *tautology*—that is, something that is always true regardless of the interpretation of these primitives. A formula is *satisfiable* if there is at least one interpretation for which it's true. A formula can also be an *axiom*; for example, "if it's snowing, then it's cold" can be represented as the assumption Implies(Var("snowing"), Var("cold")). In this example, variables are used to represent a wire in a digital circuit that may be low or high.

When you're dealing directly with the abstract syntax for Prop, it can be convenient to define infix operators to help you build abstract syntax values. Listing 12-13 shows the definition of seven operators (&&&, |||, ~~~, <=>, ===, ==>, and ^^^) that look a little like the notation you expect for propositional logic. You also define the function var for building primitive propositions and fresh for generating fresh variables. The types of these functions are as follows:

```
val var : Var -> Prop
val fresh : (string -> Var)
```

NOTE The operators in Listing 12-13 aren't overloaded and indeed outscope the default overloaded bitwise operations on integers discussed in Chapter 3. However, that doesn't matter for the purposes of this chapter. If necessary, you can use alternative operator names.

Evaluating Propositional Logic Naively

Before tackling the problem of representing hardware using propositional logic, let's look at some naive approaches for working with propositional logic formulae. Listing 12-14 shows routines that evaluate formulae given an assignment of variables and that generate the rows of a *truth table* for a Prop formula.

Listing 12-14. Evaluating Propositional Logic Formulae

```
let rec eval (env : Map<Var,bool>) inp =
    match inp with
    | Exists(v,p) -> eval (env.Add(v,false)) p || eval (env.Add(v,true)) p
    | And(p1,p2)  -> eval env p1 && eval env p2
    | Var(v)      -> if env.ContainsKey(v) then env.[v]
                     else failwithf "env didn't contain a value for %A" v
    | Not(p)      -> not (eval env p)
    | False       -> false

let rec support f =
    match f with
    | And(x,y)    -> Set.union (support x) (support y)
    | Exists(v,p) -> (support p).Remove(v)
    | Var(p)      -> Set.singleton p
    | Not(x)      -> support x
    | False       -> Set.empty

let rec cases supp =
    seq { match supp with
          | [] ->  yield Map.empty
          | v::rest ->
              yield! rest |> cases |> Seq.map (Map.add v false)
              yield! rest |> cases |> Seq.map (Map.add v true) }

let truthTable x =
    x |> support |> Set.toList |> cases |> Seq.map (fun env -> env,eval env x)

let satisfiable x =
    x |> truthTable |> Seq.exists(fun (env,res) -> res)

let tautology x =
    x |> truthTable |> Seq.forall (fun (env,res) -> res)

let tautologyWithCounterExample x =
    x |> truthTable |> Seq.tryFind (fun (env,res) -> not res) |> Option.map fst

let printCounterExample =
    (function None -> printfn "tautology verified OK"
            | Some env -> printfn "tautology failed on %A" (Seq.toList env))
```

The types of these functions are as follows:

```
val eval : Map<Var,bool> -> Prop -> bool
val support : Prop -> Set<Var>
val cases : 'a list -> seq<Map<'a,bool>> when 'a : comparison
val truthTable : Prop -> seq<Map<Var,bool> * bool>
val satisfiable : Prop -> bool
val tautology : Prop -> bool
val tautologyWithCounterExample : Prop -> Map<Var,bool> option
val printCounterExample : seq<'a> option -> unit
```

The function eval computes the value of a formula given assignments for each of the variables that occurs in the formula. support computes the set of variables that occurs in the formula. You can now use these functions to examine truth tables for some simple formulae, although first you may want to define the following functions to display truth tables neatly in F# Interactive:

```
let stringOfBit b = (if b then "T" else "F")
let stringOfEnv env =
    Map.fold (fun acc k v -> sprintf "%s=%s;" k (stringOfBit v)+acc) "" env
let stringOfLine (env,res) = sprintf "%20s %s" (stringOfEnv env) (stringOfBit res)
let stringOfTruthTable tt =
    "\n" + (tt |> Seq.toList |> List.map stringOfLine |> String.concat "\n")
```

Here are the truth tables for x, x AND y, and x OR NOT(x):

```
> fsi.AddPrinter(fun tt -> tt |> Seq.truncate 20 |> stringOfTruthTable);;

> truthTable (var "x");;
> val it : seq<Map<Var,bool> * bool>
=
                x=F;  F
                x=T;  T

> truthTable (var "x" &&&  var "y");;
> val it : seq<Map<Var,bool> * bool>
=
              x=F;y=F;  F
              x=F;y=T;  F
              x=T;y=F;  F
              x=T;y=T;  T

> truthTable (var "x" ||| ~~~(var "x"));;
> val it : seq<Map<Var,bool> * bool>
=
                x=F;  T
                x=T;  T
```

From this, you can see that x OR NOT(x) is a tautology, because it always evaluates to TRUE regardless of the value of the variable x.

From Circuits to Propositional Logic

Figure 12-4 shows a diagrammatic representation of three hardware circuits: a *half adder*, a *full adder*, and a *2-bit carry ripple adder*. The first of these has two input wires, x and y, and sets the *sum* wire high if exactly one of these is high. If both x and y are high, then the sum is low, and the carry wire is high instead. Thus, the circuit computes the 2-bit sum of the inputs. Likewise, a full adder computes the sum of three Boolean inputs, which, because it's at most three, can still be represented by 2 bits. A 2-bit carry ripple adder is formed by composing a half adder and a full adder together, wiring the carry from the first adder to one of the inputs of the second adder. The overall circuit has four inputs and three outputs.

Figure 12-4. *Three simple hardware circuits*

The following code models these circuit components. This uses *relational modeling,* where each circuit is modeled not as a function but as a propositional logic predicate that relates its input wires to its output wires:

```
let sumBit x y = (x ^^^ y)
let carryBit x y = (x &&& y)
let halfAdder x y sum carry =
    (sum === sumBit x y)   &&&
    (carry === carryBit x y)

let fullAdder x y z sum carry =
    let xy = (sumBit x y)
    (sum === sumBit xy z) &&&
    (carry === (carryBit x y ||| carryBit xy z))

let twoBitAdder (x1,x2) (y1,y2) (sum1,sum2) carryInner carry =
    halfAdder x1 y1 sum1 carryInner &&&
    fullAdder x2 y2 carryInner sum2 carry
```

Note the close relation between the diagram for the 2-bit adder and its representation as code. You can read the implementation as a specification of the diagram, and vice versa. But the types of these functions are a little less informative:

```
val sumBit : Prop -> Prop -> Prop
val carryBit : Prop -> Prop -> Prop
val halfAdder : Prop -> Prop -> Prop -> Prop -> Prop
val fullAdder : Prop -> Prop -> Prop -> Prop -> Prop -> Prop
val twoBitAdder : Prop * Prop -> Prop * Prop -> Prop * Prop -> Prop -> Prop -> Prop
```

In practice, circuits are defined largely with respect to vectors of wires, not just individual wires. You can model these using arrays of propositions; and because it's now clear that you're modeling bits via propositions, you make an appropriate type abbreviation for them as well:

```
type bit = Prop
type bitvec = bit[]

let Lo : bit = False
let Hi : bit = True
let vec n nm : bitvec = Array.init n (fun i -> var (sprintf "%s%d" nm i))
let bitEq (b1:bit) (b2:bit) = (b1 <=> b2)
let AndL l = Seq.reduce (fun x y -> And(x,y)) l
let vecEq (v1:bitvec) (v2:bitvec) = AndL (Array.map2 bitEq v1 v2)
```

These functions have types as follows:

```
type bit = Prop
type bitvec = bit []
val Lo : bit
val Hi : bit
val vec : int -> string -> bitvec
val bitEq : bit -> bit -> Prop
val AndL : #seq<Prop> -> Prop
val vecEq : bitvec -> bitvec -> Prop
```

You can now proceed to define larger circuits. For example:

```
let fourBitAdder  (x:bitvec) (y:bitvec) (sum:bitvec) (carry:bitvec) =
    halfAdder  x.[0] y.[0]              sum.[0] carry.[0] &&&
    fullAdder  x.[1] y.[1] carry.[0] sum.[1] carry.[1] &&&
    fullAdder  x.[2] y.[2] carry.[1] sum.[2] carry.[2] &&&
    fullAdder  x.[3] y.[3] carry.[2] sum.[3] carry.[3]
```

Or, more generally, you can chain an arbitrary series of adders to form an *N*-bit adder. First you define an abbreviation for the AndL function to represent the composition of multiple circuit blocks:

```
let Blocks l = AndL l
```

And here is the definition of an *N*-bit adder with a halfAdder at one end:

```
let nBitCarryRippleAdder (n:int) (x:bitvec) (y:bitvec) (sum:bitvec) (carry:bitvec) =
    Blocks [ for i in 0 .. n-1 ->
               if i = 0
               then halfAdder x.[i] y.[i] sum.[i] carry.[i]
               else fullAdder x.[i] y.[i] carry.[i-1] sum.[i] carry.[i]  ]
```

Using a similar approach, you get the following satisfying specification of a symmetric *N*-bit adder that accepts a carry as input and also gives a carry as output:

```
let rippleAdder (n:int) (x:bitvec) (y:bitvec) (sum:bitvec) (carry:bitvec)  =
    Blocks [ for i in 0 .. n-1 ->
               fullAdder x.[i] y.[i] carry.[i] sum.[i] carry.[i+1] ]
```

Let's now look at the propositional formula for a halfAdder with variable inputs and outputs:

```
> halfAdder (var "x") (var "y") (var "sum") (var "carry");;
> val it : Prop =
  And
    (Not
      (And
        (Not
          (And
            (Var "sum",
             Not
              (Not
                (And
                  (Not (And (Var "x",Var "y")),
                   Not (And (Not (Var "x"),Not (Var "y")))))))),
         Not
          (And
            (Not (Var "sum"),
             Not
              (Not
                (Not
                  (And
                    (Not (And (Var "x",Var "y")),
                     Not (And (Not (Var "x"),Not (Var "y")))))))))),
     Not
      (And
        (Not (And (Var "carry",And (Var "x",Var "y"))),
         Not (And (Not (Var "carry"),Not (And (Var "x",Var "y")))))))
```

Clearly, you don't want to be doing too much of that! You see better ways of inspecting circuits and the symbolic values of bit vectors in the section "Representing Propositional Formulae Efficiently Using BDDs."

In passing, note that the twoBitAdder uses an internal wire. You can model this using an existential formula:

```
let twoBitAdderWithHiding (x1,x2) (y1,y2) (sum1,sum2) carry =
    let carryInnerVar = fresh "carry"
    let carryInner = var(carryInnerVar)
    Exists(carryInnerVar, halfAdder x1 y1 sum1 carryInner &&&
                          fullAdder x2 y2 carryInner sum2 carry)
```

However, this brings up issues beyond the scope of this chapter. Instead, you take an approach to modeling where there are no boundaries to the circuits and where all internal wires are exposed.

Checking Simple Properties of Circuits

Now that you've modeled the initial hardware circuits, you can check simple properties of these circuits. For example, you can check that if you give a fullAdder all low (that is, false) inputs, then the output wires may be low as well, and, conversely, that you have a contradiction if one of the output wires is high:

```
> tautology (fullAdder Lo Lo Lo Lo Lo);;
val it : bool = true

> satisfiable (fullAdder Lo Lo Lo Hi Lo);;
val it : bool = false
```

It's of course much better to check these results *symbolically* by giving symbolic inputs. For example, you can check that if the same value is given to the two inputs of a halfAdder, then the sum output is low and the carry output is the same as the input:

```
> tautology (halfAdder (var "x") (var "x") Lo (var "x"));;
val it : bool = true
```

Likewise, you can check that a 2-bit adder is commutative—in other words, that it doesn't matter if you swap the *x* and *y* inputs:

```
> tautology
    (nBitCarryRippleAdder 2 (vec 2 "x") (vec 2 "y") (vec 2 "sum") (vec 3 "carry")
 === nBitCarryRippleAdder 2 (vec 2 "y") (vec 2 "x") (vec 2 "sum") (vec 3 "carry"));;
val it : bool = true
```

However, if you repeat the same for sizes of 5 or bigger, things start to slow down, and the naive implementation of checking propositional logic tautology based on truth tables begins to break down. Hence, you have to turn to more efficient techniques to process propositional formulae.

Representing Propositional Formulae Efficiently Using BDDs

In practice, propositional formulae to describe hardware can be enormous, involving hundreds of thousands of nodes. As a result, hardware companies have an interest in smart algorithms to process these formulae and check them for correctness. The circuits in the computers you use from day to day have almost certainly been verified using advanced propositional logic techniques, often using a functional language as the means to drive and control the analysis of the circuits.

A major advance in the application of symbolic techniques to hardware design occurred in the late 1980s with the discovery of *binary decision diagrams*, a representation for propositional logic formulae that is compact for many common circuit designs. BDDs represent a propositional formula via the use of if ... then ... else conditionals alone, which you write as (variable => true-branch | false-branch). Special nodes are used for true and false at the leaves: you write these as T and F. Every BDD is constructed with respect to a global variable ordering, so *x* AND NOT *y* can be represented as (x => (y => F | T) | F) if *x* comes before *y* in this ordering and as (y => F | (x => T | F)) if *y* comes before *x*. The variable ordering can be critical for performance of the representation.

BDDs are efficient because they use some of the language representation techniques you saw in Chapter 9. In particular, they work by *uniquely memoizing* all BDD nodes that are identical, which works by representing a BDD as an integer index into a lookup table that stores the real information about the node. Furthermore, negative indexes are used to represent the negation of a particular BDD node without creating a separate entry for the negated node. Listing 12-15 shows an implementation of BDDs. Fully polished BDD packages are often implemented in C. It's easy to access those packages from F#

using the techniques described in Chapter 19. Here, you have a clear and simple implementation entirely in F# code.

Listing 12-15. Implementing Binary Decision Diagrams

```
open System.Collections.Generic

let memoize f =
    let tab = new Dictionary<_,_>()
    fun x -> if tab.ContainsKey(x) then tab.[x]
             else let res = f x in tab.[x] <- res; res

type BddIndex = int
type Bdd = Bdd of BddIndex
type BddNode = Node of Var * BddIndex * BddIndex
type BddBuilder(order : Var -> Var -> int) =

    // The core data structures that preserve uniqueness
    let uniqueTab = new Dictionary<BddNode,BddIndex>()
    let nodeTab   = new Dictionary<BddIndex,BddNode>()

    // Keep track of the next index
    let mutable nextIdx = 2
    let trueIdx = 1
    let falseIdx = -1
    let trueNode = Node("",trueIdx,trueIdx)
    let falseNode = Node("",falseIdx,falseIdx)

    // Map indexes to nodes. Negative indexes go to their negation. The special
    // indexes -1 and 1 go to special true/false nodes.
    let idxToNode(idx) =
        if idx = trueIdx then trueNode
        elif idx = falseIdx then falseNode
        elif idx > 0 then nodeTab.[idx]
        else let (Node(v,l,r)) = nodeTab.[-idx]
            Node(v,-l,-r)

    // Map nodes to indexes. Add an entry to the table if needed.
    let nodeToUniqueIdx(node) =
        if uniqueTab.ContainsKey(node) then uniqueTab.[node]
        else
            let idx = nextIdx
            uniqueTab.[node] <- idx
            nodeTab.[idx] <- node
            nextIdx <- nextIdx + 1
            idx

    // Get the canonical index for a node. Preserve the invariant that the
    // left-hand node of a conditional is always a positive node
    let mkNode(v:Var,l:BddIndex,r:BddIndex) =
        if l = r then l
        elif l >= 0 then nodeToUniqueIdx(Node(v,l,r) )
        else -nodeToUniqueIdx(Node(v,-l,-r))
```

```
// Construct the BDD for a conjunction "m1 AND m2"
let rec mkAnd(m1,m2) =
    if m1 = falseIdx || m2 = falseIdx then falseIdx
    elif m1 = trueIdx then m2 elif m2 = trueIdx then m1
    else
        let (Node(x,l1,r1)) = idxToNode(m1)
        let (Node(y,l2,r2)) = idxToNode(m2)
        let v,(la,lb),(ra,rb) =
            match order x y with
            | c when c = 0 -> x,(l1,l2),(r1,r2)
            | c when c < 0 -> x,(l1,m2),(r1,m2)
            | c              -> y,(m1,l2),(m1,r2)
    mkNode(v,mkAnd(la,lb), mkAnd(ra,rb))

// Memoize this function
let mkAnd = memoize mkAnd


// Publish the construction functions that make BDDs from existing BDDs
member g.False = Bdd falseIdx
member g.And(Bdd m1,Bdd m2) = Bdd(mkAnd(m1,m2))
member g.Not(Bdd m) = Bdd(-m)
member g.Var(nm) = Bdd(mkNode(nm,trueIdx,falseIdx))
member g.NodeCount = nextIdx
```

The types of these functions are as follows:

```
val memoize : ('a -> 'b) -> ('a -> 'b) when 'a : equality
type BddIndex = int
type Bdd = Bdd of BddIndex
type BddNode = Node of Var * BddIndex * BddIndex
type BddBuilder =
    new : order:(Var -> Var -> int) -> BddBuilder
    member And : _arg1:Bdd * _arg2:Bdd -> Bdd
    member Not : _arg3:Bdd -> Bdd
    member Var : nm:Var -> Bdd
    member False : Bdd
    member NodeCount : int
```

In addition to the functions that ensure that nodes are unique, the only substantial function in the implementation is mkAnd. It relies on the following logical rules for constructing BDD nodes formed by taking the conjunction of existing nodes. Note how the second rule is used to interleave variables:

- $(x => P \mid Q)$ AND $(x => R \mid S)$ is identical to $(x => P$ AND $R \mid Q$ AND $S)$.

- $(x => P \mid Q)$ AND $(y => R \mid S)$ is identical to $(x => P$ AND $T \mid Q$ AND $T)$ where T is simply $(y => R \mid S)$.

One final important optimization in the implementation is to memoize the application of the mkAnd operation.

Given the previous implementation of BDDs, you can now add the members ToString to convert BDDs to strings, Build to convert a Prop representation of a formula into a BDD, and Equiv to check for equivalence between two BDDs:

```
type BddBuilder(order : Var -> Var -> int) =
    ...
    member g.ToString(Bdd idx) =
        let rec fmt depth idx =
            if depth > 3 then "..." else
            let (Node(p,l,r)) = idxToNode(idx)
            if p = "" then if l = trueIdx then "T" else "F"
            else sprintf "(%s => %s | %s)" p (fmt (depth+1) l) (fmt (depth+1) r)
        fmt 1 idx

    member g.Build(f) =
        match f with
        | And(x,y) -> g.And(g.Build x, g.Build y)
        | Var(p) -> g.Var(p)
        | Not(x) -> g.Not(g.Build x)
        | False -> g.False
        | Exists(v,p) -> failwith "Exists node"

    member g.Equiv p1 p2 = (g.Build(p1) = g.Build(p2))
```

You can now install a pretty-printer and inspect the BDDs for some simple formulae:

```
> let bddBuilder = BddBuilder(compare);;
val bddBuilder: BddBuilder

> fsi.AddPrinter(fun bdd -> bddBuilder.ToString(bdd));;
val it: unit = ()

> bddBuilder.Build(var "x");;
val it : Bdd = (x => T | F)

> bddBuilder.Build(var "x" &&& var "x");;
val it : Bdd = (x => T | F)

> bddBuilder.Build(var "x") = bddBuilder.Build(var "x" &&& var "x");;
val it : bool = true

> (var "x") = (var "x" &&& var "x");;
val it : bool = false

> bddBuilder.Build(var "x" &&& var "y");;
val it : Bdd = (x => (y => T | F) | F)

> bddBuilder.Equiv (var "x") (var "x" &&& var "x");;
val it : bool = true
```

Note that the BDD representations of *x* and *x* AND *x* are identical, whereas the Prop representations aren't. The Prop representation is an *abstract syntax* representation, whereas the BDD representation is more of a *semantic* or *computational* representation. The BDD representation incorporates all the logic necessary to prove propositional formula equivalent; in other words, this logic is built into the representation.

Circuit Verification with BDDs

You can now use BDDs to perform circuit verification. For example, the following verifies that you can swap the *x* and *y* inputs to an 8-bit adder:

```
> bddBuilder.Equiv
    (nBitCarryRippleAdder 8 (vec 8 "x") (vec 8 "y") (vec 8 "sum") (vec 9 "carry"))
    (nBitCarryRippleAdder 8 (vec 8 "y") (vec 8 "x") (vec 8 "sum") (vec 9 "carry"));;
val it : bool = true
```

Thirty-three variables are involved in this circuit. A naive exploration of this space would involve searching a truth table of more than eight billion entries. The BDD implementation takes moments on any modern computer. Efficient symbolic representations pay off!

A more substantial verification problem involves checking the equivalence of circuits that have substantial structural differences. To explore this, let's take a different implementation of addition called a *carry select adder*. This avoids a major problem with ripple adders caused by the fact that the carry signal must propagate along the entire length of the chain of internal adders, causing longer delays in the electrical signals and thus reducing the clock rates of a circuit or possibly increasing power consumption. A carry select adder gets around this through a common hardware trick of speculative execution. It divides the inputs into blocks and adds each block twice: once assuming the carry is low and once assuming it's high. The result is then selected *after* the circuit, when the carry for the block has been computed. Listing 12-16 shows the specification of the essence of the hardware layout of a carry select adder using the techniques developed so far. The specification uses the slicing syntax for arrays described in Chapter 4.

Listing 12-16. A Carry Select Adder Modeled Using Propositional Logic

```
let mux a b c = ((~~~a ==> b) &&& (a ==> c))

let carrySelectAdder
        totalSize maxBlockSize
        (x:bitvec) (y:bitvec)
        (sumLo:bitvec) (sumHi:bitvec)
        (carryLo:bitvec) (carryHi:bitvec)
        (sum:bitvec) (carry:bitvec) =
    Blocks
      [ for i in 0..maxBlockSize..totalSize-1 ->
          let sz = min (totalSize-i) maxBlockSize
          let j = i+sz-1
          let carryLo = Array.append [| False |] carryLo.[i+1..j+1]
          let adderLo = rippleAdder sz x.[i..j] y.[i..j] sumLo.[i..j] carryLo
          let carryHi = Array.append [| True  |] carryHi.[i+1..j+1]
          let adderHi = rippleAdder sz x.[i..j] y.[i..j]  sumHi.[i..j] carryHi
          let carrySelect = (carry.[j+1] === mux carry.[i] carryLo.[sz] carryHi.[sz])
```

```
    let sumSelect =
        Blocks [for k in i..j ->
                        sum.[k] === mux carry.[i] sumLo.[k] sumHi.[k]]
    adderLo &&& adderHi &&& carrySelect &&& sumSelect ]
```

You can now check that a carrySelectAdder is equivalent to a rippleAdder. Here's the overall verification condition:

```
let checkAdders n k =
    let x = vec n "x"
    let y = vec n "y"
    let sumA     = vec n "sumA"
    let sumB     = vec n "sumB"
    let sumLo    = vec n "sumLo"
    let sumHi    = vec n "sumHi"
    let carryA  = vec (n+1) "carryA"
    let carryB  = vec (n+1) "carryB"
    let carryLo = vec (n+1) "carryLo"
    let carryHi = vec (n+1) "carryHi"
    let adder1 = carrySelectAdder n k x y sumLo sumHi carryLo  carryHi  sumA carryA
    let adder2 = rippleAdder n x y sumB carryB
    (adder1 &&& adder2 &&& (carryA.[0] === carryB.[0]) ==>
        (vecEq sumA sumB &&& bitEq carryA.[n] carryB.[n]))
```

Ignoring the construction of the inputs, the verification condition specifies the following:

- Assume you have the two adder circuits, with the same inputs.

- Assume the input carry bits are the same.

- Then, the output sum vectors are identical, and the final output carry bits are identical.

Here is the verification condition being checked interactively, for 5-bit inputs, in chunks of 2 for the carrySelectAdder:

```
> bddBuilder.Equiv (checkAdders 5 2) True;;
val it : bool = true
```

In practice, BDDs require a good variable ordering, and the default alphabetic ordering is unlikely to be the best. Here is a larger verification using a more random ordering induced by first comparing on the hash codes of the names of the variables:

```
let approxCompareOn f x y =
    let c = compare (f x) (f y)
    if c <> 0 then c else compare x y
let bddBuilder2 = BddBuilder(approxCompareOn hash)
```

```
> bddBuilder2.Equiv (checkAdders 7 2) True;;
val it : bool = true
```

Seventy-four Boolean variables are involved in this last verification problem. You would have to generate up to 2^{74} test cases to explore this systematically via testing; that's 22 thousand billion billion test cases. By using symbolic techniques, you've explored this entire space in a matter of seconds and in only a few hundred lines of code.

■ **Note** Hardware and software verification are highly active areas of research and one of the most important applications of symbolic programming techniques in the industrial arena. The verifications performed here aim to give you a taste of how symbolic techniques can provide nontrivial results about circuits in a matter of seconds. We've omitted some simple techniques that can make these verifications scale to very large circuits; for example, we expand equivalence nodes in propositional formulae. Preserving them can lead to smaller symbolic descriptions and more efficient processing with BDDs.

Summary

This chapter looked at two applications of language-oriented symbolic programming. The first was algebraic symbolic differentiation and visualization, where you learned how to differentiate, simplify, and display algebraic expressions. The second was hardware modeling and verification using propositional logic and binary decision diagrams, where you saw how to use symbolic techniques to describe circuits as propositional logic formulae and then used brute-force and/or binary decision diagram techniques to analyze these for correctness. These examples are only two of the many in the large domain of symbolic computation problems, a domain where functional programming and F# truly excels.

CHAPTER 13

∎∎∎

Reactive, Asynchronous, and Parallel Programming

So far in this book, you've seen functions and objects that process their inputs immediately using a single thread of execution where the code runs to completion and produces useful results or state changes. In this chapter, you turn your attention to *concurrent, parallel, asynchronous,* and *reactive* programs. These represent substantially different approaches to programming from those you've seen so far. Some of the reasons for turning to these techniques are as follows:

- To achieve better responsiveness in a graphical user interface (GUI)
- To report progress results during a long-running computation and to support cancellation of these computations
- To achieve greater throughput in a reactive application or service
- To achieve faster processing rates on a multiprocessor machine or cluster
- To take advantage of the I/O parallelism available in modern disk drives or network connections
- To sustain processing while network and disk I/O operations are in process

This chapter covers some of the techniques that can help achieve these outcomes:

- Using .NET threads and the BackgroundWorker class for background computations
- Using events and messages to report results back to a GUI
- Using F# asynchronous workflows and the .NET thread pool to handle network requests and other asynchronous I/O operations
- Using F# pattern-matching to process message queues
- Using low-level .NET shared-memory primitives to implement new concurrency techniques and control access to mutable data structures

Chapter 11 looked at the most common type of reactive program: GUI programs that respond to events raised on the GUI thread. The inner loop of such an application (contained in the Windows Forms library) spends most of its time blocked and waiting for the underlying operating system to notify it of a relevant event, such as a click from the user or a timer event from the operating system. This notification is received as an event in a message queue. Many GUI programs have only a single thread of execution, so all computation happens on the GUI thread. This can lead to problems such as nonresponsive user interfaces. This is one of many reasons it's important to master some of the techniques of concurrent and asynchronous programming.

Introducing Some Terminology

Let's begin by looking more closely at some terminology:

- *Processes* are, in the context of this chapter, standard operating system (OS) processes. Each instance of the .NET Common Language Runtime (CLR) runs in its own process, and multiple instances of the .NET CLR are often running on the same machine.

- *Threads* are, in the context of this chapter, standard .NET threads. On most implementations of .NET, these correspond to operating system threads. Each .NET process has many threads running within the one process.

- *Concurrent programs* are ones with multiple threads of execution, each typically executing different code, or at different execution points within the same code. Simultaneous execution may be simulated by scheduling and descheduling the threads, which is done by the OS. For example, most OS services and GUI applications are concurrent.

- *Parallel programs* are one or more processes or threads executing simultaneously. For example, many modern microprocessors have two or more physical CPUs capable of executing processes and threads in parallel. Parallel programs can also be *data parallel*. For example, a massively parallel device such as a graphics processor unit (GPU) can process arrays and images in parallel. Parallel programs can also be a cluster of computers on a network, communicating via message passing. Historically, some parallel scientific programs have even used e-mail for communication!

- *Asynchronous programs* perform requests that don't complete immediately but are fulfilled at a later time and where the program issuing the request has to do meaningful work in the meantime. For example, most network I/O is inherently asynchronous. A web crawler is also a highly asynchronous program, managing hundreds or thousands of simultaneous network requests.

- *Reactive programs* are ones whose normal mode of operation is to be in a state of waiting for some kind of input, such as waiting for user input or for input from a message queue via a network socket. For example, GUI applications and web servers are reactive programs.

Parallel, asynchronous, concurrent, and reactive programs bring many interesting challenges. For example, these programs are nearly always *nondeterministic*. This makes debugging more challenging because it's difficult to step through a program; even pausing a running program with outstanding asynchronous requests may cause timeouts. Most dramatically, incorrect concurrent programs may *deadlock*, which means all threads are waiting on results from some other thread and no thread can make progress. Programs may also *livelock*, where processing is occurring and messages are being sent between threads but no useful work is being performed.

Using and Designing Background Workers

One of the easiest ways to get going with concurrency and parallelism is to use the
System.ComponentModel.BackgroundWorker class of the .NET Framework. A BackgroundWorker class runs
on its own dedicated operating system thread. These objects can be used in many situations but are
especially useful for coarse-grained concurrency and parallelism such as checking the spelling of a
document in the background. This section shows some simple uses of BackgroundWorker and how to
build similar objects that use BackgroundWorker internally.

Listing 13-1 shows a simple use of BackgroundWorker that computes the Fibonacci numbers on the
worker thread.

Listing 13-1. A Simple BackgroundWorker

```
open System.ComponentModel
open System.Windows.Forms

let worker = new BackgroundWorker()
let numIterations = 1000

worker.DoWork.Add(fun args ->

    let rec computeFibonacci resPrevPrev resPrev i =
        // Compute the next result
        let res = resPrevPrev + resPrev

        // At the end of the computation write the result into mutable state
        if i = numIterations then
            args.Result <- box res
        else
            // Compute the next result
            computeFibonacci resPrev res (i+1)

    computeFibonacci 1 1 2)

worker.RunWorkerCompleted.Add(fun args ->
    MessageBox.Show(sprintf "Result = %A" args.Result) |> ignore)

// Execute the worker
worker.RunWorkerAsync()
```

Table 13-1 shows the primary members of a BackgroundWorker object. The execution sequence of
the code in Listing 13-1 is as follows:

1.   The main application thread creates and configures a BackgroundWorker
     object.

2.   After configuration is complete, the main application thread calls the
     RunWorkerAsync method on the BackgroundWorker object. This causes the DoWork
     event to be raised on the worker thread.

3.   The DoWork event handler is executed in the worker thread and computes the
     one-thousandth Fibonacci number. At the end of the computation, the result is
     written into args.Result, a mutable storage location in the event arguments
     for the DoWork event. The DoWork event handler then completes.

4. At some point after the DoWork event handler completes, the RunWorkerCompleted event is automatically raised on the main application thread. This displays a message box with the result of the computation, retrieved from the args field of the event arguments.

Table 13-1. Primary Members of the BackgroundWorker Class

Member and Type	Description
RunWorkerAsync: unit -> unit	Starts the process on a separate thread asynchronously. Called from the main thread.
CancelAsync: unit -> unit	Sets the CancellationPending flag of the background task. Called from the main thread.
CancellationPending: bool	Set to true by raising CancelAsync. Used by the worker thread.
WorkerReportsProgress: bool	Set to true if the worker can support progress updates. Used by the main thread.
WorkerSupportsCancellation: bool	Set to true if the worker can support cancellation of the current task in progress. Used by the main thread.
ReportProgress: int -> unit	Indicates the progress of the operation. Used by the worker thread.
DoWork: IEvent<DoWorkEventArgs>	Fires in response to a call to RunWorkerAsync. Invoked on the worker thread.
RunWorkerCompleted: IEvent<RunWorkerCompletedEventArgs>	Fires when the background operation is canceled, when the operation is completed, or when an exception is thrown. Invoked on the main thread.
ProgressChanged: IEvent<ProgressChangedEventArgs>	Fires whenever the ReportProgress property is set. Invoked on the main thread.

■ **Note** Objects such as a BackgroundWorker are two-faced: they have some methods and events that are for use from the main thread and some that are for use on the worker thread. This is common in concurrent programming. In particular, be careful to understand which thread an event is raised on. For BackgroundWorker, the RunWorkerAsync and CancelAsync methods are for use from the GUI thread, and the ProgressChanged and RunWorkerCompleted events are raised on the GUI thread. The DoWork event is raised on the worker thread, and the ReportProgress method and the CancellationPending property are for use from the worker thread when handling this event.

The members in Table 13-1 show two additional facets of BackgroundWorker objects: they can optionally support protocols for cancellation and reporting progress. To report progress percentages, a worker must call the ReportProgress method, which raises the ProgressChanged event in the GUI thread. For cancellation, a worker computation need only check the CancellationPending property at regular intervals, exiting the computation as a result.

Building a Simpler Iterative Worker

Capturing common control patterns such as cancellation and progress reporting is an absolutely essential part of mastering concurrent programming. However, one of the problems with .NET classes such as BackgroundWorker is that they're often more imperative than you may want, and they force other common patterns to be captured by using mutable data structures shared between threads. This leads to the more difficult topic of shared-memory concurrency, discussed later in the chapter. Furthermore, the way BackgroundWorker handles cancellation means that you must insert flag-checks and early-exit paths in the executing background process. Finally, BackgroundWorker isn't useful for background threads that perform asynchronous operations, because the background thread exits too early, before the callbacks for the asynchronous operations have executed.

For this reason, it can often be useful to build abstractions that are similar to BackgroundWorker but that capture richer or different control patterns, preferably in a way that doesn't rely on the use of mutable state and that interferes less with the structure of the overall computation. Much of the rest of this chapter looks at various techniques to build these control structures.

You start with a case study in which you build a type IterativeBackgroundWorker that represents a variation on the BackgroundWorker design pattern. Listing 13-2 shows the code.

Listing 13-2. A Variation on the BackgroundWorker Design Pattern for Iterative Computations

```
open System.ComponentModel
open System.Windows.Forms

/// An IterativeBackgroundWorker follows the BackgroundWorker design pattern
/// but instead of running an arbitrary computation it iterates a function
/// a fixed number of times and reports intermediate and final results.
/// The worker is paramaterized by its internal state type.
///
/// Percentage progress is based on the iteration number. Cancellation checks
/// are made at each iteration. Implemented via an internal BackgroundWorker.
type IterativeBackgroundWorker<'T>(oneStep:('T -> 'T),
                                   initialState:'T,
                                   numIterations:int) =

    let worker =
        new BackgroundWorker(WorkerReportsProgress=true,
                             WorkerSupportsCancellation=true)


    // Create the events that we will later trigger
    let completed = new Event<_>()
    let error     = new Event<_>()
    let cancelled = new Event<_>()
    let progress  = new Event<_>()

    do worker.DoWork.Add(fun args ->
```

```
            // This recursive function represents the computation loop.
            // It runs at "maximum speed", i.e. is an active rather than
            // a reactive process, and can only be controlled by a
            // cancellation signal.
            let rec iterate state i =
                // At the end of the computation terminate the recursive loop
                if worker.CancellationPending then
                    args.Cancel <- true
                elif i < numIterations then
                    // Compute the next result
                    let state' = oneStep state

                    // Report the percentage computation and the internal state
                    let percent = int ((float (i+1)/float numIterations) * 100.0)
                    do worker.ReportProgress(percent, box state);

                    // Compute the next result
                    iterate state' (i+1)
                else
                    args.Result <- box state

            iterate initialState 0)

    do worker.RunWorkerCompleted.Add(fun args ->
        if args.Cancelled        then cancelled.Trigger()
        elif args.Error <> null then error.Trigger args.Error
        else completed.Trigger (args.Result :?> 'T))

    do worker.ProgressChanged.Add(fun args ->
        progress.Trigger (args.ProgressPercentage,(args.UserState :?> 'T)))

    member x.WorkerCompleted  = completed.Publish
    member x.WorkerCancelled  = cancelled.Publish
    member x.WorkerError      = error.Publish
    member x.ProgressChanged  = progress.Publish

    // Delegate the remaining members to the underlying worker
    member x.RunWorkerAsync()    = worker.RunWorkerAsync()
    member x.CancelAsync()       = worker.CancelAsync()
```

The types inferred for the code in Listing 13-2 are as follows:

```
type IterativeBackgroundWorker<'State> =
    new : ('State -> 'State) * 'State * int -> IterativeBackgroundWorker<'State>
    member RunWorkerAsync : unit -> unit
    member CancelAsync : unit -> unit

    member ProgressChanged : IEvent<int * 'State>
    member WorkerCompleted : IEvent<'State>
    member WorkerCancelled : IEvent<unit>
    member WorkerError     : IEvent<exn>
```

Let's look at this signature first, because it represents the design of the type. The worker constructor is given a function of type 'State -> 'State to compute successive iterations of the computation, plus an initial state and the number of iterations to compute. For example, you can compute the Fibonacci numbers using the following iteration function:

```
let fibOneStep (fibPrevPrev:bigint,fibPrev) = (fibPrev, fibPrevPrev+fibPrev);;
```

The type of this function is as follows:

```
val fibOneStep : bigint * bigint -> bigint * bigint
```

The RunWorkerAsync and CancelAsync members follow the BackgroundWorker design pattern, as do the events, except that you expand the RunWorkerCompleted event into three events to correspond to the three termination conditions and modify the ProgressChanged to include the state. You can instantiate the type as follows:

```
> let worker = new IterativeBackgroundWorker<_>( fibOneStep,(1I,1I),100);;
val worker : IterativeBackgroundWorker<bigint * bigint>

> worker.WorkerCompleted.Add(fun result ->
    MessageBox.Show(sprintf "Result = %A" result) |> ignore);;
val it : unit = ()

> worker.ProgressChanged.Add(fun (percentage, state) ->
    printfn "%d%% complete, state = %A" percentage state);;
val it : unit = ()

> worker.RunWorkerAsync();;
1% complete, state = (1I, 1I)
2% complete, state = (1I, 2I)
3% complete, state = (2I, 3I)
4% complete, state = (3I, 5I)
...
98% complete, state = (135301852344706746049I, 218922995834555169026I)
99% complete, state = (218922995834555169026I, 354224848179261915075I)
100% complete, state = (354224848179261915075I, 573147844013817084101I)
val it : unit = ()
```

One difference here is that cancellation and percentage progress reporting are handled automatically based on the iterations of the computation. This is assuming each iteration takes roughly the same amount of time. Other variations on the BackgroundWorker design pattern are possible. For example, reporting percentage completion of fixed tasks such as installation is often performed by timing sample executions of the tasks and adjusting the percentage reports appropriately.

■ **Note** You implement IterativeBackgroundWorker via delegation rather than inheritance. This is because its external members are different from those of BackgroundWorker. The .NET documentation recommends that you use implementation inheritance for this, but we disagree. Implementation inheritance can only *add* complexity to the signature of an abstraction and never makes things simpler, whereas an IterativeBackgroundWorker is in many ways simpler than using a BackgroundWorker, despite that it uses an instance of the latter internally. Powerful, compositional, simple abstractions are the primary building blocks of functional programming.

Raising Additional Events from Background Workers

Often, you need to raise additional events from objects that follow the BackgroundWorker design pattern. For example, let's say you want to augment IterativeBackgroundWorker to raise an event when the worker starts its work and for this event to pass the exact time that the worker thread started as an event argument. Listing 13-3 shows the extra code you need to add to the IterativeBackgroundWorker type to make this happen. You use this extra code in the next section.

Listing 13-3. Code to Raise GUI-Thread Events from an IterativeBackgroundWorker Object

```
open System
open System.Threading

// Pseudo-code for adding event-raising to this object
type IterativeBackgroundWorker<'T>(...) =

    let worker = ...

    // The constructor captures the synchronization context. This allows us to post
    // messages back to the GUI thread where the BackgroundWorker was created.
    let syncContext = SynchronizationContext.Current
    do if syncContext = null then failwith "no synchronization context found"

    let started = new Event<_>()

    // Raise the event when the worker starts. This is done by posting a message
    // to the captured synchronization context.
    do worker.DoWork.Add(fun args ->
        syncContext.Post(SendOrPostCallback(fun _ -> started.Trigger(DateTime.Now)),
                        state=null)
        ...

    /// The Started event gets raised when the worker starts. It is
    /// raised on the GUI thread (i.e. in the synchronization context of
    /// the thread where the worker object was created).
    // It has type IEvent<DateTime>
    member x.Started              = started.Publish
```

The simple way to raise additional events is often wrong. For example, it's tempting to create an event, arrange for it to be triggered, and publish it, as you would do for a GUI control. However, if you do that, you end up triggering the event on the background worker thread, and its event handlers run on that thread. This is dangerous, because most GUI objects (and many other objects) can be accessed only from the thread they were created on; this is a restriction enforced by most GUI systems.

■ **Note** One of the nice features of the BackgroundWorker class is that it automatically arranges to raise the RunWorkerCompleted and ProgressChanged events on the GUI thread. Listing 13-3 shows how to achieve this. Technically speaking, the extended IterativeBackgroundWorker object captures the *synchronization context* of the thread where it was created and posts an operation back to that synchronization context. A synchronization context is an object that lets you post operations back to another thread. For threads such as a GUI thread, this means that posting an operation posts a message through the GUI event loop.

Connecting a Background Worker to a GUI

To round off this section on the BackgroundWorker design pattern, Listing 13-4 shows the full code required to build a small application with a background worker task that supports cancellation and reports progress.

Listing 13-4. Connecting an IterativeBackgroundWorker to a GUI

```
open System.Drawing
open System.Windows.Forms

let form = new Form(Visible=true,TopMost=true)

let panel = new FlowLayoutPanel(Visible=true,
                                Height = 20,
                                Dock=DockStyle.Bottom,
                                BorderStyle=BorderStyle.FixedSingle)

let progress = new ProgressBar(Visible=false,
                               Anchor=(AnchorStyles.Bottom ||| AnchorStyles.Top),
                               Value=0)

let text = new Label(Text="Paused",
                     Anchor=AnchorStyles.Left,
                     Height=20,
                     TextAlign= ContentAlignment.MiddleLeft)

panel.Controls.Add(progress)
panel.Controls.Add(text)
form.Controls.Add(panel)

let fibOneStep (fibPrevPrev:bigint,fibPrev) = (fibPrev, fibPrevPrev+fibPrev)

// Run the iterative algorithm 500 times before reporting intermediate results
let rec repeatMultipleTimes n f s =
```

```
    if n <= 0 then s else repeatMultipleTimes (n-1) f (f s)

// Burn some additional cycles to make sure it runs slowly enough
let rec burnSomeCycles n f s =
    if n <= 0 then f s else ignore (f s); burnSomeCycles (n-1) f s

let step = (repeatMultipleTimes 500 (burnSomeCycles 1000 fibOneStep))

// Create the iterative worker.
let worker = new IterativeBackgroundWorker<_>(step,(1I,1I),80)

worker.ProgressChanged.Add(fun (progressPercentage,state)->
    progress.Value <- progressPercentage)

worker.WorkerCompleted.Add(fun (_,result) ->
    progress.Visible <- false;
    text.Text <- "Paused";
    MessageBox.Show(sprintf "Result = %A" result) |> ignore)

worker.WorkerCancelled.Add(fun () ->
    progress.Visible <- false;
    text.Text <- "Paused";
    MessageBox.Show(sprintf "Cancelled OK!") |> ignore)

worker.WorkerError.Add(fun exn ->
    text.Text <- "Paused";
    MessageBox.Show(sprintf "Error: %A" exn) |> ignore)

form.Menu <- new MainMenu()
let workerMenu = form.Menu.MenuItems.Add("&Worker")

workerMenu.MenuItems.Add(new MenuItem("Run",onClick=(fun _ args ->
    text.Text <- "Running";
    progress.Visible <- true;
    worker.RunWorkerAsync())))


workerMenu.MenuItems.Add(new MenuItem("Cancel",onClick=(fun _ args ->
    text.Text <- "Cancelling";
    worker.CancelAsync())))

form.Closed.Add(fun _ -> worker.CancelAsync())
```

When you run the code in F# Interactive, a window appears, as shown in Figure 13-1.

Figure 13-1. A GUI window with a BackgroundWorker reporting progress percentage

---

■ **Note** Forcibly aborting computations uncooperatively isn't recommended in .NET programming. You can attempt to do this using `System.Threading.Thread.Abort()`, but using this method may have many unintended consequences, discussed later in this chapter.

Introducing Asynchronous and Parallel Computations

The two background worker samples shown so far run at full throttle. In other words, the computations run on the background threads as active loops, and their reactive behavior is limited to flags that check for cancellation. In reality, background threads often have to do different kinds of work, either by responding to completed asynchronous I/O requests, by processing messages, by sleeping, or by waiting to acquire shared resources. Fortunately, F# comes with a powerful set of techniques for structuring asynchronous programs in a natural way. These are called *asynchronous workflows*. The next three sections cover how to use asynchronous workflows to structure asynchronous and message-processing tasks in ways that preserve the essential logical structure of your code.

Fetching Multiple Web Pages in Parallel, Asynchronously

One of the most intuitive asynchronous tasks is fetching a web page; we all use web browsers that can fetch multiple pages simultaneously. The samples in Chapter 2 showed how to fetch pages synchronously. This is useful for many purposes, but browsers and high-performance web crawlers have tens or thousands of connections in flight at once.

The type `Microsoft.FSharp.Control.Async<'T>` lies at the heart of F# asynchronous workflows. A value of type `Async<'T>` represents a program fragment that will generate a value of type `'T` at some point in the future. Listing 13-5 shows how to use asynchronous workflows to fetch several web pages simultaneously. (This example uses a method `AsyncReadToEnd` defined in the open source library called the F# Power Pack. If you like, you can replace this with a call to the synchronous method `ReadToEnd`, defined in the standard .NET libraries. Doing so may increase the thread count used by executing this code.)

Listing 13-5. *Fetching Three Web Pages Simultaneously*

```
#r "FSharp.PowerPack.dll" // contains the definition for AsyncReadToEnd
open System.Net
open System.IO

let museums = ["MOMA",            "http://moma.org/";
               "British Museum", "http://www.thebritishmuseum.ac.uk/";
               "Prado",          "http://museoprado.mcu.es"]

let fetchAsync(nm,url:string) =
    async { printfn "Creating request for %s..." nm
            let req  = WebRequest.Create(url)

            let! resp  = req.AsyncGetResponse()

            printfn "Getting response stream for %s..." nm
            let stream = resp.GetResponseStream()

            printfn "Reading response for %s..." nm
            let reader = new StreamReader(stream)
            let! html = reader.AsyncReadToEnd()

            printfn "Read %d characters for %s..." html.Length nm }

for nm,url in museums do
    Async.Start (fetchAsync(nm,url))
```

The types of these functions and values are as follows:

```
val museums : (string * string) list
val fetchAsync : string * string -> Async<unit>
```

When run on one of our machines via F# Interactive, the output of the code from Listing 13-5 is as follows:

```
Creating request for MOMA...
Creating request for British Museum...
Creating request for Prado...
Getting response for MOMA...
Reading response for MOMA...
Getting response for Prado...
Reading response for Prado...
Read 188 characters for Prado...
Read 41635 characters for MOMA...
Getting response for British Museum...
Reading response for British Museum...
Read 24341 characters for British Museum...
```

The heart of the code in Listing 13-5 is the construct introduced by async { ... }. This is an application of the workflow syntax introduced in Chapter 9.

Let's take a closer look at Listing 13-5. The key operations are the two let! operations within the workflow expression:

```
async { ...
        let! resp  = req.AsyncGetResponse()
        ...
        let! html = reader.AsyncReadToEnd()
        ... }
```

Within asynchronous workflow expressions, the language construct let! var = expr in body means "perform the asynchronous operation expr and bind the result to var when the operation completes. Then, continue by executing the rest of the computation body."

With this in mind, you can now see what fetchAsync does:

- It synchronously requests a web page.

- It asynchronously awaits a response to the request.

- It gets the response Stream and StreamReader synchronously after the asynchronous request completes.

- It reads to the end of the stream asynchronously.

- After the read completes, it prints the total number of characters read synchronously.

Finally, you use the method Async.Start to initiate the execution of a number of asynchronous computations. This works by queuing the computations in the .NET thread pool. The following section explains the .NET thread pool in more detail.

Understanding Thread Hopping

Asynchronous computations are different from normal, synchronous computations: an asynchronous computation tends to hop between different underlying .NET threads. To see this, let's augment the asynchronous computation with diagnostics that show the ID of the underlying .NET thread at each point of active execution. You can do this by replacing uses of printfn in the function fetchAsync with uses of the following function:

```
let tprintfn fmt =
    printf "[.NET Thread %d]" System.Threading.Thread.CurrentThread.ManagedThreadId;
    printfn fmt
```

After doing this, the output changes to the following:

```
[.NET Thread 12]Creating request for MOMA...
[.NET Thread 13]Creating request for British Museum...
[.NET Thread 12]Creating request for Prado...
[.NET Thread 8]Getting response for MOMA...
[.NET Thread 8]Reading response for MOMA...
[.NET Thread 9]Getting response for Prado...
[.NET Thread 9]Reading response for Prado...
```

```
[.NET Thread 9]Read 188 characters for Prado...
[.NET Thread 8]Read 41635 characters for MOMA...
[.NET Thread 8]Getting response for British Museum...
[.NET Thread 8]Reading response for British Museum...
[.NET Thread 8]Read 24341 characters for British Museum...
```

Note how each individual Async program hops between threads; the MOMA request started on .NET thread 12 and finished life on .NET thread 8. Each asynchronous computation in Listing 13-5 executes in the following way:

- It starts life as a work item in the .NET thread pool. (The .NET thread pool is explained in the "What Is the .NET Thread Pool?" sidebar.) These are processed by a number of .NET threads.

- When the asynchronous computations reach the AsyncGetResponse and AsyncReadToEnd calls, the requests are made, and the continuations are registered as I/O completion actions in the .NET thread pool. No thread is used while the request is in progress.

- When the requests complete, they trigger a callback in the .NET thread pool. These may be serviced by different threads than those that originated the calls.

What Is the .NET Thread Pool?

.NET objects such as BackgroundWorker use a single .NET background thread, which corresponds to a single Windows or other OS thread. OS threads have supporting resources such as an execution stack that consume memory and are relatively expensive to create and run.

However, many concurrent processing tasks require only the ability to schedule short-lived tasks that then suspend, waiting for further input. To simplify the process of creating and managing these tasks, the .NET Framework provides the System.Threading.ThreadPool class. The thread pool consists of two main sets of suspended tasks: a queue containing user work items and a pool of I/O completion callbacks, each waiting for a signal from the operating system. The number of threads in the thread pool is automatically tuned, and items can be either queued asynchronously or registered against a .NET WaitHandle synchronization object (for example, a lock, a semaphore, or an I/O request). This is how to queue a work item in the .NET thread pool:

```
open System.Threading

ThreadPool.QueueUserWorkItem(fun _ -> printf "Hello!") |> ignore
```

Under the Hood: What Are Asynchronous Computations?

Async<'T> values are essentially a way of writing continuation-passing or callback programs explicitly. Continuations themselves were described in Chapter 8 along with techniques to pass them explicitly. Async<'T> computations call a *success continuation* when the asynchronous computation completes and an *exception continuation* if it fails. They provide a form of *managed asynchronous computation*, where *managed* means that several aspects of asynchronous programming are handled automatically:

- *Exception propagation is added for free*: If an exception is raised during an asynchronous step, then the exception terminates the entire asynchronous computation and cleans up any resources declared using use, and the exception value is then handed to a continuation. Exceptions may also be caught and managed within the asynchronous workflow by using try/with/finally.

- *Cancellation checking is added for free*: The execution of an Async<'T> workflow automatically checks a cancellation flag at each asynchronous operation. Cancellation can be controlled through the use of cancellation tokens.

- *Resource lifetime management is fairly simple*: You can protect resources across parts of an asynchronous computation by using use inside the workflow syntax.

If you put aside the question of cancellation, values of type Async<'T> are effectively identical to the following type:

```
type Async<'T> = Async of ('T -> unit) * (exn -> unit) -> unit
```

Here, the functions are the success continuation and exception continuations, respectively. Each value of type Async<'T> should eventually call one of these two continuations. The async object is of type AsyncBuilder and supports the following methods, among others:

```
type AsyncBuilder with
    member Return : 'T -> Async<'T>
    member Delay : (unit -> Async<'T>) -> Async<'T>
    member Using: 'T * ('T -> Async<'U>) -> Async<'U> when 'T :> System.IDisposable
    member Bind: Async<'T> * ('T -> Async<'U>) -> Async<'U>
```

The full definition of Async<'T> values and the implementations of these methods for the async object are given in the F# library source code. As you saw in Chapter 9, builder objects such as async containing methods like those shown previously mean that you can use the syntax async { ... } as a way of building Async<'T> values.

Table 13-2 shows the common constructs used in asynchronous workflow expressions. For example, the following asynchronous workflow

```
async { let req  = WebRequest.Create("http://moma.org/")
        let! resp  = req.AsyncGetResponse()
        let stream = resp.GetResponseStream()
        let reader = new StreamReader(stream)
        let! html = reader.AsyncReadToEnd()
        html }
```

is shorthand for the following code:

```
async.Delay(fun () ->
    let req = WebRequest.Create("http://moma.org/")
    async.Bind(req.AsyncGetResponse(), (fun resp ->
        let stream = resp.GetResponseStream()
        let reader = new StreamReader(stream)
        async.Bind(reader.AsyncReadToEnd(), (fun html ->
            async.Return html)))
```

As you saw in Chapter 9, the key to understanding the F# workflow syntax is always to understand the meaning of let!. In the case of async workflows, let! executes one asynchronous computation and schedules the next computation for execution after the first asynchronous computation completes. This is syntactic sugar for the `Bind` operation on the `async` object.

Table 13-2. Common Constructs Used in async { ... } Workflow Expressions

Construct	Description
`let! pat = expr`	Executes the asynchronous computation expr, and binds its result to pat when it completes. If expr has type Async<'T>, then pat has type 'T. Equivalent to `async.Bind(expr,(fun pat -> ...))`.
`let pat = expr`	Executes an expression synchronously, and binds its result to pat immediately. If expr has type 'T, then pat has type 'T.
`do! expr`	Equivalent to `let! () = expr`.
`do expr`	Equivalent to `let () = expr`.
`return expr`	Evaluates the expression, and returns its value as the result of the containing asynchronous workflow. Equivalent to `async.Return(expr)`.
`return! expr`	Executes the expression as an asynchronous computation, and returns its result as the overall result of the containing asynchronous workflow. Equivalent to expr.
`use pat = expr`	Executes the expression immediately, and binds its result immediately. Calls the `Dispose` method on each variable bound in the pattern when the subsequent asynchronous workflow terminates, regardless of whether it terminates normally or by an exception. Equivalent to `async.Using(expr,(fun pat -> ...))`.

Parallel File Processing Using Asynchronous Workflows

This section shows a slightly longer example of asynchronous I/O processing. The running sample is an application that must read a large number of image files and perform some processing on them. This kind of application may be *compute bound* (if the processing takes a long time and the file system is fast) or *I/O bound* (if the processing is quick and the file system is slow). Using asynchronous techniques tends to give good overall performance gains when an application is I/O bound and can also give performance improvements for compute-bound applications if asynchronous operations are executed in parallel on multicore machines.

Listing 13-6 shows a synchronous implementation of the image-transformation program.

Listing 13-6. A Synchronous Image Processor

```
open System.IO
let numImages = 200
let size = 512
let numPixels = size * size

let makeImageFiles () =
    printfn "making %d %dx%d images... " numImages size size
```

```
    let pixels = Array.init numPixels (fun i -> byte i)
    for i = 1 to numImages  do
        System.IO.File.WriteAllBytes(sprintf "Image%d.tmp" i, pixels)
    printfn "done."

let processImageRepeats = 20

let transformImage (pixels, imageNum) =
    printfn "transformImage %d" imageNum;
    // Perform a CPU-intensive operation on the image.
    for i in 1 .. processImageRepeats do
        pixels |> Array.map (fun b -> b + 1uy) |> ignore
    pixels |> Array.map (fun b -> b + 1uy)

let processImageSync i =
    use inStream =  File.OpenRead(sprintf "Image%d.tmp" i)
    let pixels = Array.zeroCreate numPixels
    let nPixels = inStream.Read(pixels,0,numPixels);
    let pixels' = transformImage(pixels,i)
    use outStream =  File.OpenWrite(sprintf "Image%d.done" i)
    outStream.Write(pixels',0,numPixels)

let processImagesSync () =
    printfn "processImagesSync...";
    for i in 1 .. numImages do
        processImageSync(i)
```

You assume the image files are already created using the following code:

```
> System.Environment.CurrentDirectory <-  __SOURCE_DIRECTORY__;;
val it : unit = ()

> makeImageFiles();;
val it : unit = ()
```

You leave the transformation on the image largely unspecified, such as the function transformImage. By changing the value of processImageRepeats, you can adjust the computation from compute bound to I/O bound.

The problem with this implementation is that each image is read and processed sequentially, when in practice multiple images can be read and transformed simultaneously, giving much greater throughput. Listing 13-7 shows the implementation of the image processor using an asynchronous workflow.

Listing 13-7. The Asynchronous Image Processor

```
let processImageAsync i =
    async { use inStream = File.OpenRead(sprintf "Image%d.tmp" i)
            let! pixels = inStream.AsyncRead(numPixels)
            let  pixels' = transformImage(pixels,i)
            use outStream = File.OpenWrite(sprintf "Image%d.done" i)
            do! outStream.AsyncWrite(pixels')  }
```

```
let processImagesAsync() =
    printfn "processImagesAsync...";
    let tasks = [ for i in 1 .. numImages -> processImageAsync(i) ]
    Async.RunSynchronously (Async.Parallel tasks)  |> ignore
    printfn "processImagesAsync finished!";
```

On one of our machines, the asynchronous version of the code ran up to three times as fast as the synchronous version (in total elapsed time), when processImageRepeats is 20 and numImages is 200. A factor of 2 was achieved consistently for any number of processImageRepeats because this machine had two CPUs.

Let's take a closer look at this code. The call Async.Run   (Async.Parallel ...) executes a set of asynchronous operations in the thread pool, collects their results (or their exceptions), and returns the overall array of results to the original code. The core asynchronous workflow is introduced by the async { ... } construct. Let's look at the inner workflow line by line:

```
async { use inStream = File.OpenRead(sprintf "Image%d.tmp" i)
        ... }
```

This line opens the input stream synchronously using File.OpenRead. Although this is a synchronous operation, the use of use indicates that the lifetime of the stream is managed over the remainder of the workflow. The stream is closed when the variable is no longer in scope: that is, at the end of the workflow, even if asynchronous activations occur in between. If any step in the workflow raises an uncaught exception, then the stream is also closed while handling the exception.

The next line reads the input stream asynchronously using inStream.AsyncRead:

```
async { use inStream =  File.OpenRead(sprintf "Image%d.tmp" i)
        let! pixels = inStream.AsyncRead(numPixels)
        ... }
```

Stream.AsyncRead is an extension method added to the .NET System.IO.Stream class defined in the F# library and generates a value of type Async<byte[]>. The use of let! executes this operation asynchronously and registers a callback. When the callback is invoked, the value pixels is bound to the result of the operation, and the remainder of the asynchronous workflow is executed. The next line transforms the image synchronously using transformImage:

```
async { use inStream =  File.OpenRead(sprintf "Image%d.tmp" i)
        let! pixels = inStream.AsyncRead(numPixels)
        let  pixels' = transformImage(pixels,i)
        ... }
```

Like the first line, the next line opens the output stream. Using use guarantees that the stream is closed by the end of the workflow regardless of whether exceptions are thrown in the remainder of the workflow:

```
async { use inStream =  File.OpenRead(sprintf "Image%d.tmp" i)
        let! pixels = inStream.AsyncRead(numPixels)
        let  pixels' = transformImage(pixels,i)
        use outStream =  File.OpenWrite(sprintf "Image%d.done" i)
        ... }
```

The final line of the workflow performs an asynchronous write of the image. Once again, AsyncWrite is an extension method added to the .NET System.IO.Stream class defined in the F# library:

```
async { use inStream =  File.OpenRead(sprintf "Image%d.tmp" i)
        let! pixels = inStream.AsyncRead(numPixels)
        let  pixels' = transformImage(pixels,i)
        use outStream =  File.OpenWrite(sprintf "Image%d.done" i)
        do! outStream.AsyncWrite(pixels')  }
```

If you now return to the first part of the function, you can see that the overall operation of the function is to create numImages individual asynchronous operations, using a sequence expression that generates a list:

```
let tasks = [ for i in 1 .. numImages -> processImageAsync(i) ]
```

You can compose these tasks in parallel using Async.Parallel and then run the resulting process using Async.Run. This waits for the overall operation to complete and returns the result:

```
Async.Run (Async.Parallel tasks)
```

Table 13-3 shows some of the primitives and combinators commonly used to build asynchronous workflows. Take the time to compare Listings 13-7 and 13-6. Notice the following:

- The overall structure and flow of the core of Listing 13-7 is similar to Listing 13-6: that is, the synchronous algorithm, even though it includes steps executed asynchronously.

- The performance characteristics of Listing 13-7 are the same as those of Listing 13-6. Any overhead involved in executing the asynchronous workflow is easily dominated by the overall cost of I/O and image processing. It's also much easier to experiment with modifications such as making the write operation synchronous.

Table 13-3. Some Common Primitives Used to Build Async<'T> Values

Member/Type	Description
Async.FromContinuations	Builds a single primitive asynchronous step of an asynchronous computation. The function that implements the step is passed continuations to call after the step is complete or if the step fails.
Async.Parallel: seq<Async<'T>> -> Async<'T[]>	Builds a single asynchronous computation that runs the given asynchronous computations in parallel and waits for results from all to be returned. Each may either terminate with a value or return an exception. If any raise an exception, then the others are cancelled, and the overall asynchronous computation also raises the same exception.

Running Asynchronous Computations

Values of type Async<'T> are usually run using the functions listed in Table 13-4. You can build Async<'T> values using functions and members in the F# libraries.

Table 13-4. Common Methods in the Async Type Used to Run Async<'T> Values

Member/Type	Description
Async.RunSynchronously: Async<'T> -> 'T	Runs an operation in the thread pool and waits for its result.
Async.Start: Async<unit> -> unit	Queues the asynchronous computation as an operation in the thread pool.
Async.StartChild: Async<unit> -> Async<unit>	Queues the asynchronous computation, initially as a work item in the thread pool, but inherits the cancellation handle from the current asynchronous computation.

Common I/O Operations in Asynchronous Workflows

Asynchronous programming is becoming more widespread because of the use of multicore machines and networks in applications, and many .NET APIs now come with both synchronous and asynchronous versions of their functionality. For example, all web service APIs generated by .NET tools have asynchronous versions of their requests. A quick scan of the .NET API documentation on the Microsoft website reveals the asynchronous operations listed in Table 13-5. These all have equivalent Async<'T> operations defined in the F# libraries as extensions to the corresponding .NET types.

Table 13-5. Some Asynchronous Operations in the .NET Libraries and Corresponding Expected F# Naming Scheme

.NET Asynchronous Operation	F# Naming Scheme	Description
Stream.Begin/EndRead	AsyncRead	Reads a stream of bytes asynchronously. See also FileStream, NetworkStream, DeflateStream, IsolatedStorageFileStream, and SslStream.
Stream.Begin/EndWrite	AsyncWrite	Writes a stream of bytes asynchronously. See also FileStream.
Socket.BeginAccept/EndAccept	AsyncAccept	Accepts an incoming network socket request asynchronously.
Socket.BeginReceive/EndReceive	AsyncReceive	Receives data on a network socket asynchronously.

.NET Asynchronous Operation	F# Naming Scheme	Description
Socket.BeginSend/EndSend	AsyncSend	Sends data on a network socket asynchronously.
WebRequest.Begin/EndGetResponse	AsyncGetResponse	Makes an asynchronous web request. See also FtpWebRequest, SoapWebRequest, and HttpWebRequest.
SqlCommand.Begin/EndExecuteReader	AsyncExecuteReader	Executes an SqlCommand asynchronously.
SqlCommand.Begin/EndExecuteXmlReader	AsyncExecuteXmlReader	Executes a read of XML asynchronously.
SqlCommand.Begin/EndExecuteNonQuery	AsynExecuteNonQuery	Executes a nonreading SqlCommand asynchronously.

Sometimes, you may need to write a few primitives to map .NET asynchronous operations into the F# asynchronous framework. You see some examples later in this section and in Chapter 14.

Under the Hood: Implementing Async.Parallel

Async.Parallel can appear magical. Computation tasks are created, executed, and resynchronized almost without effort. Listing 13-9 shows that a basic implementation of this operator is simple and again helps you see how Async<'T> values work under the hood.

Listing 13-9. A Basic Implementation of a Fork-Join Parallel Operator

```
let forkJoinParallel(taskSeq) =
    Async.FromContinuations (fun (cont,econt,ccont) ->
        let tasks = Seq.toArray taskSeq
        let count = ref tasks.Length
        let results = Array.zeroCreate tasks.Length
        tasks |> Array.iteri (fun i p ->
            Async.Start
                (async { let! res = p
                         results.[i] <- res;
                         let n = System.Threading.Interlocked.Decrement(count)
                         if n=0 then cont results })))
```

This basic implementation first converts the input task sequence to an array and then creates mutable state count and results to record the progress of the parallel computations. It then iterates through the tasks and queues each for execution in the .NET thread pool. Upon completion, each writes its result and decrements the counter using an atomic Interlocked.Decrement operator, discussed further in the section "Using Shared-Memory Concurrency" at the end of this chapter. The last process to finish calls the continuation with the collected results.

In practice, Async.Parallel is implemented more efficiently and takes into account exceptions and cancellation; again, see the F# library code for full details.

Using async for CPU Parallelism with Fixed Tasks

One of the great advantages of F# async programming is that it can be used for both CPU and I/O parallel programming tasks. For example, you can use it for many CPU parallelism tasks that don't perform any I/O but rather carry out straight CPU-bound computations.

For optimized, partitioned CPU parallelism, this is often done by using `Async.Parallel` with a number of tasks that exactly matches the number of physical processors on a machine. For example, the following code shows parallel initialization of an array where each cell is filled by running the input function. The implementation of this function makes careful use of shared memory primitives (a topic discussed later in this book) and is highly efficient:

```
open System.Threading
open System

// Initialize an array by a parallel init using all available processors
// Note, this primitive doesn't support cancellation.
let parallelArrayInit n f =
    let currentLine = ref -1
    let res = Array.zeroCreate n
    let rec loop () =
        let y = Interlocked.Increment(&currentLine.contents)
        if y < n then res.[y] <- f y; loop()

    // Start just the right number of tasks, one for each physical CPU
    Async.Parallel [ for i in 1 .. Environment.ProcessorCount -> async { do loop()} ]
        |> Async.Ignore
        |> Async.RunSynchronously

    res
```

```
> let rec fib x = if x < 2 then 1 else fib (x - 1) + fib (x - 2)
> parallelArrayInit 25 (fun x -> fib x);;
val it : int [] =
  [|1; 1; 2; 3; 5; 8; 13; 21; 34; 55; 89; 144; 233; 377; 610; 987; 1597; 2584;
    4181; 6765; 10946; 17711; 28657; 46368; 75025; 121393; 196418; 317811;
    514229; 832040|]
```

Understanding Exceptions and Cancellation

Two recurring topics in asynchronous programming are exceptions and cancellation. Let's first explore some of the behavior of asynchronous programs with regard to exceptions:

```
> let failingTask = async { do failwith "fail" };;
val failingTask: Async<unit>

> Async.RunSynchronously failingTask;;
Microsoft.FSharp.Core.FailureException: fail
stopped due to error

> let failingTasks = [ async { do failwith "fail A" };
                       async { do failwith "fail B" }; ];;
```

```
val failingTasks: Async<unit>

> Async.RunSynchronously (Async.Parallel failingTasks);;
Microsoft.FSharp.Core.FailureException: fail A
stopped due to error

> Async.RunSynchronously (Async.Parallel failingTasks);;
Microsoft.FSharp.Core.FailureException: fail B
stopped due to error
```

From these examples, you can see the following:

- Tasks fail only when they're actually executed. The construction of a task using the async { ... } syntax never fails.

- Tasks run using Async.RunSynchronously report any failure back to the controlling thread as an exception.

- It's nondeterministic which task will fail first.

- Tasks composed using Async.Parallel report the first failure from among the collected set of tasks. An attempt is made to cancel other tasks by setting the cancellation flag for the group of tasks, and any further failures are ignored.

You can wrap a task using the Async.Catch combinator. This has the following type:

```
static member Catch : Async<'T> -> Async<Choice<'T,exn>>
```

For example:

```
> Async.RunSynchronously (Async.Catch failingTask);;
val it : Choice<unit,exn> = Choice2_2 (FailureException ())
```

You can also handle errors by using try/finally in an async { ... } workflow.

Passing and Processing Messages

A distinction is often made between *shared-memory* concurrency and *message passing* concurrency. The former is often more efficient on local machines and is covered in the section "Using Shared-Memory Concurrency" later in this chapter. The latter scales to systems where there is no shared memory—for example, distributed systems—and can also be used to avoid performance problems associated with shared memory. Asynchronous message passing and processing is a common foundation for concurrent programming, and this section looks at some simple examples of message-passing programs.

Introducing Message Processing

In a sense, you've already seen a good deal of message passing in this chapter. For example:

- In the BackgroundWorker design pattern, the CancelAsync method is a simple kind of message.

- Whenever you raise events on a GUI thread from a background thread, you are, under the hood, posting a message to the GUI's event queue. On Windows, this event queue is managed by the OS, and the processing of the events on the GUI thread is called the *Windows event loop*.

This section covers a simple kind of message processing called *mailbox processing* that's popular in languages such as Erlang. A *mailbox* is a message queue that you can scan for a message particularly relevant to the message-processing agent you're defining. Listing 13-10 shows a concurrent agent that implements a simple counter by processing a mailbox as messages arrive. The type MailboxProcessor is defined in the F# library.

Listing 13-10. Implementing a Counter Using a MailboxProcessor

```
let counter =
    new MailboxProcessor<_>(fun inbox ->
        let rec loop n =
            async { printfn "n = %d, waiting..." n
                    let! msg = inbox.Receive()
                    return! loop (n+msg) }
        loop 0)
```

The type of counter is MailboxProcessor<int>, where the type argument indicates that this object expects to be sent messages of type int:

```
val counter : MailboxProcessor<int>
```

The "Message Processing and State Machines" sidebar describes the general pattern of Listing 13-10 and the other MailboxProcessor examples in this chapter, all of which can be thought of as *state machines*. With this in mind, let's take a closer look at Listing 13-10. First, let's use counter on some simple inputs:

```
> counter.Start();;
n = 0, waiting...

> counter.Post(1);;
n = 1, waiting...

> counter.Post(2);;
n = 3, waiting...

> counter.Post(1);;
n = 4, waiting...
```

Looking at Listing 13-10, note that calling the Start method causes the processing agent to enter loop with n = 0. The agent then performs an asynchronous Receive request on the inbox for the MailboxProcessor; that is, the agent waits asynchronously until a message has been received. When the message msg is received, the program calls loop (n+msg). As additional messages are received, the internal counter (actually an argument) is incremented further.

You post messages to the agent using counter.Post. The type of inbox.Receive is as follows:

```
member Receive: unit -> Async<'Message>
```

Using an asynchronous receive ensures that no real threads are blocked for the duration of the wait. This means the previous techniques scale to many thousands of concurrent agents.

Message Processing and State Machines

Listing 13-10 shares a common structure with many of the other message-processing components you see in this chapter, all of which are *state machines*. This general structure is as follows:

```
let agent =
    MailboxProcessor.Start(fun inbox ->

        // The states of the state machine
        let rec state1(args) = async { ... }
        and     state2(args) = async { ... }
        ...
        and     stateN(args) = async { ... }

        // Enter the initial state
        state1(initialArgs))
```

That is, message-processing components typically use sets of recursive functions, each defining an asynchronous computation. Each of these functions can be thought of as a state, and one of these states is identified as the initial state. You can pass arguments between these states just as you pass them between any other set of recursive functions.

Creating Objects That React to Messages

Often, it's wise to hide the internals of an asynchronous computation behind an object, because the use of message passing can be seen as an implementation detail. Listing 13-10 doesn't show you how to retrieve information from the counter, except by printing it to the standard output. Furthermore, it doesn't show how to ask the processing agent to exit. Listing 13-11 shows how to implement an object wrapping an agent that supports Increment, Stop, and Fetch messages.

Listing 13-11. Hiding a Mailbox and Supporting a Fetch Method

```
/// The internal type of messages for the agent
type internal msg = Increment of int | Fetch of AsyncReplyChannel<int> | Stop

type CountingAgent() =
    let counter = MailboxProcessor.Start(fun inbox ->
                // The states of the message-processing state machine...
                let rec loop n =
                    async { let! msg = inbox.Receive()
                            match msg with
                            | Increment m ->
                                // increment and continue...
                                return! loop(n+m)
                            | Stop ->
                                // exit
                                return ()
                            | Fetch  replyChannel  ->
                                // post response to reply channel and continue
                                do replyChannel.Reply n
                                return! loop n }

                // The initial state of the message-processing state machine...
                loop(0))

    member a.Increment(n) = counter.Post(Increment n)
    member a.Stop() = counter.Post Stop
    member a.Fetch() = counter.PostAndReply(fun replyChannel -> Fetch replyChannel)
```

The inferred public types indicate how the presence of a concurrent agent is successfully hidden by the use of an object:

```
type CountingAgent =
    new : unit -> CountingAgent
    member Fetch : unit -> int
    member Increment : n:int -> unit
    member Stop : unit -> unit
```

Here, you can see an instance of this object in action:

```
> let counter = new CountingAgent();;
val counter : CountingAgent

> counter.Increment(1);;
val it : unit = ()

> counter.Fetch();;
val it : int = 1

> counter.Increment(2);;
val it : unit = ()
```

```
> counter.Fetch();;
val it : int = 3

> counter.Stop();;
val it : unit = ()
```

Listing 13-11 shows several important aspects of message passing and processing using the mailbox-processing model:

- Internal message protocols are often represented using discriminated unions. Here the type msg has cases Increment, Fetch, and Stop, corresponding to the three methods accepted by the object that wraps the overall agent implementation.

- Pattern matching over discriminated unions gives a succinct way to process messages. A common pattern is a call to inbox.Receive() or inbox.TryReceive() followed by a match on the message contents.

- The PostAndReply on the MailboxProcessor type gives a way to post a message and wait for a reply. A temporary *reply channel* is created and should form part of the message. A reply channel is an object of type Microsoft.FSharp.Control.AsyncReplyChannel<'reply>, which in turn supports a Post method. The MailboxProcessor can use this to post a reply to the waiting caller. In Listing 13-11, the channel is sent to the underlying message-processing agent counter as part of the Fetch message.

Table 13-6 summarizes the most important members available on the MailboxProcessor type.

Table 13-6. Some Members of the MailboxProcessor<'Message> Type

Member/Type	Description
Post: 'Message -> unit	Posts a message to a mailbox queue.
Receive: ?timeout:int -> Async<'Message>	Returns the next message in the mailbox queue. If no messages are present, performs an asynchronous wait until the message arrives. If a timeout occurs, then raises a TimeoutException.
Scan: ('Message -> Async<'T> option) * ?timeout:int -> Async<'T>	Scans the mailbox for a message where the function returns a Some(_) value. Returns the chosen result. If no messages are present, performs an asynchronous wait until more messages arrive. If a timeout occurs, then raises a TimeoutException.
TryReceive : ?timeout:int -> Async<'Message option>	Like Receive, but if a timeout occurs, then returns None.
TryScan : ('Message -> Async<'T> option) * ?timeout:int -> Async<'T option>	Like Scan, but if a timeout occurs, then returns None.

Scanning Mailboxes for Relevant Messages

It's common for a message-processing agent to end up in a state where it's not interested in all messages that may appear in a mailbox but only a subset of them. For example, you may be awaiting a reply from another agent and aren't interested in serving new requests. In this case, it's essential that you use MailboxProcessor.Scan rather than MailboxProcessor.Receive. Table 13-6 shows the signatures of both of these. The former lets you choose between available messages by processing them in order, whereas the latter forces you to process every message. Listing 13-12 shows an example of using MailboxProcessor.Scan.

Listing 13-12. Scanning a Mailbox for Relevant Messages

```
type Message =
    | Message1
    | Message2 of int
    | Message3 of string

let agent =
    MailboxProcessor.Start(fun inbox ->
        let rec loop() =
            inbox.Scan(function
                | Message1 ->
                    Some (async { do printfn "message 1!"
                                  return! loop() })
                | Message2 n ->
                    Some (async { do printfn "message 2!"
                                  return! loop() })
                | Message3 _ ->
                    None)
        loop())
```

You can now post these agent messages, including messages of the ignored kind Message3:

```
> agent.Post(Message1) ;;
message 1!
val it : unit = ()

> agent.Post(Message2(100));;
message 2!
val it : unit = ()

> agent.Post(Message3("abc"));;
val it : unit = ()

> agent.Post(Message2(100));;
message 2!
val it : unit = ()

> agent.CurrentQueueLength;;
val it : int = 1
```

When you send Message3 to the message processor, the message is ignored. However, the last line shows that the unprocessed Message3 is still in the message queue, which you examine using the backdoor property UnsafeMessageQueueContents.

Example: Asynchronous Web Crawling

At the start of this chapter, we mentioned that the rise of the Web and other forms of networks is a major reason for the increasing importance of concurrent and asynchronous programming. Listing 13-13 shows an implementation of a web crawler using asynchronous programming and mailbox-processing techniques.

Listing 13-13. A Scalable, Controlled Asynchronous Web Crawler

```
open System.Collections.Generic
open System.Net
open System.IO
open System.Threading
open System.Text.RegularExpressions

let limit = 50
let linkPat = "href=\s*\"[^\"h]*(http://[^&\"]*)\""
let getLinks (txt:string) =
    [ for m in Regex.Matches(txt,linkPat)  -> m.Groups.Item(1).Value ]

// A type that helps limit the number of active web requests
type RequestGate(n:int) =
    let semaphore = new Semaphore(initialCount=n,maximumCount=n)
    member x.AsyncAcquire(?timeout) =
        async { let! ok = Async.AwaitWaitHandle(semaphore,
                                            ?millisecondsTimeout=timeout)
                if ok then
                   return
                     { new System.IDisposable with
                         member x.Dispose() =
                             semaphore.Release() |> ignore }
                else
                   return! failwith "couldn't acquire a semaphore" }

// Gate the number of active web requests
let webRequestGate = RequestGate(5)

// Fetch the URL, and post the results to the urlCollector.
let collectLinks (url:string) =
    async { // An Async web request with a global gate
            let! html =
                async { // Acquire an entry in the webRequestGate. Release
                        // it when 'holder' goes out of scope
                        use! holder = webRequestGate.AsyncAcquire()

                        let req = WebRequest.Create(url,Timeout=5)

                        // Wait for the WebResponse
                        use! response = req.AsyncGetResponse()
```

```
                          // Get the response stream
                          use reader = new StreamReader(response.GetResponseStream())

                          // Read the response stream (note: a synchronous read)
                          return reader.ReadToEnd()   }

                // Compute the links, synchronously
                let links = getLinks html

                // Report, synchronously
                do printfn "finished reading %s, got %d links" url (List.length links)

                // We're done
                return links }

/// 'urlCollector' is a single agent that receives URLs as messages. It creates new
/// asynchronous tasks that post messages back to this object.
let urlCollector =
    MailboxProcessor.Start(fun self ->

        // This is the main state of the urlCollector
        let rec waitForUrl (visited : Set<string>) =

            async { // Check the limit
                    if visited.Count < limit then

                        // Wait for a URL...
                        let! url = self.Receive()
                        if not (visited.Contains(url)) then
                            // Start off a new task for the new url. Each collects
                            // links and posts them back to the urlCollector.
                            do! Async.StartChild
                                    (async { let! links = collectLinks url
                                             for link in links do
                                                 self.Post link }) |> Async.Ignore

                        // Recurse into the waiting state
                        return! waitForUrl(visited.Add(url)) }

        // This is the initial state.
        waitForUrl(Set.empty))
```

You can initiate a web crawl from a particular URL as follows:

```
> urlCollector <-- "http://news.google.com";;
finished reading http://news.google.com, got 191 links
finished reading http://news.google.com/?output=rss, got 0 links
finished reading http://www.ktvu.com/politics/13732578/detail.html, got 14 links
finished reading http://www.washingtonpost.com/wp-dyn/content/art..., got 218 links
finished reading http://www.newsobserver.com/politics/story/646..., got 56 links
finished reading http://www.foxnews.com/story/0,2933,290307,0...1, got 22 links
...
```

The key techniques shown in Listing 13-13 are as follows:

- The type `RequestGate` encapsulates the logic needed to ensure that you place a global limit on the number of active web requests occurring at any point in time. This is instantiated to the particular instance `webRequestGate` with limit 5. This uses a `System.Threading.Semaphore` object to coordinate access to this shared resource. Semaphores are discussed in more detail in the section "Using Shared-Memory Concurrency."

- The `RequestGate` type ensures that web requests sitting in the request queue don't block threads but rather wait asynchronously as callback items in the thread pool until a slot in the `webRequestGate` becomes available.

- The `collectLinks` function is a regular asynchronous computation. It first enters the `RequestGate` (that is, acquires one of the available entries in the `Semaphore`). After a response has been received, it reads off the HTML from the resulting reader, scrapes the HTML for links using regular expressions, and returns the generated set of links.

- The `urlCollector` is the only message-processing program. It's written using a `MailboxProcessor`. In its main state, it waits for a fresh URL and spawns a new asynchronous computation to call `collectLinks` once one is received. For each collected link, a new message is sent back to the `urlCollector`'s mailbox. Finally, you recurse to the waiting state, having added the fresh URL to the overall set of URLs you've traversed so far.

- The operator `<--` is used as shorthand for posting a message to an agent. This is a recommended abbreviation in F# asynchronous programming.

- The `AsyncAcquire` method of the `RequestGate` type uses a design pattern called a *holder*. The object returned by this method is an `IDisposable` object that represents the acquisition of a resource. This holder object is bound using `use`, and this ensures that the resource is released when the computation completes or when the computation ends with an exception.

Listing 13-13 shows that it's relatively easy to create sophisticated, scalable asynchronous programs using a mix of message passing and asynchronous I/O techniques. Modern web crawlers have thousands of outstanding open connections, indicating the importance of using asynchronous techniques in modern scalable web-based programming.

Using Shared-Memory Concurrency

The final topics covered in this chapter are the various primitive mechanisms used for threads, shared-memory concurrency, and signaling. In many ways, these are the assembly language of concurrency.

This chapter has concentrated mostly on techniques that work well with immutable data structures. That isn't to say you should *always* use immutable data structures. It is, for example, perfectly valid to use mutable data structures as long as they're accessed from only one particular thread. Furthermore, private mutable data structures can often be safely passed through an asynchronous workflow, because at each point the mutable data structure is accessed by only one thread, even if different parts of the asynchronous workflow are executed by different threads. This doesn't apply to workflows that use operators such as `Async.Parallel` and `Async.StartChild` that start additional threads of computation.

This means we've largely avoided covering shared-memory primitives so far, because F# provides powerful declarative constructs such as asynchronous workflows and message passing that often subsume the need to resort to shared-memory concurrency. However, a working knowledge of thread primitives and shared-memory concurrency is still very useful, especially if you want to implement your own basic constructs or highly efficient concurrent algorithms on shared-memory hardware.

Creating Threads Explicitly

This chapter has avoided showing how to work with threads directly, instead relying on abstractions such as BackgroundWorker and the .NET thread pool. If you want to create threads directly, here is a short sample:

```
open System.Threading
let t = new Thread(ThreadStart(fun _ ->
                printfn "Thread %d: Hello" Thread.CurrentThread.ManagedThreadId));
t.Start();
printfn "Thread %d: Waiting!" Thread.CurrentThread.ManagedThreadId
t.Join();
printfn "Done!"
```

When run, this gives the following:

```
val t : Thread

Thread 1: Waiting!
Thread 10: Hello
Done!
```

■ **Caution** Always avoid using Thread.Suspend, Thread.Resume, and Thread.Abort. These are guaranteed ways to put obscure concurrency bugs in your program. The MSDN website has a good description of why Thread.Abort may not even succeed. One of the only compelling uses for Thread.Abort is to implement Ctrl+C in an interactive development environment for a general-purpose language such as F# Interactive.

Shared Memory, Race Conditions, and the .NET Memory Model

Many multithreaded applications use mutable data structures shared between multiple threads. Without synchronization, these data structures will almost certainly become corrupt: threads may read data that has been only partially updated (because not all mutations are *atomic*), or two threads may write to the same data simultaneously (a *race condition*). Mutable data structures are usually protected by *locks*, although lock-free mutable data structures are also possible.

Shared-memory concurrency is a difficult and complicated topic, and a considerable amount of good material on .NET shared-memory concurrency is available on the Web. All this material applies to F# when you're programming with mutable data structures such as reference cells, arrays, and hash tables and the data structures can be accessed from multiple threads simultaneously. F# mutable data structures map to .NET memory in fairly predictable ways; for example, mutable references become mutable fields in a .NET class, and mutable fields of word size can be assigned atomically.

On modern microprocessors, multiple threads can see views of memory that aren't consistent; that is, not all writes are propagated to all threads immediately. The guarantees given are called a *memory model* and are usually expressed in terms of the ordering dependencies between instructions that read/write memory locations. This is, of course, deeply troubling, because you have to think about a huge number of possible reorderings of your code, and it's one of the main reasons why shared mutable data structures are difficult to work with. You can find further details on the .NET memory model at www.expert-fsharp.net/topics/MemoryModel.

Using Locks to Avoid Race Conditions

Locks are the simplest way to enforce mutual exclusion between two threads attempting to read or write the same mutable memory location. Listing 13-14 shows an example of code with a race condition.

Listing 13-14. Shared-Memory Code with a Race Condition

```
type MutablePair<'T,'U>(x:'T,y:'U) =
    let mutable currentX = x
    let mutable currentY = y
    member p.Value = (currentX,currentY)
    member p.Update(x,y) =
        // Race condition: This pair of updates is not atomic
        currentX <- x;
        currentY <- y

let p = new MutablePair<_,_>(1,2)
do Async.Start (async { do (while true do p.Update(10,10)) })
do Async.Start (async { do (while true do p.Update(20,20)) })
```

Here is the definition of the F# lock function:

```
open System.Threading
let lock (lockobj : obj) f  =
    Monitor.Enter lockobj;
    try
        f()
    finally
        Monitor.Exit lockobj
```

The pair of mutations in the Update method isn't atomic; that is, one thread may have written to currentX, another then writes to both currentX and currentY, and the final thread then writes to currentY, leaving the pair holding the value (10,20) or (20,10). Mutable data structures are inherently prone to this kind of problem if shared between multiple threads. Luckily, F# code tends to have fewer mutations than imperative languages, because functions normally take immutable values and return a calculated value. However, when you do use mutable data structures, they shouldn't be shared between threads, or you should design them carefully and document their properties with respect to multithreaded access.

Here is one way to use the F# lock function to ensure that updates to the data structure are atomic. Locks are also required on uses of the property p.Value:

```
do Async.Start (async { do (while true do lock p (fun () -> p.Update(10,10))) })
do Async.Start (async { do (while true do lock p (fun () -> p.Update(20,20))) })
```

■ **Caution** If you use locks inside data structures, then do so only in a simple way that uses them to enforce the concurrency properties you've documented. Don't lock just for the sake of it, and don't hold locks longer than necessary. In particular, beware of making indirect calls to externally supplied function values, interfaces, or abstract members while a lock is held. The code providing the implementation may not be expecting to be called when a lock is held and may attempt to acquire further locks in an inconsistent fashion.

Using ReaderWriterLock

It's common for mutable data structures to be read more than they're written. Indeed, mutation is often used only to initialize a mutable data structure. In this case, you can use a .NET ReaderWriterLock to protect access to a resource. For example, consider the following two functions:

```
open System.Threading

let readLock (rwlock : ReaderWriterLock) f  =
  rwlock.AcquireReaderLock(Timeout.Infinite)
  try
      f()
  finally
      rwlock.ReleaseReaderLock()

let writeLock (rwlock : ReaderWriterLock) f  =
  rwlock.AcquireWriterLock(Timeout.Infinite)
  try
      f();
      Thread.MemoryBarrier()
  finally
      rwlock.ReleaseWriterLock()
```

Listing 13-15 shows how to use these functions to protect the MutablePair class.

Listing 13-15. Shared-Memory Code with a Race Condition

```
type MutablePair<'T,'U>(x:'T,y:'U) =
    let mutable currentX = x
    let mutable currentY = y
    let rwlock = new ReaderWriterLock()
    member p.Value =
        readLock rwlock (fun () ->
            (currentX,currentY))
    member p.Update(x,y) =
        writeLock rwlock (fun () ->
            currentX <- x;
            currentY <- y)
```

Some Other Concurrency Primitives

Table 13-7 shows some of the other shared-memory concurrency primitives available in the .NET Framework.

Table 13-7. .NET Shared-Memory Concurrency Primitives

Type	Description
System.Threading.WaitHandle	A synchronization object for signaling the control of threads.
System.Threading.AutoResetEvent	A two-state (on/off) WaitHandle that resets itself to "off" automatically after the signal is read. Similar to a two-state traffic light.
System.Threading.ManualResetEvent	A two-state (on/off) WaitHandle that requires a call to ManualResetEvent.Reset() to set it "off."
System.Threading.Mutex	A lock-like object that can be shared between operating system processes.
System.Threading.Semaphore	Used to limit the number of threads simultaneously accessing a resource. However, use a mutex or lock if at most one thread can access a resource at a time.
System.Threading.Interlocked	Atomic operations on memory locations. Especially useful for atomic operations on F# reference cells.

Summary

This chapter covered concurrent, reactive, and asynchronous programming, which is a set of topics of growing importance in modern programming because of the widespread adoption of multicore microprocessors, network-aware applications, and asynchronous I/O channels. It discussed in depth background processing and a powerful F# construct called asynchronous workflows. Finally, the chapter covered applications of asynchronous workflows to message-processing agents and web crawling, and examined covered some of the shared-memory primitives for concurrent programming on the .NET platform. The next chapter looks at web programming, from serving web pages to delivering applications via web browsers.

CHAPTER 14

■■■

Building Smart Web Applications

Delivering content and applications via web browsers is one of the most important aspects of modern software development. This chapter examines how you can build web applications using F#. The topics covered are as follows:

- Serving static files and dynamic content by directly responding to HTTP requests

- Using the ASP.NET framework to develop page-based, server-side web applications that use input controls and read data from a database using F# LINQ

- A walk-through of the ASP.NET essentials: organizing web forms and sites, understanding the various types of server controls (web and HTML), user creating controls, and configuring and debugging web applications

- The fundamentals of the ASP.NET event model: page and control events, the page life cycle, posting information from a page (postback and cross-page posting), and maintaining state

- A look at techniques to build client-based web applications, including the use of the WebSharper project

- Consuming web services to deliver programmatic services via web connections

Serving Static Web Content

When you point your browser at a web page or call a web service from your application, you're effectively issuing one or more requests (commands) to a web (HTTP) server. HTTP commands are simple text-based instructions that are automatically generated by your web browser. For instance, when your browser goes to a particular URL, it does the following:

- Requests the page from the web server and waits for the response

- Analyzes the contents of the page in the response for further content to be fetched (images, for example), and issues the appropriate requests if necessary

- Displays the results, and executes any dynamic scripts and content contained in the page

A response can be a verbatim copy of a resource found on the web server (most often a static file such as an image, a style sheet, or a media file) or can be generated on the fly. This section shows how you can use F# to serve content directly.

Listing 14-1 shows a simple web server written directly in F#.

391

Listing 14-1. A Simple Web Server

```
open System.Net
open System.Net.Sockets
open System.IO
open System.Text.RegularExpressions
open System.Text

/// A table of MIME content types
let mimeTypes =
    dict [".html", "text/html";
          ".htm",  "text/html";
          ".txt",  "text/plain";
          ".gif",  "image/gif";
          ".jpg",  "image/jpeg";
          ".png",  "image/png"]

/// Compute a MIME type from a file extension
let getMimeType(ext) =
    if mimeTypes.ContainsKey(ext) then mimeTypes.[ext]
    else "binary/octet"

/// The pattern Regex1 uses a regular expression to match
/// one element
let (|Regex1|_|) (patt: string) (inp: string) =
    try Some(Regex.Match(inp, patt).Groups.Item(1).Captures.Item(0).Value)
    with _ -> None

/// The root for the data we serve
let root = @"c:\inetpub\wwwroot"

/// Handle a TCP connection for an HTTP GET. We use an
/// asynchronous task in case any future actions in
/// handling a request need to be asynchronous.
let handleRequest(client: TcpClient) =
    async {
        use stream = client.GetStream()
        let out = new StreamWriter(stream)
        let inp = new StreamReader(stream)
        match inp.ReadLine() with
        | Regex1 "GET (.*?) HTTP/1\\.[01]$" fileName ->
            let fname = root + @"\" + fileName.Replace("/", @"\")
            let mimeType = getMimeType(Path.GetExtension(fname))
            let content = File.ReadAllBytes fname
            fprintfn out "HTTP/1.0 200 OK"
            fprintfn out "Content-Length: %d" content.Length
            fprintfn out "Content-Type: %s" mimeType
            fprintfn out ""
            out.Flush()
            stream.Write(content, 0, content.Length)
        | line ->
            ()
    }
```

```
/// The server as an asynchronous process. We handle requests
/// sequentially.
let server =
    async {
        let socket = new TcpListener(IPAddress.Parse("127.0.0.1"), 8090)
        socket.Start()
        while true do
            use client = socket.AcceptTcpClient()
            try
                Async.Start (handleRequest client)
            with _ ->
                ()
    }
```

You can use this code as follows, where http is the function defined in Chapter 2 for requesting web pages and where you assume the directory c:\inetpub\wwwroot contains the file iisstart.htm:

```
> Async.Start server;;
val it : unit = ()

> http "http://127.0.0.1:8090/iisstart.htm";;
val it : string = "..."    // the text of the iisstart.htm file will be shown here
```

This HTTP request (you can also open the previous URL in a browser) ultimately sends the following text down the TCP socket connection:

```
GET iisstart.htm HTTP/1.1
```

When started, the server in Listing 14-1 attaches itself to a given port (8090) on the local machine (which has IP 127.0.0.1) and listens for incoming requests. These requests are line-based, so when one comes in, you read the full input line and attempt to parse a valid GET request using regular expression matching. Other commands and error recovery aren't dealt with.

The server's actions in response are simple: it locates the requested file relative to a root web directory, determines the MIME type from a fixed table, and sends the necessary response header and the content of the file through the client TCP connection. When all this is done, the connection is disposed, and the session ends. The main loop of the server task is a busy waiting loop—you wait for requests indefinitely and handle them one by one.

Listing 14-1 uses two techniques not directly related to web programming:

- Regex1 is a very simple and common *active pattern* for regular expression pattern matching. You learned about active patterns in Chapter 9. This example is particularly interesting because it also shows how to use a parameterized active pattern.

- The value server is an asynchronous task, as is the handleRequest function. You learned about asynchronous tasks in Chapter 13. Many web servers handle multiple requests simultaneously, and high-performance web servers use asynchronous techniques extensively. In this example, the server task serves requests sequentially using a single thread, but you can just as well start a dedicated thread for the server using more explicit threading techniques from System.Threading.

While the above example may look simple, many common server-side applications are primarily TCP-based, and you can use the pattern shown above to implement many of these. For example, the following encapsulates an arbitrary TCP server:

```
type AsyncTcpServer(addr,port,handleServerRequest) =
    let socket = new TcpListener(addr, port)
    member x.Start() = async { do x.Run() } |> Async.Start
    member x.Run() =
        socket.Start()
        while true do
            let client = socket.AcceptTcpClient()
            Async.Start (async { try // Client has lifetime equal to the async request
                                    use _holder = client
                                    do! handleServerRequest client
                                 with e -> () })
```

This class can now be instantiated and developed in many ways, including more interesting applications than simple HTTP servers. For example, the code below is a simulation of a "quote server" that serves "quotes" (represented here as a blob of bytes) to a TCP client every 1 second. Because serving each quote is very simple (simply writing a few bytes to the socket), you can serve many thousands of clients simultaneously using this technique.

```
let quoteSize = 512 // one quote
let quote = Array.init<byte> quoteSize (fun i -> 1uy)

let handleRequest (client: TcpClient) =
    async {
        // Cleanup the client at the end of the request
        let stream = client.GetStream()
        do! stream.AsyncWrite(quote, 0, 1)  // write header
        while true do
            do! stream.AsyncWrite(quote, 0, quote.Length)
            // Mock an I/O wait for the next quote
            do! Async.Sleep 1000

        stream.Close()
    }
```

```
let server() =
    AsyncTcpServer(IPAddress.Loopback, 10003, handleRequest)
```

Additionally, you should consider using secure sockets (https) for your application. Secure network programming is a big topic, beyond the scope of this book, but the code below indicates the basic shape of an SSL server, built compositionally using a non-secure one, and indicates the .NET types you can use to implement authentication-related functionality:

```
type AsyncTcpServerSecure(addr,port,handleServerRequest) =

    let getCertficate() =
        // Instantiate the x509Store object to represent the Certificate Store
        // that contains the certificate to use for server authentication.
        let store = new X509Store(StoreName.My, StoreLocation.CurrentUser);
```

```
// Open the store for read-only access.
store.Open(OpenFlags.ReadOnly);

// Extract all the certificates that match your certificate criteria.
// Return all certificates that have the identifying value in their name.
let cert = store.Certificates.Find(X509FindType.FindBySubjectName,
                                   "localhost", true);

// This assumes the collection contains one certificate,
// based on the search criteria.
cert.[0];

let handleServerRequestSecure (client: TcpClient) =
    async {
        let stream = new SslStream(client.GetStream());
        do! stream.AsyncAuthenticateAsServer(getCertficate());

        if (stream.IsAuthenticated) then
            Console.WriteLine("IsAuthenticated: {0}", stream.IsAuthenticated);

            // In this example only the server is authenticated.
            Console.WriteLine("IsEncrypted: {0}", stream.IsEncrypted);
            Console.WriteLine("IsSigned: {0}", stream.IsSigned);

            // Indicates whether the current side of the connection
            // is authenticated as a server.
            Console.WriteLine("IsServer: {0}", stream.IsServer);

        return! handleServerRequest stream
    }

let server = AsyncTcpServer(addr,port,handleServerRequestSecure)

member x.Start() = server.Start()
```

TCP-based applications achieve excellent scaling, and cloud-computing solutions such as Azure allow you to host your TCP-based services on a load-balanced set of machines dedicated to serving requests, under one common TCP address. The modern web is built with server-side programs following the architectures similar to those laid out above.

Serving Dynamic Web Content with ASP.NET

In practice, it's rare to develop and implement a web server manually as you did in the previous section. Instead, most web development adds an extension to an existing web server via a web development framework such as ASP.NET, PHP, or JavaServer Pages (JSP). This section covers how you can use F# to write server-side applications using ASP.NET.

ASP.NET is a fully compiled dynamic server technology that allows you to write web applications as a set of dynamic pages and to describe how the pages should interact via a rich object model and an abundance of server-side controls. The resulting web applications are easy to deploy—they're independent of the hosting environment and the system registry—and can be configured through an integrated web application configuration tool or via XML-based configuration files. ASP.NET was originally designed by Microsoft and is often used with Microsoft's Internet Information Services (IIS) web server but can also be used with Apache and others via the Mono implementation of ASP.NET and the Common Language Infrastructure (CLI).

■ **Note** Modern web-development frameworks allow you to put together sophisticated web sites with many useful features and almost no coding. Code is often used as glue between the incoming requests and back-end databases. For this reason, web programmers often need a variety of design, security, database, and system skills in addition to mastery of one or more programming languages.

About Dynamic Page-Based Web Development Frameworks

You may already be familiar with various web scripting languages and technologies that allow you to embed bits of code (usually in certain metatags or inside special markers) in your pages. When a request is made to such pages (which typically have a different file extension, such as `.asp`, `.aspx`, `.php`, `.jsp`, and so on), the web server invokes a preprocessor that consumes the page script and outputs the resulting HTML after evaluating each dynamic block. Depending on your web-server architecture, such processors can be plugged in on demand (as with Apache's modules) or tied directly to the server technology (as with the Java-based web server Tomcat or as with ASP.NET).

Roughly speaking, there are two main types of dynamic content generation. In the first, the scripting type, requests for the same scripted resource produce the same actions: the source page is pumped through the preprocessor every time, and each dynamic construct is distilled to HTML. Typically, this type of content generation is limited to using special tags and local code expressions that may refer only to a set of built-in features and occasionally a set of global state variables such as the server response. The problem with this approach is inherent: the dynamic functionality is often too limited, although it's simple to use. Most important, no caching or compilation is done, and as such it's much slower than the compiled alternatives. Furthermore, as dynamic functionality is added to a page, it becomes progressively more complex and more difficult to maintain, often leading to spaghetti code. Tying the dynamic content to the presentation layer in this way is well recognized as a significant drawback.

The second approach is the one taken by ASP.NET and JSP. A page-scripting model is combined with an underlying compiled language (Java for JSP, and any .NET language for ASP.NET) and the speed of serving static content. In this model, pages are composed of objects with complex life cycles and are generated/maintained by compiled programs, so a scripted page is translated to a program that generates the final HTML page and as a result can contain arbitrary logic expressed in the source language. These programs are produced on the fly and maintained by the web container. A change to a web page results in updating the server-side resource responsible for creating that web page. This compilation causes a one-time penalty, but subsequent requests are served without any processing by sending the result of the new page-behind code.

Understanding the Languages Used in ASP.NET

Web development frameworks such as ASP.NET can be a little bewildering at first. One reason is the number of languages involved in even simple web sites. For example, developing a minimal web site using ASP.NET involves using at least five different languages to represent the necessary information:

- *ASP.NET page markup (ASPX):* Used for the declarative construction and configuration of server controls that form the page
- *HTML:* Used for the basic presentation content embedded in the ASP.NET markup
- *Cascading Style Sheets (CSS):* Used for declarative control over visual characteristics of the presentation content
- *XML:* Used for the web site's configuration files
- *F# and/or another .NET language:* Used for expressing the web site's logic

In contrast, the programs you've seen so far in this book have used only one language (F#) with only one kind of file (source code files with the suffix .fs). Furthermore, a fully fledged web site can involve additional languages and schemas:

- *SQL:* For queries and commands used for database access and management
- *JavaScript:* For dynamic client-side behavior, a topic discussed later in this chapter
- *Further XML schemas:* For files specifying additional web-site data or security and configuration information
- *Database connection strings:* For configuring access to underlying databases

This has the effect of making simple web site projects seem quite complex. To help you through this, Table 14-1 shows the most common file types used when writing web applications using F# and ASP.NET. Table 14-2 shows some additional file types you should be aware of.

Table 14-1. *The Most Common File Types for F# and ASP.NET*

Extension	Type	Language	Characteristics
.aspx	Web form (web page)	ASPX	The presentation layer, often authored using visual editing tools. These files include ASP.NET control declarations and embedded HTML tags. They may also include fragments of other languages such as CSS and scripts written in F#.
.ascx	User control	ASPX	Similar to the .aspx file but is used for writing elementary building blocks that can be reused on multiple pages in the application.
.fs	Server-side code	F#	The programmatic portion of the web-site logic. Typically makes extensive use of the System.Data and System.Web namespaces.

Extension	Type	Language	Characteristics
.dll	Precompiled server-side code	Binary	Compiled DLLs referenced by your server-side code.
web.config	Configuration	XML	Configuration files that may be located in every application directory and are used to specify aspects such as security or compilation options.

Table 14-2. *Additional File Types Used with ASP.NET*

Extension	Type	Language	Characteristics
.resx	Resource	XML	Resources such as bitmaps and error strings, often used for localizing web sites to multiple languages. Resources were described in passing in Chapter 7. These files use the .NET resource schema.
.sql	Database scripts and stored procedures	T-SQL	Many web sites use relational databases heavily. Operations on these databases are typically described using scripts written in database scripting languages such as T-SQL.
.css	Style	CSS	Cascading Style Sheets, a W3C standard for declarative configuration of the HTML presentation layer. CSS fragments can also appear in HTML and ASPX documents.
.master	Master page	ASPX	Similar to the .aspx file but used as a template for other pages in the web site. When used with a page, the content page must fill the placeholders declared in the master page.
.sitemap	Site map	XML	Defines the structure of the web site and can be used with ASP.NET navigation controls to generate content like a menu bar, a breadcrumb, or a site map.
.mdf	Database file	Binary	Many web sites use databases accessed via SQL Server Express 2005. The .mdf format is a detached, file-based database used by SQL Server Express.

Understanding the Structure of an ASP.NET Web Site

ASP.NET files of the types shown in Tables 14-1 and 14-2 are located in the web application's *web root directory* and the various subfolders within. The standard ASP.NET folders are as follows:

- App_Code: Utility, application, and data access layer code—basically, all source files that aren't code-behind files

- App_Data: Database and XML files

- App_GlobalResources: Global resource files, such as those related to localization

- App_LocalResources: Resource files associated with specific controls or pages

- App_WebReferences: Web reference discovery files and service descriptions (wsdl)

- Bin: Third-party binaries, libraries—these are automatically referenced in the web application

A Simple ASP.NET Web Application

The simplest web sites use only HTML static content. This book doesn't consider these, although we assume you're familiar with authoring HTML. Beyond this, the building blocks of the *dynamic* content on ASP.NET web sites are .aspx web forms (web pages). These are essentially HTML files that contain ASPX markup for server-side controls, although they aren't processed as embedded scripts; instead, the page should be viewed as an object type that produces the final HTML based on the declarative markup and the behavior expressed as code inside standard HTML <script> blocks or in code-behind files. Listing 14-2 shows a simple web form that uses the server to compute the current time and allows the user to refresh the page. Listing 14-3 (later in this chapter) shows an ASP.NET web.config web site configuration file suitable for use with all the examples in this chapter.

Listing 14-2. Time.aspx: A Simple ASP.NET Web Form with an Embedded F# Server-Side Script

```
<%@ Page Language="F#" %>

<!DOCTYPE html PUBLIC "-//W3C//DTD XHTML 1.0 Transitional//EN"
                "http://www.w3.org/TR/xhtml1/DTD/xhtml1-transitional.dtd">

<script language="F#" runat="server">
    /// F# scripts embedded in ASPX pages must be a set of 'member' declarations.
    /// ASP.NET inserts these into the code generated for the page object type.

    /// This member is invoked on the server when the page is loaded. It tests
    /// whether the page was loaded for the first time and updates the content of
    /// the this.Time control.
    member this.Form1_Load(sender: obj, e: EventArgs) =
        if not this.Page.IsPostBack then
            this.Time.Text <- DateTime.Now.ToString()

    /// This member is invoked on the server when the Reload button is clicked.
    member this.Reload_Click(sender: obj, e: EventArgs) =
```

```
            this.Time.Text <- "(R) " + DateTime.Now.ToString()
</script>

<html xmlns="http://www.w3.org/1999/xhtml">
<head runat="server">
    <title>Current time</title>
    <style type="text/css">
        body { font-family:calibri,verdana,sans-serif; }
    </style>
</head>
<body>
    <form id="Form1" runat="server" OnLoad="Form1_Load">
        The current time is:
        <asp:Label  runat="server" id="Time" />
        <asp:Button runat="server" id="Reload" text="Reload" OnClick="Reload_Click" />
    </form>
</body>
</html>
```

■ **Note** You need to make sure the F# compiler is referenced in `web.config`, as shown in Listing 14-3. Check that the version number (the listing uses 1.9.9.9) matches the one reported by F# Interactive and that the other information matches what is used in the ASP.NET samples in your F# distribution.

Let's take a closer look at Listing 14-2. ASP.NET files can initially look like a sea of strange symbols. Table 14-3 shows the meanings of some of the symbolic forms you see in ASP.NET files.

Table 14-3. The Primary Symbolic and HTML Directives in ASP.NET .aspx Files

Example Directive	What It Means
`<%@ ... %>`	ASP.NET directives. See Table 14-4 for a list of commonly used ASP.NET directives.
`<!-- ... -->`	HTML comment.
`<!DOCTYPE ... >`	HTML meta-information. Usually generated when the file is first created. Can be ignored.
`<script language="F#" runat="server">...</script>`	Inserts F# or other scripting code as part of the generated code for the page. The F# code should be a portion of an object type definition.
`<form id="Form1" runat="server">`	Indicates that the given HTML element is treated as an ASP.NET control and generated dynamically on the server as part of the page object (with the ID as its name).

Example Directive	What It Means
<%= ... %>	Inserts F# or other scripting code into a rendering of the page as an expression. For example, `<%= let a = 40+2 in a.ToString() %>`.
<%# ... %>	Data-binding expression: inserts F# code as the current item of an ASP.NET data control. A convenient shortcut for referring to a given data field is via the Eval method. For example, `<%# this.Eval("Rgb") %>`.

Beyond the HTML and ASP.NET controls, the key code in Listing 14-2 is the embedded F# script beginning with `<script language="F#" runat="server">`. F# scripts embedded in .aspx pages must be a set of member declarations—in other words, fragments of an F# type definition. ASP.NET inserts these into the code generated for the page object.

The embedded F# script contains two members. The first is as follows:

```
member this.Form1_Load(sender: obj, e: EventArgs) =
    if not this.Page.IsPostBack then
        this.Time.Text <- DateTime.Now.ToString()
```

This member is associated with the Form1 control and is invoked on the server when the page is loaded—in other words, as part of the process of generating the final HTML for the page. You can see this because the event callback for the control mentions this event handler:

```
<form id="Form1" runat="server" onload="Form1_Load">
```

The implementation of Form1_Load uses the IsPostBack property of the page object to detect whether the page is loaded for the first time or whether it's loaded in reaction to some event invoked by a control. The reaction to an event that involves executing server-side code is called a *postback*, and it's triggered by sending data from the client back to the current page. When the page is loaded for the first time, this event handler sets the content of this.Time. This is the label element of the page being presented to the user (note the close correspondence between ASP.NET elements and HTML elements).

The second part of the script is the following member:

```
member this.Reload_Click(sender: obj, e: EventArgs) =
    this.Time.Text <- "(R) " + DateTime.Now.ToString()
```

This member is associated with the Reload button control and is invoked when the button is clicked. Because the event handler associated with the button must be executed on the server, the page is reloaded, and the event is triggered. Note that the entire page is reloaded, so the Form1_Load handler is called as well; but for this and subsequent reloads, the IsPostBack property is set to true and the label isn't updated by that event handler.

■ **Note** When ASP.NET serves the page, it generates F# code using the F# CodeDOM dynamic code generator. The text of embedded script fragments is added verbatim to the generated code, indented to an appropriate position. The generated code may appear in error messages including syntax errors, so you may occasionally need to look at the details of the generated ASP.NET code.

Deploying and Running the Application

Figure 14-1 shows the simple web application from Listing 14-2 accessed via a web browser on the local machine. You can deploy and run web applications like this in three ways.

- You can create an ASP.NET project inside Visual Studio, add the Time.aspx file to the project, and adjust the web.config file in the project to contain the given compiler entry. Visual Studio comes with its own built-in web server so that when you run the web application using F5 from inside Visual Studio, a browser is automatically opened with a reference to this web server.

- You can deploy the application to your local web server. For example, copy Time.aspx and web.config to an application directory in an ASP.NET-enabled web server. When using IIS, you can copy them to a directory inside your default web root such as c:\inetpub\wwwroot\Time and reference the web site via http://localhost/Time/Time.aspx, or you can set up IIS virtual directories and copy to their corresponding folders. Ensure that your web server is ASP.NET-enabled as described later in the sidebar "Serving ASP.NET Pages Locally."

- You can deploy the files to a live web server. Again, copy Time.aspx and web.config to an application directory in an ASP.NET-enabled web server. Ensure that the F# compiler has been installed on the web server, or deploy the F# binaries as part of the bin directory of your web application.

Figure 14-1 shows the results of launching the application via the second technique.

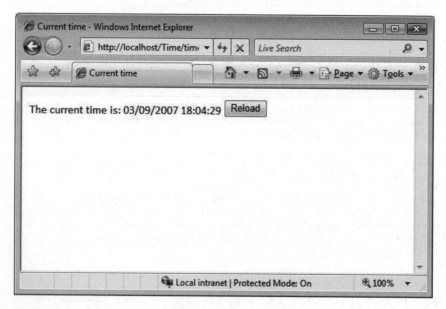

Figure 14-1. The simple web application from Listing 14-1

Serving ASP.NET Pages Locally

You need to enable a number of configuration settings in order to ensure that you can use your local machine as an experimental development web server.

When using Visual Studio, by far the easiest way to get going with developing web applications is to use the local web server built into Visual Studio, which is invoked when you run ASP.NET projects using F5. This starts the built-in web server using a random port and opens the default page by constructing a URL such as `http://localhost:59120/Time/time.aspx`.

Another option is using Microsoft's IIS web server; you can deploy web applications under separate folders in the main web root folder—for instance, `c:\inetpub\wwwroot\Time`—and these can then be accessed via URLs such as `http://localhost/Time/time.aspx`. Here are some tips for doing this:

- Ensure that ASP.NET support is enabled in IIS. On Windows 7, you do so using Control Panel ➤ Programs ➤ Programs and Features ➤ Turn Windows features on or off. Be sure the check box at Internet Information Services ➤ World Wide Web Services ➤ Application Development Features ➤ ASP.NET is selected.

- Ensure that the default web root folder `c:\inetpub\wwwroot` exists and that you've copied your `.aspx` and `web.config` files to that directory.

- Ensure that the `web.config` file contains an entry for the F# compiler, as shown in Listing 14-3. If not, ASP.NET can't invoke the compiler dynamically. This is automatically done if you use the F# Website project type.

- Check that you can access other local URLs such as `http://localhost/iisstart.htm`, the default starting page for IIS. If not, check the settings for IIS under Control Panel ➤ Administrative Tools ➤ Internet Information Services (IIS) Manager.

- Add a debug entry to your `web.config` file, as shown in Listing 14-3, to ensure that verbose debugging information is generated for your F# code. Otherwise, errors reported by ASP.NET will be difficult to diagnose.

A number of application settings are relevant to web applications, but most of them are beyond the scope of this book. The easiest way to get some guidance is to look at the `web.config.comments` file. For Microsoft .NET, you can find this file in your Windows directory and the `Microsoft.Net\Framework\{your .NET version}\CONFIG` folder within. This same directory also contains a configuration file called `machine.config`, which has settings that apply to all web applications on the host machine. Many of the common, default settings are stored in this file.

Listing 14-3. `web.config`: An ASP.NET Web Site Configuration File for Listing 14-2

```
<?xml version="1.0"?>
<configuration>
  <system.web>
    <compilation debug="true" />
  </system.web>
```

```
<system.codedom>
  <compilers>
    <compiler language="F#;f#;fs;fsharp"
              extension=".fs"
              type="Microsoft.FSharp.Compiler.CodeDom.FSharpAspNetCodeProvider,
                    FSharp.Compiler.CodeDom,
                    Version=1.9.9.9,
                    Culture=neutral,
                    PublicKeyToken=a19089b1c74d0809"/>
  </compilers>
</system.codedom>
</configuration>
```

Using Code-Behind Files

Embedded scripts in web applications tend to create spaghetti code that confuses details of the presentation layer with the underlying logic of the application. However, embedding scripts is a useful way of trying new features.

The normal practice for ASP.NET web site development is for each Page.aspx file to have backing code in a particular language, such as Page.aspx.fs for F# code. Listing 14-4 shows the code from Listing 14-2 but without the embedded script and with ASP.NET directives at the top of the file indicating that a code-behind file is being used.

Listing 14-4. Time2.aspx: A Simple ASP.NET Web Form with F# Code-Behind

```
<%@ Page Language="F#"
        AutoEventWireup="true"
        CodeFile="Time2.aspx.fs"
        Inherits="FSharpWeb.Time2" %>


<!DOCTYPE html PUBLIC "-//W3C//DTD XHTML 1.0 Transitional//EN"
                      "http://www.w3.org/TR/xhtml1/DTD/xhtml1-transitional.dtd">

<html xmlns="http://www.w3.org/1999/xhtml">
<head runat="server">
    <title>Current time</title>
    <style type="text/css">
        body { font-family:calibri,verdana,sans-serif; }
    </style>
</head>
<body>
    <form runat="server">
      The current time is:
      <asp:Label  runat="server" id="Time" />
      <asp:Button runat="server" id="Reload" text="Reload" OnClick="Reload_Click" />
    </form>
</body>
</html>
```

In turn, Listing 14-5 shows the accompanying F# code placed in a code-behind file. To place F# code in the code-behind file, you do the following:

- Place the code in a namespace.

- Define a page type with the same base name as the .aspx page. The code generated from the .aspx file uses implementation inheritance to merge with the type defined here (see Chapter 6 for a description of implementation inheritance). This is standard practice for ASP.NET and matches the Inherits directive in Listing 14-4.

- Place the implementation of the callback members into the page.

Listing 14-5. Time2.aspx.fs: The F# Code-Behind for Time2.aspx

```
namespace FSharpWeb

open System
open System.Web
open System.Web.UI
open System.Web.UI.WebControls

type Time2() =
    inherit Page()

    [<DefaultValue>]
    val mutable Time : Label
    [<DefaultValue>]
    val mutable Reload : Button

    member this.Page_Load(sender: obj, e: EventArgs) =
        if not this.Page.IsPostBack then
            this.Time.Text <- DateTime.Now.ToString()

    member this.Reload_Click(sender: obj, e: EventArgs) =
        this.Time.Text <- "(R) " + DateTime.Now.ToString()
```

Using ASP.NET Input Controls

The minimalist application shown in Listing 14-2 and Figure 14-1 does nothing but use the server to compute the time, something easily done on the local machine. Listing 14-6 shows the .aspx code for a web application shown in Figure 14-2 that computes a list of prime numbers for a selected range. The web.config file for this application remains the same.

Listing 14-6. Computing and Displaying a Range of Prime Numbers Using the Web Server

```
<%@ Page Language="F#" %>

<!DOCTYPE html PUBLIC "-//W3C//DTD XHTML 1.0 Transitional//EN"
                    "http://www.w3.org/TR/xhtml1/DTD/xhtml1-transitional.dtd">

<script language="F#" runat="server">
    member page.GenerateData_Click(sender: obj, e: EventArgs) =
        let isPrime(i: int) =
            let lim = int(sqrt(float(i)))
```

```
            let rec check j =
                j > lim or (i % j <> 0 && check (j+1))
            check 2

        let lowerLimit = System.Convert.ToInt32(page.LowerLimit.Text)
        let upperLimit = System.Convert.ToInt32(page.UpperLimit.Text)
        let data =
            [ let previousTime = ref System.DateTime.Now
              for i in lowerLimit..upperLimit do
                  if isPrime(i) then
                      let time = System.DateTime.Now
                      yield (i, time-previousTime.Value)
                      do previousTime := time ]
        page.Repeater.DataSource <- data
        page.Repeater.DataBind()
</script>

<html xmlns="http://www.w3.org/1999/xhtml">
<head id="Head1" runat="server">
    <title>Current time</title>
    <style type="text/css">
        body { font-family:calibri,verdana,sans-serif; }
    </style>
</head>
<body>
    <form id="Form1" runat="server">
        <h2>Displaying data</h2>
        <p>
            Compute primes
            from <asp:TextBox runat="server" id="LowerLimit" />
            to   <asp:TextBox runat="server" id="UpperLimit" />.
        </p>
        <asp:Button runat="server"
                    id="GenerateData"
                    text="Generate" OnClick="GenerateData_Click" />
        <p>
        Results:

        <ul>
        <asp:Repeater id="Repeater" runat="server">
            <ItemTemplate>
                <li style="color:blue">
                    n = <%# this.Eval("Item1") %>,
                    time since previous: <%# this.Eval("Item2") %></li>
            </ItemTemplate>
            <AlternatingItemTemplate>
                <li style="color:green">
                    n = <%# this.Eval("Item1") %>,
                    time since previous: <%# this.Eval("Item2") %></li>
            </AlternatingItemTemplate>
        </asp:Repeater>
        </ul>
```

```
      </p>
   </form>
</body>
</html>
```

The application in Listing 14-6 consists of two input controls with the ASP.NET names `LowerLimit` and `UpperLimit` and an ASP.NET data-listing control called `Repeater`. The rest of the code is HTML markup and the F# embedded script to naively compute a sequence of prime numbers in the given range:

- The function `isPrime` implements the basic naive primality test.

- The computed value `data` is a list of tuples containing the prime numbers found in the given range. The type of each entry of this data list is (int * System.TimeSpan).

This code demonstrates how to acquire input data from forms filled in by the client and how to display data grids back to the client. The input data is acquired by using `page.LowerLimit.Text` and `page.UpperLimit.Text` in the server-side event handlers.

The data grid is generated by using the `Repeater` control to iteratively generate HTML; conceptually, this is somewhat like a `for` loop that prints HTML at each step. Here is the relevant snippet:

```
<asp:Repeater id="Repeater" runat="server">
    <ItemTemplate>
        <li style="color:blue">
            n = <%# this.Eval("Item1") %>,
            time since previous: <%# this.Eval("Item2") %></li>
    </ItemTemplate>
    <AlternatingItemTemplate> ... </AlternatingItemTemplate>
</asp:Repeater>
```

The repeater control contains two templates that define the HTML code that is generated during the iteration. It's common that subsequent lines use different formatting, and `Repeater` automatically switches between `ItemTemplate` and `AlternatingItemTemplate`. The body of the template uses somewhat cryptic ASP.NET constructs such as `<%# this.Eval("Item1") %>`. These are instances of one of the ASP.NET-embedded F# expression forms from Table 14-3. ASP.NET textually evaluates this element at each step of the repeated iteration.

The repeater iterates over a data source. The data source can be specified either declaratively as you see later or programmatically as in this example using the following lines:

```
page.Repeater.DataSource <- data
page.Repeater.DataBind()
```

Figure 14-2. Computing a data table using Listing 14-4

Displaying Data from Databases

Now that you've been introduced to the ASP.NET framework and the usual organization of the code in ASP.NET web applications, you're ready for a more complicated example. The next few pages present a web application that displays data from the standard sample AdventureWorks database.

If you don't have the AdventureWorks database installed, you can grab a copy following the instructions at

```
http://msftdbprodsamples.codeplex.com/wikipage?title=Installing%20Databases
```

The Visual Studio solution has three projects: a C# library project for the Data Access Object (DAO) layer, an F# library project for the backend logic, and a C# web application project for the web-application user interface. This organization encourages a better separation of concerns by breaking the parts of the application into separate projects, each of the type that is best suited for the purpose.

The Dao project contains a single class representing the AdventureWorks database. You can follow the steps described in Chapter 15 and generate the LINQ bindings with the SqlMetal tool, or you can use the Visual Studio support to do the same. To do the latter, create a new C# library project called Dao and a LINQ to SQL Classes item called Dao.dbml to it. Under Server Explorer, you can add a new or select an existing data connection—use the one that points to the AdventureWorks database. Open this connection, browse down to the data tables, select all, and move them to the Object Relational Designer surface. Make sure that in the Project Properties, the assembly name and the default namespace are set to Dao. At this point, you can save the project and compile it to create the library for the DAO.

Next, implement an F# module in the Backend F# library project, DataSource.fs, as shown in Listing 14-7; it contains functions for accessing the database. To do this, you use F# LINQ, which is described in more detail in Chapter 15. In short, F# LINQ makes it possible to use F# sequence expressions and quotations to write database queries and thus reduces the number of languages you need to master when writing data-aware web applications. To compile this project, add a project reference to the Dao project and the System.Configuration, System.Data, System.Data.Linq, and the FSharp.PowerPack.Linq libraries. The first three are standard .NET libraries; you need to reference the last one from the F# Power Pack (and download it if you don't have it installed).

Listing 14-7. Backend/DataSource.fs: The F# Module for Accessing Data from the AdventureWorks Database

```
namespace FSharpWeb

open System.Configuration
open Microsoft.FSharp.Linq.Query

type Category =
    val mutable _Name : string
    val mutable _CategoryID : int

    member this.Name
        with get () = this._Name
        and  set name = this._Name <- name

    member this.CategoryID
        with get () = this._CategoryID
        and  set name = this._CategoryID <- name

    new (categoryID, name) = { _CategoryID=categoryID; _Name=name }

type Product =
    val mutable _Name : string
    val mutable _Price : System.Decimal

    member this.Name
        with get () = this._Name
        and  set name = this._Name <- name

    member this.Price
        with get () = this._Price
        and  set name = this._Price <- name

    new (name, price) = { _Name=name; _Price=price }

module DataSource =
    let cs = ConfigurationManager.ConnectionStrings
                    .Item("AdventureWorks").ConnectionString
    let db = new Dao.DaoDataContext(cs)
    let GetCategories () =
        query <@ seq { for c in db.ProductCategories
                         -> new Category(c.ProductCategoryID, c.Name) } @>
```

```
let GetProducts categoryId =
    query <@ seq {  for p in db.Products do
                       if p.ProductCategoryID = categoryId then
                           yield new Product(p.Name, p.ListPrice) } @>
```

The code in Listing 14-7 first declares two simple class types Category and Product that are used in the helper functions to return results from the database queries. You could use tuples or records for these results, but class types are easier to work with when accessing the information stored using ASP.NET markup. The database itself is referenced by the Dao.DaoDataContext type (provided that you named the LINQ to SQL Classes item Dao.dbml and set the default namespace as described earlier). The constructor of this type takes the connection string as an argument, which you can read via the ConfigurationManager provided by ASP.NET from the web.config file (discussed shortly). Note that the named connection string you're referencing is called AdventureWorks. Finally, the module contains two functions, both implemented using F# LINQ. Both database queries are written as a sequence expression and are wrapped in F# quotations as discussed in Chapter 9. The queries are executed (or, to be more precise, translated to the underlying LINQ mechanism to be executed on demand) using the query function, which is discussed in more detail in Chapter 15. The GetCategories function returns the IDs and names of all the product categories in the database; the GetProducts function returns information about products in a specified category that is passed as a parameter. Note that when referring to a concrete variable in the F# LINQ query, you can splice it as is into the query representation.

Now, let's look at the Category.aspx file, shown in Listing 14-8, which contains the ASP.NET markup for viewing products in a specified category. You can specify the category that is displayed as an argument in the URL: for example, Category.aspx?id=18.

Listing 14-8. Category.aspx: The ASP.NET Page for Displaying Products in a Category

```
<%@ Page Language="F#" %>
<html>
<head runat="server">
    <title>Category Listing</title>
</head>
<body>
    <form runat="server">
        <!-- Unordered list of products using ASP.NET Repeater -->
        <ul>
        <asp:Repeater runat="server" id="rptProducts"
                    DataSourceID="awProducts">
            <ItemTemplate>
                <li><%# this.Eval("Name") %>
                    (price: <%# this.Eval("Price") %>)</li>
            </ItemTemplate>
        </asp:Repeater>
        </ul>

        <!-- ASP.NET DataSource control for loading the data -->
        <asp:ObjectDataSource id="awProducts" runat="server"
            TypeName="FSharpWeb.DataSource" SelectMethod="GetProducts">
            <SelectParameters>
                <asp:QueryStringParameter Name="categoryId" Type="Int32"
                    QueryStringField="id" DefaultValue="0"/>
            </SelectParameters>
        </asp:ObjectDataSource>
    </form>
</body>
</html>
```

The ASP.NET markup in Listing 14-8 doesn't use any code-behind code, because all you need to access the data is already available in the module you wrote in Listing 14-7. The first part of the markup declares the ASP.NET Repeater control including an ItemTemplate that is used to render a single product. Similar to the earlier examples, you use the Eval construct to access the data; but in this example, the product is represented using the Product class type declared earlier, so you can use the appropriate labels as an argument to the Eval function.

The second part of the markup is far more interesting; it declares an ASP.NET ObjectDataSource control, which is a nonvisual control, meaning it doesn't generate any HTML code. It serves as a source of data for the Repeater control in the first part: these two are linked together using the DataSourceID attribute of the Repeater control, which is set to the ID of the data source control. The ObjectDataSource is configured using the TypeName attribute, which specifies the .NET type that implements the functionality (in this case, you're using an F# module instead of an object type). The attribute SelectMethod sets a name of the method (or a function in this case) that should be called when the data is required. Because the method has one argument, you also need to use SelectParameters to specify what value should be passed as an argument to the function. You want to take the argument from the URL query string so you can use QueryStringParameter provided by ASP.NET. It has several attributes; the most important are QueryStringField, which sets the name of the argument in the URL address (id in this example), and Name, which has to match the parameter name of the GetProducts function in the F# module.

You looked only at the ASP.NET page for displaying the products in a specified category; but to make the application complete, you also need a page that lists all the categories using the GetCategories function. To do this, you must create a page similar to Category.aspx and modify a few details, so the page isn't shown here. As the last step, Listing 14-9 shows the web configuration file.

Listing 14-9. web.config: Configuration of the Sample Database Viewing Application

```
<?xml version="1.0"?>
<configuration>
  <connectionStrings>
    <!-- Connection string for the AdventureWorks database -->
    <add name="AdventureWorks" providerName="System.Data.SqlClient"
        connectionString=".. database connection string .." />
  </connectionStrings>
  <system.web>
    <compilation debug="true" />
  </system.web>
  <system.codedom>
    <compilers>
      <compiler language="F#;f#;fs;fsharp"
                extension=".fs"
                type="Microsoft.FSharp.Compiler.CodeDom.FSharpAspNetCodeProvider,
                    FSharp.Compiler.CodeDom,
                    Version=1.9.9.9,
                    Culture=neutral,
                    PublicKeyToken=a19089b1c74d0809"/>
    </compilers>
  </system.codedom>
</configuration>
```

In the configuration file, you first configure the connection string referenced by name as AdventureWorks, which you used earlier in the module that contains the data-access functionality. Connection strings describe the connection details to a database and are discussed in Chapter 15. A number of libraries are required to run your web application. You can properly track them by adding a project reference to Backend, which carries along its dependencies on the Dao project and the library references required to run F# LINQ queries. Finally, the web.config file must also include a configuration of the F# CodeDOM provider, which is referenced from the global assembly cache (GAC).

Going Further with ASP.NET

So far, you've seen some very simple kinds of web applications with ASP.NET and F#. In practice, ASP.NET offers an enormously powerful framework for all aspects of server-side web development. The following sections explore additional aspects; for full details, consult some of the excellent books dedicated to the topic of ASP.NET.

ASP.NET Directives

The first line of an .aspx file usually contains special markup embedded inside <%@ ... %> ... %> containing a number of ASP.NET directives. These are instructions given to the processing environment, indicating, among other things, which scripting language is used. Table 14-4 explains the most important directives and some of their attributes.

Table 14-4. Some ASP.NET Directives and Their Attributes

Directive/Attribute	Description
Page or Control	
AutoEventWireup	Wires page events that follow the Page_ naming convention automatically if true (default). If false, event handlers need to be wired explicitly.
CodeFile	Specifies the path to the code-behind file.
Inherits	Specifies the name of the class that goes together with the page.
Language	Specifies the language used for writing inline code in the page.
Import	Opens a namespace specified by the Namespace attribute and makes it available to all code in the page.
Register	Registers a user control for use with the page. See the section "Creating Custom ASP.NET Server Controls" later in this chapter.
OutputCache	Declaratively controls caching; if present, ASP.NET keeps the rendered output of a page or a control in a cache for a specified amount of time.
Assembly	References an external assembly. You can use the Name attribute to specify the name of the assembly (without the extension).
Implements	Specifies that the page implements the interface specified in the Interface attribute.
Reference	Associates another page or user control with the current one. You can use the Control, Page, or VirtualPath attribute to identify the component to be referenced, causing it to be compiled together.

Server Controls

In web forms, ordinary HTML markup such as `<strong>`, `<ul>`, and `<h2>` is treated as text and is passed to the browser verbatim (via the `LiteralControl` server control class). On the other hand, explicit server controls (those with the `runat="server"` attribute) are processed on the server and translated to HTML markup (just to illustrate, there are server controls that equate to hundreds of HTML tags, and many can be mapped nearly one to one). All server controls can be programmatically managed, which typically means you customize the way they respond to various events or how they appear or behave visually. Categorically speaking, there are two main types of server controls: HTML server controls that directly correspond to an HTML element and web server controls. The second type can be divided into several groups depending on the use of the control. For example, validation controls ensure that entered values fulfill some criteria, data source controls are similar to the `ObjectDataSource` mentioned earlier, membership controls handle user login and registration, and so on.

In Listing 14-2, you saw server controls such as labels and buttons, both of which are web-server controls. It's beyond the scope of this book to discuss the great number of web-server controls available in ASP.NET 2.0 and above. As a reference, Table 14-5 shows some of the ones most commonly used.

Table 14-5. Common ASP.NET Server Controls

Type	Controls
Basic	Button, TextBox, Label, Panel, CheckBox, ListBox, RadioButton, PlaceHolder, DropDownList
Data viewing/editing	Repeater, DataList, GridView, DetailsView
Data sources	ObjectDataSource, SqlDataSource
Membership	Login, LoginView
Validation	RequiredFieldValidator, CompareValidator, RegularExpressionValidator

HTML server controls correspond to a given HTML tag and are applied by adding the `runat="server"` attribute. This turns the standard HTML tag into a server control, allowing you to change its appearance or behavior programmatically. Because web-server controls offer a more robust object model, they're almost always preferable to HTML server controls.

Validation controls are a special type of web controls that perform typical validation patterns on your web form input fields and display error messages where appropriate. The Validation section of the Visual Studio Toolbox contains the available validation controls, as summarized in Table 14-6.

Table 14-6. Common ASP.NET Validation Controls

Control Name	Description
RequiredFieldValidator	Ensures that the associated input control isn't empty.
RangeValidator	Validates that the user input is in a given range.
RegularExpressionValidator	Checks whether the user input matches a regular expression pattern. See Chapter 10 for a description of using .NET regular expressions.

Control Name	Description
CompareValidator	Compares the user input against a given value or another control.
CustomValidator	Validates the user input based on custom, user-specified logic.
ValidationSummary	Lists all validation error messages.

Each validator has an ErrorMessage and a Text property that you can set in conjunction with displaying an error message. When the validator fails, it displays the content of the Text property at the place where it's inserted in your page markup. A typical scenario ensures that a given user-input control has a value entered. Here, all you need to do is add your input control and a RequiredFieldValidator next to it, set its ControlToValidate property to the ID of the associated input control, and set the Text property to *. This shows an asterisk when no value is entered in the input control at the time the page is submitted. Using another validator is just as easy, except you need to customize different properties. Table 14-7 summarizes the main properties for each validator.

Table 14-7. The Main Customizable Validator Properties

Control Name	Main Properties
RequiredFieldValidator	InitialValue
RangeValidator	MinimumValue, MaximumValue, Type
RegularExpressionValidator	ValidationExpression
CompareValidator	ControlToCompare, Operator, ValueToCompare, Type
CustomValidator	ClientValidationFunction, ServerValidate (event)
ValidationSummary	DisplayMode, HeaderText, ValidationGroup

You may end up working with complex web pages that have many, even dozens, of input controls that belong to different forms on the page (for instance, a web page with a search form, a user registration form, and a contact form). By default, all validators defined on the page run and most likely prohibit your end user from moving to the next page because of validation errors that are seemingly unrelated to the user's chosen action. To solve this problem, you can use validation groups, which specify a set of related controls and their validators. You form a validation group by specifying a common group name (as a string) for the ValidationGroup property of each validator and the input control that triggers a page submission. Doing so ensures that only validators related to the control initiating the page submission run. Finally, you can disable any validation by setting the CausesValidation property of a postback control to false.

Debugging, Profiling, and Tracing

Debugging ASP.NET applications is easy when you use a tool such as Visual Studio. You can set breakpoints in your F# code that let you break into the middle of code executing when server requests are performed. Chapter 18 discusses debugging techniques for regular F# code.

During development, it's often necessary to trace what happens on a page, as well as during the process of serving that page. You can enable page tracing by adding the Trace="true" page attribute to your web form. This appends the information shown in Table 14-8 to the page displayed. Figure 14-3 shows an example of this information for the application from Listing 14-4.

Table 14-8. Information Generated by Tracing an ASP.NET Page

Section	Information Collected
Request Details	Shows the session ID, request type, time of request, status code, and request/response encoding for the request
Trace Information	Shows the various page life-cycle events and the time spent on processing each
Control Tree	Shows each server control and its type, render size, view state size, and control state size in a parent-child tree
Session State	Shows the various keys, their associated values, and their types defined in the page's session state
Application State	Shows the various keys, their associated values, and their types defined in the server's application state
Request/Response Cookies Collection	Shows the name/value/size of each cookie
Headers Collection	Shows the name and value of each page header
Response Headers Collection	Shows the name and value for the server response
Server Variables	Shows the various server variables and their values at the time of processing

Figure 14-3. Debugging and tracing an ASP.NET web page

Understanding the ASP.NET Event Model

In the previous sections, you saw various server controls triggering events, submitting pages with form data, validating input controls, and so on. These all involve events. ASP.NET has an event-driven architecture: each web form and server control supports a number of events that it can respond to, and these events can be attached to various event handlers. As you'd expect, these events fall into two categories: page and control events, respectively. Consider what happens as you interact with a simple SayHello.aspx page that has a text box for a name, an empty label, and a submit button:

1. An HTTP GET request is made for *SayHello.aspx* to the server.

2. On receiving this request, the server processes the page (doing compilation if necessary), calls the appropriate page event handlers (Page_Load, and so on), and ultimately returns an HTML response.

3. This HTML response, along with the state/content of the HTML controls (the view state: an empty text box and label), is sent back to the browser, and the page is displayed.

4. You fill in your name and click the submit button. This causes the form containing the text box and button controls to post back to the server, passing the view state with it.

5. The server executes the appropriate page handlers and the control event handler(s) for the button click, and an HTML response is generated (the same page with the label now greeting you by name).

6. This HTML response is sent back to the browser and displayed.

As this simple but representative example shows, the server controls on a given page are in constant contact with the server: they catch events and pass them onto the server where they're handled and responded to accordingly.

Page events occur when a page is requested from the server, via either the GET (the first time) or POST (when data is posted to the page) HTTP methods. For instance, there are events for page initialization (PreInit, Init), page loading (Load), rendering (Render), and so on. These page events are always handled in a given order as defined by the ASP.NET page life cycle (see the sidebar "The ASP.NET Page Life Cycle"). Although you can programmatically bind a delegate to a given page event, ASP.NET makes it even easier. As you saw it in Listing 14-5, you can add page event handlers by declaring members of the form Page_XXX, where XXX is the name of the page event. This works because by default, the AutoEventWireup page attribute is true, and this causes wiring of the intended event handler (using this naming convention) to the appropriate event automatically.

Control events are triggered by the end user: clicking a button, selecting an item in a list box, and so on. Unlike page events, control events can't be automatically wired, and thus you need to establish the link between the handler and the event manually. This is quite easy to do: set the OnXXX attribute of the server control to the event handler, as you did with the Reload button in the first example.

Not all control events are immediately posted back to the server; only a few are, such as button clicks. All other control events are so-called *change events* (because they're triggered as a control undergoes some changes: the selected item in a drop-down list changes, or a check box or radio button is selected) and as such aren't posted to the server automatically for efficiency reasons. You can, on the other hand, enable postback in such situations by overriding the control's AutoPostBack property to true. This technique can be useful; for instance, a page can respond directly to a change in a drop-down list without the end user having to click a submit button, thus saving valuable clicks and time in the appropriate situations.

The ASP.NET Page Life Cycle

The ASP.NET page life cycle consists of a few dozen steps and as such is beyond the scope of this book to discuss in detail. However, it's important to understand the main steps involved in this life cycle. For a complete reference, you can refer to books devoted to ASP.NET. Here we give a brief and simplified description, sufficient enough for most situations.

Given a request for a page, and assuming that the appropriate page class exists in a compiled form on the server (if not, the ASP.NET runtime kicks in and performs a number of code compilation steps), a page instance is created with all server controls declared but not yet initialized. At this point, there are three main life-cycle phases: initialization, loading, and rendering. Initialization starts with determining whether the page requested is in postback mode (in which case the view state is encoded in the page request) or is being requested for the first time. The PreInit handler is executed, and the page theme and master page are applied. Next, the Init handler is called, initializing all server controls and the page itself, and then the InitCompleted event is triggered.

The loading phase involves loading any view state (in the case of a postback request) from the page request and loading it into the server controls. When the view state is restored, the PreLoad event is triggered, followed by the Load event. This is where you normally put page-processing logic that runs on every page request. Following this event, loading the view state is executed again to catch any dynamically added controls (for instance, those created in the Load event handler). Then, any control-change events and postback events are handled, and finally the LoadComplete event is raised.

The rendering phase starts by performing all data binding (which involves the DataBinding and DataBound events for each data-bound control); then, the PreRender event is triggered. Next, any asynchronous tasks (registered via RegisterAsyncTask) are fired off, and the PreRenderComplete event is called. Before the actual rendering takes place, the view state is saved back to the page (by default to the default hidden input field). Finally, the page's Render method is called: it produces HTML by recursively invoking the same method on each server control. Before this HTML is passed to the client, the Unload event is triggered, and every object involved in the page creation is disposed.

Both page and control events are executed on the server. When they're triggered, the parent page and its view state are posted to the server, where the event is handled and a response (the same or another page) is sent back to the client. A *postback* occurs if a page posts information to the server requesting the same page back. This round-trip scenario is common: the Reload button in Listing 14-2 and the Generate button in Listing 14-4 are examples of triggering a postback.

In both of these cases, you have a postback because you remain on the same page; for example, the originating page handles the data submission by updating the content of a label (an HTML <span> element) in the button click handler. More often, though, data is posted to another page, in which case it's referred to as *cross-page posting*. You can easily enable cross-page posting by setting the PostBackUrl property of the submitting control. For instance, a SayHello button can be declared as follows:

```
<asp:Button ID="btnSayHello" runat="server" Text="Greet" PostBackUrl="SayIt.aspx" />
```

There is a significant difference between how data submissions are handled via postback and cross-page posting: whereas the former is done in the submitting control's click event handler (for example, Reload_Click in the timer example), with cross-page posting, the submission event is handled in the Load event handler of the page to which the postback URL points. What slightly complicates matters is that the form data submitted isn't available directly on the receiving page: instead, you have to reference it through the page's PreviousPage property.

Because you often place initialization or cross-page posting code in a page event (typically for the Load event), you need to make sure this code is executed only for initialization or when data is being posted to the page. You can do so by checking the IsPostBack property of the Page object, which returns false if the page is requested the first time.

Maintaining the View State

HTTP is a stateless protocol, so you must take special care to preserve the state of a given page. For instance, suppose a visitor fills out a long form and, as sometimes happens, makes an error. After posting the page, this visitor expects to see all entered data preserved, with an indication of where the missing or incorrect entry is. Recovering form values after a postback is possible because ASP.NET maintains the *view state*: the state of all server controls on the page. These values are passed as HTTP form variables on a post and returned as hard-wired HTML.

View state is automatically encoded as a hidden <input> element in your pages, and no special handling is needed to enable it. You can, on the other hand, disable it by adding EnableViewState="false" to your Page directive, or disable it partially on the control level by setting the same control property for any control for which no view state is to be maintained. This may be necessary if your page displays large amounts of data with no possibility of a postback or the data on the page can't be modified, thus making the page source considerably smaller and quicker to download to your clients.

Understanding the Provider Model

ASP.NET comes with a number of built-in application services that you can use and customize as you build your web applications. These encapsulate much of the core functionality common to most web sites, such as membership and role management, profiles and personalization, and site navigation, and you can easily plug them into your web-site logic out of the box.

These services interact with service-specific data (the users registered, the different user roles your site is programmed for, various data associated with the authenticated users, and so on) via *providers*, which are classes that implement the appropriate interfaces to fulfill contracts for various services. ASP.NET comes with a number of built-in providers; for instance, it has a SQL and an Active Directory membership provider. The provider model allows you to plug in your own providers (by specifying them in the appropriate section of your web.config), so you may write an Oracle or a custom membership provider to your existing user/membership database or a role service provider based on simple XML files.

Table 14-9 shows some common provider-based services in ASP.NET.

Table 14-9. ASP.NET Provider-Based Services

Service	Description
Encryption	Handles the encryption and decryption of ASP.NET configuration files and sections within
Membership	Manages users and their accounts
Profile	Adds user information (for instance, user preferences) that is to be collected and stored for each user
Role Management	Manages roles and their associated access rights
Session Management	Manages session state for a user visit
Site Map	Stores information about each page and its place in the site's structure
Web Events	Allows the monitoring of an application for control purposes
Web Parts	Manages a set of controls and their content and appearance that make up a portal

Configuring the Provider Database

By default (as guided by the server's machine.config file), the data-aware services use SQL providers that work against a SQL Express database (by default, aspnetdb.mdf in the App_Data folder). The relevant part of the machine.config containing the default connection strings is as follows:

```
<connectionStrings>
    <clear />
    <add name="LocalSqlServer"
        connectionString="data source=.\SQLEXPRESS;Integrated Security=SSPI;
AttachDBFilename=|DataDirectory|aspnetdb.mdf;User Instance=true"
        providerName="System.Data.SqlClient" />
</connectionStrings>
```

This defines a LocalSqlServer connection string that all data-centric providers use by default, which points to the aspnetdb.mdf SQL Express database in the web data directory. (Note how the database server is set to be running as a SQL Express named instance.) This database file is automatically created on first use or by triggering the web-site administration console. It's important to remember that these default settings work only with SQL Express; but on a typical development machine with a standard SQL Express installation, everything works like a charm out of the box.

Even if you're using SQL Express and all the default providers, you should (re)define the connection string settings in your site web.config file, mostly because it's more portable that way and because this becomes necessary if you use a different database server, say SQL Server. At the time of writing, SQL Server doesn't let you attach database files to the server using the AttachDBFilename property, so you need to use a regular database and refer to it using the Initial Catalog or Database keyword in your connection string.

If for some reason you can't automatically generate the default database when using SQL Server, you can build it by hand by first creating an empty database (for instance, by right-clicking Server Explorer/Data Connections and selecting Create New SQL Server Database) and running aspnet_regsql.exe (found in your .NET installation folder) in wizard mode with the information about your newly created database. This tool generates all the data tables and stored procedures needed by the default providers. You can then change your web.config file to include a reference to this new database:

```
<connectionStrings>
    <remove name="LocalSqlServer" />
    <add name="LocalSqlServer"
         connectionString="Data Source=localhost;Integrated Security=SSPI;
Initial Catalog=YourDatabase"
         providerName="System.Data.SqlClient" />
</connectionStrings>
```

Here you use localhost for SQL Server and the YourDatabase database. You may need to change the host when you deploy your application to point to the right database server. Furthermore, be aware that SQL Server doesn't support detached databases (.mdf files); if you're migrating from a SQL Express instance (for example, when your hosting provider supports only SQL Server), you need to manually import the contents of the detached database file into a SQL Server database (either by attaching it from the hosting provider's administrative console or creating a backup from the Express database and importing it). In other words, there is no way to use the .mdf database with SQL Server directly.

Creating Custom ASP.NET Server Controls

You can create new server controls for ASP.NET on two conceptual levels: user controls and custom (web) server controls. User controls are similar to web forms: they're a collection of server control and/or HTML markup, which is named (declared) and then used via reference. They can also expose public properties that you can set to control various aspects of the user control. This chapter considers only user controls.

User controls are contained in .ascx files. You can create a new user control in Visual Studio by selecting the Web User Control template from the New/File menu option. The new user control is empty except for a Control directive that acts similarly to the Page directive of a web form. You can add any additional markup as needed. As an example, consider a user control that repeats a given text fragment a specified number of times.

This user control (RepeatText.ascx in Listing 14-10) contains a single control: a placeholder label. The code-behind file is located in RepeatText.ascx.fs, shown in Listing 14-11.

Listing 14-10. RepeatText.ascx: A Simple User Control Implemented in F#

```
<%@ Control Language="F#"
            AutoEventWireup="true"
            CodeFile="RepeatText.ascx.fs"
            Inherits="MyUserControl.RepeatText" %>

<asp:Label ID="Place" runat="server"/>
```

Listing 14-11. RepeatText.ascx.fs: The Implementation of an ASP.NET User Control

```
namespace MyUserControl

open System
open System.Web.UI.WebControls

type RepeatText() =
    inherit System.Web.UI.UserControl()

    /// This is the internal state and parameters of the control
    let mutable text = ""
    let mutable count = 0

    /// This internal control is initialized by ASP.NET
    [<DefaultValue>]
    val mutable Place : Label


    /// These properties allow the state to be used from the page
    member self.Text        with get() = text  and set(v) = text <- v
    member self.RepeatCount with get() = count and set(v) = count <- v

    /// This event is automatically wired up through the use of the
    /// AutoEventWireup ASP.NET directive (true by default)
    member self.Page_Load (sender: obj, e: EventArgs) =
        let acc = new Text.StringBuilder()
        for i in 1..count do
            acc.Append(self.Text) |> ignore
        self.Place.Text <- acc.ToString()
```

The state and parameters of the control are ultimately held in the variables text and count. Note how you define public properties (Text and RepeatCount) that are available when you use the control from a page. All you need to do to use this user control from a page is to register it using the Register directive, giving a tag prefix and a tag name by which you can refer to it. For example, the code in Listing 14-12 results in an HTML label element containing the text "Monkey!" 10 times.

Listing 14-12. TestRepeat.aspx: Using the Control from Listing 14-4

```
<%@ Page AutoEventWireup="true" %>
<%@ Register Src="RepeatText.ascx" TagName="Repeater" TagPrefix="text" %>
<!DOCTYPE html PUBLIC "-//W3C//DTD XHTML 1.0 Transitional//EN"
                      "http://www.w3.org/TR/xhtml1/DTD/xhtml1-transitional.dtd">
<html xmlns="http://www.w3.org/1999/xhtml">
```

```
<head runat="server">
    <title>My User Control Test</title>
</head>
<body>
    <form runat="server">
        <text:Repeater id="chart" runat="server" RepeatCount="10" Text="Monkey!" />
    </form>
</body>
</html>
```

Building Ajax Rich Client Applications

So far in this chapter, you've looked at programming server-side web applications. In recent years, a new class of rich-client web applications has emerged, leading to what is commonly called the *Ajax* development paradigm. This is a general term for any web application that incorporates substantial amounts of code executed on the client side of the application by running JavaScript in the web browser.

You can develop Ajax applications in at least three ways using F#:

- You can manually write and serve additional JavaScript files as part of your web application. This isn't hard, but you don't benefit from existing frameworks.

- You can use the Ajax support via ASP.NET and develop Ajax web applications with F# code-behind files or F# library code exposed via C# or VB code-behind.

- You can use the WebSharper platform to write both client and server code in F#.

Developing Ajax applications with the first two techniques follows a fairly standard path mostly independent of F#. The remainder of this section gives a brief overview of some of the core WebSharper features, including *pagelets, formlets,* and *flowlets.*

More on the WebSharper Platform

WebSharper enables robust, rapid, client-based web application development with F# and provides a wealth of composable primitives to build web applications from small to large-scale. These represent an extremely powerful way of writing robust, efficient, integrated client/server applications in a single, type-checked framework. In particular, WebSharper employs several advanced features of F#, the combination of which offers a unique programming experience for web applications:

- Client-side and server-side code are marked with custom attributes and can be authored in a single F# project. Client-side code, called *pagelets*, is automatically translated to JavaScript using F# quotations and reflection and is served to the client on demand. (See Chapter 9 for details on F# quotations and reflection.)

- The program runs initially as a server-side application, generating JavaScript code to populate and handle the interactions of the web user interface.

- Web forms can be expressed in an extraordinarily compact form as first-class, type-safe values and are represented as *formlets*. They can be composed and enhanced with just a few lines of code, including adding validation and complex user interactions, and defining *dependent* formlets.

- Sequences of web forms, *flowlets*, are first-class values, providing an elegant and concise way to express larger-than-page functionality, yet remaining in Ajax space.

- The client-side code can use functionality from many .NET and F# libraries. The calls are mapped to corresponding JavaScript functionality through sophisticated techniques. You can also provide custom proxies to any .NET type, describing how to translate it to JavaScript.

- The client side may make calls to any JavaScript technology via WebSharper stubs implemented for that technology. At the time of writing, WebSharper comes with a number of extensions to various JavaScript libraries, including JQuery, Google Maps, Google Visualization, Yahoo UI, JQuery UI, and JQuery Tools, among others.

- The client side may make asynchronous calls to the server using variations on the techniques described in Chapter 13.

- The resulting web applications are dramatically shorter and easier to maintain and extend, and can be readily deployed under IIS on the top of ASP.NET.

Getting Started with WebSharper

WebSharper is available free of charge for noncommercial purposes, and it's the recommended way of developing Rich Internet Applications (RIAs) with F#. You can grab the latest WebSharper from www.websharper.com.

WebSharper installs as a set of tools, most notably the F# to JavaScript compiler, and a new Visual Studio project type that provides a template to build WebSharper applications. At the time of writing, this Visual Studio template creates two projects: an F# library project that contains WebSharper application code, and a web application project that exposes WebSharper site functionality via ASPX markup and includes the settings and post-processing hooks to make compiling, running, and deploying a pleasant experience. This WebSharper template also includes a quick sample application; after you create a new WebSharper project, you can press F5 to start it using ASP.NET.

WebSharper Pagelets

As you've seen in the previous sections, handling user input in ASP.NET applications involves declaring server-side controls that are rendered to HTML to take input from the end user, and defining various event handlers to handle that input. You can add validators by declaring further server-side controls and connecting them with the controls they're to validate against. Similarly, the ASP.NET controls defined in ASPX markup are paired with their event handlers either by a predefined naming convention or by connecting them via strings in the markup.

The earlier examples of loose coupling between the various ASP.NET components easily lead to problems when you need to code more complex web applications. Furthermore, the server-centric view requires that all components be rendered to code on the server side, which then executes to produce HTML with any submission/processing event delegated to the server again, leaving little opportunity to customize interaction on the client side.

WebSharper takes a fundamentally different approach and views web applications from a client-based perspective. WebSharper applications are made up of pagelets, annotated F# code that is automatically translated to JavaScript to run on the client on demand. You can combine pagelets to form larger pagelets; you can develop web pages and even entire web sites in a single pagelet. Pagelets that create DOM nodes can be exposed as ASP.NET server controls and composed into ASPX markup seamlessly.

Consider the following simple example:

```
open IntelliFactory.WebSharper
open IntelliFactory.WebSharper.Html

[<JavaScript>]
```

```
let HelloWorld =
    let welcome = P [Text "Welcome"]
    Div [
        welcome
        Input [Type "Button"; Value "Click me!"]
        |> OnClick (fun e args ->
            welcome.Text <- "Hello, world!")
    ]
```

HelloWorld defines a pagelet that returns a DOM node: a DIV tag with two child nodes. The first child node is a paragraph containing welcome text, and the second is an HTML button with "Click me!" as its title. The key thing to note here is the use of the [<JavaScript>] attribute, which defines a particular code element to be available in JavaScript and thus on the client side. The button's click event handler is attached using OnClick, a shorthand function for the On Events.Click sequence. Additional HTML combinators are available in the IntelliFactory.WebSharper.Html namespace. Each combinator takes a sequence of DOM nodes or a sequence of attributes. If both are required, you can use the -< combinator, such as

```
Div [Class "your-css-class"] -< [ … ]
```

Calling Server Code from the Client

You can define server-side functionality such as functions to fetch data from server files or databases as easily as you define client-side code. Server-side functions, such as those defined to execute over RPC, can be called from client-code seamlessly; the communication protocol is implemented by the WebSharper runtime as JavaScript code. The following is example skeleton code:

```
module YourWebApplication =
    open IntelliFactory.WebSharper
    ...
    [<Rpc.Callable>]
    let YourServerFunction (...) = ...

    [<JavaScript>]
    let YourClientFunction () =
        let data = YourServerFunction (...)
        ...
```

WebSharper Formlets

Nearly all web pages need to take user input in one way or another. For example, the user may click buttons or links, or enter values in a web form. Furthermore, web forms typically impose various limitations for the values entered: many fields are required and must be supplied a value, date fields can only be set using date values, fields that expect numeric values reject alpha and special characters, and so on.

WebSharper formlets provide an elegant, type-safe, robust way to build web forms and represent the structural make-up, the validations involved, and the layout and other presentation details as a single F# value. They're composable building blocks that can be enhanced and customized to an arbitrary complexity.

The IntelliFactory.WebSharper.Formlet namespace contains various formlet controls and enhancements that you can apply, along with important formlet combinators such as Formlet.Run, which renders a formlet into a DOM node. A simple example is a text-box formlet that takes a string input from the user:

```
let snippet1 = Controls.Input "initial value"
```

You can test this and other formlets quickly by writing a short wrapper function that takes a render function that translates values to DOM nodes and a formlet that supplies those values:

```
[<JavaScript>]
let RunInBlock f formlet =
    let output = Div []
    formlet
    |> Formlet.Run (fun res ->
        let (elem: Element) = f res
        output -< [ elem ] |> ignore)
    |> fun form ->
        Div [
            form
            output
        ]
```

Another helper function takes simple string formlets and echoes what has been accepted by those formlets:

```
[<JavaScript>]
let RunSnippet formlet =
    formlet
    |> RunInBlock (fun name ->
        Div [
            P ["Hi " + name + "!" |> Text]
        ])
```

RunSnippet returns a DOM node so you can wrap it in an ASP.NET server control:

```
[<JavaScriptType>]
type Snippet1() =
    inherit Web.Control()

    [<JavaScript>]
    override this.Body = snippet1 |> RunSnippet
```

Adding this ASP.NET server control to an ASPX markup displays a text box to write text into and an empty echo message. Each time you press a key, an event is triggered, and the formlet enters an accepting state; subsequently it displays a new echo message that is appended to the previous ones.

To remove the initial empty echo message, you can add a validator that doesn't accept values with fewer than three characters by enhancing the plain input formlet:

```
[<JavaScript>]
let Snippet1a =
    Formlet.Yield (fun name -> name)
    <*> (Controls.Input ""
        |> Validator.Is (fun s -> s.Length > 3) "Enter a valid name")
```

This is a slightly more elaborate version of the input formlet, enhanced with a particular validator and wrapped in a Formlet.Yield combinator. This function defines how the values collected in the formlet are returned from the formlet and comes in handy for larger formlets that carry multiple fields.

You can equip your formlets with a visual form container by adding a further enhancement, this time with a validator that accepts any non-empty string:

```
[<JavaScript>]
let Snippet1b =
    Formlet.Yield (fun name -> name)
    <*> (Controls.Input ""
        |> Validator.IsNotEmpty "Enter a valid name"
        |> Enhance.WithFormContainer)
```

You can also cause the formlet not to submit until a submit button is pressed. In addition, you can supply a reset button that resets the formlet to its original state. This example adds both:

```
[<JavaScript>]
let Snippet1c =
    Formlet.Yield (fun name -> name)
    <*> (Controls.Input ""
        |> Validator.IsNotEmpty "Enter a valid name"
        |> Enhance.WithFormContainer
        |> Enhance.WithSubmitAndResetButtons)
```

The accepting status of the formlet and any validation error messages can be revealed to the user via a validation icon or an error summary enhancement. You can do the former, and move the submit and reset buttons into the form container, as follows:

```
[<JavaScript>]
let Snippet1d =
    Formlet.Yield (fun name -> name)
    <*> (Controls.Input ""
        |> Validator.IsNotEmpty "Enter a valid name"
        |> Enhance.WithValidationIcon
        |> Enhance.WithSubmitAndResetButtons
        |> Enhance.WithFormContainer)
```

Adding a label for the input control is yet another enhancement:

```
[<JavaScript>]
let Snippet1e =
    Formlet.Yield (fun name -> name)
    <*> (Controls.Input ""
        |> Validator.IsNotEmpty "Enter a valid name"
        |> Enhance.WithValidationIcon
        |> Enhance.WithTextLabel "Name"
        |> Enhance.WithSubmitAndResetButtons
        |> Enhance.WithFormContainer)
```

And finally, you can add an information icon before the label:

```
[<JavaScript>]
let Snippet1f =
    Formlet.Yield (fun name -> name)
    <*> (Controls.Input ""
        |> Validator.IsNotEmpty "Enter a valid name"
```

```
    |> Enhance.WithValidationIcon
    |> Enhance.WithLabelAndInfo "Name" "Enter your name"
    |> Enhance.WithSubmitAndResetButtons
    |> Enhance.WithFormContainer)
```

These formlets are shown in Figure 14-4. Although these examples contain a single input field, you can create further input formlets as shown in the following example:

```
[<JavaScript>]
let input (label: string) (err: string) =
    Controls.Input ""
    |> Validator.IsNotEmpty err
    |> Enhance.WithValidationIcon
    |> Enhance.WithTextLabel label
```

```
[<JavaScript>]
let inputInt (label: string) (err: string) =
    Controls.Input ""
    |> Validator.IsInt err
    |> Enhance.WithValidationIcon
    |> Enhance.WithTextLabel label
```

```
[<JavaScript>]
let Snippet2 : Formlet<string * int> =
    Formlet.Yield (fun name age -> name, age |> int)
    <*> input "Name" "Please enter your name"
    <*> inputInt "Age" "Please enter a valid age"
    |> Enhance.WithSubmitAndResetButtons
    |> Enhance.WithFormContainer
```

Note how this formlet returns a string-int pair for the name and age obtained from the user, in essence providing a type-safe and robust way to collect and handle the input values.

Figure 14-4. Various formlet snippets using WebSharper

Another useful formlet combinator is `Formlet.Many`. It gives you the ability to collect a list of values and visuals:

```
[<JavaScript>]
let Snippet3a =
    Formlet.Yield (fun name age -> name, age |> int)
    <*> input "Name" "Please enter your name"
    <*> inputInt "Age" "Please enter a valid age"
    |> Enhance.WithLegend "Person"
    |> Enhance.WithTextLabel "Person"
    |> Formlet.Many
    |> Enhance.WithLegend "People"
    |> Enhance.WithSubmitAndResetButtons
    |> Enhance.WithFormContainer
```

.NET Proxies and JavaScript Stubs

WebSharper enables you to use F# in your client-side coding and gives you nearly the entire F# language to develop client code including powerful language features such as pattern matching, active patterns, discriminated unions and records, classes, interfaces, exceptions, and asynchronous computations, among others. It also comes with proxies for a large part of the F# core libraries and .NET namespaces, enabling you to use those seamlessly in your WebSharper applications without having to worry about how to map them to JavaScript.

WebSharper also lets you map additional .NET libraries and enlist them in the WebSharper space by writing proxies for them. Similarly, you can provide stubs for existing JavaScript libraries and technologies and write F# code to access them, freeing you from developing untyped JavaScript code. For more information about writing .NET proxies and JavaScript stubs, please refer to the documentation available on the WebSharper project site. At the time of writing, WebSharper comes with a number of extensions to various JavaScript technologies, including JQuery, Google Maps and Visualization, Yahoo UI, JQuery UI, JQuery Tools, and others.

Automated Resource Tracking and Handling

Pagelets can define their own resource dependencies, such as style sheets, JavaScript code, and other artifacts that they need to work properly. These dependencies are automatically referenced by the WebSharper script manager tag in ASPX markup when those pagelets are used in the page. For instance, the formlet examples in the preceding section came with a dependency on the main formlet style sheet provided by WebSharper (along with additional skins), giving the appearance shown in Figure 14-4.

Dependent Formlets and Flowlets

Often, web forms need more elaborate considerations. For instance, a given part of a web form may depend on what is entered in another. You can express these dependencies using *dependent formlets*, which you can create most conveniently using the formlet computation expression builder. As plain formlets, dependent formlets are also first-class values and further encode linear dependencies between the various form parts. Consider the following simple example in which the name and age are obtained one after the other; a name must be entered before the input field for the age is displayed:

```
[<JavaScript>]
let Snippet4 =
    formlet {
        let! name = input "Name" "Please enter your name"
        let! age = inputInt "Age" "Please enter a valid age"
        return name, age |> int
    }
    |> Enhance.WithSubmitAndResetButtons
    |> Enhance.WithFormContainer
```

The IntelliFactory.WebSharper.Formlet namespace provides additional combinators you can use to express nonlinear dependencies and build complex user interface interactions and forms.

Similar to dependent formlets, *flowlets* provide a slightly different visual experience and enable you to serve various formlets as a sequence of steps, collecting and accumulating the composite result of the entire flowlet. The following example dresses up each primitive formlet step in a form container with reset and submit buttons:

```
[<JavaScript>]
    let Snippet4b =
        flowlet {
            let! name = input "Name" "Please enter your name"
                        |> Enhance.WithSubmitAndResetButtons
                        |> Enhance.WithFormContainer
            let! age =  inputInt "Age" "Please enter a valid age"
                        |> Enhance.WithSubmitAndResetButtons
                        |> Enhance.WithFormContainer
            return name, age |> int
        }
```

Using WSDL Web Services

You can use web services to implement *service-oriented architectures*, a popular application integration strategy where the interacting software components and services are loosely coupled in a distributed environment. The benefits of such integration include offering services as independent entities that can be used and reused from different systems within an organization or around the world. Consuming web services is a great way to expand the functionality of your application.

A *web service* is a set of functionality that is offered through a platform-independent interface. Applications can explore the pieces of functionality offered by a web service by examining its Web Services Description Language (WSDL) signature. This WSDL definition uses XML to describe the signature of each operation by declaring the data types of the parameters and optional return values. Communicating with a web service occurs via the Simple Object Access Protocol (SOAP), which encodes service invocations and return values in an XML envelope over HTTP. Because web services are invoked over HTTP, they can be used by any application with Internet connectivity.

Communicating with web services is usually performed via so-called *proxy classes*. A proxy performs all the grunge work involved in calling the service and deciphering the results, freeing you from a lot of work. A typical workflow when calling a web service is as follows:

1. The client instantiates the proxy and calls the desired operation on it.

2. The proxy creates a SOAP XML request and sends it to the web service via HTTP.

3. The web service receives the request and performs the requested operation.

4. The web service packages the return value from the operation (or any exception that occurred) into a SOAP XML response and returns it to the proxy via HTTP.

5. The proxy deserializes the response into a .NET data type and returns it to the calling class.

Consuming Web Services

Many great web services are available on the Internet. For instance, Microsoft's TerraService is a free web service at msrmaps.com; it enables you to integrate USGS images and data into your applications. webservicex.net is another great source for web services; for instance, its WeatherForecast web service can supply weather information for any given U.S. location. Calling these and other web services in your .NET applications is painless using F# web references. Finally, www.programmableweb.com is an excellent online directory with a huge number of well-documented web services, using both SOAP and other protocols such as REST.

All web services are called via generated proxy code. The easiest way to generate this code is to add a web reference to Visual Studio, which automatically generates a .NET proxy class for the given web service. Figure 14-5 shows the available operations for the web service from http://terraservice.net/TerraService.asmx.

Figure 14-5. Adding a web service reference

You can also generate code using the .NET command-line tool wsdl.exe. The following example generates C# code for TerraService and WeatherForecast and compiles it explicitly:

```
C:\fsharp> wsdl /namespace:WebReferences http://webservicex.net/WeatherForecast.asmx
Microsoft (R) Web Services Description Language Utility
Writing file 'C:\fsharp\WeatherForecast.cs'.

C:\fsharp> csc /target:library /r:System.dll /r:System.Web.Services.dll
          /r:System.Xml.dll WeatherForecast.cs

C:\fsharp> wsdl /namespace:WebReferences http://terraservice.net/terraservice.asmx
Microsoft (R) Web Services Description Language Utility
Writing file 'C:\fsharp\TerraService.cs'.

C:\fsharp> csc /target:library /r:System.dll /r:System.Web.Services.dll
          /r:System.Xml.dll TerraService.cs

C:\fsharp> dir *.dll
```

```
...
03/09/2010  00:18        10,752 WeatherForecast.dll
03/09/2010  00:18        47,616 TerraService.dll
```

■ **Note** You can also use `wsdl.exe` to generate F# code by adding a command-line option that gives an explicit reference to the F# CodeDOM dynamic code generator, part of the F# Power Pack on `www.codeplex.com`. For example, you can use an option such as `/language:"Microsoft.FSharp.Compiler.CodeDom. FSharpCodeProvider, FSharp.Compiler.CodeDom, Version=1.9.9.9, Culture=neutral, PublicKeyToken=a19089b1c74d0809"`. Note the similarity to the CodeDOM reference used in the `web.config` file in Listing 14-2. The generated file can then be compiled as normal, although we have found that small adjustments sometimes need to be made to the generated code.

You can reference these two generated DLLs from F# Interactive using the following references:

```
> #r @"C:\fsharp\WeatherForecast.dll";;
> #r @"C:\fsharp\TerraService.dll";;
```

You can now use these web services directly from F# Interactive:

```
> open System;;
> open WebReferences;;

> let ws = new WeatherForecast();;
val ws : WeatherForecast = WebReferences.WeatherForecast

> let weather = ws.GetWeatherByPlaceName("Los Angeles");;
val weather : WeatherForecasts

> let today = weather.Details.[0];;
val today : WeatherData

> printf "Temperature: %sF/%sC\n" today.MaxTemperatureF today.MaxTemperatureC;;
Temperature: 72F/22C
val it : unit = ()

> let ts = new TerraService();;
val ts : TerraService = WebReferences.TerraService

> let place = new Place(City="Los Angeles", State="CA", Country="USA");;
val place : Place

> let facts = ts.GetPlaceFacts(place);;
```

```
val facts : PlaceFacts

> printfn "Lat/Lon: %f/%f" facts.Center.Lat facts.Center.Lon;;
Lat/Lon: 33.833000/-118.217003
```

Calling Web Services Asynchronously

If you put a timer on these web service calls, you'd see that they take significant time to execute—even seconds, depending on your network connection. This can be serious idle time for your application. To remedy this problem, you can either minimize the number of web-service calls through some sort of caching (for instance, in a web application you can store web-service data in the session or the application state and reuse it instead of making new calls) or make these calls in parallel, *asynchronously*. For example, it makes sense to connect to two web services simultaneously and wait for both responses to come back before proceeding with the rest of an operation.

The easiest and most compositional way to access a web service asynchronously is to use the *asynchronous workflows* discussed in Chapter 13. The proxy code generated for the web service includes methods such as BeginGetWeatherByPlaceName and EndGetWeatherByPlaceName, which follow the style for .NET library asynchronous invocations described in Chapter 13. You first map these pairs of operations into methods that construct asynchronous tasks. As in Chapter 13, you do this by defining extension members to the types in the generated code:

```
type WebReferences.WeatherForecast with
    member ws.GetWeatherByPlaceNameAsyncr placeName =
        Async.FromBeginEnd(placeName,
                            ws.BeginGetWeatherByPlaceName,
                            ws.EndGetWeatherByPlaceName)


type WebReferences.TerraService with
    member ws.GetPlaceFactsAsyncr place =
        Async.FromBeginEnd(place,
                            ws.BeginGetPlaceFacts,
                            ws.EndGetPlaceFacts)
```

These have the following types:

```
member ws.GetWeatherByPlaceNameAsyncr : placeName:string -> Async<WeatherForecast>
member ws.GetPlaceFactsAsyncr: place:Place -> Async< PlaceFacts>
```

You can now define various asynchronous tasks using these primitives. For example, you can define a function getWeather that collects both the weather and position data for a given location but executes the two calls simultaneously:

```
type Microsoft.FSharp.Control.Async with
    static member Parallel2 (a1, a2) =
        async { let! job1 = Async.StartChild a1
                let! job2 = Async.StartChild a2
                let! res1 = job1
```

```
                    let! res2 = job2
                    return res1, res2 }

let getWeather(city,state,country) =
    async { let ws = new WeatherForecast()
            let ts = new TerraService()
            let place = new Place(City=city, State=state, Country=country)
            let! weather,facts =
                Async.Parallel2 (
                        ws.GetWeatherByPlaceNameAsyncr(city),
                        ts.GetPlaceFactsAsyncr(place))
            let today = weather.Details.[0]
            return (today.MinTemperatureF,today.MaxTemperatureC,
                    facts.Center.Lat,facts.Center.Lon) }
```

The type of this function is as follows:

```
val getWeather : string * string * string -> Async<string * string * float * float>
```

One simple use of this task is to run it and print the results when the operation completes:

```
Async.RunSynchronously (
    async { let! (maxF, maxC, lat, lon) = getWeather("Los Angeles", "CA", "USA")
            do printfn "Temperature: %sF/%sC" maxF maxC
            do printfn "Lat/Lon: %f/%f" lat lon })
```

With an active web connection, this results in output such as the following (after a short delay while the connections are resolved):

```
Temperature: 72F/22C
Lat/Lon: 33.833000/-118.217003
```

Summary

In this chapter, you've seen how to use F# to perform a range of web programming tasks. You started by using sockets and TCP/IP to implement a web server and other TCP-based services directly, an example of a system or web network programming task. You can learned how to use ASP.NET to implement web applications involving HTML and input server controls and how to use embedded scripts and code-behind files. We also showed how you can query a database and display its data. You then looked briefly at web applications that incorporate significant client-side scripting using the WebSharper Platform, the recommended way to develop Rich Internet Applications (RIAs) with F#. Finally, you saw how to use web services from F#, including making compositional asynchronous invocations of web services.

Data access is a topic that complements web programming and often forms a major part of server-based web applications. The next chapter discusses how to access relational databases from F# programs and also examines other aspects of working with data from F#.

CHAPTER 15

■■■

Working with Data

Software applications deal with data in a wide array of forms: single values such as integers or strings; composite values paired together as tuples, records, or objects; collections of smaller pieces of data represented as lists, sets, arrays, or sequences; XML strings with tags describing the shape and kind of data; and data coming from relational or object-oriented databases, just to name a few.

This chapter looks at ways of working with some common data sources:

- In Chapter 3, you saw that sequences, similar to other enumerable data types such as lists, arrays, maps, and sets, have various aggregate iteration, query, and transform operators. This chapter first looks at how you can use these operators in a straightforward manner to form SQL-like operations over in-memory collections. This mechanism can be further tuned and applied to other data sources where the original data source is mapped to a sequence.

- We cover how you can work with relational databases from F# programs using the ADO.NET libraries. You learn how to connect to a database; create, update, and delete tables and records using simple SQL statements; access database data sequentially; and work with parts of tables using disconnected in-memory representations. You also learn how to manage database connections and data sources; create databases; add new tables; and work with relationships, constraints, and stored procedures using Visual Studio.

- We cover how you can use the Language Integrated Query (LINQ) infrastructure in combination with F# metaprogramming to bring relational data query logic into reach without explicit use of SQL. The essential goal is to write database queries in F# itself using the same techniques you use to query in-memory data structures.

- Finally, the chapter looks at the use of XML as a generic data format. You saw in Chapter 9 how to work with the XML Document Object Model (DOM), and we briefly survey how to desugar XML into sequences using LinqToXml.

Querying In-Memory Data Structures

Query languages are often made up of building blocks that transform and filter data. Functional programming gives you the basic tools that allow you to apply standard query logic on all F# types that are compatible with the F# sequence type, such as F# lists, arrays, sequences, and anything else that implements the IEnumerable<'a>/seq<'a> interface.

Select/Where/From Queries Using Aggregate Operators

Consider the following aggregate operators described in Chapter 3:

```
let select = Seq.map
let where  = Seq.filter
```

Here you rename the operations in the F# Seq module to correspond to more standard database query terminology: the select operator is defined as a transform operation, because in a selection you take sequence elements and map (often narrow) them to new values. Similarly, the where operator is defined as a filter applied on a sequence that takes an 'a -> bool predicate to filter out the desired elements. You can use these aggregate operators in a straightforward manner to query and transform in-memory data. The only other piece you need is the glue that makes the query and transform operators work together: the standard pipe operator (|>). Recall that this operator flips the order of its arguments; being an infix operator, it feeds the left-side argument into the function on the right. This is useful because the argument to the function is seen before the function itself, propagating important typing information into the function.

For instance, given a string * int * string array representing the name, age, and department of various employees, you can select those names that start with the letter *R* as follows:

```
let people = [| ("Joe", 27, "Sales");  ("Rick", 35, "Marketing");
                ("Mark", 40, "Sales"); ("Rob", 31, "Administration");
                ("Bob", 34, "Marketing") |]

let namesR =
    people |> select (fun (name, age, dept) -> name)
           |> where  (fun name -> name.StartsWith "R")
```

Note that the types of name, age, and dept are inferred from people, and no type annotation is necessary. Finding those people who work in sales and are older than 30 years old is also straightforward:

```
> let namesSalesOver30 =
    people |> where  (fun (_, age, _)  -> age >= 30)
           |> where  (fun (_, _, dept) -> dept = "Sales")
           |> select (fun (name, _, _) -> name);;
val namesSalesOver30 : seq<string>

> namesSalesOver30;;
val it : seq<string> = seq ["Mark"]
```

Using Aggregate Operators in Queries

In the previous section, you used alternative names such as select and where for some standard F# operations such as Seq.map and Seq.filter. This is for illustrative purposes to show the connection between these operators and SQL-like querying. In most F# code, you should continue to use the standard F# operators from the Seq module.

In addition to the restriction (filter/where) and projection (map/select) operators, the Seq module contains other useful functions, many of which were described in Chapter 3; and you can easily define further operators. For instance, you can define sorting over sequences by using a custom sorting function together with Seq.sortBy.

Another useful query-like function is Seq.truncate, which takes the first *n* elements and truncates the rest. Using these new operators—given, for example, an unbounded stream of random numbers— you can extract the first three even numbers and return a pair of those numbers and their square in reverse order, as the following example shows:

```
let rand = System.Random()
let numbers = seq { while true do yield rand.Next(1000) }

numbers |> Seq.filter (fun i -> i % 2 = 0)  // "where"
        |> Seq.truncate 3
        |> Seq.sort                          // sort ascending
        |> Seq.map (fun i -> i, i*i)         // "select"
```

```
// random - results will vary!
val it : seq<int * int> = seq [(814, 662596); (686, 470596); (242, 58564)]
```

Accumulating Using Folding Operators

Some of the most general operators supported by most F# data structures are reduce, fold, and foldBack. These apply a function to each element of a collection and accumulate a result. For fold and foldBack, the function is applied in left-to-right or right-to-left order, respectively. If you use the name fold, then typically the ordering is left to right. Both functions also take an initial value for the accumulator. For example:

```
> List.fold (fun acc x -> acc + x) 0 [4; 5; 6];;
val it : int = 15

> Seq.fold (fun acc x -> acc + x) 0.0 [4.0; 5.0; 6.0];;
val it : float = 15.0

> List.foldBack (fun x acc -> min x acc) [4; 5; 6; 3; 5] System.Int32.MaxValue;;
val it : int = 3
```

The following are equivalent, but no explicit anonymous function values are used:

```
> List.fold (+) 0 [4; 5; 6];;
val it : int = 15

> Seq.fold (+) 0.0 [4.0; 5.0; 6.0];;
val it : float = 15.0

> List.foldBack min [4; 5; 6; 3; 5] System.Int32.MaxValue;;
val it : int = 3
```

If used carefully, the various `foldBack` operators are pleasantly compositional, because they let you apply a selection function as part of the accumulating function:

```
> List.foldBack (fst >> min) [(3, "three"); (5, "five")] System.Int32.MaxValue;;
val it : int = 3
```

The F# library also includes more direct accumulation functions such as `Seq.sum` and `Seq.sumBy`. These use a fixed accumulation function (addition) with a fixed initial value (zero).

■ **Caution** Folding operators are very powerful and can help you avoid many explicit uses of recursion or loops in your code. However, they're sometimes overused in functional programming and can be hard for novice users to read and understand. Take the time to document uses of these operators, or consider using them to build simpler operators that apply a particular accumulation function.

Expressing Some Queries Using Sequence Expressions

Using aggregate operators to form queries is closely related to the sequence expression notation described in Chapter 3 and is used frequently in this book. For example, `namesSalesOver30` defined previously can also be defined as follows:

```
seq { for (name, age, dept) in people do
        if age >= 30 && dept = "Sales" then
          yield name }
```

This is a different notation for the same computation. For very simple queries, F# sequence expressions also support an even more compact form where `if`/`then` clauses are replaced by `when`, the final `do` is dropped from the `for` statement, and `yield` is replaced by `->`:

```
seq { for (name, age, dept) in people do
        if age >= 30 && dept = "Sales" then
          yield name }
```

There is no difference between these two sequence expressions—it's just a matter of syntax.

You can use sequence expressions in conjunction with the `|>` operator. For example:

```
seq { for i in numbers do
        if i % 2 = 0 then
            yield (i, i*i) }
|> Seq.truncate 3
|> Seq.sort
```

There are pros and cons to using sequence-expression syntax for some parts of queries:

- Sequence expressions are very good for the subset of queries expressed using iteration (`for`), mapping (`select`/`yield`), and filtering (`if`/`then`/`when`/`where`). They're particularly good for queries containing multiple nested `for` statements.

- Other query constructs such as ordering, truncating, grouping, and aggregating must be expressed directly using aggregate operators such as `Seq.sortBy` and `Seq.groupBy`.

- Some queries depend on the index position of an item within a stream. These are best expressed directly using aggregate operators such as `Seq.mapi`.

- Many queries are part of a longer series of transformations chained by `|>` operators. Often, the type of the data being transformed at each step varies substantially through the chain of operators. These queries are best expressed using aggregate operator chains.

■ **Note** It's likely that in the future, the F# sequence-expression syntax will include support for specifying grouping and aggregation operations within the expression syntax. However, at the time of writing, it's necessary to explicitly use operators such as `Seq.sortBy` and `Seq.groupBy` for these operations.

In-Memory Queries and LINQ

In this section, you've seen how you can use aggregate sequence operators and sequence expressions to query and manipulate in-memory data structures using a SQL-like syntax. This is essentially the idea behind Microsoft's LINQ technology. You apply the same techniques to queries over relational data (LINQ to SQL) later in this chapter.

In Chapter 3, you saw that sequences can be used to wrap collections and that a number of collection data types implement the sequence interface. It's possible to provide parallel implementations for the iteration, aggregation, and transformation operations of these data types—for instance, a parallel list implementation that uses worker threads—and assume independence between the transformation steps. This idea forms the basis of Parallel LINQ, a parallel version of LINQ. This library can be accessed using the F# Power Pack library `FSharp.PowerPack.Parallel.Seq.dll`, for parallel sequence operations.

Using Databases to Manage Data

Storing data in various files, reading them into memory, and querying and manipulating the resulting in-memory data collection is a sufficient approach for many applications working with data, but there comes a point where more persistent data handling is required.

For example, consider a business that has two applications that need to access the same set of data about employees. One way to do this is to store data in a text file and work with this data file from both applications. But this approach is vulnerable; you'd quickly realize how redundant text files can get when adding new pieces of data (say you wanted to add an address next to the name, department, and age of each employee) or if you wanted to group your employee data by introducing various relationships (say, multiple addresses per employee). Even if you managed to find a good storage alternative, you'd still have to modify both applications to read and write this new data format. Databases make scenarios like these much easier to cope with by enforcing centralized control of persistent data (data that is more persistent than what appears in a single application) and by giving you the freedom to define, manipulate, and query this data in an application-neutral way.

Databases provide many benefits. Some of the more important ones are listed here:

- *Data security:* When you have centralized control of your data, you can erect a full security system around the data, implementing specific access rules for each type of access or parts of the database.

- *Sharing data*: Any number of applications with the appropriate access rights can connect to your database and read the data stored within—without needing to worry about containing the logic to extract this data. As you see shortly, applications use various query languages (most notably SQL) to communicate with databases.

- *A logical organization of data*: You can write new applications that work with the same data without having to worry about how the data is physically represented and stored. On the basic level, this logical structure is provided by a set of entities (data tables) and their relationships.

- *Avoiding data redundancy*: Having all requirements from each consuming application up front helps to identify a logical organization for your data that minimizes possible redundancy. For instance, you can use foreign keys instead of duplicating pieces of data. *Data normalization* is the process of systematically eliminating data redundancy, a large but essential topic that we don't consider in this book.

- *Transactions*: Reading from and writing to databases occurs atomically, and as a result, two concurrent transactions can never leave data in an inconsistent, inaccurate state. *Isolation levels* refer to specific measures taken to ensure transaction isolation by locking various parts of the database (fields, records, tables). Higher isolation levels increase locking overhead and can lead to a loss of parallelism by rendering concurrent transactions sequential; on the other hand, no isolation can lead to inconsistent data.

- *Maintaining data integrity*: Databases make sure the data stored within is accurate. Having no redundancy is one way to maintain data integrity (if a piece of data is changed, it's changed in the only place it occurs; thus, it remains accurate); on the other hand, data security and transaction isolation are needed to ensure that the data stored is modified in a controlled manner.

The Relational Model: Data Relations

A relational database table is essentially a two-dimensional matrix with rows (records) and columns (fields). A *primary key* is a column that uniquely identifies each row, and that means you can't store the same value in a primary-key column of any two records (so it's also a *unique key*). The primary key is usually a single numeric or GUID column, but it can also be composed as a set of columns, in which case it's called a *composite primary key*.

Tables can be linked or related to one another using relationships. To set up a relationship, you need *foreign keys*, which are columns that store primary key values in a host table. For instance, in a *one-to-one relationship*, a record in table A can be associated with a record in table B by A containing a foreign key to B's primary key column, or vice versa, or both, depending on the *navigability* of the relationship. A one-to-one relationship is rare because it makes more sense to merge the two tables, unless the foreign key is allowed to be null. On the other hand, *one-to-many* (1..*) relationships are ubiquitous, allowing records in table A to be associated with multiple records in table B. For instance, a Customers table is likely to be associated with an Orders table this way, allowing each customer to have multiple orders. This can be modeled by storing a foreign key in Orders that refers to a Customers primary key. By moving two (or more) foreign keys into a separate *association table*, you obtain a *many-to-many* relationship between those tables.

Referential integrity refers to the fact that only valid primary key values are allowed in a foreign-key column—that is, the rows these keys reference are present in the related table.

Choosing Your Database Engine

Table 15-1 shows some of the most common database engines, all of which can be used from F# and .NET.

Table 15-1. Common Databases

Name	Type	Description	Available From
PostgreSQL	Open source	Open source database engine	http://postgresql.org/
SQLite	Open source	Small, embeddable, zero-configuration SQL database engine	www.sqlite.org/
DB2	Commercial	IBM's database engine	www-01.ibm.com/software/data/db2/ad/dotnet.html
Firebird	Open source	Based on Borland Interbase	www.firebirdsql.org/
MySQL	Open source	Reliable and popular database	www.mysql.com/
Mimer SQL	Commercial	Reliable database engine	www.mimer.com/
Oracle	Commercial	One of the most popular enterprise database engines	www.oracle.com/
SQL Server	Commercial	Microsoft's main database engine	www.microsoft.com/sql/default.mspx
SQL Server Express	Commercial	Free and easy-to-use version of SQL Server	www.microsoft.com/express/database/default.aspx
Sybase iAnywhere	Commercial	Mobile database engine	www.ianywhere.com/

Applications communicate with relational databases using Structured Query Language (SQL). Each time you create tables, create relationships, insert new records, or update or delete existing ones, you're explicitly or implicitly issuing SQL statements to the database. The examples in this chapter use a dialect of Standard SQL called Transact-SQL (T-SQL), used by SQL Server and SQL Server Express.

SQL has syntax to define the structure of a database schema (loosely speaking, a collection of data tables and their relations) and also syntax to manage the data within. These subsets of SQL are called *Data Definition Language* (DDL) and *Data Manipulation Language* (DML), respectively. The most important DDL statements are the following:

```
CREATE/ALTER/DROP TABLE
CREATE/DROP VIEW
```

Understanding ADO.NET

ADO.NET is the central database-access machinery in the .NET Framework, and it provides full XML support, disconnected and typed datasets, scalability, and high performance. This section gives a brief overview of the ADO.NET fundamentals.

With ADO.NET, data is acquired through a *connection* to the database via a provider. This connection serves as a medium against which to execute a *command*; this can be used to fetch, update, insert, or delete data from the data store. Statements and queries are articulated as SQL text (CREATE, SELECT, UPDATE, INSERT, and DELETE statements) and are passed to the command object's constructor. When you execute these statements, you obtain data (in the case of queries) or the number of affected rows (in the case of UPDATE, INSERT, and DELETE statements). The data returned can be processed via two main mechanisms: sequentially in a read-only fashion using a DataReader object or by loading it into an in-memory representation (a DataSet object) for further disconnected processing. DataSet objects store data in a set of table objects along with metadata that describes their relationships and constraints in a fully contained model.

ADO.NET 2.0 comes with four data providers: SQLClient, OleDb, Oracle, and Odbc. Table 15-2 describes them and a couple of more commonly used providers. These providers act as the main gateway to the database.

Table 15-2. Common Data Providers

Name	Namespace	Available From
SQLClient	System.Data.SqlClient	.NET 2.0
OleDb	System.Data.OleDb	.NET 2.0
Oracle	System.Data.OracleClient	.NET 2.0
ODBC	System.Data.Odbc	.NET 2.0
PostgreSQL	Npgsql	http://npgsql.projects.postgresql.org/
MySql	MySql.Data.MySqlClient	http://dev.mysql.com/downloads/

The OleDb and ODBC data providers are provided for compatibility with earlier database-access technologies. All ADO.NET connection and command classes have the data provider name as the prefix to their class name, as in OdbcConnection and OdbcCommand or OleDbConnection and OleDbCommand.

Establishing Connections to a Database Engine

Before you can do any work with a database, you need to establish a connection to it. For instance, you can connect to a locally running instance of SQL Server 2005 Express using the following code:

```
open System.Data
open System.Data.SqlClient

let connString = @"Server='.\SQLEXPRESS';Integrated Security=SSPI"
let conn = new SqlConnection(connString)
```

The value connString is a connection string. Regardless of how you created your connection object, to execute any updates or queries on it, you need to open it first:

```
> conn.Open();;
val it : unit = ()
```

If this command fails, then you may need to do one of the following:

- Install SQL Server 2005 Express or a newer version.

- Consult the latest SQL Server Express samples for alternative connection strings.

- Add UserInstance='true' to the connection string. This starts the database engine as a user-level process.

- Change the connection string if you have a different database engine installed and running (for instance, if you're using SQL Server instead of SQL Server Express).

Connections established using the same connection string are pooled and reused depending on your database engine. Connections are often a limited resource and should generally be closed as soon as possible within your application.

■ **Tip** The "More on Connection Strings" sidebar contains details about creating and managing connection strings. A useful web site for complete connection strings is www.connectionstrings.com.

Creating a Database

Now that you've established a connection to the database engine, you can explicitly create a database from F# code by executing a SQL statement directly. For example, you can create a database called company as follows:

```
open System.Data
open System.Data.SqlClient

let execNonQuery conn s =
    let comm = new SqlCommand(s, conn, CommandTimeout = 10)
    comm.ExecuteNonQuery() |> ignore

execNonQuery conn "CREATE DATABASE company"
```

You use execNonQuery in the subsequent sections. This method takes a connection object and a SQL string and executes it as a SQL command, ignoring its result.

■ **Note** If you try to create the same database twice, you receive a runtime exception. However, if you intend to drop an existing database, you can do so by issuing a DROP DATABASE company SQL command. The DROP command can also be used for other database artifacts, including tables, views, and stored procedures.

More on Connection Strings

Before a connection can be opened, its ConnectionString property must be initialized, typically by passing it to the connection constructor. Although you can assemble this connection string by hand, doing so is error prone because it's subject to various insertion traps; and the exact keys that various providers accept are many and hard to remember.

For these reasons, it's common to either externalize entire connection strings in configuration files (discussed next) or use a ConnectionStringBuilder object from the appropriate provider namespace. This object contains all the known connection keys as properties that can be safely set, avoiding the passing of values of incorrect type or misspelling key names. Consider the following example (this time, using SQL Server running on localhost and referencing the company database; before that database is created, you should remove or comment out the InitialCatalog reference from your connection string):

```
open System.Data
open System.Data.SqlClient

let connStr = new SqlConnectionStringBuilder(DataSource="localhost",
                                             IntegratedSecurity=true,
                                             InitialCatalog="company")
```

On the other hand, not all keys accepted by the various providers are contained in these builder objects, and it's sometimes necessary to add custom key/value pairs. You can do this by using the Add method. For instance, for an OleDb provider, user credentials can be given as follows:

```
connStr.Add("User Id",  "your_user_id")
connStr.Add("Password", "your_password")
```

This naturally requires extra care to ensure that the proper keys are assigned. You can now access the resulting connection string by reading the ConnectionString property and use it to create a connection object:

```
let conn = new SqlConnection(connStr.ConnectionString)
```

You can also store your connection strings in configuration files (web.config for web applications or YourProgram.exe.config for regular applications). The main advantage is that connection details can be configured without affecting the application. Consider the following configuration file:

```
<?xml version='1.0' encoding='utf-8'?>
<configuration>
  <connectionStrings>
```

```
    <add name="MyCS"
         connectionString="Data Source='localhost';Initial Catalog='company'" />
  </connectionStrings>
</configuration>
```

This defines a new connection string called MyCS. From within your application, you can read the value of this connection string using the ConfigurationManager class:

```
#r "System.Configuration.dll"
open System.Configuration
open System.Data.SqlClient

let cs = ConfigurationManager.ConnectionStrings.Item("MyCS")
let conn = new SqlConnection(cs.ConnectionString)
```

For this to work, make sure you reference System.Configuration.dll in your project properties using the -r option, or use the #r directive in your code as shown here, because this DLL isn't automatically included at compile time.

Creating Tables and Inserting and Fetching Records

You can execute a simple SQL command to create a table; all you need to do is specify its data fields and their types and whether null values are allowed. The following example creates an Employees table with a primary key EmpID and FirstName, LastName, and Birthday fields:

```
execNonQuery conn "CREATE TABLE Employees (
    EmpID int NOT NULL,
    FirstName varchar(50) NOT NULL,
    LastName varchar(50) NOT NULL,
    Birthday datetime,
    PRIMARY KEY (EmpID))"
```

You can now insert two new records as follows

```
execNonQuery conn "INSERT INTO Employees (EmpId, FirstName, LastName, Birthday)
    VALUES (1001, 'Joe', 'Smith', '02/14/1965')"
```

```
execNonQuery conn "INSERT INTO Employees (EmpId, FirstName, LastName, Birthday)
    VALUES (1002, 'Mary', 'Jones', '09/15/1985')"
```

and retrieve two columns of what was inserted using a fresh connection and a data reader:

```
let query() =
    seq { use conn = new SqlConnection(connString)
          do conn.Open()
          use comm = new SqlCommand("SELECT FirstName, Birthday FROM Employees",
                                    conn)
          use reader = comm.ExecuteReader()
          while reader.Read() do
              yield (reader.GetString 0, reader.GetDateTime 1)  }
```

When you evaluate the query expression in F# Interactive, a connection to the database is created and opened, the command is built, and the reader is used to read successive elements:

```
> fsi.AddPrinter(fun (d: System.DateTime) -> d.ToString());;
val it : unit = ()

> query();;
val it : seq<string * System.DateTime> =
    seq [("Joe", 14/02/1965 00:00:00); ("Mary", 15/09/1985 00:00:00)]
```

The definition of query uses sequence expressions that locally define new IDisposable objects such as conn, comm, and reader using declarations of the form use var = expr. These ensure that the locally defined connection, command, and reader objects are disposed after exhausting the entire sequence. See Chapters 4, 8, and 9 for more details about sequence expressions of this kind.

F# sequences are on-demand (that is, lazy), and the definition of query doesn't open a connection to the database. This is done when the sequence is first iterated; a connection is maintained until the sequence is exhausted.

Note that the command object's ExecuteReader method returns a DataReader instance that is used to extract the typed data returned from the query. You can read from the resulting sequence in a straightforward manner using a sequence iterator. For instance, you can use a simple anonymous function to print data on the screen:

```
> query() |> Seq.iter (fun (fn, bday) -> printfn "%s has birthday %O" fn bday);;
Joe has birthday 14/02/1965 00:00:00
Mary has birthday 15/09/1985 00:00:00
val it : unit = ()
```

The query brings the data from the database in-memory, although still as a lazy sequence. You can then use standard F# in-memory data transformations on the result:

```
> query()
    |> Seq.filter (fun (nm, bday) -> bday < System.DateTime.Parse("01/01/1985"))
    |> Seq.length;;
val it : int = 1
```

However, be aware that these additional transformations are happening in-memory and not in the database.

The command object has different methods for executing different queries. For instance, if you have a nonselect query, you need to use the ExecuteNonQuery method (for UPDATE, INSERT, and DELETE statements, as previously in execNonQuery), which returns the number of rows affected (updated, inserted, or deleted), or the ExecuteScalar method, which returns the first column of the first row of the result, providing a fast and efficient way to extract a single value, such as the number of rows in a table or a result set.

In the previous command, you extracted fields from the result rows using GetXXX methods on the reader object. The particular methods have to match the types of the fields selected in the SQL query, and a mismatch results in a runtime InvalidCastException. For these and other reasons, DataReader tends to be suitable only in situations when the following items are true:

- You need to read data only in a sequential order (as returned from the database). DataReader provides forward-only data access.

- The field types of the result are known, and the query isn't configurable.

- You're reading only and not writing data. DataReader provides read-only access.

- Your use of the DataReader is localized. The data connection is open throughout the reader loop.

Command Behaviors

Database connections are precious resources, and you should always release them as soon as possible. In the previous case, you did this by using a locally defined connection. It's also sufficient to implicitly close the reader by constructing it with the CloseConnection option that causes it to release and close the data connection upon closing the reader instance.

Common options include SchemaOnly, which you can use to extract field information only (without any data returned); SingleResult to extract a single value only (the same as using the ExecuteScalar method discussed earlier); SingleRow to extract a single row; and KeyInfo to extract additional columns (appended to the end of the selected ones) automatically that uniquely identify the rows returned.

Using Untyped Datasets

Datasets allow applications to work in a *disconnected mode*, which means the application connects to the database, loads relevant data to an in-memory representation, and processes the data locally. When the processing is completed, the data in the in-memory dataset can be synchronized with the database.

ADO.NET datasets are compact in-memory databases and provide similar functionality to real databases; however, they're designed to work with a limited amount of data. A DataSet contains a collection of tables, the relationships between those tables, and various constraints. Tables are represented by the DataTable type. And as in a SQL server, tables are defined by their columns (DataColumn objects), and the data is stored in rows (DataRow objects).

In ADO.NET, the loading of data into the dataset and the synchronization to the database are coordinated by *data adapters*—for instance, SqlDataAdapter objects. Consider the following example, which defines a buildDataSet function that takes a connection and a SQL SELECT query and returns the resulting DataSet object:

```
let dataAdapter = new SqlDataAdapter()

let buildDataSet conn queryString =
    dataAdapter.SelectCommand <- new SqlCommand(queryString, conn)
    let dataSet = new DataSet()
    // This line is needed to configure the command
    let _ = new SqlCommandBuilder(dataAdapter)
    dataAdapter.Fill(dataSet) |> ignore  // ignore the number of records returned
    dataset
```

The inferred types are as follows:

```
val dataAdapter : SqlDataAdapter
val buildDataSet : SqlConnection -> string -> DataSet
```

When setting up the data adapter, you initialize its SelectCommand property to the query string that was passed as an argument. This SQL query is used to populate the DataSet when the Fill method is called. The somewhat mysterious line let _ = new SqlCommandBuilder(dataAdapter) creates a command-builder object, which has the side effect of building the INSERT, UPDATE, and DELETE commands automatically from the query in SelectCommand, making the dataset capable of persisting changes. Also, note that you don't have to worry about opening or closing connections, because this is taken care of with the data adapter; all you need is the connection object itself:

```
let dataSet =
    buildDataSet conn "SELECT EmpID, FirstName, LastName, Birthday from Employees"
```

The resulting DataSet contains a single table; you obtain it by index and print its content. This table is assembled based on the query and contains the columns that are part of the SELECT statement:

```
let table = dataSet.Tables.Item(0)
for row in table.Rows do
    printfn "%O, %O - %O"
        (row.Item "LastName")
        (row.Item "FirstName")
        (row.Item "Birthday")
```

When run in F# Interactive, this produces the following output:

```
Smith, Joe - 14/02/1965 00:00:00
Jones, Mary - 15/09/1985 00:00:00
```

You can refer to each column of a row by the same field name used in the SELECT query. Adding a new row to table is treated similarly:

```
let row = table.NewRow()
row.Item("EmpID") <- 1003
row.Item("FirstName") <- "Eve"
row.Item("LastName") <- "Smith"
row.Item("Birthday") <- System.DateTime.Today
table.Rows.Add row
dataAdapter.Update(dataSet) |> ignore  // ignore the number of affected rows
```

Repeating the SQL query from the previous section reveals the addition of the new entry to the database table:

```
> query();;
val it : seq<string * System.DateTime> =
    seq [("Joe", 14/02/1965 00:00:00);
         ("Mary", 15/09/1985 00:00:00);
         ("Eve", 27/09/2007 00:00:00)]
```

Note that you use the INSERT statement that was built by the command-builder object based on the selection query. Using untyped datasets is a great way to execute dynamic queries and to provide ad hoc access to your data. On the other hand, the lack of strong typing means it suffers from possible type mismatches or incorrect field names.

Generating Typed Datasets Using xsd.exe

Typed datasets are derived from ordinary datasets and allow you to work with data in a type-safe manner. This means that instead of (row.Item "FirstName" :?> string), you can write row.FirstName. You can create typed datasets using the xsd.exe command-line tool included in the .NET SDK. Among other things, this tool generates source code from XML schema documents; to use it, you must obtain an XSD document for the tables for which you want data objects. (You can quickly generate an XML schema document using Visual Studio; select File ➤ New ➤ File ➤ XML Schema, and drag the needed data tables onto the design canvas.)

Alternatively, you can extract this schema definition using code:

```
open System.IO

let dataSet2 = buildDataSet conn "SELECT * FROM Employees"
let file name = Path.Combine(@"c:\fsharp", name)

File.WriteAllText(file "employees.xsd", dataSet2.GetXmlSchema())
```

Using this extracted XSD document, you can now fire up xsd.exe from the command-line shell:

```
C:\fsharp> xsd.exe employees.xsd /d /l:CS /n:Employees.Data
Writing file 'C:\fsharp\Employees.cs'.
C:\fsharp> csc /target:library Employees.cs
```

This generates a C# file Employees.cs in the Employees.Data namespace, containing a typed dataset for the Employees table, which you then compile to Employees.dll. You can now reference this DLL and create an instance of a typed dataset:

```
> #r @"employees.dll";;
Binding session to 'C:\fsharp\Employees.dll'...

> let employeesTable = new Employees.Data.NewDataSet();;
val employeesTable : Employees.Data.NewDataSet

> dataAdapter.Fill(employeesTable) |> ignore;;  // ignore the number of records
val it : unit = ()

> for emp in employeesTable._Table do
    printfn "%s, %s - %O" emp.LastName emp.FirstName emp.Birthday;;
Smith, Joe - 14/02/1965 00:00:00
Jones, Mary - 15/09/1985 00:00:00
Smith, Eve - 27/09/2007 00:00:00
```

Note that in the iteration emp is known to have a strong type that allows you to access the fields LastName, FirstName, and Birthday.

Finally, it's very easy to dump out XML for your data:

```
> printf "%s" (employeesTable.GetXml());;
<NewDataSet>
  <Table>
    <EmpID>1001</EmpID>
    <FirstName>Joe</FirstName>
    <LastName>Smith</LastName>
    <Birthday>1965-02-14T00:00:00+00:00</Birthday>
  </Table>
  <Table>
    <EmpID>1002</EmpID>
    <FirstName>Mary</FirstName>
    <LastName>Jones</LastName>
    <Birthday>1985-09-15T00:00:00+01:00</Birthday>
  </Table>

  <Table>
    <EmpID>1003</EmpID>
    <FirstName>Eve</FirstName>
    <LastName>Smith</LastName>
    <Birthday>2007-09-27T00:00:00+01:00</Birthday>
  </Table>
</NewDataSet>
```

You can also write it to a file:

```
> System.IO.File.WriteAllText(file "employees.xml", employeesTable.GetXml());;
val it : unit = ()
```

Using Stored Procedures

Stored procedures are defined and stored in your relational database and provide a number of benefits over literal SQL. First, they're external to the application and thus provide a clear division of the data logic from the rest of the application. This enables you to make data-related modifications without having to change application code or having to redeploy the application. Second, they're stored in the database in a prepared or compiled form and thus are executed more efficiently than literal SQL statements (although those can be prepared as well at a one-time cost, but they're still contained in application space, which is undesirable). Supplying arguments to stored procedures instantiates the compiled formula.

In Visual Studio, you can add stored procedures just like any other database artifacts using the Server Explorer window: right-click the Stored Procedures item in the appropriate database, and select Add New Stored Procedure. Doing so creates a stored procedure template that you can easily customize. Alternatively, you can add stored procedures programmatically using the CREATE PROCEDURE SQL command. Consider the following stored procedure that returns the first and last names of all employees whose last name matches the given pattern:

```
execNonQuery conn "
CREATE PROCEDURE dbo.GetEmployeesByLastName
        (
        @Name nvarchar(50)
        )
AS
    SELECT
        Employees.FirstName, Employees.LastName
    FROM Employees
    WHERE Employees.LastName LIKE @Name"
```

You can wrap this stored procedure in a function as follows:

```
let GetEmployeesByLastName (name: string) =
    use comm = new SqlCommand("GetEmployeesByLastName", conn,
                            CommandType=CommandType.StoredProcedure)

    comm.Parameters.AddWithValue("@Name", name) |> ignore
    use adapter = new SqlDataAdapter(comm)
    let table = new DataTable()
    adapter.Fill(table) |> ignore
    table
```

You can execute the stored procedure as follows to find employees with the last name Smith:

```
> for row in (GetEmployeesByLastName "Smith").Rows do
    printfn "row = %O, %O" (row.Item("FirstName")) (row.Item("LastName"));;
row = Joe, Smith
row = Eve, Smith
val it : unit = ()
```

Using Data Grids

You saw in Chapter 14 how data tables can be visualized in web applications. The return value of GetEmployeesByLastName from the previous section is a DataTable. These objects can also be directly bound to a Windows Forms data grid, a visual data control that supports the DataSource property and that can display data in a tabular format (Windows Forms controls were discussed in Chapter 11):

```
open System.Windows.Forms

let emps = GetEmployeesByLastName "Smith"
let grid = new DataGrid(Width=300, Height=200, DataSource=emps)
let form = new Form(Visible=true, TopMost=true)
form.Controls.Add(grid)
```

Figure 15-1 shows what you see when you run this code.

Figure 15-1. Calling the GetEmployeesByLastName stored procedure

Stored procedures can also perform deletions or updates (executed via the ExecuteNonQuery() method of the command object) or return data through *out* parameters. You can define these using the OUTPUT keyword after a single parameter definition in the stored procedure. When calling the stored procedure, the out parameter's direction must be set to ParameterDirection.Output; after the stored procedure executes, its return value can be read using the Value property of the given parameter.

Working with Databases in Visual Studio

Many of the database tasks you saw earlier in this chapter can be easily performed using the built-in capabilities of Visual Studio. It also provides good tools for working with stored procedures and views, building SQL queries, and designing entity models.

Creating a Database

Assuming you have a version of SQL Server installed, you can create a new SQL Server database in Visual Studio's Server Explorer (Ctrl+Alt+S, or View ➤ Server Explorer) by right-clicking Data Connections and selecting the Create New SQL Server Database menu item. In the screen shown in Figure 15-2, you can configure your connection details and specify the name of the new SQL Server database.

Figure 15-2. Creating a new Microsoft SQL Server database

In addition to creating a new database, this process also creates a Server Explorer connection to the new database, which you can use in Visual Studio to browse, create, manipulate, and delete tables, triggers, views, stored procedures, functions, and other database artifacts.

Visual Data Modeling: Adding Relationships

Various tools exist to assist application architects in designing the data layer. On a logical level, entity-relationship (ER) models provide a visual representation of data tables and their relationships, showing table fields, primary and foreign keys, and various constraints. Visual Studio simplifies the design process and supports visual modeling; let's take a brief look at how you can exploit its capabilities.

In the previous section, you used Visual Studio to create an SQL Server database called company; and earlier, you saw how to create a table to store data about employees. Let's extend this database with a new table that stores addresses. You can then link the existing Employees table to it to store an optional address record for each employee. This means you allow multiple employees to live at the same address, but not multiple addresses for a given employee.

Start by creating the Addresses table: right-click Add New Table in the Tables list item in Server Explorer ➤ Data Connections under the company database. Add the columns shown in Figure 15-3.

Column Name	Data Type	Allow Nulls
AddID	int	☐
Street	varchar(50)	☑
City	varchar(50)	☑
State	varchar(50)	☑
Zip	varchar(10)	☑
		☐

Figure 15-3. The Addresses table in the designer mode

Note that you designate AddID as a non-null primary key (right-click, select Set Primary Key, and clear the Allow Nulls flag). Also, under Column Properties and Identity Specification, you should set the

Is Identity property to Yes; this takes care of automatically incrementing the primary-key value when inserting new records.

Next, create a new database diagram, and add/drag your existing two tables, Employees and Addresses, onto it. Before you can add a relationship between these two tables, you must create a new nullable field in the Employees table to store the address foreign key; call it AddressID.

Now you're ready to link the two tables. First, right-click the Employees table, and select Relationships. Next, click Add to add a new foreign-key relationship, name it FK_Employee_Address under Identity, and then click the ellipsis icon next to Tables and Columns Specification under General to configure the relationship. The foreign-key table (the table that stores references to rows in another table) is Employees, which is grayed out because you started by adding a relationship to the Employees table; but you can select the foreign-key field to be AddressID. Then, select the primary-key table to be Addresses, with the field AddID. Doing so links the two tables by storing unique address IDs in the AddressID field of the Employees table records, giving you a one-to-many relationship between addresses and employees. Figure 15-4 shows the table design canvas after you're finished. Similarly, linking two primary keys yields a one-to-one relationship.

■ **Note** Linking tables via explicit relationships and controlling the nullability of the foreign-key columns gives you fine control of referential integrity. For instance, you run into a foreign-key violation if you try to remove a record that is linked to another by a foreign-key constraint. On the other hand, storing raw primary-key values without an explicit constraint in related tables loses these benefits.

Figure 15-4. Adding a one-to-many relationship between Employees and Addresses

In the previous example, you made the `AddressID` field nullable, meaning it's possible that not every employee has an address. You can also control what happens if employees or addresses are removed or updated. (However, as a design decision, you need to carefully consider one-to-many relationships such as those shown earlier: should a change in one employee's address cause the same change in the addresses of all other employees with the same address? Probably, if it's the same address; otherwise, a particular employee should be updated with a different address record.) Placing a cascade on deletes removes all records that are linked to a record that is deleted; naturally, you should treat this option with care.

Accessing Relational Data with Linq Queries

The following sections show how to perform relational database queries using FLinq, the F# way of doing LinqToSql queries. FLinq uses F# quotation metaprogramming to represent SQL queries. These are then translated across to SQL and executed using the Microsoft LINQ libraries that are part of .NET Framework 3.5 or higher. At the time of writing, you can work with FLinq as part of the F# Power Pack; be sure to check the latest samples in that distribution for full details and updates.

We assume you're working with the `Northwnd.mdf` database, a common database used in many LINQ samples. You can download this sample database as part of the F# Power Pack, or from many other sources on the Web.

Generating the Object/Relational Mapping

The first step in using LINQ with F# is to generate the code that implements the *object/relational* (O/R) mapping for the database tables to which you're connecting. Let's first look at why you want to do this. You learned previously how to create simple tables and store and retrieve data using SQL code. However, this approach doesn't work well for large data schemas with multiple related tables and constraints. For instance, creating a hierarchy of records in a number of related tables connected by foreign keys involves issuing multiple SQL statements to create the base data and to connect them in ways that obey the foreign-key and other constraints that may be in place. Instead, it can often be much better to view records in tables as if they were objects. This is part of what an O/R mapping provides.

You already saw that datasets can be used to fetch and manipulate data in a disconnected way. These datasets are managed by data adapters that handle the gory details of producing the appropriate SQL statements and issuing them to the underlying database when fetching records or synchronizing the changes made to the dataset back to the database. The main goal of a separate Data Access Layer (DAL) is to bridge the gap between two disparate domains: the database and your application logic. Practically speaking, this frees you from having to write SQL code and mingle it with your application code.

O/R mappings use smart data objects that can load and persist record-level data. Underneath, they use objects such as ADO.NET datasets that are filled and flushed on demand.

The tool this section focuses on is SqlMetal, which computes the O/R mapping for LINQ, part of the .NET Framework 3.5. For example, to use SqlMetal to generate bindings for the `Northwnd.mdf` database, you can use this:

```
sqlmetal /code:northwind.cs /namespace:Nwind /server:.\SQLExpress Northwnd.mdf
```

This assumes you're running SQL Server Express on your machine as a named instance. Further options are available when you run SqlMetal without parameters. You may want to use the `/code` and `/xml` flags to specify a different output file of the object bindings and to create a schema definition, respectively. The resulting code by default uses C#, which you can change using the `/language` option. You can easily add the generated mappings under a separate DLL project in your F# solution and reference it from your F# project.

The remainder of this section uses the generated data object layer for the classic Northwind database, as used by the F# LINQ samples in the F# distribution. This C# source file contains classes for each data table in the Northwind database, and the relationships between those tables are strongly typed.

■ **Tip** Regardless of your choice to work with SQL explicitly or implicitly, in applied database scenarios you frequently want to separate data definitions entirely from application code. DDL scripts that create schemas, tables, triggers, and views and scripts that create seed data should be managed as separate artifacts that are executed prior to application deployment.

Building the DataContext Instance

One of the classes (with the same name as your database) generated by SqlMetal represents the entire database. This class inherits from the DataContext class and carries with it all the connection details that are used when accessing the data contained in the database through the mapped objects. You can supply a connection string when you instantiate this main database object, as the following code snippet shows (to run this, you need the Northwnd.mdf file in your source directory):

```
#I @"c:\Program Files\Reference Assemblies\Microsoft\Framework\v3.5"
#r "System.Core.dll"
#r "System.Data.Linq.dll"
#r "FSharp.PowerPack.Linq.dll"
#r "Northwind.dll"

open System
open System.Data.SqlClient
open Nwind

let db =
    let connB = new SqlConnectionStringBuilder()
    connB.AttachDBFilename <- __YOUR_SOURCE_DIRECTORY__ + @"\Northwnd.mdf"
    connB.IntegratedSecurity <- true
    connB.Enlist <- false
    connB.DataSource <- @".\SQLExpress"
    new Northwnd(connB.ConnectionString)
```

Using LINQ from F#

So far, you've seen how you can perform LINQ-style queries using a set of aggregate operators that work on enumerable objects, and you see these same operators query and manipulate XML data in the coming section. Performing querying and manipulation on relational data is done almost the same way, except that these are implemented under the hood by calling LINQ. Assuming you've mapped your employees database with SqlMetal and created the main database object as db, here is an example similar to those in earlier sections using FLinq syntax:

```
open Microsoft.FSharp.Linq.Query

let res =
    query <@ seq { for emp in db.Employees do
                        if emp.BirthDate.Value.Year > 1960
                            && emp.LastName.StartsWith "S" then
                            yield (emp.FirstName, emp.LastName) }
              |> Seq.take 5 @>

for (first, last) in res do
  printfn "%s %s" first last
```

One notable difference between this and previous queries is the use of F# quotations inside <@ and @>. As shown in Chapter 9, quotations are reified syntax trees that can be read and manipulated by F# programs. Quoted expressions (provided by the Microsoft.FSharp.Quotations namespace) are of type Expr<'a>, where 'a is the type of the unquoted expression. You can read more about metaprogramming via F# quotations in depth in Chapter 9.

Note that in F# quotations, you can splice values bound to identifiers into the quotation expression tree. This allows quotations to reference defined objects and values such as those representing the database.

The type of the previous query function is as follows:

```
val query: Quotations.Expr<'T> -> 'T
```

This function works on F# quotations. These are converted to LINQ Expression objects and passed to the underlying LINQ mechanism to produce SQL that is then executed on demand.

■ **Note** When writing embedded queries using F# LinqToSql, you can use only a limited subset of operators to express your queries, in particular those defined in the F# LinqToSql library. Check the latest F# LINQ documentation for more details.

How LINQ appears from F#

You can make LINQ-style queries on two types of objects: those implementing the IEnumerable<'a> / seq<'a> and IQueryable<'a> interfaces. The former is used for in-memory objects or those that can be iterated one by one to provide a uniform way to query and transform, whereas the latter provides more customization in terms of the deriving object's identity and enables you to control how those operations are actually carried out.

Much of the LINQ architecture relies on representing query expressions using reified expression trees through the System.Expressions.Expression type. This type is used to encode lambda expressions in C#, thus giving a straightforward syntax embedding for LINQ-style queries. In F#, metaprogramming is built around a similar mechanism—F# quotations, discussed in Chapter 9. A bridge is used to convert between F# quotations and LINQ expression trees. LINQ queries on queryable objects are encoded as expression trees and translated to the underlying LINQ machinery at runtime.

Working with XML as a Generic Data Format

XML provides a way to represent data in plain-text format that is independent of the platform, operating system, and application. Nowadays, XML is ubiquitous; it's widely used to describe application configuration data, as an output format for applications such as Microsoft Word and Excel, to wrap data that is sent across networks, and as a way to interact with the new generation of database servers, including Oracle 8*i* and newer, as well as Microsoft SQL Server 2000 and above. These database servers can work with XML data directly, allowing you to update the database from XML documents or extract data in XML.

Data represented as XML carries various tags and metainformation that help to identify what sort of data is contained within. This results in a larger size, but typically this can be compensated for by applying compression on the XML text.

As an example, consider the following classic XML example (`contacts.xml`):

```
<contacts>
  <contact>
    <name>John Smith</name>
    <phone type="home">+1 626-123-4321</phone>
  </contact>
</contacts>
```

One way to represent and work with XML documents is via the XML Document Object Model (DOM) contained in the System.Xml namespace; you saw how to work with this model in Chapter 9. Using the XML DOM constructors and methods, you can create the previous XML as follows:

```
open System.Xml

let doc = new XmlDocument()
let rootNode = doc.CreateElement "contacts"
doc.AppendChild rootNode |> ignore
let contactNode = doc.CreateElement "contact"
let nameNode = doc.CreateElement "name"
let nameText = doc.CreateTextNode "John Smith"
let phoneNode = doc.CreateElement "phone"
phoneNode.SetAttribute("type", "home")
let phoneText = doc.CreateTextNode "+1 626-123-4321"
nameNode.AppendChild nameText |> ignore
contactNode.AppendChild nameNode |> ignore
contactNode.AppendChild phoneNode |> ignore
phoneNode.AppendChild phoneText |> ignore
rootNode.AppendChild contactNode |> ignore
```

Here, you build an XML document in a bottom-up fashion via a series of method calls that mutate the main XML document object. This means various XML elements can't be constructed without this document container object. In addition, construction by mutation makes the shape of the XML hard to read.

Using XmlWriter, the result is a bit more readable:

```
let doc = new XmlDocument()
let writer = doc.CreateNavigator().AppendChild()
writer.WriteStartElement "contacts"
writer.WriteStartElement "contact"
writer.WriteElementString ("name", "John Smith")
```

```
writer.WriteStartElement "phone"
writer.WriteAttributeString ("type", "home")
writer.WriteString "+1 626-123-4321"
writer.WriteEndElement()
writer.Close()
```

Here, you don't have to worry about creating the structure of the document; instead, you output each element in a sequence. XmlWriter also takes care of the closing tags, even if you forget them before closing the writer.

Constructing XML via LINQ

LINQ to XML (LinqToXml) offers a new and easier way to work with XML than using the traditional XML DOM. The System.Xml.Linq namespace contains everything you need to construct, load and save, manipulate, and query over XML documents. You can reference the DLL containing this namespace as follows:

```
#I @"c:\Program Files\Reference Assemblies\Microsoft\Framework\v3.5"
#r "System.Xml.Linq.dll"
```

Being a data format for tree-like structures, XML trees are made up of a collection of XNode objects. Structurally, two XNode descendants can contain other nodes (and thus inherit from XContainer, a subclass of XNode): XDocument and XElement. Therefore, all XML documents are represented either as an XDocument with nested XElement objects or as a collection of nested XElements.

A fully qualified XML document (an instance of XDocument) contains metainformation such as declarations (added as a child XDeclaration object) and a DTD (added as an XDocumentType) and may contain various XML processing instructions (instances of XProcessingInstruction). Typically, you need an XDocument only if the XML you produce is exchanged with the external world (information passed through a web service, for instance); in any other case, you're working with a collection of nested XElement objects. These can have other XNode objects such as XText for storing text, which often represents binary data encoded using Base64 encoding mentioned in Chapter 10, or XComment for embedding comments. On the other hand, XElements typically have attributes (XAttribute)—key/value pairs, which are non-XNode objects. Both the XElement names (the tags themselves) and the XAttribute keys are XName objects.

The easiest way to construct an XML document is to call the Parse method of the XDocument or XElement class on a string:

```
open System.Xml.Linq

let xml =
    "<contacts>
      <contact>
         <name>John Smith</name>
         <phone type=\"home\">+1 626-123-4321</phone>
      </contact>
    </contacts>"
let doc = XDocument.Parse xml
```

LinqToXml makes *functional construction* of XML possible. It does so by making all XML constituents first-class values that can be created and embedded in each other. The functional construction also requires that you treat these values uniformly. Let's assume you create a few shorthand functions for various XML constructors:

```fsharp
open System.Xml.Linq

let xname n                   = XName.op_Implicit(n)
let xdoc (el: seq<XElement>)  = new XDocument(Array.map box (Array.ofSeq el))
let xelem s el                = new XElement(xname s, box el)
let xatt  a b                 = new XAttribute(xname a, b) |> box
let xstr  s                   = box s
```

Using these functions, you can construct the XML from the beginning of this section as follows:

```fsharp
let doc =
    xdoc
        [ xelem "contacts"
            [ xelem "contact"
                [ (xelem "name" (xstr "John Smith"))
                  (xelem "phone"
                      [ xatt "type" "home"
                        xstr "+1 626-123-4321" ])
                ]
            ]
        ]
```

This also includes the default document header (`<?xml version="1.0" encoding="utf-8"?>`). If this header isn't needed, you can omit the top-level call to xdoc.

Storing, Loading, and Traversing LinqToXml Documents

Loading an existing XML document is straightforward; you can call the Load static method on either an XDocument or an XElement:

```fsharp
let file name = Path.Combine(__YOUR_SOURCE_DIRECTORY__, name)

XElement.Load (file "contacts.xml")
```

Saving is just as easy, reusing doc from earlier:

```fsharp
doc.Save (file "contacts.xml")
```

LinqToXml considers an XML document as a collection of XElement objects, each in a parent/child relationship. The root XElement's Parent property is null, even if it's embedded in an XDocument, which can be ignored as far as the data in the XML is concerned. You can obtain XElement children using the Elements() method, or its override, which expects an XName argument and returns all elements with a given name:

```fsharp
let contacts = doc.Element(xname "contacts")  // Get the first contact
for elem in contacts.Elements() do
    printfn "Tag=%s, Value=%A" elem.Name.LocalName elem.Value
```

Querying XML

Queries on XML are often expressed using the XPath query language, which this book doesn't cover in detail but which is supported by the types in the System.Xml namespace. As a good alternative to XPath, you can use the standard sequence operators to perform queries over XML data. The following example uses the helper functions and the file contacts.xml created in the previous section:

```
open System
open System.Xml.Linq

let elem (e: XElement) s       = e.Element(xname s)
let elemv e s                  = (elem e s).Value

let contactsXml = XElement.Load(file "contacts.xml")
let contacts = contactsXml.Elements ()
```

```
> contacts |> Seq.filter (fun e -> (elemv e "name").StartsWith "J")
          |> Seq.map (fun e -> (elemv e "name"), (elemv e "phone"));;
val it : seq<string * string> = seq [("John Smith", "+1 626-123-4321")]
```

This example also defines some helper functions: elem to extract from an XElement object the first child element with a given name, and elemv to convert that to a string value.

You can also use the query operators in building new XML:

```
xelem "results"
   [ contacts |> Seq.filter  (fun e -> (elemv e "name").StartsWith "J")  ]
```

This creates a <results> tag and inserts all employees whose last name starts with the letter *J*. You can also use sequence expressions to achieve the same result:

```
xelem "results"
   [ for e in contacts do
        if (elemv e "name").StartsWith "J" then
           yield e ]
```

Summary

In this chapter, you saw how the functional programming techniques from Chapter 3 are often used to implement in-memory queries similar to those used to access databases. You also learned how to use sequence expressions as an alternative notation for these query expressions. We then turned to databases themselves and covered how to use ADO.NET to access relational databases. You saw how to perform a variety of database-related tasks from Visual Studio. You next learned how to perform simple, typed queries using F# LinqToSql, taking particular advantage of the object/relational data objects generated by the LINQ tool SqlMetal.exe. Finally, you saw how to use XML as a generic data format, partly by using functionality from the LINQ libraries.

The next chapter covers parsing techniques, including using the lexer and parser generator tools that come with the F# distribution.

Lexing and Parsing

In this chapter, you take a closer look at lexing and parsing, topics introduced briefly in Chapters 9 and 11. In particular, the chapter introduces the lexer and parser generators, fslex and fsyacc, that come with the F# distribution. A typical scenario when these techniques and tools can come in handy is the following:

- You want to read user-readable input that has a well-defined syntax.

- You have a type (often an *abstract syntax tree* [AST] type) to represent this input.

The typical task is to parse the user input into your internal representation by breaking down the input string into a sequence of tokens (a process called *lexical analysis*) and then constructing an instance of your internal representation based on a grammar (via *syntactic analysis*). Lexing and parsing don't have to be separated, and there are often convenient .NET methods for extracting information from text in particular formats, as shown in this chapter. Nevertheless, it's often best to treat the two processes separately.

The goal of this chapter is to provide the background you need to use the built-in lexing and parsing facilities of .NET and F# effectively and to understand the options for lexing and parsing other input formats:

- For lexing, we cover simple line-based techniques to crack data formats using the .NET libraries directly. You then learn how to use fslex to break text into simple tokens, strings with escape characters, and nested comments, and you see table-based token generation and *stateful lexing* (passing state as a parameter as opposed to using mutable state).

- For parsing, we cover the core parsing topics of languages, grammar formalisms, and various parser types. We explain the typical problems for recursive-descent parsing and introduce fsyacc by giving a parser for Kitty, a small BASIC-like language. This highlights how to parse lists of symbols, how to assign precedence andassociativity to your tokens and production rules, and how you can recover from parsing errors. You also learn about conflicts that can arise in the fsyacc specifications and how to resolve them.

Finally, the chapter covers combinator-based techniques, which are particularly useful for writing parsers for binary formats without relying on fslex and fsyacc.

Syntax vs. Semantic Analysis

Lexical analysis is concerned with identifying those tokens that make up a given input. A *token* is a piece of the input text that constitutes a word from the lexer's perspective. This can be a number, an identifier, a special word, or any sequence of characters deemed to make a unit.

During syntax analysis, you check whether the input (a series of tokens) is structured according to a set of grammar rules that make up your language. For instance, the F# construct `let a = b*2 in ..` is syntactically correct, but it's a semantically valid expression only if the variable b is bound in the preceding scope. The notion of scope and binding depends on the semantics of your language, and these are the topics of interest for *semantic* analysis. In a typical compiler, for instance, source programs go through the following stages:

Lexing ➤ Parsing ➤ Semantic analysis ➤ Optimization(s)/Transformations ➤ Code generation

Chapters 9 and 11 cover examples of semantic analysis and optimization/transformation.

Processing Line-Based Input

A common, simple case of parsing and lexing occurs when you're working with an existing line-based text-file format. In this case, parsing is often as easy as splitting each line of input at a particular separator character and trimming whitespace off the resulting partial strings:

```
> let line = "Smith, John, 20 January 1986, Software Developer";;
val line : string = "Smith, John, 20 January 1986, Software Developer"

> line.Split [| ',' |];;
val it : string [] = [|"Smith"; " John"; " 20 January 1986"; " Software Developer"|]

> line.Split [| ',' |] |> Array.map (fun s -> s.Trim());;
val it : string [] = [|"Smith"; "John"; "20 January 1986"; "Software Developer"|]
```

You can then process each column in the data format:

```
let splitLine (line: string) =
    line.Split [| ',' |] |> Array.map (fun s -> s.Trim())

let parseEmployee (line: string) =
    match splitLine line with
    | [| last; first; startDate; title |] ->
        last, first, System.DateTime.Parse(startDate), title
    | _ ->
        failwithf "invalid employee format: '%s'" line
```

The type of this function is as follows:

```
val parseEmployee : string -> string * string * System.DateTime * string
```

Here is an example use:

```
> parseEmployee line;;
val it : string * string * System.DateTime * string
      = ("Smith", "John", 20/01/1986 00:00:00 { ... }, "Software Developer")
```

On-Demand Reading of Files

You can turn a file into an on-demand sequence of results using a sequence builder:

```
open System.IO

let readEmployees (fileName : string) =
    seq {
        use reader = File.OpenText fileName
        while not reader.EndOfStream do
            yield reader.ReadLine() |> parseEmployee
    }
```

The following example takes the first three entries from an artificially generated file containing 10,000 copies of the same employee:

```
> File.WriteAllLines("employees.txt", Array.create 10000 line);;
val it : unit

> let firstThree = readEmployees("employees.txt") |> Seq.take 3;;
val firstThree : (string * string * System.DateTime * string) list

> for (last,first,startDate,title) in firstThree do
      printfn "%s %s started on %A" first last startDate;;
John Smith started on 20/01/1986 00:00:00
John Smith started on 20/01/1986 00:00:00
John Smith started on 20/01/1986 00:00:00
```

This technique is often used to do exploratory analysis of large data files. After the algorithm is refined using a prefix of the data, the analysis can then easily be run directly over the full data file.

Using Regular Expressions

Another technique that's frequently used to extract information from strings is to use regular expressions. The System.Text.RegularExpressions namespace provides convenient string-matching and -replacement functions. For example, let's say you have a log file containing a record of HTML GET requests. Here is a sample request:

```
GET /favicon.ico HTTP/1.1
```

The following code captures the name of the requested resource (`favicon.ico`) and the lower version number of the HTML protocol (1) used:

```
open System.Text.RegularExpressions

let parseHttpRequest line =
    let result = Regex.Match(line, @"GET (.*?) HTTP/1\.([01])$")
    let file = result.Groups.[1].Value
    let version = result.Groups.[2].Value
    file, version
```

The relevant fields are extracted by using the Groups attribute of the regular expression match to access the matched strings for each parenthesized group in the regular expression.

Tokenizing with FsLex

Although it's possible to hand-code lexers by using a range of ad hoc techniques such as those discussed in the previous section or by writing functions that explicitly manipulate lists of characters, doing so can be boring and time consuming. Instead, it's often easier to rely on a *lexer generator* to do this job for you. This section looks at how to use the `fslex` tool that comes with the F# Power Pack to perform lexical analysis. The F# Power Pack also includes `fsyacc`, which is also available as a separate download from MSDN and CodePlex. When you use `fslex` or `fsyacc` generated code in your projects, you must include a library reference to `FSharp.PowerPack.dll` from the F# Power Pack.

Let's start with a simple example. Listing 16-1 shows a lexer that replaces all < and > characters in an input stream with their HTML equivalents, < and >. Listing 16-2 shows a small program that uses this generated lexer.

Listing 16-1. Replacing Characters with Their HTML Equivalents: text2htmllex.fsl

```
{
module Text2HtmlLex

let lexeme = Lexing.LexBuffer<_>.LexemeString

(* You can add your helper functions here *)
}
rule convertHtml chan = parse
  | '<'    { fprintf chan "&lt;"
             convertHtml chan lexbuf }
  | '>'    { fprintf chan "&gt;"
             convertHtml chan lexbuf }
  | eof    { () }
  | _      { fprintf chan "%s" (lexeme lexbuf)
             convertHtml chan lexbuf }
```

Listing 16-2. Replacing Characters with Their HTML Equivalents: text2html.fs

```
open System.IO
open System.Text

let main() =
```

```
let args = System.Environment.GetCommandLineArgs()
if args.Length <= 2 then
    let exe = Path.GetFileName(args.[0])
    eprintfn "Usage: %s dir pattern" exe
    exit 1
let directory = args.[1]
let pattern = args.[2]

for fileName in Directory.GetFiles(directory, pattern) do

    // Open a file stream for the file name
    use inputReader = File.OpenText fileName

    // Create a lex buffer for use with the generated lexer. The lex buffer
    // reads the inputReader stream.
    let lexBuffer = Lexing.LexBuffer<_>.FromTextReader inputReader

    // Open an output channel
    let outputFile = Path.ChangeExtension(fileName,"html")
    use outputWriter = (new StreamWriter(outputFile) :> TextWriter)

    // Write the header
    fprintfn outputWriter "<html>\n<head></head>\n<pre>"

    // Run the generated lexer
    Text2htmllex.convertHtml outputWriter lexBuffer

    // Write the footer
    fprintfn outputWriter "</pre>\n</html>\n"

main()
```

You can produce an F# source file from the previous lexer definition by running the following command at the Windows command prompt:

```
fslex text2htmllex.fsl --unicode
```

This produces text2htmllex.fs, which contains the implementation of the lexer convertHtml. This lexer is *imperative*, in that it prints to an output stream instead of returning tokens. The signature of the entry point to the generated lexer is as follows:

```
val Text2HtmlLex.convertHtml: System.IO.TextWriter -> Lexing.Lexbuffer<char> -> unit
```

You can now compile the driver and the lexer together:

```
fsc text2htmllex.fs text2html.fs -r FSharp.PowerPack.dll
```

You can run the resulting program as follows, giving a source directory and a file pattern and producing an .html version of each file that matches by applying the HTML conversion:

```
text2html . *.txt
```

Let's look at the previous example more closely. The `rule` section of `text2htmllex.fsl` defines the lexer, which takes the output channel as an argument before the lexing buffer. It says that if you encounter the < or > character, you should output its HTML equivalent and recursively call your lexer to process the remaining input. If you find the end of the file, you stop; and for any other character, you print it to the output channel. In each rule, you can refer to a predefined variable (visible only inside the rule) named `lexbuf` that is the instantiation of the `Microsoft.FSharp.Text.Lexing.LexBuffer` type. You can access various bits of information through this variable about the lexing state; some of these are collected in Table 16-1.

The driver is all F# code. You check the input arguments and then iterate through files in the directory given by the first argument whose name matches the pattern given by the second argument. You then open each file and instantiate your generated lexer with the following lines:

```
use inputReader = File.OpenText fileName
let lexBuffer = Lexing.LexBuffer<_>.FromTextReader inputReader
...
Text2HtmlLex.convertHtml outputWriter lexBuffer
```

This code uses some important functions from the `LexBuffer` type. Table 16-1 shows the notable static members and some of the properties in this type.

Table 16-1. *Some Static Members and Properties of the LexBuffer Type*

Member	Type	Description
FromString	string -> LexBuffer<char>	Makes a LexBuffer for the given string
FromTextReader	TextReader -> LexBuffer<char>	Makes a LexBuffer for the given text reader
FromBinaryReader	BinaryReader -> LexBuffer<byte>	Makes a LexBuffer for the given binary reader
LexemeString	LexBuffer<char> -> string	Returns the matched string
this.EndPos	Lexing.Position	Gets/sets the current position associated with the end of the matched token
this.IsPastEndOf Stream	bool	True if the LexBuffer has exhausted the available input
this.StartPos	Lexing.Position	Gets/sets the current position associated with the start of the matched token

■ **Note** FsLex works by constructing a table-driven finite automaton that is executed to consume the input character sequence one by one until a full token can be returned. The automaton blocks until further input is received. The states of this machine are derived from the regular expressions defined by each rule. Single-character literals advance the machine to a new state, and repetitions cause it to remain in the same state. These states form a graph, and the edges between the states are those symbols that advance between the states.

The FsLex Input in More Detail

You saw the basic structure of lexer files in the preceding example, which contained only a handful of rules. In general, `fslex` input files have the following simple structure:

```
// Preamble - any user code you need for the lexer, such as opening modules, etc.
{ [Code] }

// Definitions - named patterns that you can use in the rules or other definitions
let [Ident_1] = [Pattern]
let ...

// Rules - text patterns that trigger certain actions
rule [Rule_1] [arg1... argn] = parse
    | [Pattern] { [Action] }
    | ...
    | [Pattern] { [Action] }
and [Rule_2] [arg1... argn] = parse
    ...
rule [Rule_3] ...

// Epilogue - code that can call the lexer rules defined above
{ [Code] }
```

Each rule defined in the lexer becomes an F# function that can be accessed from other modules and the lexer itself. You can place comments between (* and *), and you can also use // comments in the actions just like in any other F# code. Patterns can be any of the forms listed in Table 16-2.

Lexical actions are pieces of F# code enclosed in braces; they're executed when a lexer match is made. You can put any logic here that you like; typically, you construct a token. Tokens are specified in the parser definition using the %token directive (you see this later in this chapter); if you don't have a parser, any user-defined type will do. If your lexer rules don't construct tokens, or if your lexer is simple enough, often you may want to put all driver code in the epilogue section to create a stand-alone lexer.

Table 16-2. Patterns in Lexer Rules

Pattern Form	Description
`'c'`	Character constants; in single quotes, such as `'+'` and `'.'`
`['a' 'b' 'c']`	Character sets; matches any character in the given set
`['a'-'z']`	Character ranges; matches any character in the given range, in ASCII ordering
`[^'a' 'b' 'c']`	Complementary character sets; matches any character except those in the given character set
`"abc"`	Matches the given string of characters
`_`	Matches any character

Pattern Form	Description
eof	Matches the end of the stream
identifier	A predefined named regular expression (named earlier in the file using a let binding)
pattern?	Zero or one occurrences of pattern
pattern+	One of more occurrences of pattern
pattern*	Zero or more occurrences of pattern
pattern1 | pattern2	Either pattern1 or pattern
pattern1 pattern2	Concatenation; pattern1 followed by pattern2

Generating a Simple Token Stream

Listing 16-3 shows a lexer that constructs a list of tokens that then is printed. It can recognize integers, floats, identifiers, and the symbols ^, *, -, and +. Any other character causes a runtime exception.

Listing 16-3. SimpleTokensLex.fsl: Lexing Simple Tokens: Integers, Floats, and Identifiers

```
{
module SimpleTokensLex

open System

type token =
    | INT    of int
    | FLOAT  of float
    | ID     of string
    | STRING of string
    | PLUS | MINUS | TIMES | HAT
    | EOF

let lexeme = Lexing.LexBuffer<_>.LexemeString
}

let num         = ['0'-'9']+
let intNum      = '-'? num
let floatNum    = '-'? num ('.' num)? (['e' 'E'] num)?
let ident       = ['a'-'z']+
let whitespace  = ' ' | '\t'
let newline     = '\n' | '\r' '\n'

rule token = parse
    | intNum      { INT (Convert.ToInt32 (lexeme lexbuf)) }
```

```
| floatNum    { FLOAT (Convert.ToDouble (lexeme lexbuf))  }
| ident       { ID (lexeme lexbuf)  }
| '+'         { PLUS }
| '-'         { MINUS }
| '*'         { TIMES }
| '^'         { HAT }
| whitespace  { token lexbuf }
| newline     { token lexbuf }
| eof         { EOF }
| _           { failwithf "unrecognized input: '%s'" (lexeme lexbuf) }
```

You can generate the lexer using this:

```
fslex simpleTokensLex.fsl --unicode
```

The generated lexer contains a single module SimpleTokensLex with one entry-point function for each rule. In this case, the type of this function is as follows:

```
val token: Lexing.LexBuffer<char> -> SimpleTokensLex.token
```

The following indicates how you can imperatively generate a simple token stream from a string and print the results in F# Interactive:

```
> #r "FSharp.PowerPack.dll";;
...
> #load "SimpleTokensLex.fs";;
> let lexbuf = Lexing.LexBuffer<_>.FromString "3.4 x 34 xyx";;
val lexbuf : Lexing.LexBuffer<char>

> SimpleTokensLex.token lexbuf;;
val it : SimpleTokensLex.token = FLOAT 3.4

> SimpleTokensLex.token lexbuf;;
val it : SimpleTokensLex.token = ID "x"

> SimpleTokensLex.token lexbuf;;
val it : SimpleTokensLex.token = INT 34

> SimpleTokensLex.token lexbuf;;
val it : SimpleTokensLex.token = ID "xyx"

> SimpleTokensLex.token lexbuf;;
val it : SimpleTokensLex.token = EOF

> SimpleTokensLex.token lexbuf;;
System.Exception: End of file on lexing stream
```

Tracking Position Information Correctly

Lexers generated by fslex keep track of partial information about the position of the most recently accepted token within the source stream of characters. In particular, the StartPos and EndPos properties on the LexBuffer type return Lexing.Position values. A partial signature of this position type is as follows:

```
type Position with
    // The file name associated with the input stream.
    member FileName : string

    // The line number in the input stream, assuming fresh
    // positions have been updated modifying the
    // EndPos property of the LexBuffer.
    member Line : int

    // The character number in the input stream
    member AbsoluteOffset : int

    // Return the column number marked by the position, e.g. the
    // difference between the AbsoluteOffset and the StartOfLineAbsoluteOffset.
    member Column : int

    // Convert a position just beyond the end of a line to a
    // position at the start of the next line.
    member NextLine : Position
    ...
end
```

In some cases, certain lexer actions must perform extra bookkeeping. In particular, the lexer should update the EndPos property of the LexBuffer each time a newline marker is processed (this is left up to the lexer because the interpretation of newline characters can differ between various lexers). In particular, you can change the endOfLine rule in the lexer in Listing 16-3 to make this update:

```
| newline     { lexbuf.EndPos <- lexbuf.EndPos.NextLine;
                  token lexbuf }
```

You can now experiment with this updated lexer in F# Interactive and examine the StartPos and EndPos properties after fetching each token:

```
> let lexbuf = Lexing.LexBuffer<_>.FromString "3.4 \n 34 xyx";;
val lexbuf : Lexing.LexBuffer<char>

> SimpleTokensLex.token lexbuf;;
val it : SimpleTokensLex.token = FLOAT 3.4

> (lexbuf.StartPos.Line, lexbuf.StartPos.Column);;
val it : int * int = (0,0)

> (lexbuf.EndPos.Line, lexbuf.EndPos.Column);;
```

```
val it : int * int = (0,3)

> SimpleTokensLex.token lexbuf;;
val it : SimpleTokensLex.token = INT 34

> (lexbuf.StartPos.Line, lexbuf.StartPos.Column);;
val it : int * int = (1,1)
```

Often, you may need to attach position information to each lexer token. However, when you use lexers in conjunction with fsyacc parser generators, the position information is automatically read after each token is processed and then stored in the parser's state. We return to this topic later in this chapter.

Handling Comments and Strings

So far, you've seen examples with one lexing rule only. This is because the main lexer rule was sufficient for all tokens and you haven't yet come across the need to lex input that can't be described by a regular expression. To illustrate this point, for instance, say you want to lex comments enclosed by (* and *). Formally, you have an opening delimiter, followed by the body of the comment, and finally enclosed by the closing delimiter. The first attempt, shown here

```
"(*" _* "*)"
```

fails because the middle pattern matches everything and you never reach the closing *). So, the best compromise could be as follows

```
"(*" [^ '*']* "*)"
```

where you match the inside of the comment as long as you don't see an asterisk, and then you try to match the closing *). This of course fails on any comment that contains an asterisk. You can play with this regular expression a little more. The inside of the comment is either anything but an asterisk or all asterisks that aren't followed by another asterisk or right parenthesis:

```
"(*" ([^ '*'] | ('*'+ ([^ '*' ')'])))* '*'+ ')'
```

This is about as close as you can get, and yet even this pattern has a problem: it can't match nested comments; it always stops at the first closing delimiter, ignoring all nested comment openers.

You can handle this problem by using a multirule lexer. The following rules show the additions you can make to the SimpleTokensLex.fsl lexer from Listing 16-3 in order to properly handle comments and strings:

```
rule token =
    ...
    | "(*"        { comment lexbuf; token lexbuf }
    | "\""        { STRING (string lexbuf.StartPos "" lexbuf) }
    | _           { failwith "unrecognized input: '%s'" (lexeme lexbuf) }

and comment = parse
    | "(*"        { comment lexbuf; comment lexbuf  }
    | "*)"        { () }
    | "\n"        { lexbuf.EndPos <- lexbuf.EndPos.NextLine
```

```
                    comment lexbuf }
    | eof           { failwith "Unterminated comment" }
    | _             { comment lexbuf }

and string pos s = parse
    | "\\" ('"' | 'n' | 'r' | 't')
                    { let s' = s + (match lexeme lexbuf with
                                    | "\\\"" -> "\""
                                    | "\\n" ->  "\n"
                                    | "\\r" ->  "\r"
                                    | "\\t" ->  "\t"
                                    | "\\\\" -> "\\"
                                    | _ ->      "")
                      string pos s' lexbuf }
    | "\""          { s }
    | "\n"          { lexbuf.EndPos <- lexbuf.EndPos.NextLine
                      string pos (s + "\n") lexbuf }
    | eof           { failwithf "end of file in string started at or near %A" pos }
    | _             { string pos (s + (lexeme lexbuf)) lexbuf }
```

Comment processing begins when you encounter (* in the token rule. When the closing *) is encountered, you exit one invocation of the comment rule. The idea is that you deal with nested comments by recursively applying the lexer when a nested comment is reached. Note the double invocation of comment lexbuf for nested comment delimiters: once to tokenize the comment that belongs to the opener and again to tokenize the rest of the enclosing comment. There are also two further matches within the comment rule. If you hit the end of the source stream, you have an unterminated comment, and you raise an exception; in every other case, you move forward inside the comment.

In the example, strings are also handled by a separate lexer rule string that is invoked by the token lexer when you encounter the double-quote character. This rule takes two parameters: the string consumed so far and the start position of the string. The latter is used to report a nicer error for an unterminated string (you could also use this technique for the matching case for comments). You can also check whether you have an escaped character in the input. If so, you append the appropriate escape sequence to the string already accumulated and advance the current position. Upon encountering the closing character, you return the overall string. An imperative System.Text.StringBuffer object can also be used to accumulate the string, which is more efficient if strings get very long.

■ **Note** Because lexer rules can pass arguments, there is little need to use mutable state in a lexer—instead, pass additional arguments.

Recursive-Descent Parsing

You can now turn your attention to parsing. Let's assume for the moment that you're writing an application that performs simple symbolic differentiation, say on polynomials only. You want to read polynomials such as x^5-2x^3+20 as input from your users, which in turn is converted to your internal polynomial representation so that you can perform symbolic differentiation and pretty-print the result to the screen. One way to represent polynomials is as a list of terms that are added or subtracted to form the polynomial:

```
type Term =
    | Term  of int * string * int
    | Const of int

type Polynomial = term list
```

For instance, the polynomial in this example is as follows:

```
[Term (1,"x",5); Term (-2,"x",3); Const 20]
```

In Listing 16-3, you built a lexer and a token type suitable for generating a token stream for the input text (shown as a list of tokens here):

```
[ID "x"; HAT; INT 5; MINUS; INT 2; ID "x"; HAT; INT 3; PLUS; INT 20]
```

Listing 16-4 shows a *recursive-decent parser* that consumes this token stream and converts it into the internal representation of polynomials. The parser works by generating a lazy list for the token stream. Lazy lists are a data structure in the F# library module `Microsoft.FSharp.Collections.LazyList`, and they're a lot like sequences with one major addition: lazy lists effectively allow you to pattern-match on a sequence and return a residue lazy list for the tail of the sequence.

***Listing 16-4.** Recursive-Descent Parser for Polynomials*

```
open SimpleTokensLex
open Microsoft.FSharp.Text.Lexing

type Term =
    | Term  of int * string * int
    | Const of int

type Polynomial = term list
type TokenStream = LazyList<token * Position * Position>

let tryToken (src: TokenStream ) =
    match src with
    | LazyList.Cons ((tok, startPos, endPos), rest) -> Some(tok, rest)
    | _ -> None

let parseIndex src =
    match tryToken src with
    | Some (HAT, src) ->
        match tryToken src with
        | Some (INT num2, src) ->
            num2, src
        | _ -> failwith "expected an integer after '^'"
    | _ -> 1, src

let parseTerm src =
    match tryToken src with
    | Some (INT num, src) ->
        match tryToken src with
        | Some (ID id, src) ->
            let idx, src = parseIndex src
```

```
            Term (num, id, idx), src
        | _ -> Const num, src
    | Some (ID id, src) ->
        let idx, src = parseIndex src
        Term(1, id, idx), src
    | _ -> failwith "end of token stream in term"

let rec parsePolynomial src =
    let t1, src = parseTerm src
    match tryToken src with
    | Some (PLUS, src) ->
        let p2, src = parsePolynomial src
        (t1 :: p2), src
    | _ -> [t1], src
```

The functions here have the following types (using the type aliases you defined):

```
val tryToken        : TokenStream -> (token * TokenStream ) option
val parseIndex      : TokenStream -> int * TokenStream
val parseTerm       : TokenStream -> Term * TokenStream
val parsePolynomial : TokenStream -> Polynomial * TokenStream
```

You can turn the fslex-generated lexer for the lexer specification in Listing 16-3 into a TokenStream using the following code:

```
let getTokenStream  inp : TokenStream  =
    // Generate the token stream as a seq<token>
    seq { let lexbuf = LexBuffer<_>.FromString inp
          while not lexbuf.IsPastEndOfStream do
              match SimpleTokensLex.token lexbuf with
              | EOF -> yield! []
              | token -> yield (token, lexbuf.StartPos, lexbuf.EndPos) }

    // Convert to a lazy list
    |> LazyList.ofSeq

let parse input =
    let src = getTokenStream  input
    let result, src = parsePolynomial src
    match tryToken src with
    | Some _ -> failwith "unexpected input at end of token stream!"
    | None -> result
```

These functions have the following types:

```
val getTokenStream : string -> TokenStream
val parse: string -> polynomial
```

Note in the previous examples that you can successfully parse either constants or complete terms; but after you locate a HAT symbol, a number must follow. This sort of parsing, in which you look only at the next token to guide the parsing process, is referred to as *LL(1)*, which stands for left-to-right, leftmost derivation parsing; 1 means that only one look-ahead symbol is used. The parser approach you used earlier is called *recursive-descent*. This has various advantages and disadvantages, and we discuss those in a bit. To conclude, you can look at the parse function in action:

```
> parse "1+3";;
val it : term list = [Const 1; Const 3]

> parse "2x^2+3x+5";;
val it : term list = [Term (2,"x",2); Term (3,"x",1); Const 5]
```

More on Grammars and Their Notations

LL parsers such as the recursive-descent parser in the previous example are based on a subset of the *context-free grammars* (CFGs). These can be defined by giving their corresponding grammar as a set of *production rules*. For context-free languages, each rule has a single nonterminal symbol (the head) on the left side, defining a substitution of the nonterminal and/or terminal symbols on the right side. A terminal symbol is part of the concrete string that is parsed. A convenient notation for describing context-free languages is the Backus-Naur Form (BNF). Here, nonterminals are inside brackets (<>), and terminal symbols are either named (such as ID) or quoted. The Extended BNF (EBNF) notation provides further convenient operators to express optionality (inside brackets) and repetition (using the +, ?, and * symbols with the same meaning as in regular expressions), thus providing a more succinct and readable description.

The recursive-descent parser from this section parses each nonterminal in the following simple grammar expressed in EBNF:

```
<polynomial> ::= <term> ['+' <polynomial>]
<idxterm> ::=  ID '^' NUM | ID
<term> ::=  NUM [ <idxterm> ] | <idxterm>
```

Grammars give rise to corresponding derivations; for instance, consider how 2x^3+1 is derived:

```
<polynomial> ➤ <term> '+' <polynomial>
             ➤ NUM <idxterm> '+' <polynomial>
             ➤ NUM ID '^' NUM '+' <polynomial>
             ➤ NUM ID '^' NUM '+' <term>
             ➤ NUM ID '^' NUM '+' NUM
             ➤ 2x^3 + 1
```

You can produce different derivations depending on which nonterminal you expand at each step. In the previous derivation, you chose to always expand the leftmost nonterminals, but you can just as easily expand from the right or even mix the two strategies. Usually, you stick to either left or rightmost derivation using LL or LR parsers, respectively; and if your grammar is written in a well-defined way, you get the same parse tree. On the other hand, if, given a particular derivation strategy, you get more than one parse tree for a given input, the grammar is said to be *ambiguous*.

477

As mentioned in the example, recursive-descent parsers are LL(*n*) parsers; in other words, they perform leftmost derivation. Typically, only a single look-ahead symbol is used to drive parsing—these are LL(1) parsers—but the example can be extended to LL(*n*) for some *n*>1, because inside a given parsing function you can retrieve several look-ahead symbols and make the appropriate parsing decisions. This is possible because the look-ahead calculation is nondestructive; in other words, there is no global parsing state. Instead, you pass around the particular input string (the remaining token stream) instance on which you want to base your parsing.

LR parsers are a special subset of bottom-up parsers; they read their input from left to right and produce a rightmost derivation (that is, the rightmost nonterminal is always expanded during parsing). Special subsets include Simple LR (SLR) and Look-Ahead LR (LALR; as generated by the `yacc` family of parser generators, including `fsyacc`, as you see in the coming sections); and extensions include LR(1), (where the parse tables are typically larger because of the one symbol look-ahead) and Generalized LR (GLR), which can handle nondeterminism and ambiguous grammars.

Limitations of Recursive-Descent Parsers

There are various limitations that you can't handle with recursive-descent parsers. For instance, if you translate a left-recursive production into code, you get an infinite recursion, like so:

```
<polynomial> ::= <polynomial> '+' <term> | <term>
```

This corresponds to the following:

```
let rec parsePolynomial src =
    let poly, src = parsePolynomial src
    ...
```

Another common problem with LL(*k*) parsing for some *k*>=1 is that the grammar rules for a given nonterminal can't start with the same symbols, or else there is no easy way to decide which rule to apply (because each is determined to be applicable upon checking *k* number of symbols). In such cases, *left-factoring* can be applied. For example, you can move the symbols after the common part into another production, as shown here:

```
<polynomial> ::= <term> | <term> '+' <polynomial>
```
can be refactored as
```
<polynomial> ::= <term> <polymomialTail>
<polynomialTail> ::= EPSILON | '+' <polynomial>
```

Here, EPSILON is the empty symbol, so the function that parses polynomialTail both checks for a plus symbol and issues a call to parse a polynomial or exit in the absence of an initial plus symbol, leaving the input unchanged. Although this case is relatively simple (you can parse terms until they're followed by a plus sign iteratively), coding such grammar rules in the general case is cumbersome.

Problems such as these arise because you have to make parsing decisions early on (such as deciding which grammar rule you're pursuing if there are multiple choices for a given nonterminal), because they construct the parse tree from the top and proceed downward. LR parsers, on the other hand, postpone these decisions as much as possible and construct the parse tree bottom-up, resulting in much more flexibility both in terms of how naturally grammar rules can be expressed and how they can be mapped into code.

Parsing with FsYacc

The tool fsyacc generates LALR(1) parsers, which are a special subset of LR(1) parsers where the state table is compressed by merging similar states. This in practice doesn't limit the languages that can be parsed, but it does result in significant savings over the parse-table size. The generated parser automaton performs one of four distinct operations in any state based on the look-ahead token, and these are important to understand if you have various grammar conflicts to fix. It can *shift* the look-ahead (always a terminal symbol) to its stack, *reduce* a number of stack entries by a grammar rule leaving the head symbol in their place, *accept* the input as syntactically correct, or *reject* in the opposite case. Parsing proceeds until an accept or a reject state is reached.

You first see how to develop a parser for a simple programming language. A sample fragment of the BASIC-like language you want to parse is shown here:

```
a := 1;
b := 0;
if a then d := 20 + 20;
if b then d := 40 * 20 + 20;
print d;
while d do
    begin
        d := d + 1;
        print d
    end;
print d
```

For simplicity, let's call this language Kitty. As the previous example shows, Kitty supports naming values, printing values, basic arithmetic operators, and a while and conditional construct. The Ast module (shown in Listing 16-5) defines the internal representation for Kitty programs.

Listing 16-5. KittyAst.fs: Defining the AST for Kitty Programs

```
module Ast

type expr =
    | Val    of string
    | Int    of int
    | Plus   of expr * expr
    | Minus  of expr * expr
    | Times  of expr * expr

type stmt =
    | Assign     of string * expr
    | While      of expr * stmt
    | Seq        of stmt list
    | IfThen     of expr * stmt
    | IfThenElse of expr * stmt * stmt
    | Print      of expr

type prog = Prog of stmt list
```

The Lexer for Kitty

Listing 16-6 shows a lexer for the language in the file `KittyLexer.fsl`. It's similar to lexers developed earlier in this chapter. The one exception is that you use a *keyword table*. Matching against lexemes to identify tokens is a sensible solution only if there are relatively few cases. Tokenizing a large set of keywords and operators using explicit rules can lead to large lexers. This situation is often handled using tables that contain the possible lexeme matches and the tokens to be returned. Listing 16-6 uses simple dictionaries (maps).

Listing 16-6. `KittyLexer.fsl`: Lexer for Kitty

```
{
module KittyLexer

open System
open KittyParser
open Microsoft.FSharp.Text.Lexing

let lexeme = LexBuffer<_>.LexemeString

let ids = [ ("while",    WHILE);
            ("begin",    BEGIN);
            ("end",      END);
            ("do",       DO);
            ("if",       IF);
            ("then",     THEN);
            ("else",     ELSE);
            ("print",    PRINT);]

let idsMap = Map.ofList ids

let ident lexbuf tokenText =
    if Map.containsKey tokenText idsMap then Map.find tokenText idsMap
    else ID tokenText
}

let num        = ['0'-'9']+
let alpha      = ['a'-'z' 'A'-'Z']
let ident      = alpha+ (alpha | ['_' '$'])*
let integer    = '-'? num
let whitespace = ' ' | '\t'
let newline    = '\n' | '\r' '\n'

rule token = parse
    | whitespace { token lexbuf }
    | newline    { lexbuf.EndPos <- lexbuf.EndPos.NextLine; token lexbuf }
    | "("        { LPAREN }
    | ")"        { RPAREN }
    | "+"        { PLUS }
    | "-"        { MINUS }
    | "*"        { TIMES }
    | ";"        { SEMI }
    | ":="       { ASSIGN }
    | ident      { ident lexbuf (lexeme lexbuf) }
    | integer    { INT (Int32.Parse(lexeme lexbuf)) }
    | eof        { EOF }
```

Note that at compilation time, the lexer depends on the parser defined later in Listing 16-7. This is because the lexer must return the type of tokens required by the parser.

You can generate the lexer by calling `fslex`:

```
fslex KittyLexer.fsl --unicode
```

This produces `KittyLexer.fs`, which contains the implementation of the lexer.

The Parser for Kitty

Listing 16-7 shows the parser specification for the Kitty language in the file `KittyParser.fsy`.

Listing 16-7. KittyParser.fsy: Parser for Kitty

```
%{
open Ast
%}

// The start token becomes a parser function in the compiled code.
%start start

// These are the terminal tokens of the grammar along with the types of
// the data carried by each token:
%token <string> ID
%token <int> INT
%token PLUS MINUS TIMES LPAREN RPAREN IF THEN ELSE
%token WHILE DO BEGIN END PRINT SEMI ASSIGN EOF

// Associativity and Precedences - Lowest precedence comes first
%left PLUS MINUS
%left TIMES

// This is the type of the data produced by a successful reduction
// of the 'start' symbol:
%type <prog> start

%%

start: Prog                    { $1 }

Prog: StmtList                 { Prog (List.rev $1) }

Expr: ID                       { Val $1 }
    | INT                      { Int $1 }
    | Expr PLUS Expr           { Plus ($1, $3) }
    | Expr MINUS Expr          { Minus ($1, $3) }
    | Expr TIMES Expr          { Times ($1, $3) }
    | LPAREN Expr RPAREN       { $2 }


Stmt: ID ASSIGN Expr              { Assign ($1, $3) }
    | WHILE Expr DO Stmt          { While ($2, $4) }
```

```
    | BEGIN StmtList END         { Seq (List.rev $2) }
    | IF Expr THEN Stmt          { IfThen ($2, $4) }
    | IF Expr THEN Stmt ELSE Stmt { IfThenElse ($2, $4, $6) }
    | PRINT Expr                 { Print $2 }

StmtList:
    | Stmt                 { [$1] }
    | StmtList SEMI Stmt { $3 :: $1  }
```

You can generate the parser by calling fsyacc:

```
  fsyacc KittyParser.fsy --module KittyParser
```

This produces KittyParser.fs, which contains the implementations of the parser, along with a signature file KittyParser.fsi. The generated parser has one entry point for each %start symbol (here there is only one). The type of this entry point is as follows:

```
val start : (LexBuffer<'a> -> token) -> LexBuffer<'a> -> Ast.prog
```

You see how to use this function a little later in this chapter. In a roundabout way, the type says, "If you give me a lexing function that generates tokens and give me a LexBuffer to supply to that lexing function, then I'll generate you an Ast.prog." The generic type variable indicates that the parser is independent of the characters manipulated by the LexBuffer.

We now cover in more detail the different aspects of fsyacc parsing illustrated by this example.

The fsyacc Input in More Detail

The general structure of fsyacc input files is as follows:

```
// Preamble - any code you need for the parser, such as opening modules, etc.
%{ [Code] %}

// Tokens and their types - each line may contain several tokens
%token <[Type]> [TokenName] ... [TokenName]
...
// Associativity and precedences - where tokens associate (left, right,
// nonassoc) and how strongly they bind (in the order of their declaration)
%left      [TokenName]
%right     [TokenName]
%nonassoc  [TokenName]
...


// Start symbols and their types
%start [StartSymbol]
%type <[Type]> [StartSymbol]
%%

// Productions - defining how non-terminals are derived
[Symbol] : [Symbols_1] { [Code_1] }
```

```
        | [Symbols_2] { [Code_2] }
...
```

The preamble can contain F# code, typically opening various modules and defining helper functions. You define the tokens (terminal symbols) of the grammar with the %token directive, giving the name of the token(s) preceded by its type enclosed in <>. The type can be omitted if a token carries no data. There must be at least one start symbol defined using the %start; you give its type with the %type directive. The resulting parser exposes only those parsing functions that were designated as start symbols. The productions for the same nonterminal can be merged into the same rule, separated by an | character.

Parsing Lists

In Kitty, statements can be separated by semicolons. This is handled in the StmtList grammar production, whose semantic extract is a list of statements. Note that you could have written this rule in a head-recursive way:

```
StmtList:
    | Stmt               { [$1] }
    | Stmt SEMI StmtList { $1 @ [ $3 ] }
```

Unlike in recursive-descent or any other LL parsing technique, the previous rule doesn't pose a problem for fsyacc, and thus no left-factoring is needed. However, it does create a copy of the statement list each time a new expression is appended to it. You eliminate this by using the following productions

```
StmtList:
    | Stmt               { [$1] }
    | StmtList SEMI Stmt { $3 :: $1 }
```

combined with a List.rev where the rule is used. This rule consumes all statements and inserts them, one by one, into the singleton list that contains the first statement. As a result, the return list is in reverse order, which is why you need to apply List.rev. You may want to define a separate rule to perform this operation. Another feature that is often needed is the ability to parse empty or optional lists. This can be easily accomplished using an empty (epsilon) symbol, as in the following example:

```
StmtListOpt:
              { [] }
    | StmtList { $1 }
```

This rule matches an optional list of statements and returns an empty list if no statements can be parsed.

Resolving Conflicts, Operator Precedence, and Associativity

As usual with arithmetic operators, division and multiplication should take precedence over addition and subtraction: 1+2*3 should be parsed as 1+(2*3). With fsyacc, this can be expressed easily using the associativity directives—or, to be more precise, their ordering:

```
// Associativity and Precedences - Lowest precedence comes first
%left PLUS MINUS
%left TIMES
```

By specifying what tokens associate and where (how strongly they bind), you can control how parse derivations are performed. For instance, giving left-associativity to the addition operator (PLUS), given an input 1+2+3, the parser automatically generates a nonambiguous derivation in the form of (1+2)+3. The basic arithmetic operators are left-associative and should be listed from the lowest precedence to the highest; in the example, the addition and subtraction operators have lower precedence than multiplication—the way it should be. Other associativity specifications include %nonassoc and %right, which are used to denote that a given symbol doesn't associate or associates to the right, respectively. The former is useful for relational and equality operators such as <, >, or !=, where the operator isn't applicable if applied multiple times: 1 > 2 > 3 yields a syntax error.

You can also give precedence to a rule by using %prec at the end of the rule and giving a token whose precedence is to be applied. You can list arbitrary tokens in the associativity and precedence declarations, even if they haven't been declared as tokens, and use them in such situations. You can find more details about specifying precedence at www.expert-fsharp.com/Topics/FsYacc.

■ **Tip** One option for fsyacc.exe is -v, which causes fsyacc to produce a readable extract of the parser's states. This is useful when there are various conflicts to resolve.

Each state in this extract corresponds to one or more *items*, which are productions that indicate what has been seen while parsing them. This current position with respect to a rule is marked with a period (.). Furthermore, to each state belong various actions that are triggered by certain look-ahead symbols. For instance, the action in some state as follows

```
action 'ID' (noprec):   shift 7
```

indicates that if the ID token, which has no defined precedence, is encountered as look-ahead, the parser pushes this token to the parsing stack and shifts to state 7. For reduce actions, the rule that is reduced is shown. An error (reject) or accept action is shown for tokens that trigger a syntax error or acceptance, respectively.

The parser state extract also provides useful information about conflicts in your grammar. Conflicts arise when your grammar is ambiguous (which translates to having more than one choice for a parser action at any time), ultimately meaning more than one derivation can accept a given input. You can do a number of things to disambiguate your grammar. You can apply precedence to various tokens or rules, or rewrite your rules to be consistent and unambiguous. There are two main sources of grammar conflicts: reduce-reduce and shift-reduce conflicts. Reduce-reduce conflicts are considered really bad because there are multiple rules to reduce by at a given situation. Although fsyacc applies a disambiguation strategy (reducing by the grammar rule that was defined earlier), you should avoid reduce-reduce conflicts as much as possible.

Shift-reduce conflicts arise when the parser has the choice to shift a token or reduce by a rule. Unless you fix this conflict, fsyacc favors the shift action and defers the reduction to a later point. In some situations (for instance, the dangling-else problem), this yields the expected behavior; but in general, any such conflict is also considered a serious problem.

Putting It Together

You can generate the parsers and lexers by calling fslex and fsyacc:

```
fslex KittyLexer.fsl --unicode
fsyacc KittyParser.fsy --module KittyParser
```

This produces KittyLexer.fs and KittyParser.fs, which contain the implementations of the parser and lexer. You can test these using F# Interactive by loading the files directly using the #load directive. The following code creates a LexBuffer called lexbuf. It then calls the KittyParser.start entry point for the parser, passing KittyLexer.token as the lexical analysis engine and lexbuf as the LexBuffer. This connects the parser and the lexer:

```
open Ast
open KittyParser
open KittyLexer

let parseText text =
    let lexbuf = Lexing.LexBuffer<_>.FromString text
    try
        KittyParser.start KittyLexer.token lexbuf
    with e ->
        let pos = lexbuf.EndPos
        failwithf "Error near line %d, character %d\n" pos.Line pos.Column
```

You can now test this function interactively:

```
> let sample = "counter := 100; accum := 0; \n\
                while counter do \n\
                begin \n\
                    counter := counter - 1; \n\
                    accum := accum + counter \n\
                end; \n\
                print accum";;
val sample : string = "..."

> parseText sample;;
val it : Ast.prog
= Prog
    [Assign ("counter",Int 100); Assign ("accum",Int 0);
     While
       (Val "counter",
        Seq
          [Assign ("counter",Minus (Val "counter",Int 1));
           Assign ("accum",Plus (Val "accum",Val "counter"))]); Print Val "accum"]
```

Writing an evaluator for Kitty is straightforward. Here, you use an environment that maps variable names to the integer values they store. As expected, assignments in the source language add a binding for a given variable, and evaluating variables reads a value from this environment. Because of the lack of other types in Kitty, you use a nonzero value for the Boolean true and zero for false and wire the logic of the conditional and looping construct accordingly:

```
let rec evalE (env: Map<string, int>) = function
    | Val v          -> if env.ContainsKey v then env.[v]
                        else failwith ("unbound variable: " + v)
    | Int i          -> i
    | Plus  (e1, e2) -> evalE env e1 + evalE env e2
    | Minus (e1, e2) -> evalE env e1 - evalE env e2
```

```
    | Times (e1, e2) -> evalE env e1 * evalE env e2

and eval (env: Map<string, int>) = function
    | Assign (v, e) ->
        env.Add(v, evalE env e)
    | While (e, body) ->
        let rec loop env e body =
            if evalE env e <> 0 then
                loop (eval env body) e body
            else env
        loop env e body
    | Seq stmts ->
        List.fold eval env stmts
    | IfThen (e, stmt) ->
        if evalE env e <> 0 then eval env stmt else env
    | IfThenElse (e, stmt1, stmt2) ->
        if evalE env e <> 0 then eval env stmt1 else eval env stmt2
    | Print e ->
        printf "%d" (evalE env e); env
```

With these at hand, continuing the same interactive session, you can now evaluate the sample Kitty program:

```
> match parseText sample with
    | Prog stmts ->
        eval Map.empty (Seq stmts) |> ignore;;
4950
val it : unit = ()
```

Binary Parsing and Pickling Using Combinators

One final case of parsing is common when working with binary data. That is, say you want to work with a format that is conceptually relatively easy to parse and generate (such as a binary format) but where the process of actually writing the code to crack and encode the format is somewhat tedious. This section covers a useful set of techniques to write readers and writers for binary data quickly and reliably.

The running example shows a set of *pickling* (also called *marshalling*) and *unpickling* combinators to generate and read a binary format of our design. You can easily adapt the combinators to work with existing binary formats such as those used for network packets. Picklers and unpicklers for different data types are function values that have signatures as follows:

```
type outstate = System.IO.BinaryWriter
type instate  = System.IO.BinaryReader

type pickler<'T> = 'T -> outstate -> unit
type unpickler<'T> = instate -> 'T
```

Here, instate and outstate are types that record information during the pickling or parsing process. In this section, these are just binary readers and writers; but more generally, they can be any type that can collect information and help compact the data during the writing process, such as by ensuring that repeated strings are given unique identifiers during the pickling process.

At the heart of every such library lies a set of primitive leaf functions for the base cases of aggregate data structures. For example, when you're working with binary streams, this is the usual set of primitive read/write functions:

```
let byteP (b: byte) (st: outstate) = st.Write(b)
let byteU (st: instate) = st.ReadByte()
```

You can now begin to define additional pickler/unpickler pairs:

```
let boolP b st = byteP (if b then 1uy else 0uy) st
let boolU st = let b = byteU st in (b = 1uy)

let int32P i st =
    byteP (byte (i &&& 0xFF)) st
    byteP (byte ((i >>> 8) &&& 0xFF)) st
    byteP (byte ((i >>> 16) &&& 0xFF)) st
    byteP (byte ((i >>> 24) &&& 0xFF)) st

let int32U st =
    let b0 = int (byteU st)
    let b1 = int (byteU st)
    let b2 = int (byteU st)
    let b3 = int (byteU st)
    b0 ||| (b1 <<< 8) ||| (b2 <<< 16) ||| (b3 <<< 24)
```

These functions have the following types:

```
val byteP  : pickler<byte>
val byteU  : unpickler<byte>
val boolP  : pickler<bool>
val boolU  : unpickler<bool>
val int32P : pickler<int>
val int32U : unpickler<int>
```

So far, so simple. One advantage of this approach comes as you write combinators that put these together in useful ways. For example, for tuples

```
let tup2P p1 p2 (a, b) (st: outstate) =
    (p1 a st : unit)
    (p2 b st : unit)

let tup3P p1 p2 p3 (a, b, c) (st: outstate) =
    (p1 a st : unit)
    (p2 b st : unit)
    (p3 c st : unit)

let tup2U p1 p2 (st: instate) =
    let a = p1 st
    let b = p2 st
    (a, b)
```

```
let tup3U p1 p2 p3 (st: instate) =
    let a = p1 st
    let b = p2 st
    let c = p3 st
    (a, b, c)
```

and for lists:

```
// Outputs a list into the given output stream by pickling each element via f.
let rec listP f lst st =
    match lst with
    | [] ->      byteP 0uy st
    | h :: t -> byteP 1uy st; f h st; listP f t st

// Reads a list from a given input stream by unpickling each element via f.
let listU f st =
    let rec ulist_aux acc =
        let tag = byteU st
        match tag with
        | 0uy -> List.rev acc
        | 1uy -> let a = f st in ulist_aux (a::acc)
        | n ->    failwithf "listU: found number %d" n
    ulist_aux []
```

These functions conform to the following types:

```
val tup2P : 'a pickler -> 'b pickler -> ('a * 'b) pickler
val tup3P : 'a pickler -> 'b pickler -> 'c pickler -> ('a * 'b * 'c) pickler
val tup2U : 'a unpickler -> 'b unpickler -> ('a * 'b) unpickler
val tup3U : 'a unpickler -> 'b unpickler -> 'c unpickler -> ('a* 'b* 'c) unpickler
val listP : 'a pickler -> 'a list pickler
val listU : 'a unpickler -> 'a list unpickler
```

It's now beginning to be easy to pickle and unpickle aggregate data structures using a consistent format. For example, imagine that the internal data structure is a list of integers and Booleans:

```
type format = list<int32 * bool>

let formatP = listP (tup2P int32P boolP)
let formatU = listU (tup2U int32U boolU)

open System.IO

let writeData file data =
    use outStream = new BinaryWriter(File.OpenWrite(file))
    formatP data outStream

let readData file  =
    use inStream = new BinaryReader(File.OpenRead(file))
    formatU inStream
```

You can now invoke the pickle/unpickle process as follows:

```
> writeData "out.bin" [(102, true); (108, false)] ;;
val it : unit = ()

> readData "out.bin";;
val it : (int * bool) list = [(102, true); (108, false)]
```

Combinator-based pickling is a powerful technique and can be taken well beyond what has been shown here. For example, it's possible to do the following:

- Ensure data is compressed and shared during the pickling process by keeping tables in the input and output states. Sometimes this requires two or more phases in the pickling and unpickling process.

- Build in extra-efficient primitives that compress leaf nodes, such as writing out all integers using `BinaryWriter.Write7BitEncodedInt` and `BinaryReader.Read7BitEncodedInt`.

- Build extra combinators for arrays, sequences, and lazy values and for lists stored in other binary formats than the 0/1 tag scheme used here.

- Build combinators that allow dangling references to be written to the pickled data, usually written as a symbolic identifier. When the data is read, the identifiers must be resolved and relinked, usually by providing a function parameter that performs the resolution. This can be a useful technique when processing independent compilation units.

Combinator-based pickling is used mainly because it allows data formats to be created and read in a relatively bug-free manner. It isn't always possible to build a single pickling library suitable for all purposes, and you should be willing to customize and extend code samples such as those listed previously in order to build a set of pickling functions suitable for your needs.

■ **Note** Combinator-based parsing borders on a set of techniques called *parser combinators* that we don't cover in this book. The idea is very much the same as the combinators presented here; parsing is described using a compositional set of functions. You also can write parser combinators using the workflow notation described in Chapter 9.

Summary

This chapter covered *lexing* and *parsing*, which are tasks that can be tiresome if you don't use the right tools and techniques for the job. You learned about working with simple line-oriented formats, including on-demand reading of large data files, and then with the fslex and fsyacc tools, which are particularly suited for parsing programming languages and other languages with structured, rather than line-oriented, formats. Finally, we covered some combinator-based approaches for generating and reading binary data, which is also a form of parsing. The next chapter switches to a different area of programming and looks at how to write F# code that interoperates with native code.

CHAPTER 17

■■■

Interoperating with C and COM

Software integration and reuse is becoming one of the most relevant activities of software development nowadays. This chapter discusses how F# programs can interoperate with the outside world, accessing code available in the form of DLLs and COM components.

Common Language Runtime

Libraries and binary components provide a common way to reuse software; even the simplest C program is linked to the standard C runtime to benefit from core functions such as memory management and I/O. Modern programs depend on a large number of libraries that are shipped in binary form, and only some of them are written in the same language as the program. Libraries can be linked statically during compilation into the executable or can be loaded dynamically during program execution. Dynamic linking has become significantly common to help share code (dynamic libraries can be linked by different programs and shared among them) and adapt program behavior while executing.

Interoperability among binaries compiled by different compilers, even of the same language, can be a nightmare. One of the goals of the .NET initiative was to ease this issue by introducing the Common Language Runtime (CLR), which is targeted by different compilers and different languages to help interoperability among software developed in those languages.

The CLR is a runtime designed to run programs compiled for the .NET platform. The binary format of these programs differs from the traditional one adopted by executables; Microsoft terminology uses *managed* for the first class of programs and *unmanaged* otherwise (see Figure 17-1).

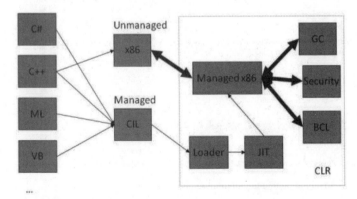

Figure 17-1. Compilation scheme for managed and unmanaged code

A Deeper Look Inside .NET Executables

Programs for the .NET platform are distributed in a form that is executed by the CLR. Binaries are expressed in an intermediate language that is compiled incrementally by the Just-In-Time (JIT) compiler during program execution. A .NET assembly, in the form of a `.dll` or an `.exe` file, contains the definition of a set of types and the definition of the method bodies, and the additional data describing the structure of the code in the intermediate language form is known as *metadata*. The intermediate language is used to define method bodies based on a stack-based machine, where operations are performed by loading values on a stack of operands and then invoking methods or operators.

Consider the following simple F# program in the `Program.fs` source file:

```
open System
let i = 2
Console.WriteLine("Input a number:")
let v = Int32.Parse(Console.ReadLine())
Console.WriteLine(i * v)
```

The F# compiler generates an executable that can be disassembled using the `ildasm.exe` tool distributed with the .NET Framework. The following screenshot shows the structure of the generated assembly. Because everything in the CLR is defined in terms of types, the F# compiler must introduce the class `$Program$Main` in the `<StartupCode$applicationname>` namespace. In this class, the definition of the `main@` static method is the entry point for the execution of the program. This method contains the intermediate language corresponding to the example F# program. The F# compiler generates several elements that aren't defined in the program, whose goal is to preserve the semantics of the F# program in the intermediate language.

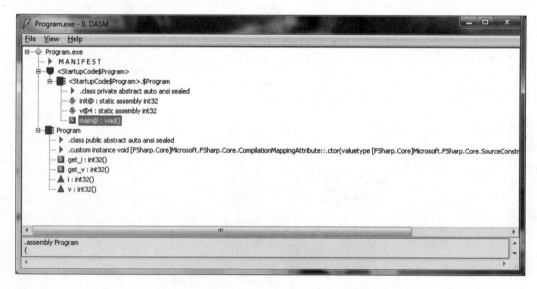

If you open the main@ method, you find the following code, which is annotated here with the corresponding F# statements:

```
.method public static void  main@() cil managed
{
  .entrypoint
  // Code size       38 (0x26)
  .maxstack  4

  // Console.WriteLine("Input a number:")
  IL_0000:  ldstr      "Input a number:"
  IL_0005:  call       void [mscorlib]System.Console::WriteLine(string)

  // let v = Int32.Parse(Console.ReadLine())
  IL_000a:  call       string [mscorlib]System.Console::ReadLine()
  IL_000f:  call       int32 [mscorlib]System.Int32::Parse(string)
  IL_0014:  stsfld     int32 '<StartupCode$ConsoleApplication1>'.$Program::v@4

  // Console.WriteLine(i * v) // Note that i is constant and its value has been inlined
  IL_0019:  ldc.i4.2
  IL_001a:  call       int32 Program::get_v()
  IL_001f:  mul
  IL_0020:  call       void [mscorlib]System.Console::WriteLine(int32)

// Exits
  IL_0025:  ret
} // end of method $Program$Main::main@
```

The ldxxx instructions are used to load values onto the operand stack of the abstract machine, and the stxxx instructions store values from that stack in locations (locals, arguments, or class fields). In this example, a static field is used for v, and the value of i is inlined using the ldc instruction. For method invocations, arguments are loaded on the stack, and a call operation is used to invoke the method.

The JIT compiler is responsible for generating the binary code that runs on the actual processor. The code generated by the JIT interacts with all the elements of the runtime, including external code loaded dynamically in the form of DLLs or COM components.

Because the F# compiler targets the CLR, its output is managed code, allowing compiled programs to interact directly with other programming languages targeting the .NET platform. Chapter 10 showed how to exploit this form of interoperability, when you saw how to develop a graphic control in F# and use it in a C# application.

Memory Management at Runtime

Interoperability of F# programs with unmanaged code requires an understanding of the structure of the most important elements of a programming language's runtime. In particular, you must consider how program memory is organized at runtime. Memory used by a program is generally classified in three classes depending on the way it's handled:

- *Static memory*: Allocated for the entire lifetime of the program
- *Automatic memory*: Allocated and freed automatically when functions or methods are executed

- *Dynamic memory:* Explicitly allocated by the program, and freed explicitly or by an automatic program called the *garbage collector*

As a rule of thumb, top-level variables and static fields belong to the first class, function arguments and local variables belong to the second class, and memory explicitly allocated using the new operator belongs to the last class. The code generated by the JIT compiler uses different data structures to manage memory and automatically interacts with the operating system to request and release memory during program execution.

Each execution thread has a stack where local variables and arguments are allocated when a function or method is invoked (see Figure 17-2). A stack is used because it naturally follows the execution flow of method and function calls. The topmost record contains data about the currently executing function; below that is the record of the caller of the function, which sits on top of another record of its caller, and so on. These *activation records* are memory blocks used to hold the memory required during the execution of the function and are naturally freed at the end of its execution by popping the record off the stack. The stack data structure is used to implement the automatic memory of the program; and because different threads execute different functions at the same time, a separate stack is assigned to each of them.

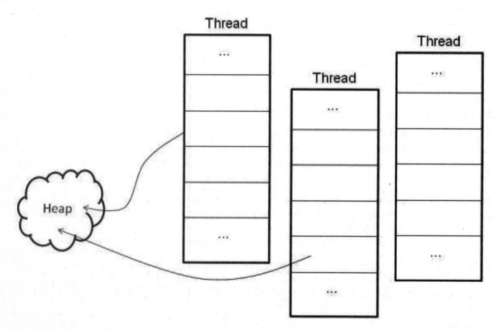

Figure 17-2. Memory organization of a running CLR program

Dynamic memory is allocated in the *heap*, which is a data structure where data resides for an amount of time not directly related to the events of program execution. The memory is explicitly allocated by the program, and it's deallocated either explicitly or automatically depending on the strategy adopted by the runtime to manage the heap. In the CLR, the heap is managed by a *garbage collector*, which is a program that tracks memory usage and reclaims memory that is no longer used by the program. Data in the heap is always referenced from the stack—or other known areas such as static memory—either directly or indirectly. The garbage collector can deduce the memory potentially reachable by program execution in the future, and the remaining memory can be collected. During garbage collection, the running program may be suspended because the collector may need to manipulate objects needed by its execution. In particular, a garbage collector may adopt a strategy called *copy collection* that can move objects in memory; during this process, the references may be inconsistent. To avoid dangling references, the memory model adopted by the CLR requires that methods access the heap through object references stored on the stack; objects in the heap are forbidden to reference data on the stack.

Data structures are the essential tool provided by programming languages to group values. A data structure is rendered as a contiguous area of memory in which the constituents are available at a given offset from the beginning of the memory. The actual layout of an object is determined by the compiler (or by the interpreter for interpreted languages) and is usually irrelevant to the program because the programming language provides operators to access fields without having to explicitly access the memory. System programming, however, often requires explicit manipulation of memory, and programming languages such as C let you control the in-memory layout of data structures. The C specification, for instance, defines that fields of a structure are laid out sequentially, although the compiler is allowed to insert extra space between them. Padding is used to align fields at word boundaries of the particular architecture in order to optimize the access to the fields of the structure. Thus, the same data structure in a program may lead to different memory layouts depending on the strategy of the compiler or the runtime, even in a language such as C where field ordering is well defined. By default, the CLR lays out structures in memory without any constraint, which gives you the freedom of optimizing memory usage on a particular architecture, although it may introduce interoperability issues if a portion of memory must be shared among the runtimes of different languages.[1]

Interoperability among different programming languages revolves mostly around memory layouts, because the execution of a compiled routine is a jump to a memory address. But routines access memory explicitly, expecting that data is organized in a certain way. The rest of this chapter discusses the mechanisms used by the CLR to interoperate with external code in the form of DLLs or COM components.

COM Interoperability

Component Object Model (COM) is a technology that Microsoft introduced in the 1990s to support interoperability among different programs possibly developed by different vendors. The Object Linking and Embedding (OLE) technology that lets you embed arbitrary content in a Microsoft Word document, for instance, relies on this infrastructure. COM is a binary standard that allows code written in different languages to interoperate, assuming that the programming language supports this infrastructure. Most of the Windows operating system and its applications are based on COM components.

The CLR was initially conceived as an essential tool to develop COM components, because COM was the key technology at the end of 1990s. It's no surprise that the Microsoft implementation of CLR interoperates easily and efficiently with the COM infrastructure.

This section briefly reviews the main concepts of the COM infrastructure and its goals in order to show you how COM components can be consumed from F# (and vice versa) and how F# components can be exposed as COM components.

A COM component is a binary module with a well-defined interface that can be dynamically loaded at runtime by a running program. The COM design was influenced by CORBA and the Interface Definition Language (IDL) to describe a component as a set of interfaces. In the case of COM, however, components are always loaded inside the process using the dynamic loading of DLLs. Even when a component runs in a different process, a stub is loaded as a DLL, and it's responsible for interprocess communication.

---

[1] Languages targeting .NET aren't affected by these interoperability issues because they share the same CLR runtime.

When you create an instance of a COM component, you obtain a pointer to an IUnknown interface that acts as the entry point to all interfaces implemented by the component. The QueryInterface method of this interface allows you to get pointers to additional interfaces.

Interface pointers in COM are pointers to tables of pointers defining the method's location. The program must know the layout of the table in order to read the desired pointer and invoke the corresponding method. This knowledge can be compiled into the program (interfaces must be known at compile time) or acquired at runtime by accessing component metadata in the form of an interface named IDispatch or a database called *type library*.

Because COM components can be compiled by any compiler supporting the generation of memory layouts compatible with the standard, it's necessary for the client to share the same layout for data structures that must be passed or returned by the component methods. The standard type system for COM, defined in ole.dll, defines a simple and restricted set of types. COM types correspond to the Variant type of Visual Basic and provide only basic types and arrays. For structured types, COM requires a custom marshaller to be developed, but this has been rarely used in components that are widely available.

The COM infrastructure provides a memory manager that uses reference counting to automatically free components when they aren't used anymore. Whenever a copy of a pointer to an interface is copied, you must invoke the AddRef method of the IUnknown interface (every interface inherits from IUnknown); and when the pointer is no longer required, you should call the Release method to decrement the counter inside the component. When the counter reaches zero, the component is automatically freed. This strategy of memory management, although more automatic than the traditional malloc/free handling of the heap, has proven to be error prone, because programmers often forget to increment the counter when pointers are copied (risk of dangling pointers) or decrement when a pointer is no longer needed (risk of memory wasted in the garbage).

When Microsoft started developing the runtime that has become the CLR, which was destined to replace the COM infrastructure, several design goals addressed common issues of COM development:

- *Memory management*: Reference counting has proven to be error prone. A fully automated memory manager was needed to address this issue.

- *Pervasive metadata*: The COM type system was incomplete, and the custom marshaller was too restrictive. A more complete and general type system whose description was available at runtime would have eased interoperability.

- *Data and metadata separation*: The separation between data and metadata has proven to be fragile because components without their description are useless, and vice versa. A binary format containing both components and their descriptions avoids these issues.

- *Distributed components*: DCOM, the distributed COM infrastructure, has proven to be inefficient. The CLR was designed with a distributed memory management approach to reduce the network overhead required to keep remote components alive.

The need for a better component infrastructure led Microsoft to create the CLR, but the following concepts from COM proved so successful that they motivated several aspects of the CLR:

- *Binary interoperability*: The ability to interoperate at the binary level gives you the freedom to develop components from any language supporting the component infrastructure. For instance, Visual Basic developers can benefit from C++ components, and vice versa.

- *Dynamic loading*: The interactive dynamic loading of components is an essential element to allow scripting engines such as Visual Basic for Applications to access the component model.

- *Reflection*: The component description available at runtime allows programs to deal with unknown components. This is especially important for programs featuring scripting environments, as witnessed by the widespread use of IDispatch and type libraries in COM.

COM Metadata and the Windows Registry

COM components are compiled modules that conform to well-defined protocols designed to allow binary interoperability among different languages. An essential trait of component architectures is the ability to dynamically create components at runtime. It's necessary for an infrastructure to locate and inspect components in order to find and load them. The Windows registry holds this information, which is why it's such an important structure in the operating system.

The HKEY_CLASSES_ROOT registry key holds the definition of all the components installed on the local computer. It's helpful to understand the basic layout of the registry in this respect when you're dealing with COM components. The following is a simple script in JScript, executed[2] by the Windows Scripting Host, which is an interpreter used to execute Visual Basic and JScript scripts on Windows:

```
w = WScript.CreateObject("Word.Application");
w.Visible = true;
WScript.Echo("Press OK to close Word");
w.Quit();
```

This simple script creates an instance of a Microsoft Word application and shows its window programmatically by setting the Visible property to true. Assuming that the script is executed using the wscript command (the default), its execution is stopped until the message box displayed by the Echo method is closed, and then Word is closed.

How can the COM infrastructure dynamically locate the Word component and load it without prior knowledge about it? The COM infrastructure is accessed through the ubiquitous CreateObject method, which accepts as input a string containing the *program ID* of the COM component to be loaded. This is the human-readable name of the component; but the COM infrastructure was conceived as a foundation of a potentially large number of components and therefore adopted globally unique identifier (GUID) strings to define components. GUIDs are often displayed during software installation and are familiar for their mysterious syntax of a sequence of hexadecimal digits enclosed in curly braces. GUIDs are also used to identify COM classes; these IDs are known as CLSIDs and are stored in the Windows registry as subkeys containing further metadata about the COM object. When CreateObject is invoked, the code infrastructure looks for the key:

```
HKEY_CLASSES_ROOT\Word.Application\CLSID
```

The default value for the key in this example (on one of our computers) is as follows:

```
{000209FF-0000-0000-C000-000000000046}
```

Now, you can access the registry key defining the COM component and find all the information relative to the component. The following screenshot shows the content of the LocalServer32 subkey, which says

---

[2] To execute the script, save the text in a file with .js extension (for instance, StartWord.js) and then double-click the Windows Explorer icon.

that `winword.exe` is the container of the `Word.Application` component. If a COM component should be executed in a process different from that of the creator, `LocalServer32` contains the location of the executable. Components are often loaded in-process in the form of a DLL; in this case, the `InprocServer32` key indicates the location of the library.

To get a feel for the number of COM components installed on a Windows system, you can use a few lines of F# using `fsi.exe` as a shell:

```
> open Microsoft.Win32;;
> let k = Registry.ClassesRoot.OpenSubKey("CLSID");;
val k : RegistryKey
> k.GetSubKeyNames().Length;;
val it : int = 9237
> k.Close();;
val it : unit = ()
```

The registry is also responsible for storing information (that is, the metadata associated with COM components that describes their interfaces) about type libraries. Type libraries are also described using registry entries and identified by GUIDs available under the registry key:

```
HKEY_CLASSES_ROOT\TypeLib
```

COM components can be easily consumed from F# programs, and the opposite is also possible by exposing .NET objects as COM components. The following example is similar to the one discussed in the "COM Metadata and the Windows Registry" sidebar; it's based on the Windows Scripting Host but uses F# and `fsi.exe`:

```
> open System;;
> let o = Activator.CreateInstance(Type.GetTypeFromProgID("Word.Application"));;
val o : obj
> let t = o.GetType();;
val t : Type = System.__ComObject
> t.GetProperty("Visible").SetValue(o, (true :> Object), null);;
val it : unit  = ()
> let m = t.GetMethod("Quit");;
val m : Reflection.MethodInfo
> m.GetParameters().Length;;
val it : int = 3
> m.GetParameters();;
val it : ParameterInfo []
      = [|System.Object& SaveChanges
            {Attributes = In, Optional, HasFieldMarshal;
             DefaultValue = System.Reflection.Missing;
             IsIn = true;
             IsLcid = false;
             IsOptional = true;
             IsOut = false;
             IsRetval = false;
             Member =
                Void Quit(System.Object ByRef,
                            System.Object ByRef, System.Object ByRef);
             MetadataToken = 134223449;
             Name = "SaveChanges";
             ParameterType = System.Object&;
             Position = 0;
             RawDefaultValue = System.Reflection.Missing;};
          ... more ... |]
> m.Invoke(o, [| null; null; null |]);;
val it : obj = null
```

Because F# imposes type inference, you can't use the simple syntax provided by an interpreter. The compiler should know in advance the number and type of arguments of a method and the methods exposed by an object. Remember that even though fsi.exe allows you to interactively execute F# statements, it's still subject to the constraints of a compiled language. Because you're creating an instance of a COM component dynamically in this example, the compiler doesn't know anything about this component. Thus, it can be typed as System.Object. To obtain the same behavior as an interpreted language, you must resort to .NET runtime's reflection support. Using the GetType method, you can obtain an object describing the type of the object o. Then, you can obtain a PropertyInfo object describing the Visible property, and you can invoke the SetValue method on it to show the Word main window. The SetValue method is generic; therefore, you have to cast the Boolean value to System.Object to comply with the method signature.

In a similar way, you can obtain an instance of the MethodInfo class describing the Quit method. Because a method has a signature, you ask for the parameters; there are three of them, and they're optional. You can invoke the Quit method by calling the Invoke method and passing the object target of the invocation and an array of arguments that you set to null because arguments are optional.

■ **Note** Although COM technology is still widely used for obtaining so-called automation, .NET is quietly entering the picture, and several COM components are implemented using the CLR. Whenever a reference to `mscoree.dll` appears in the `InprocServer32` registry key, the .NET runtime is used to deliver the COM services using the specified assembly. Through COM interfaces, native and .NET components can be composed seamlessly, leading to very complex interactions between managed and unmanaged worlds. Microsoft Word 2010, for instance, returns a .NET object instead than a COM wrapper, which provides access to Word services without the need for explicit use of reflection.

How can the runtime interact with COM components? The basic approach is based on the *COM callable wrapper* (CCW) and the *runtime callable wrapper* (RCW), as shown in Figure 17-3. The former is a chunk of memory dynamically generated with a layout compatible with the one expected from COM components, so that external programs—even legacy Visual Basic 6 applications—can access services implemented as managed components. The latter is more common and creates a .NET type dealing with the COM component, taking care of all the interoperability issues. It's worth noting that although the CCW can always be generated because the .NET runtime has full knowledge about assemblies, the opposite isn't always possible. Without `IDispatch` or type libraries, there is no description of a COM component at runtime. Moreover, if a component uses custom marshalling, it can't be wrapped by an RCW. Fortunately, for the majority of COM components, it's possible to generate an RCW.

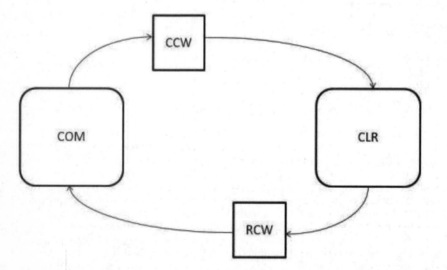

Figure 17-3. The wrappers generated by the CLR to interact with COM components

Programming patterns based on event-driven programming are widely adopted, and COM components have a programming pattern to implement callbacks based on the notion of a *sink*. The programming pattern is based on the delegate event model, and the sink is where a listener can register a COM interface that should be invoked by a component to notify an event. The Internet Explorer Web Browser COM component (implemented by shdocvw.dll), for instance, provides a number of events to notify its host about various events such as loading a page or clicking a hyperlink. The RCW generated by the runtime exposes these events in the form of delegates and takes care of handling all the details required to perform the communication between managed and unmanaged code.

Although COM components can be accessed dynamically using .NET reflection, explicitly relying on the ability of the CLR to generate CCW and RCW, it's desirable to use a less verbose approach to COM interoperability. The .NET runtime ships with tools that allow you to generate RCW and CCW wrappers offline, which lets you use COM components as .NET classes and vice versa. These tools are as follows:

- `tlbimp.exe`: This is a tool for generating an RCW of a COM component given its type library.

- `aximp.exe`: This is similar to `tlbimp.exe` and supports the generation of ActiveX components[3] that have graphical interfaces (and that need to be integrated with Windows Forms).

- `tlbexp.exe`: This generates a COM type library describing a .NET assembly. The CLR is loaded as a COM component and generates the appropriate CCW to make .NET types accessible as COM components.

- `regasm.exe`: This is similar to `tlbexp.exe`. It also performs the registration of the assembly as a COM component.

To better understand how COM components can be accessed from your F# programs and vice versa, let's consider two examples. In the first, you wrap the widely used Flash Player into a form interactively; and in the second, you see how an F# object type can be consumed as if it were a COM component.

The Flash Player you're accustomed to using in everyday browsing is an ActiveX control that is loaded by Internet Explorer using an `OBJECT` element in the HTML page (it's also a plug-in for other browsers, but here you're interested in the COM component). By using a search engine, you can easily find that an HTML element similar to the following is used to embed the player in Internet Explorer:

```
<OBJECT
      classid ="clsid:D27CDB6E-AE6D-11cf-96B8-444553540000"
      codebase="http://download.macromedia.com/pub/shockwave/cabs/flash/swflash.cab"
      width   ="640" height="480"
      title   ="My movie">
   <param name="movie"   value="MyMovie.swf" />
   <param name="quality" value="high" />
</OBJECT>
```

From this tag, you know that the CLSID of the Flash Player ActiveX component is the one specified with the `classid` parameter of the `OBJECT` element. You can now look in the Windows registry under `HKEY_CLASSES_ROOT\CLSID` for the subkey corresponding to the CLSID of the Flash ActiveX control. If you look at the subkeys, you notice that the `ProgID` of the component is `ShockwaveFlash.ShockwaveFlash`, and `InprocServer32` indicates that its location is `C:\Windows\system32\Macromed\Flash\Flash10d.ocx`. You can also find the GUID relative to the component type library—which, when investigated, shows that the type library is contained in the same OCX file.

---

[3] ActiveX components are COM components implementing a well-defined set of interfaces. They have a graphical interface. Internet Explorer is well known for loading these components, but ActiveX can be loaded by any application using the COM infrastructure.

■ **Note** With a 64-bit version of Windows and the 32-bit version of the Flash Player, you should look for the key CLSID under HKEY_CLASSES_ROOT\Wow6432Node, which is where the 32-bit component's information is stored. In general, all references to the 32-bit code are stored separately from the 64-bit information. The loader tricks old 32-bit code to see different portions of the registry. In addition, executable files are stored under %WinDir%\SysWow64 instead of %WinDir%\system32. Moreover, to wrap 32- or 64-bit components, you need the corresponding version of the .NET tool.

Because Flash Player is an ActiveX control with a GUI, you can rely on aximp.exe rather than just tlbimp.exe to generate the RCW for the COM component:

```
C:\> aximp c:\Windows\System32\Macromed\Flash\Flash10d.ocx
Generated Assembly: C:\ShockwaveFlashObjects.dll
Generated Assembly: C:\AxShockwaveFlashObjects.dll
```

If you use ildasm.exe to analyze the structure of the generated assemblies, notice that the wrapper of the COM component is contained in ShockwaveFlashObjects.dll and is generated by the tlbimp.exe tool. The second assembly contains a Windows Forms host for ActiveX components and is configured to host the COM component, exposing the GUI features in terms of the elements of the Windows Forms framework.

You can test the Flash Player embedded in an interactive F# session as follows:

```
> #I @"c:\";;
--> Added 'c:\ ' to library include path
> #r "AxShockwaveFlashObjects.dll";;
--> Referenced 'c:\AxShockwaveFlashObjects.dll'
> open AxShockwaveFlashObjects;;
> open System.Windows.Forms;;
> let f = new Form();;
val f : Form
> let flash = new AxShockwaveFlash();;
val flash : AxShockwaveFlash
Binding session to 'c:\AxShockwaveFlashObjects.dll'...
> f.Show();;
val it : unit = ()
> flash.Dock <- DockStyle.Fill;;
val it : unit = ()
> f.Controls.Add(flash);;
val it : unit = ()
> flash.LoadMovie(0, "http://laptop.org/img/meshDemo18.swf");;
val it : unit = ()
```

You first add to the include path of the fsi.exe directory containing the assemblies generated by aximp.exe using the #I directive, and then you reference the AxShockwaveFlashObjects.dll assembly using the #r directive. The namespace AxShockwaveFlashObjects containing the AxShockwaveFlash class is opened; this is the managed class wrapping the ActiveX control. You create an instance of the Flash Player that is now exposed as a Windows Forms control; then, you set the Dock property to DockStyle.Fill to let the control occupy the entire area of the form. Finally, you add the control to the form.

When you're typing the commands into F# Interactive, it's possible to test the content of the form. When it first appears, a right-click on the client area is ignored. After the ActiveX control is added to the form, the right-click displays the context menu of the Flash Player. You can now programmatically control the player by setting the properties and invoking its methods; the generated wrapper takes care of all the communications with the ActiveX component.

The Running Object Table

Sometimes you need to obtain a reference to an out-of-process COM object that is already running. This is useful when you want to automate some task of an already-started application or reuse an object model without needing to start a process more than once. The easiest way to achieve this is through the GetActiveObject method featured by the Marshal class:

```
#r "EnvDTE"
open System.Runtime.InteropServices
let appObj =Marshal.GetActiveObject("VisualStudio.DTE") :?> EnvDTE80.DTE2
printfn "%s" appObj.ActiveDocument.FullName
```

In this example, you obtain a reference to one of the most important interfaces of Visual Studio's COM automation model. An interesting experiment is to print the name of the active document open in the editor and try to run different instances of Visual Studio, opening different documents. The COM infrastructure connects to one instance of the COM server without being able to specify a particular one.

You can find a specific instance by accessing a system-wide data structure called the Running Object Table (ROT), which provides a list of running COM servers. Because the name of a running server must be unique within the ROT, many servers mangle the PID with the COM ProgID so it's possible to connect to a given instance; this is the case for Visual Studio. The following F# function connects to a specific Visual Studio instance:

```
#r "EnvDTE"
open System.Runtime.InteropServices
open System.Runtime.InteropServices.ComTypes

[<DllImport("ole32.dll")>]
extern int internal GetRunningObjectTable(uint32 reserved, IRunningObjectTable& pprot)

[<DllImport("ole32.dll")>]
extern int internal CreateBindCtx(uint32 reserved, IBindCtx& pctx)

let FetchVSDTE (pid:int) =
  let mutable (prot:IRunningObjectTable) = null
  let mutable (pmonkenum:IEnumMoniker) = null
  let (monikers:IMoniker[]) = Array.create 1 null
  let pfeteched = System.IntPtr.Zero
  let mutable (ret:obj) = null
  let endpid = sprintf ":%d" pid

  try
```

```
        if (GetRunningObjectTable(0u, &prot) <> 0) || (prot = null) then
            failwith "Error opening the ROT"
    prot.EnumRunning(&pmonkenum)
    pmonkenum.Reset()
    while pmonkenum.Next(1, monikers, pfeteched) = 0 do
      let mutable (insname:string) = null
      let mutable (pctx:IBindCtx) = null
      CreateBindCtx(0u, &pctx) |> ignore
      (monikers.[0]).GetDisplayName(pctx, null, &insname);
      Marshal.ReleaseComObject(pctx) |> ignore
      if insname.StartsWith("!VisualStudio.DTE") && insname.EndsWith(endpid) then
          prot.GetObject(monikers.[0], &ret) |> ignore
  finally
    if prot <> null then Marshal.ReleaseComObject(prot) |> ignore
    if pmonkenum <> null then Marshal.ReleaseComObject(pmonkenum) |> ignore
  (ret :?> EnvDTE.DTE)
```

You use two `PInvoke` declarations to import functions from the `ole.dll` COM library where the ROT is defined. After you get a reference to the table, you perform an enumeration of its elements, retrieving the display name and looking for any Visual Studio DTE with a specific PID at its end. The `GetObject` method is used to finally connect to the desired interface.

This example shows the flexible control .NET and F# can provide over COM infrastructure. The ability to access specific COM object instances is widely used on the server side to implement services made available through web pages.

Next, let's see an example of exposing an F# object type as a COM component. There are several reasons it can be useful to expose a managed class as a COM component, but perhaps the most important is interoperability with legacy systems. COM has been around for a decade and has permeated every aspect of Windows development. Systems have largely used COM infrastructures, and they can be extended using this technology. COM components are heavily used by applications based on the Active Scripting architecture, such as ASP and VBA in Microsoft Office. The ability to expose F# code to existing applications is useful because it allows you to immediately start using this new language and integrate it seamlessly into existing systems.

■ **Note** Version 4 of CLR introduced a new set of tools for .NET. You must pay attention to which version you're using. If you compile an assembly targeting a framework older than version 4, use the tools located in the directory `C:\Program Files (x86)\Microsoft SDKs\Windows\v7.0A\Bin`. Otherwise, use the tools in `C:\Program Files (x86)\Microsoft SDKs\Windows\v7.0A\Bin\NETFX 4.0 Tools`.

Suppose you're exposing a simple F# object type as a COM component, and you invoke a method of this object type from a JScript script. You define the following type in the `hwfs.fs` file:

```
namespace HelloWorld

open System

type FSCOMComponent() =
    member x.HelloWorld() = "Hello world from F#!"
```

The assembly that must be exposed as a COM component should be added to the global assembly cache (GAC), which is where shared .NET assemblies are stored. Assemblies present in the GAC must be strongly named, which means a public key cryptographic signature must be used to certify the assembly. To perform the test, you generate a key pair to be used to sign the assembly using the sn.exe command available with the .NET SDK:

```
C:> sn -k testkey.snk

Microsoft (R) .NET Framework Strong Name Utility  Version 4.0.30319.1
Copyright (c) Microsoft Corporation.  All rights reserved.

Key pair written to testkey.snk
```

You can compile the program in a DLL called hwfs.dll:

```
C:\> fsc -a --keyfile:testkey.snk hwfs.fs
```

Note that you use the --keyfile switch to indicate to the compiler that the output should be signed using the specified key pair. Now, you can add the assembly to the GAC (note that under Windows Vista and 7, the shell used should run with administrator privileges):

```
C:\ > gacutil /i hwfs.dll
Microsoft (R) .NET Global Assembly Cache Utility.  Version 4.0.30319.1
Copyright (c) Microsoft Corporation.  All rights reserved.

Assembly successfully added to the cache
```

Use the regasm.exe tool to register the hwfs.dll assembly as a COM component:

```
C:\ > regasm hwfs.dll
Microsoft (R) .NET Framework Assembly Registration Utility 4.0.30319.1
Copyright (C) Microsoft Corporation 1998-2004.  All rights reserved.

Types registered successfully
```

Next, you must write the script using the JScript language to test the component. The script uses the CreateObject method to create an instance of the F# object type, with the CCW generated by the CLR taking care of all the interoperability issues. But what is the ProgID of the COM component? You use regasm.exe with the /regfile switch to generate a registry file containing the keys corresponding to the registration of the COM component instead of performing it. The generated registry file contains the following component registration (we've included only the most relevant entries):

```
[HKEY_CLASSES_ROOT\HelloWorld.FSCOMComponent]
@="HelloWorld.FSCOMComponent"
[HKEY_CLASSES_ROOT\HelloWorld.FSCOMComponent\CLSID]
@="{30094EBA-CDCB-3C57-9297-49C724421ACB}"
[HKEY_CLASSES_ROOT\CLSID\{30094EBA-CDCB-3C57-9297-49C724421ACB}]
```

```
@="HelloWorld.FSCOMComponent"
[HKEY_CLASSES_ROOT\CLSID\{30094EBA-CDCB-3C57-9297-49C724421ACB}\InprocServer32]
@="mscoree.dll"
"ThreadingModel"="Both"
"Class"="HelloWorld.FSCOMComponent"
"Assembly"="hwfs, Version=0.0.0.0, Culture=neutral, PublicKeyToken=d25287aa2b2b0de6"
"RuntimeVersion"="v4.0.30319"
```

The InprocServer32 subkey indicates that the COM component is implemented by mscoree.dll, which is the CLR. The additional attributes indicate the assembly that should be run by the runtime.

Note that the ProgID and the class name of the component are HelloWorld.FSCOMComponent. You can now write the following script in the hwfs.js file:

```
o = WScript.CreateObject("HelloWorld.FSCOMComponent");
WScript.Echo(o.HelloWorld());
```

If you execute the script (here using the command-based host cscript), you obtain the expected output:

```
C:\ > cscript foo.js
Microsoft (R) Windows Script Host Version 5.8
Copyright (C) Microsoft Corporation. All rights reserved.

Hello world from F#!
```

Using the fully qualified .NET name to name a COM component isn't always a good idea. Names are important, especially in a component infrastructure, because they're used for long time. So far, you've used only the basic features of COM interoperability, but a number of custom attributes can give you finer control over the CCW generation. These attributes are defined in the System.Runtime.InteropServices namespace; and among these classes you find the ProgIdAttribute class, whose name hints that it's related to the ProgID. You can annotate your F# object type using this attribute:

```
namespace HelloWorld

open System
open System.Runtime.InteropServices

[<ProgId("Hwfs.FSComponent")>]
type FSCOMComponent() =
    member x.HelloWorld() = "Hello world from F#!"
```

First, unregister the previous component:

```
C:\> regasm hwfs.dll /unregister
Microsoft (R) .NET Framework Assembly Registration Utility 4.0.30319.1
Copyright (C) Microsoft Corporation 1998-2004.  All rights reserved.

Types un-registered successfully
C:\> gacutil /u hwfs
Microsoft (R) .NET Global Assembly Cache Utility.  Version 4.0.30319.1
```

Now you can update the script as follows and register everything again after recompiling the F# file:

```
o = WScript.CreateObject("Hwfs.FSComponent");
WScript.Echo(o.HelloWorld());
```

Using other attributes, it's possible to specify the GUIDs to be used and several other aspects that are important in some situations. When a system expects a component implementing a given COM interface, the COM component is expected to return the pointer to the interface with the appropriate GUID. In this case, the ability to explicitly indicate a GUID is essential to defining a .NET interface that should be marshalled as the intended COM interface.

Complex COM components can be tricky to wrap using these tools, and official wrappers are maintained by component developers. Microsoft provides the managed version of the Office components, the managed DirectX library, and the Web Browser control to spare programmers from having to build their own wrappers.

In conclusion, it's possible to use COM components from F# and vice versa. You can expose F# libraries as COM components, which allows you to extend existing systems using F# or use legacy code in F# programs.

Platform Invoke

COM interoperability is an important area in F#, but it's limited to Windows and to the Microsoft implementation of the ECMA and ISO standards of the Common Language Infrastructure (CLI). The CLI standard, however, devises a standard mechanism for interoperability that is called Platform Invoke (PInvoke to friends); it's a core feature of the standard available on all CLI implementations, including Mono.

The basic model underlying PInvoke is based on loading DLLs into the program, which allows managed code to invoke exported functions. DLLs don't provide information other than the entry point location of a function; this isn't enough to perform the invocation unless additional information is made available to the runtime.

The invocation of a function requires the following:

- The address of the code in memory

- The calling convention, which is how parameters, return values, and other information are passed through the stack to the function

- Marshalling of values and pointers so that the different runtime support can operate consistently on the same values

You obtain the address of the entry point using a system call that returns the pointer to the function given a string. You must provide the remaining information to instruct the CLR about how the function pointer should be used.

Calling Conventions

Function and method calls (a method call is similar to a function call but with an additional pointer referring to the object passed to the method) are performed by using a shared stack between the caller and the callee. An activation record is pushed onto the stack when the function is called, and memory is allocated for arguments, the return value, and local variables. Additional information is also stored in the activation record, such as information about exception handling and the return address when the execution of the function terminates.

The physical structure of the activation record is established by the compiler (or by the JIT in the case of the CLR), and this knowledge must be shared between the caller and the called function. When the binary code is generated by a compiler, this isn't an issue; but when code generated by different compilers must interact, it may become a significant issue. Although each compiler may adopt a different convention, the need to perform system calls requires that the calling convention adopted by the operating system is implemented, and it's often used to interact with different runtimes. Another popular approach is to support the calling convention adopted by C compilers, because it's widely used and has become a fairly universal language for interoperability. Note that although many operating systems are implemented in C, the libraries providing system calls may adopt different calling conventions. This is the case with Microsoft Windows: the operating system adopts the *stdcall* calling convention rather than *cdecl*, which is the C calling convention.

A significant dimension in the arena of possible calling conventions is the responsibility for removing the activation record from the thread stack. At first glance, it may seem obvious that before returning, the called function resets the stack pointer to the previous state. This isn't the case for programming languages such as C that allow functions with a variable number of arguments, such as `printf`. When variable arguments are allowed, the caller knows the exact size of the activation record; therefore, it's the caller's responsibility to free the stack at the end of the function call. Apart from being consistent with the chosen convention, there may seem to be little difference between the two choices; but if the caller is responsible for cleaning the stack, each function invocation requires more instructions, which leads to larger executables. For this reason, Windows uses the stdcall calling convention instead of the C calling convention. It's important to notice that the CLR uses an array of objects to pass a variable number of arguments, which is very different from the variable arguments of C: the method receives a single pointer to the array that resides in the heap.

It's important to note that if the memory layout of the activation record is compatible, as it is in Windows, using the cdecl convention instead of the stdcall convention leads to a subtle memory leak. If the runtime assumes the stdcall convention (which is the default), and the callee assumes the cdecl convention, the arguments pushed on the stack aren't freed, and at each invocation the height of the stack grows until a stack overflow happens.

The CLR supports a number of calling conventions. The two most important are stdcall and cdecl. Other implementations of the runtime may provide additional conventions to the user. In the PInvoke design, nothing restricts the supported conventions to these two (and in fact the runtime uses the *fcall* convention to invoke services provided by the runtime from managed code).

The additional information required to perform the function call is provided by custom attributes that are used to decorate a function prototype and inform the runtime about the signature of the exported function.

Getting Started with PInvoke

This section starts with a simple example of a DLL developed using C++, to which you add code during your experiments using PInvoke. The CInteropDLL.h header file declares a macro defining the decorations associated with each exported function:

```
#define CINTEROPDLL_API __declspec(dllexport)
extern "C" {
void CINTEROPDLL_API HelloWorld();
}
```

The __declspec directive is specific to the Microsoft Visual C++ compiler. Other compilers may provide different ways to indicate the functions that must be exported when compiling a DLL.

The first function is HelloWorld; its definition is as expected:

```
void CINTEROPDLL_API HelloWorld()
{
    printf("Hello C world invoked by F#!\n");
}
```

Say you now want to invoke the HelloWorld function from an F# program. You have to define the prototype of the function and inform the runtime how to access the DLL and the other information needed to perform the invocation. The program performing the invocation is the following:

```
open System.Runtime.InteropServices

module CInterop =
    [<DllImport("CInteropDLL", CallingConvention=CallingConvention.Cdecl)>]
    extern void HelloWorld()

CInterop.HelloWorld()
```

The extern keyword informs the compiler that the function definition is external to the program and must be accessed through the PInvoke interface. A C-style prototype definition follows the keyword, and the whole declaration is annotated with a custom attribute defined in the System.Runtime.InteropServices namespace. The F# compiler adopts C-style syntax for extern prototypes, including argument types (as you see later), because C headers and prototypes are widely used; this choice helps in the PInvoke definition. The DllImport custom attribute provides the information needed to perform the invocation. The first argument is the name of the DLL containing the function; the remaining option specifies the calling convention chosen to make the call. Because you don't specify otherwise, the runtime assumes that the name of the F# function is the same as the name of the entry point in the DLL. It's possible to override this behavior using the EntryPoint parameter in the DllImport attribute.

It's important to note the declarative approach of the PInvoke interface. No code is involved in accessing external functions. The runtime interprets metadata in order to automatically interoperate with native code contained in a DLL. This is a different approach from the one adopted by different virtual machines, such as the Java virtual machine. The Java Native Interface (JNI) requires that you define a layer of code using types of the virtual machine and invoke the native code.

PInvoke requires high privileges in order to execute native code, because the activation record of the native function is allocated on the same stack containing the activation records of managed functions and methods. Moreover, as discussed shortly, it's also possible to have the native code invoking a delegate marshalled as a function pointer, allowing stacks with native and managed activation records to be interleaved.

The HelloWorld function is a simple case because the function doesn't have input arguments and doesn't return any value. Consider this function with input arguments and a return value:

```
int CINTEROPDLL_API Sum(int i, int j)
{
    return i + j;
}
```

Invoking the Sum function requires integer values to be marshalled to the native code and the value returned to managed code. Simple types such as integers are easy to marshal because they're usually passed by value and use types of the underlying architecture. The F# program using the Sum function is as follows:

```
module CInterop =
    [<DllImport("CInteropDLL", CallingConvention=CallingConvention.Cdecl)>]
    extern int Sum(int i, int j)

printf "Sum(1, 1) = %d\n" (CInterop.Sum(1, 1));
```

Parameter passing assumes the same semantics of the CLR, and parameters are passed by value for value types and by the value of the reference for reference types. Again, you use the custom attribute to specify the calling convention for the invocation.

Data Structures

Let's first cover what happens when structured data is marshalled by the CLR in the case of nontrivial argument types. Here you see the SumC function responsible for adding two complex numbers defined by the Complex C data structure:

```
typedef struct _Complex {
    double re;
    double im;
} Complex;

Complex CINTEROPDLL_API SumC(Complex c1, Complex c2)
{
    Complex ret;
    ret.re = c1.re + c2.re;
    ret.im = c1.im + c2.im;
    return ret;
}
```

To invoke this function from F#, you must define a data structure in F# corresponding to the Complex C structure. If the memory layout of an instance of the F# structure is the same as that of the corresponding C structure, then values can be shared between the two languages. But how can you control the memory layout of a managed data structure? Fortunately, the PInvoke specification helps with custom attributes that let you specify the memory layout of data structures. The StructLayout custom attribute indicates the strategy adopted by the runtime to lay out fields of the data structure. By default, the runtime adopts its own strategy in an attempt to optimize the size of the structure, keeping fields aligned to the machine world in order to ensure fast access to the structure's fields. The C standard ensures that fields are laid out in memory sequentially in the order they appear in the structure definition; other languages may use different strategies. Using an appropriate argument, you can indicate that a C-like sequential layout strategy should be adopted. It's also possible to provide an explicit layout for the structure, indicating the offset in memory for each field of the structure. This example uses the sequential layout for the Complex value type:

```
module CInterop =
    [<Struct; StructLayout(LayoutKind.Sequential)>]
    type Complex =
        val mutable re:double
        val mutable im:double

        new(r,i) = { re = r; im = i; }

    [<DllImport("CInteropDLL")>]
    extern Complex SumC(Complex c1, Complex c2)

let c1 = CInterop.Complex(1.0, 0.0)
let c2 = CInterop.Complex(0.0, 1.0)

let mutable c3 = CInterop.SumC(c1, c2)
printf "c3 = SumC(c1, c2) = %f + %fi\n" c3.re c3.im;
```

The SumC prototype refers to the F# Complex value type. But because the layout of the structure in memory is the same as the corresponding C structure, the runtime passes the bits that are consistent with those expected by the C code.

Marshalling Parameters

A critical aspect of dealing with PInvoke is ensuring that values are marshalled correctly between managed and native code and vice versa. A structure's memory layout doesn't depend only on the order of the fields. Compilers often introduce padding to align fields to memory addresses so that access to fields requires fewer memory operations, because CPUs load data into registers with the same strategy. Padding may speed up access to the data structure, but it introduces inefficiencies in memory usage: there may be gaps in the structures, leading to allocated but unused memory.

Consider, for instance, the following C structure:

```
struct Foo {
    int i;
    char c;
    short s;
};
```

Depending on the compiler decision, it may occupy from 8 to 12 bytes on a 32-bit architecture. The most compact version of the structure uses the first 4 bytes for i, a single byte for c, and 2 more bytes for s. If the compiler aligns fields to addresses that are multiples of 4, then the integer i occupies the first slot, 4 more bytes are allocated for c (although only one is used), and the same happens for s.

Padding is a common practice in C programs; because it may affect performance and memory usage, directives instruct the compiler about padding. It's possible to have data structures with different padding strategies running within the same program.

The first step you face when using PInvoke to access native code is finding the definition of data structures, including information about padding. Then, you can annotate F# structures to have the same layout as the native ones, and the CLR can automate the marshalling of data. Note that you can pass parameters by reference; thus, the C code may access the memory managed by the runtime, and errors in memory layout may result in corrupted memory. For this reason, you should keep PInvoke code to a minimum and verify it accurately to ensure that the execution state of the virtual machine is preserved. The declarative nature of the interface is a great help in this respect because you must check declarations and not interop code.

Not all the values are marshalled as is to native code; some values may require additional work from the runtime. Strings, for instance, have different memory representations between native and managed code. C strings are arrays of bytes that are null terminated, whereas runtime strings are .NET objects with a different layout. Also, function pointers are mediated by the runtime: the calling convention adopted by the CLR isn't compatible with external conventions, so code stubs are generated that can be called by native code from managed code and vice versa.

In the SumC example, arguments are passed by value, but native code often requires data structures to be passed by reference to avoid the cost of copying the entire structure and passing only a pointer to the native data. The ZeroC function resets a complex number whose pointer is passed as an argument:

```
void CINTEROPDLL_API ZeroC(Complex* c)
{
    c->re = 0;
    c->im = 0;
}
```

The F# declaration for the function is the same as the C prototype:

```
[<DllImport("CInteropDLL")>]
extern void ZeroC(Complex* c)
```

Now you need a way to obtain a pointer given a value of type Complex in F#. You can use the && operator to indicate a pass by reference; this results in passing the pointer to the structure expected by the C function:

```
let mutable c4 = CInterop.SumC(c1, c2)
printf "c4 = SumC(c1, c2) = %f + %fi\n" c4.re c4.im

CInterop.ZeroC(&&c4)
printf "c4 = %f + %fi\n" c4.re c4.im
```

In C and C++, the notion of objects (or struct instances) and the classes of memory are orthogonal: an object can be allocated on the stack or on the heap and share the same declaration. In .NET, this isn't the case; objects are instances of classes and are allocated on the heap, and value types are stored in the stack or wrapped into objects in the heap.

Is it possible to pass objects to native functions through PInvoke? The main issue with objects is that the heap is managed by the garbage collector, and one possible strategy for garbage collection is *copy collection* (a technique that moves objects in the heap when a collection occurs). Thus, the base address in memory of an object may change over time, which can be a serious problem if the pointer to the object has been marshalled to a native function through a PInvoke invocation. The CLR provides an operation called *pinning* that prevents an object from moving during garbage collection. Pinned pointers are assigned to local variables, and pinning is released when the function performing the pinning exits. It's important to understand the scope of pinning: if the native code stores the pointer somewhere before returning, the pointer may become invalid but still usable from native code.

Now, let's define an object type for Complex and marshal F# objects to a C function. The goal is to marshal the F# object to the ZeroC function. In this case, you can't use the pass-by-reference operator, and you must define everything so that the type checker is happy. You can define another function that refers to ZeroC but with a different signature involving ObjComplex, which is an object type similar to the Complex value type. The EntryPoint parameter maps the F# function onto the same ZeroC C function, although in this case the argument is of type ObjComplex rather than Complex:

```
module CInterop =
    [<StructLayout(LayoutKind.Sequential)>]
    type ObjComplex =
        val mutable re:double
        val mutable im:double

        new() as x = { re = 0.0; im = 0.0 }
        new(r:double, i:double) as x = { re = r; im = i }

    [<DllImport("CInteropDLL", EntryPoint="ZeroC")>]
    extern void ObjZeroC(ObjComplex c)

let oc = CInterop.ObjComplex(2.0, 1.0)
printf "oc = %f + %fi\n" oc.re oc.im
CInterop.ObjZeroC(oc)
printf "oc = %f + %fi\n" oc.re oc.im
```

In this case, the object reference is marshalled as a pointer to the C code, and you don't need the && operator in order to call the function. The object is pinned to ensure that it doesn't move during the function call.

Marshalling Strings

PInvoke defines the default behavior for mapping common types used by the Win32 API. Table 17-1 shows the default conversions. Most of the mappings are natural, but note that there are several entries for strings. This is because strings are represented in different ways in programming language runtimes.

Table 17-1. Default Mapping for Types of the Win32 API Listed in Wtypes.h

Unmanaged Type in Wtypes.h	Unmanaged C Type	Managed Class	Description
HANDLE	void*	System.IntPtr	32 bits on 32-bit Windows operating systems, 64 bits on 64-bit Windows operating systems
BYTE	unsigned char	System.Byte	8 bits
SHORT	short	System.Int16	16 bits

Unmanaged Type in Wtypes.h	Unmanaged C Type	Managed Class	Description
WORD	unsigned short	System.UInt16	16 bits
INT	int	System.Int32	32 bits
UINT	unsigned int	System.UInt32	32 bits
LONG	long	System.Int32	32 bits
BOOL	long	System.Int32	32 bits
DWORD	unsigned long	System.UInt32	32 bits
ULONG	unsigned long	System.UInt32	32 bits
CHAR	char	System.Char	Decorate with ANSI
LPSTR	char*	System.String or System.Text.StringBuilder	Decorate with ANSI
LPCSTR	const char*	System.String or System.Text.StringBuilder	Decorate with ANSI
LPWSTR	wchar_t*	System.String or System.Text.StringBuilder	Decorate with Unicode
LPCWSTR	const wchar_t*	System.String or System.Text.StringBuilder	Decorate with Unicode
FLOAT	Float	System.Single	32 bits
DOUBLE	Double	System.Double	64 bits

To see how strings are marshalled, start with a simple C function that echoes a string on the console:

```
void CINTEROPDLL_API echo(char* str)
{
    puts(str);
}
```

The corresponding F# PInvoke prototype is as follows:

```
[<DllImport("CInteropDLL", CallingConvention=CallingConvention.Cdecl)>]
extern void echo(string s);
```

What happens when the F# function echo is invoked? The managed string is represented by an array of Unicode characters described by an object in the heap; the C function expects a pointer to an array of single-byte ANSI characters that are null terminated. The runtime is responsible for performing the conversion between the two formats, and it's performed by default when mapping a .NET string to an ANSI C string.

It's common to pass strings that are modified by C functions, yet .NET strings are immutable. For this reason, it's also possible to use a System.Text.StringBuilder object instead of a string. Instances of this class represent mutable strings and have an associated buffer containing the characters of the string. You can write a C function in the DLL that fills a string buffer given the size of the buffer:

```
void CINTEROPDLL_API sayhello(char* str, int sz)
{
    static char* data = "Hello from C code!";
    int len = min(sz, strlen(data));
    strncpy(str, data, len);
    str[len] = 0;
}
```

Because the function writes into the string buffer passed as an argument, you must take care and use a StringBuilder rather than a string to ensure that the buffer has the appropriate room for the function to write. You can use the following F# PInvoke prototype:

```
[<DllImport("CInteropDLL", CallingConvention=CallingConvention.Cdecl)>]
extern void sayhello(StringBuilder sb, int sz);
```

Because you have to indicate the size of the buffer, you can use a constructor of the StringBuilder class that allows you to do so:

```
let sb = new StringBuilder(50)
```

```
CInterop.sayhello(sb, 50)
printf "%s\n" (sb.ToString())
```

You've used ANSI C strings so far, but this isn't the only type of string. Wide-character strings are becoming widely adopted and use 2 bytes to represent a single character; following the C tradition, the string is terminated by a null character. Consider a wide-character version of the sayhello function:

```
void CINTEROPDLL_API sayhellow(wchar_t* str, int sz)
{
    static wchar_t* data = L"Hello from C code Wide!";
    int len = min(sz, wcslen(data));
    wcsncpy(str, data, len);
    str[len] = 0;
}
```

How can you instruct the runtime that the StringBuilder should be marshalled as a wide-character string rather than an ANSI string? The declarative nature of PInvoke helps by providing a custom attribute to annotate function parameters of the prototype and to inform the CLR about the marshalling strategy to be adopted. The sayhellow function is declared in F# as follows:

```
[<DllImport("CInteropDLL", CallingConvention=CallingConvention.Cdecl)>]
extern void sayhellow([<MarshalAs(UnmanagedType.LPWStr)>]StringBuilder sb, int sz);
```

In this case, the MarshalAs attribute indicates that the string should be marshalled as LPWSTR rather than LPSTR.

Function Pointers

Another important data type that often should be passed to native code is a function pointer. Function pointers are widely used to implement callbacks and provide a simple form of functional programming; think for instance of a sort function that receives as input the pointer to the comparison function. Graphical toolkits have widely used this data type to implement event-driven programming, and they often have to pass a function that is invoked by another one.

PInvoke can marshal delegates as function pointers; again, the runtime is responsible for generating a suitable function pointer callable from native code. When the marshalled function pointer is invoked, a stub is called, and the activation record on the stack is rearranged to be compatible with the calling convention of the runtime. Then, the delegate function is invoked.

Although in principle the generated stub is responsible for implementing the calling convention adopted by the native code receiving the function pointer, the CLR supports only the stdcall calling convention for marshalling function pointers. Thus, the native code should adopt this calling convention when invoking the pointer; this restriction may cause problems, but in general on the Windows platform the stdcall calling convention is widely used.

The following C function uses a function pointer to apply a function to an array of integers:

```
typedef int (CALLBACK *TRANSFORM_CALLBACK)(int);

void CINTEROPDLL_API transformArray(int* data, int count, TRANSFORM_CALLBACK fn)
{
    int i;
    for (i = 0; i < count; i++)
        data[i] = fn(data[i]);
}
```

The TRANSFORM_CALLBACK type definition defines the prototype of the function pointer you're interested in here: a function taking an integer as the input argument and returning an integer as a result. The CALLBACK macro is specific to the Microsoft Visual C++ compiler and expands to __stdcall in order to indicate that the function pointer, when invoked, should adopt the stdcall calling convention instead of the cdecl calling convention.

The transformArray function takes as input an array of integers with its length and the function to apply to its elements. You now have to define the F# prototype for this function by introducing a delegate type with the same signature as TRANSFORM_CALLBACK:

```
type Callback = delegate of int -> int

[<DllImport("CInteropDLL", CallingConvention=CallingConvention.Cdecl)>]
extern void transformArray(int[] data, int count, Callback transform);
```

Now, you can increment all the elements of an array by using the C function:

```
let data = [| 1; 2; 3 |]
printf "%s\n" (string.Join("; ", (Array.map any_to_string data)))

CInterop.transformArray(data, data.Length, new CInterop.Callback(fun x -> x + 1))
printf "%s\n" (string.Join("; ", (Array.map any_to_string data)))
```

PInvoke declarations are concise, but you must pay attention to the fact that for data types such as function pointers, parameter passing can be expensive. In general, libraries assume that crossing the language boundary causes a loss of efficiency and callbacks are invoked at a price different from ordinary functions. In this respect, the example represents a situation where the overhead of PInvoke is significant: a single call to transformArray causes a number of callbacks without performing any real computation into the native code.

PInvoke Memory Mapping

As a more complicated example of PInvoke usage, this section shows you how to benefit from memory mapping into F# programs. Memory mapping is a popular technique that allows a program to see a file (or a portion of a file) as if it was in memory. This provides an efficient way to access files, because the operating system uses the machinery of virtual memory to access files and significantly speed up data access on files. After proper initialization, which is covered in a moment, the program obtains a pointer into the memory, and access to that portion of memory appears the same as accessing data stored into the file.

You can use memory mapping to both read and write files. Every access performed to memory is reflected in the corresponding position in the file.

This is a typical sequence of system calls in order to map a file into memory:

1. A call to the CreateFile system call to open the file and obtain a handle to the file.

2. A call to the CreateFileMapping system call to create a mapped file object.

3. One or more calls to MapViewOfFile and UnmapViewOfFile to map and release portions of a file into memory. In a typical usage, the whole file is mapped at once in memory.

4. A call to CloseHandle to release the file.

The PInvoke interface to the required functions involves simple type mappings as is usual for Win32 API functions. All the functions are in kernel32.dll, and the signature can be found in the Windows SDK. Listing 17-1 contains the definition of the F# wrapper for memory mapping.

The SetLastError parameter informs the runtime that the called function uses the Windows mechanism for error reporting and that the GetLastError function can be read in case of error; otherwise, the CLR ignores such a value. The CharSet parameter indicates the character set assumed, and it's used to distinguish between ANSI and Unicode characters; with Auto, you delegate the runtime to decide the appropriate version.

You can define the generic class MemMap that uses the functions to map a given file into memory. The goal of the class is to provide access to memory mapping in a system where memory isn't directly accessible because the runtime is responsible for its management. A natural programming abstraction to expose the memory to F# code is to provide an array-like interface where the memory is seen as a homogeneous array of values.

Listing 17-1. Exposing Memory Mapping in F#

```
module MMap =

    open System
    open System.IO
    open System.Runtime.InteropServices
    open Microsoft.FSharp.NativeInterop
    open Printf
```

```
type HANDLE = nativeint
type ADDR   = nativeint

[<DllImport("kernel32", SetLastError=true)>]
extern bool CloseHandle(HANDLE handler)

[<DllImport("kernel32", SetLastError=true, CharSet=CharSet.Auto)>]
extern HANDLE CreateFile(string lpFileName,
                         int dwDesiredAccess,
                         int dwShareMode,
                         HANDLE lpSecurityAttributes,
                         int dwCreationDisposition,
                         int dwFlagsAndAttributes,
                         HANDLE hTemplateFile)

[<DllImport("kernel32", SetLastError=true, CharSet=CharSet.Auto)>]
extern HANDLE CreateFileMapping(HANDLE hFile,
                                HANDLE lpAttributes,
                                int flProtect,
                                int dwMaximumSizeLow,
                                int dwMaximumSizeHigh,
                                string lpName)

[<DllImport("kernel32", SetLastError=true)>]
extern ADDR MapViewOfFile(HANDLE hFileMappingObject,
                          int dwDesiredAccess,
                          int dwFileOffsetHigh,
                          int dwFileOffsetLow,
                          int dwNumBytesToMap)

[<DllImport("kernel32", SetLastError=true, CharSet=CharSet.Auto)>]
extern HANDLE OpenFileMapping(int dwDesiredAccess,
                              bool bInheritHandle,
                              string lpName)

[<DllImport("kernel32", SetLastError=true)>]
extern bool UnmapViewOfFile(ADDR lpBaseAddress)

let INVALID_HANDLE = new IntPtr(-1)
let MAP_READ     = 0x0004
let GENERIC_READ = 0x80000000
let NULL_HANDLE = IntPtr.Zero
let FILE_SHARE_NONE = 0x0000
let FILE_SHARE_READ = 0x0001
let FILE_SHARE_WRITE = 0x0002
let FILE_SHARE_READ_WRITE = 0x0003
let CREATE_ALWAYS  = 0x0002
let OPEN_EXISTING   = 0x0003
let OPEN_ALWAYS  = 0x0004
let READONLY = 0x00000002

type MemMap<'a> (fileName) =
```

```
let ok =
    match typeof<'a>) with
    | ty when ty = typeof<int>)      -> true
    | ty when ty = typeof<int32>)    -> true
    | ty when ty = typeof<byte>)     -> true
    | ty when ty = typeof<sbyte>)    -> true
    | ty when ty = typeof<int16>)    -> true
    | ty when ty = typeof<uint16>)   -> true
    | ty when ty = typeof<int64>)    -> true
    | ty when ty = typeof<uint64>)   -> true
    | _ -> false

do if not ok then failwithf
   "the type %s is not a basic blittable type" ((typeof<'a>).ToString())
let hFile =
    CreateFile (fileName,
                GENERIC_READ,
                FILE_SHARE_READ_WRITE,
                IntPtr.Zero, OPEN_EXISTING, 0, IntPtr.Zero  )
do if ( hFile.Equals(INVALID_HANDLE) ) then
    Marshal.ThrowExceptionForHR(Marshal.GetHRForLastWin32Error());
let hMap = CreateFileMapping (hFile, IntPtr.Zero, READONLY, 0,0, null )
do CloseHandle(hFile) |> ignore
do if hMap.Equals(NULL_HANDLE) then
    Marshal.ThrowExceptionForHR(Marshal.GetHRForLastWin32Error());

let start = MapViewOfFile (hMap, MAP_READ,0,0,0)

do  if ( start.Equals(IntPtr.Zero) ) then
      Marshal.ThrowExceptionForHR(
          Marshal.GetHRForLastWin32Error())


member m.AddressOf(i: int) : 'a nativeptr  =
    NativePtr.of_nativeint(start + (nativeint i))

member m.GetBaseAddress (i:int) : int -> 'a =
    NativePtr.get (m.AddressOf(i))

member m.Item
    with get(i : int) : 'a = m.GetBaseAddress 0 i

member m.Close() =
   UnmapViewOfFile(start) |> ignore;
   CloseHandle(hMap) |> ignore

interface IDisposable with
  member m.Dispose() =
    m.Close()
```

The class exposes two properties: Item and Element. The former returns a function that allows access to data in the mapped file at a given offset using a function; the latter allows access to the mapped file at a given offset from the origin.

The following example uses the MemMap class to read the first byte of a file:

```
let mm = new MMap.MemMap<byte>("somefile.txt")

printf "%A\n" (mm.[0])

mm.Close()
```

Memory mapping provides good examples of how easy it can be to expose native functionalities into the .NET runtime and how F# can be effective in this task. It's also a good example of the right way to use PInvoke to avoid calling PInvoked functions directly and build wrappers that encapsulate them. Verifiable code is one of the greatest benefits provided by virtual machines, and PInvoke signatures often lead to nonverifiable code that requires high execution privileges and risks corrupting the runtime's memory.

A good approach to reduce the amount of potentially unsafe code is to define assemblies that are responsible for accessing native code with PInvoke and that expose functionalities in a .NET verifiable approach. This way, the code that should be trusted by the user is smaller, and programs can have all the benefits provided by verified code.

Wrapper Generation and Limits of PInvoke

PInvoke is a flexible and customizable interface, and it's expressive enough to define prototypes for most libraries available. However, in some situations it can be difficult to map directly the native interface into the corresponding signature. A significant example is function pointers embedded into structures, which are typical C programming patterns that approximate object-oriented programming. Here, the structure contains a number of pointers to functions that can be used as methods; but you must take care to pass the pointer to the structure as the first argument to simulate the this parameter. Oracle's Berkeley Database (BDB) is a popular database library that adopts this programming pattern. The core structure describing an open database is as follows:

```
struct __db {
        /* ... */
        DB_ENV *dbenv;                  /* Backing environment. */
        DBTYPE type;                    /* DB access method type. */
        /* ... */
        int  (*close)  __P((DB *, u_int32_t));
        int  (*cursor) __P((DB *, DB_TXN *, DBC **, u_int32_t));
        int  (*del)  __P((DB *, DB_TXN *, DBT *, u_int32_t));
        // ...
}
```

This was impossible to access directly from the PInvoke interface until .NET 2.0, because function pointers in managed structures were impossible to describe. With version 2 of the runtime, the System.Runtime.InteropServices.Marshal class features the GetFunctionPointerForDelegate for obtaining a pointer to a function that invokes a given delegate. The caller of the function must guarantee that the delegate object will remain alive for the lifetime of the structure, because stubs generated by the runtime aren't moved by the garbage collector but can still be collected. Furthermore, callbacks must adopt the stdcall calling convention: if this isn't the case, the PInvoke interface can't interact with the library.

When PInvoke's expressivity isn't enough for wrapping a function call, you can still write an adapter library in a native language such as C. This is the approach followed by the BDB# library, where an intermediate layer of code has been developed to make the interface to the library compatible with PInvoke. The trick has been, in this case, to define a function for each database function, taking as input the pointer to the structure and performing the appropriate call:

```
DB *db;
// BDB call
db->close(db, 0);
// Wrapper call
db_close(db, 0);
```

The problem with wrappers is that they must be maintained manually when the signatures of the original library change. The intermediate adapter makes it more difficult to maintain the code's overall interoperability.

Many libraries have a linear interface that can be easily wrapped using PInvoke, and of course wrapper generators have been developed. At the moment, there are no wrapper generators for F#, but the C-like syntax for PInvoke declarations makes it easy to translate C# wrappers into F# code. An example of such a tool is SWIG, which is a multilanguage wrapper generator that reads C header files and generates interop code for a large number of programming languages such as C#.

Summary

In this chapter, you saw how F# can interoperate with native code in the form of COM components and the standard Platform Invoke interface defined by the ECMA and ISO standards. Neither mechanism is dependent on F#, but the language exposes the appropriate abstractions built into the runtime. You studied how to consume COM components from F# programs and vice versa, and how to access DLLs through PInvoke.

CHAPTER 18

∎∎∎

Debugging and Testing F# Programs

Anecdotal evidence indicates that functional programming frequently leads to a substantially reduced bug rate for good programmers. This is primarily because programs built using functional techniques tend to be highly compositional, building correct programs out of correct building blocks. The functional programming style avoids or substantially reduces the use of side effects in the program, one property that makes programs more compositional. However, debugging and testing are still essential activities to ensure that a program is as close as possible to its specifications. Bugs and misbehaviors are facts of life, and F# programmers must learn techniques to find and remove them.

As a result, software testing is an important activity when you're developing large systems. Tests are initially carried out by writing small programs and interactively running them, but a larger infrastructure quickly becomes necessary as a system grows and as new functionalities must preserve the existing ones. This chapter discusses how you can perform testing with F# using F# Interactive, using the debugging facilities provided by Visual Studio and the .NET infrastructure, and using the NUnit framework for unit testing.

A widely adopted debugging technique is the "do-it-yourself-by-augmenting-your-program-with-printf" approach. However, this technique suffers from several problems; although it's useful, it shouldn't be the only technique you're prepared to apply to the complexities associated with program testing and debugging.

You can use several strategies to test programs and ensure that they behave as expected. The testing theory developed by software engineering has introduced several techniques used every day in software development. This chapter focuses on three aspects of program debugging and testing with F#:

- Using the Visual Studio debugger and the .NET debugging framework

- Using F# Interactive for testing and debugging

- Doing unit testing using NUnit, a freely available framework for unit testing

Alternative tools for debugging and unit testing are available, such as the .NET debugger that ships with the .NET Framework and the testing framework included in some Visual Studio flavors. The concepts behind these tools are similar to those presented here, and the techniques discussed in this chapter can be easily adapted when using them. All these techniques and tools are very helpful, but it's important to remember that these are just tools and you must use them in the appropriate way.

■ **Note** Visual Studio 2008 Team System introduced support for unit testing integrated in the UI for programming languages shipping with the IDE (C#, VB.NET, and C++). Visual Studio 2010 doesn't provide support for unit testing in F#, even though the language ships with the environment. Nevertheless, you can develop unit tests for F# programs using one of the available languages.

Debugging F# Programs

Programming systems such as .NET support debugging as a primary activity through tools to help you inspect programs for possible errors. The debugger is one of the most important of these tools, and it allows you to inspect the program state during execution. You can execute the program stepwise and analyze its state during execution.

Debuggable Programs

The debugger requires support from debugged programs in order to work properly. For interpreted languages, the interpreter supervises program execution, and the debugger must interact with it. Compiled languages, on the other hand, must include this support during compilation so that the debugger can properly interact with the running program.

The CLR provides support for program debugging, and compiled programs provide information to the debugger via a file with a .pdb file extension, which is the program debugging database. Because the compilation process maps high-level programming constructs into equivalent ones in a less expressive language (in this case, the intermediate language), some information gets lost during this process even if the semantics of the program are preserved. For example, in the intermediate language, the names of local variables are referred to as indexes into an array rather than names. A database is used to preserve the information about the correspondence between the program instructions and the intermediate language instructions. The debugging infrastructure uses it to create the illusion that the program is interpreted at the language level, showing the current line of execution in the source code rather than the one in the compiled—and actually running—program. The database retains correspondence among intermediate language instructions (and those that have been used to generate them) and other important information, such as local variable names, that is lost during compilation. The program database is language independent so the debugger tool can be shared among programming languages and you can analyze the program execution even when a program has been developed with different languages. It's also possible to step through unmanaged code from managed code and vice versa.

Debugging without the .pdb file is possible, although the debugger is incapable of showing the source code; instead, the intermediate code or the machine code is shown to the user.

Let's start with the following simple function, which is in principle meant to return true if the input string is a palindrome and false otherwise:

```
let isPalindrome (str:string) =
    let rec check(s:int, e:int) =
        if s = e then true
```

```
    elif str.[s] <> str.[e] then false
    else check(s + 1, e - 1)

check(0, str.Length - 1)
```

The function appears correct at first sight. However, it works only for strings with an odd number of characters and strings with an even length that aren't palindromes. In particular, the program raises an exception with the "abba" string as input.

Let's see how to use the Visual Studio debugger to figure out the problem with this simple function. The algorithm recursively tests the characters of the string pair-wise at the beginning and at the end of the string, because a string is a palindrome if the first and last characters are equal and the substring obtained by removing them is a palindrome too. The s and e variables define the boundaries of the string to be tested and initially refer to the first and last characters of the input string. Recursion terminates when the outermost characters of the string to be tested differ or when you've tested the whole string and the indexes collide.

Figure 18-1 shows the debugging session of the simple program. You set a breakpoint at the instruction that prints the result of the isPalindrome function for the "abba" string by clicking where the red circle is shown, which indicates the location of the breakpoint. When you start the program in debug mode, its execution stops at the breakpoint, and you can step through the statements. The current instruction is indicated by the yellow arrow, and the current statement is highlighted, as shown in Figure 18-1.

Figure 18-1. The Visual Studio debugger

You can access the state of the program through a number of windows that show different aspects of the running program and that are usually docked at the bottom of the debugging window. For instance, you can inspect the state of the local variables of the current method (the Locals window shows the local variables and arguments, e and s in this example) or the state of the call stack to see the sequence of method calls (the Call Stack window). The Watch view lets you write variable names and simple expressions and watch them change during execution. You can also evaluate expressions in the Immediate window and invoke methods, as shown in Figure 18-1, where the simple expressions e and s are used. More views are available through the Debug menu, including the state of executing threads and the memory.

This simple example examines why isPalindrome misbehaves for an input string of even length. As shown in Figure 18-1, the Watch window is used to monitor the s and e variables intended to define the bounds of the substring that has yet to be checked; in this case, the two indexes cross without ever becoming equal, which is the criterion used to successfully stop the recursion. This happens when s has value 2 and e has value 1 in the example. The symptom of the function misbehavior is that an exception is thrown; this is frequently where debugging starts. In this example, the exception is thrown a few steps forward when e gets value -1, which is an invalid index for accessing a character in a string. If you used str[e] as the watch expression or in the Immediate window, the problem would be evident. In more complicated situations, the ability to inspect the application state when the exception is raised makes it possible to determine what conditions to break on and where to set breakpoints before a bug occurs. Now that you've found the bug, you can fix it by extending the test from s = e to s >= e to ensure that even if the end index becomes smaller than the starting index, you deal with the situation appropriately.

■ **Note** In Visual Studio and other Microsoft .NET debugging tools, debugger expressions follow the C# syntax, and arrays don't require the dot before the square braces. The most noticeable differences between C# and F# expression syntax are that access to arrays uses [ ] rather than .[ ] and the equality operator is == rather than =.

Using Advanced Features of the Visual Studio Debugger

This section focuses on relevant aspects of the debugging facilities that the CLR provides to managed applications and via tools such as the Visual Studio debugger.

Consider the notion of a *breakpoint*—an essential tool to mark a statement in a program where you want to suspend execution and inspect the program state. Often, a bug appears only under very specific conditions. Trivial bugs such as the one discussed earlier are the easiest to track and the first to be fixed in a program. It can be difficult or even impossible to selectively suspend program execution at a statement only when certain conditions are met. Many programmers introduce an if statement with a dummy statement for the body and set the breakpoint to the statement to suspend the program under the defined condition; this requires a recompilation of the program and a change to the source code, which may lead to further problems, particularly when several points of the program must be kept under control. A more effective strategy is to use *conditional breakpoints*, a powerful tool offered by the debugger. When you right-click a breakpoint in the editor window or in the Breakpoints window (accessible through the Debug menu), a number of additional options become available.

For each breakpoint you can indicate the following:

- *A condition*: An expression that must be satisfied by the program state in order to suspend program execution

- *A hit count*: The number of times the breakpoint should be hit before suspending execution

- *A filter*: A mechanism to filter the machine, process, and thread to select the set of threads that will be suspended when the breakpoint is hit

- *An action*: Something to be executed when the breakpoint is hit

Breakpoint conditions and hit counts are the most frequently used options. A hit count is useful when a bug appears only after a significant period of execution. For instance, when you're debugging a search engine, a bug may occur only after indexing gigabytes of data; the number of hits of the breakpoint can be determined.[1] Conditional expressions are more useful when it's difficult to reproduce the exact circumstances that trigger a bug, and when the number of times the breakpoint is hit is variable. For expressions entered in the Immediate window, conditional expressions are expressed as in C#; this is true for all languages, because the debugger infrastructure within the CLR is designed to deal with compiled programs and ignores the source language.

Sometimes you need to debug a running program that has been started without the debugger; a typical situation is when you're debugging a service started through the Service snap-in of the Management Console or debugging a web application live that is executed by IIS rather than by the web server used for development by Visual Studio. In these situations, you can attach the debugger to a running process by selecting Tools ➤ Attach to Process and selecting the process to debug. There are standard processes that are generally known to programmers: w3p.exe is used by IIS to run application pools where ASP.NET applications run, and the svchost.exe process generally hosts Windows services. However, sometimes it can be difficult to find out which process is running the code to debug, because several of these generic process hosts run applications.

Debugging a program significantly slows down its execution speed because the debugger infrastructure injects code to monitor program execution. Conditional breakpoints tend to worsen the situation because every time the breakpoint is hit, the condition must be tested before standard execution resumes.

The CLR debugging infrastructure operates at the level of compiled assemblies; this has several implications. The objects and types that are visible to the debugger are those generated by the compiler and aren't always explicitly defined by you in the source code. The program database information tends to preserve the mapping between the source and the compiled program, but sometimes the underlying structure surfaces to the user. On the other hand, you can debug programs written in different programming languages, even when managed and unmanaged code must interoperate.

■ **Note** One tricky problem with F# programs is debugging *tail calls*. (Chapter 8 described tail calls.) In particular, when a tail call is executed, the calling stack frame is removed prior to the call. This means the calls shown in the Visual Studio call stack window may not be complete. Entries may be missing that should, logically speaking, be present, according to the strict call sequence that caused a program to arrive at a particular point. Likewise, the debugger commands step-into and step-out can behave a little unusually when stepping into a tail call. This behavior may be absent for programs compiled for debugging because many optimizations are disabled, but it appears when you're debugging a program compiled for release.

---

[1] One of the authors became a fan of this approach when a program he was writing crashed only after crunching 2GB of input data. The ability to stop the program immediately before the crash made it possible to find a particular input sequence that was unexpected. It would have been very difficult to find this bug by printing the state of the application.

Figure 18-2 shows a debugging session for the program discussed in Chapter 17; you've stepped into the HelloWorld method, which is a C function accessed through the PInvoke interface as witnessed by the Call Stack window. To enable cross-language debugging, you indicate in the project options' Debug section that the debugging scope is the whole program rather than the current project.

Figure 18-2. Cross-language debugging with the Visual Studio debugger

Instrumenting Your Program with the System.Diagnostics Namespace

A managed application can programmatically access the debugging services of the CLR through the types contained in the System.Diagnostics namespace. Several types in the namespace encompass aspects of the runtime, including stack tracing, communicating with the debugger, accessing performance counters to read statistics about the computer state (memory and CPU usage are typically available using them), and handling operating system processes.

This section focuses on the classes related to debugging and the debugger. You can interact with the debugging infrastructure in three primary ways:

- The Debug class programmatically asserts conditions in the program and outputs debugging and tracing information to debuggers and other listeners.

- The Debugger class interacts with the debugger, checks whether it's attached, and triggers breaks explicitly from the program.

- The debugging attributes are a set of custom attributes that you can use to annotate the program to control its behavior (see Chapters 9 and 10 for more information about custom attributes).

The Debug class provides a way to output diagnostic messages without assuming that the program has been compiled as a console application; the debug output is collected by one or more *listeners* that receive the output notifications and do something with them. Each listener is an instance of a class inherited from the TraceListener class and typically sends the output to the console or to a file, or notifies the user with a dialog box (you can find more information about how to write a listener in the class library documentation). The following example instruments the isPalindrome function with tracing statements:

```
let isPalindrome (str:string) =
    let rec check(s:int, e:int) =
        Debug.WriteLine("check call")
        Debug.WriteLineIf((s = 0), "check: First call")
        Debug.Assert((s >= 0 || s < str.Length), sprintf "s is out of bounds: %d" s)
        Debug.Assert((e >= 0 || e < str.Length), sprintf "e is out of bounds: %d" e)
        if s = e || s = e + 1 then true
        else if str.[s] <> str.[e] then false
        else check(s + 1, e - 1)
  check(0, str.Length - 1)
```

The Write*XXX* methods of the Debug class output data of a running program and are a sophisticated version of the printf debugging approach, where the program is enriched with print statements that output useful information about its current state. In this case, however, you can redirect all the messages to different media rather than just print them to the console. You can also conditionally output messages to reduce the number of messages sent to the debug output. The example outputs a message each time the check method is invoked and uses the conditional output to mark the first invocation.

■ **Note** By default, the diagnostic output isn't sent to the console on Windows. When a program is executed in debugging mode in Visual Studio, the output is sent to the Output window. Otherwise, you need a tool such as DebugView, available on Microsoft TechNet. F# Interactive doesn't output any debug assertions being compiled for release.

Assertions are a well-known mechanism to assert conditions about the state of a running program, ensuring that at a given point in the program, certain preconditions must hold. For instance, assertions are often used to ensure that the content of an option-valued variable isn't None at some point in the program. During testing, you should ensure that if this precondition isn't satisfied, program execution is suspended as soon as possible. This avoids tracing back from the point where the undefined value of the variable would lead to an exception. The Assert method lets you specify a Boolean condition that must hold; otherwise, the given message is displayed, prompting the user with the failed assertion.

Both debug output and assertions are statements that typically are useful during program development; but when a release is made, these calls introduce unnecessary overhead. Often, the program compiled with these extra checks is called the *checked version* of the program. The .NET Framework designers devised a general mechanism to strip out the calls to methods under a particular condition with the help of the compiler. The ConditionalAttribute custom attribute is used to label methods whose calls are included in the program only if a given compilation symbol is defined; for the methods in the Debug type, it's the DEBUG symbol. The F# compiler supports this mechanism, making it possible to use these tools to instrument the F# program in a way that is supported by the .NET infrastructure.

The Debugger type lets you check whether the program is attached to a debugger and to trigger a break if required. You can also programmatically launch the debugger using this type and send log messages to it. This type is used less often than the Debug type, but it may be useful if a bug arises only when there is no attached debugger. In this case, you can programmatically start the debugging process when needed.

Another mechanism that lets you control the interaction between a program and the debugger is based on a set of custom attributes in the System.Diagnostics namespace. Table 18-1 shows the attributes that control in part the behavior of the debugger.

Table 18-1. Attributes Controlling Program Behavior Under Debug

Attribute	Description
DebuggerBrowsableAttribute	Determines whether and how a member is displayed in the Debug window.
DebuggerDisplayAttribute	Indicates how a type or field should be displayed in the Debug window.
DebuggerHiddenAttribute	The debugger may interpret this attribute and forbid interaction with the member annotated by it.
DebuggerNonUserCodeAttribute	Marks code that isn't user written (for instance, designer-generated code) and that can be skipped to avoid complicating the debugging experience.
DebuggerStepperBoundaryAttribute	Locally overrides the use of DebuggerNonUserCodeAttribute.
DebuggerStepThroughAttribute	The debugger may interpret this attribute and disallow stepping into the target method.
DebuggerTypeProxyAttribute	Indicates a type that is responsible for defining how a type is displayed in the Debug window. It may affect debugging performance and should be used only when it's really necessary to radically change how a type is displayed.
DebuggerVisualizerAttribute	Indicates for a type the type that defines how to render it while debugging.

These attributes allow you to control two aspects of debugging: how data is visualized by the debugger and how the debugger should behave with respect to the visibility of members.

The ability to control how types are displayed by the debugger can help you produce customized views of data that may significantly help you inspect the program state in an aggregate view. The easiest way is to use DebuggerDisplayAttribute, which supports customizing the text associated with a value in the Debug window; an object of that type can still be inspected in every field. Consider the following simple example:

```
[<DebuggerDisplay("{re}+{im}i")>]
type MyComplex=
    { re : double
      im : double }
let c = { re = 0.0; im = 0.0 }
Console.WriteLine("{0}+{1}i", c.re, c.im)
```

Here, you introduce a record named MyComplex with the classic definition of a complex number. The DebuggerDisplayAttribute attribute is used to annotate the type so that the debugger displays its instances using the mathematical notation rather than just displaying the type name. The syntax allowed assumes that curly braces are used to indicate the name of a property whose value should be inserted in the format string. Figure 18-3 shows the result in the Visual Studio debugger: on the left is how the debugger window appears when MyComplex is without the DebuggerDisplay annotation; on the right, the custom string appears, with the properties in the string in curly braces. As you can see, the difference is in the value field, and the structure can still be inspected. You can use a custom visualizer to fully customize the appearance of the data in the debugger, but it may affect debugging performance.

Figure 18-3. The MyComplex type shown by the debugger without and with DebuggerDisplay

Figure 18-3 is also interesting because it shows how the debugger displays information from the compiled program. In this case, the association between the name c and the runtime local variable has been lost, and the record appears because it has been compiled by the compiler as a pair of fields and public properties.

The rest of the namespace contains classes to interact with the runtime: the event-logging infrastructure, process and thread management, and the representation of a thread's stack. Stack manipulation can be useful if you need to know the call sequence that leads to executing a particular method. The StackTrace type exposes a list of StackFrame objects that provide information about each method call on the stack.

Debugging Concurrent and Graphical Applications

Although a debugger is a fundamental tool for inspecting applications, it isn't the Holy Grail, and it must be used carefully: be aware that the process interferes with an application's normal execution. The most relevant impact of the debugging process on a running program is the influence on execution timing; and graphical and concurrent programs are much more prevalent these days. Sometimes, a bug disappears while the debugger is being used, due to these changes in execution timing.

Debugging and testing concurrent applications can be particularly difficult because using a debugger is guaranteed to alter execution timing. There is no general rule for debugging concurrent applications, but this section briefly discusses how you can use the debugger in these cases. Consider this simple example of a multithreaded application:

```
open System
open System.Threading

let t1 = Thread(fun () ->
    while true do
        printf "Thread 1\n"
)
let t2 = Thread(fun () ->
    while true do
        printf "Thread 2\n"
)
t1.Start()
t2.Start()
```

■ **Note** If you run this example in F# Interactive, you must abort the thread explicitly by calling the Abort method, right-clicking the F# Interactive window, and choosing Cancel Evaluation. If it doesn't resume, you may have to kill the fsi.exe process that is using the CPU most. This is a common solution when a computation gets out of control during interactive sessions.

Threads t1 and t2 access the console, which is a shared resource; when you run the program without a debugger attached, the string printed by the two threads appears interleaved on the console. If you set a breakpoint on the two printf statements and start a debugging session, stepping automatically moves from one thread to the other; the output of the program is completely different from that obtained without debugging. This is true also if you disable the breakpoints. The output is even more unbalanced if you set the breakpoint in only one of the two threads.

Chapter 13 discussed shared-memory multithreaded applications. In such applications, shared objects accessed by different threads are critical resources that may be viewed in the debugger. If the debug of a single thread fails, setting breakpoints in different threads may help you study the dynamic of the application, even if the full interaction of the threads can't be fully simulated. If this approach fails, it may be useful to introduce tests inside the application and use the Debugger type only when a given condition occurs. Channel-based message-passing applications are generally easier to debug than those that rely on shared memory, because you can monitor the communication end points using breakpoints or logging messages. Although careful use of the debugger may help when you're debugging concurrent applications, sometimes external observation is enough to influence a running program. In these cases, tracing through debug output becomes a viable alternative; large systems have different levels of traces to monitor program execution.

Graphical applications also present issues when you're debugging. As discussed in Chapter 11, a GUI application's event loop is handled by a single thread; if this is blocked, the application's GUI ceases working while it's suspended in the debugger. Consider the following simple application:

```
open System
open System.Windows.Forms

let f = new Form(Text="Hello world")
let b = new Button(Text="Click me!", Dock=DockStyle.Fill)
b.Click.Add(fun _ ->
    b.Text <- "Click me again"
```

```
    MessageBox.Show("Hello world") |> ignore
)
f.Controls.Add(b)

f.Show()

Application.Run(f)
```

If you set a breakpoint at the MessageBox statement and debug the application, then when the button is clicked, the debugger suspends execution, and the form stops responding. The text of the button doesn't change until execution resumes, because the thread suspended by the debugger is responsible for handling GUI events, including the paint event that refreshes the button's content and updates the button label.

More specifically, event handlers can affect the appearance of a form in two ways: by setting properties of graphical controls and by explicitly drawing using a Graphics object. In the first case, the change isn't noticed until execution resumes; the property change usually asks for a refresh of the control's appearance, which eventually results in a paint event that must be processed by the thread that is suspended in the debugger. In the second case, updates are immediately visible when a statement involving drawing primitives is executed (unless double buffering has been enabled on the window).

For example, consider the following program, which displays a window with a number of vertical lines:

```
open System
open System.Windows.Forms
open System.Drawing

let f = new Form(Text="Hello world")
f.Paint.Add(fun args ->
    let g = args.Graphics

    for i = 0 to f.Width / 10 do
        g.DrawLine(Pens.Black, i*10, 0, i*10, f.Height)

)
f.Show()
Application.Run(f)
```

Set a breakpoint at the DrawLine statement and start debugging the application, moving the debugger window in order to make the application form visible. If you continue the execution one statement at a time, you can see the lines appear on the form. In this case, the interaction with the graphical system doesn't trigger an event but interacts directly with the Graphics object by emitting graphic primitives that are rendered immediately.

This discussion of debugging graphical applications uses examples based on Windows Forms. The same considerations apply to all event systems where a thread is responsible for event notification. For graphical systems such as WPF, based on the retention of graphic primitives, things work slightly differently, but there are analogous considerations.

Debugging and Testing with F# Interactive

Functional programming languages have traditionally addressed many debugging and testing issues through the ability to interactively evaluate program statements and print the values of variables, inspecting the program state interactively. F# Interactive allows you to execute code fragments and quickly test them; you can also inspect the state of the fsi script by querying values from the top level.

Development and testing using F# Interactive can effectively reduce development time, because you can evaluate code fragments more than once without having to recompile the entire system. The Visual Studio project system for F# makes this process even more productive because code is edited in the development environment with type checking and IntelliSense; you can send code to F# Interactive by selecting it and pressing the Alt+Enter shortcut. In this scenario, the isPalindrome function from the previous section could have been developed incrementally and tested by invoking it with a test input argument. After you found and fixed the issue, you could them evaluate the function definition again and test it for further bugs.

During software development, it's common practice to write simple programs to test specific features (the "Unit Testing" section discuses this topic more extensively). With F# Interactive, you can define tests as functions stored in a file and selectively evaluate them in Visual Studio. This approach can be useful in developing and defining new tests, but you can use more specific tools to run tests in a more organic way.

Controlling F# Interactive

As you saw in Chapter 9, programs run in F# Interactive have access to an object called fsi that lets you control some aspects of the interactive execution. It's contained in the assembly FSharp.Interactive.Settings.dll, which is automatically referenced in files ending with .fsx and in F# Interactive sessions.

Table 18-2 shows some of the methods supported by this object.

Table 18-2. Members of the fsi Object

Member	Type	Description
fsi.FloatingPointFormat	string	Gets or sets the format used for floating-point numbers, based on .NET Formatting specifications
fsi.FormatProvider	System.IFormat Provider	Gets or sets the cultural format used for numbers, based on .NET Formatting specifications
fsi.PrintWidth	int	Gets or sets the print width used for formatted text output
fsi.PrintDepth	int	Gets or sets the depth of output for tree-structured data
fsi.PrintLength	int	Gets or sets the length of output for lists and other linear data structures
fsi.ShowProperties	bool	Gets or sets a flag indicating whether properties should be printed for displayed values
fsi.ShowDeclarationValues	bool	Gets or sets a flag indicating whether declaration values should be printed
fsi.ShowIEnumerable	bool	Gets or sets a flag indicating whether sequences should be printed in the output of the interactive session

Member	Type	Description
fsi.AddPrinter	('a -> string) -> unit	Adds a printer for values compatible with the specific type 'a
fsi.AddPrintTransformer	('a -> obj) -> unit	Adds a printer that shows any values compatible with the specific type 'a as if they were values returned by the given function
fsi.CommandLineArgs	string[]	Gets the command-line arguments after ignoring the arguments relevant to the interactive environment and replacing the first argument with the name of the last script file

Some Common F# Interactive Directives

Table 18-3 shows several common directives accepted by F# Interactive, some of which correspond to options for the F# command-line compiler.

Table 18-3. Some Commonly Used F# Interactive Directives

Directive	Description
#r path	References a DLL. The DLL is loaded dynamically when first required.
#I path	Adds the given search path to that used to resolve referenced DLLs.
#load file ... file	Loads the given file(s) as if it had been compiled by the F# command-line compiler.
#time	Toggles timing information on/off.
#quit	Exits F# Interactive.

Understanding How F# Interactive Compiles Code

Although F# Interactive is reminiscent of the read-eval-print loops of interpreted languages, it's substantially different because it compiles code rather than interprets it. Whenever a code fragment is typed at the top level, it's compiled on the fly as part of a dynamic assembly and evaluated for side effects. This is particularly important for types because you can create new ones at the top level and their dependencies may be tricky to understand fully.

Let's start with an example of a nontrivial use of F# Interactive that shows these intricacies. You define the class APoint, which represents points using an angle and a radius:

```
type APoint(angle,radius) =
    member x.Angle = angle
    member x.Radius = radius
    new() = APoint(angle=0.0, radius=0.0)
```

If you create an instance of the class using F# Interactive, you can inspect the actual type by using the GetType method. The output is as follows:

```
> let p = APoint();;
val p : APoint

> p.GetType();;
val it : System.Type
= FSI_0002+APoint
      {Assembly = FSI-ASSEMBLY, Version=0.0.0.0, Culture=neutral, PublicKeyToken=null;
       AssemblyQualifiedName = "FSI_0002+APoint, FSI-ASSEMBLY, Version=0.0.0.0, ... }
```

Now, suppose you want to extend the APoint class with an additional member that stretches the point radius a given amount; it's natural to type the new definition of the class into the top level and evaluate it. F# Interactive doesn't complain about the redefinition of the type:

```
type APoint(angle,radius) =
    member x.Angle = angle
    member x.Radius = radius
    member x.Stretch (k:double) = APoint(angle=x.Angle, radius=x.Radius + k)
    new() = APoint(angle=0.0, radius=0.0)
```

Because you've redefined the structure of APoint, you may be tempted to invoke the stretch method on it, but doing so results in an error:

```
> p.Stretch(22.0);;
  p.Stretch(22.0);;
  --^^^^^^^^

stdin(2,2): error: FS0039: The field, constructor or member 'Stretch' is not defined.
```

To understand what's happening, create a new instance p2 of the class APoint and ask for the type:

```
> let p2 = APoint();;
val p2 : APoint

> p2.GetType();;
val it : System.Type
= FSI_0005+APoint
      {Assembly = FSI-ASSEMBLY, Version=0.0.0.0, Culture=neutral, PublicKeyToken=null;
       AssemblyQualifiedName = "FSI_0005+APoint, FSI-ASSEMBLY, Version=0.0.0.0, ... }
```

As you can see, the name of p2's type is FSI_0005+APoint, whereas p's type is FSI_0002+APoint. Under the hood, F# Interactive compiles types into different modules to ensure that types can be redefined; it also ensures that the most recent definition of a type is used. The older definitions are still available, and their instances aren't affected by the type redefinition.

Understanding the inner mechanisms of F# Interactive is useful when you use it to test F# programs, because interactive evaluation isn't always equivalent to running code compiled using the command-line compiler. On the other hand, the compiled nature of the system guarantees that the code executed by F# Interactive performs as well as compiled code.

F# Interactive and Visual Studio

The relation between Visual Studio and F# Interactive is different from typical Visual Studio add-ins. It's useful to understand because the state of an F# Interactive session is separate from the Visual Studio state and can affect the process of testing and debugging in many subtle ways. You can also manage external resources through .NET and COM interfaces, including automating Visual Studio tasks, but accessing its interfaces is less easy than it may appear at first.

F# Interactive is a Visual Studio tool window[2] that lets you interact with an fsi.exe process like a standard console. You communicate with the fsi.exe process using standard streams. This design choice ensures that a code mistake that causes the F# Interactive to hang doesn't affect the Visual Studio editor that contains the data. You can restart F# Interactive from the tool window and obtain a fresh new instance without having to restart Visual Studio.

Restarting F# Interactive during testing and debugging ensures a clean environment. Consider, for example, a class whose instances open the same file. During a test, the file may be locked by an instance and become inaccessible due to variable redefinition; at some point, the garbage collector runs the finalizer and may close the file, slowing the iterative process of testing with F# Interactive. Sometimes, redefinition causes problems too: a class definition may be evaluated before you make additional changes, and the interface may then behave differently than the one in the program editor; you may continue to evaluate code that refers to the older version. In these cases, restarting F# Interactive is an option and returns you to a clean state.

Using Visual Studio automation, you can use F# Interactive to access objects exposing functionalities of the programming environment. The DTE and the DTE2 interfaces are the entry points to the entire Visual Studio object model. For instance, you can print the full path of the active document window:

```
#r @"EnvDTE.dll"
#r @"EnvDTE80.dll"
open System.Runtime.InteropServices
let appObj =Marshal.GetActiveObject("VisualStudio.DTE") :?> EnvDTE80.DTE2
printfn "%s" (appObj.ActiveDocument.FullName)
```

You use the GetActiveObject method to obtain a reference to the Visual Studio object model, and then you use the .NET assembly containing the interface generated from the COM types to access the object model. In this example, you connect to a running instance of Visual Studio (usually the first one started), not necessarily the same one associated with the F# Interactive executing the code. To attach to a specific instance of Visual Studio, you need to access the COM Running Object Table and associate with the desired instance.

Using Visual Studio automation, you can automate several tasks during testing and debugging, including building temporary configurations within Visual Studio for testing purposes. Manipulation of Visual Studio elements isn't restricted to F# projects, but it can affect any area also affected by the macro system.

---

2   Tool windows in Visual Studio are dockable, like the Solution Explorer window.

VSLab

VSLab is an open source project developed at the University of Pisa under contract by Microsoft. Its aim is to permit F# Interactive to interactively define and control Visual Studio tool windows. The project is available on CodePlex (http://vslab.codeplex.com). It defines an environment similar to MatLab and Mathematica, in which data can be interactively manipulated by using F# Interactive capabilities and displayed using tool windows containing graphics.

The system is a sophisticated example of Visual Studio interoperability and object-oriented programming with F#. Tool windows (*viewlets*, in VSLab terminology) are created by an add-in communicating with the running instance of F# Interactive. A viewlet is a special kind of Windows Forms control that draws its content into an associated tool window even if it belongs to a different process.

Chapter 11 discussed how you can achieve similar results by opening Forms from F# Interactive. But viewlets are tool windows, so they fully integrate with the Visual Studio windowing system and support the docking and effective management that are necessary to orchestrate many different data views.

Unit Testing

Software testing is an important task in software development; its goal is to ensure that a program or a library behaves according to the system specifications. It's a significant area of software-engineering research, and tools have been developed to support increasing efforts in software verification. Among a large number of testing strategies, unit testing has rapidly become popular because of the software tools used to support this strategy. The core idea behind this approach involves writing small programs to test single features of a system during development. When bugs are found, new unit tests are added to ensure that a particular bug doesn't occur again. Recently, it's been proposed that testing should drive software development, because tests can be used to check new code and later to conduct regression tests, ensuring that new features don't affect existing ones.

This section discusses how you can develop unit tests in F# using the freely available NUnit tool (www.nunit.com). The tool was inspired by JUnit, a unit-testing suite for the Java programming language, but the programming interface has been redesigned to take advantage of the extensible metadata that the CLR provides by means of custom attributes.

Let's start with an example and develop a very simple test suite for the isPalindrome function. The first choice you face is whether tests should be embedded in the application. If you create tests as a separated application, you can invoke only the public interface of your software; features internal to the software can't be tested directly. On the other hand, if you embed unit tests in the program, you introduce a dependency from the nunit.framework.dll assembly, and the unit tests are available at runtime even where they aren't needed. Because the NUnit approach is based on custom attributes, performance isn't affected in either case. If you use tests during program development, it's more convenient to define them inside the program; in this case, conditional compilation may help to include them only in checked builds.

Listing 18-1 shows a *test fixture* for the isPalindrome function—that is, a set of unit tests. Test fixtures are represented by a class annotated with the TestFixture custom attribute; tests are instance methods with the signature unit -> unit and annotated with the Test custom attribute. Inside a test case, you use methods of the Assert class to test conditions that must be satisfied during the test. If one of these fails, the entire test is considered a failure, and it's reported to the user by the tool that coordinates test execution.

Listing 18-1. A Test Fixture for the isPalindrome Function

```
open System
open NUnit.Framework
open IsPalindrome

[<TestFixture>]
type Test() =

    let posTests(strings) =
        for s in strings do
            Assert.That(isPalindrome s, Is.True,
                            sprintf "isPalindrome(\"%s\") must return true" s)

    let negTests(strings) =
        for s in strings do
            Assert.That(isPalindrome s, Is.False,
                            sprintf "isPalindrome(\"%s\") must return false" s)

    [<Test>]
    member x.EmptyString () =
        Assert.That(isPalindrome(""), Is.True,
                        "isPalindrome must return true on an empty string")

    [<Test>]
    member x.SingleChar () = posTests ["a"]

    [<Test>]
    member x.EvenPalindrome () = posTests [ "aa"; "abba"; "abaaba" ]

    [<Test>]
    member x.OddPalindrome () = posTests [ "aba"; "abbba"; "abababa" ]

    [<Test>]
    member x.WrongString () = negTests [ "as"; "F# is wonderful"; "Nice" ]
```

Test units are methods that invoke objects of the program and test return values to be sure their behavior conforms to the specification. This example also introduces the posTests and negTests functions used in several tests.

Developing unit tests is a matter of defining types containing the tests. Although you can write a single test for a program, it's a good idea to have many small tests that check various features and different inputs. In this case, you introduce five tests: one for each significant input to the function. You could develop a single test containing all the code used for the individual tests; but as you see shortly, doing so would reduce the test suite's ability to spot problems in the program. In general, the choice of the test suite's granularity for a program is up to you; it's a matter of finding a reasonable tradeoff between having a large number of unit tests checking very specific conditions and having a small number of unit tests checking broader areas of the program.

To compile the project, you must reference the nunit.framework.dll assembly. After the program has been compiled, you can start NUnit and open the executable.

As shown in Figure 18-4, the assembly containing the unit tests is inspected using the CLR's reflection capabilities, classes annotated with the TestFixture attribute are identified by NUnit, and searched-for methods are annotated with the Test attribute. Initially, all the fixtures and the tests are marked with gray dots. When you run tests, the dot is colored green or red depending on the outcome of the particular test.

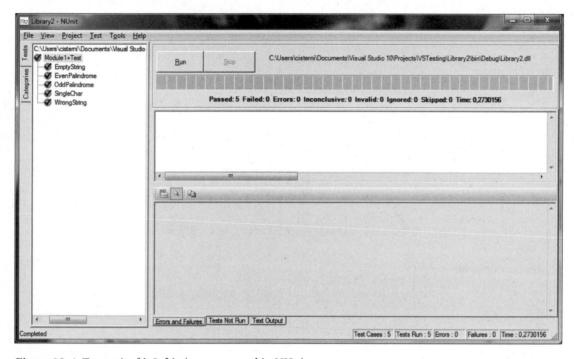

Figure 18-4. *Test unit of* isPalindrome *executed in NUnit*

If you reintroduce the original bug in the isPalindrome function and run NUnit again, EmptyString and EvenPalindrome fail, the corresponding dots are marked red, and the Errors and Failures tabs contain details about the test failure. This is the main benefit of having a large number of small unit tests: tools can run them automatically to identify problems in a program as well as the area potentially involved in the problem. Even in this simple example, a single test for the entire function would indicate the problem with the function, although it would fail to spot the kind of input responsible for the issue.

Like every other piece of software, unit tests must be maintained, documented, and updated to follow the evolution of the software for which they're designed. The number of test cases, organized in fixtures, tends to grow with the system during development, and a large system may have thousands of these tests. Tools such as NUnit have features to control tests and allow you to run subsets of the entire set of test cases for a system. Test fixtures are a form of grouping: a test suite may contain different test fixtures that may group test cases for different aspects to be tested.

NUnit features a number of additional attributes to support the documentation and classification of test cases and test fixtures. The Description attribute lets you associate a description with annotated test fixtures and test cases. You can use the Category and Culture attributes to associate a category and a culture string with test fixtures and test cases; in addition, to provide more information about tests, NUnit lets you filter tests to be run using the content of the attributes. The ability to select the tests that must be run is important, because running all tests for a system may require a significant amount of time. Other mechanisms to control the execution of tests are offered by the Ignore and Explicit attributes; you can use the former to disable a test fixture for a period without having to remove all the annotations, and the latter indicates that a test case or a fixture should only be run explicitly.

Another important aspect of testing nontrivial software is the test fixture's life cycle. Test cases are instance methods of a class; and with a simple experiment, you can easily find that NUnit creates an instance of the class and runs all the tests it contains. To verify this, it's enough to define a counter field in the class annotated as a fixture and update its value every time a test is run; the value of the counter is incremented for each test in the suite. Although you may rely on the standard life cycle of the class, NUnit provides additional annotations to indicate the code that must be run to set up a fixture and the corresponding code to free the resources at the end of the test; you can also define a pair of methods that are run before and after each test case. The TestFixtureSetUp and TestFixtureTearDown attributes annotate methods to set up and free a fixture; SetUp and TearDown are the attributes for the corresponding test cases.

Listing 18-2 shows a test fixture for the isPalindrome function that includes most of the attributes discussed and one test case.[3] You mark the category of this test case as a "Special case." You also include a description for each test case and the methods invoked before and after the fixture and single test cases are run. NUnit's graphical interface includes a tab that reports the output sent to the console; when tests run, the output shows the invocation sequence of the setup and teardown methods.

Listing 18-2. A Refined Test Fixture for the isPalindrome Function

```
open System
open NUnit.Framework

[<TestFixture;
  Description("Test fixture for the isPalindrome function")>]
type Test() =
    [<TestFixtureSetUp>]
    member x.InitTestFixture () =
        printfn "Before running Fixture"

    [<TestFixtureTearDown>]
    member x.DoneTestFixture () =
        printfn "After running Fixture"

    [<SetUp>]
    member x.InitTest () =
        printfn "Before running test"

    [<TearDown>]
    member x.DoneTest () =
        Console.WriteLine("After running test")

    [<Test;
      Category("Special case");
      Description("An empty string is palindrome")>]
    member x.EmptyString () =
        Assert.That(isPalindrome(""), Is.True,
                        "isPalindrome must return true on an empty string")
```

The ability to set up resources for test cases may introduce problems during unit testing; in particular, you must treat the setup and teardown methods of test fixtures carefully, because the state shared by different test cases may affect the way they execute. Suppose, for instance, that a file is open during the setup of a fixture. This may save time because the file is opened only once and not for each test case. If a test case fails and the file is closed, subsequent tests may fail because they assume the file

---

[3]   To run the example, you must include the definition of the isPalindrome function.

has been opened during the fixture's setup. Nevertheless, in some situations, preloading resources only once for a fixture may save significant time.

NUnit comes with two versions of the tool: one displaying the graphical interface shown in Figure 18-4, and a console version that prints results to the console. Both versions are useful; the windowed application is handy to produce reports about tests and interactively control test processing, and the console version can be used to include the test process in a chain of commands invoked via scripts. Also, other programs can read the tool's output to automate tasks after unit tests. A large number of command-line arguments are available in the console version to specify all the options available, including test filtering based on categories.

When a unit test fails, you must set up a debugging session to check the application state and the reason for the failure. You can debug tests with the Visual Studio debugger by configuring the Debug tab in the project properties in a similar way, as shown in Figure 18-5. After it's configured, you can set breakpoints in the code and start the debugging session as usual. This is important when code development is driven by tests, because new features can be implemented alongside test cases. It's a good way to capitalize on the small test programs that developers frequently write: these small programs become test cases and can be collected without having to develop a new test program each time.

The example shown in Figure 18-5 passes a single argument to nunit-console.exe, the assembly containing the tests to be executed. You can also specify an additional argument to filter the tests that must be run. In this example, if you set a breakpoint in one of the test cases annotated explicitly, the debugger doesn't stop, because by default these tests are skipped.

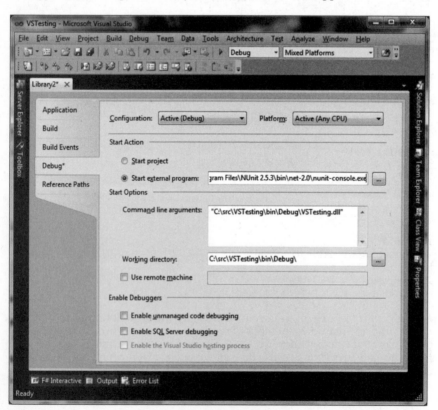

Figure 18-5. Configuring an F# project for debugging NUnit test fixtures

■ **Note** This section shows how you can use NUnit to define test cases using F#. However, NUnit isn't the only tool for unit testing that's available for .NET. For example, Visual Studio includes powerful unit-testing tools.

Summary

This chapter introduced techniques and tools you can use to debug F# programs and automate the execution of unit tests. Because testing and debugging activities relate to the execution of programs, these tools tend to work on the compiled version of a program, relying on additional information such as metadata exposed through the reflection API or program debug database information files generated by compilers. Programming languages such as F# that feature programming abstractions don't map directly to the CLR intermediate language and type system; as a result, compilation details may surface when you use tools that operate on compiled assemblies. Nevertheless, these are valuable tools for developing large systems.

The next chapter covers another set of software engineering issues for F# code: library design in the context of F# and .NET.

CHAPTER 19

■ ■ ■

Designing F# Libraries

This book deals with F#, a language situated in the context of .NET-based software construction and engineering. As an expert F# programmer, you need more than knowledge of the F# language; you also need to use a range of software-engineering tools and methodologies wisely to build software that is truly valuable for the situation where it's deployed. The previous chapter touched on some important tools. This final chapter looks at some of the methodological issues related to F# library design:

- Designing vanilla .NET libraries that minimize the use of F#-specific constructs, according to existing .NET design conventions

- Elements of *functional programming design methodology*, which offers important and deep insights into programming but doesn't address several important aspects of the library or component design problems

- Specific suggestions for designing .NET and F# libraries, including naming conventions, how to design types and modules, and guidelines for using exceptions

F# is often seen as a functional language; but as this book emphasizes, it's really a multiparadigm language. The OO, functional, imperative, and language-manipulation paradigms are all well supported. That is, F# is a *function-oriented* language—many of the defaults are set up to encourage functional programming, but programming in the other paradigms is effective and efficient, and a combination is often best of all. Nonetheless, a multiparadigm language brings challenges for library designs and coding conventions.

It's a common misconception that the functional and OO programming methodologies compete; in fact, they're largely orthogonal. However, it's important to note that functional programming doesn't directly solve many of the practical and prosaic issues associated with library design—for solutions to these problems, you must look elsewhere. In the context of .NET programming, this means turning first to the *.NET Library Design Guidelines*, published online by Microsoft and as a book by Addison-Wesley.

In the official documents, the .NET library design is described in terms of conventions and guidelines for the use of the following constructs in public framework libraries:

- Assemblies, namespaces, and types (see Chapters 6 and 7 in this book)

- Classes and objects, containing properties, methods, and events (see Chapter 6)

- Interfaces (in other words, object interface types; see Chapter 6)

- .NET delegate types (mentioned briefly in Chapters 5 and 6)

- Enumerations (that is, enums from languages such as C#; mentioned briefly in Chapter 6)

- Constants (that is, constant literals from languages such as C#)

- Type parameters (that is, generic parameters; see Chapter 5)

From the perspective of F# programming, you must also consider the following constructs:

- Discriminated union types and their tags (Chapters 3 and 9)

- Record types and their fields (Chapter 3)

- Type abbreviations (Chapter 3)

- Values and functions declared using let and let rec (Chapter 3)

- Modules (Chapter 6)

- Named arguments (Chapter 6)

- Optional arguments (Chapter 6)

Framework library design is always nontrivial and often underestimated. F# framework and library design methodology is inevitably strongly rooted in the context of .NET OO programming. This chapter gives our opinions about how you can approach library design in the context of F# programming. These opinions are neither proscriptive nor official. More official guidelines may be developed by the F# team and community at some future point, although ultimately the final choices lie with F# programmers and software architects.

■ **Note** Some F# programmers choose to use library and coding conventions much more closely associated with OCaml, Python, or a particular application domain such as hardware verification. For example, OCaml coding uses underscores in names extensively, a practice avoided by the .NET Framework guidelines but used in places by the F# library. Some also choose to adjust coding conventions to their personal or team tastes.

Designing Vanilla .NET Libraries

One way to approach library design with F# is to design libraries according to the .NET Library Design Guidelines. This implicitly can mean avoiding or minimizing the use of F#-specific or F#-related constructs in the public API. We call these libraries *vanilla .NET libraries*, as opposed to libraries that use F# constructs without restriction and are mostly intended for use by F# applications.

Designing vanilla .NET libraries means adopting the following rules:

- Apply the .NET Library Design Guidelines to the public API of your code. Your internal implementation can use any techniques you want.

- Restrict the constructs you use in your public APIs to those that are most easily used and recognized by .NET programmers. This means avoiding the use of some F# idioms in the public API.

- Use the Microsoft FxCop quality-assurance tool to check the public interface of your assembly for compliance. Use FxCop exemptions where you deem necessary.

At the time of writing, here are some specific recommendations from the authors of this book:

- Avoid using F# list types 'T list in vanilla .NET APIs. Use seq<'T> or arrays instead of lists.

- Avoid using F# function types in vanilla .NET APIs. F# function values tend to be a little difficult to create from other .NET languages. Instead, consider using .NET delegate types such as the overloaded System.Func<...> types available from .NET 3.5 onward.

- Avoid using F#-specific language constructs such as discriminated unions and optional arguments in vanilla .NET APIs.

For example, consider the code in Listing 19-1, which shows some F# code that you intend to adjust to be suitable for use as part of a .NET API.

Listing 19-1. An F# Type Prior to Adjustment for Use as Part of a Vanilla .NET API

```
namespace global
open System
type APoint(angle,radius) =
    member x.Angle = angle
    member x.Radius = radius
    member x.Stretch(l) = APoint(angle=x.Angle, radius=x.Radius * l)
    member x.Warp(f) = APoint(angle=f(x.Angle), radius=x.Radius)
    static member Circle(n) =
        [ for i in 1..n -> APoint(angle=2.0*Math.PI/float(n), radius=1.0) ]
    new() = APoint(angle=0.0, radius=0.0)
```

The inferred F# type of this class is as follows:

```
type APoint =
    new : unit -> APoint
    new : angle:double * radius:double -> APoint
    static member Circle : n:int -> APoint list
    member Stretch : l:double -> APoint
    member Warp : f:(double -> double) -> APoint
    member Angle : double
    member Radius : double
```

Let's look at how this F# type appears to a programmer using C# or another .NET library. The approximate C# signature is as follows:

```
// C# signature for the unadjusted APoint class of Listing 19-1

public class APoint {
    public APoint();
    public APoint(double angle, double radius);
    public static Microsoft.FSharp.Collections.List<APoint> Circle(int count);
    public APoint Stretch(double factor);
    public APoint Warp(Microsoft.FSharp.Core.FastFunc<double,double> transform);
    public double Angle { get; }
    public double Radius  { get; }
}
```

There are some important points to notice about how F# has chosen to represent constructs here. For example:

- Metadata such as argument names has been preserved.

- F# methods that take tupled arguments become C# methods that take multiple arguments.

- Functions and lists become references to corresponding types in the F# library.

The full rules for how F# types, modules, and members are represented in the .NET Common Intermediary Language are explained in the F# language reference on the F# web site.

To make a .NET component, you place it in a file component.fs and compile this code into a strong-name signed DLL using the techniques from Chapter 7:

```
C:\fsharp> sn -k component.snk
C:\fsharp> fsc --target:library --keyfile:component.snk  component.fs
```

Figure 19-1 shows the results of applying the Microsoft FxCop tool to check this assembly for compliance with the .NET Framework Design Guidelines. This reveals a number of problems with the assembly. For example, the .NET Framework Design Guidelines require the following:

- Types must be placed in namespaces.

- Public identifiers must be spelled correctly.

- Additional attributes must be added to assemblies related to .NET Security and Common Language Specification (CLS) compliance.

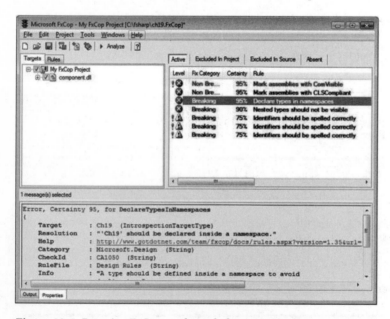

Figure 19-1. Running FxCop on the code from Listing 19-1

Listing 19-2 shows how to adjust this code to take these things into account.

Listing 19-2. An F# Type After Adjustment for Use As Part of a Vanilla.NET API

```
namespace ExpertFSharp.Types

open System

module AssemblyAttributes =
    [<assembly: System.Runtime.InteropServices.ComVisible(false);
      assembly: System.CLSCompliant(true)>]
    do()

type RadialPoint(angle,radius) =
    member x.Angle = angle
    member x.Radius = radius
    member x.Stretch(factor) = RadialPoint(angle=x.Angle, radius=x.Radius * factor)
    member x.Warp(transform:Converter<_,_>) =
        RadialPoint(angle=transform.Invoke(x.Angle), radius=x.Radius)
    static member Circle(count) =
        seq { for i in 1..count ->
                    RadialPoint(angle=2.0*Math.PI/float(count), radius=1.0) }
    new() = RadialPoint(angle=0.0, radius=0.0)
```

The inferred F# type of the code in Listing 19-2 is as follows:

```
type RadialPoint =
    new : unit -> RadialPoint
    new : angle:double * radius:double -> RadialPoint
    static member Circle : count:int -> seq<RadialPoint>
    member Stretch : factor:double -> RadialPoint
    member Warp : transform:System.Converter<double,double> -> RadialPoint
    member Angle : double
    member Radius : double
```

The C# signature is now as follows:

```
// C# signature for the unadjusted RadialPoint class of Listing 19-2

public class RadialPoint {
    public RadialPoint();
    public RadialPoint(double angle, double radius);
    public static System.Collections.Generic.IEnumerable<RadialPoint> Circle(int count);
    public RadialPoint Stretch(double factor);
    public RadialPoint Warp(System.Converter<double,double> transform);
    public double Angle { get; }
    public double Radius  { get; }
}
```

The fixes you make to prepare this type for use as part of a vanilla .NET library are as follows:

- You add several attributes as directed by the FxCop tool. You can find the meaning of these attributes in the MSDN documentation referenced by the FxCop warning messages.

- You adjust several names: `APoint` , `n`, `l`, and `f` became `RadialPoint`, `count`, `factor`, and `transform`, respectively.

- You use a return type of `seq<RadialPoint>` instead of `RadialPoint list` by changing a list construction using `[ ... ]` to a sequence construction using `seq { ... }`. An alternative option would be to use an explicit upcast (`[ ... ] :> seq<_>`).

- You use the .NET delegate type `System.Converter` instead of an F# function type.

After applying these, the last remaining FxCop warning tells you that namespaces with two to three types aren't recommended.

The last two previous points aren't essential, but, as mentioned, delegate types and sequence types tend to be easier for C# programmers to use than F# function and list types (F# function types aren't compiled to .NET delegate types, partly for performance reasons). Note that you can use FxCop exemptions to opt out of any of the FxCop rules, either by adding an exemption entry to FxCop itself or by attaching attributes to your source code.

■ **Tip** If you're designing libraries for use from any .NET language, then there's no substitute for actually doing some experimental C# and Visual Basic programming to ensure that uses of your libraries look good from these languages. You can also use tools such as .NET Reflector and the Visual Studio Object Browser to ensure that libraries and their documentation appear as expected to developers. If necessary, enroll the help of a C# programmer and ask them what they think.

Understanding Functional Design Methodology

So far, this chapter has looked at how to do vanilla .NET library design with F#. However, frequently F# programmers design libraries that are free to make more sophisticated use of F# and more or less assume that client users are using F# as well. To make the best use of F# in this situation, it's helpful to use functional programming design techniques as part of the library design process. For this reason, this section covers what functional programming brings to the table with regard to design methodology.

Understanding Where Functional Programming Comes From

Let's recap the origins of the major programming paradigms from a design perspective:

- *Procedural programming* arises from the fundamentally imperative nature of processing devices: microprocessors are state machines that manipulate data using side effects.

- *Object-oriented programming* arises from the need to encapsulate and reuse large objects and associated behaviors such as those used for GUI applications.

- *Functional programming* differs in that it arises from one view of the *mathematics* of computation. That is, functional programming, in its purest form, is a way of describing computations using constructs that have useful mathematical properties, independent of their implementations.

For example, the functional programming design methodology places great importance on constructs that are *compositional*. For example, in F#, you can map a function over a list of lists as follows:

```
let map2 f inp = List.map (List.map f) inp
```

This is a simple example of the inherent compositionality of generic functions: the expression List.map f produces a new function that can in turn be used as the argument to List.map. Understanding compositionality is the key to understanding much of what goes by the name of functional programming. For example, functional programmers aren't interested in a lack of side effects just for the sake of it—instead, they like programs that don't use side effects because such program tend to be more compositional than those that do.

Functional programming often goes further by emphasizing *transformations that preserve behavior*. For example, you expect to be able to make the following refactorings to your code regardless of the function f or of the values inp, x, or rest:

```
List.hd (x :: rest) ➤ x
```

```
List.concat (List.map (List.filter f) inp) ➤ List.filter f (List.concat inp)
```

Equations like these can be a source of useful documentation and test cases, and in some situations they can even be used to specify entire programs. Furthermore, good programmers routinely manipulate and optimize programs in ways that effectively assume these transformations are valid. If these transformations are *not* valid, then it's easy to accidentally insert bugs when you're working with code. That said, many important transformation equations aren't guaranteed to *always* be valid—they typically hold only if additional assumptions are made—for example, in the first example, the expression rest shouldn't have side effects.

Transformational reasoning works well for some kinds of code and badly for others. Table 19-1 lists some of the F# and .NET constructs that are highly compositional and for which transformational reasoning tends to work well in practice.

Table 19-1. Some Compositional F# Library Constructs Amenable to Equational Reasoning

Constructs	Examples	Explanation
Base types	int, float	Code using immutable basic types is often relatively easy to reason about. There are some exceptions to the rule: the presence of NaN values and approximations in floating-point operations can make it difficult to reason about floating-point code.
Collections	Set<'T>, Map<'Key,'Value>	Immutable collection types are highly amenable to equational reasoning. For example, you expect equations such as Set.union Set.empty x = x to hold.

Constructs	Examples	Explanation
Control types	Lazy<'T>, Async<'T>	Control constructs are often highly compositional and have operators that allow you to combine them in interesting ways. For example, you expect equations such as (lazy x).Force() = x to hold.
Data abstractions	seq<'T>	F# sequences aren't pure values, because they may access data stores using major side effects such as network I/O. However, in practice, uses of sequences tend to be very amenable to equational reasoning. This assumes that the side effects for each iteration of the sequence are isolated and independent.

Understanding Functional Design Methodology

Functional design methodology is rooted in compositionality and reasoning. In practice, it's largely about the following steps:

1. Deciding what values you're interested in representing. These values may range from simple integers to more sophisticated objects such as expression trees from Chapter 9 or the asynchronous tasks from Chapter 13.

2. Deciding what operations are required to build these values, extracting information from them, and combining them and transforming them.

3. Deciding what equations and other algebraic properties should hold between these values, and assessing whether these properties hold the implementation.

Steps 1 and 2 explain why functional programmers often prefer to define operations separately from types. As a result, functional programmers often find OO programming strange because it emphasizes operations on *single* values, whereas functional programming emphasizes operations that *combine* values. This carries over to library implementation in functional programming, where you often see types defined first and then modules containing operations on those types.

Because of this, one pattern that is common in the F# library is the following:

• The type is defined first.

• Then, a module defines the functions to work over the type.

• Finally, a with augmentation adds the most common functions as members. Chapter 6 describes augmentations.

One simple example of functional programming methodology in this book appears in Chapter 12, where you saw how a representation for propositional logic is defined using a type:

```
type Var = string
type Prop =
    | And of Prop * Prop
    | Var of Var
    | Not of Prop
    | Exists of Var * Prop
    | False
```

Operations were then defined to combine and analyze values of type Prop. It wouldn't make sense to define all of these operations as intrinsic to the Prop type, an approach often taken in OO design. In that same chapter, you saw another representation of propositional logic formulae where two logically identical formulae were normalized to the same representations. This is an example of step 3 of the functional design methodology: the process of designing a type involves specifying the equations that should hold for values of that type.

You've seen many examples in this book of how OO programming and functional programming can work very well together. For example, F# objects are often immutable but use OO features to group together some functionality working on the same data. Also, F# object interface types are often used as a convenient notation for collections of functions.

However, some tensions exist between functional programming and OO design methodology. For example, when you define operations independently of data (that is, the functional style), it's simple to add a new operation, but modifying the type is more difficult. In OO programming using abstract and virtual methods, it's easy to add a new inherited type, but adding new operations (that is, new virtual methods) is difficult.

Similarly, functional programming emphasizes *simple but compositional* types: for example, functions and tuples. OO programming tends to involve creating many (often large and complex) types with considerable amounts of additional metadata. These are often less compositional but sometimes more self-documenting.

Finally, although functional programming doesn't provide a complete software design methodology, it's beautiful and powerful when it works, creating constructs that can be wielded with amazing expressivity and a very low bug rate. However, not all constructs in software design are amenable to compositional descriptions and implementations, and an over-reliance on pure programming can leave you bewildered and abandoned when the paradigm doesn't offer useful solutions that scale in practice. This is the primary reason why F# is a multiparadigm language: to ensure that functional techniques can be combined with other techniques where appropriate.

■ **Note** Some functional languages such as Haskell place strong emphasis on equational reasoning principles. In F#, equational reasoning is slightly less important; however, it still forms an essential part of understanding what functional programming brings to the arena of design methodology.

Applying the .NET Library Design Guidelines to F#

This section presents some additional recommendations for applying the .NET Library Design Guidelines to F# programming. We do this by making a series of recommendations that can be read as extensions to these guidelines.

Recommendation: Use the .NET Naming and Capitalization Conventions Where Possible

Table 19-2 summarizes the .NET guidelines for naming and capitalization in code. We've added our own recommendations for how these should be adjusted for some F# constructs. This table refers to the following categories of names:

- *PascalCase*: LeftButton and TopRight, for example
- *camelCase*: leftButton and topRight, for example
- *Verb*: A verb or verb phrase; performAction or SetValue, for example

- *Noun*: A noun or noun phrase; `cost` or `ValueAfterDepreciation`, for example

- *Adjective*: An adjective or adjectival phrase; `Comparable` or `Disposable`, for example

In general, the .NET guidelines strongly discourage the use of abbreviations (for example, "use `OnButtonClick` rather than `OnBtnClick`"). Common abbreviations such as `Async` for `Asynchronous` are tolerated. This guideline has historically been broken by functional programming; for example, `List.iter` uses an abbreviation for iterate. For this reason, using abbreviations tends to be tolerated to a greater degree in F# programming, although we discourage using additional abbreviations beyond those found in existing F# libraries.

Acronyms such as XML aren't abbreviations and are widely used in .NET libraries, although in uncapitalized form (Xml). Only well-known, widely recognized acronyms should be used.

The .NET guidelines say that casing can't be used to avoid name collisions and that you must assume that some client languages are case insensitive. For example, Visual Basic is case insensitive.

Table 19-2. *Conventions Associated with Public Constructs in .NET Frameworks and Author-Recommended Extensions for F# Constructs*

Construct	Case	Part	Examples	Notes
Concrete types	PascalCase	Noun/ adjective	`List`, `DoubleComplex`	Concrete types are structs, classes, enumerations, delegates, records, and unions. Type names are traditionally lowercase in OCaml, and F# code has generally followed this pattern. However, as F# matures as a language, it's moving much more to follow standardized .NET idioms.
DLLs	PascalCase		`Microsoft.FSharp.Core.dll<Company>.<Component>.dll`	
Union tags	PascalCase	Noun	`Some`, `Add`, `Success`	Don't use a prefix in public APIs. Optionally use a prefix when internal, such as `type Teams = TAlpha | TBeta | TDelta`.
Event	PascalCase	Verb	`ValueChanged`	
Exceptions	PascalCase		`WebException`	
Field	PascalCase	Noun	`CurrentName`	
Interface types	PascalCase	Noun/ adjective	`IDisposable`	
Method	PascalCase	Verb	`ToString`	

Construct	Case	Part	Examples	Notes
Namespace	PascalCase		`Microsoft.FSharp.Core`	Generally use `<Organization>.<Technology>[.<Subnamespace>]`, but drop the organization if the technology is independent of organization.
Parameters	camelCase	Noun	`typeName`, `transform`, `range`	
let values (internal)	camelCase	Noun/ verb	`getValue`, `myTable`	
let values (external)	camelCase or PascalCase	Noun	`List.map`, `Dates.Today`	let-bound values are often public when following traditional functional design patterns. However, generally use PascalCase when the identifier can be used from other .NET languages.
Property	PascalCase	Noun/ adjective	`IsEndOfFile`, `BackColor`	Boolean properties generally use `Is` and `Can` and should be affirmative, as in `IsEndOfFile`, not `IsNotEndOfFile`.
Type parameters	Any	Noun/ adjective	`'T, 't, 'Key, 'Value`	

We generally recommend using lowercase for variable names, unless you're designing a library:

```
✓ let x = 1
✓ let now = System.DateTime.Now
```

We recommend using lowercase for all variable names bound in pattern matches, function definitions, and anonymous inner functions. Functions may also use uppercase:

```
✗ let add I J = I+J
✓ let add i j = i + j
```

Use uppercase when the natural convention is to do so, as in the case of matrices, proper nouns, and common abbreviations such as I for the identity function:

```
✓ let f (A:matrix) (B:matrix) = A+B
✓ let Monday = 1
✓ let I x = x
```

We recommend using camelCase for other values, including the following:

- Ad hoc functions in scripts
- Values making up the internal implementation of a module
- Locally bound values in functions

```
✓ let emailMyBossTheLatestResults = ...
✓ let doSomething () =
      let firstResult = ...
      let secondResult = ...
```

Recommendation: Avoid Using Underscores in Names

In some older F# code, you see the frequent use of underscores to qualify some names. For example:

- Suffixes such as _left and _right

- Prefix verbs such as add_, remove_, try_, and is_, do_

- Prefix connectives such as to_, of_, from_, and for_

We recommend avoiding this style because it clashes with .NET naming conventions.

■ **Note** No rules are hard and fast. Some F# programmers ignore this advice and use underscores heavily, partly because functional programmers often dislike extensive capitalization. Furthermore, OCaml code uses underscores everywhere. But be aware that the style is often disliked by others who have a choice about whether to use it. It has the advantage that abbreviations can be used in identifiers without them being run together.

Recommendation: Follow the .NET Guidelines for Exceptions

The .NET Framework Design Guidelines give good advice about the use of exceptions in the context of all .NET programming. Some of these guidelines are as follows:

- Don't return error codes. Exceptions are the main way of reporting errors in frameworks.

- Don't use exceptions for normal flow of control. Although this technique is often used in languages such as OCaml, it's bug-prone and slow on .NET. Instead, consider returning a None option value to indicate failure.

- Document all exceptions thrown by your code when a function is used incorrectly.

- Where possible, throw existing exceptions in the System namespaces.

- Use invalidOp and invalidArg to throw exceptions where possible

---

■ **Note** Other exception-related topics covered by the .NET guidelines include advice on designing custom exceptions, wrapping exceptions, choosing exception messages, and special exceptions to avoid throwing (OutOfMemoryException, ExecutionEngineException, COMException, SEHException, StackOverflowException, NullReferenceException, AccessViolationException, and InvalidCastException).

Recommendation: Consider Using Option Values for Return Types Instead of Raising Exceptions

The .NET approach to exceptions is that they should be exceptional: that is, they should occur relatively infrequently. However, some operations (for example, searching a table) may fail frequently. F# option values are an excellent way to represent the return types of these operations.

Recommendation: Follow the .NET Guidelines for Value Types

The .NET guidelines give good guidance about when to use .NET value types (that is, structs, introduced in Chapter 6). In particular, they recommend using a struct in a public API only when the following are all true:

- A type logically represents a single value similar to a primitive type.

- It has an instance size smaller than 16 bytes.

- It's immutable.

- It won't have to be boxed frequently (that is, converted to/from the type System.Object).

Some programmers are much stricter and almost never use structs in public APIs.

Recommendation: Consider Using Explicit Signature Files for Your Framework

Chapter 7 describes explicit signature files. Using explicit signatures files for framework code ensures that you know the full public surface of your API and can cleanly separate public documentation from internal implementation details.

Recommendation: Consider Avoiding the Use of Implementation Inheritance for Extensibility

Chapter 6 describes implementation inheritance. In general, the .NET guidelines are agnostic with regard to the use of implementation inheritance. In F#, implementation inheritance is used more rarely than in other .NET languages. The main rationale for this is given in Chapter 6, which also presents many alternative techniques for designing and implementing OO types using F#. However, implementation inheritance is used heavily in GUI frameworks.

■ **Note** Other OO extensibility topics discussed in the .NET guidelines include events and callbacks, virtual members, abstract types and inheritance, and limiting extensibility by sealing classes.

Recommendation: Use Properties and Methods for Attributes and Operations Essential to a Type

Here's an example:

```
✓ type HardwareDevice with
      ...
      member ID: string
      member SupportedProtocols: seq<Protocol>
```

Consider using methods for the intrinsic operations essential to a type:

```
✓ type HashTable<'Key,'Value> with
      ...
      member Add           : 'Key * 'Value -> unit
      member ContainsKey   : 'Key -> bool
      member ContainsValue : 'Value -> bool
```

Consider using static methods to hold a Create function instead of revealing object constructors:

```
✓ type HashTable<'Key,'Value> with
      static member Create : IHashProvider<'Key> -> HashTable<'Key,'Value>
```

Recommendation: Avoid Revealing Concrete Data Representations Such as Records

Where possible, avoid revealing concrete representations such as records, fields, and implementation inheritance hierarchies in framework APIs.

The rationale is that one of the overriding aims of library design is to avoid revealing concrete representations of objects, for the obvious reason that you may want to change the implementation later. For example, the concrete representation of System.DateTime values isn't revealed by the external, public API of the .NET library design. At runtime, the Common Language Runtime knows the committed implementation that will be used throughout execution. However, compiled code doesn't pick up dependencies on the concrete representation.

Recommendation: Use Active Patterns to Hide the Implementations of Discriminated Unions

Where possible, avoid using large discriminated unions in framework APIs, especially if you expect there is a chance that the representation of information in the discriminated union will undergo revision and change. For frameworks, you should typically hide the type or use active patterns to reveal the ability to pattern-match over language constructs. Chapter 9 describes active patterns.

This doesn't apply to the use of discriminated unions internal to an assembly or to an application. Likewise, it doesn't apply if the only likely future change is the addition of further cases, and you're willing to require that client code be revised for these cases. Finally, active patterns can incur a performance overhead, and this should be measured and tested, although their benefits frequently outweigh this cost.

■ **Note** Using large, volatile discriminated unions freely in APIs encourages people to use pattern-matching against these discriminated union values. This is appropriate for unions that don't change. However, if you reveal discriminated unions indiscriminately, you may find it very hard to version your library without breaking user code.

Recommendation: Use Object Interface Types Instead of Tuples or Records of Functions

In Chapter 5, you saw various ways to represent a dictionary of operations explicitly, such as using tuples of functions or records of functions. In general, we recommend that you use object interface types for this purpose, because the syntax associated with implementing them is generally more convenient.

Recommendation: Understand When Currying Is Useful in Functional Programming APIs

Currying is the name used when functions take arguments in the iterated form—that is, when the functions can be partially applied. For example, the following function is curried:

```
let f x y z = x + y + z
```

This isn't:

```
let f (x,y,z) = x + y + z
```

Here are some of our guidelines for when to use currying and when not to use it:

- Use currying freely for rapid prototyping and scripting. Saving keystrokes can be very useful in these situations.

- Use currying when partial application of the function is highly likely to give a useful residual function (see Chapter 3).

- Use currying when partial application of the function is necessary to permit useful precomputation (see Chapter 8).

- Avoid using currying in vanilla .NET APIs or APIs to be used from other .NET languages.

When using currying, place arguments in order from the least varying to the most varying. Doing so makes partial application of the function more useful and leads to more compact code. For example, List.map is curried with the function argument first because a typical program usually applies List.map to a handful of known function values but many different concrete list values. Likewise, you saw in Chapters 8 and 9 how recursive functions can be used to traverse tree structures. These traversals often carry an environment. The environment changes relatively rarely—only when you traverse the subtrees of structures that bind variables. For this reason, the environment is the first argument.

When you use currying, consider the importance of the pipelining operator; for example, place function arguments first and object arguments last.

F# also uses currying for let-bound binary operators and combinators:

```
✓ let divmod n m = ...
✓ let map f x = ...
✓ let fold f z x = ...
```

However, see Chapters 6 and 8 for how to define operators as static members in types, which aren't curried.

Recommendation: Use Tuples for Return Values, Arguments, and Intermediate Values

Here is an example of using a tuple in a return type:

✓ `val divmod : int -> int -> int * int`

Some Recommended Coding Idioms

This section looks at a small number of recommendations for writing implementation code, as opposed to library designs. We don't give many recommendations on formatting, because formatting code is relatively simple for #light indentation-aware code. We do make a couple of formatting recommendations that early readers of this book asked about.

Recommendation: Use the Standard Operators

The following operators are defined in the F# standard library and should be used wherever possible instead of defining equivalents. Using these operators tends to make code much easier to read, so we strongly recommend it. This is spelled out explicitly because other languages similar to F# don't support all of these operators, and thus some F# programmers aren't aware that these operators exist:

```
f >> g    -- forward composition
g << f    -- reverse composition
x |> f    -- forward pipeline
f <| x    -- reverse pipeline

x |> ignore   -- throwing away a value

x + y    -- overloaded addition (including string concatenation)
x - y    -- overloaded subtraction
x * y    -- overloaded multiplication
x / y    -- overloaded division
x % y    -- overloaded modulus

x <<< y  -- bitwise left shift
x >>> y  -- bitwise right shift
x ||| y  -- bitwise left shift, also for working with enumeration flags
x &&& y  -- bitwise right shift, also for working with enumeration flags
x ^^^ y  -- bitwise left shift, also for working with enumeration flags

x && y   -- lazy/short-circuit and
x || y   -- lazy/short-circuit or
```

Recommendation: Place the Pipeline Operator |> at the Start of a Line

People often ask how to format pipelines. We recommend this style:

```
let methods =
    System.AppDomain.CurrentDomain.GetAssemblies
    |> List.ofArray
    |> List.map (fun assem -> assem.GetTypes())
    |> Array.concat
```

Recommendation: Format Object Expressions Using the member Syntax

People often ask how to format object expressions. We recommend this style:

```
let thePlayers =
        { new Organization() with
            member x.Chief = "Peter Quince"
            member x.Underlings =
                [ "Francis Flute"; "Robin Starveling";
                    "Tom Snout"; "Snug"; "Nick Bottom"]
          interface IDisposable with
            member x.Dispose() = ()  }
```

■ **Note** The discussion of F# design and engineering issues in Chapters 18 and 19 is necessarily limited. In particular, we haven't covered topics such as aspect-oriented programming, design and modeling methodologies, software quality assurance, or software metrics, all of which are outside the scope of this book.

Summary

This chapter covered some of the rules you may apply to library design in F#, particularly taking into account the idioms and traditions of .NET. It also considered some of the elements of the functional programming design methodology, which offers many important and deep insights. Finally, we gave some specific suggestions for use when you're designing .NET and F# libraries.

That concludes our tour of F#. We hope you enjoy a long and productive career coding in the language.

F# Brief Language Guide

This appendix describes the essential constructs of the F# language in a compact form. You can find a full guide to the F# language in the F# Language Specification on the F# website.

Comments and Attributes

Comments (Chapter 2)

```
// comment

(* comment *)

/// XML doc comment
let x = 1
```

Attaching Attributes (Chapter 9)

```
[<Obsolete("Deprecated at 1.2")>]
type Type =
    ...
[<Conditional("DEBUG")>]
let Function(x) =

[<assembly: Note("argument")>]
do ()
```

Basic Types and Literals

Basic Types and Literals (Chapter 3)

```
sbyte       = System.SByte      76y
byte        = System.Byte       76uy
int16       = System.Int16      76s
uint16      = System.UInt16     76us
int32       = System.Int32      76
uint32      = System.UInt32     76u
int64       = System.Int64      76L
uint64      = System.UInt64     76UL
string      = System.String     "abc", @"c:\etc"
single      = System.Single     3.14f
double      = System.Double     3.14, 3.2e5
char        = System.Char       '7'
nativeint   = System.IntPtr     76n
unativeint  = System.UIntPtr    76un
bool        = System.Boolean    true, false
unit        = Microsoft.FSharp.Core.Unit  ()
```

Basic Type Abbreviations

```
int8    = sbyte
uint8   = byte
int     = int32
float32 = single
float   = double
```

Types

Types (Chapter 3 and 5)	
ident	Named type
ident<type,...,type>	Type instantiation
type * ... * *type*	Tuple type
type[]	Array type
#type	Flexible type (accepts any subtype)
'ident	Variable type
type -> type	Function type

Type instantiations can be postfix:`int list`

Patterns and Matching

Patterns (Chapter 3 and 9)	
_	Wildcard pattern
literal	Constant pattern
ident	Variable pattern
(pat, ..., pat)	Tuple pattern
[pat; ...; pat]	List pattern
[| pat; ...; pat |]	Array pattern
{ id=pat; ...; id=pat }	Record pattern
id(pat, ..., pat)	Union case pattern
id expr ... expr (pat, ..., pat)	Active pattern
*pat	pat*	"Or" pattern
pat & pat	"Both" pattern
pat as id	Named pattern
:? type	Type test pattern
:? type as id	Type cast pattern
null	Null pattern

Matching (Chapter 3)
`match` *expr* `with`
`|` *pat* `->` *expr*
...
`|` *pat* `->` *expr*
Note: Rules of a match may use
`|` *pat* `when` *expr* `->` *expr*

Active Patterns (Chapter 9)
`let (|`*Tag1*`|`*Tag2*`|)` `inp = ...`
`let (|`*Tag1*`|_|)` `inp = ...`
`let (|`*Tag1*`|)` `inp = ...`

Functions, Composition, and Pipelining

Function values (Chapter 3)	
`fun` *pat* `...` *pat* `->` *expr*	Function
`function`	Match
`function`	
`|` *pat* `->` *expr*	
...	
`|` *pat* `->` *expr*	

Application and Pipelining (Chapter 3)	
`f x`	Application
`x |> g`	Forward pipe
`f >> g`	Function composition

Binding and Control Flow

Control Flow (Chapter 3 and 4)	
expr expr	Sequencing
do expr expr	Sequencing
for id = expr to expr do expr	Simple loop
for pat in expr do expr	Sequence loop
while expr do expr	While loop

Binding and Scoping (Chapter 3)	
let pat = expr expr	Value binding
let id args = expr expr	Function binding
let rec id args = expr expr	Recursive binding
use pat = expr expr	Auto dispose binding

Syntax Forms Without Indentation

```
let pat = expr in expr
while expr do expr done
for pat in expr do expr done
expr ; expr
do expr in expr
```

Exceptions

Exception Handling	

try
    expr
with
    | pat -> expr
    | pat -> expr
	Handling

try
    expr
finally
    expr
	Compensation

use id = expr	Automatic Dispose

Some Exceptions (Chapter 4)

```
Microsoft.FSharp.Core.FailureException
System.MatchFailureException
System.InvalidArgumentException
System.StackOverflowException
```

Raising Exceptions (Common Forms)

raise expr	Throw exception
failwith expr	Throw FailureException

Catch and Rethrow

```
try expr
with
    | :? ThreadAbortException ->
        printfn "thrown!"
        rethrow ()
```

Tuples, Arrays, Lists, and Collections

Tuples (Chapter 3)	
`(expr, ..., expr)`	Tuple
`fst expr`	First of pair
`snd expr`	Second of pair

F# Lists (Chapter 3)	
`[ expr; ...; expr ]`	List
`[ expr..expr ]`	Range list
`[ comp-expr ]`	Generated list
`expr :: expr`	List cons
`expr @ expr`	List append

Arrays (Chapter 4)	
`[| expr; ...; expr |]`	Array literal
`[| expr..expr |]`	Range array
`[| comp-expr |]`	Generated array
`Array.create size expr`	Array creation
`Array.init size expr`	Array init
`arr.[expr]`	Lookup
`arr.[expr] <- expr`	Assignment
`arr.[expr..expr]`	Slice
`arr.[expr..]`	Right slice
`arr.[..expr]`	Left slice

See Chapter 4 for multi-dimensional operators.

F# Options (Chapter 3)	
`None`	No value
`Some(expr)`	With value

Some Other Collection Types
`System.Collections.Generic.Dictionary`
`System.Collections.Generic.List`
`System.Collections.Generic.SortedList`
`System.Collections.Generic.SortedDictionary`
`System.Collections.Generic.Stack`
`System.Collections.Generic.Queue`
`Microsoft.FSharp.Collections.Set`
`Microsoft.FSharp.Collections.Map`

Operators

Overloaded Arithmetic (Chapter 3)

```
x + y   Addition
x - y   Subtraction
x * y   Multiplication
x / y   Division
x % y   Remainder/modulus
-x      Unary negation
```

Overloaded Math Operators

```
abs, acos, atan, atan2,
ceil, cos, cosh, exp,
floor, log, log10, pow,
pown, sqrt, sin, sinh,
tan, tanh
```

Overloaded Conversion Operators

```
byte, sbyte, int16, uint16,
int, int32, uint32, int64,
uint64, float32, float, single,
double, nativeint,
unativeint
```

Mutable Locals (Chapter 4)

```
let mutable var = expr   Declare
var                      Read
var <- expr              Update
```

Mutable Reference Cells (Chapter 4)

```
ref expr        Allocate
!expr           Read
expr.Value      Read
expr := expr    Assign
```

Booleans

```
not expr          Boolean negation
expr && expr      Boolean "and"
expr || expr      Boolean "or"
```

Overloaded Bitwise Operators (Chapter 3)

```
x >>> y   Shift right
x <<< y   Shift left
x &&& y   Bitwise logical and
x ||| y   Bitwise logical or
x ^^^ y   Bitwise exclusive or
~~~ x     Bitwise logical not
```

Generic Comparison and Hashing

```
hash x            Generic hashing
x = y             Generic equality
x <> y            Generic inequality
compare x y       Generic comparison
x >= y, x <= y,
x > y, x < y,
min x y, max x y
```

```
Note: Records, tuples, arrays and unions
automatically implement structural equality
and hashing (see Chapters 5 and 8).
```

Indexed Lookup (Chapter 4)

```
expr.[idx]           Lookup
expr.[idx] <- expr   Assignment
expr.[idx..idx]      Slice
expr.[idx..]         Right slice
expr.[..idx]         Left slice
```

```
See Chapter 4 for multidimensional operators
```

Object-Related Operators and Types

```
type obj = System.Object
box(x)            Convert to type obj
unbox<type>(x)    Extract from type obj
typeof<type>      Extract Sytem.Type
x :> type         Static cast to supertype
x :?> type        Dynamic cast to subtype
```

Type Definitions and Objects

Union Types: Chapters 3 and 6

```
type UnionType =
  | TagA of type * ... * type
  | TagB of type * ... * type
```

Record Types: Chapters 3 and 6

```
type Record =
  { Field1: type
    Field2: type }
```

Object Expressions: Chapter 6

```
{ new IObject with
    member x.Prop1 = expr
    member x.Meth1 args = expr }

{ new Object() with
    member x.Prop1 = expr
    interface IObject with
      member x.Meth1 args = expr
    interface IWidget with
      member x.Meth1 args = expr }
```

Implementation Inheritance

```
type ObjectType(args) as x =
  inherit BaseType(expr) as base
```

Constructed Class Types: Chapter 6

```
type ObjectType(args) =
  let internalValue = expr
  let internalFunction args = expr
  let mutable internalState = expr
  member x.Prop1 = expr
  member x.Meth2 args = expr
```

Object Interface Types: Chapter 6

```
type IObject =
  interface ISimpleObject
  abstract Prop1 : type
  abstract Meth2 : type -> type
```

Some Special Members

```
member x.Prop                setter property
  with get() = expr
  and  set v = expr

member x.Item                indexer property
  with get idx = expr
  and  set idx v = expr

static member (+) (x,y) = expr operator
```

Named and Optional Arguments for Members

```
member obj.Method(?optArgA)          Declaring optional arg

new Object(x=expr, y=expr)           Call with named args
obj.Method(optArgA=expr, PropB=expr) Call with optional args and properties
```

Namespaces and Modules

Namespaces: Chapter 7

`namespace Org.Product.Feature`
 	
`type TypeOne =`
   `...`
 	
`module ModuleTwo =`
   `...`

Files As Modules: Chapter 7

`module Org.Product.Feature.Module`
 	
`type TypeOne =`
   `...`
 	
`module ModuleTwo =`
   `...`

Sequence Expressions and Workflows

Sequence Expressions and Workflows: See Chapters 3, 9, and 13

`[ comp-expr ]`	Generated list
`[| comp-expr |]`	Generated array
`seq { comp-expr }`	Generated sequence
`async { comp-expr }`	Asynchronous workflow
`ident { comp-expr }`	Arbitrary workflow

Syntax for Workflows

`let! pat = expr` `comp-expr`	Execute and bind computation
`let pat = expr` `comp-expr`	Execute and bind expression
`do! expr` `comp-expr`	Execute computation
`do expr` `comp-expr`	Execute expression
`if expr then comp-expr else comp-expr`	Conditional workflow
`if expr then comp-expr`	Conditional workflow
`while expr do comp-expr`	Repeated workflow
`for pat in expr do comp-expr`	Enumeration loop
`try comp-expr with pat -> expr`	Workflow with catch
`try comp-expr finally expr`	Workflow with compensation
`use pat = expr in comp-expr`	Workflow with auto dispose
`return expr`	Return expression
`return! expr`	Return computation
`yield expr`	Yield expression (for sequences only)
`yield! expr`	Yield sequence (for sequences only)

Index

■ H

I

■ N

■ T

■ U

You Need the Companion eBook

Your purchase of this book entitles you to buy the companion PDF-version eBook for only $10. Take the weightless companion with you anywhere.

We believe this Apress title will prove so indispensable that you'll want to carry it with you everywhere, which is why we are offering the companion eBook (in PDF format) for $10 to customers who purchase this book now. Convenient and fully searchable, the PDF version of any content-rich, page-heavy Apress book makes a valuable addition to your programming library. You can easily find and copy code—or perform examples by quickly toggling between instructions and the application. Even simultaneously tackling a donut, diet soda, and complex code becomes simplified with hands-free eBooks!

Once you purchase your book, getting the $10 companion eBook is simple:

❶ Visit **www.apress.com/promo/tendollars/**.

❷ Complete a basic registration form to receive a randomly generated question about this title.

❸ Answer the question correctly in 60 seconds, and you will receive a promotional code to redeem for the $10.00 eBook.

eBookshop

233 Spring Street, New York, NY 10013

Offer valid through 11/10.